Bible Interpreters
of the Twentieth Century
A Selection of Evangelical Voices

Walter A. Elwell, editor

J. D. Weaver, editor

 Baker Books

A Division of Baker Book House Co
Grand Rapids, Michigan 49516

Published by Baker Books
a division of Baker Book House Company
P.O. Box 6287, Grand Rapids, MI 49516-6287

Printed in the United States of America

Library of Congress Cataloging-in-Publication Data

Bible interpreters of the twentieth century / Walter A. Elwell, editor; J. D. Weaver, editor.
   p. cm.
Includes bibliographical references.
ISBN 0-8010-2073-5 (pbk.)
  1. Biblical scholars—Biography. 2. Bible—Criticism, interpretation, etc.—History—
  20th century. 3. Evangelists—Biography. I. Elwell, Walter A.
  II. Weaver, J. D. (Jim D.)
BS501.A1B53 1999
220.6′092′2—dc21   99-43138

Scripture quotations are from the King James Version (KJV), the New International Version (NIV), and the Revised Standard Version (RSV).

For information about academic books, resources for Christian leaders, and all new releases available from Baker Book House, visit our web site:
               http://www.bakerbooks.com

Contents

Preface

The history of the church is the history of the church's interpretation of the Bible. So in order to understand and appreciate contemporary evangelicalism one must become acquainted with modern evangelical biblical interpreters. With that belief in view this volume features thirty-five twentieth-century evangelical scholars. Its purpose is to provide basic information about certain influential evangelical interpreters of the Bible. This includes biographical facts, theological development, scholarly contribution, and personal evaluation.

The reader may be curious to know what criteria were used in making the selections. Before stating the criteria, we need to answer the more fundamental question, What is evangelicalism anyway? This movement is the subject of much study,[1] and no simple answer will do.

Everyone seems to know, in some intuitive kind of way, what evangelicalism is. But when it comes to articulating the essence of this movement, no two definitions are exactly alike. They run the spectrum from the very broad understanding of evangelicalism as synonymous with Protestantism to some very specific formulations that entail acceptance of a lengthy list of precise theological statements. Various middle positions define evangelicalism as commitment to the tenets of historical orthodoxy.

---

1. See, for example, Bernard Ramm, *The Evangelical Heritage: A Study in Historical Theology* (Waco: Word, 1973); Donald G. Bloesch, *The Evangelical Renaissance* (Grand Rapids: Eerdmans, 1973); *The Gospel in America: Themes in the Story of America's Evangelicals*, ed. John D. Woodbridge, Mark A. Noll, and Nathan O. Hatch (Grand Rapids: Zondervan, 1979); *Evangelicalism and Modern America*, ed. George M. Marsden (Grand Rapids: Eerdmans, 1984); Mark A. Noll, *Between Faith and Criticism: Evangelicals, Scholarship, and the Bible in America* (San Francisco: Harper and Row, 1986; 2d ed., Grand Rapids: Baker, 1991); George M. Marsden, *Reforming Fundamentalism: Fuller Seminary and the New Evangelicalism* (Grand Rapids: Eerdmans, 1987); James Davison Hunter, *Evangelicalism: The Coming Generation* (Chicago: University of Chicago Press, 1987); Donald W. Dayton, *Discovering an Evangelical Heritage* (Peabody, Mass.: Hendrickson, 1988); George M. Marsden, *Understanding Fundamentalism and Evangelicalism* (Grand Rapids: Eerdmans, 1990); Donald W. Dayton and Robert K. Johnson, *The Variety of American Evangelicalism* (Downers Grove, Ill.: InterVarsity, 1991); Alister McGrath, *Evangelicals and the Future of Christianity* (Downers Grove, Ill.: InterVarsity, 1995); Joel A. Carpenter, *Revive Us Again: The Reawakening of American Fundamentalism* (New York: Oxford University Press, 1997); and Christian Smith, *American Evangelicalism: Embattled and Thriving* (Chicago: University of Chicago Press, 1998). For a comprehensive survey of materials relating to evangelicalism, see *Twentieth-Century Evangelicalism: A Guide to the Sources*, ed. Edith L. Blumhofer and Joel A. Carpenter (New York: Garland, 1990); *Researching Modern Evangelicalism: A Guide to the Holdings of the Billy Graham Center, with Information on Other Collections*, comp. Robert D. Shuster et al. (Westport, Conn.: Greenwood, 1990).

David Bebbington, in an excellent volume titled *Evangelicalism in Modern Britain,* speaks of the "enormous variation in Evangelicalism over time" in his country.[2] The same holds true for America as well.[3] For along the way considerations in the areas of sociology, economics, philosophy, and even matters of personal style have made a single comprehensive definition of evangelicalism even more elusive.

For all of the complicating factors, however, a feeling remained that evangelicalism could still be roughly defined and understood. The uncertainties obviously did not stop books from being written on the subject! Having to make a decision, we opted for a middle-of-the-road definition.[4]

Too broad a definition would have meant that almost anyone could be included. Too narrow a definition would have meant that certain people would be left out. So rather than enter into a complex and, for our purposes, unnecessary discussion as to the exact nature of evangelicalism, we opted for a definition somewhat more on the broad rather than on the narrow side. That we have included biblical interpreters who by some definitions are not solidly evangelical goes without saying, but our purpose has been to allow for the inclusion of biblical interpreters who have had a marked influence on the evangelical movement and considered themselves evangelical, even if not everyone agreed. In the end, the reader will have to decide.

Once the basic question was for all practical purposes settled, we established some criteria for deciding which biblical interpreters to include in our list:

1. Twentieth-century figures (i.e., for a biblical interpreter to be included, at least part of his career must have taken place in the twentieth century)
2. Representatives from both halves of the century (i.e., pre- and post-1950)
3. Identification with the evangelical movement
4. Significant influence on or in the evangelical movement
5. Representatives of various denominational points of view; these include (a) Arminian/Wesleyan, (b) Calvinist/Reformed, (c) charismatic, (d) dispensationalist, (e) Lutheran, (f) Baptist, and (g) Anglican (of course, some of these categories may overlap)
6. Major interest in biblical studies rather than systematic theology

2. David Bebbington, *Evangelicalism in Modern Britain: A History from the 1730s to the 1980s* (Grand Rapids: Baker, 1992), 276.
3. Timothy Smith uses the terms *mosaic* and *kaleidoscope* (see *Evangelicalism and Modern America,* ed. Marsden, viii). Robert Webber has found fourteen varieties (*Common Roots: A Call to Evangelical Maturity* [Grand Rapids: Zondervan, 1978], 32).
4. For a good discussion see *Evangelicalism and Modern America,* ed. Marsden, vii–xix; and Kenneth S. Kantzer, "Unity and Diversity in Evangelical Faith," in *The Evangelicals: What They Believe, Who They Are, Where They Are Changing,* ed. David F. Wells and John D. Woodbridge, rev. ed. (Grand Rapids: Baker, 1977), 50–87.

By using these criteria we were able to come up with a fairly good cross section of evangelicalism in the twentieth century. We knew at the outset that not everyone could be included and that some systematic theologians would eminently qualify. (And some declined to be featured in this volume.) But our criteria were set, and the choices made. There might be legitimate discussion about some biblical scholars who have not been included in this volume, but we doubt that many would exclude those who have been.

The next task was to choose writers for the various articles. It would have made excellent sense to have some of our subjects write on the earlier biblical interpreters. But that seemed too ingrown an idea. So we decided, with but one exception, not to have anyone who was being written about write on someone else. That settled, where it was possible we chose people who were in one way or another close to the scholar being written about. For example, Donald Hagner had revised George Ladd's *Theology of the New Testament,* and Walter Elwell's position at Wheaton College made Merrill Tenney's literary output readily accessible. We hoped that this would provide a sense of immediacy and freshness to the essays.

It is a sad fact that our biblical interpreters are probably little more than names to members of the younger generation. This volume can introduce them to venerable scholars now gone, but also to those of our own generation, who are shaping biblical studies today. Such is our aim at any rate. We offer these essays with the hope that the evangelical biblical interpreters will be understood better, and that evangelicalism will be strengthened as a result.

Contributors

Alexander, Patrick H. M.A., Gordon-Conwell Theological Seminary. Editorial Director, Hendrickson Publishers, Peabody, Massachusetts.

Beckwith, Roger. B.D., Oxford University; D.D. (honorary), Lambeth.

Belcher, Richard P. Th.D., Concordia Theological Seminary. Director of Pastoral Ministry Program, Columbia International University, Columbia, South Carolina.

Brooks, James A. D.Phil., Oxford University. Professor of New Testament, Bethel Seminary, St. Paul, Minnesota.

Calvert, Kenneth R. Th.M., Harvard Divinity School. Assistant Professor of History, Hillsdale College, Hillsdale, Michigan.

Dennison, James T., Jr. Th.M., Pittsburgh Theological Seminary. Lecturer in Church History, Westminster Theological Seminary, San Diego, California.

Dockery, David S. Ph.D., University of Texas at Arlington. President, Union University, Jackson, Tennessee.

Elwell, Walter A. Ph.D., University of Edinburgh. Professor of Biblical and Theological Studies, Wheaton College Graduate School, Wheaton, Illinois.

Eslinger, Lyle. Ph.D., McMaster University. Professor of Religious Studies, University of Calgary, Alberta, Canada.

Griffiths, Valerie. M.A., Oxford University; Th.M., Regent College.

Hagner, Donald A. Ph.D., University of Manchester. George Eldon Ladd Professor of New Testament, Fuller Theological Seminary, Pasadena, California.

Hannah, John. Ph.D., University of Texas at Dallas. Chairman and Senior Professor of Historical Theology, Dallas Theological Seminary, Dallas, Texas.

Harmon, Allan. Th.D., Westminster Theological Seminary. Professor of Old Testament and Principal, Presbyterian Theological College, Melbourne, Australia.

Harris, Murray J. Ph.D., University of Manchester. Professor of New Testament Exegesis and Theology, emeritus, Trinity Evangelical Divinity School, Deerfield, Illinois.

Hartmann, John J. Ph.D. candidate, Cambridge University. Lecturer in New Testament, Covenant Theological Seminary, St. Louis, Missouri.

Hubbard, David Allan. Ph.D., St. Andrews University. Late president, Fuller Theological Seminary, Pasadena, California.

Kaiser, Walter C., Jr. Ph.D., Brandeis University. President and Colman M. Mockler Distinguished Professor of Old Testament, Gordon-Conwell Theological Seminary, South Hamilton, Massachusetts.

Kiehl, Erich H. Th.D., Concordia Seminary. Professor Emeritus, Concordia Seminary, St. Louis, Missouri.

Kistemaker, Simon J. Ph.D., Free University of Amsterdam. Professor of New Testament, Reformed Theological Seminary, Orlando, Florida.

Köstenberger, Andreas J. Ph.D., Trinity Evangelical Divinity School. Associate Professor of New Testament and Greek, Southeastern Baptist Theological Seminary, Wake Forest, North Carolina.

McCartney, Dan G. Ph.D., Westminster Theological Seminary. Professor of New Testament, Westminster Theological Seminary, Philadelphia, Pennsylvania.

McKnight, Edgar V. Ph.D., Southern Baptist Theological Seminary. Research Professor and William R. Kenan, Jr., Professor Emeritus of Religion, Furman University, Greenville, South Carolina.

Motyer, Steve. Ph.D., King's College. Lecturer in New Testament, London Bible College, Northwood, Middlesex, England.

Payne, Philip Barton. Ph.D., University of Cambridge. President, Linguist's Software, Inc., and Adjunct Professor of New Testament, Fuller Theological Seminary, Seattle, Washington.

Rosin, Robert. Ph.D., Stanford University. Professor and Chairman of Historical Theology, Concordia Seminary, St. Louis, Missouri.

Sailhamer, John H. Ph.D., University of California at Los Angeles. Arthur B. Whiting Professor of Old Testament Languages and Literature, Western Seminary, Portland, Oregon.

Selman, Martin J. Ph.D., University of Wales. Deputy Principal, Spurgeon's College, London, United Kingdom.

Skilton, John H. Ph.D., University of Pennsylvania. Late Professor Emeritus, Westminster Theological Seminary, Philadelphia, Pennsylvania.

Stewart, David G. Th.D., Auckland College of Theology. Principal Emeritus, The Bible College of New Zealand.

Taylor, J. Glen. Ph.D., Yale University. Associate Professor of Old Testament and Dean, Wycliffe College, University of Toronto, Ontario, Canada.

Taylor, Marion Ann. Ph.D., Yale University. Associate Professor of Old Testament, Wycliffe College, University of Toronto, Ontario, Canada.

Toon, Peter. D.Phil., Oxford University. Executive President of the Prayer Book Society of the Episcopal Church, USA.

Wilkins, Michael J. Ph.D., Fuller Theological Seminary. Professor of New Testament Language and Literature, Talbot School of Theology, Biola University, La Mirada, California.

Williams, David John. Ph.D., University of Melbourne. Former Vice Principal, Ridley College, Melbourne.

Yarbrough, Robert W. Ph.D., University of Aberdeen. Associate Professor of New Testament and New Testament Department Chair, Trinity Evangelical Divinity School, Deerfield, Illinois; New Testament Department Chair, Emanuel Bible Institute, Oradea, Romania.

John Charles Ryle

Peter Toon

John Charles Ryle ended his long service in the ordained ministry in the Church of England as the first bishop of the new diocese of Liverpool (1880–1900). Though he had a fine mind and preached at Oxford and Cambridge Universities, he was not an academic theologian at heart. He deliberately cultivated a popular and simple style of presentation in order to teach and defend the biblical faith of the Church of England as it is expressed in the Thirty-nine Articles. He was perfectly content to use the Book of Common Prayer (1662) and to defend as thoroughly biblical this form of public worship and daily prayer. He wrote many tracts and books; several of the latter, containing biblical exposition and Calvinist theology, have remained in print for a century or more, used not only by Anglicans but by readers of a variety of denominational allegiances.

The Early Years

Ryle was born in Macclesfield, Cheshire, into an upper-middle-class family on May 10, 1816. After education at a local school, from 1828 to 1834 he attended the famous Eton College, across the river from Windsor Castle. Here the nominal religion was that of the Church of England, the education was based upon the Greek and Latin classics, and the social context was that of the aristocracy and the rich. Apart from gaining a thorough knowledge of classical languages, he also learned to get on with other people and not to expect to have his own way!

From Eton College, Ryle went on to Christ Church, Oxford, the college where John Owen had been the dean in the 1650s. One of his tutors was Henry Liddell, famous for his Greek lexicon. In the years 1834–37 Ryle excelled at the game of cricket and in his studies. He gained a first-class degree and could have stayed on at Oxford with a fellowship at one of the colleges, and become an academic. However, thinking that he would follow his father in banking and business, he did not accept any Oxford appointment but returned home.

Ryle was at Oxford during the early years of the Oxford (Anglo-Catholic) Movement, but it did not attract him then or during later life. In fact he was to become an opponent of the ceremonialism introduced by the clerical members of the movement. Yet it was towards the close of his Oxford career that he began to think seriously about Christ and Christianity. In his incomplete autobiography he wrote that "the circumstances which led to a complete change in my character were very many and very various. . . . It was not a sudden change but very gradual. I cannot trace it to one person, or any one event or thing, but to a singular variety of persons and things. In all of them I believe now the Holy Ghost was working though I did not know it at the time."[1] Amongst the influences on Ryle were several evangelical clergy at Macclesfield, compulsory study of the Thirty-nine Articles (both at Eton and at Oxford), and the reading of *A Practical View,* the evangelical classic by William Wilberforce.

During this period when he felt himself being drawn into a committed (in contrast to a nominal) Christianity, Ryle developed very clear doctrinal views:

> The leading things which seemed to flash out before my mind, as clearly and sharply as the picture of a photographic plate when the developing liquid is poured over it, were such as these.
>
> The extreme sinfulness of sin, and my own personal sinfulness, helplessness, and spiritual need: the entire suitableness of the Lord Jesus Christ by his sacrifice, substitution, and intercession to be the Savior of a sinner's soul: the absolute necessity of anybody who would be saved being born again or converted by the Holy Ghost: the indispensable necessity of holiness of life, being the only evidence of a true Christian: the absolute need of coming out from the world and being separate from its vain customs, recreation, and standards of what is right, as well as from its sins: the supremacy of the Bible as the only rule of what is true in faith, or right in practice, and the need of regular study and reading of it: the absolute necessity of daily, private prayer and communion with God if anyone intends to live the life of a true Christian: the enormous values of what are called Protestant principles as compared to Romanism: the unspeakable excellence and beauty of the doctrine of the Second Advent of our Lord and Saviour, Jesus Christ: [and] the unutterable folly of supposing that baptism is regeneration, or formal-going-to-church [is] Christianity, or taking the sacrament [is] a means of wiping away sins, or clergymen to know more of the Bible than other people or to be mediators between God and men by virtue of their office.[2]

Though he had been baptized as a baby and regularly attended the parish church and the college chapels, it was only when he reached the age of twenty-one that he was inwardly converted to Jesus Christ and came to a very clear understanding of the faith. He would later recall: "Nothing I can remember to this day appeared to me so clear and distinct, as my own sinfulness, Christ's preciousness, the value of the Bible, the need of being born

---

1. John Charles Ryle, *A Self-Portrait,* ed. Peter Toon (Swengel, Pa.: Reiner, 1976), 38–39.
2. Ibid., 41–42.

again, and the enormous folly of the whole doctrine of baptismal regeneration. All these things . . . seemed to flash upon me like a sunbeam in the winter of 1837 and have stuck in my mind from that time down to this."[3] Not surprisingly, Ryle's conversion caused the loss of some friends and the gaining of new ones, who shared his evangelical faith.

Tragedy

From 1837 to 1841 Ryle lived in London and at home in Cheshire, where he worked in his father's bank. His parents tolerated his evangelical faith but did not encourage him. All seemed to be going well until the bank unexpectedly collapsed. "In the month of June, 1841," he wrote, "I had to pass through the greatest change in a temporal point of view that I ever went through in my life." Recounting the disaster in a different way, Ryle wrote: "We got up one summer's morning with all the world before us as usual, and went to bed that same night completely and entirely ruined." The family lost the house, servants, and income! Though his external reaction was exemplary, Ryle suffered much inwardly and for the rest of his life found it difficult to get over the great humiliation. Reflecting upon this terrible experience from the perspective of his Christian faith he wrote: "I believe that God never expects us to feel no suffering or pain when it pleases him to visit us with affliction. There are great mistakes upon this point. Submission to God's will is perfectly compatible with intense and keen suffering under the chastisement of his will. Troubles not felt are in fact not troubles at all. To feel trouble deeply and yet submit to it patiently is that which is required of a Christian."[4] And he quoted Richard Baxter, who said, "I groan but I do not grumble."

On December 12, 1841, Ryle was ordained in the private chapel of the evangelical bishop of Winchester, Charles Sumner. He became a clergyman not because of any special calling, but simply because to do so meant he had an income! That is, he received enough to live in a humble way—but not in the style to which he was accustomed. Ryle served as an assistant curate in the parish of Fawley, in the New Forest, Hampshire, for two years. With his usual commitment he gave himself wholeheartedly to the work and thus learned by experience the art of preaching and of visitation. But illness forced him to take a break before he became rector in the parish of St. Thomas, Winchester, in December 1843.

Ryle had not been in Winchester long before he received from the lord chancellor the offer of the rectory of Helmingham in Suffolk. The major attraction of Helmingham was that it paid a much better stipend than did Winchester. Since Ryle wanted to be financially independent and in a position to marry, he accepted the offer. Before he left the city he did, however, have

3. Ibid., 42–43.
4. Ibid., 58.

some friendly and long conversations on the topic of baptismal regeneration with a leading High Churchman of the day, Bishop Samuel Wilberforce, who was then a canon of Winchester Cathedral.

East Anglia

From 1844 to 1861 Ryle lived in Helmingham as rector of the parish. He married Matilda Charlotte Louisa Plumptre on October 29, 1844; and their child, Georgina Matilda, was born in April 1846. She was named Georgina in memory of Lady Georgina Tollemache of Tollemache Hall in the parish, who had died a year earlier. Regrettably, Mrs. Ryle took ill after the birth of her daughter and remained sick until her death in June 1847. On February 21, 1850, Ryle married Jessie Elizabeth Walker, who was Georgina's godmother. Their marriage lasted ten years before she died of Bright's disease in 1860. She gave birth to one daughter (Jessie Isabell) and three sons (Reginald John, Herbert Edward, and Arthur Johnston). In October 1861, soon after his move to Stradbroke (where he remained from 1861 until 1880), Ryle married Henrietta Legh-Clowes, who proved a fine mother to his five children.

As rector of Helmingham, Ryle developed a simple and effective way of both speaking and writing. Increasingly he was called upon to speak at the meetings of evangelical societies in Suffolk and London. Further, he began to write tracts which were published in Ipswich by William Hunt. By 1859 Hunt could offer seven volumes of tracts under the title of *Home Truths*. Ryle had the writer's gift of a judicious use of the imagination, and this is what made his evangelical writings so popular. Hunt also published two collections of hymns for Ryle in 1849 and 1860. Apart from tracts and pamphlets, Ryle also did more sustained and serious writing in East Anglia—biblical commentary, biographies of spiritual leaders, expositions of doctrine, and calls to sanctification.

After the move to Stradbroke in 1861, Ryle became more involved in the ecclesiastical and doctrinal issues of the day, and was in even greater demand as a speaker and preacher. He was acutely aware of the progress of the Anglo-Catholic movement with its growing stress on ritualism and ceremonialism. Not only did he preach and write against these innovations (see his booklet *What Do We Owe to the Reformation?*), but he raised money to restore Stradbroke parish church so that his successors would have no excuse to introduce "ornaments or fittings of an un-Protestant character."

Ryle was also greatly concerned about the lack of unity and common purpose amongst those in the Church of England who called themselves evangelicals. He took part in various activities to bring about a working union. But there were all kinds of forces pulling the movement apart. One was a disagreement over the way to holiness. Ryle followed the traditional Puritan and Calvinist approach, and thus could not appreciate what seemed to him the new and truncated forms of holiness taught by those influenced by Robert Pearsall Smith and his book *Holiness through Faith* (1870).

In the eyes of his fellow evangelicals, Ryle's most controversial activity was his attendance at the church congress, which met annually in different cities, and which evolved into the church assembly (now the general synod). Here he boldly spoke for the Protestant principles of the national church. Defending his attendance he wrote: "I do not particularly like Congresses. I never expect them to do very much for the Church, or add much to our stock of knowledge. I have attended them purely as a matter of duty. I have advised others to attend them for the same reason. But one good thing I am convinced they do. They help churchmen to understand one another and in this way they are useful."[5] On a personal level this exposure to the comprehensiveness of the church prepared Ryle for the call which came to him at the age of sixty-four to become the first bishop of the new diocese of Liverpool, a growing city and the nation's busiest port.

Liverpool

Oxford University recognized its first-class-honors graduate of 1837 by conferring on Ryle the degree of doctor of divinity in May 1880. He was consecrated bishop in York Minster on June 11, 1880, and sat in his "cathedral" in Liverpool on July 1. In "A Pastoral Letter" issued that day he asked for the prayers of his clergy and urged them to preach the Word and administer the sacraments with faithfulness. And, bearing in mind that his new diocese had a variety not only of evangelical clergy, but also of High Church and Broad Church clergy as well, he wrote: "I ask you, in the last place, to assist me by cultivating and encouraging a spirit of brotherly love, charity and forbearance among Churchmen. In a fallen world like ours, and in a free country like England, it is vain to expect all men to see things alike and to interpret the language of the formularies precisely in the same way. Let us on no account be colourless Churchmen destitute of any distinct opinions. But so long as any brother walks loyally within the limits of the *Articles* and the *Prayer Book,* let us respect him and treat him courteously, even when we do not altogether agree with him." Ryle was not only calling upon his clergy, but was making a resolution as to how he himself would behave. It was not going to be easy, given the tensions caused by the growth of the Anglo-Catholic and ritualist movements.

Therefore one matter on which Ryle spent more time than he desired was his attempt to stop or to minimize the presence of ceremonialism and ritualism in the High Church parishes of the diocese. Towards the end of his episcopate he issued a pastoral letter on "lawlessness" in public worship (1897). Though only a few were being lawless, he was well aware of the spread of the ritualist movement in the national church. So he requested his clergy to abstain from the use of incense, of lighted candles on the communion table, of priestly vestments, of catechisms which taught Mariolatry, of prayers for

5. John Charles Ryle, *Principles for Churchmen* (Ipswich: William Hunt, 1884), 78.

the departed, of the reserved sacrament (retention of a portion of the elements either for adoration in the church or for administration to the sick), of auricular confession, and of the word *mass*.

In a more positive key, the bishop made the recruitment and use of "more living agents," ordained and lay, to be a priority. In his first charge to the diocese he described the great but desperately needy city of Liverpool and then went on to say: "If the Established Church of this country claims to be 'the Church of the people,' it is her bounden duty to see that no part of the people are left like sheep without a shepherd. If she claims to be a territorial and not a congregational church, she should never rest until there is neither a street, nor a lane, nor a house, nor a garret, nor a cellar, nor a family, which is not regularly looked after, and provided with the offer of means of grace by her officials." Accordingly, Ryle encouraged the building of mission halls and churches as well as the recruitment of caring and evangelical people for ministry.

Though he had little time to write material other than that required for his diocesan work, Ryle did raise contemporary theological issues in his charges. In 1893 he spoke about the higher criticism of the Old Testament and publicly rejected the current Germanic theories on the origin of the Pentateuch and the Psalter. This meant that he had taken a position very different from that of his brilliant son Herbert, who as a professor at Cambridge had adopted and commended such theories both in his teaching and in his writings. In fact, while staying with his father in Liverpool, Herbert once noted, "I write in a land where . . . German criticism has not obtained much foothold, even in the bookshelves." However, father and son remained good friends, especially so after the death of Mrs. Ryle in 1889.[6]

Of course as a bishop Ryle was obliged to take part in a host of meetings, but he sought to keep these to a minimum—often because of his age and poor health. Sometimes he missed important events such as the Lambeth Conference of 1888, which issued the so-called Chicago-Lambeth Quadrilateral as a basis for Christian reunion. He refused to accept it because he believed that it was not true to the Reformed character of the Church of England. In this refusal he was in a minority.

Old age and ill health caused Ryle to resign the bishopric in early 1900. In his farewell to the diocese he said: "Almost the last words of the great apostle to the Gentiles are before the eyes of my mind today: 'I have finished the course: the time of my departure is at hand.' After filling unexpectedly the office of your bishop for nearly twenty years, I am about to resign a post which years and failing health at the age of eighty-three told me I was not longer able to fill with advantage to the diocese or to the Church of England." After describing the approaching separation as a great wrench to his soul, he continued:

6. M. H. FitzGerald, *H. E. Ryle* (London, 1928), 131–34.

Before I leave you I ask you to accept a few parting words from an old minister who has had more than fifty-eight years' experience, and during that time has seen and heard many things. It is written: "Days should speak, and multitude of years should teach wisdom" (Job 32:7). Let me, then, charge all the clergy whom I am about to leave behind me never to neglect their preaching. Your districts and population may be comparatively small or large, but the minds of your people are thoroughly awake. They will not be content with dull, tame sermons; they want life, and light, and fire and love in the pulpit, as well as in the parish. Let them have plenty of it. Never forget that a lively, Christ-exalting minister will always have a church-going people."

Then in closing he urged all the people of God to "cling to the old Church of England . . . cling to its Bible, its Prayer Book and its Articles," to "consider the many poor and needy," and never to forget "that the principles of the Protestant Reformation made this country what she is, and let nothing ever tempt you to forsake them."[7]

Ryle died soon after his retirement. Speaking at the memorial service, Richard Hobson said: "A great man has just now fallen in Israel in the decease of the dear Bishop. Yes, he was great through the abounding grace of God. He was great in stature; great in mental power; great in spirituality; great as a preacher and expositor of God's most Holy Word; great in hospitality; great in winning souls to God; great as a writer of Gospel tracts; great as an author of works which will live long; great as a Bishop of the Reformed Evangelical Church of England of which he was a noble defender; great as first Bishop of Liverpool."[8] He was buried with his hand clasping his Bible in the same grave as that of his third wife. On his gravestone were inscribed two texts: "For by grace are ye saved through faith" (Eph. 2:8), and "I have fought the good fight, I have finished the course, I have kept the faith" (2 Tim. 4:7).

Biblical Theologian

Ryle's son Herbert, as we have seen, became a Cambridge professor and a bishop of the Church of England. Had John Charles stayed at Oxford in 1837 and taken up a fellowship, he too would have had an academic career. But in the providence of God, John Charles became a parish clergyman who used his brilliant mind and great energy both in pastoral work and in distilling the best of conservative theology and biblical interpretation for a hungry public.

Anyone who carefully looks over Ryle's seven-volume *Expository Thoughts on the Gospels,* and who is familiar with commentaries and theological movements, will recognize that beneath the simple style there is great learning. Since he was able to read Latin and Greek fluently, he made use of

7. Peter Toon and Michael Smout, *John Charles Ryle* (Swengel, Pa.: Reiner, 1976), 99–100.
8. M. G. Clark, *J. C. Ryle* (London: Church Book Room, 1947), 33.

many commentaries in the classical languages. Further, he consulted all the
major conservative commentaries written in English. However, he paid little
attention to the works of the new higher critics because they told him little
or nothing about the meaning of the sacred text.

It is instructive to read in the preface to the volumes on John the list of
commentaries Ryle consulted and his views of them and their usefulness. For
example, he wrote: "The Fathers appear to me greatly overrated, as commentators and expositors. Cyril and Chrysostom are far the most valuable of
them, in my judgment, on St. John."[9] By the time he published the three volumes on John he very clearly held to plenary verbal inspiration. Yet he did
not also hold that all parts of the Bible are equally important. That verses are
equally inspired does not mean of necessity that they are equally important.
In interpretation Ryle followed the historical-grammatical exegesis of traditional Protestantism, allowing for typology but not the fourfold pattern of
the medieval interpreters (the literal, moral, allegorical, and eschatological
senses).

Ryle brought the fruit of his biblical study, together with his reading of the
writings and the theology of the Protestant Reformers, the English and Scottish Puritans, and the evangelical leaders of the eighteenth century, to his expositions of the nature of the church, of baptism and the Lord's Supper, of
justification, of conversion, of faith, of practical doctrines, and of the pursuit
of holiness. This is seen very clearly in such books as *Knots Untied, Old
Paths,* and *Holiness,* as well as in the hundreds of tracts and sermons he published. He is still eminently readable today because of his simple style and his
commitment to applying the plain grammatical sense of Scripture to the
human heart. A perusal of his writings reveals Ryle's chief concerns and interests—evangelism and sound teaching, biblical exposition, the pursuit of
personal holiness, devotional material, Christian biography, together with
controversial doctrinal and liturgical issues (e.g., ritualism) in the Church of
England. What we miss in his writings are expositions of the very basic dog-
mas of Christianity—the holy, blessed, and undivided Trinity, and the person
and nature of our Lord Jesus Christ, who is one person with two natures.
Ryle took these for granted, and perhaps that was a mistake. This said, it may
be claimed that there is no finer exposition of a moderate biblical Calvinism
in accessible English than the writings of John Charles Ryle.

Primary Sources

Ryle, John Charles. *Expository Thoughts on the Gospels.* 7 vols. Ipswich: William
    Hunt, 1856–73. *Expository Thoughts on Matthew* (1856); *Expository Thoughts
    on Mark* (1857); *Expository Thoughts on Luke,* 2 vols. (1858–59); *Expository
    Thoughts on John,* 3 vols. (1873). 7 vols in 4. Grand Rapids: Baker, 1990.

9. John Charles Ryle, *Expository Thoughts on the Gospels,* 7 vols. in 4 (Grand Rapids: Baker,
1990), 3:x.

————. *Holiness: Its Nature, Hindrances, Difficulties, and Roots.* Ipswich: William Hunt, 1877. 2d ed., Grand Rapids: Baker, 1979.

————. *Home Truths: Miscellaneous Addresses and Tracts.* 8 vols. Ipswich: William Hunt, 1854–71.

————. *Knots Untied: Plain Statements on Disputed Points in Religion.* Ipswich: William Hunt, 1864.

————. *Old Paths: Plain Statements on Some of the Weightier Matters of Christianity.* Ipswich: William Hunt, 1877.

————. *Principles for Churchmen.* Ipswich: William Hunt, 1884.

————. *Shall We Go? Thoughts about Church Congresses.* Ipswich: William Hunt, 1878.

————. *What Do We Owe to the Reformation?* Ipswich: William Hunt, 1877.

Secondary Sources

Balleine, G. R. *A History of the Evangelical Party in the Church of England.* New ed. London: Church Book Room, 1951.

Bebbington, David W. *Evangelicalism in Modern Britain: A History from the 1730s to the 1980s.* London: Unwin Hyman/Routledge, 1989.

Clark, M. G. *J. C. Ryle.* London: Church Book Room, 1947.

Hylson-Smith, Kenneth. *Evangelicals in the Church of England, 1734–1984.* Edinburgh: T. and T. Clark, 1989.

Loane, Marcus L. *John Charles Ryle, 1816–1900.* London: Hodder and Stoughton, 1983.

Ryle, John Charles. *A Self-Portrait: A Partial Autobiography.* Edited by Peter Toon. Swengel, Pa.: Reiner, 1976.

Toon, Peter, and Michael Smout. *John Charles Ryle: Evangelical Bishop.* Swengel, Pa.: Reiner, 1976.

William Henry Green

Marion Ann Taylor

A very learned Old Testament scholar at Princeton Theological Seminary, William Henry Green has long been remembered as the great naysayer against radical higher criticism and as a strong defender of traditional views about the authorship, integrity, and inspiration of the Old Testament. Green was born on January 27, 1825, in Groveville, a small town near Princeton, New Jersey.[1] Brought up in a family which had long-standing ties to the Presbyterian church, the academic institutions in Princeton, and the judiciary of the state of New Jersey, Green was given a very fine education. At the age of ten, he was sent to live with his maternal grandparents in Easton, Pennsylvania, so that he could attend a renowned classical school. Two years later, he entered Lafayette College. In 1840, at the age of fifteen, Green graduated with honors. He then worked as a tutor in mathematics at Lafayette before beginning his first year of theological studies at Princeton Theological Seminary in 1842. Green interrupted his theological education to assume the position of adjunct professor of mathematics at Lafayette for the academic year 1843–44. In 1846, upon the completion of two years of further study at the seminary, Green accepted a scholarship for a year of graduate study at the seminary and the offer of a teaching assistantship in Hebrew.

Green's appointment as an instructor in Hebrew at the age of twenty-one marked the beginning of his lifelong teaching career at Princeton Seminary. During the second and third years of his appointment, he gained some practical experience by working as a supply minister for the First and Second

---

1. Although a full biography of Green has not been written, much information about his life can be gleaned both from the various addresses given in 1896 to celebrate the fiftieth anniversary of his appointment to a teaching position at Princeton and from the numerous notices and memorials of his death in 1900. See especially *Celebration of the Fiftieth Anniversary of the Appointment of Professor William Henry Green as an Instructor in Princeton Theological Seminary* (New York: Scribner, 1896); John D. Davis, *The Life and Work of William Henry Green* (Philadelphia: MacCalla, 1900); idem, "Professor William Henry Green," *Biblical World* 15.6 (June 1900): 406–13; idem, "William Henry Green," *Presbyterian and Reformed Review* 11, no. 43 (July 1900): 377–96; Marion Ann Taylor, *The Old Testament in the Old Princeton School (1812–1929)* (San Francisco: Mellen Research University Press, 1992), 167–251. Also helpful is the "Scrapbook of Obituary Notices, Condolences, etc.," presented by Dr. and Mrs. P. M. Stimson, and located in the archives of Princeton Theological Seminary.

Presbyterian Churches of Princeton. In 1849, he accepted a call from the Central Presbyterian Church of Philadelphia, where he gained the reputation of being "a laborious, faithful and sympathetic pastor."[2] Then in 1851 the General Assembly of the Presbyterian Church elected Green to the chair of biblical and Oriental literature at Princeton Seminary, a position which he held until his death on February 10, 1900.[3]

Green's education at Princeton Seminary under the tutelage of Archibald Alexander, Samuel Miller, and Charles Hodge had a profound influence on him. But it was the brilliant yet eccentric Joseph Addison Alexander who became Green's personal mentor.[4] Alexander, the son of the seminary's founder Archibald Alexander, had received his education at Princeton under the direction of his father and Charles Hodge. He then studied in Europe, where he was especially drawn to the work of the critically informed yet orthodox German confessionalists E. W. Hengstenberg and Friedrich A. G. Tholuck. The training which Green received from Alexander in Hebrew, comparative Semitic languages and Old Testament history, literature, and interpretation was the finest available in the United States at that time. Then in 1858 Green traveled to Germany to study under Alexander's mentor Hengstenberg. Alexander's influence on Green can be traced throughout his career, although as Green matured and as the issues in the field of Old Testament studies changed, he developed his own areas of expertise and a distinctive role in both the church and the academy.

When Green was inaugurated as professor of biblical and Oriental literature in 1851, it was already recognized that a battle over the Scriptures was impending, a battle which would be fought on the grounds covered by Green's department.[5] The charge given to Green at his inauguration centered on his responsibilities for fighting the intellectual battles of the church and the seminary. Green was directed to follow the model of Christian scholarship established by his predecessors. He was to use the beneficial aspects of modern critical studies, to take a leadership role in the battle against such enemies as "traditionists" and "advocates of a mere nominal inspiration," and to train his students to do the same.[6] Green faithfully carried out these directives in the classroom, in the pulpit, in public debates, and in the articles

2. Davis, "William Henry Green," 379.
3. This chair had previously been held by Joseph Addison Alexander, who was at this time appointed professor of biblical and ecclesiastical history. In 1859, when Alexander decided to teach New Testament instead of history, Green's title was changed to the Helena Professor of Oriental and Old Testament Literature.
4. For a biography of Alexander see Henry Carrington Alexander, *The Life of Joseph Addison Alexander, D.D.*, 2 vols. (New York: Scribner, 1870). That Alexander read Hebrew when he was ten and the Koran in Arabic at twelve and would eventually master more than twenty languages attests to both his brilliance and his eccentricity.
5. See *Discourses at the Inauguration of the Rev. William Henry Green as Professor of Biblical and Oriental Literature in the Theological Seminary at Princeton, N.J.* (Philadelphia: C. Sherman, 1851). It is noteworthy that Green chose the authority of the Scriptures as the subject of his inaugural speech. His convictions about the nature of the Scriptures undergirded everything he did.
6. Ibid., 22–27.

and books he wrote for academic and popular audiences throughout his life.[7]

Among the most significant evidences of Green's contributions to biblical studies are his influence on his students (who numbered more than three thousand) and the many publications which developed out of his work in the classroom. As a teacher of Hebrew and Oriental languages, Green was very exacting yet understanding. His students gained a thorough knowledge of the Hebrew language and were influenced by his passion for Old Testament texts, his confidence that linguistic studies would support the Princetonian confessional stance, and his commitment to discipline and hard work. Green's particularly keen students also learned Aramaic, Syriac, Arabic, and Sanskrit. At the celebration of the fiftieth anniversary of his appointment as a teaching assistant at the seminary, Green was lauded as "the Hebrew teacher of his generation . . . in fact, the most influential Hebrew teacher of his time among English-speaking men."[8] Students at Princeton and far beyond benefited from his two Hebrew grammars (1861, 1866) and his *Hebrew Chrestomathy* (1863). Green's work in Hebrew grammar, especially in the early sixties, represented a major contribution to the field of Hebrew studies in America. The later revisions of his grammars did not have the same impact on the discipline.[9]

General Introduction to the Old Testament

Green's teaching responsibilities included courses in general introduction, which dealt with the canon and text of Scripture and hermeneutics. Questions about the canon were of special interest to Green throughout his career in view of the new and ever-changing critical issues that challenged the traditional understanding of the canon as an inspired and authoritative collection of books. In 1898 Green published his *General Introduction to the Old Testament: The Canon,* which treated the topic "not theologically, but historically."[10] Curiously, Green began the volume with a "History of Introduction to the Old Testament," a brief sketch extracted from an unpublished lecture of J. A. Alexander from 1843. Although this decision suited Green's historical predilections, it set an extremely negative tone for the book.[11]

7. Green wrote eleven books and more than two hundred articles. Some of his books went through a number of editions and revisions, and some were translated into other languages. For a list of Green's published writings from 1846 to 1896 see Joseph H. Dulles, "Bibliography," in *Celebration,* 181–93.
8. James F. McCurdy, "Green's Contribution to Semitic Scholarship," in *Celebration,* 33.
9. Commenting on the 1888 revision of Green's 1861 grammar, John D. Davis said: "The revision is an improvement on the first edition, but the original work is the greater of the two. In several respects it stood ahead of all the Hebrew grammars of the day, and through it he distinctly advanced a forward movement in the grammatical exhibition of the Hebrew language" ("William Henry Green," in *Presbyterian and Reformed Review* 11 [1900]: 385).
10. William Henry Green, *General Introduction to the Old Testament: The Canon* (New York: Scribner, 1898), vii.
11. T. Witton Davies, review of *General Introduction to the Old Testament: The Canon,* by William Henry Green, *American Journal of Theology* 3 (1899): 765, writes: "Had Dr. Alexander written in 1898, and not in 1843, he would not have described German exegesis as having an infidel character, nor would he have spoken of the general principles of unbelief as taught with great skill and talent by De Wette."

Green followed the approach of what he referred to as the Christian or believing school of such scholars as E. W. Hengstenberg, C. F. Keil, Johann Kurtz, and Karl Noesgen. He defended this position against the views of the extreme critical school of scholars like Eduard Reuss, Julius Wellhausen, and Abraham Kuenen, and of the more moderate critical school of scholars like Friedrich Bleek, Johann Stähelin, Hermann Strack, Eduard König, William Robertson Smith, and S. R. Driver.[12] On the issue of the formation of the canon, for example, Green argued against the views of scholars like Heinrich Ewald, August Dillmann, and Johann Eichhorn, who rejected the traditional consensus that the books in the Old Testament were written by inspired writers.[13] Thus he declared: "It is not the religious profit derived from these books which led to their admission into the canon, but it is their being inspired of God to guide the faith and practice of the church—in other words, their canonicity—which makes them profitable to the religious life."[14]

Similarly, Green attempted to show fallacies in the various critical arguments for the late dating of such books as Chronicles, Nehemiah, and Daniel. For example, in response to the growing support for a second-century dating of Daniel, Green agreed with Franz Delitzsch that the principal argument mounted against the authenticity of the Book of Daniel centered on the issues of miracles and predictive prophecy. Then he outlined and attempted to respond to Driver's arguments for a late dating based on literary, linguistic, and historical rather than dogmatic grounds. Green remained unconvinced by Driver. He was also frustrated by Driver's mediating position which, while adopting the critical conclusions for a second-century dating, at the same time held the book to have inspired and revelatory character.[15] For Green, the options seemed much more clear-cut: one either embraced the critical methodology and its presuppositions wholeheartedly, or else one held on tenaciously to a traditional understanding of the biblical texts as the inspired and revealed Word of God.

Green's volume on the canon was lauded by many for its timely, clear, and learned defense of the traditional views on the canon of the Old Testament.[16] Others deemed Green's work to be outmoded and inadequate.[17] Charles Briggs, however, labeled Green's position a highly dangerous "modern

---

12. Green, *Canon*, vii–viii, 4–5.

13. Ibid., 26–36.

14. Ibid., 31.

15. Ibid., 73: "It is surely very inconsistent in those who admit the reality of a divinely inspired foresight of the future, to prescribe in advance the limits and bounds within which alone this may be exercised, and to refuse to acknowledge the genuineness of any prophecy which exceeds the restrictions that they have arbitrarily imposed upon it."

16. E.g., George C. M. Douglas, review of *General Introduction to the Old Testament: The Canon*, by William Henry Green, *Presbyterian and Reformed Review* 10 (1899): 334–37.

17. In the judgment of Edward Curtis (review of *General Introduction to the Old Testament: The Canon*, by William Henry Green, *Biblical World* 14 [1899]: 459), "to one who believes on dogmatic grounds, with Professor Green, in the Mosaic authorship of the Pentateuch and the historical inerrancy of the Old Testament, his work may seem a cogent presentation of his subject, but to all others it will reveal the utter inadequacy of the old traditional views historically to explain biblical facts."

American theory of canonicity" which had neither "the stamp of antiquity upon it," nor "ecclesiastical authority behind it," and yet made "loud claims of orthodoxy itself."[18] Briggs felt that Green's position "forced American Presbyterianism [into] a serious and unreasonable war against the higher criticism."[19] Briggs's insight that Green's book had significance far beyond academic questions regarding the canon was undoubtedly true, since it also dealt with timely issues relating to the use of higher criticism in the church.

In 1899 Green published a sequel, his *General Introduction to the Old Testament: The Text.*[20] Like his book on the canon, the sequel presents a scholarly, conservative assessment of the subject matter. The book evaluates both carefully and positively the character and condition of the text of the Old Testament.[21] Specifically, Green sets forth the conservative approach which he had advocated as chairman of the American Bible Revision Committee: "The Masoretic text is on the whole vastly superior to [the Septuagint], and should not be corrected by it. . . . In the great majority of cases where a divergence exists, the presumption is strongly in favor of the correctness of the Hebrew and against the Septuagint."[22] Green's preference for the Hebrew text was opposed by text critics who placed more confidence in the Septuagint text. Thus Briggs charged Green and his school as representing "the same spirit of hostility" toward textual criticism that Keil had shown in Germany.[23]

Green also addresses various critical issues relating to the text. His approach and position become evident through his engagement with the critics. For example, against those who, on the assumption that the Hebrew language changed over the course of eight centuries, argue that the Pentateuch was late, Green contends that all Semitic languages had a fixed and stationary quality, that the Israelites were isolated and relatively stable during this period, that their language was fixed through the influence of the books of Moses, and that there are not enough data to trace the developments in Hebrew from the time of Moses.[24] More specifically, Green admits that "at first glance" the attempt of Friedrich Giesebrecht and others to show the lateness of the language of the supposed priestly source (P) of the Pentateuch seems plausible and logical; there are, however, serious flaws in the methodology and argumentation.[25] Green's engagement with the critics demonstrates his

---

18. Charles Augustus Briggs, *General Introduction to the Study of Holy Scripture* (New York: Scribner, 1899), 158.

19. Ibid., 159.

20. William Henry Green, *General Introduction to the Old Testament: The Text* (New York: Scribner, 1899).

21. While Green's positive attitude toward the Old Testament text is evident throughout, he avoids discussing whether the original autographs were inerrant, as had been proposed by his colleagues A. A. Hodge and B. B. Warfield, "Inspiration," *Presbyterian Review* 2 (1881): 225–60.

22. Green, *Text*, 174.

23. Briggs, *General Introduction*, 229.

24. Green, *Text*, 22–24.

25. Ibid., 29.

genuine interest in new proposals, his penchant for history and questions relating to the history of the Hebrew language, and his tendency to attack specific problems by using general arguments against the presuppositions or methodology of historical criticism.

Special Introduction to the Old Testament

Green's courses in special introduction examined the authorship, integrity, and structure of the individual Old Testament books as well as questions relating to hermeneutics. Green's extant lectures on individual books are most significant in that they show his commitment to a supernaturalist approach to the Old Testament texts, his remarkable sensitivity to the literary shape and organic structure of the books, his historical predilections, and his constant engagement with new critical ideas. For example, Green's lectures on Job (as well as his popular book on Job) show his awareness of the artistic features and literary shape of the book.[26] Using a comprehensive hermeneutical or literary approach (as opposed to a fragmentary approach) to the Book of Job, he examined its plan and structure and considered it in its fuller canonical context.[27] Although Green's work on Job was not polemical, he realized that a comprehensive approach which presupposes the unity of a book is an effective tool for staying the hand of the critic. As the battle over the Scriptures intensified, Green made more use of the comprehensive approach as a defensive tool.

Green's lectures and unpublished notes on individual Old Testament books also reveal his human side as he honestly grapples with the methods and results of modern critical and historical studies. An example of a personal struggle with the evidence that forced him to change his position on authorship and dating is found in an 1884 lecture on Ecclesiastes. Following a systematic refutation of the various arguments that had been mounted against the traditional view of Solomonic authorship, Green briefly addresses the issue of language and style: "It is alleged, and the fact seems to be, that the Hebrew of this book is so Aramean that it must belong to a period later than Solomon; and the style is unlike that of any other of the writings of Solomon."[28] Green does not go into details, but refers his students to the writings of Delitzsch, Hengstenberg, and Keil, who flesh out the arguments against Solomonic authorship that are based on language and style. He then suggests a possible answer to the problem of the presence of Aramean words and the diversity of style, but concludes the lecture with the

26. See *Syllabus of Dr. Green's Lectures: Special Literature of the Old Testament* (Princeton, N.J.: Blanchard's Print, 1866); William Henry Green, *The Argument of the Book of Job Unfolded* (New York: Carter, 1874).
27. Green, *Job*, 1–2.
28. William Henry Green, *Old Testament Literature: Lectures on the Poetical Books of the Old Testament: Psalms, Song of Solomon, Proverbs, Ecclesiastes*, ed. G. F. Greene and D. W. Woods (Trenton: Edwin Fitzgeorge, 1884), 51.

honest admission that he cannot see how the argument from language can adequately be met: "We conclude, therefore, that it is decisive. We agree with Delitzsch that if the book is Solomon's we must give up everything like a history of the Hebrew language. This is the uniform opinion of scholars at the present time."[29] A student's candid notation that "Dr. Green does not see how to answer objections from style against this being by Solomon"[30] and Green's use of words like "puzzling" and "exceedingly perplexing" to describe the Book of Ecclesiastes suggest that Green's shift from his earlier traditional position regarding Solomonic authorship was difficult.[31] However, in spite of the shift, Green still seems to tie the interpretation of the book to the person and life of Solomon.[32]

In later discussion of the dating of the Book of Ecclesiastes, Green strongly implies that Solomon did not write the book. Against Driver's late-third- or early-second-century dating, he argues that the book may have been composed in the century after the Babylonian exile.[33] Green's dating accords both with the position of the early Jewish historian Josephus, who associated the closing of the canon with the end of Artaxerxes Longimanus's reign, and with the traditional Jewish consensus that after the last prophet, Malachi, the Holy Spirit departed from Israel.[34] Green's willingness to change his position on the issue of the authorship of Ecclesiastes shows that there were times when his intellectual attraction to the scholarly consensus overruled his deep sense of loyalty to tradition and his general conservatism, although this was not generally the case.

The Pentateuch and Higher Criticism

Green's publications and lecture notes indicate a very early interest in battling over fundamental issues like the integrity and Mosaic authorship of the Pentateuch.[35] His first serious defense of the Pentateuch was *The Pentateuch Vindicated from the Aspersions of Bishop Colenso* (1863). Green's analysis and critique of each of Colenso's aspersions against the integrity of the Old Testament were logical, commonsensical, and filled with sarcasm. His apologetic defense of the Pentateuch was effective. During the sixties and seventies, Green kept abreast of the latest developments in Continental scholarship and continued to publish reviews of important books. However, it was not

---

29. Ibid., 56.
30. Ibid., 55.
31. Ibid., 49, 51.
32. See, e.g., ibid., 61, where in Green's analysis of the structure of Ecclesiastes his heading for chapters 1 and 2 is "Argument from Solomon's own experience." Cf. Green's earlier article "The Scope and Plan of the Book of Ecclesiastes," *Biblical Repertory and Princeton Review* 29 (1857): 419–40, where he assumes Solomonic authorship.
33. Green, *Canon*, 53–55.
34. Ibid., 78.
35. See, e.g., William Henry Green, review of *History of the Old Covenant*, vol. 1, by Johann H. Kurtz, *Biblical Repertory and Princeton Review* 23 (1851): 451–86.

until the last decade of the nineteenth century, when the controversies over higher criticism intensified dramatically and moved to the American shores, that Green took up a frontline position in the battle over the higher criticism and emerged as "the Nestor of the conservative Old Testament School," an "Athanasius against the world."[36]

During this period of heightened warfare, Green recruited and trained students to defend the integrity of the Old Testament against its many critics. In the church, he battled over the issue of the appropriateness of the use of higher criticism. His engagements with Briggs, whom Green increasingly viewed as an enemy within the ranks, peaked with the infamous Briggs case, which did much to heighten awareness of historical criticism and the battle over the Pentateuch.[37] Moreover, in both academic and popular presses, Green continuously and extensively battled with the proponents of radical and moderate higher criticism, whom he viewed as enemies of the traditional understanding of the Scriptures. These people included, most notably, Robertson Smith, Kuenen, Wellhausen, Driver, Briggs, and William Rainey Harper.[38]

Green's 1895 publication, *The Higher Criticism of the Pentateuch,* was his final attempt to defend what he felt was the unanimous testimony of inspired and uninspired tradition regarding the unity and Mosaic authorship of the Pentateuch. The book was not a new work, but a compilation of addresses and essays that over a thirty-year period had attempted to prove the traditional understanding and to disprove all other views. Chapter 1 is a slightly abridged form of an article published originally in 1865 under the title "The Structure of the Old Testament."[39] Similarly, chapter 2, "The Plan and Contents of the Pentateuch," is an adaptation of a lecture written in 1866 for his course in special introduction. As early as 1866, Green had taught that the theme of the Pentateuch is "the establishing of Israel as the people of God."[40] In the battle in 1895 he used this unifying theme in combination with evidence of a unifying plan to argue for the unity of the composition of the Pentateuch as a whole. This overarching unity, he writes, "creates a presumption that these books are, as they have been traditionally believed to be, the prod-

---

36. Such laudatory titles were common at the celebration of the fiftieth anniversary of Green's appointment as a teaching assistant at Princeton Seminary (1846); see *Celebration.*

37. See Lefferts A. Loetscher, *The Broadening Church: A Study of Theological Issues in the Presbyterian Church since 1869* (Philadelphia: University of Pennsylvania Press, 1954), 29–37; C. R. Jeschke, "The Briggs Case: The Focus of a Study of Nineteenth Century Presbyterian History" (Ph.D. diss., University of Chicago, 1966); Mark S. Massa, *Charles Augustus Briggs and the Crisis of Historical Criticism* (Minneapolis: Augsburg Fortress, 1990).

38. For an account of Green's battles with the various critics see Taylor, *Old Testament,* 225–38.

39. William Henry Green, "The Structure of the Old Testament," *Biblical Repertory and Princeton Review* 37 (1865): 161–87. Green had also lectured on this subject in his course in special introduction (*Syllabus,* 5). There is no indication in his *Higher Criticism of the Pentateuch* (New York: Scribner, 1895) that any of its portions had been published earlier.

40. Green, *Syllabus,* 10. In 1895 Green wrote essentially the same thing: "The Pentateuch has one theme, which is consistently pursued from first to last, viz., the theocracy in Israel, or the establishment of Israel to be the people of God" (*Higher Criticism,* 19).

uct of a single writer; and the presumption thus afforded must stand unless
satisfactory proof can be brought to the contrary."[41]

In the third chapter Green begins his full defense of Mosaic authorship
with a discussion about the nature of the Pentateuch.[42] In view of its importance as a historical record, the contents of which stand "in intimate relation
to the problems of physical and ethnological science, to history and archaeology and religious faith," the critical question is whether or not the Pentateuch is "a veritable, trustworthy record."[43] Green ties this question into
the issue of Mosaic authorship. Although the credibility of the Pentateuch is
"not absolutely dependent upon its Mosaic authorship," for all intents and
purposes it is, since a better case can be made for verity if the authorship of
the Pentateuch is Mosaic: "If it was written by Moses, then the history of the
Mosaic age was recorded by a contemporary and eyewitness . . . and it must
be confessed that there is in this fact the highest possible guaranty of the accuracy and truthfulness of the whole."[44] In his defense of Mosaic authorship,
Green cites the following evidence: (1) support from tradition and the New
Testament (those who accept Jesus "as an infallible teacher" will, like him,
assume Mosaic authorship); (2) "the firm faith of Israel" as attested to in the
Old Testament; (3) the testimony in the pentateuchal legislation (and by extension of the narrative) that it was written by Moses; (4) the style, language,
and nature of the laws themselves; (5) direct and indirect allusions in the rest
of the Old Testament; (6) the recognition of the Pentateuch's authority by the
northern kingdom; (7) the elementary character of the Pentateuch's teachings; and (8) the Pentateuch's familiarity with Egyptian words and customs.[45]

Although the internal evidence alone convinced Green that Moses wrote
the Pentateuch, he also recognized the serious need to counter the criticisms
that had been leveled against this position. Thus he presented a comprehen-

41. Green, *Higher Criticism,* 29–30. See also Green's defense of the unity of the Book of Genesis
(*The Unity of the Book of Genesis* [New York: Scribner, 1895], 1–3).

42. The first part of this chapter was given as an address to the Sixth Annual Interdenominational
Seaside Bible Conference, August 1893, and published as "The Mosaic Origin of the Pentateuch," in
Anti–Higher Criticism, or Testimony to the Infallibility of the Bible, ed. L. W. Munhall (New York:
Hunt and Eaton, 1894), 71–85. For earlier examples of Green's work in this area see *Syllabus,* 6, 8,
and "Was Moses the Author of the Pentateuch?" in *Schaff-Herzog Encyclopedia of Religious Knowl-
edge,* 3 vols. (New York: Funk and Wagnalls, 1883), 3:1796–1801.

43. Green, *Higher Criticism,* 31. This was the fundamental question for Green. In a sermon on
higher criticism he stated: "The actual issue . . . is vital and fundamental. It is a question of the historical truth and the Divine authority of the Old Testament from beginning to end. Are the statements
trustworthy? Can they be depended upon, not in minor and unessential matters, but in the great body
of its contents? And has it any just claim to be regarded as really the Word of God?" (cited by N. L.
Walker, "Professor Green on the Pentateuch," *Expository Times* 3 [1891–92]: 316).

44. Green, *Higher Criticism,* 32. Along the same line Green disagrees with those who regard the
issue of Mosaic authorship as of no importance: "If you detach these books from Moses as their author, you thereby detach them likewise from the endorsement of our Lord and His apostles. They bid
us accept what Moses taught and what Moses commanded. If these are not the teachings of Moses,
and these commands are not his, their sanction is withdrawn" (cited by Walker, "Green on the Pentateuch," 316).

45. Green, *Higher Criticism,* 32–46.

sive analysis and refutation of a variety of these criticisms: (1) the presence of anachronisms, inconsistencies, and incongruities in the text; (2) evidence of composite origin; (3) evidence of distinction and development in the law codes; and (4) evidence for the late dating of laws.[46] In his discussion of the earliest objections to the tradition of Mosaic authorship, which were based on anachronisms, Green made one of his few concessions to his critics: "It is far easier to assume that some slight additions may here and there have been made to the text, than to set aside the multiplied and invincible proofs that the Pentateuch was the production of Moses."[47]

Green's treatment of the more difficult issue of evidence of a composite authorship was quite detailed. He countered the critics point by point with arguments that he had rehearsed many times before. In dealing with this issue his primary interest was not the prehistory of the text. For him the critical matter was the choice between Mosaic authorship, "whatever may have been the sources from which the materials were taken," and composite authorship.[48]

Green's treatment of the classic evidence for composite authorship (i.e., the alternation of divine names, parallel passages, and diversity in diction, style, and ideas) focused on the critical method itself rather than on the interpretation of data. For example, he parodied the critical method by applying to stories such as the prodigal son and the good Samaritan a critical analysis along the lines of Charles Mead's dissection of the Book of Romans into four sources on the basis of differences in diction, style, and doctrine.[49] On the basis of the evident absurdity of these illustrations, Green concluded that "no dependence can be placed upon a process that leads to palpably erroneous conclusions in other cases. An argument that will prove everything, proves nothing."[50]

Green included a separate chapter on the developmental hypothesis regarding Israelite law. Again his critique focused on the assumptions and arguments that were used to support the critical position. Basic to Green's aversion to the developmental hypothesis was his belief that it not only goes against "explicit statements of the Pentateuch itself, but is utterly inconsistent with the history on which it is professedly based."[51] Green concluded

---

46. See also Green's defense of Mosaic authorship and his critique of the documentary hypothesis in *Unity of the Book of Genesis.*

47. Green, *Higher Criticism*, 51–52.

48. Ibid., 61.

49. See ibid., 118–30, for other examples of the "precarious character of the methods and results of this style of subjective criticism." See also William Henry Green, review of *Romans Dissected,* by Charles Marsh Mead [E. D. McRealsham, pseud.], *Presbyterian and Reformed Review* 2 (1891): 679–80; idem, *Unity of the Book of Genesis,* 7–9.

50. Green, *Higher Criticism,* 125.

51. Ibid., 156. Parts of this chapter had been presented at the Sixth Annual Interdenominational Seaside Bible Conference, August 1893, and published as "The Mosaic Origin of the Pentateuch," in *Anti-Higher Criticism,* ed. Munhall, 86–95. In his treatise *The Hebrew Feasts in Their Relation to Recent Critical Hypotheses concerning the Pentateuch* (New York: Carter, 1885), Green had attempted to come to terms with one specific aspect of the developmental theory.

that there is "no good reason" for abandoning the biblical statements regarding the Mosaic authorship of the law.[52]

As we noted earlier, in *The Higher Criticism of the Pentateuch* Green added little to the painstaking efforts he had already made in defense of the Mosaic authorship of the Pentateuch and in opposition to higher-critical reconstructions. And yet one senses that for Green the book represented a crystalization of his position in the 1890s. In the final chapter, Green gets to the heart of his personal polemic against higher criticism. First, he claims that the pernicious critical theories contain a bias against the supernatural which manifests itself in the rejection of "the reality of miracles and prophecy and immediate divine revelation in their genuine and evangelical sense."[53] Second, since biblical religion is necessarily a historical religion based on palpable facts, the documentary hypothesis is untenable.[54] Third, he points out that modern pentateuchal criticism undermines the theological unity of the Testaments. Fourth, he argues against the more moderate critics like Delitzsch, Robertson Smith, and Briggs that there is no middle ground on the issue of Mosaic authorship. Mosaic authorship and historical veracity—and by extension, inspiration and all of the other doctrines of faith—were inextricably linked for Green. His final word to those who professed faith and higher criticism was an invitation to "revise their own ill-judged alliance with the enemies of evangelical truth" and reconsider whether "Christ's view of the Old Testament may not, after all, be the true view."[55]

In 1895 Green published *The Unity of the Book of Genesis,* in which he argues similarly that the literary unity of the book attests to unity of authorship. While much of Green's volume consists of a rehearsal and critique of the critics' diachronic approach to consecutive sections of Genesis, his arguments for the unity of the book based on his sensitive observations about its present shape and meaning are significant, for they adumbrate an approach to the study of Genesis which has only recently been discovered by postcritical Old Testament scholars. Concerning the literary function of the *tôlĕdôt* formula ("these are the generations of") in Genesis 2:4a, Green cogently ob-

---

52. Green, *Higher Criticism,* 144.

53. Ibid., 157. Later on (p. 166) Green suggests that the critics have a passion to eliminate the supernatural: "While the discussion seemingly turns on words and phrases and the supposed peculiarities of individual writers, the bent of the whole thing is to rivet the conclusion which the framers of the hypothesis have tacitly though steadily contemplated, a conclusion irrefragable on their philosophical principles, viz., that the supernatural must be eliminated from the Scriptures."

54. Ibid., 163. In his *Unity of the Book of Genesis* Green gives detailed consideration to critical reconstructions of patriarchal history. In his disapprobation of this enterprise, he stands in continuity with his mentor J. A. Alexander, whom he quotes at length on the subject. For instance, Alexander had said in an unpublished lecture: "It is plain that this ingenious child's play could be carried on *ad infinitum;* and this very facility deprives it of all force as proof that the imaginary process was a real one, or that the stream of history flows backward from its estuary to its source. In spite of all sophistical refinements the common sense of mankind will still cleave to the lesson taught by all analogy, that primitive history must deal with individualities, and that philosophical myths can only be obtained from them by generalizing combination" (cited by Green, *Unity of the Book of Genesis,* 565 n. 1).

55. Green, *Higher Criticism,* 178.

serves that, functioning as a heading for the section which follows, "it plainly declares the subject of [that] section to be not the creation of the world, but the formation of man and the first stage of human history."[56] Green argues further that Genesis 2 is not to be regarded as a parallel account of creation that came about through the arbitrary juxtaposition of the J (Yahwist source) account of creation and the P (priestly source) account in chapter 1, but rather as a supplement and "natural sequence . . . the next act, so to speak, in the divine drama . . . of the unfolding plan of God."[57] In this way Green uses his comprehensive hermeneutical approach to defend the unity of the book and Mosaic authorship.

Green's *Unity of the Book of Genesis* together with his classic *Higher Criticism of the Pentateuch* constitutes his ultimate defense of the unity and Mosaic authorship of Genesis and of the Pentateuch. Green's defense, particularly his arguments against the documentary hypothesis and the presuppositions undergirding the entire critical enterprise, has never been superseded in the eyes of those who continue to share many of his theological presuppositions and to promote his negative assessment of classic higher criticism. Indeed many of his spiritual heirs have either simply used Green's works or updated and reformulated his views.[58] Unfortunately, because Green's genuine insights into the literary shape of the text were tied inextricably into his highly polemical apologetic regarding the historicity and Mosaic authorship of the Pentateuch, they were lost to many of his generation. Those who rejected his conclusion that literary intentionality can be explained only through single authorship and historicity also ignored his insights into the literary nature of the texts. On the other hand, those who were attracted to his apologetic defense were primarily interested in his conclusions, not his mode of argumentation.

The Reaction to Green's Publications

Responses to Green's 1895 publications were mixed. One reviewer of *The Higher Criticism of the Pentateuch* described Green as a warrior: "The Pentateuch and nothing but the Pentateuch—that is Dr. Green's battle-flag."[59] Another spoke of his book as a work of "the chief of staff of the army of

---

56. Green, *Unity of the Book of Genesis*, 14. Green also suggests that the genealogies point to the "main design" of the book, which is "to trace the line of descent of the chosen race from the beginning to the point where it was ready to expand to a great nation, whose future organization was already foreshadowed, its tribes being represented in the twelve sons of Jacob, and its tribal divisions in their children" (p. 2). Cf. Brevard Childs's discussion of the canonical function of the *tôlĕdôt* formulae in Genesis (*Introduction to the Old Testament as Scripture* [Philadelphia: Fortress, 1979], 145–50, 152–53).

57. Green, *Unity of the Book of Genesis*, 15–16.

58. In the preface to the reprint of Green's *Unity of the Book of Genesis* (Grand Rapids: Baker, 1979), Ronald Youngblood characterizes himself and other evangelicals of like mind as "we who are his spiritual heirs and who find his views eminently compatible with our own" (p. viii).

59. John A. Selbie, review of *The Higher Criticism of the Pentateuch*, by William Henry Green, *Expository Times* 7 (1895–96): 227.

American Hebraists and Old Testament students . . . a survey of the whole field of battle, of the points of attack and defense," and a guide to "the only roads by which the victory is won."[60] To "all those in America who believe the Bible to be God's Word," the same reviewer commended Green as "a champion, a leader, whose reverent spirit towards God and His Word, whose learning and knowledge and strong common sense, whose fairness to opponents and clear perception of the impregnable rock, abundantly qualify him for that position."[61] Green's work as an apologist was appreciated by many in the church who felt confused and somewhat overwhelmed by the information that they had about higher criticism. Many in the church looked to Green for answers.[62]

However, Green was certainly not without critics. The caustic interchange in the *Expository Times* between a German reviewer, Carl Steuernagel, and Dunlop Moore, a supporter of Green, is quite revealing.[63] Steuernagel wrote disparagingly that "there is now but one Old Testament scholar who rejects the results of criticism."[64] He also charged Green with superficiality, gross misrepresentation of the critical position and of the motives of critics, failure to recognize the human factor in the development of Scripture, lest the possibility of human error be introduced, and poor scholarship.[65] Both Steuernagel and Green recognized that their differences pointed to a serious impasse in terms of scholarly method. Steuernagel's expression of it was quite accurate: "On this point, moreover [namely, that Green used specious reasoning to explain the alternations in the divine names in the Pentateuch], the possibility of coming to an understanding is quite excluded. One who rejects criticism as a very principle will find a way satisfactory to himself over every difficulty; one, on the other hand, who in principle accepts the critical position, needs no guidance from me in order to discover the inadequacy of Moore's explanations."[66] If Green had responded to Steuernagel, he would probably have defended the hermeneutical method of harmonization, which he felt was in accord with the principles of common sense. Addressing this very issue in 1895, Green had stated:

60. Howard Osgood, review of *The Higher Criticism of the Pentateuch,* by William Henry Green, *Presbyterian and Reformed Review* 7 (1896): 134.
61. Ibid., 136.
62. Edwin C. Bissell, "The Pentateuchal Discussion—Present Outlook," *Homiletic Review* 22 (1891): 201–2, notes that anyone desiring "to see how the arguments usually urged in favor of this theory are met in detail, at once with the utmost candor and clearness and with the most decisive results, should consult the series of papers now appearing in *Hebraica* from the pen of Professor Green, of Princeton."
63. John A. Selbie, the editor of the *Expository Times,* initially expressed Steuernagel's views; later Steuernagel himself defended the charges that he had made against Green and that Moore had judged to be unfair.
64. See Selbie, review of *Higher Criticism,* 227.
65. See Dunlop Moore, "Critics and Apologists," *Presbyterian and Reformed Review* 10 (1899): 533–42; Carl Steuernagel, "Dr. W. H. Green of Princeton: A Reply to Dr. Dunlop Moore," *Expository Times* 10 (1898–99): 476–80.
66. Steuernagel, "Dr. W. H. Green," 476–77.

There is nothing for which the critics seem to have such an aversion as a harmonizing interpretation; and very naturally, for it annuls all their work. And yet it is the plain dictate of common sense that the different parts of the same instrument should be interpreted in harmony, provided the language employed will in fairness admit of such an interpretation.

The simple observation of this obvious rule, together with the principle . . . that things which are really distinct should be treated as distinct, will not only relieve all the critical doubts and perplexities relative to the chapters now before us, but the great majority of those which are raised in the rest of Genesis and of the Pentateuch as well.[67]

The gulf that separated Green from the growing majority of Old Testament scholars was indeed real. Moreover, Steuernagel's characterization of Green as a lonely naysayer to higher criticism would become more accurate over time.

Indeed, even as the century drew to a close, Green sensed that he was losing the battle that he had been fighting for so long. Green stood for a type of scholarship which had become increasingly outmoded in America in the nineteenth century. Against those who advocated studying the Old Testament with a scientific and objective approach like that used for other literature, Green believed that such objectivity was impossible. Hence he defended a distinctively Christian or supernaturalist approach which used the tools of modern scholarship to the extent that they did not clash with one's precommitments to the Scriptures as the revealed and inspired Word of God. In coming to a study of the Scriptures a believing critic would presuppose their inspiration, integrity, and genuineness, and trust in revered traditions about their authorship, canonical ordering, and in some cases their interpretation. Green's vision called for "a race of critics . . . of equal learning, ingenuity, and patient toil, who shall have some reverence for what is sacred, some respect for historical testimony, and some regard for the dictates of common sense."[68] While his particular approach was rejected by many, most contemporaries still felt themselves "under lasting obligation to Dr. Green for presenting the most scholarly arguments which support the traditional views."[69]

More positively, the postcritical phase of twentieth-century Old Testament scholarship with its emphasis on such issues as canon, text, authority, and the Bible as literature and Scripture, has in many ways vindicated the scholarship of William Henry Green. For besides his work as an apologist, Green correctly focused his scholarly energies on issues which have proven to be of fundamental importance to the study of the Old Testament. Moreover, he correctly identified fundamental weaknesses in the critical approach. However, because of the conservative theological stance of the Old

67. Green, *Unity of the Book of Genesis*, 8–9.
68. William Henry Green, review of *Historico-Critical Inquiry into the Origin and Composition of the Hexateuch*, by Abraham Kuenen, *Presbyterian Review* 8 (1887): 147.
69. George S. Duncan, "Rev. Professor William Henry Green, D.D., LL.D.," *Biblical World* 8 (1896): 46.

Princeton School with which Green was associated, his genuine insights were lost to many of his contemporaries and of the next generation of Old Testament scholars. Old Testament scholarship has only recently begun to shift its focus to the issues which Green realized were of fundamental importance.

Primary Sources

Green, William Henry. *The Argument of the Book of Job Unfolded*. New York: Carter, 1874.

————. *An Elementary Hebrew Grammar*. New York: Wiley, 1866. 2d ed., 1871.

————. *General Introduction to the Old Testament: The Canon*. New York: Scribner, 1898; Grand Rapids: Baker, 1980.

————. *General Introduction to the Old Testament: The Text*. New York: Scribner, 1899.

————. *A Grammar of the Hebrew Language*. New York: Wiley, 1861.

————. *The Hebrew Feasts in Their Relation to Recent Critical Hypotheses concerning the Pentateuch*. New York: Carter, 1885.

————. *The Higher Criticism of the Pentateuch*. New York: Scribner, 1895; Grand Rapids: Baker, 1978.

————. *Moses and the Prophets*. New York: Carter, 1883.

————. *The Pentateuch Vindicated from the Aspersions of Bishop Colenso*. New York: Wiley, 1863.

————. *The Unity of the Book of Genesis*. New York: Scribner, 1895; Grand Rapids: Baker, 1979.

Secondary Sources

Celebration of the Fiftieth Anniversary of the Appointment of Professor William Henry Green as an Instructor in Princeton Theological Seminary. New York: Scribner, 1896.

Davis, John D. *The Life and Work of William Henry Green*. Philadelphia: MacCalla, 1900.

————. "Professor William Henry Green." *Biblical World* 15.6 (June 1900): 406–13.

————. "William Henry Green." *Presbyterian and Reformed Review* 11, no. 43 (July 1900): 377–96.

"Scrapbook of Obituary Notices, Condolences, etc." Presented by Dr. and Mrs. P. M. Stimson. Archives of Princeton Theological Seminary. Princeton, N.J.

Taylor, Marion Ann. *The Old Testament in the Old Princeton School (1812–1929)*. San Francisco: Mellen Research University Press, 1992.

John Albert Broadus

David S. Dockery

John Albert Broadus was born on January 24, 1827, in Culpeper County, Virginia. When he died on March 16, 1895, he was regarded as one of North America's most capable biblical scholars and certainly one of the world's greatest preachers. Almost three decades after Broadus's death, his prize student, A. T. Robertson, reflected:

> The world has never seemed the same to me since Broadus passed on. For ten years I was enthralled by the witchery of his matchless personality. For three years I was his student. For seven years I was his assistant and colleague and for part of the last year an inmate of his home. It was my sacred and sad privilege to see the passing of this prince in Israel. No man has ever stirred my nature as Broadus did in the classroom and in the pulpit. It has been my fortune to hear Beecher and Phillips Brooks, Maclaren, Joseph Parker and Spurgeon, John Hall and Moody, John Clifford and David Lloyd George. At his best and in a congenial atmosphere Broadus was the equal of any man that I have ever heard.[1]

It comes as little surprise, then, that Robertson's first major publication was a tribute to the mentor whom he so greatly loved. *The Life and Letters of John Albert Broadus* was first published in 1901. Robertson's esteem was reflected both in the length of the original manuscript—over one thousand pages!—and its content. Typical was Robertson's characterization of his friend and mentor as "one of the finest fruits of modern Christianity."[2]

Life and Influence

The Early Years

The Broadus family was of Welsh extraction (the name was originally Broadhurst) and had long been rooted in the soil of the Old Dominion. They were a farming family, but several of Broadus's ancestors had devoted them-

---

1. A. T. Robertson, "Broadus as Scholar and Preacher," in *The Minister and His Greek New Testament* (New York: George H. Doran, 1923; Nashville: Broadman, 1977 reprint), 118.
2. A. T. Robertson, *Life and Letters of John Albert Broadus* (Philadelphia: American Baptist Publication Society, 1901), x.

selves to teaching, and others had become ministers of the gospel, some of them having attained great distinction and influence. Most members of this deeply spiritual family belonged to the country Baptist churches of Virginia.

John's father, Major Edmund Broadus, was a man of high character, ability, and independence of judgment that expressed itself in a variety of ways. Not only was he a farmer and major in the Culpeper County militia, but he was also a miller, a teacher, a leader in the Whig Party, and a member of the Virginia legislature for eighteen years. He was gifted with strong common sense and keen insight into the character and motives of people. Above all he was a deeply spiritual man, an ardent Baptist, and a strong leader in his church and local association. His life and work demonstrated that it was indeed possible for a public figure of his day to be an active Christian.

The extraordinary accomplishments of John Broadus can in many ways be traced to the marvelous model, love, and wisdom exhibited by his father. That a variety of social, political, and religious leaders frequented the Broadus home was also of great influence. In addition, Major Broadus had offered much support to Thomas Jefferson in the development of the University of Virginia, with which his famous son was to be intimately associated. And Broadus's mother was likewise a woman of godly character and a competence that admirably suited her to be the wife of her notable husband and the mother of her remarkable children.

John Broadus was educated in the private subscription schools of Culpeper County. His preparatory schooling was completed at the Black Hill Boarding School under the capable tutelage of his uncle, Albert G. Simms. Here young John was well prepared for his years at the University of Virginia.

While still at his uncle's school, John attended a lengthy revival meeting conducted at the Mt. Poney Church by Charles Lewis and Barnett Grimsley. Sensing John's inability to take hold of the promises of God, his close friend James G. Field quoted to him John 6:37: "All that the Father giveth me shall come to me; and him that cometh to me I will in no wise cast out." Field pleaded, "Can you take hold of this, John?" Somehow the Spirit used this passage, and young Broadus experienced the gift of regeneration at that moment. Field later recalled:

> I knew him quite intimately from 1842 to 1847. We were youths of about the same age, he going to school to his uncle, Albert G. Simms, and I living in the store of Thomas Hill & Son, at Culpeper. Our fathers had been opposing candidates for the legislature. In May, 1843, at a protracted meeting conducted by Elder Charles Lewis with the Mt. Poney Church, at Culpeper, we both professed conversion . . . and were baptized by Rev. Cumberland George. . . . [John] did not remain in the Mt. Poney Church very long, but took his letter and joined New Salem, the church where his father and family had their membership.[3]

3. Ibid., 33–34.

The University of Virginia Years

Following the advice of his teachers and pastors, Broadus began the study of Greek when he entered the University of Virginia in 1846. This eager and dedicated student was endowed with great and rich gifts of mind as well as heart, which he never allowed to substitute for intense and persistent study. Broadus was a toiler, the apostle of hard work throughout life, which he had learned in the farm country of Virginia. It was later said of Broadus that if genius is the ability and willingness to do hard work, he was a genius. This diligent work ethic characterized him all his days. Professor F. H. Smith of the University of Virginia observed that while a student at the university Broadus "cultivated a great power of application and grew to have a great ability to work, and was not ashamed that others should know it. . . . The wonderful result of this steady, methodical industry was that in later years he could do unheard-of things in the briefest time. His disciplined faculties were so under his will that the result, while natural, was surprising."[4]

While at the University of Virginia Broadus continued to mature in his Christian faith. Considering his conversion a call to service, he sought throughout the rest of his life to bring others to Christian belief. Robertson tells of the first evangelistic effort, an experience that Broadus frequently shared with his students in later days: "In a meeting a few months after John's conversion, the preacher urged all Christians at the close of the service to move about and talk to the unconverted. John looked anxiously around to see if there was anybody present he could talk to about his soul's salvation. He had never done anything of the kind before. Finally he saw a man . . . named Sandy. He thought he might venture to speak to him . . . and Sandy was converted."[5] Thereafter, whenever Sandy happened to see Broadus, he would run up to him and say: "Howdy, John! thankee, John. Howdy, John! thankee, John." As Broadus retold the story in later years, he would add: "And if I ever reach the heavenly home and walk the golden streets, I know the first person to meet me will be Sandy, coming and saying again: 'Howdy, John! thankee, John.'"[6]

Another event typical of the university years warrants mention. Broadus once wrote a note in Greek to a fellow student: "*Hen se hysterei* (one thing thou lackest)." This simultaneous compliment and delicate admonition eventually bore fruit in his friend's conversion. Broadus frequently utilized his everyday contacts and relationships to communicate the truths of the gospel.

These events and others like them confirmed Broadus's call to ministry. It was not unexpected that he should consider ministry as a possible lifework. An uncle who was a notable preacher took special interest in his gifted nephew. Several other members of the Broadus family had been ministers. John began to manifest serious interest in Christian service at the time of his

---

4. Quoted in W. J. McGlothlin, "John Albert Broadus," *Review and Expositor* 27 (April 1930): 147.
5. Robertson, *Life and Letters*, 35.
6. Ibid.

conversion. He regularly attended church services on Sunday as well as Wednesday and Saturday. His work in Sunday school convinced him that he was called to preach. Yet he struggled with the call because he could not speak well in public. But in 1846, the year he entered the university, Broadus surrendered to the ministry; never again for one moment did he waver.

The years at the University of Virginia had a profound effect. Broadus was particularly influenced by two professors: Gessner Harrison, professor of Greek; and W. H. McGuffey, professor of moral philosophy. Though he initially struggled with the high demands of the University of Virginia curriculum, he was regarded as a promising scholar by the time he graduated with the A.M. degree in 1850. Following graduation he set for himself a broad self-study course in the Old and New Testaments, church history, and theology. On August 12 of that same year he was ordained at the New Salem Church, which he had joined soon after his conversion. If all of this were not enough for one year, he also (in 1850) married the daughter of Gessner Harrison, his esteemed professor and friend.

Numerous opportunities for teaching and preaching soon came to Broadus, and would follow him the rest of his life. Yet he held few positions during his lifetime. His only pastorate began in September 1851 at Charlottesville, Virginia, which enabled him simultaneously to accept the invitation from his alma mater to serve as an assistant professor of Latin and Greek. Thus he was able at once to combine his dual loves of preaching and teaching. Broadus served the church for eight years. From 1855 to 1857 he also served as the university chaplain.

The Southern Baptist Theological Seminary Years

Broadus never attended a seminary. His university education provided an outstanding background in the classical languages and philosophy, but his theological preparation, like so many other Baptist preachers in the South, came about through self-study. The freestanding theological seminary was a distinctively American idea, and was by this time becoming recognized in the American educational system. Newton Theological Institute had been in operation in the North since 1825, but there was no Baptist seminary in the South. The vision for such a seminary came largely through James Petigru Boyce. While Boyce is generally credited with the founding of the Southern Baptist Theological Seminary, he could not have built the institution without Basil Manly, Jr., and especially John A. Broadus.[7] In 1856 Broadus was appointed by the Southern Baptist Convention to serve on a study committee to prepare a plan for the new seminary. This introduced Broadus to what was to be his life's work. When Broadus and Manly were asked to join the original

---

7. For the story of Broadus's crucial role in the providential founding of the Southern Baptist Theological Seminary see William Mueller, *A History of the Southern Baptist Theological Seminary* (Nashville: Broadman, 1959); and Roy L. Honeycutt, "Heritage Creating Hope: The Pilgrimage of the Southern Baptist Theological Seminary," *Review and Expositor* 81 (Fall 1984): 367–91.

seminary faculty, both responded to one another, "I'll go if you will go." Still Broadus wrestled with leaving the Charlottesville pastorate and his beloved Virginia homeland. When the time came for him to respond to the invitation from the seminary, it took a year for him to decide to tear himself away from his first love; when he did agree to go to the new seminary in Greenville, South Carolina, the decision brought great sorrow both to him and to the church.

Even though Manly and Boyce had been educated in northern seminaries, Broadus was given the assignment to organize the curriculum. Not surprisingly, his proposal was based largely on a University of Virginia model: heavy emphasis was placed on study of the English Bible, and the students were given freedom in their selection of course work. It was a creative proposal that was fifty years ahead of most theological education in North America. While offering something for every student, the plan emphasized rigorous scholarship for the most able. The seminary opened its doors in 1859 to twenty-six students. Only three years later, however, the Civil War forced the new institution to suspend its course of study.

Apprised of the young professor's gifts, Stonewall Jackson asked J. William Jones, an associate of Broadus, to help secure his services as a chaplain: "Write to him by all means and beg him to come. Tell him that he never had a better opportunity for preaching the gospel than he would have right now in these camps."[8] So, during the years of the Civil War, Broadus served as a preacher to the Army of Northern Virginia.

After the war the seminary reopened in the fall of 1865. At this time Broadus began his celebrated commentary on the Gospel of Matthew. He labored for twenty years on this project, which was ultimately published in 1886.

Another significant achievement received its impetus when the seminary recommenced classes after the Civil War. Broadus had only one student in his homiletics class, and this student was blind. The lectures that Broadus used to teach him were published in 1870. For decades this volume, *On the Preparation and Delivery of Sermons*, was widely used throughout the world, and it is still employed today in some settings. Without question it is Broadus's most famous work.[9] The publication of the volume is clear evidence of God's providential oversight. Here is a book that came about through lectures to one blind student in a small, at that time almost anonymous, institution in Greenville, South Carolina. In this influential volume Broadus, who was already widely known as a preacher of rare ability and power, fleshes out the ideals of preaching that he had pursued over the past two decades. These ideals had been shaped by his study of the great masters of the art of preaching throughout the history of the church.[10]

8. Robertson, *Life and Letters*, 197.

9. See R. Albert Mohler, "Classic Texts Deserve Valued Spot on the Preacher's Bookshelf," *Preaching* 4.5 (March-April 1989): 33–34.

10. James W. Cox, review of *On the Preparation and Delivery of Sermons*, by John A. Broadus, *Review and Expositor* 81 (Fall 1984): 464–66; and idem, "The Pulpit and Southern," *Review and Expositor* 82 (Winter 1985): 77–78.

When the seminary faced seemingly insurmountable financial obstacles in the mid-1870s, a decision was made to move the institution to Louisville, Kentucky, a more centrally located site. Broadus, too, moved to Louisville, his home until his death in 1895. The move was successful largely because of Boyce's courageous vision, Broadus's unrelenting will, and their common trust in God. Challenging his colleagues not to give up their efforts in behalf of the struggling seminary, Broadus uttered his famous words, "The seminary may die, but let us die first."

Although Broadus was offered the pastorates of several prominent churches as well as the presidency of Brown University and Crozer Theological Seminary, all of which entailed significantly higher salaries, he chose to remain in his faculty position at the seminary. Following Boyce's death, Broadus was elected president of the Southern Baptist Theological Seminary in 1889. In the same year Broadus delivered the prestigious Lyman Beecher Lectures on preaching at Yale University. Unfortunately, the lectures were never written down, and their contents can be reconstructed only from newspaper articles that appeared in the *Examiner* and the *Christian Inquirer*.[11] (Broadus never took notes into the pulpit and discouraged the transcribing of his messages.) As his fame continued to spread, Broadus was invited to deliver other prestigious lectures around the country, including a presentation on "Textual Criticism of the New Testament" at Newton and on "Jesus of Nazareth" at Johns Hopkins University.

Broadus had no greater impact than his influence on his prize student and son-in-law, A. T. Robertson. A special bond formed between them, especially during Robertson's years on the Southern faculty. Robertson affectionately called Broadus his "truest earthly friend." And Broadus served as a model for the young professor in two disciplines for which Robertson became equally, if not more, famous: New Testament interpretation and preaching.

Broadus modeled for Robertson an interpretive method that took into account the recent developments in critical scholarship but still remained true to the authority of Holy Scripture. The critical textual notes Robertson contributed to Broadus's *Harmony of the Gospels* reveal continuity with, and addition to, the Broadus legacy. One of the finest compliments Robertson ever received was from J. H. Farmer of McMaster University: "Professor Robertson has worthily maintained the Broadus tradition."[12] Robertson's mammoth *Grammar of the Greek New Testament* and *Word Pictures in the New Testament* clearly reflect Broadus's impact.

The death of Boyce and the added responsibility of presidential leadership had a considerable toll on Broadus. Robertson observed that after 1889

---

11. See Steve Reagles, "The Century after the 1889 Yale Lectures: A Reflection on Broadus's Homiletical Thought," *Preaching* 5.3 (Nov.-Dec. 1989): 32–36; and A. T. Robertson, "Broadus the Preacher," *Methodist Quarterly Review* 69 (April 1920): 152. E. C. Dargan, Broadus's successor in teaching homiletics at Southern, attempted to incorporate portions of the Yale lectures in a revised edition of *On the Preparation and Delivery of Sermons.*

12. Quoted in Everett Gill, *A. T. Robertson: A Biography* (New York: Macmillan, 1943), 198.

Broadus never regained the buoyancy of life he had once had. In his final year as president Broadus's health grew weaker. Yet his standing as a national Baptist leader continued to build the seminary in terms of financial support as well as national and international recognition. The great Baptist leader, preacher, and scholar died on March 16, 1895. On that day the *Louisville Courier-Journal* reported, "There is no man in the United States whose passing would cause more widespread sorrow than that of Doctor Broadus."[13]

New Testament Scholar and Preacher

Many elements make up a person who is successful as both scholar and preacher. Obviously he is blessed by divine enablement and multigiftedness. On the human level such a person is a complex force. The natural endowment must be there to begin with, and then there must be tireless energy and much preparation. Many persons gifted as scholars or preachers are not successful. Broadus excelled because of his strong work ethic, the focus of his work, the subject matter explored, the drive for excellence, and his rigorous pursuit to handle the material accurately.

Broadus authored tracts; articles for newspapers, popular magazines, and scholarly journals; major volumes; and an untold number of sermons. As we have seen, his first major publication was *On the Preparation and Delivery of Sermons* (1870). Broadus was, of course, not the first to address the subject of preaching. The incredible success of the book can be attributed to his marvelous ability to communicate complex material in a popular way. He presented similar material in *The History of Preaching,* a more challenging and scholarly treatise based on five lectures given at Newton in 1876.

The volume that gained Broadus a reputation as an evangelical biblical interpreter was his twenty-year effort on the Gospel of Matthew. While not as well known as *On the Preparation and Delivery of Sermons,* this volume in the American Commentary series is generally considered the greatest of all his works. Just as significant volumes on preaching preceded Broadus's 1870 publication, so there were hundreds of works on the Gospel of Matthew. Yet for over a century Broadus's effort has clearly remained the most notable volume in the American Commentary series, and one of the truly scholarly volumes on the first Gospel.

Three other works on the Gospels are worthy of note. Shortly after the publication of the Matthew commentary, Broadus penned a brief work on *Jesus of Nazareth,* which was a revision of the lectures given at Johns Hopkins. In 1893 he completed his *Harmony of the Gospels,* which Robertson would revise several times over the years. The *Commentary on the Gospel of Mark* was published posthumously in 1905. Several other works on New

---

13. Quoted in Robertson, *Life and Letters,* 431. See also Bernard R. DeRemer, "The Life of John Albert Broadus," *Christianity Today,* 13 April 1962, 22–23; E. Y. Mullins, "One Hundred Years: A Retrospect," *Review and Expositor* 24 (April 1927): 129–31; and Claude W. Duke, "Memorial Address of Dr. John A. Broadus," *Review and Expositor* 24 (April 1927): 167–76.

Testament themes were never published. When biblical authority and historical criticism became a major issue on the Southern campus, Broadus defended the full truthfulness of Scripture in *Three Questions as to the Bible* (1883) and *The Paramount and Permanent Authority of the Bible* (1887). Finally, following the death of his beloved colaborer, Broadus authored *The Memoir of James Petrigru Boyce* (1893).

With every publication Broadus sought to edify his readers, to expand their knowledge, and to build up the church of Jesus Christ. The conclusion to the preface of *The History of Preaching* could serve as the motto and prayer of all his writings: "God grant that the little volume may be of some real use!" Each work reflects commitment to careful scholarship, industrious research, accuracy, and conscientiousness in communication. Whatever Broadus did was, in his favorite phrase, "worth working at." His works have retained their place over the years because they were not the effusions of mere ambition to be a published author.

Those who heard Broadus said he was even a better preacher than writer. Here he combined the scholarly commitment to New Testament exegesis so evident in his commentaries with a masterful understanding of the art of preaching. The skillful yet simple touch of a craftsman was evident to all who heard him proclaim the message of God's Word.

Belief in Biblical Inspiration

To have an accurate understanding of Broadus's interpretive method and his distinctive contributions to interpretation in the evangelical tradition, we need to examine his view on the inspiration of the Bible. Inspiration became a major issue on the campus of Southern Seminary in the 1870s and 1880s as the faculty attempted to respond to their colleague C. H. Toy, who resigned over his acceptance of historical-critical conclusions. The major treatise was produced by Basil Manly, Jr., and titled *The Bible Doctrine of Inspiration* (1888). The key to understanding Manly and Broadus is to recognize their common opposition to Toy's doctrine of Scripture and its practical implications.[14] While affirming plenary inspiration, Manly carefully refuted any theory of mechanical dictation. Broadus also refuted mechanical dictation, but was more cautious in his theorizing as to verbal inspiration.[15] Both clearly affirmed every aspect of Scripture as infallible truth and divine authority.

In *Three Questions as to the Bible*, Broadus's answer to the question "To what extent ought we regard the sacred writings of the Old and New Testaments as inspired?" was "Completely." But while unhesitatingly defending the trustworthiness and authority of the Bible, he was cautious in asserting a definition of inspiration. Thus he wrote, "But whatever these [biblical] writers meant to say, or whatever we learn from subsequent revelation that God

14. For an account of the Toy controversy see Mueller, *History*.
15. John A. Broadus, *Commentary on the Gospel of Matthew* (Philadelphia: American Baptist Publication Society, 1886), 58.

meant to say through their words, though not by themselves fully under-stood, that we hold to be true, thoroughly true, not only in substance but in statement. . . . Even today I know of no discrepancies in the Bible which im-pair its credibility."[16] Similarly, his work *The Paramount and Permanent Au-thority of the Bible* took seriously the human authorship of the Bible as well as its divine origin. He contended for the complete truthfulness of Holy Scrip-ture in a manner reflective of other great Christian leaders of the nineteenth century like Boyce, Manly, J. L. Dagg, and Alvah Hovey, yet with an inde-pendence and creativity characteristic of all of his work.[17] Perhaps most tell-ing is Broadus's wish that the young seminarians in a New Testament class he addressed a few days before his death be "mighty in the scriptures."[18]

Broadus attributed the doctrinal unity among Baptists and other evangel-icals during the nineteenth century to their emphasis on the authority of the Bible in matters of faith and practice.[19] Accordingly, in *The Paramount and Permanent Authority of the Bible* he addressed himself "to people who be-lieve that the Bible is the Word of God; not merely that it contains the Word of God, which wise persons may disentangle from other things in the book, but that it is the Word of God. . . . It is entirely possible that we may have no creed or system of theology, no professors or even preachers, nor even news-paper writers, nor writers of tracts, that can always interpret the Bible with infallible success. But our persuasion is that the real meaning of the Bible is true."[20] Here he explicitly affirms that the Bible, apart from human interpre-tation, has objective meaning and value.

While Broadus was at the forefront of American biblical scholarship in the nineteenth century and was a pacesetter in certain areas, he denied that all the progress of the nineteenth century made it "superior to all previous cen-turies in thinking, for in some respects our age has not time to be wiser."[21] Thus his careful and wise scholarship remained faithful to the authority of Holy Scripture as the only sufficient revelation of God. In his view "a 'pro-gressive orthodoxy' that forsakes or adds to the teaching of Christ becomes heterodoxy."[22] Broadus's words on the archeological, philosophical, and sci-entific debates of his time are equally applicable today. "The great principle, in all such inquiries," he declared, "is that while it is lawful to reinvestigate the Scripture in the light of current opinion and feeling, it is not lawful to put anything as authority above God's Word."[23] This foundational commitment

---

16. John A. Broadus, *Three Questions as to the Bible* (Philadelphia: American Baptist Publication Society, 1883), 9, 34.
17. See David S. Dockery, *Christian Scripture: An Evangelical Perspective on Inspiration, Author-ity, and Interpretation* (Nashville: Broadman and Holman, 1995), 177–99.
18. Robertson, *Life and Letters*, 430.
19. John A. Broadus, *The Paramount and Permanent Authority of the Bible* (Philadelphia: Amer-ican Baptist Publication Society, 1887), 1–2.
20. Ibid., 3.
21. Ibid., 5.
22. Ibid., 8.
23. Ibid., 13.

undergirded the painstaking and evenhanded exegesis that characterized his lifework.

Method of Biblical Interpretation

Broadus's work, which reveals his broad exposure and up-to-date reading not only in his two major fields of New Testament and preaching, but in many other areas as well, has been concisely summarized by William Mueller as "honest, critical in the best sense, and reverent."[24] That he neither wholeheartedly accepted nor rejected the conclusions of nineteenth-century biblical criticism shows his general good sense as well as his understanding of the many pendulum swings throughout history.

To explain his interpretive method, Broadus offered five guiding steps in answer to the question, "How ought the inspired writings be treated by us?"[25]

1. *Ascertain the text.* Convinced that a high view of inspiration should lead to great zeal for textual criticism, Broadus began with the work of textual criticism.
2. *Procure the best possible translation.* An accurate rendition of the original languages is indispensable. (Of course, translations can never fully bring out the exact meaning of the original text because they must seek a balance between accuracy and readability.)
3. *Personally study the Bible.* Simply reading a translation does not suffice as genuine biblical interpretation. Using historical and contextual helps, each Christian must make personal study of the Scriptures a priority.
4. *Teach the Bible truth to others.* Broadus's strong commitment to preaching led him to insist that Christians share with others the instruction they receive from Scripture.
5. *Act out the Bible in everyday life.* Broadus urged his students and readers to put the Bible into practical service by displaying a missionary spirit.

Moving from the critical apparatus to practical application, these steps link textual and historical methodologies with actually living out the message of the Bible. Here we see Broadus as both scholar and preacher, academic and churchman.

Broadus's commentaries put his method into practice. He began with a full commitment to historical-grammatical exegesis. His scholarly work was creative, but he was not infatuated with the novel. Accepted interpretations were set aside only when they seemed to be clearly wrong, and then only in a tender, respectful manner. He preferred accuracy to speculation.[26] In ap-

24. Mueller, *History,* 61.
25. Broadus, *Three Questions,* 58–67.
26. J. Estill Jones, "The New Testament and Southern," *Review and Expositor* 82 (Winter 1985): 21–22.

plying his exegesis, he provided helpful sermonic material for younger preachers. These applications were not overly simplistic, amorphously pietistic, nor fanciful in any way, but short, suggestive, and faithful to the text's original meaning.

In examining Broadus's *Commentary on the Gospel of Matthew*, we note that the preface thoroughly discusses textual matters, including various viewpoints, comparisons, evaluations, and conclusions. For example, he states that "the general contributions to textual criticism made by Westcott and Hort are invaluable, and most of their judgments as to particular passages seem to me correct. But in a number of cases I have felt bound to dissent, and to give the reasons as fully and strongly as the character and limits of this work allowed."[27] The commentary itself, with its copious footnotes, proceeds to offer insights on Greek grammar and syntax. Yet the direct word-by-word, phrase-by-phrase exposition makes the work useful for the Sunday school teacher as well as for the scholar.

Broadus did not sidestep the tough questions impacting the veracity and accuracy of the biblical text. He addressed seeming contradictions and errors simply and directly, reflecting his conviction of and trust in the Bible's truthfulness.[28] And after wrestling to determine the historical meaning of the text, Broadus completed his five-step approach with his "homiletical and practical" comments, wedding exacting exegesis with solid application. By focusing on the practical aspects as well, Broadus brilliantly combined his two specialties, showing that biblical interpretation must ultimately be done in the service of the church.

We ought also note that the theological conclusions in the commentary on Matthew evidence Broadus's Reformed convictions, the confessional traditions that gave birth to Southern Seminary. For example, he contended for the virgin birth (see the comments on 1:21), affirmed that Jesus claimed to be the Messiah (see the comments on 13:10–17), and expounded the need for God to take the initiative to make himself known to depraved humans (see the comments on 22:14).

Overall, Broadus's work on Matthew is a model commentary, and in many ways ushered in a new era of commentary writing within evangelical scholarship.[29] Significant advances included the incorporation of historical,

---

27. Broadus, *Gospel of Matthew*, x.
28. See, e.g., Broadus, *Gospel of Matthew*, 6–7, where he deals with the variations in the genealogies in Matthew and Luke.
29. The publication of the New American Commentary series (ed. David S. Dockery and E. Ray Clendenen, 40 vols. [Nashville: Broadman, 1991–]) is in many ways a tribute to Broadus's legacy. The preface of each volume states that "in one sense *The New American Commentary* is not new, for it represents the continuation of a heritage rich in biblical and theological exposition. The title of this forty-volume set points to the continuity of this series with an important commentary project published at the end of the nineteenth century called *An American Commentary*, edited by Alvah Hovey. The older series included, among other significant contributions, the outstanding volume on Matthew by John A. Broadus, from whom the publisher of the new series, Broadman Press, partly derives its name." (Broadman Press is named after John A. Broadus [Broad-] and Basil Manly, Jr. [-man].)

textual, and grammatical research that was being done during his lifetime. He demonstrated an awareness of and conservative openness to European critical scholarship, but he was not willing to unreservedly subject Holy Scripture to the antisupernatural biases of many of the German critics. The inclusion of grammatical, exegetical, theological, and practical comments make the work valuable to a very wide readership.

Commentaries are not the only place where Broadus made original contributions. In the *Harmony of the Gospels,* as Robertson notes, "Dr. Broadus was the first one to depart from the traditional division of the ministry of Christ by the Passovers rather than the natural unfolding of the ministry itself. . . . Dr. Broadus's work is the ripe fruit of a lifetime of rich study and reflection by one of the rarest teachers of the New Testament that any age or country has ever seen."[30] Here, too, Broadus's firm theological foundation and level-headed explorations allowed him to employ the best of European critical scholarship without embracing the conclusions. His openness has been misinterpreted by some. For example, Roger Finke and Rodney Stark claim that "Broadus was extremely impressed with the application of critical methods to biblical studies that was going on in European universities, especially in Germany."[31] On the other hand, J. M. Carter's notes on Broadus's lectures on New Testament introduction make it clear that while Broadus was certainly open to new advances, his interpretive method cannot be considered progressive.[32] He rejected recent critical notions that the Gospel of John is in conflict with the other Gospels. He clearly held to a Johannine authorship of the fourth Gospel. And he affirmed both the supernatural origin of the Gospels and their legitimacy as eyewitness accounts.

At the same time Broadus recognized the pitfalls in harmonizing the Gospels. It could fail to recognize and distinguish the unique emphases of each Gospel. He warned that the Gospels are not a mere mass to be artificially reconstructed, for each one is a living and independent whole. Yet he saw the values of harmonization as providing an overall look at the life of Christ and a way to reconcile apparent discrepancies in the Gospels.

Whether in his classroom lectures, in his scholarly treatises, or in his preaching, the striking feature of all of Broadus's work is the pervasive tone of solemn reverence and deep spirituality. His thoroughgoing scholarship and devotional spirit are a worthy model for all who have had the privilege of learning from him, whether as his contemporaries in the nineteenth century or as Bible students preparing for the twenty-first century. John A.

30. A. T. Robertson, preface to John A. Broadus, *A Harmony of the Gospels in the Revised Version,* 7th ed. (New York: George H. Doran, 1903); see also Martin E. Marty, *Pilgrims in Their Own Land* (New York: Penguin, 1984), 304.

31. Roger Finke and Rodney Stark, *The Churching of America, 1776–1990: Winners and Losers in Our Religious Economy* (New Brunswick, N.J.: Rutgers University Press, 1992), 179.

32. These unpublished notes are housed in the James P. Boyce Library on the campus of the Southern Baptist Theological Seminary. I am indebted to Greg Thornbury for his research help at this point in particular, and for his help with other aspects of this chapter.

Broadus practiced what he taught his students, for indeed he was a man "mighty in the Scriptures."

Primary Sources

Broadus, John A. *Commentary on the Gospel of Mark*. Philadelphia: American Baptist Publication Society, 1905.

———. *Commentary on the Gospel of Matthew*. Philadelphia: American Baptist Publication Society, 1886.

———. *A Harmony of the Gospels*. New York: George H. Doran, 1893.

———. *Memoir of James Petigru Boyce*. New York: A. C. Armstrong and Son, 1893.

———. *On the Preparation and Delivery of Sermons*. Philadelphia: Smith, English, 1870; New York: Harper and Row, 1979.

———. *The Paramount and Permanent Authority of the Bible*. Philadelphia: American Baptist Publication Society, 1887.

———. *Three Questions as to the Bible*. Philadelphia: American Baptist Publication Society, 1883.

Secondary Sources

Cox, James W. "The Pulpit and Southern." *Review and Expositor* 82 (Winter 1985): 77–78.

———. Review of *On the Preparation and Delivery of Sermons*, by John A. Broadus. *Review and Expositor* 81 (Fall 1984): 464–66.

DeRemer, Bernard R. "The Life of John Albert Broadus." *Christianity Today*, 13 April 1962, 22–23.

Jones, J. Estill. "The New Testament and Southern." *Review and Expositor* 82 (Winter 1985): 21–22.

McGlothlin, W. J. "John Albert Broadus." *Review and Expositor* 27 (April 1930): 141–68.

Mohler, R. Albert. "Classic Texts Deserve Valued Spot on the Preacher's Bookshelf." *Preaching* 4.5 (March-April 1989): 33–34.

Mueller, William. *A History of the Southern Baptist Theological Seminary*. Nashville: Broadman, 1959.

Reagles, Steve. "The Century after the 1889 Yale Lectures: A Reflection on Broadus's Homiletical Thought." *Preaching* 5.3 (Nov.-Dec. 1989): 32–36.

Robertson, A. T. "Broadus as Scholar and Preacher." In *The Minister and His Greek New Testament*, 118–39. New York: George H. Doran, 1923; Nashville: Broadman, 1977 reprint.

———. *Life and Letters of John Albert Broadus*. Philadelphia: American Baptist Publication Society, 1901.

Whitsett, W. H. "John Albert Broadus." *Review and Expositor* 4 (1907): 339–51.

Theodor Zahn

Erich H. Kiehl

Theodor Zahn was an eminent New Testament and patristic scholar of the nineteenth and the early decades of the twentieth century. He was a careful and dedicated conservative theologian. His extensive writings are characterized by great erudition and thoroughness. A leader of conservative scholars in New Testament studies at a time when higher criticism was dominant, Zahn's long and fruitful activity reflects the careful and dedicated training received during his childhood and youth from his gifted Christian parents. Some detail on this is necessary to arrive at a well-informed understanding of his intellectual and theological stature.[1]

The Formative Years

Theodor Zahn was born on October 10, 1838, in Mörs, west of the Rhine between Düsseldorf and Wesel. He was the eighth son of Franz L. Zahn and Anna Zahn, née Schlatter. Three brothers had died before his birth. Two sisters were born after him.

Theodor's great-grandfather was Johann Michael Zahn, who served on the faculty at Wittenberg in philosophy. After four years he turned to study theology, and at the age of thirty-four was assigned to a parish in his home territory.

Theodor's grandfather, Gottlieb Zahn, was an outspoken rationalist who grieved that his children became dedicated Christians. Two of his sons became pastors and a third served as a missionary to South Africa.

Theodor's father noted that in his childhood he experienced love only from his mother. He did not receive any Christian training but only the rationalistic views of his father and teacher. Later he studied law at the University of Jena, where through the influence of G. H. Schubert he experienced the joy of the Christian faith. After four years in legal practice and ongoing inner religious conflict, Franz Zahn began theological studies. Then serving first as an instructor in an institution for training elementary teachers and later as the director of such an institution, he received a call to pastor a

---

1. Most of the biographical information is drawn from Zahn's autobiographical essay "Theodor Zahn: Mein Werdegang und meine Lebensarbeit," in *Die Religionswissenschaft der Gegenwart in Selbstdarstellungen,* ed. Erich Stange (Leipzig: Felix Meiner, 1925), 221–45.

church in Mörs. After ten years he left the church at Mörs to begin his own private educational institution.

Theodor recorded in his autobiography that he never attended what we would term a public school, but received his training and preparation for higher education in private schools. From his fifth to his ninth year he together with two older brothers was taught by a "house-teacher." In the winter of 1847–48 he translated the eight books of Caesar's *Gallic Wars* into German. Aside from the usual classes, he received instruction in religion from his father. Under the guidance of a Frenchman, he also spent two years learning French. In the summer of 1854, he passed the secondary school examinations.

Theodor's father sent him to Basel to begin university studies in theology. He stayed in a boarding house for theological students. In addition to working in classical languages, he spent two years learning Hebrew. He also began a study of church history under Karl Rudolf Hagenbach, who compelled his students to make purposeful use of the library of about ten thousand volumes. Hagenbach's requirement of careful research on given topics resulted in Zahn's growing interest and later expertise in church history as reflected in his writings.

In New Testament studies Zahn was especially influenced by Christoph Johannes Riggenbach, Immanuel Stockmeyer, and Johann Christian Konrad von Hofmann. In a study of the Gospels under Riggenbach, who through much struggle had become a dedicated Christian, Theodor learned that it is important to discover the unique message of each of the Synoptics rather than stress only their similarities. In classes on the Sermon on the Mount and on Galatians he learned much about proper exegetical methodology. He also sat in on presentations on divine revelation, including John's Book of Revelation. While at home in the winter of 1855–56, he studied with growing interest Hofmann's careful theological study of *Prophecy and Fulfilment.*

At Easter in 1856 Zahn went for three semesters to the University at Erlangen and studied under Hofmann. He enjoyed Hofmann's concerned and winsome attention to individual students, which had a long-lasting effect on Zahn in his later years. Enriched and much influenced by the lectures of Franz Delitzsch, he spent a good deal of time making a careful study of detailed commentaries on both the Old and the New Testament. Then he went to Berlin to complete his theological, homiletical, and practical studies.

From the fall of 1858 to 1861 Zahn lived at home, preparing for the various licentiate and *pro ministerio* examinations. During this period he suffered from a serious eye condition, necessitating an operation. For a year he was not to read and write; then his eyesight improved.

The Years of Service

In 1861 Zahn began three-and-a-half years of service as a teacher at the gymnasium at Neustrelitz. During his last two years there he taught religion as well as world history and German literature.

In the spring of 1865 Zahn became a lecturer at the University of Göttingen, where lecturers were required to teach both Old and New Testament, church history, dogmatics, and ethics. At that time Albrecht Ritschl served as the dean of the theological faculty. In the spring of 1868 Zahn became a privatdozent, graduated with a doctorate, and passed several other requirements. He also served as a university preacher. On April 1, 1871, he was promoted to associate professor.

Zahn expressed a desire to the theological faculty to begin lecturing on the books of the New Testament and the literature of the early church to around A.D. 450. This necessitated that he learn Syriac. During his twelve-year service at Göttingen, he wrote books on Marcellus of Ancyra, the Shepherd of Hermas, and Ignatius of Antioch. He also edited in collaboration with Oskar von Gebhardt and Adolf von Harnack the three-volume *Patrum apostolicorum opera,* to which he contributed *Ignatii et Polycarpi epistulae, martyria, fragmenta.*

Zahn's life as a lecturer at Göttingen became more difficult when colleagues began to teach his courses in New Testament exegesis. The curator of the university informed him of the general view of the faculty: "As preacher you are absolutely necessary but as a professor superfluous." Zahn's name was on a number of lists of potential professors, but he invariably received negative comments from those who did not share his approach.

Through the commendation of the curator at Göttingen, who did not share the general view, Zahn received a call in January 1877 to serve as a professor of New Testament at the University of Kiel. On December 20, 1877, his former professor Johann von Hofmann died. On December 30, in fulfilment of Hofmann's wishes Zahn was offered and accepted the position of dean of the theological faculty at Erlangen. He was asked to teach the course in introductory knowledge and New Testament exegesis. This subject area included both what we today term New Testament introduction and the principles of New Testament exegesis. His second teaching area centered on the history of the New Testament canon and a deeper understanding of New Testament history.

Zahn's ongoing research from 1881 to 1916 resulted in a nine-volume work, *Forschungen zur Geschichte des neutestamentlichen Kanons und der altkirchlichen Literatur.* A number of the studies in this set were contributed by colleagues. In Zahn's view the most helpful studies were the collection of Tatian's Diatessaron in the first volume and the *Urausgabe der Apostelgeschichte des Lukas* in the last volume.

At Erlangen Zahn presented lectures and seminars on the exegesis of Matthew through Revelation and stressed the educational and historical content of the New Testament. Because of the large number of students, he began meeting with private groups in homes. Some of the more gifted students later became colleagues at Erlangen and co-workers on commentaries on the books of the New Testament.

During his years of service at Göttingen, Kiel, and Erlangen, Zahn frequently preached in local churches. He also made presentations on various facets of life in the church. In doing so, he went beyond the usual boundaries of church history but without arousing negative reactions. For example, he made a presentation on "Sklaverei and Christentum in der alten Welt" and published the book *Cyprian von Antiochien und die deutschen Fasttage.*

At the end of his first tenure at Erlangen, the first part of Zahn's *Geschichte des neutestamentlichen Kanons* (viz., *Das Neue Testament vor Origenes*) appeared. In the fall of 1888 he became a member of the faculty at Leipzig, where he remained until Easter of 1892. The final volume of the *Geschichte* appeared soon after his return to Erlangen in 1892. Here he continued his teaching and writing activities, including a two-volume *Einleitung in das Neue Testament*. He retired in 1909 but continued his study and writing. He died at the age of ninety-five in 1933.

Scholarly Visits Abroad

Zahn made a number of trips abroad to make personal contact with scholars and institutions in various parts of Europe.[2] In the fall of 1879 he traveled to "Venedy," seemingly an old-German term for Venice, to do research in the Library of St. Mark on manuscripts of the *Acta Joannis,* legends about John. He studied Constantin Tischendorf's copies of the *Acta* and excerpts from the Paris manuscripts. During the Easter holiday in 1883 he examined manuscripts on Cyprian of Antioch among others. He visited the Ambrosian Library at Milan and the Benedictine Library at Monte Cassino, south of Rome. Only in September 1913, however, was he given the opportunity to study manuscripts at the Vatican.

As part of his ongoing research in various areas of patristics, Zahn carefully investigated the authenticity of the shortest Syrian translation of the letters of Ignatius and then wrote his monograph *Ignatius von Antiochien*. This received a favorable reaction from J. B. Lightfoot, who remained in collegial contact with Zahn for some years.

In 1897 William Sanday was influential in arranging for Cambridge University to give special recognition to Zahn's achievements. This permitted him to reestablish his relationship with James Armitage Robinson, A. E. Brooke, and A. E. Burn. It also afforded the privilege of getting to know James Rendel Harris and Francis Crawford Burkitt personally.

Views on the Canon of Scripture

Zahn's study of the canon of Scripture resulted in major publications: *Geschichte des neutestamentlichen Kanons* and *Forschungen zur Geschichte des neutestamentlichen Kanons und der altkirchlichen Literatur.* This study involved very extensive research in patristics, in some instances the interrela-

2. Ibid., 245–48.

tionships between some of the writings of the early church. Also of concern was the effect that the theological views of the writers had on what they wrote. These topics were matters of ongoing debate in church history and theology at that time.

Zahn's research included a careful study of the Muratorian Canon, the oldest extant list of the writings of the New Testament. The beginning and probably the end of the manuscript are missing, as a study of the content suggests. In addition to most of the New Testament books it mentions the Apocalypse of Peter with a caveat; it rejects the Shepherd of Hermas, some of the Marcionite epistles, and other writings reflecting Gnosticism and Montanism. The status of some of these works was being debated at the time of Zahn's studies and therefore needed careful review.

Among Zahn's sources in this research were the writings of Origen, including his canon; the Syriac Doctrine of Addai (the traditional founder of the church at Edessa); the Diatessaron of Tatian; the Acts of Paul; the canon of the Codex Claromontanus; the canon of Cyril of Jerusalem (c. A.D. 350), the Cheltenham Canon (c. A.D. 360), the African canon (c. 360); the Roman canon of 382; the Syrian canon of 400; the thirty-ninth festal letter of Athanasius, which includes a list of the canonical writings of the Old and the New Testaments; and the writings of Eusebius.[3] Bruce Metzger comments:

> Still an indispensable mine of information are Theodor Zahn's two volumes on the history of the New Testament canon, as well as the nine volumes of "Investigations" that he edited on various problems bearing on the canon. A concise summary of Zahn's mature views on the canon, namely, that it came into existence by the end of the first century, is provided in his *Grundriss der Geschichte des neutestamentlichen Kanons*.[4]

Harnack criticized Zahn's reconstruction of the development of the canon. According to Harnack, the role of the church in the process of canonization was one of selection, whereas Zahn stressed the concept of growth. He understood the collection of the books of the New Testament to possess authority, but not on the grounds that the New Testament as such is Holy Scripture. He felt, for example, that the four Gospels are authoritative because they contain the sayings of Jesus. Hence in Zahn's view a New Testament canon was possible a century earlier than in Harnack's view.[5]

3. Theodor Zahn, *Grundriss der Geschichte des neutestamentlichen Kanons: Eine Ergänzung zu der Einleitung in das Neue Testament* (Leipzig: Deichert, 1901).
4. Bruce M. Metzger, *The Canon of the New Testament: Its Origin, Development, and Significance* (New York: Oxford University Press, 1987), 23–24.
5. Ibid., 24. For an extensive and informative article reflecting Zahn's careful ongoing research into the canon see Theodor Zahn, "Canon of Scripture," in *New Schaff-Herzog Encyclopedia of Religious Knowledge*, ed. Samuel Macauley Jackson et al., 13 vols. (New York: Funk and Wagnalls, 1908–14), 2:388–400.

Views on the Gospels and Acts

Zahn edited a seventeen-volume commentary series on the New Testament, *Kommentar zum Neuen Testament,* to which a number of scholars contributed. He himself wrote on seven of the New Testament books: Matthew (1903), Luke (1913), John (1908), Acts (2 vols., 1919, 1921), Romans (1910), Galatians (1905), and Revelation (2 vols., 1924, 1926). Some of these are in the second or third edition. None of them is available in English translation.

In discussing the Synoptic Gospels, Zahn adopted a position that was accepted by Augustine and is common today. The Gospel according to Matthew was written by Jesus' disciple, who, before his call, had served as a tax collector. Zahn's view was that the Greek version of Matthew is a translation of the original Aramaic form of the Gospel. This translation was influenced by the Greek Gospel of Mark, which had previously been produced from the Aramaic form of Matthew.[6]

Zahn held that the lack of chronological order in Mark was due to dependence on the witness of Peter, who was concerned to meet the needs of his hearers rather than to follow strict chronological sequence.[7] Zahn also felt that the "young man" who followed Jesus from Gethsemane (Mark 14:51–52) is a reference to Mark.[8]

In his discussion of Luke 1:1–4 Zahn contends that Theophilus was not yet a Christian when Luke wrote his Gospel account. On the other hand, the address to Theophilus in Acts 1:1 may be an indication that in the interim he had become a Christian.[9] Zahn also suggests that Luke in his Gospel account and in Acts purposefully connected events with specific places in order to impress Theophilus with the trustworthiness of the Christian history.[10] Another intriguing suggestion, this one based on the considerable differences between the Western text of Acts and the early texts, is that Luke himself may have prepared two editions of the Book of Acts.[11]

In the light of his extensive studies of the writings of John and the history of the early church, Zahn underlines that the Gospel account of John, the Epistles of John, and Revelation are the work of the apostle John:

> The Johannine writings . . . originated in the province of Asia, and for this information we are not dependent upon tradition alone. It is unmistakably affirmed in Revelation, and the tradition is entirely confirmed in this point by the contents of the Gospel and the Epistles. In the same province also we find living until far on in the second century personal disciples of the John of Ephe-

6. Theodor Zahn, *Introduction to the New Testament,* 3 vols. (Grand Rapids: Kregel, 1953), 2:601–17.
7. Ibid., 2:439–40.
8. Ibid., 2:429.
9. Ibid., 3:41–44.
10. Ibid., 3:68–69.
11. Ibid., 3:8–41; see also Theodor Zahn, *Die Urausgabe der Apostelgeschichte des Lukas* (Leipzig: Deichert, 1916), 1–10.

sus to whom these writings are ascribed. Some of these are bishops, as Papias in Hierapolis and Polycarp in Smyrna; others are not mentioned by name, but [are] associated by Irenaeus, the personal disciple of Polycarp, with Papias and Polycarp, and called "the elders." . . . The fact that John lived to an extreme age and was still alive at the beginning of Trajan's reign (98–117), dying, therefore, about the year 100, and the fact that Polycarp died in the year 155 (Feb. 23) at a very great age—86 years after his baptism, which must have taken place, therefore, in the year 69—give us an unbroken tradition from Jesus to Irenaeus, i.e., from 30 to 180, with only two links between them, namely, John of Ephesus and Polycarp of Smyrna.[12]

This clear witness unfortunately is often ignored by some today, who posit instead the activity of a redactor. Zahn notes that one of the starting points for this view is the fact that the pericope about the adulterous woman (John 7:53–8:11) is not found in a number of the early manuscripts (P66, P75, Sinaiticus, and Vaticanus).[13] Zahn's view was that John wrote this Gospel account for the benefit of Christians who were members of the churches under his care. The intention of the Gospel of John was not to convert Gentiles and Jews to the Christian faith. Rather, the purpose was to emphatically underline (e.g., through the references to Jesus' miracles as signs) that Jesus truly is the Son of God, and that faith in him brings life in his name.[14]

Views on the Epistles

In his opening comments on Paul's Letter to the Romans, Zahn stresses that Paul's first concern is to establish a proper connection between himself and the church in Rome. Thus he begins by noting that he has been called to be an apostle set apart to proclaim God's message of salvation, and that his readers' conversion to faith in Christ has become known throughout the whole world. He prays that his visit with them will result in strengthening their faith.

Zahn points out that the church in Rome was dominantly Jewish. Since Rome was also a center of the Judaistic propaganda that had plagued Paul in his previous missionary activity, the moral support of the Roman church was essential if his intended outreach in Spain (Rom. 15:24, 28) was to be successful.[15] Zahn cites the Acts of Peter as clearly implying that Paul visited Spain between his two imprisonments.[16]

Zahn's late dating of some of Paul's epistles causes him some trouble. For example, he holds to the view that Paul's so-called captivity letters were written in Rome in the early 60s during what he terms Paul's first imprisonment. Yet his careful analysis of all the evidence indicates that these letters were most likely written during Paul's stay in Ephesus between 52 and 55.[17]

12. Zahn, *Introduction*, 3:175.
13. Ibid., 3:334, 346–47.
14. Ibid., 3:207–8, 299–333.
15. Ibid., 1:352–69, 434–38.
16. Ibid., 2:63.
17. Ibid., 1:439–564.

Who was the author of the Letter to the Hebrews? Zahn carefully analyzes the suggestions that either Paul or Barnabas may have written this book. He carefully demonstrates that both of these hypotheses are without proper evidence. He feels that Luther's suggestion of Apollos has some merit, but in the end he concludes with Origen that only God knows the answer.[18]

That Jesus' half-brother James was the author of the Letter of James has been questioned by some on the grounds that James would not have had the knowledge of Greek evidenced in this letter. But Zahn argues that the reign of the Seleucids brought Greek to Palestine and hence to Galilee, through which ran the great trade routes of that time. He concludes as have later historians that the people of Galilee were bilingual. He joins others who place the writing of this letter before A.D. 50.[19]

Whereas Zahn believed that Peter wrote his first letter to Gentiles in Asia Minor, he held that the readers of 2 Peter were for the most part Jewish Christians in Palestine and in the adjoining regions. He ruled out the areas north and northwest of Syrian Antioch. In addition, denying that 2 Peter 3:1 refers to 1 Peter, he suggested that 2 Peter was written earlier than 1 Peter.[20] And on the basis of close resemblances between the Letter of Jude and 2 Peter (cf. Jude 4 and 17–18 with 2 Peter 3:2–3), Zahn also suggested that Jude cited 2 Peter.[21]

In Zahn's view the apostle John is the author of 1–3 John.[22] Church tradition has generally held that the term *presbyteros* in 2 John 1 refers to the apostle John. Eusebius, however, argued that Papias's reference to the truth as it had been declared by disciples of the Lord, including "the elder John," had in view a person other than the apostle. In a detailed analysis Zahn maintains that Papias in using the term *presbyteros* was indeed referring to the apostle. In this instance the term is perhaps best translated as "the ancient one," for the apostle John reached a very old age.[23]

The tradition that the apostle John wrote the Book of Revelation is very strong. Zahn points out that the apocalyptic language of Revelation is not a problem. Because Revelation is a book of prophecy and visions, it is deeply influenced by Old Testament models. Its style is necessarily different from that of John's Gospel.[24]

Zahn also provides very helpful information on what at times is a subject of intense debate, namely, whether the events described in Revelation are to be interpreted as historical and contemporary with the writing or as futuristic in nature.[25] He points out that Irenaeus discarded the view that the number 666 should be interpreted as referring to a former or future Roman em-

18. Ibid., 2:341–56.
19. Ibid., 1:34–72.
20. Ibid., 2:194–221.
21. Ibid., 2:250–66.
22. Ibid., 3:355–74.
23. Ibid., 2:435–45.
24. Ibid., 3:428–35.
25. Ibid., 3:436–49.

peror. "Genuine prophecy," declares Zahn, "contains much which lies outside the consciousness of the prophet himself, and will first become clear through its fulfillment."[26]

A leader of conservative New Testament critics, Zahn seems to have been overlooked by many who did not share his view of Scripture as the inspired Word of God. An additional problem is that his theological German is very elegant but at times very challenging to read. Not surprisingly, then, most of his writings have not been translated into English. But though most of his writings are challenging and have not been translated into English, Zahn had a very great influence on the conservative theologians of his day. And his students, through their teaching and writing on Scripture, especially the New Testament, as well as on the church fathers, later shared their inheritance from Zahn's teaching and writing. Through their efforts many theologians of our day have been enriched by Zahn's achievements.

Primary Sources

Zahn, Theodor. *Cyprian von Antiochien und die deutschen Fasttage.* Erlangen: Deichert, 1882.

———. *Der Hirt des Hermas untersucht.* Gotha, 1868.

———. *Die bleibende Bedeutung des neutestamentlichen Kanons.* Leipzig: Deichert, 1898.

———. *Einleitung in das Neue Testament.* 2 vols. Leipzig: Deichert, 1897, 1900.

———. *Forschungen zur Geschichte des neutestamentlichen Kanons und der altkirchlichen Literatur.* 9 vols. Erlangen: Deichert, 1881–1916.

———. *Geschichte des neutestamentlichen Kanons.* 2 vols. Erlangen: Deichert, 1888, 1892.

———. *Grundriss der Geschichte des neutestamentlichen Kanons: Eine Ergänzung zu der Einleitung in das Neue Testament.* Leipzig: Deichert, 1901.

———. *Ignatius von Antiochien.* Gotha, 1873.

———. *Introduction to the New Testament.* 3 vols. Grand Rapids: Kregel, 1953.

———. *Kommentar zum Neuen Testament.* Leipzig: Deichert, 1903–26. *Matthew* (1903); *Luke* (1913); *John* (1908); *Acts* (2 vols., 1919, 1921); *Romans* (1910); *Galatians* (1905); and *Revelation* (2 vols., 1924, 1926).

———. *Marcellus von Ancyra.* Gotha, 1867.

———. "Mein Werdegang und meine Lebensarbeit." In *Die Religionswissenschaft der Gegenwart in Selbstdarstellungen*, ed. Erich Stange, 221–48. Leipzig: Felix Meiner, 1925.

———, ed. *Ignatii et Polycarpi epistulae, martyria, fragmenta.* Leipzig: Deichert, 1876.

———, Adolf von Harnack, and Oskar von Gebhardt, eds. *Patrum apostolicorum opera.* 3 vols. Leipzig: Deichert, 1875–78.

26. Ibid., 445.

Adolf Schlatter

Robert W. Yarbrough

Although hardly a household name even among specialists, Adolf Schlatter ranks as one of the most productive and profound biblical scholars of modern times. He was once relatively unknown in the English-speaking world because only a few of his writings had been translated. But this situation is rapidly changing. For sheer volume of output (he is credited with over 420 publications, 50 of them longer than a hundred pages) and breadth of expertise Schlatter takes a back seat to few biblical scholars. A brief survey of his life will clarify the often difficult settings in which he carried out his work. It will also set the stage for assessment of Schlatter's significance for both church and academy today.

Biographical Sketch

Family Background and Schooling

Adolf Schlatter was born in Saint Gall, Switzerland, on August 16, 1852, the seventh of nine children. His godly and theologically astute paternal grandmother, Anna Bernet Schlatter (1773–1826), bequeathed to her family a rich heritage: by 1935 six of her nine hundred descendants had become missionaries, and sixty-six had taken up theological study or other ministry-related vocations. Besides Schlatter, one of them was the well-known New Testament and patristics scholar Theodor Zahn (1838–1933).

Schlatter's own parents set a high example of Christian devotion. Schlatter's father Stephan (1805–80), disillusioned with the nominalism and increasing liberalism of the Swiss state church, helped found an independent evangelical church in the late 1830s. Adolf's mother Wilhelmine (1819–94) remained in the Swiss Reformed Church, where Schlatter himself was confirmed and eventually ordained. His parents' loyalty to Christ and each other despite differing ecclesial commitments encouraged an ecumenical openness in Schlatter that would mark his entire life.

In the home Schlatter received not only spiritual nurture but also intellectual encouragement. His father, who had studied pharmaceutics, passed on his interest in the natural world to his children. Late in life the outdoors-loving Schlatter was still able to give a public discourse on Alpine flora, so solid was his early exposure to botany. In school he received the highest possible marks in all subjects. These included five foreign languages, among them Latin, Greek, and Hebrew. Schlatter's Greek teacher Franz Misteli encouraged his gifted young charge to become a professional philologist. But in the end, encouraged by his mother and challenged by his sister Lydia, Schlatter selected theology as his major field of university study.

His first four semesters at the University of Basel (1871–73) were largely devoted to philosophy, as was the custom in pastoral training of the day. Intellectual problems posed by the Christian faith weighed heavily on Schlatter, whose letters home alarmed his family. He joined an academically oriented student group, not the pietistic one recommended by his mother. His letters from that time hint at a crisis of conviction familiar to many students. The tempered faith that emerged following those years was not cheaply won.

Schlatter took special interest in Spinoza and Aristotle. Kant and Hegel were likewise focal points of study. He heard Friedrich Nietzsche lecture on Plato, but the impression was not positive. Years later he recalled chiefly Nietzsche's "offensive haughtiness. He treated his listeners like despicable peons. He convinced me of the principle that to throw out love is to despoil the business of teaching—only genuine love can really educate." For three semesters Schlatter moved to the famous university town of Tübingen in Germany, where he was especially struck by the intense lectures of biblical theologian Johann Tobias Beck. He then returned to Basel, where in 1875 he passed all his oral and written exams with the highest possible marks. His basic preparation for the ministry was complete.

Pastor-Scholar

Although encouraged by a Basel professor to pursue further academic work leading to a teaching chair, Schlatter felt called to parish ministry. From 1875 to 1880 he served with distinction in several Swiss state churches. In 1878 he married Susanna Schoop; they would eventually have five children. In 1880, reluctant to leave the pastorate, Schlatter responded with trepidation to a request that he pursue a university post in the Swiss city of Bern. He knew that the liberal university faculty would seek to block the appointment of a conservative candidate like him. Indeed, when Schlatter arrived and paid a courtesy visit to an influential faculty member, he was brusquely informed that he might as well pack his bags and leave town. But he persevered, submitting as his doctoral dissertation a study of John the Baptist which showed a high level of technical mastery. The faculty, hoping to bar his way despite his acceptable dissertation, responded by amassing a special set of exams for Schlatter. But he never faltered in the course of the eight written and five oral exams to which he was subjected. No other faculty candidate had to endure this ordeal either before or after Schlatter's candidacy. He was appointed to lecture in New Testament exegesis and historical theology.

Faculty relations were much less strained in the northern German university at Greifswald, to which Schlatter was called in 1888. In fact, Schlatter here enjoyed an idyllic five years of service in close cooperation with the renowned Greek lexicographer Hermann Cremer (1834–1903). His appointment was to teach both New Testament and systematic theology. His publications attracted job offers from universities in Bonn, Basel, Heidelberg, and Marburg, but he remained in Greifswald until 1893. At that time he accepted a call to the University of Berlin, where controversy raged over Adolf von Harnack's criticism of the Apostles' Creed. Schlatter, who accepted a systematics chair with permission to teach New Testament topics as well, was expected to provide a theological counterweight. Despite their contrasting outlooks, Schlatter and Harnack enjoyed a friendly relationship. During his Berlin years (1893–98) Schlatter was also active in church and mission work, serving on the board of the Berlin East Africa (later Bethel) Mission and assisting various Christian student organizations.

Professor in Tübingen (1898–1922)

In 1898 Schlatter with his wife and five children made their last major move—to Tübingen in southwest Germany. He was assigned to lecture in New Testament and systematics. His practical involvement in conference speaking and student ministries grew steadily. Shunned at first by the local students, who followed Schlatter's colleagues in considering him too pious and uncritical, he eventually gained respect and even favor with his gripping lectures (delivered without notes), numerous publications, and popularity among students from elsewhere who flocked to hear him. Archival sources abound with details from these years; a recurring theme is student awe at Schlatter's ability to quote lengthy biblical texts from memory—in the original languages. It is reported that he knew the Greek text of the New Testament by heart.

As Schlatter neared the usual years of peak academic productivity, his wife Susanna died suddenly in 1907 at the age of fifty-one. Schlatter was devastated but continued his work with the help of daughters Hedwig and Dora, who with their mother's passing took over household responsibilities for their father, remaining unmarried till their deaths. They were ably assisted by Schlatter's older son, Theodor. Life's end was suddenly palpably near to Schlatter as he approached sixty, and books began to stream from his pen with astonishing speed. In the seven years after his wife's death he wrote four major works totaling two thousand pages, to say nothing of fifty more articles and essays. Large numbers of students crowded into his lectures; in 1912–13 class records put attendance at 231 for his Matthew lectures, 141 for his theological introduction, and 123 for Romans. And he had by no means reached the peak of his Tübingen popularity.

The opening months of the First World War brought the bitter news of the battlefield death of Schlatter's son Paul, who at the war's onset was writing a dissertation on Napoleon. The years of the war and its aftermath saw the volume of Schlatter's literary activity slacken, in part because of sorrow over his son, in part because of grief over the mounting battlefield slaughter, and in part because of heavy involvement in practical student, lay, and civic ministry. More than two thousand letters from pastors, students, and laypersons of all ages who wrote to him after hearing him preach or teach at various conferences have survived. Schlatter was privately sickened by the war, in whose bloody glare his academic work seemed to him for a time like a sacrilege. Yet with war-torn Germany, like all of Europe, suddenly overwhelmed with large numbers of grieving mothers and widows, Schlatter spoke often to women's groups, and in 1921 he was the supervisor for Lydia Schmidt, the first woman to achieve the rank of theological licentiate in the German Protestant church.

Active Retirement (1922–38)

Retirement was mandatory for Schlatter in 1922 at age seventy. In that same year he penned a review of Karl Barth's Romans commentary, which marked the beginning of a new theological era. It was an era in which Schlatter remained active. He made use of his right to offer university lectures and seminars as professor emeritus and continued to teach until 1930, when he ceased after exactly one hundred consecutive semesters of classroom labor. His emeritus lectures drew sufficient numbers of students to fill a hall seating more than seven hundred. He spoke at various annual meetings and conferences. He was also active politically, attempting to give biblical direction to his country's desperate attempts to piece together a better social order in the difficult Weimar years (1919–33). While Schlatter's theology did not conflate church and state, he urged a vibrant, bold, and well-informed participation of Christians in social and political matters.

Capping a life of remarkable productivity, Schlatter's publications from 1929—when he turned seventy-seven—till his death in 1938 bespeak the joy of living, remarkable energy, and iron discipline. In rapid succession he produced nine critical commentaries that together amount to more than four thousand pages. Schlatter published two thousand pages, most of a scholarly nature, in 1930–32 alone. (See figure 1 for English translations of the titles of some of his major works, including the nine New Testament critical commentaries.)

In addition, ministry to students continued unabated, not only in public lectures but in small groups that met weekly in Schlatter's home. These "open evenings" were a fixture in Schlatter's life for forty-eight years (1888–1936). Students from any field of study were invited and encouraged to raise pressing issues. Schlatter would enter the living room promptly at eight, cigar box in hand, greet each student, and then begin fielding questions. At ten o'clock the evening was over. Schlatter was known for his gentleness toward the meek and struggling. He likewise dealt with insincerity and cheek in an appropriate manner.

Figure 1: Schlatter's Major Works

Title in English	Date of Original Publication	Approximate Number of Pages
Faith in the New Testament	1885	600
New Testament Expositions (lay-level commentary on the entire New Testament)	1887–1910	3,430
Introduction to the Bible	1889	500
The Topography and History of Palestine	1893	430
The Days of Trajan and Hadrian	1897	100
The Church of Jerusalem, A.D. 70–130	1898	90
The History of Israel from Alexander the Great to Hadrian	1901	340
The Language and Provenance of the Fourth Gospel	1902	180
The History of Philosophy since Descartes	1906	255
The Theology of the New Testament	1909–10	1,200
Christian Dogmatics	1911	660
Hebrew Names in Josephus	1913	120
Christian Ethics	1914	380
The Corinthian Theology	1914	125
The Grounds for Christian Certainty	1917	110
Luther's Interpretation of Romans	1917	90
The History of Earliest Christianity (English trans. 1955)	1926	387
Devotionals	1927	379
*Matthew the Evangelist	1929	800
*John the Evangelist	1930	400
*The Gospel of Luke	1931	720
The Theology of Judaism according to Josephus	1932	270
*The Letter of James	1932	300
*Paul, Jesus' Messenger (1 and 2 Corinthians commentary)	1934	700
*Mark, Gospel for the Greeks	1935	280
*God's Righteousness (Romans commentary)	1935	400
*Paul's View of the Hellenistic Church (Pastoral Epistles commentary)	1936	270
*Peter and Paul (1 Peter commentary)	1937	180
Do We Know Jesus?	1937	550

*critical New Testament commentaries

Schlatter also made time for one-on-one talks. Though in his last two years he was virtually homebound, he conferred with individual visitors until the last semester before his death. This continued a practice, unheard of for a German university professor, that had always been a part of Schlatter's academic schedule: he was available one hour *each day* to meet with students. German theologian Karl Heinrich Rengstorf suggests that in this custom

Schlatter was utterly unique among his peers, for whom one hour *per week* would have been typical.

Schlatter's last major work was a penetrating devotional guide called *Kennen wir Jesus?* (Do we know Jesus?) containing 366 meditations (Feb. 29 is included). First published in 1937, it bears the stamp of Schlatter's opposition to the National Socialist (Nazi) ideology that had by then inundated his adopted homeland. It also highlights his conviction of Jesus Christ's central significance for both individual and social survival: "Do we know Jesus? If we lose the knowledge of him, we have lost track of our own identity."[1] On the same page Schlatter makes it clear that he fears his German countrymen have indeed traded their culture's Christian heritage for a mess of neopagan pottage. He thus ended his life in the same fashion that he had tirelessly expended it: calling hearers and readers to the sovereign reality of God's presence in the world and the redemptive necessity of the gospel of Christ. He died peacefully on May 19, 1938.

Modern Neglect of Schlatter

A striking picture emerges from even a cursory survey of Schlatter's life and thought. Along with this picture emerges a pressing question: why did Schlatter's voluminous and painstaking academic work have so little impact on German theological thought?

One reason is the difficulty of Schlatter's language. His Swiss accent and often energetic style of delivery made for difficult listening. His general policy of never composing two sentences when he could get by with one renders his writings dauntingly complex at times. Another reason is his failure to have built personal bridges to academic opponents as effectively as he might: in personal writings he confessed that perhaps his greatest sin was his poor relations with colleagues. In fairness to Schlatter, his writings were attacked and sometimes cheaply ridiculed by peers, among them the influential Emil Schürer. But Schlatter's own perception that his response, especially in his younger years, was not always as measured as it might have been was not groundless.

Yet it was the content, not the mode, of his communication that caused many of his academic peers to neglect Schlatter's studies and proposals. Werner Neuer lists ten ways in which Schlatter's scholarship ran against the grain of his times:

1. He affirmed metaphysics and proofs for God's existence as constituent parts of Christian dogmatics.
2. He rejected Kantian epistemology and ethics.
3. He proposed instead a theology and ethics that were empirical, realist, and biblical in nature, not rationalist and idealist as had been prevalent in post-Enlightenment liberal Protestantism.

---

1. Adolf Schlatter, *Kennen wir Jesus?* (Stuttgart: Calwer, 1937), v.

4. He had high regard for creation and nature as revelatory components of God's self-disclosure; he also affirmed the concept of natural law.
5. Accordingly, he rejected the Barthian reduction of the scope of God's self-disclosure to the solitary point of Jesus Christ.
6. He carefully criticized post-Reformation theology for succumbing to intellectualism and failing to move beyond the admittedly all-important doctrine of faith alone to the equally crucial ethical results of vital faith. He traced the roots of these unfortunate developments back to the Reformation itself.
7. He sharply demarcated his own theological outlook from the successive critical orthodoxies of his lifetime: rationalistic liberalism, Ritschlian liberalism, Troeltschian *Kulturprotestantismus,* dialectical theology.
8. He did not facilely join himself to an existing theological school, nor did he found one.
9. He resisted the move of many of his conservative contemporaries toward a simplistic repristination of confessionalism.
10. He incorporated many insights of the obscure early neo-Thomist, Roman Catholic philosopher Franz von Baader (1765–1841), whose insights (gleaned in part from Kant's nemesis Johann Hamann) were of considerable importance to Schlatter in the years immediately following his university training.[2]

Schlatter was by no means without influence or followers in his time. Two generations of pastors gleaned guidance from his teaching. And academicians like Paul Althaus and Wilhelm Lütgert, former Schlatter students, contributed greatly to theological scholarship. Consider also that Hans Emil Weber, Emil Brunner, Dietrich Bonhoeffer, and more recently Otto Michel owed much to Schlatter. A modern theologian has called Schlatter's writings a *Steinbruch* (quarry) from which many have freely borrowed. And he remains the most-read German theologian of his generation—no one else born in the 1830–60 time span even approximates the number of his works in print.

Yet to some degree Schlatter was coolly received by both critical and conservative forces because his creatively independent outlook made each camp suspect him of supporting the other. Conservatives who might have had the will to push Schlatter's views were fragmented and ineffective (in twentieth-century Germany and North America, conservatives lost their determinative influence in their cultures' major intellectual institutions), while certain influential critical thinkers of the 1920s rushed onto the bandwagon of dialectical theology. To the present hour Schlatter remains a marginal figure on the German theological scene—not because his ideas have been sifted and proven unworkable, but because the clamor of dialectical theology and subsequent

2. Werner Neuer, *Die Zusammenhang von Dogmatik und Ethik bei Adolf Schlatter* (Giessen: Brunnen, 1986), 21–22.

movements, along with the passing of several decades, has made it convenient to proceed as if Schlatter's pointed criticisms of modernism's theological implications have been discredited. But these criticisms retain force in the postmodern setting.

Thus it is that Schlatter's achievement remains virtually unappropriated, and largely unacknowledged, even on the German-speaking scene, though scholars like the late Klaus Bockmühl, Peter Stuhlmacher, Werner Neuer, and Rainer Riesner have begun to strip back the prevailing veil of ignorance. Schlatter's pioneering insights continue to hold promise for future hermeneutical and theological initiatives.

Schlatter as Biblical Scholar

Without detracting from Schlatter's importance in such fields as theology, ethics, and philosophy, it must be said that he was primarily an exegete. About 75 percent of his fifty longer writings (over one hundred pages) are devoted to the study of the New Testament or its historical setting, especially Judaism of the intertestamental, New Testament, and post–New Testament eras. A number of characteristics of Schlatter's exegetical contribution deserve mention.

Philological Rigor

Philology is the detailed study of literature, language, and linguistics. While liberal theological colleagues attacked Schlatter's exegesis for its alleged lack of scholarly depth, the philosophy faculty of the University of Berlin was closer to the mark. In 1932, on the occasion of Schlatter's eightieth birthday, when a number of his critical commentaries had already appeared, it granted Schlatter an honorary doctorate with the following commendation: "The faculty honors in Professor von Schlatter the proponent and upholder of a *Philologia sacra* [sacred philology] in the venerable ancient sense, which [philology] moves upward from a precise and accurate understanding of the linguistic and historical to a vital and enlivening overarching conception of the New Testament tradition."[3]

Evidence of Schlatter's command of philological detail may be found in both the text and appendix of his commentary on Matthew, where hundreds of Semitic parallels to Matthew's usage are cited. The commentary on John is even more striking with its nineteen pages of painstakingly detailed wordlists: Semitic parallels to John's Gospel, parallels to Josephus in John's Gospel, Johannine words absent from Josephus, parallels between John's Gospel and John's Apocalypse (both of which Schlatter held were written by John the son of Zebedee), and Johannine words absent from John's Apocalypse (Schlatter counts a total of twenty). Also notable in this connection are the twenty (unpublished but preserved in archives) volumes of Schlatter's hand-

3. *Adolf-Schlatter-Archiv* (Stuttgart: Landeskirchliches Archiv/Adolf-Schlatter-Archiv, 1988), 230.

written notes on Josephus, including a two-volume concordance that he compiled from his own reading, further evidence of the philological rigor for which Schlatter strove.

Focus on the Primary Text

Until late in life when his critical commentaries appeared, Schlatter was accused of ignoring the work of other scholars. The ground for this charge lay in the fact that his writings (with the exception of his dogmatics volume) were not packed with the dense masses of footnotes conventional in modern scholarly monographs. Schlatter's response to this charge was twofold. First, he self-effacingly claimed that early in his career he realized he would have to choose between being expert in the ancient sources and being expert in modern critical opinion. He chose the former. Second, he stated repeatedly that his passion was to examine the historical, philological, and theological details of the texts he studied, not to grope for direction in the obscuring fog that the antitheological conjectures of his colleagues produced. He conceded the obvious value of familiarity with current theories—and his writings bristle with implicit evidence that he was aware of his colleagues' views. But he was also aware that our "hearing [of the text] is imperiled when at the same time we are stormed by a jumble of voices. Stillness is the condition for hearing; it demands restricting our communion to the one who now speaks to us."[4] Secondary sources can broaden the interpreter's horizon, but they can as easily becloud it.[5]

Scholarship in Service of the Gospel

Schlatter lived in the heyday of liberal Protestantism. Institutions that had once served the church—for example, university theology faculties that trained pastors—now tended to see their task as freeing the church from old-fashioned beliefs like Jesus' divinity, his substitutionary atonement, his bodily resurrection, and the Bible's entire and normative veracity. In many cases pastors were trained accordingly. Schlatter resisted this trend, not in a reactionary but in a progressive manner. He placed his literary ability at the service of lay and pastoral readers as he wrote his best-known works, *Erläuterungen zum Neuen Testament* (New Testament expositions), a ten-volume (often bound in three volumes) running commentary on the entire New Testament. Schlatter is the sole New Testament scholar of stature to achieve—some would say stoop to—this feat in the twentieth century. He toiled to let Scripture, not just modern dismissals of it, be heard, refusing to enthrone as the church's normative leaders academicians sporting unsatisfactory innovations: "Leadership of the church does not belong to the theologians; they are not the sole agent of the one who alone rules and builds churches."[6]

4. Werner Neuer, *Adolf Schlatter: Ein Leben für Theologie und Kirche* (Stuttgart: Calwer, 1995), 435.
5. Ibid., 501.
6. Ibid., 481.

This does not mean that trained academicians have no role in the church—their service is desperately needed—but they must be willing to cultivate contacts with pastoral and lay leaders and to labor at practical acts of Christian love.[7] And they must not be overly enamored of the fashions that sweep academe and sometimes subvert Christian scholarship. (Already in the late 1920s Schlatter's exposure to Rudolf Bultmann's books and at least one lecture led him to fear that Bultmann was headed in the direction of "an atheistic interpretation of Jesus.")[8]

In theological education Schlatter believed in engaging the hearts, not just the minds of students. His goal was to train them in "independent reading of Holy Scripture and theological literature" rather than in swallowing whole the opinions of their teachers.[9] The pastoral office calls for "wide-awake observers . . . not men who are blinded by their fixed ideas."[10] Schlatter also emphasized that a healthy fear of God is requisite to theological training and discussion; theology is "not only a matter of intellectual precision but also, and even more, of the inner disposition of the person toward God."[11]

In all of this Schlatter maintained the highest academic standards and methodological rigor. In serving church interests he did not dilute the legitimate demands of scholarship. He refused to allow dogmatic liberalism, or existentialist-oriented dialectical theology, to dictate the content and significance of the ancient biblical sources. And he just as adamantly refused to let dogmatic conservatism short-circuit the need for perennial scholarly scrutiny of the biblical sources historically understood as a basis for ongoing personal, doctrinal, and ultimately social renewal.

Attention to Jewish Backgrounds

One of the most important hallmarks of Schlatter's biblical scholarship was his attention to Jewish backgrounds. Many of his academic peers were heavily indebted to philosophical idealism and tended to see ancient Judaism and pure Christianity in antithetical terms. Historical research sometimes became a matter of finding parallels to the New Testament in non-Jewish sources, and then theorizing how these non-Jewish ideas, however remote temporally or geographically, came to appear in the Semitic-sounding books of the New Testament. A whole interpretive school formed around this enterprise: the *Religionsgeschichtliche Schule* (history-of-religions school). Typical of its approach were its explanations of central aspects of John's Gospel on the basis of ideas found in Greek and Hellenistic sources such as Plato and Philo.

Schlatter demurred: "If we surround [the New Testament] with pieces of background which contradict its clear statements, we are making historical

---

7. Ibid., 256.
8. Ibid., 472.
9. Ibid., 279.
10. Ibid., 286.
11. Ibid., 444–45.

research into a work of fiction. In my view, New Testament theology only fulfills its obligations by observation, not by free creation."[12] Schlatter argued for a Palestinian origin of John's Gospel. In both technical monographs and his critical commentary on John, Schlatter advanced extensive linguistic and historical arguments to support his view. He went largely unheeded in his lifetime—but was vindicated after Dead Sea Scroll discoveries in the late 1940s bore out his contentions about the Palestinian flavor of the fourth Gospel.

Schlatter's attention to the Semitic dimensions of the New Testament did not, however, cause him to ignore Hellenism's ubiquitous presence in first-century Palestine. For example, the first volume of his New Testament theology details the similarities and differences between Jesus' and Hellenistic thought.[13] Volume 2 likewise carefully notes the distinctives of Greek culture in its interplay with the gospel.[14] To say that Schlatter paid attention to Jewish thought is not to say that he gave short shrift to Greek ideas. It is simply to point out that he noted not only *similarities* between New Testament language and Hellenistic sources, but also *differences*. These differences had to be accounted for, and Schlatter found that the most likely sources were often Jewish and Old Testament background material.

In recent years E. P. Sanders has called attention to the distortions of ancient Judaism that plagued New Testament scholarship in the past. Today both Gospel and Pauline studies are marked by pronounced emphasis on, and positive assessment of, the New Testament's Jewish features. While the pendulum has swung too far in this direction in some quarters, the current trend is an improvement over the covert, and sometimes overt, anti-Semitism of past scholarship. Schlatter deserves credit for anticipating this trend. His laborious and, at the time, lonely forays into the labyrinths of rabbinic thought and Jewish history mark him as a true pioneer. Modern New Testament historians like the late F. F. Bruce and Martin Hengel have continued to show the fruitfulness of this approach, enlarging the foundation that Schlatter laid.

A Method Open to the Transcendent

In the past two hundred years scholars have embarked on various quests for the historical Jesus. This means the Jesus found by applying certain critical theories to the Gospel traditions. These theories have tended to deny that the New Testament writings—taken as unified wholes—have as much in-

---

12. Adolf Schlatter, "The Theology of the New Testament and Dogmatics," in *The Nature of New Testament Theology*, ed. and trans. Robert Morgan (London: SCM, 1973), 135. This seminal essay also appears as an appendix in Werner Neuer, *Adolf Schlatter*, trans. Robert Yarbrough (Grand Rapids: Baker, 1996), 169–210 (the quote is found on p. 185).

13. Adolf Schlatter, *Die Geschichte des Christus* (Stuttgart: Calwer, 1922), 41–47 (this volume was originally published in 1909 under the title *Das Wort Jesu*); idem, *The History of the Christ*, trans. Andreas Köstenberger (Grand Rapids: Baker, 1997), 48–52.

14. Adolf Schlatter, *Die Theologie der Apostel* (Stuttgart: Calwer, 1910), 209–17, 292–98, 550–62, which appears in English as *The Theology of the Apostles*, trans. Andreas Köstenberger (Grand Rapids: Baker, 1998).

sight to offer into the historical Jesus as do modern scholars with their latest claims and methods. On the basis of isolated New Testament (or extrabiblical) passages the real Jesus is argued to have been a political revolutionary, a wandering sage, a cynical social critic, or even a magician, instead of the Son of God, the sacrifice for sin, and giver of eternal life—in a word, the Messiah—that the New Testament writings in their entirety present.

Schlatter, on the other hand, believed that "there is no ground for the hope that we can arrive at a 'historical' Jesus after we have rejected the statements of all his disciples—Matthew, John, Paul, and with them the entirety of early Christendom."[15] His researches confirmed for him that Jesus was indeed the messianic deliverer of Old Testament promise. This led him to argue that scholarship goes astray in dogmatically rejecting the material presence of God in the space-time world. Such banning of God from the phenomenal realm has dominated Protestant theology since Kant. But by adamantly rejecting even the *possibility* of such Christian affirmations as the incarnation, Jesus' ontological unity with God, and history's capacity to serve as vehicle for the transcendent, scholars, instead of soberly observing and investigating the realities to which the New Testament writers point, risk embarking on a blind and partisan dispute with them.

It is acceptable, Schlatter conceded, to employ a method informed by the theory that certain data can be accounted for without resorting to God or divine causation as an essential explanatory factor. This is the classic *etsi Deus non daretur* (as if God did not exist) premise, the assumption that phenomena can be explained solely with reference to immanent causation. As a heuristic tool this premise has value, even for biblical studies. The trouble arises when the tool moves from a methodological premise, a consciously adopted angle of vision, to a dogmatically held postulate. Then the danger of rationalism arises: "Where judgment cuts loose from the perception which is indispensable to it, where the intellect's productive power tries to be in command and play the creator so that what we produce is no longer connected with a prior receiving, where thought circles around one's own self, as though this could create from itself the material from which knowledge comes and the rules by which it is to be judged, there we have rationalism. It stands in irreconcilable hostility to the very basis of the New Testament, because acknowledging God is the direct opposite of rationalism. But this rationalism is at the same time the road to dreamland and the death of intellectual integrity."[16]

Schlatter opposed such rationalism on both theological and scientific grounds. While *methodological* atheism is reasonable in the pluralistic sphere of academic inquiry, *dogmatic* atheism is the enemy of true science, to say nothing of religion. Much of Schlatter's work represents a challenge,

---

15. Schlatter, *Geschichte*, 17–18; idem, *History of the Christ*, 31.
16. Schlatter, "Theology of the New Testament," 150; Neuer, *Adolf Schlatter*, trans. Yarbrough, 196–97.

and constructive alternative, to the covert intellectual totalitarianism that results when dogmatic atheism prevails, causing damage to both scholarship and church interests.[17] One of the most important potential results of the renewed attention to Schlatter is that current biblical scholarship may develop a sharper awareness of the ideological underpinnings that inform allegedly neutral methods.

In Germany, Schlatter studies, while not a torrent, are appearing with gratifying frequency. In English-speaking circles familiarity with Schlatter is rapidly growing. A recent monograph by Stephen Dintaman and a translation of Werner Neuer's important short biography are promising signs. So is the appearance of his hefty two-volume New Testament theology.[18]

Schlatter's writings hold rich potential for summoning serious biblical scholarship back to its classic sources, methods, and aims. In today's fragmented academic climate a voice of informed and independent moderation based on comprehensive and sympathetic observation of the Bible is much needed. Schlatter's work instructively upholds the historic Christian ideal of balanced erudition committed to the task of letting Christ and Scripture grace lost humankind and rule the church with their truth and light. Time marches on; but Schlatter's observations, proposals, and methodological insights—many still waiting to be recovered—will retain their relevance for the foreseeable future.

Primary Sources

Schlatter, Adolf. *Atheistische Methoden in der Theologie*. Edited by Heinzpeter Hempelmann. Wuppertal: Brockhaus, 1985.

———. *The Church in the New Testament Period*. Translated by Paul P. Levertoff. London: S.P.C.K., 1955.

———. *Das Evangelium des Lukas*. Stuttgart: Calwer, 1931.

———. *Der Brief des Jakobus*. Stuttgart: Calwer, 1932.

———. *Der Evangelist Johannes*. Stuttgart: Calwer, 1930.

———. *Der Evangelist Matthäus*. Stuttgart: Calwer, 1929.

———. *Der Glaube im Neuen Testament*. Stuttgart: Calwer, 1885.

———. *Die Geschichte des Christus*. Stuttgart: Calwer, 1922. Eng. trans., *The History of the Christ*. Translated by Andreas Köstenberger. Grand Rapids: Baker, 1997.

———. *Die Kirche der Griechen im Urteil des Paulus* [Pastoral Epistles]. Stuttgart: Calwer, 1936.

———. *Die Theologie der Apostel*. Stuttgart: Calwer, 1910. Eng. trans., *The Theology of the Apostles*. Translated by Andreas Köstenberger. Grand Rapids: Baker, 1998.

17. See Adolf Schlatter, *Atheistische Methoden in der Theologie*, ed. Heinzpeter Hempelmann (Wuppertal: Brockhaus, 1985), translated into English in Neuer, *Adolf Schlatter*, trans. Yarbrough, 211–25.
18. See nn. 13–14.

————. *Erläuterungen zum Neuen Testament*. 10 vols. in 3. Stuttgart: Calwer, 1887–1910.

————. *Gottes Gerechtigkeit*. Stuttgart: Calwer, 1935. Eng. trans., *Romans: The Righteousness of God*. Translated by Siegfried Schatzmann. Peabody, Mass.: Hendrickson, 1995.

————. *Kennen wir Jesus?* Stuttgart: Calwer, 1937.

————. *Markus, Evangelium für die Griechen*. Stuttgart: Calwer, 1935.

————. *Paulus, der Bote Jesu* [1 and 2 Corinthians]. Stuttgart: Calwer, 1934.

————. *Petrus und Paulus* [1 Peter]. Stuttgart: Calwer, 1937.

————. Review of *Epistle to the Romans*, 2d ed., by Karl Barth. Translated by Keith R. Crim. In *The Beginnings of Dialectic Theology*, edited by James M. Robinson, vol. 1. Richmond: John Knox, 1968.

————. "The Theology of the New Testament and Dogmatics." In *The Nature of New Testament Theology*, edited by Robert Morgan, 117–66. Studies in Biblical Theology, 2d ser., vol. 25. London: SCM, 1973.

Secondary Sources

Adolf-Schlatter-Stiftung. *Das Schrifttum Adolf Schlatters* [bibliography of Schlatter's published writings]. Neustettin: Spengler, n.d.

Bock, Ernst. *Adolf-Schlatter-Archiv* [inventory of Schlatter's unpublished writings]. Stuttgart: Landeskirchliches Archiv/Adolf-Schlatter-Archiv, 1988.

Dintaman, Stephen. *Creative Grace: Faith and History in the Theology of Adolf Schlatter*. New York: Peter Lang, 1993.

Neuer, Werner. *Adolf Schlatter: A Biography of Germany's Premier Biblical Theologian*. Translated by Robert W. Yarbrough. Grand Rapids: Baker, 1996.

————. *Adolf Schlatter: Ein Leben für Theologie und Kirche*. Stuttgart: Calwer, 1995.

————. "Schlatter, Adolf (1852–1938)." In *Theologische Realenzyklopädie* 30:135–43. New York: Walter deGruyter, 1998.

————. *Die Zusammenhang von Dogmatik und Ethik bei Adolf Schlatter*. Giessen: Brunnen, 1986.

Stuhlmacher, Peter. "Adolf Schlatter's Interpretation of Scripture." *New Testament Studies* 24 (1978): 433–46.

————. "Jesus of Nazareth as Christ of Faith." In Peter Stuhlmacher, *Jesus of Nazareth—Christ of Faith*, 1–38. Translated by Siegfried S. Schatzmann. Peabody, Mass.: Hendrickson, 1993.

Yarbrough, Robert. "Adolf Schlatter." In *Historical Handbook of Major Biblical Interpreters*, edited by Donald McKim, 518–22. Downers Grove, Ill.: InterVarsity, 1998.

————. "Adolf Schlatter's 'The Significance of Method for Theological Work': Translation and Commentary." *Southern Baptist Journal of Theology* 1.2 (Summer 1997): 64–76.

Robert Dick Wilson

Walter C. Kaiser, Jr.

Robert Dick Wilson was born on February 4, 1856. Perhaps what Robert was to become could be seen in part from the fact that his father, a leading merchant in the town of Indiana, Pennsylvania, was a man of culture and taste. He was president of the board of trade in his county and president of the local school board. He was able to give his attention to all of these ventures along with the ten children in his home.

Already at the age of four Robert Dick could read. He began school at the age of five, and at eight he had read, among many other books, the *Five Great Monarchies of the Ancient Eastern World,* a ponderous work by the archeologist George Rawlinson. Further evidence of a great appetite for learning and books is an episode that occurred when he was nine. He and his brother accompanied their father on a rather long journey for those days from their home near Pittsburgh to Philadelphia. As Robert Dick later recounted, the most exciting part of that trip was a visit to a bookstore on Chestnut Street, where their father left the boys for a while so that they could select their own books. He was startled to discover, upon returning, that they had gathered about fifty volumes, including such "light reading" as Prescott, Robertson, J. S. C. Abbott, and similar standard works.[1]

Having completed public school in Indiana, Pennsylvania, Robert was ready at the age of fourteen to begin his collegiate experience at the College of New Jersey (later renamed Princeton University). However, he did not enter that year, but waited until he was seventeen years old. He later explained the reason for this delay: "I had a good deal of headache[s] between my fourteenth and twentieth years, and then typhoid. After that my headache[s] disappeared. I really couldn't half do my work before that."[2]

In college Robert specialized in language study, psychology, and mathematics. He would one day in retrospect express embarrassment that a low grade of 90 in one of his Bible courses had pulled down his average. His real love seemed to be language study. He had prepared himself for college by studying French, German, and Greek.

---

1. Philip E. Howard, foreword to *Is the Higher Criticism Scholarly?* by Robert Dick Wilson (Philadelphia: Sunday School Times, 1922), 5–6.
2. Ibid., 6.

Because Wilson had made up his mind that he wanted to study the classics in the original languages, his habit was to take a grammar book with him when he went on a walk. When he stopped for a rest, he would study for a bit and learn what he could. His friends claimed he had a remarkably retentive memory. His procedure for working through a grammar proved remarkably successful:

> I would read a grammar through, look up the examples, making notes as I went along, and I wouldn't pass by anything until I could explain it. I never learned long lists of words, but I would read a page through, recall the words I didn't know, and then look them up. I read anything I thought would be interesting to me if it were in English. I got so interested in the story that I was unconscious of the labor—as a man is interested in his roses, and he doesn't think of the thorns. So I learned Greek, Latin, French, German, Hebrew, Italian, Spanish, Portuguese, Biblical Aramaic, Syriac, Arabic, and so on.[3]

Using this method, he eventually mastered twenty-six languages and dialects.

Wilson graduated from the College of New Jersey in 1876 with an A.B.; in 1879 he received his A.M. Having in the meantime been licensed by the Kittanning Presbytery, he began holding evangelistic services in places like Cherry Tree, Burnside, Bethel, Mechanicsburg, and Armagh. During most of this time, Wilson was an assistant to Alexander Donaldson of Elder's Ridge, Pennsylvania. Prior to his entering seminary, Wilson and his brother devoted approximately a year and a half to the work of evangelism in the town of Indiana. The response was so encouraging that Robert would have taken up the work of an evangelist had not his studies caused him to perceive that there was a great need for a type of biblical scholarship that would deal objectively with the evidence. While holding meetings at Cherry Tree, he purchased a Hebrew Bible and a Hebrew dictionary and grammar that were written in Latin. Through studying these books, he won a prize for Hebrew upon entering Western Theological Seminary (Pittsburgh).

In the years 1881–83 Wilson did research in Semitic languages at the University of Berlin. There he concentrated on Assyriology under Eberhard Schrader, August Dillmann, and Eduard Sachau. It was during his student days in Germany that Wilson designed a plan for his life. He believed it would be well for him to divide his career into three blocks of fifteen years each. Not many young men would design a forty-five-year program for themselves, but that is another indication of the unique quality of the man. The first fifteen years would be spent studying the original languages of the Bible and various cognate tongues. During the second fifteen years he would focus on biblical textual matters in the light of his philological studies. His hope was to spend the last fifteen years in writing what he had learned.

3. Ibid., 7.

After Berlin, Wilson returned to Western Theological Seminary, where he served as an instructor (1883–85) and then as a professor of Old Testament (1885–1900). He was ordained in 1885, and received his Ph.D. from the College of New Jersey in 1886. Having risen to the position of head of the Department of Old Testament History and Hebrew, he left in 1900 to take a similar position at Princeton Theological Seminary.

Wilson served at Princeton until 1929. He loved the classroom; his material was fresh, and his pedagogical methods were never stereotyped. Whether the subject was Hebrew or a refutation of some new theory of the higher critics, Wilson threw himself into the lectures with enthusiasm. "For a number of years at Princeton he gave the new students a lecture on the importance of Hebrew. He called it his 'Cui Bono?' (i.e., 'What's the Use [of Hebrew]?') lecture. And it became an institution; upperclassmen who had heard the lecture once or twice already would come to hear Dr. Wilson enlarge upon a theme so dear to his heart."[4]

Writings

By the time Wilson died in his seventy-fifth year, most of his forty-five-year program had been achieved. He had familiarized himself with twenty-six languages, including Assyrian and Babylonian cuneiform, Ethiopic, Phoenician, various Aramaic dialects, Egyptian, Coptic, Persian, Arabic, Syriac, and Hebrew. He also had published thirty-six major articles and fifteen book reviews in the *Princeton Theological Review* and at least four monographs on key critical issues of the day. Wilson's scholarship was often extremely technical, and therefore had little appeal to the general audience. He did very little work in exegesis per se and did not much enter into theological discussion. Serious students of the Bible who are acquainted with his written legacy are, however, quick to acknowledge that his defense of the Word of God remains challenging and instructive even to this day.

While still at Western Theological Seminary, Wilson published his *Introductory Syriac Method and Manual* (1891), which was modeled after William Rainey Harper's *Introductory Hebrew Method and Manual*. The brief *Notes on Hebrew Syntax* (1892) soon followed. Wilson's inaugural address upon being appointed by Princeton Seminary to the prestigious chair named after William Henry Green was delivered on September 21, 1900, and published the next year under the title *The Lower Criticism of the Old Testament as a Preparation for the Higher Criticism* (1901). Next came his *Illustrations of Gesenius' Hebrew Grammar with Vocabularies* (1906) and his *Hebrew Grammar for Beginners* (1908).

Even though Wilson had not been trained at Princeton Seminary, he became a champion of its theology and a defender of its conservative stance on

4. Oswald T. Allis, "Robert Dick Wilson—Defender of God's Word," *Christianity Today* 1.7 (Nov. 1930): 4.

critical matters. Given his expertise in Semitic philology, in ancient Near Eastern history, literature, and archeology, and in the general movements of contemporary Old Testament scholarship, he was able to mount one of the most successful defenses of the conservative position on many of the critical issues that were in the forefront of Old Testament scholarship in the first third of the twentieth century.

Wilson recognized that some of the most significant battles centered on the Book of Daniel: its miracles, history, and prophecies. It was his conviction that if one maintained a clear conservative view on this book of the Bible, one would remain conservative on other matters as well.[5] Not surprisingly, then, it was for his Daniel studies that Wilson earned his reputation as one of the leading conservative voices of Old Testament scholarship. In the first volume of *Studies in the Book of Daniel* (1917) he concludes that the charges and methods of the critics are "illogical, irrational, and *unscientific*. They are illogical because they beg the question at issue. They are irrational because they assume that historic facts are self-evident, and that they can set limits to the possible. They are unscientific because they base their conclusions on incomplete inductions and on a practical claim of omniscience."[6] The second planned volume, which was to have dealt specifically with the linguistic problems of Daniel, was never written, but the third planned volume was published first as a series of articles in the *Princeton Theological Review* and then as volume 2 of *Studies in the Book of Daniel* (1938).

By this time most scholars had already accepted a Maccabean date for the Book of Daniel as set forth by S. R. Driver's *Book of Daniel* (1900).[7] However, Wilson's early dating of Daniel did attract the attention of Semitic philologists and some Old Testament scholars. A clear example of Wilson's approach is the hard linguistic argument that he aimed directly at Driver's thesis that the Persian, Greek, and Aramaic words in the Book of Daniel either presuppose, permit, or demand a date after the conquest of Palestine by Alexander the Great (332 B.C.).[8]

So stung was Driver by the challenge that he included a rejoinder to Wilson in the ninth edition of his *Introduction to the Literature of the Old Testament*. Driver was most incensed that Wilson had not represented his position fairly: Driver had not claimed that the Aramaic of Daniel "proved" the book to be a product of the second century B.C.; he had said only that the Ar-

5. Wilson made this assertion to his students in the academic year 1925–26; see Marion A. Taylor, *The Old Testament in the Old Princeton School (1812–1929)* (San Francisco: Mellen Research University Press, 1992), 267 n. 67.

6. Robert Dick Wilson, *Studies in the Book of Daniel*, 2 vols. in 1 (Grand Rapids: Baker, 1979), 1:xiii.

7. S. R. Driver, *The Book of Daniel*, Cambridge Bible for Schools and Colleges (Cambridge: Cambridge University Press, 1900).

8. Robert Dick Wilson, "The Aramaic of Daniel," in *Biblical and Theological Studies*, by the members of the faculty of Princeton Theological Seminary (New York: Scribner, 1912), 261–306.

amaic "permitted" it to be from that date. H. H. Rowley, feeling that Wilson's learned article required a fuller response than that offered by Driver, produced *The Aramaic of the Old Testament*, which was vicious at points in its assessment of Wilson, accusing him of inaccuracy, blindness, and prejudice in handling his data.[9] Wilson spent his last summer studying Rowley's book, but the materials found after his death were insufficient to be pieced together into publishable form.[10]

In a series of essays published in 1919 in the *Princeton Theological Review* Wilson set forth the method that he followed during his years at Western and Princeton. These essays were later revised and enlarged for his *Scientific Investigation of the Old Testament* (1926). He called his method "scientific" to emphasize that he based his conclusions on the evidence of facts rather than on the status of some recognized authority. Wilson appealed to textual, grammatical, linguistic, and historical evidences as well as comparable texts from cognate languages and cultures. He would apply the evidence in the same way that documents are admitted in our courts of law, that is, to demonstrate what is reasonable to accept, given the weight of the facts. He was consumed with a deep desire to remove the subjective intrusions into Old Testament studies in order that the objective facts could be given their proper prominence.

Wilson's wide-ranging argument was most clearly expressed in a booklet entitled *Is the Higher Criticism Scholarly?* (1922). This forerunner of *A Scientific Investigation of the Old Testament* claims to present "clearly attested facts showing that the destructive 'assured results of modern scholarship' are indefensible." Wilson begins by asserting that "there is no good reason for doubting that the Biblical narrative is derived from *written* sources."[11] Evidence for this statement is that Abraham came from Babylonia, where writing had been in use for hundreds of years before his time. Since Egypt also had by Abraham's time been using writing for some two thousand years, it would not be unreasonable to think that the patriarch conducted his business there in writing as well. It is also possible to prove that the Hebrew language was used in Palestine before the time of Moses. For example, embedded in the Amarna correspondence between the pharaohs of the Eighteenth Dynasty in Egypt (fourteenth century B.C.) and various princes in Palestine and Syria are more than one hundred common Hebrew words and more than thirty Hebrew names for cities in Palestine and Syria.

    9. H. H. Rowley, *The Aramaic of the Old Testament: A Grammatical and Lexical Study of Its Relations with Other Early Aramaic Dialects* (London: Oxford University Press, 1929).
    10. Allis, "Robert Dick Wilson," 5, leaves the reverse impression: "It is fortunate that [Rowley's work] came to Dr. Wilson's hands in time for him to devote part of the last summer of his life to examining it. His reply was nearly ready when he died; and it will probably appear in *The Evangelical Quarterly* (Edinburgh) in the not too distant future." On the other hand, Taylor, *Old Testament*, 271, says, "In spite of Wilson's promises that his rejoinder to Rowley was almost ready for publication, neither his reply nor enough material to piece together his response was found after his death in 1930."
    11. Wilson, *Is the Higher Criticism Scholarly?* 15.

Wilson then proceeds to point out that "the general scheme of *chronology* and *geography* presented to us in the Hebrew records corresponds with what we can learn from other documents of the same period."[12] That is to say, the annals of various foreign nations accord with what the Bible presents as the framework of world history. Equally noteworthy is that the scriptural transliterations of "twenty-four names of kings of Egypt, Assyria, Babylon, *et al.*, contain 120 consonantal letters, of which all are found in the same order in the transcriptions of the kings themselves or in those of their contemporaries."[13] This is remarkable, judges Wilson, when compared to the transliteration of foreign words in other documents from comparable periods. The Bible's success in this area is unequaled in the history of literature.

Wilson then turns to the critics' argument that the intrusion of foreign words into the Bible disproves the traditional claims regarding date and authenticity. Also particularly vulnerable are the fifteen hundred words that appear only once in the Old Testament, and possibly the three thousand words that occur no more than five times in the Hebrew text. Wilson's rejoinder to those who used many of these words as evidence for late dating of the biblical documents is unswerving: "In each stage of the literature the foreign words in the documents are found to belong to the language of the peoples that the Scriptures and the records of the nations surrounding Israel unite in declaring to have influenced and affected the Israelites at that time."[14] As for those words that occur nowhere else in Scripture, it is pointless to find such a word in a much later extrabiblical document and then assign to that word's biblical context an equally late date. That a word occurs but once in Scripture demonstrates only the uniqueness of the author's style, but nothing particular about the date of his writing.

Turning from the language of the Old Testament to its literature, Wilson notes that the text exhibits all of the literary forms observed in the cognate literatures. The legal forms are of particular interest, since the critics claim that the law as it is presented in the Old Testament did not come from the Mosaic era, but clearly was written later. Wilson has some tough questions for these critics to face. First, if the covenant code of Exodus 20–24 and the main part of Deuteronomy actually came from the period of the kingdoms of Israel and Judah, why is the king mentioned only once, and that in a passage (Deut. 17) that only anticipates the kingly office? And why is Zion or Jerusalem, the capital of the Judean kingdom, never mentioned if these laws were written hundreds of years later as many scholars claim? Furthermore, why is there no mention of the temple, but only of what the critical scholars consider a mythical tabernacle? Finally, how did the so-called priestly code's emphasis on the shedding of blood come about, given that the Baby-

12. Ibid., 16.
13. Ibid., 19.
14. Ibid., 26.

lonian religion, its alleged source, does not seem to have assigned any importance or usefulness to the concept of blood. In fact, the vocabulary bearing on the ceremonial observances is entirely different from that of the Babylonian system, from which the priestly aspects of the Torah were supposedly borrowed.

Wilson applies the same scrutiny to the critics' claims about the books of Chronicles, Psalms, Ezra and Nehemiah. He concludes with the complaint that the critics "cut up the books and doctor the documents and change the text and wrest the meaning, to suit the perverted view of their own fancy. They seem to think that they know better what the Scriptures ought to have been than the prophets and apostles and even the Lord himself!"[15]

In sum, Wilson championed the conservative position on many of the crucial issues of the day: the completion of the Old Testament canon before the last of the prophets (fifth century B.C.); the historicity and Mosaic authorship of the Pentateuch (even though it may have later been revised by inspired editors); the trustworthiness of the sources on which the earlier prophets depended (Joshua, Judges, Samuel, and Kings); the legitimacy of the titles in the Book of Psalms; the Solomonic authorship of Ecclesiastes, Song of Songs, and most of Proverbs; the traditional dating of the prophetical books; a fifth-century (or earlier) dating for Job; and a completion date for Esther, Ezra-Nehemiah, and Chronicles no later than 400 B.C.

The Last Years

On April 11, 1927, the Kittanning Presbytery passed the following resolutions on the occasion of Wilson's fiftieth anniversary in the ministry:

Resolved, First: That the Presbytery of Kittanning acknowledge with gratitude that kind Providence that established the parental home of Robert Dick Wilson within our bounds; that has smiled on him in the midst of varying scenes of his life of eminent scholarship, and has placed within his left hand length of days, and in his right, riches of learning and the manifold honors of our glorious Church.

Resolved, Second: That this Presbytery extend to Robert Dick our heartiest congratulations upon his fifty years of service to our beloved Church and upon his conspicuously successful achievements in the Department of the Old Testament Criticism.

Resolved, Third: That, since a large proportion of the members of this Presbytery have been students of Robert Dick Wilson at the Western and the Princeton Theological Seminaries, this Presbytery express its appreciation of Dr. Wilson's example, sympathy, efficiency, and comradeship.

Resolved, Fourth: That the Presbytery of Kittanning extend to Dr. Robert Wilson its grateful appreciation of his continuance as a member in this Presbytery, although his home, for the greater part of the year, and his work have been elsewhere, and we cherish the hope that many years of life and health and

15. Ibid., 61.

happiness may be in store for him and that often we may be honored with his presence and blessed by his gracious influence.

It was also noted in the same set of minutes that Wilson's service extended far beyond the classroom and his publications. In the preceding five years he had delivered about five hundred lectures in defense of the Bible. His itinerary had included Japan, Korea, China, England, Wales, Scotland, Canada, and many of the larger cities of the United States. And in that very year he had also addressed the two opening sessions of the Ninth International Congress of the World's Christian Fundamentals Association.

On May 23, 1929, the General Assembly of the Presbyterian Church in the U.S.A. met in St. Paul with the election of a new moderator the most controversial item on the agenda. The two men who had considerable backing were Cleland McAfee, a professor of systematic theology at McCormick Theological Seminary in Chicago, and Robert Dick Wilson. Wilson's candidacy was sponsored by a group of "fundamentalists" who yearned for the Old School Presbyterianism that had prevailed prior to its reunion with the New School in 1870. The Old School advocates also objected to the policies of J. Ross Stevenson, Princeton Seminary's president, who desired to place the management of the school under a single board instead of two bodies, a board of directors and a board of trustees. Despite being in his seventy-fourth year, with an honorable retirement awaiting him in a comfortable home, Wilson chose to leave Princeton Seminary after its reorganization to help J. Gresham Machen and Oswald T. Allis start Westminster Theological Seminary in Philadelphia. Wilson had been at Princeton nearly thirty years.

On Saturday, October 11, 1930, Robert Dick Wilson, professor of Semitic philology and Old Testament criticism at Westminster Theological Seminary, entered into his heavenly reward. His last public appearance was on October 1, 1930, at the opening exercises of the second year of Westminster Theological Seminary. Two weeks later his body was laid to rest in the cemetery in Indiana, Pennsylvania.

It happened that the Board of Trustees of Princeton Seminary was meeting on Tuesday, October 14, 1930, the very day of Wilson's funeral. In the minutes was recorded the following: "The hour of four o'clock having arrived, and having been informed that at this hour the funeral services of the Rev. Robert Dick Wilson, D.D., were being held in Philadelphia, Pa., the Board of Trustees suspended its regular order of business to stand in solemn tribute to him who had served the Seminary so long and faithfully as a teacher. The President, Dr. McEwan, led the Board of Trustees in prayer." The board included in the minutes a unanimous motion "to express to [Robert Dick's] family the sincere sympathy of its members, and to express its appreciation of the long and faithful service he rendered the Seminary and the whole Church in a most distinguished way."[16]

16. *Princeton Seminary Bulletin* 24.3 (Nov. 1930): 26–27.

Primary Sources

Wilson, Robert Dick. "The Aramaic of Daniel." In *Biblical and Theological Studies*, by the members of the faculty of Princeton Theological Seminary, 261–306. New York: Scribner, 1912.

———. *A Hebrew Grammar for Beginners*. Leipzig: W. Drugulin, 1908.

———. *Illustrations of Gesenius' Hebrew Grammar with Vocabularies*. Princeton, N.J.: Princeton Theological Seminary, 1906.

———. *Introductory Syriac Method and Manual*. New York: Scribner, 1891.

———. *Is the Higher Criticism Scholarly?* Philadelphia: Sunday School Times, 1922.

———. *The Lower Criticism of the Old Testament as a Preparation for the Higher Criticism*. Princeton, N.J.: C. S. Robinson, 1901.

———. *Notes on Hebrew Syntax*. Allegheny, Pa.: N.p., 1892.

———. *The Radical Criticism of the Psalter*. London: Victoria Institute, 1927.

———. *A Scientific Investigation of the Old Testament*. Philadelphia: Sunday School Times, 1926.

———. *Studies in the Book of Daniel*. 2 vols. Vol. 1, New York: Putnam, 1917; vol. 2, New York: Revell, 1938. 2 vols. in 1, Grand Rapids: Baker, 1979.

Secondary Sources

Allis, Oswald T. "Robert Dick Wilson—Defender of God's Word." *Christianity Today* 1.7 (Nov. 1930): 4–6.

Haines, G. L. "The Princeton Theological Seminary, 1925–1960." Ph.D. diss., New York University, 1966.

Hart, John W. "Princeton Theological Seminary: The Reorganization of 1929." *Journal of Presbyterian History* 58 (Summer 1980): 124–40.

Noll, Mark A. *Between Faith and Criticism*. 2d ed. Grand Rapids: Baker, 1991.

Taylor, Marion A. *The Old Testament in the Old Princeton School (1812–1929)*. San Francisco: Mellen Research University Press, 1992.

Geerhardus Vos

James T. Dennison, Jr.

The so-called father of Reformed biblical theology, Geerhardus Vos was born in Heerenveen, Friesland, the Netherlands, on March 14, 1862. His father, Jan Hendrik Vos (1826–1913), was trained at Kampen and pastored six churches of the Christelijke Gereformeerde Kerk before emigrating to the United States. Educated at the gymnasium at Schiedam and then at Amsterdam, Geerhardus graduated with honors in 1881. His nineteen-year-old world changed abruptly when his father, eager to quit Europe and the rise of German nationalism, sought a call to the New World. Following a trail pioneered by Dutch immigrants, Jan Vos accepted the pastorate of the Spring Street Christian Reformed Church (now the First Christian Reformed Church) of Grand Rapids, Michigan. Geerhardus enrolled in the Theologische School (now Calvin Theological Seminary) and for the next two years devoted himself to theological studies. When he completed the requirements in 1883, he bypassed an appointment as assistant docent at his Grand Rapids alma mater in order to enrol at the bastion of Old School Reformed orthodoxy, Princeton Theological Seminary in New Jersey.

At Princeton, Vos sat at the feet of two sons of the celebrated Charles Hodge: Archibald Alexander (systematic theology) and Caspar Wistar (New Testament). Francis Landey Patton (apologetics and ethics) and Vos's esteemed Old Testament mentor, William Henry Green, were also members of the faculty. For Green, Vos wrote *The Mosaic Origin of the Pentateuchal Codes* as part of the competition for a Hebrew fellowship. Vos won that competition and applied the fellowship to study abroad, first in Berlin, then in Strasbourg.

From October 1885 to August 1886, Vos took postgraduate courses at the University of Berlin. He was both challenged and stimulated by the lectures of Christian Friedrich August Dillmann ("Old Testament Introduction," "Exilic Passages of the Book of Isaiah"), Carl Philipp Bernhard Weiss ("The Epistle to the Galatians"), and Hermann Strack ("The Book of Proverbs"). It was during the spring of 1886 that Vos made his first known contact with Abraham Kuyper, founder of the Free University of Amsterdam. Kuyper urged Vos to consider an appointment as professor of Old Testament theology. Vos, however, could not disappoint his parents in Grand Rapids by remaining in the homeland. Perhaps to further incline him to return to America, in the summer of 1886 the Synod of the Christian Reformed Church (Hollandsche Christelijke Gereformeerde Kerk in Amerika) appointed him professor of theology at the Theologische School. Ostensibly to build a bridge to the emerging English-speaking Dutch community, the trustees of the Theologische School specified that Vos deliver his lectures in English and preach weekly in English in the churches of Grand Rapids and its environs. Seemingly undaunted by these inordinate demands, the dutiful son accepted the appointment, although his "sorrow" at declining the invitation to the Free University was plainly stated in personal correspondence with Kuyper and Herman Bavinck. This same correspondence indicates that Vos was already under considerable strain. His health broke on at least two occasions, necessitating curtailment of his doctoral program on orders from his physicians. The synod in North America indulged these delays, patiently postponing his appointment and inauguration.

Vos moved from Berlin to Strasbourg in the fall of 1886 in order to complete his Ph.D. studies (Oct. 1886–April 1888). The move was apparently motivated by Vos's desire to be involved with a smaller, more intimate faculty. Here Vos encountered the liberal Heinrich Julius Holtzmann (New Testament), Wilhelm Gustav Hermann Nowack (Old Testament), Wilhelm Windelband (philosophy), and Theodor Nöldeke (Oriental languages). It was Nöldeke who supervised his dissertation. This rather uninspiring work ("Die Kämpfe und Streitigkeiten zwischen den Banū 'Umajja und den Banū Hāšim") amounted to a textual collation of an Arabic manuscript by Tagi-al-Din Ahmad Maqrizi (1364–1442) that describes the conflict between the Umayyads and the Hashimites.

Doctoral degree in hand, Vos returned at age twenty-six to Grand Rapids, where he took up his duties as professor of didactic and exegetical theology at the Theologische School. On September 4, 1888, he delivered his inaugural address, "De uitzichten der theologie in Amerika" (The prospects of theology in America), which, characteristically, had a future orientation. For the next five years, Vos taught philosophy, dogmatics, systematics, and non-Christian religions *(Idololatrie)* up to twenty-five hours a week. He wrote several of his own textbooks: a five-volume *Dogmatiek* (later published in three volumes), a *Systematische theologie,* and *Geschiedenis der idololatrie.*

In 1890, Vos's contacts with Abraham Kuyper resumed. Kuyper was seeking an English translator for his *Encyclopaedie der heilige godgeleerdheid* (Encyclopedia of sacred theology). Vos's facility in both tongues had caught the attention of the future prime minister. During this exchange of letters Vos indicated his alarm that the Presbyterian Church in the U.S.A. was moving toward revision of the Westminster Confession of Faith. Vos's high Calvinism balked at this veiled attempt to substitute Arminianism for the Reformed doctrine of double predestination. Credal revision was an expression of the downgrade of historic Calvinism, and Vos feared its insidious penetration into Dutch Reformed circles. Modification of the doctrine of election and reprobation inevitably reflected a modified view of the covenant of grace. Vos met this challenge head-on in his rectoral address of 1891—"De verbondsleer in de gereformeerde theologie" (The doctrine of the covenant in Reformed theology). But this brilliant address was not sufficient to quell the controversy swirling around Vos's own views of the *ordo salutis*. Evidently a moderate supralapsarian, Vos ran afoul of a vigorous group of infralapsarians in the Grand Rapids classis. He even wrote to Kuyper for his views on the matter in an attempt to justify his position in the face of the infralapsarianism of the Canons of Dort.

By the summer of 1891, Vos was clearly unhappy with his position in Grand Rapids. To earlier inquiries from Princeton Theological Seminary he had pleaded parental loyalties and theological ties to the Dutch rather than the American Presbyterian tradition. But the workload, the poorly educated students, the carping criticisms ("useless bickering" Vos called it), the parochial Dutch community—all made his old friend and mentor's persistent invitations very attractive. In the spring of 1892, William Henry Green urged Vos to weigh an offer to teach at Princeton as "the turning point of your life."

Green was cognizant of the mode of the times. Traditional conservative positions with respect to the inspiration, authenticity, and historicity of the Bible were being undermined by a new phenomenon—critical biblical theology. In 1892 the Presbytery of New York tried Charles Augustus Briggs on a charge of heresy. The underlying issue was the role of biblical theology in the theological encyclopedia. For Briggs, biblical theology determined all, for it was the theology in tune with the times. Briggs marked the acme of the liberal, higher-critical assault on the inspiration, inerrancy, and historicity of the Word of God. Briggs had popularized a new tool in this battle for the Bible. In his hands and the hands of his higher-critical allies, biblical theology married post-Enlightenment philosophy ("scientific theology") with history (actually, history reconstructed via Enlightenment reductionism). The result was a desupernaturalizing of the Scriptures in the interest of progressive, philosophically determined historicism. This emerging liberalism was sweeping virtually every theological faculty—it had already captured Germany, Scotland, and England. Green realized that if Old Princeton was going to provide an informed answer to critical biblical theology, an advocate with firsthand knowledge of the critical sources would have to be recruited. Vos was the prime candidate (Green described him as the "one competent engineer . . . who is summoned to check the dangerous influx of devastating . . . rationalism in theology and criticism"). Green officially offered him the newly conceived chair of biblical theology at Princeton. Vos declined. But Green persisted, playing Farel to Calvin, and in September 1893 Geerhardus Vos took up residence in Hodge Hall as the Charles T. Haley Professor of Biblical Theology. Grand Rapids complained and lamented, but Kuyper said that Vos had saved himself from academic suicide by heading east. Ironically,

Vos's successor in Grand Rapids was Henricus Beuker, a brother of Vos's mother, Aaltje Beuker Vos.

For the next thirty-nine years, Vos would labor in the halls of Old School orthodoxy. Among his colleagues were Benjamin Breckenridge Warfield, J. Gresham Machen, Robert Dick Wilson, William Park Armstrong, William Brenton Greene, Jr., James Oscar Boyd, and Oswald Thompson Allis. He received ordination as an evangelist from the Presbytery of New Brunswick (Presbyterian Church in the U.S.A.) on April 24, 1894, at the Second Presbyterian Church of Princeton. On May 8 he delivered his inaugural address ("The Idea of Biblical Theology as a Science and as a Theological Discipline") to a full audience at the First Presbyterian Church. On September 7 he married Catherine Frances Smith of Grand Rapids. They were to be the parents of four children: Johannes G. (b. 1903), Bernhardus (b. 1905), Marianne (Mrs. William Radius) (b. 1906), and Geerhardus, Jr. (b. 1911).

Vos's teaching load at Princeton included courses in Arabic, Syriac, Old Testament eschatology, Pauline eschatology, the theology of Hebrews, the prophets of the eighth century B.C., the Petrine discourses in Acts, the messianic consciousness of Jesus, and, of course, the staple, Old and New Testament biblical theology. Each summer the Vos family left their home at 52 Mercer Street and traveled to Roaring Branch in central Pennsylvania. Here, in a roomy yet quiet setting, the family read together, walked together, and worshiped together (in the lone Methodist church). Geerhardus studied, wrote, created—articles, lectures, reviews, books, sermons, poems. It was here, in this secluded mountain village, that Vos penetrated the Word of God as no other before him in the Reformed tradition. *Biblical Theology: Old and New Testaments* (1948), *The Pauline Eschatology* (1930), *The Teaching of the Epistle to the Hebrews* (1956), *The Self-Disclosure of Jesus: The Modern Debate about the Messianic Consciousness* (1926), *Grace and Glory: Sermons Preached in the Chapel of Princeton Theological Seminary* (1922), *Redemptive History and Biblical Interpretation: The Shorter Writings of Geerhardus Vos* (1980)—all testify to his unique insights which matured in those quiet summer days. And it was in a hillside cemetery in this summer retreat that Vos's body was laid to rest beside his wife. Catherine (author of the *Child's Story Bible*) had died on September 14, 1937, in Santa Ana, California, where the couple had retired at the close of the Princeton years. Geerhardus then returned to the place of his American beginning—Grand Rapids—and the home of his daughter, with whom he resided until his death on Saturday, August 13, 1949. Henry Meeter of Calvin College conducted the funeral service in Grand Rapids on the following Monday. On Wednesday, August 17, 1949, Cornelius Van Til of Westminster Theological Seminary in Philadelphia and John DeWaard of the Memorial Orthodox Presbyterian Church in Rochester, New York, officiated at the interment in Roaring Branch. But no one from Princeton or the Presbyterian Church in the U.S.A. was present.

Unique Emphasis: The Inbreaking of the Eschatological

Vos formulated a distinctively evangelical and Reformed approach to biblical theology. Positioning himself over against every form of liberal reductionism, he affirmed the supernatural character and integrity of the Word of
God. This antithetical stance was not merely the affirmation of a son of the
historical orthodox church against Gotthold Lessing's ugly ditch and Immanuel Kant's epistemological divide. Vos's adherence to the objectivity of
supernatural revelation was anchored in the objectivity of God himself. The
God who is has spoken in history. That revelation is not mere witness *(Zeug-
nis)*, not mere religious insight, not mere idealism or rationalism, not mere
developmental comparison of Semitic and Hellenistic religions *(Religions-
geschichte)*. Rather, that revelation is the objective self-communication of
the very words of God *(ipsissima verba Dei)* from his throne room, his arena,
his heavenly domain, his very being. In other words, Vos eschatologizes revelation. His biblical theology is theocentric because in his view revelation is
the very word from the above to the below. The arena in which God himself
dwells is the arena from which he speaks. And that speech is intended to reveal that eschatological arena to the listening creature.

Even before the fall, even before Eve, Adam was invited by God to come
up a little higher—to enter into the eschatological arena. The earth was never
intended to be the locus of man's eschatological rest. It was an arena of pro-
bation, protologically oriented to the eschatological heavens. In his magnum
opus *Biblical Theology: Old and New Testaments,* Vos teaches us that eschatology is prior to soteriology, even as heaven is prior to Adam's fall. The implication of this observation profoundly alters one's view of revelation in history. The earth is temporal and temporary. This world will pass away. God's
dwelling place is permanent, eternal (in the heavens), never to fade away.

If the protological Adam failed, the eschatological Adam will not. If the first
Adam dissolved to his dusty origins, the second Adam will not see corruption,
but is raised a life-giving spirit. Vos taught his students (and continues to teach
his readers) that to understand the Bible, one must begin with God. And to
begin with God is to begin with the eschatological arena. Every word from
God is a summons to that heavenly arena. In this postlapsarian world, the only
ladder to that arena is the Son of man himself. Christ Jesus, the man from
heaven, covenantally binds himself to bring heaven down to earth in order
that the sons and daughters of the earth may be brought to heaven.

The progress of the history of revelation is, for Vos, the outworking of this
protological/eschatological pattern ("eschatology becomes the mother of
theology and that first of all theology in the form of a philosophy of redemptive history"). Using his favorite analogy, Vos traces the unfolding history of
redemption from the Garden of Eden to the New Jerusalem in terms of a
flower developing from bud to blossom. Inherent in the earlier stages of the
flower are the later. Indeed, retrospectively and prospectively the flower, at
every stage of growth, is organically related to history past, history present,

and history future. This linear or horizontal dimension in the development of the history of redemption has been called the typological. But for Vos, typology is not enough. The dynamic of a theocentric (and christocentric) revelation must recognize the vertical dimension. Vos transforms traditional biblical study by introducing a hermeneutic with an intersecting plane: the vertical intrudes into the horizontal; the eternal penetrates the temporal; the protological and the eschatological intersect. His diagram of the two-age construction of the New Testament Era (see figure 1) pictures the overarching "age to come" (above) interpenetrating this "present evil age" (below). The church thus finds itself in a semieschatological tension—between the now and the not yet. Even while yearning for the consummation and the resurrection of the body (the not yet), the believer is now seated in heavenly places in Christ Jesus (Eph. 2:6). The believer, "hidden with Christ in God" (Col. 3:3 NIV), possesses even now the status of the sons and daughters of God as an indication of what is yet to come.

I. The Original Scheme

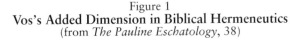

II. The Modified Scheme

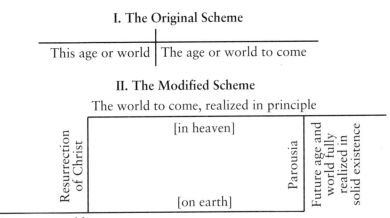

Figure 1
Vos's Added Dimension in Biblical Hermeneutics
(from *The Pauline Eschatology*, 38)

Vos carefully delineated his method of biblical theology at the inauguration of his career at Princeton (his 1894 address). This method was also evident in the final manuscript (as yet unpublished) to flow from his pen *(Old Testament Eschatology)*. In between, each essay, each sermon, each book, each review, each article explored the intersection of the eschatological with the temporal. His rectoral address of 1891 (see p. 84) positioned covenant as the subsidiary organizing principle of the history of redemption. In Reformed doctrine covenant becomes an archetypal pattern for the disclosure of God's words and deeds. Revelation is primary, but occurs in history. How can we maintain at once the transcendent unity and developmental diversity of that self-disclosure? The relationship which binds creature and Creator throughout time and space, the relationship which draws the creature into union with the Creator, the relationship which breathes the mutuality of our being chosen and being grateful, is covenant: the covenant between the Father and the Son, the covenant of works between the Creator and his protological creation, the covenant of grace between the Creator and his eschatological (un)creation.

When the covenant reached its semieschatological climax at the inbreaking of the kingdom of heaven, the church became the heir to the fullness of the promises. She is nothing less than the new Israel in which the sojourners (the "Hebrews") at the end of the age live out their odyssey to the New Jerusalem, the heavenly Zion, the land of eschatological Sabbath rest. The Pauline eschatology is but a species of this sublime drama conceived in the encounter with the risen Christ on the Damascus Road. The Pharisee is transformed by the encounter with eschatological life. Now Saul, bondslave of the law of Judaism, must be the servant of the Messiah for the Gentiles. Old is displaced with new—the law does not justify; the blood of Abraham does not save; the mysteries of the seers do not enlighten. Only Christ Jesus justifies as he himself has been justified by resurrection from the dead (1 Tim. 3:16). Only faith in Christ saves as he himself has been faithful up to and through death. Only the mystery of Christ enlightens as he himself is the effulgence and radiance of the Father.

The eschatological lifestyle is dramatically rehearsed in the church which Paul planted. In Christ, the church has died to the law that she may be raised to reflect the moral character of heaven itself. In Christ, the church walks by faith because she even now possesses the reality of the heavenly arena. In Christ, the church sees the light of glory and reflects that radiance to a dark and dreary world.

Four Revolutionary Volumes

Vos penned four revolutionary volumes after his appointment to the faculty of Princeton Seminary. Each volume accents Vos's unique emphasis on the priority of eschatology. Their perspectives are, respectively, eschatology and the kingdom, eschatology and the homiletic moment, eschatology and the messianic self-consciousness of Jesus, and eschatology and the Pauline theology.

Vos's first book-length contribution to the biblical theology of his day was *The Teaching of Jesus concerning the Kingdom of God and the Church* (1903). Vos's exegesis contrasts the kingdom of God proclaimed by Jesus with (1) first-century Jewish expectations; (2) nineteenth-century liberal views of the kingdom of God according to which Jesus is not the bringer of the kingdom (God is!), but rather the one who prepares humans for the appearance of the kingdom (which he mistakenly expected in his own lifetime); and (3) the early-twentieth-century apocalyptic-eschatological view (e.g., of Albert Schweitzer) that Jesus attempted to extort the kingdom from God only to die in dereliction when God abandoned him. The fundamental error of all three views is the desupernaturalizing of the kingdom. For Vos, the coming of the kingdom which Jesus announced entailed supernatural events both visible (e.g., the miracles) and hidden (e.g., the underlying referents of the parables). This kingdom begins for us in regeneration (supernatural rebirth) and continues with gifts derived from the spiritual person and work of Christ. Our incorporation into this spiritual aspect of the kingdom is the ongoing function of the Spirit of Christ, who brought it with his very own advent. And yet there is a not yet. The kingdom which Jesus announced has a future eschatological dimension. It will be consummated in a sudden crisis so cosmic and visible in scope that the outcome will be utterly and totally final. Supernatural incorporation into the kingdom now; supernatural consummation of the kingdom in the future. The now and not yet (the two ages) of Jesus' kingdom proclamation surpass Judaism with its nationalistic, political, sensual kingdom hopes. The present and future aspects of the kingdom which Jesus brings contravene classic liberalism, which immanentizes the eschaton. And Vos's presentation of Christ's kingdom avoids the dereliction of Schweitzer's (non)historical Jesus because it presumes the credibility and historicity of the Gospel records.

In 1922, Vos published six sermons which he had delivered in the chapel of Princeton Theological Seminary. These sermons represent the craft of the biblical theologian applied to the homiletical moment. Each sermon highlights the priority of God's invitation to his creature to dwell with him. It is as if Vos reverses the traditional preaching event by drawing his listeners into the living text of Scripture rather than extracting truths from the text and imposing them upon the listeners. *Grace and Glory* exemplifies a homiletical method encouraging and enabling God's people to identify and unite with the life of Christ revealed in a particular word of God. In other words, the goal of preaching for Vos is not primarily application, nor is it fundamentally introspection—it is supremely identification with and incorporation into Christ. The eschatological perspective dominates even the sermons Vos preached.

Vos published *The Self-Disclosure of Jesus: The Modern Debate about the Messianic Consciousness* in 1926. In a scintillating survey of various views of Christ's messianic self-consciousness, Vos examines the evolution of the modern critical discussion from (1) denial of messianic consciousness in Jesus (Gustav Volkmar, James Martineau, and Nathaniel Schmidt) to (2) an agnostic conclusion derived from Jesus' prohibition, especially in Mark's Gospel, of the disciples' revealing his messiahship (William Wrede's *Messiasgeheimnis*) to (3) the belief that Jesus grew from not being conscious of being the Messiah to *thinking* he was the Messiah (David Friedrich Strauss, Ernest Renan, and Heinrich J. Holtzmann). Always hovering in the background is the eschatological (actually noneschatological) Jesus of Albert Schweitzer and Johannes Weiss.[1] At heart, each liberal reduction is an attempt to elimi-

---

1. See Geerhardus Vos, review of *The Quest of the Historical Jesus*, by Albert Schweitzer, *Princeton Theological Review* 9 (1911): 132–41.

nate the eschatological element from the person of Jesus. In other words, de-supernaturalize Jesus of Nazareth, and religion becomes "a movement taking its departure from Christ and addressing itself to the world, rather than a movement seeking the Person of Christ in order to occupy itself with him. A religion intended to be first of all centripetal has become alarmingly centrifugal."[2] What Vos brilliantly points out is that to reduce Jesus to the level of human religion, liberalism must make him part of the world, not distinct from the world. But supernatural and eschatological messiahship sets him apart from the world (while yet in the world) as wholly unique. All liberalism must re-create Jesus of Nazareth in its own immanentistic image.

After surveying modern critical views, Vos spends the bulk of the volume in an exegetical tour de force with the messianic titles: Christ, the Lord, the Son of God, the Son of man, Savior. He concludes with an exposition of the messianic death, which, in itself, is not only exegetical of the prophetic projection (notably Isa. 53), but revelatory of the glory of the passion of Jesus. Vos's legacy with regard to the messianic consciousness of Jesus is a rehabilitation of the orthodox supernatural view. Jesus of Nazareth is the Messiah because he is the supernatural Son of God anointed to be the Savior of his people. To patronize Jesus as a moral example while one rejects his supernatural person is pathological.

The final volume from the Princeton years was *The Pauline Eschatology* (1930). Vos has his eye primarily on the critical reduction of eschatology and Paul, but he casts a glance at burgeoning premillennialism (chiliasm) and its competitor (postmillennialism). The lengthy first chapter on the structure of the Pauline eschatology repristinates a Vosian emphasis—"to unfold the Apostle's eschatology means to set forth his theology as a whole."[3] It is the end (of history) that shapes the beginning of Paul's estimate of Christ. In particular, as Richard B. Gaffin, Jr., has demonstrated, the resurrection of the dead is the central motif of Paul's system. With the resurrection of Christ, the future eon has burst in upon the present (see figure 1 on p. 87). Believing Christians are even now in possession of the eschatological arena because they too have been raised up together with Christ. Their life in this world is dominated by the age to come; their walk reflects the character of heaven's Lord. The Pauline church is conscious of living in the heavenlies even now as she sojourns towards the consummation. In soteriology Vos demonstrates that for Paul and his churches the ultimate is determinative of the present, not vice versa. Likewise, eschatology is prior to and determinative of ethics. All moralism, whether liberal or conservative, is unbiblical because it is fundamentally anthropocentrism religiously conditioned.

Vos's contribution to the centennial celebration of Princeton Seminary in 1912 ("The Eschatological Aspect of the Pauline Conception of the Spirit") should be integrated at this point, for it forms the backbone of chapter 6 of

2. Geerhardus Vos, *The Self-Disclosure of Jesus* (New York: George H. Doran, 1926), 37.
3. Geerhardus Vos, *The Pauline Eschatology* (Princeton, N.J.: Princeton University Press, 1930), 11.

The Pauline Eschatology. The function of the Holy Spirit after the glorification of the risen Lord Jesus is to incorporate the believer now into the life of the age to come. The down payment *(arrabōn)* of the life of heaven is displayed in the life of the believer. This is so because the Holy Spirit unites Christians to their ascended Lord and energizes their existence in the world.

Vos's sermons, essays, books, and poems were a constant litany of the difference Christ makes. That difference is anticipated in the eschatological intrusion evident in the biblical theology of the Old Testament. That christocentric difference is inaugurally semirealized in the eschatological intrusion evident in the biblical theology of the New Testament. That difference will be fully realized in face-to-face consummation at the death of the believer and the second advent of the Son of glory.

This litany has been a legacy precious to many. Most notably John Murray, Cornelius Van Til, and Ned Stonehouse of Westminster Theological Seminary embraced Vos's biblical theology and attempted to articulate it in the classroom, pulpit, and publications. Richard B. Gaffin, Jr., Herman Ridderbos, Meredith G. Kline, and James, Charles, and William Dennison have attempted further extensions of Vos's original insights. In 1986 *Kerux: A Journal of Biblical-Theological Preaching* was launched to nurture the contemporary expression of Vos's biblical theology. Each proponent has realized that the practice of biblical theology in Vos's sense draws the believer into union with the Christ of Scripture as he is displayed from heaven from Genesis to Revelation. And life in Christ is of course the most practical form of Christianity for the New Testament church. Geerhardus Vos has provided us with the key for this preeminently biblical lifestyle.

Primary Sources

Vos, Geerhardus. *Biblical Theology: Old and New Testaments.* Grand Rapids: Eerdmans, 1948.

―――. *Grace and Glory: Sermons Preached in the Chapel of Princeton Theological Seminary.* Grand Rapids: Reformed, 1922; Edinburgh: Banner of Truth Trust, 1994.

―――. *Letters to Abraham Kuyper and Herman Bavinck, 1886–1907.* Translated by Nicolaas Van Dam and Fritz and Brenda Harms. Forthcoming.

―――. *The Mosaic Origin of the Pentateuchal Codes.* New York: A. C. Armstrong, 1886.

―――. *Old Testament Eschatology.* Edited by James T. Dennison, Jr. Forthcoming.

―――. *The Pauline Eschatology.* Princeton, N.J.: Princeton University Press, 1930; Grand Rapids: Baker, 1979.

―――. *Redemptive History and Biblical Interpretation: The Shorter Writings of Geerhardus Vos.* Edited by Richard B. Gaffin, Jr. Phillipsburg, N.J.: Presbyterian and Reformed, 1980.

―――. *The Self-Disclosure of Jesus: The Modern Debate about the Messianic Consciousness.* New York: George H. Doran, 1926; Nutley, N.J.: Presbyterian and Reformed, 1976.

———. *The Teaching of Jesus concerning the Kingdom of God and the Church.* New York: American Tract Society, 1903; Nutley, N.J.: Presbyterian and Reformed, 1972.

———. *The Teaching of the Epistle to the Hebrews.* Edited by Johannes G. Vos. Grand Rapids: Eerdmans, 1956; Nutley, N.J.: Presbyterian and Reformed, 1974.

Secondary Sources

Biographical Catalogue of Princeton Theological Seminary, 1815–1954. Princeton, N.J.: The Trustees, 1955.

De Klerk, Peter. *A Bibliography of the Writings of the Professors of Calvin Theological Seminary.* Grand Rapids: Calvin Theological Seminary, 1980.

Dennison, Charles G. "Preaching and Application." *Kerux* 4.3 (Dec. 1989): 44–52.

Dennison, James T., Jr. "The Bible and the Second Coming." In *The Book of Books: Essays on the Scriptures in Honor of Johannes G. Vos,* edited by John H. White, 55–65. Phillipsburg, N.J.: Presbyterian and Reformed, 1978.

———. "A Bibliography of the Writings of Geerhardus Vos (1862–1949). In *Redemptive History and Biblical Interpretation: The Shorter Writings of Geerhardus Vos,* edited by Richard B. Gaffin, Jr., 547–59. Phillipsburg, N.J.: Presbyterian and Reformed, 1980.

———. "What Is Biblical Theology? Reflections on the Inaugural Address of Geerhardus Vos." *Kerux* 2.1 (May 1987): 33–41.

Dennison, William D. *Paul's Two-Age Construction and Apologetics.* Lanham, Md.: University Press of America, 1985.

Gaffin, Richard B., Jr. *The Centrality of the Resurrection: A Study in Paul's Soteriology.* Grand Rapids: Baker, 1978.

———. "Geerhardus Vos and the Interpretation of Paul." In *Jerusalem and Athens,* edited by E. R. Geehan, 228–37. Nutley, N.J.: Presbyterian and Reformed, 1971.

———. Introduction to *Redemptive History and Biblical Interpretation: The Shorter Writings of Geerhardus Vos,* edited by Richard B. Gaffin, Jr., ix–xxiii. Phillipsburg, N.J.: Presbyterian and Reformed, 1980.

"Geerhardus Vos." *Princeton Seminary Bulletin* 43.3 (Winter 1950): 41–42, 44–46.

Jansen, John F. "The Biblical Theology of Geerhardus Vos." *Princeton Seminary Bulletin* 66.2 (Summer 1974): 23–34.

Meeter, H. Henry. "Professor Geerhardus Vos." *The Banner* 84 (2 Sept. 1949): 1046–47.

Princeton Seminary Bulletin 26 (June 1932): 1, 15–16.

Semi-Centennial Volume: Theological School and Calvin College, 1876–1926. Grand Rapids: Tradesman, 1926.

Vanden Bosch, Jacob G. "Geerhardus Vos." *Reformed Journal* 4.10 (Nov. 1954): 11–14.

Webster, Ransom L. "Geerhardus Vos (1862–1949): A Biographical Sketch." *Westminster Theological Journal* 40.2 (Spring 1978): 304–17.

A. T. Robertson

Edgar V. McKnight

A. T. (Archibald Thomas) Robertson for nearly fifty years occupied a significant position in American New Testament scholarship. A consequence of his forty-six years of teaching at Southern Baptist Theological Seminary was that his influence was particularly strong among Southern Baptists.

Background

Robertson was born on November 6, 1863, two years before the Civil War in America ended. For the first twelve years of his life he lived at the family home near Chatham, Virginia. These twelve years saw the defeat of the Confederacy, the loss of the family's large number of slaves, and eventually his father's bankruptcy. In September of 1875, with the two oldest boys left behind to harvest the corn and tobacco, the Robertson family moved to Statesville, North Carolina, where Robertson lived until November of 1879 when he left for Wake Forest College.

After almost six years at Wake Forest (the lack of a full high school course made this necessary) Robertson graduated in the spring of 1885. He then went to Southern Baptist Theological Seminary in Louisville, Kentucky, completing his student work in the spring of 1888, but remaining as a member of the faculty until his death in September of 1934.

The greatest influence on Robertson was John A. Broadus, a member of the original faculty and professor of New Testament interpretation and homiletics. Broadus had graduated from the University of Virginia, where he had studied Greek under Gessner Harrison. Harrison emphasized the historical method of language study that was being developed in Germany. A novelty then but increasingly accepted, this method was passed on by Broadus and adopted by Robertson.

Also evident in Robertson's career is the influence of Basil Manly, Jr., the most conservative of the four original faculty members of the seminary. Manly's courses in Old Testament interpretation and biblical introduction helped Robertson to formulate the critical framework in which he was to study, teach, and write. Robertson is usually and correctly thought of as the successor to Broadus, but before he succeeded Broadus in New Testament interpretation, he had succeeded Manly in biblical introduction.

The Period of Beginnings (1888-94)

In the spring of 1888 Robertson was engaged by the seminary to work alongside John R. Sampey in correcting papers and carrying out various other duties in the areas of Hebrew, Greek, and homiletics. Sampey, who became well known in Old Testament studies, acknowledged that Robertson was the more competent in Greek. Accordingly, Robertson went into New Testament interpretation and Sampey into Old Testament interpretation. For two years Robertson served as assistant to Broadus and did research in the New Testament. Then in May of 1890 he was made an assistant professor of Greek and homiletics.

Robertson made rapid strides in those early years. In the summer of 1890 a trip to Europe enabled him to study the German language and hear lectures by leading German scholars. He was asked to take part in the Baptist Congress of 1892 held in Philadelphia. And in May of 1892, after Manly's death, Robertson was appointed professor of biblical introduction and promoted to associate professor of New Testament interpretation.

Immediately upon his appointment to the faculty Robertson began his long writing career. He contributed articles to the *Seminary Magazine* and to various Baptist state papers in the North and South. Four particularly controversial subjects appeared and reappeared in the Baptist state papers: the nature of the Bible and its inspiration, the role of women in the church, the nature of the church in the New Testament, and the Whitsitt dispute. The editors encouraged running debates between Robertson and various individuals who disagreed with him. These occasional articles "he dashed . . . off with amazing rapidity and skill. Not a few of these were produced on whatever paper he might have at hand while at stations between trains, at intervals between engagements where he might be lecturing or preaching."[1]

The Period of Concentration on Greek Grammar (1895-1914)

In March of 1895 Broadus died, and two months later Robertson was asked to succeed his colleague as professor of New Testament interpretation. The Whitsitt controversy immediately caught up the new professor. W. H. Whitsitt, president and professor of church history at Southern, had written that Roger Williams had probably been sprinkled rather than immersed, and that among English Baptists the immersion of believers was begun by Edward Barber in 1641. Southern Baptist reactions were seen in the denominational press and at various association meetings and state conventions. Sides were taken, and from 1896 to 1899 the battle raged. Robertson and Sampey were among Whitsitt's most loyal supporters; and after Sampey left on a trip to Europe and Palestine, Robertson became the leader of the Kentucky group defending Whitsitt.

1. W. O. Carver, unpublished notes, Southern Baptist Theological Seminary Library, 38.

Insofar as the teaching at Southern Seminary was concerned, Robertson continued the undergraduate courses of study much as Broadus had organized them. But in postgraduate work—which had been instituted in 1892 when the board of trustees set up new curricula including a Th.D. program requiring at least five special courses and the preparation of a thesis—Robertson made some changes. He gradually dropped all of the required special courses except Greek exegesis, the area in which he and all his advanced students now began to major.

Robertson's method of teaching developed naturally within the framework provided by his teachers and colleagues at the seminary. He would begin class with prayer and then quickly move to questioning the students on the lesson for the day. The questions called for specific facts, not opinions or interpretations. This questioning would sometimes continue for the majority of the class period. The recitation method was a fearful thing in the hands of Robertson. Grades were recorded for the answers given, and sharp statements to the student were frequent. Robertson became known as the faculty member to whom was delegated the task of puncturing students' conceit.[2] The advanced classes were handled quite differently, however. Although Robertson was characterized as a "near tyrant" in his courses in the English New Testament, he was a "friendly teacher" in senior Greek and a "genial comrade in scholarship" in his seminars.

The real beginning of Robertson's career as an author of books came in 1901 when his *Life and Letters of John Albert Broadus* was published. Robertson wrote the book in longhand and then, as his custom continued to be, had a seminary student type it in a form acceptable to the publisher.

The vast majority of Robertson's energy during this period was spent in the field of Greek grammar. In 1898 he began a series of articles on Greek syntax for the *Seminary Magazine.* By 1900 these articles had grown into a little book of ninety-nine pages entitled *New Testament Greek Syllabus for Junior Greek Class.* Its series of lessons in syntax reflected the historical method that Broadus had championed. Soon Robertson began the gigantic task of writing the *Grammar of the Greek New Testament in the Light of Historical Research,* which was to be his chief task for twelve years. While this work was progressing, Robertson wrote his *Short Grammar of the Greek New Testament* to replace his *Greek Syllabus.* By 1931, when *The Short Grammar* was completely rewritten, there had been eight English editions and translations into Italian, French, German, and Dutch. The volume popularly called the "Big Grammar" was finally published on June 12, 1914, and met with immediate success in the scholarly world. In the following nine years it was to go through four editions and grow from 1,360 to 1,454 pages.

2. Robertson's son compared his father with H. L. Mencken: "Each was honest and opinionated, and delighted in exposing sham and hypocrisies" (A. T. Robertson, Jr., *That Old-Time Religion* [Boston: Houghton Mifflin, 1950], 22).

Although the majority of Robertson's interest and energy was spent on Greek grammar during this period, he found time to write nine other books in different fields. In 1902 he published a *Syllabus for New Testament Study*, which was designed to be used in his course in the English New Testament. By the time of the fifth edition (1923) the syllabus had expanded from 129 to 274 pages and was used by a variety of institutions. It was even brought out by a British publisher. In 1904 came *The Teaching of Jesus concerning God the Father*, which was written for the Teaching of Jesus series published by the American Tract Society. Having seen a need for a volume that would present the New Testament books in general chronological order along with an introductory sketch for each book, Robertson published *The Student's Chronological New Testament* in the same year.

Several books grew out of popular lectures. *Keywords in the Teaching of Jesus* resulted from lectures in June 1904 to the Jackson Springs (N.C.) Summer Assembly. *Epochs in the Life of Jesus* (1907) grew out of 1906 lectures on the career of Jesus to an assembly at Pertle Springs, Missouri. The response to this book was so favorable that Robertson wrote a companion volume on Paul which was published in 1909 as *Epochs in the Life of Paul*. Robertson considered this his best volume after his "Big Grammar."[3]

In 1911 Robertson published three books. *The Gospel according to Matthew* was one of a series of commentaries written under the editorship of Shailer Mathews and designed for popular consumption. Robertson supported the two-source theory of Gospel relationships. *John the Loyal* was a study of the ministry of John the Baptist. *The Glory of the Ministry* was a series of lectures on Paul's concept of ministry.

Robertson's reputation as a New Testament scholar grew to such an extent in this period that he was requested to assist in the writing of several Bible reference books, including *The Cross-Reference Bible* and *The 1911 Bible,* which commemorated the original publication of the Authorized Version three hundred years earlier. He also continued to contribute articles to popular and professional journals *(Baptist Argus, Watchman-Examiner, Sunday School Times, Bible Student, Bible Student and Teacher, Record of Christian Work, Review and Expositor, Presbyterian and Reformed Review, Biblical World,* and *Homiletical Review).*

The Period of Diverse Production (1915-34)

Very early in his career Robertson had organized his courses in New Testament so well that in his later years he needed little time to prepare for them. Instead, he spent a great deal of time in preparing and delivering popular lectures, for various religious groups coveted him as a speaker. Perhaps the Northfield (Mass.) and Winona Lake (Ind.) assemblies were those to which

---

3. Carver, unpublished notes, 38; Carver described the book as being "for its purpose a truly remarkable work, for its size unsurpassed by anything ever written about Paul."

he most appealed and those that most appealed to him. In the summer of 1912 Robertson began a practice at Northfield which he was to follow regularly. With Greek text in hand, he taught the Bible to large groups. This proved so successful that twelve of the next twenty-one summers found him teaching at Northfield directly from the Greek text of the New Testament. Some of his other lectures proved just as successful. Between 1917 and 1929, for example, he delivered a series entitled "The Sermon on the Mount and Modern Life" thirty-one times.

Robertson was also in demand as a speaker at colleges and seminaries. Twice he was invited to deliver the Stone Lectures at Princeton. In February 1915 he delivered his first series, "The Pharisees and Jesus," and in November 1926 his second series, "Paul and the Intellectuals."

The majority of Robertson's labors during the period of diverse production, however, was spent in writing. After the great work of 1914, his literary contribution in the field of New Testament Greek did not cease, although it took forms other than volumes on Greek grammar. While continuing to revise and put out new editions of his grammars, he published some works in the area of textual criticism of the New Testament, translated the Gospel of Luke, and began a translation of the entire New Testament. He also produced a sort of commentary on the whole New Testament in his *Word Pictures*. But Robertson's work in Greek during this period was minor compared to his work in other fields. From 1914 to his death in 1934 there were only two years in which he failed to publish; in eleven of those years he published two or more books. Of the thirty-three books produced, twenty-two are in areas other than Greek—although Robertson's knowledge of Greek is evident throughout.

In 1915 two books appeared. One of them, *Practical and Social Aspects of Christianity,* was basically a running commentary on the Epistle of James. It was republished several years later as *Studies in the Epistle of James,* a title that the publisher thought would increase the sales. The other book, *Studies in the New Testament,* was a teacher-training manual requested by the Southern Baptist Sunday School Board.

Robertson published one book during each of the next three years. *The Divinity of Christ in the Gospel of John,* five lectures delivered before a group of Sunday school teachers in Atlanta, was published in 1916. A series of expository talks on Philippians was published in 1917 under the title *Paul's Joy in Christ.* In 1918 appeared a book on John Mark, *Making Good in the Ministry.*

Two of Robertson's books were published in 1919. One dealt with the Gospel of Mark and the other with the general subject of Christian citizenship. *Studies in Mark's Gospel* was composed of various articles which had originally been published in scholarly journals. *The New Citizenship* grew out of a month's lectures at the Y.M.C.A. Army Camp at Blue Ridge, North Carolina.

During 1920 two more series of Robertson's lectures were put into book form. The 1915 Stone Lectures at Princeton became *The Pharisees and Jesus,* and a series at Northfield became *Luke the Historian in the Light of Research*. *Paul the Interpreter of Christ*, the sole book published by Robertson in 1921, contained his opening lecture at Southern Seminary in 1911 ("Paul as an Interpreter of Christ") and various articles previously contributed to journals.

In 1922 Robertson again offered two new books to the public. *A Harmony of the Gospels for Students of the Life of Christ* was a reworking of Broadus's *Harmony*. *Types of Preachers in the New Testament* was composed of articles that had appeared in various scholarly journals.

In the year of his sixtieth birthday, 1923, Robertson published two books: *The Minister and His Greek New Testament* and *A Translation of Luke's Gospel*. The following year also saw two new books. *New Testament History: Airplane View* was prepared as a student textbook for the Keystone Series of the International Graded Lessons system of the American Baptist Publication Society. *The Christ of the Logia* was composed mainly of articles previously written for various journals. The year 1925 was the fourth straight year in which two books by Robertson appeared: *Introduction to Textual Criticism* and a short book entitled *The Mother of Jesus*.

After *Studies in the Text of the New Testament* in 1926, a year passed before Robertson published again. But in 1928 two books came out. A running commentary on the Epistle to the Colossians, *Paul and the Intellectuals* had been delivered as the Stone Lectures in 1926. *Some Minor Characters in the New Testament* was another collection of articles previously published in religious journals.

After another yearlong pause Robertson offered three volumes of his *Word Pictures* to the public in 1930 and an additional volume in each of the following three years. In 1931 Robertson and W. Hersey Davis, his younger colleague in New Testament interpretation, produced *A New Short Grammar of the Greek Testament*. In 1933 came *Epochs in the Life of Simon Peter*; in 1934, *Passing On the Torch*; and in 1935 (the year after his death), *Epochs in the Life of the Apostle John*.

During this period of diverse productivity Robertson was called on to contribute to various volumes that promoted general understanding of the Bible. Among these volumes were the *Dictionary of the Apostolic Church, System Bible Study, Master Bible, Standard Bible Dictionary*, and *Abingdon Bible Commentary*.

Robertson also contributed essays to two volumes that honored fellow New Testament scholars. For the *Festgabe für Adolf Deissmann*, published in 1927, he wrote "New Testament Grammar after Thirty Years." For *Studies in Early Christianity*, which honored Frank Chamberlin Porter and Benjamin Wisner Bacon, he wrote "The Causal Use of "INA."

Robertson's activities as correspondent from Kentucky for the *Watchman-Examiner*, a role he had undertaken in 1895, continued into this period. He also wrote for nearly all the Baptist state papers in the South; at least 119 of his articles appeared in the *Christian Index*. In addition, scholarly essays by Robertson appeared in such journals as *Homiletic Review, Expositor, Review and Expositor, Expositor and Current Anecdotes, Biblical Review, Methodist Quarterly Review,* and *Expository Times.*

A Conservative Stance on the Nature and Interpretation of the New Testament

A continuing concern throughout Robertson's career was the nature of the Bible. During his early teaching years as professor of biblical introduction he expressed in numerous articles views in accord with the position of Manly. Later he turned to other matters, but his basic ideas about the nature of the Bible never changed. Because of inspiration the Bible is the divinely authoritative Word of God. "I am sure," he affirmed, "that the New Testament will retain its hold on men because of the power in it, rather than because of any theory of inspiration. The theories have come after the fact. The hold will stay in spite of all the theories. God is in the New Testament books whether we can tell how or not."[4]

Maintaining a critical stance, Robertson introduced his readers to detailed questions and arguments concerning authorship and authenticity. But he always ended up on the conventional conservative side, for he saw beyond these questions to the basic message and purpose of the New Testament. "That purpose is to put the soul in touch with God through Christ."[5] The Bible is a presentation of truth concerning Christ which purposes "to regenerate the heart, to make a new man out of the old man, to save him, soul and body." It reveals "truths that determine life and character and the eternal destiny of the soul." It is, chiefly, "a plan of rescue for the soul."[6]

Because he saw the evangelical purpose in the Bible as primary, Robertson became through the years more concerned with interpreting the Bible than with defending it as infallible and inerrant. And yet he remained convinced of its infallibility. This conviction was well expressed in a paper delivered at the Baptist Congress in Philadelphia in 1892. He declared that the Bible is the Word of God because here God speaks as nowhere else. God does not speak with infallible authority in the conscience of human beings, Christian experience, the church, or human reason. God speaks with infallible authority only in the Bible. It is, then, the sole authority in the realm in which it speaks. This is true because "Scripture speaks in a realm which is above that of reason; Scripture speaks where reason could never have spoken."[7] Not that Scripture and reason are inconsistent, but that humans have been given a supernatural revelation above reason; therefore, when the Bible speaks on a subject, it is the end of the matter, for reason cannot go higher. Humans

---

4. A. T. Robertson, "Presuppositions of New Testament Criticism," *Bible Student and Teacher* 5 (1906): 455.

5. Ibid.

6. A. T. Robertson, "Christian Truth and Heathen Truth," *Baptist Courier* 25 (June 21, 1894): 1.

7. A. T. Robertson, "The Relative Authority of Scripture and Reason," in *Proceedings of the Baptist Congress* (New York: Baptist Congress, 1892), 193.

are to exercise their reason in this realm only by coming to the Word and listening. "It is the noblest exercise of the human intellect to sit at the feet of the Nazarene and learn of him what human hearts most need to know and can learn nowhere else."[8] Thirty years later Robertson made a similar affirmation about the authority of the Bible:

> I must think of the authority of the Bible as being the authority of God. . . . The essential problem about the Bible is not[, then,] whether this detail of history has been established by research or whether this allusion in popular language to matters in nature is in harmony with modern scientific theory. . . . That is quite beside the problem of the Bible. The authority relates to God's revelation of himself to men and to man's relation to God.[9]

Contribution to the Study of Greek Grammar

As we have seen, Robertson is most noted for his work in Greek grammar. Almost everything he wrote reflects his knowledge of Greek. The recent discovery of new resources for the study of the Greek New Testament along with the development of new methods of grammatical study caused Robertson to recognize early in his career the need for a complete rewriting of the grammar of New Testament Greek. And yet a number of years before he became aware of the new discoveries, he was already in the process of mastering what would prove to be one of the most important foundations of his achievements in the field of grammar. This was the old Greek writings which he read at Wake Forest. He declared, "I could not have carried on my studies in New Testament Greek on the scale undertaken without the broad and secure foundation in the Old Greek writers."[10] He used the works of classical authors repeatedly throughout his writings on Greek grammar. As we would expect, he used the writings of the Koine period more frequently. He included in this group all of the writers from the Greek poets of the third century B.C. through the Christian writers of the early Christian centuries. He also made wide use of various Jewish writings. Especially prominent was his use of the Septuagint, which he saw as an example of Koine and, therefore, as having affinities with the Greek of the New Testament at many points. The New Testament itself, of course, was the basic source of Robertson's study. While remaining in touch with the important points in the general history of the Greek language, he always attempted to "keep the Greek of the N.T. out in the middle."[11]

The new resources which demanded a "new grammar on a new plan" were discoveries in the areas of comparative philology and the study of the

8. Ibid.

9. A. T. Robertson, "The Bible as Authority," *Homiletic Review* 83 (1922): 102–3.

10. A. T. Robertson, "Recollections of My Early Life," A. T. Robertson Papers, Southern Baptist Theological Seminary Library, 100.

11. A. T. Robertson, *A Grammar of the Greek New Testament in the Light of Historical Research* (Nashville: Broadman, 1934), viii.

papyri. Then too there was the historical method of grammatical study, which was based on comparative philology. Robertson adopted this method from Broadus before the turn of the century and stated that "historical grammar is the only sensible grammar."[12] He saw Sir William Jones's study of Sanskrit as revolutionizing grammatical research. Franz Bopp had used the knowledge of Sanskrit to found comparative philology, but Robertson found most useful the work of Karl Brugmann and B. Delbrück, who at the end of the nineteenth century organized all the earlier study and research into a coherent form. Robertson commented, "In common with all modern linguists I have leaned upon Brugmann and Delbrück as masters in linguistic learning."[13] Similarly, William Dwight Whitney's *Sanskrit Grammar* is cited throughout the "Big Grammar," for Robertson saw that "constant use of the Sanskrit must be made by one who wishes to understand the historical developments of the Greek tongue."[14]

By the time Robertson had written his earliest articles on Greek grammar for the *Seminary Magazine,* he had determined the historical framework that would underlie his "Big Grammar." However, one problem still existed. What is the exact relationship of New Testament Greek to the language as a whole? In 1900 Robertson had characterized New Testament Greek as "a variety of the current Greek of the first century A.D., with a strong Semitic influence. . . . There is a slight Latin tinge, a distinctively Christian character, and various dialectical marks."[15] It is evident that the uniqueness of the Greek of the New Testament gave Robertson a little trouble in fitting it into the framework of historical grammar. Robertson's determination to solve this problem led to one of his greatest contributions, his delineation of the precise nature of New Testament Greek.

By comparing the phonology, onomatology, vocabulary, inflections, syntax, and style of the New Testament with a great variety of inscriptions, papyri, and ostraca, Adolf Deissmann had showed that the New Testament is late colloquial Greek. Deissmann's position was that "for the most part, the pages of our sacred Book are so many records of popular Greek, in its various grades."[16] James Hope Moulton, carrying Deissmann's work over into the grammatical sphere, concluded from his investigation of papyri that the Greek of the New Testament is the vernacular Greek of the period. Deissmann's and Moulton's investigations convinced Robertson that the grammar of the Greek of the New Testament is the grammar of the vernacular Koine of the first century A.D. Robertson did not agree with them, however, that

12. A. T. Robertson, "Some Points on Greek Syntax—Remarks on the Greek Article," *Seminary Magazine,* 1892, 82.

13. Robertson, *Grammar,* ix.

14. Ibid., 39.

15. A. T. Robertson, *New Testament Greek Syllabus for Junior Greek Class* (Louisville: Charles T. Dearing, 1900), 3.

16. Gustav Adolf Deissmann, *Light from the Ancient East* (New York: George H. Doran, 1927), 143.

New Testament Greek is merely the vernacular: "The joy of new discovery has to some extent blurred the vision of Deissmann and Moulton to the remaining Hebraisms which do not indeed make Hebraic Greek or a peculiar dialect. But enough remain to be noticeable and appreciable."[17]

Robertson's presuppositions concerning the New Testament gave a unique emphasis to his work in Greek grammar and in New Testament interpretation. He considered the Bible as God's Word in a sense that extended to the particular shades of meaning in the Greek. Hence a minute study of the Greek is necessary for a correct understanding of God's Word. While recognizing that the Greek of the New Testament is basically the common dialect of the Hellenistic world, and that the various writers of the New Testament used it correctly, he also maintained that New Testament Greek is characterized by fine distinctions which must be carefully investigated.

Robertson's method of close investigation coordinated study of words, phrases, and sentences with judgments concerning the major themes of larger sections:

> Read the epistle several times, seek the occasion and purpose of its writing. Analyze it carefully. Then take it up section by section, slowly, painstakingly, conscientiously, digging out everything from Thayer and the commentaries. Make the section cover only what falls under one leading idea. By the time you have done this one section, go back and start over again.[18]

But for Robertson interpretation was not only an intellectual matter. Indeed, "the head cannot get all the meaning out of God's Word." So he stressed that it is sometimes necessary to rely upon faith to help clarify the truths of the Bible. Through this "experiential reliance" and pious living many passages of Scripture can be opened up. "After all our study and experience," Robertson said, "we need the help of the Holy Spirit to understand properly the Word of God. . . . He will help us if we ask him."[19]

Robertson's grammatical study and his work of interpretation fall together under the comprehensive vocation of preaching. It will be recalled that Broadus was not only professor of New Testament interpretation but also professor of homiletics. And Robertson's initial faculty appointment was as an assistant professor of Greek and homiletics. Robertson thought of himself first and foremost as a preacher. So when asked whether preaching, teaching, or writing was the highest kind of service, he replied, "Preaching! Yes, preaching is the greatest work in the world. The element in the other two that makes them worthwhile is the preaching that they contain."[20] He went on to declare that he had never considered himself as anything other

17. Robertson, *Grammar*, 91.
18. A. T. Robertson, "The Preacher and His Greek New Testament," *Seminary Magazine*, 1893, 414.
19. A. T. Robertson, "On Learning the New Testament," *Christian Index* 80 (Aug. 16, 1900): 1.
20. A. T. Robertson, interview by Frank H. Leavell, *Baptist Student* 10 (May 1932): 3.

than a preacher. Indeed, the major purpose in writing the "Big Grammar" was to help others to preach the Word. In later editions he expressed particular gratitude that preachers were finding it helpful: "It is gratifying to know that ministers are using it in their studies as one of the regular tools in the shop. My own reward for the long years of devotion to this grammar is found in the satisfaction that scholarly ministers are using the book for their own enrichment."[21]

Grounded in the most current methods and sources, Robertson's contributions to the study of New Testament Greek transcended ideological boundaries. For that reason they continue to be of use. His mastery of Greek grammar combined with his conventional conservative approach to critical and interpretative questions makes him a valuable resource for conservative and evangelical Christians even today.

Primary Sources

Robertson, A. T. *The Christ of the Logia*. New York: George H. Doran, 1924.

———. *The Divinity of Christ in the Gospel of John*. New York: Revell, 1916.

———. *Epochs in the Life of Jesus*. New York: Scribner, 1907.

———. *Epochs in the Life of Paul*. New York: Scribner, 1909.

———. *Epochs in the Life of Simon Peter*. New York: Scribner, 1933.

———. *Epochs in the Life of the Apostle John*. New York: Revell, 1935.

———. *The Glory of the Ministry*. New York: Revell, 1911.

———. *A Grammar of the Greek New Testament in the Light of Historical Research*. New York: Hodder and Stoughton, 1914; Nashville: Broadman, 1934.

———. *A Harmony of the Gospels for Students of the Life of Christ*. New York: Harper, 1922.

———. *John the Loyal*. New York: Scribner, 1911.

———. *Keywords in the Teaching of Jesus*. Philadelphia: American Baptist Publication Society, 1906.

———. *Life and Letters of John Albert Broadus*. Philadelphia: American Baptist Publication Society, 1901.

———. *Luke the Historian in the Light of Research*. New York: Scribner, 1920.

———. *Making Good in the Ministry*. New York: Revell, 1918.

———. *The Minister and His Greek New Testament*. New York: George H. Doran, 1923.

———. *The Mother of Jesus*. New York: George H. Doran, 1925.

———. *The New Citizenship*. New York: Revell, 1919.

———. *New Testament Greek Syllabus for Junior Greek Class*. Louisville: Charles T. Dearing, 1900.

———. *Passing On the Torch*. New York: Revell, 1934.

———. *Paul and the Intellectuals*. Garden City, N.Y.: Doubleday, Doran, 1928.

———. *Paul's Joy in Christ*. New York: Revell, 1917.

———. *Paul the Interpreter of Christ*. New York: George H. Doran, 1921.

21. Robertson, *Grammar,* xvii–xviii.

————. *Practical and Social Aspects of Christianity.* New York: George H. Doran, 1915.

————. *Short Grammar of the Greek New Testament.* New York: Armstrong, 1908.

————. *Some Minor Characters in the New Testament.* Garden City, N.Y.: Doubleday, Doran, 1928.

————. *The Student's Chronological New Testament.* New York: Revell, 1904.

————. *Studies in Mark's Gospel.* New York: Macmillan, 1919.

————. *Studies in the Epistle of James.* Rev. ed. Nashville: Broadman, 1959.

————. *Studies in the New Testament.* New York: Revell, 1915.

————. *Studies in the Text of the New Testament.* New York: George H. Doran, 1926.

————. *Syllabus for New Testament Study.* Louisville: Charles T. Dearing, 1902.

————. *The Teaching of Jesus concerning God the Father.* New York: American Tract Society, 1904.

————. *A Translation of Luke's Gospel.* New York: George H. Doran, 1923.

————. *Types of Preachers in the New Testament.* New York: George H. Doran, 1922.

————. *Word Pictures in the New Testament.* 6 vols. New York: R. R. Smith, 1930–33.

————, and W. Hersey Davis. *A New Short Grammar of the Greek Testament.* New York: Harper, 1931.

Richard C. H. Lenski

Robert Rosin

"Swiftly and silently the angel of death addressed the final summons to Dr. Richard Charles Henry Lenski at an early hour on Friday, August 14. And the soul of this weary and worn laborer in the Lord's kingdom answered the angel's bidding without a struggle and peacefully followed the heavenly messenger into the realms of eternal glory." So read the opening lines of the obituary run in the *Church News* of Columbus, Ohio, in the summer of 1936. Purple prose by modern standards, but those who have come to appreciate the contributions of Richard Lenski will find more drama than melodrama in those words, which capture the richness, the sense of purpose, and the devotion that marked his life and career. We no longer write obituaries that way, just as biblical scholars no longer write commentaries in Lenski's style, but both impress us with a measured grace from a bygone era that can still teach today.

Richard Lenski was acknowledged to be a man of principle and conviction, and there was little doubt about where he stood when it came to efforts at cooperation between different Lutheran groups. How he went about voicing those convictions proved problematic for people both within his own church body and in wider Lutheran circles. That he was in a position to make his voice heard is testimony to his bearing and to his scholarship, which crossed disciplines and left a legacy that continues to influence Evangelical Lutherans. Lenski was an educated pastor and a pastoral educator. Especially from his post at Capital University, where he became a fixture as he taught and wrote, he clearly influenced both his close associates and the wider sweep of Lutheranism.

About thirty-five miles northeast of Berlin in the small Prussian town of Greiffenberg,[1] Richard Lenski was born on September 14, 1864. Like so many others in Prussia and territories under its shadow, Lenski's parents became part of the German *Auswanderung*, emigrating to Jackson, Michigan,

---

1. The modern spelling has "ff," while older records sometimes read Greifenberg—not to be confused with the village of the same spelling in Bavaria—or occasionally Greisenberg, clearly a misprint coming from misreading the "f" for the "s" often found in older German print and handwriting. Ironically, the *Church News*, edited by Lenski's seminary colleague G. C. Gast, had it wrong. We have opted for the newer spelling in order to mesh with modern atlases.

where his father supported the family as a tailor. Although they had left their homeland, the Germans brought much of their educational structures and curriculum with them. So at age fourteen Lenski began his preparatory studies and continued at Capital University in Columbus, Ohio.[2] He received his B.A. in 1885 and stayed for seminary.

When Lutherans in America decided to train their own pastors rather than rely on Europe, the basic options were to adopt individual tutorial education or to found schools. Since the former produced uneven and often inadequate results, theological schools became the choice. So a program was begun as Hartwick Seminary in New York City in 1797, followed by the Lutheran seminary in Gettysburg in 1826. The Evangelical Lutheran Theological Seminary was founded in 1830 in Canton by the Ohio Synod.[3] When the lone faculty member moved to Columbus in 1831, the school—a handful of students—went with him. After a two-year start-up period the time came to find a permanent home; Columbus won a bidding war of sorts, and property was bought.[4]

By the time Lenski was a student, the tiny beginning had grown to include both a seminary program and college studies, although the student body was still not large.[5] The curriculum was strongly marked by languages, with other elements of the liberal arts added in later years. Lenski would typically have studied Latin (grammar along with readings in Caesar, Ovid, Virgil, Livy, Horace, Cicero, Tacitus), Greek (grammar, the *Iliad*, Herodotus, Aeschylus, and the New Testament), Hebrew grammar, algebra, geometry, trigonometry, history, rhetoric, speech, composition (German and English), literature (German and English), logic, natural philosophy, and catechism. The curriculum certainly made sure that serious students would be prepared for

2. For the history of Capital see David B. Owens, *These Hundred Years: The Centennial History of Capital University* (Columbus: Capital University Press, 1950).

3. The term "Ohio Synod" is used to keep matters simple. By the mid-1840s "Joint Synod" was also commonly used because the body had been divided into two districts—eastern and western—that met jointly in convention. Trying to follow the variety of names that were used over the years can be confusing. As congregations and pastors came and went as members, the church body was called the General Conference of the Evangelical Lutheran Preachers in Ohio and the Adjacent States (1818–29), the German Evangelical Lutheran Ministerium in Ohio and the Neighboring States (1818–49), the Synod and Ministerium of the Evangelical Lutheran Church in the State of Ohio (1830–43), and the Evangelical Lutheran Joint Synod of Ohio and Other States (1844–).

4. Sparked by the three hundredth anniversary of the Augsburg Confession (the pivotal statement of faith presented in 1530 to Holy Roman Emperor Charles V at the Diet of Augsburg), the Ohio Synod politely declined an invitation from New York to send their students to Hartwick and decided to start a program in Ohio instead. The problems of manpower and resources were answered in the short run when Canton pastor Wilhelm Schmidt volunteered to handle the instruction gratis for two years while several pastors and laymen prevailed on friends in Germany to donate books. Pastor Schmidt began instruction in the parsonage with two students. When he took a call the next year to Columbus, the seminary and its six students moved to his church building there. The Ohio Synod decided to make Columbus the permanent home when the people of that city contributed $2,500 (more than $1 per person—good money then) to fund the school.

5. Capital did not have four classes of students until 1867, when there were two seniors, four juniors, four sophomores, and twenty freshmen. Like other schools and with its decided tilt toward seminary, the student body was exclusively male (Owens, *These Hundred Years*, 104).

seminary.[6] In fact, readying students for seminary was what the college was virtually all about. Preparation for other careers was not emphasized; for, as can be plainly seen from the curriculum, there was nothing to point students toward the sciences.

When Lenski entered seminary in 1885, the theological faculty had a grand total of three professors.[7] Matthias Loy was the "first professor," that is to say, the dean. In 1881 he also had been thrust into the presidency of the entire Capital operation despite his objections, and when C. A. Frank resigned that same year, Loy found himself the only professor in the seminary program.[8] Help arrived when C. H. L. Schuette moved from the college to the seminary faculty, and Frederick W. Stellhorn came over from the Missouri Synod after a theological dispute.[9] The trio shaped Lenski's seminary education.[10] Loy continued as dean and concentrated on systematics, which

6. The operative phrase is "serious students," since everyone who attended for four years received a degree (Owens, *These Hundred Years*, 106–7). But given what Lenski did with his life, he certainly was not simply taking up a chair for four years.

7. While Owens's *These Hundred Years* comments on the seminary education, a more thorough source is Donald L. Huber, *Educating Lutheran Pastors in Ohio, 1830–1980: A History of Trinity Lutheran Seminary and Its Predecessors*, Studies in American Religion 33 (Lewiston, N.Y.: Edwin Mellen, 1989). One obvious advantage is that Huber carries the history of the school closer to the present day. For an account of the seminary during Lenski's student days see pp. 119–33.

8. When President William Lehmann died in 1880, the board elected Loy as his successor. Loy was still professor of theology and had just been elected president of the Joint Synod. Although the presidency of Capital was not considered a full-time position, he argued that he already had too much to handle and declined the appointment. The board refused to take no for an answer and adjourned, leaving Loy with the keys to the office, so to speak. Someone had to function as Capital's president, so for the first year Loy did the job while insisting that he had not accepted it. When he realized that the board was satisfied with the situation and was not about to elect someone else, he accepted the title that went with the work he had been doing. (The position also brought an additional $300 to his annual salary of $1,200.) Loy's shouldering what had been assigned served as a model for Lenski.

9. Stellhorn had been teaching at Concordia College in Fort Wayne. The dominating force in the Missouri Synod at that time was Carl F. W. Walther, who served on occasion as president of both the synod and Concordia Seminary in St. Louis. In the 1880s, controversy arose over a fundamental question: Did God elect people to salvation purely on the basis of grace and Christ's merit, or did he elect them also *intuitu fidei*, that is, "in view of faith," seeing something good to come and knowing that the Spirit's call would be positively answered? Walther argued the former, and Stellhorn (who happened to be married to Walther's niece) the latter. On a broader level, Missouri backed Walther, and the Ohio Synod went the other way. As a result, Ohio withdrew from the Synodical Conference, an organization founded in 1872 by the Missouri and Ohio Synods along with other groups in the hope of multiplying their influence by working together. There was some realignment of pastors as they found more comfortable theological homes. Ohio accepted men like Stellhorn while C. A. Frank left Columbus. Actually, Frank was a Missourian on loan, having come to teach at Capital's seminary during the early days of cooperation in the Synodical Conference. He had never felt at home and took the occasion of the controversy to leave, first to organize the Concordia Synod in Pennsylvania, and then to return to the Missouri Synod when his little group was absorbed.

While Lenski admired much about the Missouri Synod, he disagreed when it rejected *intuitu fidei* on the grounds that it was a synergistic position. As Lenski would later explain, *intuitu fidei* does not give people credit for contributing something to their salvation; rather, the expression means "in view of the all-sufficient merits of Christ perseveringly apprehended by faith" (quoted in his obituary in *The Lutheran Standard* 93.35 [Aug. 29, 1936]: 3).

10. Not only were Loy, Stellhorn, and Schuette the faculty for Lenski, they were the only professors at the seminary from 1881 until 1894. At least the overworked faculty could depend on some routine there.

included catechetics, dogmatics, and pastoral theology. Stellhorn offered courses in hermeneutics (the principles of interpretation), exegesis (the actual interpretation of biblical books), isagogics (the background of biblical books; i.e., matters like authorship and date), and church history. Schuette taught practical theology, which included homiletics and symbolics (the official statements and doctrines of various church bodies).[11]

The three-man faculty proceeded to revise teaching methods and curriculum. Rather than deliver each lecture in both German and English, they alternated languages from lecture to lecture, saving them double work and forcing the students to learn how to think theologically in both languages. A decade earlier a move had already begun to make more use of textbooks and end the old dictation style where students simply copied notes read in class. That trend continued under Loy as professors offered comments as they moved through the reading material that consisted of classic German titles. Lenski benefited from the recently revised curriculum. The oddest feature of the three-year curriculum was that a student did not take courses with just his own class. That would have meant offering every course each year. Instead the entire student body sat together and took a given year's courses. Students would begin with whatever happened to be offered at the time; thus each course would have beginners together with students finishing their seminary training. That is hardly ideal. But the seminary had only three professors, and with extracurricular expectations laid on them by the synod, that was the way it had to be. Still, substantial progress had been made by the time Lenski arrived, with Capital becoming a "theoretical seminary" whose entering students were expected to have a good classical background. Those seminarians could then explore theology in depth rather than worry about developing practical skills. The languages learned in the preparatory college years were particularly important, for students in Lenski's era could be expected to do exegesis based on Greek and Hebrew.

At the same time, the high level of expectation collided with the needs of the synod. Strict requirements whittled down the number of potential students, and as the enrollment dropped, the synod had fewer graduates for vacant congregations. A possible solution was to start a "practical seminary" like the Missouri Synod's school in Springfield, Illinois, where students would work with the German Bible—not as desirable as the Capital curriculum, but something had to be done.[12] Yet a second seminary would take several years to get off the ground. In the meantime the shortage of pastors forced the adoption of a second solution, namely, abbreviating the three-year

11. Huber, *Educating Lutheran Pastors*, 125–26, includes a chart of each year's courses and professors—First year: theological encyclopedia (Loy), catechetics (Loy), church history (Stellhorn), exegesis (Stellhorn), ethics (Schuette), Augsburg Confession (Loy); Second year: dogmatics (Loy), isagogics (Stellhorn), exegesis (Stellhorn), homiletics (Schuette); Third year: pastoral theology (Loy), hermeneutics (Stellhorn), exegesis (Stellhorn), symbolics (Schuette).

12. A practical program had begun as a department at Capital in 1882; it was soon moved to the synod's northwest district and eventually to St. Paul, where it became Luther Seminary.

plan. So after only his second year Lenski's studies were broken off, and he was on his way to a congregation in Baltimore—a church outside the Midwest but still a member of the Joint Synod. In the next few years Lenski returned to the state of Ohio to serve synodical congregations at Trenton, Springfield, and Anna. He also was elected president of the western district of the synod. Along the way in 1890 he received an M.A. from the Columbus seminary, which would also award him a D.D. in 1915.

Professorship at the Evangelical Lutheran Theological Seminary (Capital University)

In 1911 Lenski returned to Columbus as a member of the seminary faculty. He remained at his alma mater for twenty-five years. Although he taught some exegesis during his years there, and his name would become associated primarily with his commentary series, he was also a professor of dogmatics and homiletics, a combination that helps explain his approach to exegesis. The dogmatic outlook colors the texts of his commentaries.

Lenski returned at a time when Capital was undergoing significant changes. Throughout its history the college and seminary had shared space and, to some degree, faculty as well. But the seminary faculty had become convinced that this mixture was not good for the students' social and educational development. Moreover, the seminary suffered because of the professors' heavy involvement in the college program. The school's need for some new facilities gave the synod the opportunity to separate the two programs and to curtail some of the seminary faculty's involvement in the college program. Ironically, one of Lenski's duties upon arriving at the seminary was to teach Greek at the college. At least this was something that fed directly into his seminary teaching.

The move toward new buildings got off to an uneven start as funding stalled, but the effort to bring in new faculty went well. Lenski was one of those new appointments. Loy had retired in 1902, making Stellhorn senior faculty member. Now Stellhorn's health forced him to reduce his load and prompted a search for help. Lenski was a natural choice: a graduate of Capital with extensive experience in the parish and church administration; a protégé of Stellhorn; and the editor of the synod's German language periodical, the *Lutherische Kirchenzeitung*. Stellhorn remained officially the first professor, but Lenski was the one who made things perk, in the classroom and beyond.

Lenski's energy was brought to bear on efforts to improve Capital's curriculum. He himself had been a student when the school was geared exclusively to pastoral education. Now Lenski supported the teaching of science at the college. Since 1894 there had been feeble efforts at introducing courses in science, but there had been tepid response, so Schuette, now Capital's president, suggested at the 1912 Joint Synod meeting that science be dropped since it did not pay for itself. Lenski, however, editorialized in the *Kirchenzeitung* in behalf of the courses, noting that science credits earned at Capital were accepted at Ohio State University, so the program must be respectable and ought to be retained to give the college a better balance. Lenski's side won out when the convention referred the matter back to the school's administration and board. Lenski thus demonstrated that there was more to him than narrow theology.[13]

A year after Lenski's arrival in 1911, Otto Mees was installed as Capital's new president. The son of faculty member Theophilus Mees, the new president was said to have a progressive outlook, while Lenski was known as an "old Lutheran" with a traditional, conservative, confessional perspective. Since Lenski's student days, the seminary had grown and the faculty now numbered five full-time members. But in terms of outlook and attitude the seminary was settling into a calm, which was already evident during Loy's last years at the helm. As the new century moved forward, it was imperative that the seminary not be left in its wake. For a while, distractions with the First World War stood in the way, but the seminary faculty and Mees soon had their opportunity. With the school in need of a curricular shot in the arm, both Mees and Lenski brought much-needed energy to the task, but their different outlooks produced friction along the way.[14] It must be noted that the heat that was generated came not from substantial theological differences but from differences in style, from what each thought important to accent. Later, when Mees was under fire from the more conservative elements, Lenski showed integrity by making sure that they understood where the problems lay and that Mees was not pilloried for what he had not done or said.

Ever since his return, Lenski had acted as the virtual dean because of Stellhorn's poor health. Outside the classroom he provided additional leadership by fostering theological discussion in an extracurricular student group that he served as an advisor.[15] Yet when it came time to formally replace Stellhorn as dean in 1919, Mees did not want Lenski. The board of directors, however, overruled the president on this matter. In the decade that followed, the seminary seemed to follow Lenski's lead in displaying an "old Lutheran" spirit. Two faculty members who died were not immediately replaced, a situation that put a strain on the three men left and forced college faculty to fill in. But in 1927 the board moved to ease the strain and restructured the seminary into four chairs or departments. Lenski was assigned systematics, P. H. Beuhring exegesis, and G. C. Gast historical theology, while a new man, Jacob Dell, was brought in to handle practical theology. In 1929 more help arrived

13. Owens, *These Hundred Years*, 142.
14. Huber, *Educating Lutheran Pastors*, 155.
15. In years past the Schmidt Theological Society, named for the seminary's first professor, had become more of a social club. When the independently organized group resisted faculty efforts to rein in their activities, the faculty simply dissolved the society. Lenski was willing to become involved with the new group both to prevent a repeat of past problems and to promote the positive endeavor of students' interacting on theology apart from class assignments (see Huber, *Educating Lutheran Pastors*, 81, 128, 155).

in the area of exegesis: when the Buffalo Synod closed its seminary after merging with the Iowa Synod, Herbert Leupold moved over to Capital as professor of Old Testament. That made a full complement of five again, most of whom were generally in step with Lenski's old Lutheran views.[16] Lenski was especially impressed by the Missouri Synod's confessional intensity as were some of his faculty.[17]

Still, Dean Lenski found his faculty's integrity challenged at times in the 1920s.[18] The Ohio Synod certainly ranked among the theologically conservative Lutheran bodies, while there was no doubt that the United Lutheran Church in America (ULCA) had staked out the liberal end of the spectrum, especially if one were to ask an old Lutheran like Lenski. Conservatives were particularly rankled by unionism and the tendency to look the other way when church members joined secret societies.[19] At the start of the decade, Ohio Synod President C. C. Hein, who may have been more conservative than Lenski (if that were possible), upset the dean when in public he rather nastily termed Capital "the best seminary of the ULCA." At a meeting that Lenski arranged between Hein and the faculty, it became clear that the progressive Otto Mees was the focus of Hein's comments. (This is the case where Lenski made sure that Mees was not unjustly condemned.) No notes were made, but in the end Hein apparently was satisfied that Mees was basically conservative although relatively progressive in his style and methods. Since the seminary was keen to defend its reputation, a statement was drafted maintaining that there was no problem between Hein and Mees, that the faculty's conservatism was not in question, and that they had no interest in en-

16. Owens, *These Hundred Years*, 201.
17. In the *Kirchenzeitung* of May 20, 1922, Lenski wrote: "If there ever was a strictly conservative Lutheran body, it surely is the Missouri Synod. Nevertheless, this growth! Here is a historical fact that refutes all talk trying to persuade us that we must be liberal, accommodate ourselves to the spirit of the time, etc., in order to win men and grow externally. The very opposite is seen in the Missouri Synod. Missouri has at all times been unyielding; it is so still. In this body the Scriptures and the Confessions have been, and still are, valued to their full import. There was no disposition to surrender any part of them. With this asset Missouri has been working in free America, which abounds in sects and religious confusion, and now exhibits its enormous achievements. What so many regard as Missouri's weakness has in reality been its strength. This fact we might write down for our own remembrance. It is a mark of the pastors and leaders of the Missouri Synod that they never, yes never, tire of discussing doctrine on the basis of the Confessions and of the Scriptures. That is one trait that may be called 'the spirit of Missouri'" (quoted in Walter A. Baepler, *A Century of Grace: A History of the Missouri Synod, 1847–1947* [St. Louis: Concordia, 1947], 13).
18. Huber, *Educating Lutheran Pastors*, 191–92.
19. Unionism denoted joint activities with another church body with which a group was not in confessional agreement. Unionism was viewed as putting the lie to the group's own confessional interest and integrity by acting as if the other body's position was just as acceptable. The matter of secret societies or lodges was similar: conservatives argued that the societies' ceremonies included ritual statements that were, in effect, confessions of faith in and obedience to a god other than the true God of the Bible. Lodge members were thus in an idolatrous relationship, serving both the Christian God and the deity of the secret ritual. Echoing Joshua, conservative critics declared, "Choose you this day whom you will serve." For some Lutherans these remain serious issues. Others, believing them overblown, either are glad that the issues have eroded or have redefined the standards so that the activities in question are no longer considered so serious.

tertaining liberalism. Hein was to publicize the statement to make sure that Capital was not wrongly criticized.

The episode typifies Lenski. Staunch confessional Lutheranism was essential to him, as was his seminary's reputation as a voice thereof. When a challenge arose, Lenski reacted decisively. The matter was especially serious because the critic was the synod's president. Principle prevented Lenski from letting the remark pass. Rather than fret in private or wage a counter-campaign through third parties and backdoor channels, Lenski confronted the matter bluntly yet with propriety: a private meeting in which the concerned parties could be honest with each other was arranged. All that shows integrity on his part.

In addition, the summary statement speaks well of Lenski's role. First, any notion of a personal rift was put to rest, so the synod would not whisper about any supposed problem between Mees and Hein. Any tension between Mees and Lenski was also set aside. Then, too, the faculty's good name was defended. Because those involved were satisfied that there was no substantial problem and wanted to ensure that no reputations would be ruined, it was necessary to "put the best construction on everything," as Martin Luther had phrased it in his Small Catechism explanation of the commandment against false witness. But there was no hollow posturing for Lenski just to save face and smooth the matter over. He insisted on substance behind the words. He also expected people to step forward for principle and bear witness plainly. That blunt, straight-arrow approach worked here, and in the end all concerned seemed satisfied.

At the same time Lenski's traits could bring some grief. Of course, we would not prefer equivocation or laud duplicity, but there are times when a certain diplomacy might in the long run serve truth better. Lenski seemed intent on always being direct. But was he always right? It might have been better sometimes to pause and check before pressing ahead. Lenski's intensity could compound problems when, as later events would prove, he was wrong. Examples include his 1924 quarrel with local pastor Charles Pflueger and his criticism of the National Lutheran Council.

The Penchant for Controversy

Lenski's blunt manner triggered the incident with Pflueger.[20] Lenski had claimed that the president of Wittenberg College, R. E. Tulloss, belonged to the Masons, a secret society. After Pflueger's defense of the man had proved Lenski wrong, Lenski published an apology that was blunt but, in Pflueger's opinion, inadequate. Lenski expressed regret for any harm done to Tulloss's reputation, but he also suggested that he bore no blame since he had acted honestly on wrong information. He did not acknowledge that he should have been better informed before going public. Unsatisfied with the apology,

20. Huber, *Educating Lutheran Pastors*, 192–94.

Pflueger challenged Lenski's integrity. Efforts by church-appointed mediators did not placate Pflueger, who then launched charges of his own, claiming Lenski had maligned yet another pastor and was a money-grubber. Lenski had been preaching at a church while its pastor was on sick leave. When the congregation suggested that they might engage someone else to help out as well, Lenski allegedly implied some problem with the man's theology—hence the charge of maligning another pastor. And by blocking the man from the pulpit Lenski assured that he would continue to be paid for preaching—hence Pflueger's claim of greed. If there were truth to Pflueger's charge, it was made to look ridiculous when he argued that Lenski not only was well paid as a professor whose income was augmented by book royalties, but also made money on the side by selling flower bulbs. (Lenski was known for his gladiolus collection of some 450 varieties—his hobby.)

Though this was serious business at first with its accusation of Masonry, the situation quickly degenerated and might even have been funny if so much time had not been wasted and the contending parties not been so petty. Pflueger would not quit until he proved Lenski wrong and forced a public admission, though several mediation committees, trying to end the fray, dismissed his complaints. On the other side, Lenski did not help matters with his attitude. His original editorial attack had his typical vigor. But when he realized that he had been careless and had something to apologize for, he could not bring himself to admit personal fault. And his dismissive attitude only infuriated Pflueger. In the greater scheme of things, this was a small matter, but it illustrates the downside of Lenski's authoritarian manner. Having rushed into an error, he had deflected the blame so that he could also claim to be a victim.

The same pattern drew Lenski into a much larger argument that affected whole synods associated with the National Lutheran Council (NLC). Along with teaching and administrative duties, Lenski continued to edit the *Lutherische Kirchenzeitung,* one of the Joint Synod's publishing outlets and the vehicle through which he had made his charge against Wittenberg's president. In a series of editorials, Lenski also attacked the NLC. The NLC had been formally launched in 1918 as a combined effort of several Lutheran bodies. The year before, they had joined in an ad hoc effort to publicize the four hundredth anniversary of the posting of Luther's Ninety-five Theses. In addition, the national Lutheran Commission for Soldiers' and Sailors' Welfare was formed in 1917 to minister to those in the armed forces, and the Lutheran Bureau was established as a publicity agency. Those efforts evolved into the NLC, organized in Chicago in October 1918. No formal constitution was adopted, perhaps to keep the support of more reluctant, conservative participants. The organization operated instead with a simple statement of purpose. Among the functions were the provision of statistical information on Lutheran bodies, publicity, public relations, coordination of the activities of the constituent groups, encouragement of a national interest in Christianity, and the monitoring of church-state relations.

From the beginning some groups were uneasy about how much their involvement in the NLC linked them to church bodies with which they were not in close fellowship or communion vis-à-vis the Word and sacraments. There was debate within the more conservative church bodies about what could be done in good conscience and what constituted unionism. Though not the most reluctant member, the Joint Synod was troubled by the convictions of some other members. And among the Ohioans Lenski was a prominent critic, voicing his complaints in the pages of the *Kirchenzeitung*. While Lenski was not so extreme as to say that because everything has worship overtones, there could be no intersynodical efforts, he did editorialize against what he thought was a lax attitude that did not sufficiently test the spirits. In short, he did not rule cooperative activities out on principle but had problems with the practice. A similar evaluation might be made of his critics: they admired Lenski's staunch orthodoxy, but they objected to the way he launched his assault.[21]

In 1919 the NLC sent observers to take note of the physical needs of Europe in the wake of the Great War. As a result, financial aid was channeled to a variety of countries (except Germany, which was still closed by order of the Allies). Congregations were supported and pastors' salaries were supplemented in the hope that Lutheranism might be strengthened. But back in America some Lutherans wondered if this sort of assistance might let in fellowship via the back door. They thought the confessional position of these churches and pastors was inadequate. They would not have funded them in normal circumstances, but here they were offering support. Was this fellowship in a roundabout way? A related question was whether all the members of the NLC had to be in full agreement before they acted as a unit.

At this point the difference between *res externae*, matters external to the basic purpose of the church in its use of Word and sacraments, and *res internae*, matters essential or integral to the church's mission and ministry, came into play. There was a debate as to whether the NLC's activities were no more than external matters. Johann Michael Reu of the Iowa Synod and Richard Lenski were two of the sharper critics. They preferred that the NLC confine its activities to identifying needs and then let others provide funding. The NLC ought not give the money itself, thus supporting the ministry of some who were more liberal. Within the NLC, caution was sounded lest such critics be given more ammunition: "[We] must try to keep the Council's record very clear indeed, so that we may be in a position to make our real fight against the reactionaries with a prospect of success."[22]

21. For a summary see Huber, *Educating Lutheran Pastors,* 194–95. Copies of notes from meetings held with Lenski concerning allegations of editorial overkill and of Lenski's personal statement offered in defense were provided from the archives of the Evangelical Lutheran Church in America, Region 6, and from the archives of Trinity Lutheran Seminary (Lenski's old school now renamed).

22. See E. Clifford Nelson, ed., *The Lutherans in North America* (Philadelphia: Fortress, 1975), 407. The quotation comes from a letter written by Charles Jacobs to Lauritz Larsen (Nov. 29, 1919), which is now part of the NLC files in the Archives of Cooperative Lutheranism. On the NLC's activities and the criticism see pp. 405–9.

Lenski, one of the "reactionaries" mentioned, feared unionism and would not be deterred in his criticism. In 1920 he published a series of editorials targeting the NLC as being not simply weak but anticonfessional. Complaints against Lenski prompted his colleague C. H. L. Schuette to call a joint meeting of the seminary faculty and the pastors on the synodical publication board. Lenski objected, noting there were no constitutional grounds for such an inquiry. Nevertheless, the meeting took place on March 5, 1921.

The minutes of the meeting are quite revealing.[23] At one point Schuette challenged Lenski: "I ask you on your honor, is it not in your mind to discredit the NLC?" Lenski replied, "What is in my mind is between myself and God. He who interprets my words must also answer to God for his interpretation." That exchange suggests a great deal. It seems that the problem was not only with the substance of what Lenski wrote—a misrepresentation of the NLC, some believed—but also with how he went about voicing his objections. Lenski was not about to be drawn into that discussion. It was enough to consider his conduct and actions, not inner, private thoughts.[24] Lest anyone want to press the matter, he asserted defiantly, God waits as judge. That was true enough, but Lenski's reply was sure to grate.

Later in the meeting Pastor H. J. Schuh noted that Lenski had criticized the way in which money was being spent (or, more precisely, *not* being spent), even though he had yet to see a full public report on how funds were being managed. Lenski replied that he had acted on the basis of the minutes of meetings to which he was privy; minutes, he argued, were more honest than later public reports that would be sanitized and couched to obtain maximum support from church members who were honest and trusting but essentially ignorant. So he was doing the NLC a service by giving early warning and precluding the necessity of recouping favor through public relations.

This episode has echoes of Lenski's apology for the charge against Tulloss: he had acted on the basis of the information he had and thus was not culpable, even though later information mitigated matters. In this instance Schuh noted that the funds held back by the NLC—funds Lenski wanted spent—were being kept in reserve lest the NLC be caught without resources should some dire emergency suddenly come to light. Lenski countered by arguing that he was not at fault for prematurely criticizing; rather, the NLC was responsible because of the impression it had created. By amassing so much money the NLC had forced him to be critical. As Lenski told Schuh, "In my opinion that sum was entirely too large—that is my impression. I can only publish my impressions." Other participants in the meeting then reminded Lenski that the *Kirchenzeitung* was not his personal vehicle but belonged to

---

23. The minutes of the March 5, 1921, meeting were provided from the archives of the Evangelical Lutheran Church, Region 6.

24. One wonders how this exchange might go if it were held today, for Lenski would probably not be able to fend off attempts to get inside his private thoughts. In the postmodern age intent has become the focus, convicting or acquitting at least in the court of public opinion, while actions have become secondary, unless they are deconstructed to get back to the intent.

the church, so he ought to show more responsibility. Said Schuette, "The *Kirchenzeitung* is not your personal property. We want facts, not your personal impressions." The committee pointed out that Lenski had discredited the NLC because of his personal conclusions, not because of any official judgment or opposition from the synod. They objected to Lenski's refusal to print information disseminated by the NLC for publication in official periodicals. Moreover, whenever he did agree to print some of this information, he sometimes edited in or out what he wanted and so gave an impression different from what was intended. In reference to a specific instance came the question, "Why do you omit that last clause? That is dishonest. Missourian policies." Though this statement was intended as a rebuke, old-style Lenski would have taken it as a compliment.[25]

Lenski came close to an admission when he stated, "All you have said I appreciate, and I interpret it without casting any reproach on you. But what you brethren have just heard, if translated into acts, will work harm. . . . Men in our Synod will go into open unionism under the guidance of the NLC. . . . What we wish to do is to save the situation. Of course one may be overzealous in a good cause." Asked for proof of unionism, Lenski replied, "Its [the NLC's] work has led into unionistic directions." The notes make it clear that the committeemen were not pleased with this response. Yet they were unwilling to say too much since, as Lenski had noted, the meeting itself was constitutionally irregular. Their final statement acknowledged his editorial privilege, but noted that editorial privilege did not grant him the right to misrepresent the NLC or the ULCA. They had no power to order change, but they urged the Joint Synod president to do so.

Throughout the exchange Lenski's orthodoxy was never challenged. In the committee's view he certainly knew what was right doctrinally. But how he interpreted the actions of others—here the NLC—and how he then went about voicing criticism were both weaknesses. Lenski should have been pleased that the committee differentiated between doctrine and practice, and he ought to have conceded that people can differ honestly on the latter and that he might have acted otherwise. But not only did he see no real problem with his practice, he mixed his practice up with doctrine, saying that had he not acted as he did, he would have failed the cause of doctrine, failed to defend the truth. A personal statement filed a week later on March 12 solidly defended his position. His objections to the proceedings were repeated, followed by detailed justifications of the judgments rendered in his editorials. The statement added up to a rejection of the charge that he had misrepresented the NLC and its representatives.

At the meeting and in his subsequent statement Lenski made no concession that he could be wrong. His views, he contended, should have been given more consideration, especially his concern that well-intentioned efforts

25. For Lenski's opinion of Missouri see n. 17.

that seem to present no problem in the short term may lead to erosion in the long run. He was concerned about denominational integrity.

It is ironic that some years later when a local Columbus congregation in the United Lutheran Church asked Capital Seminary for a student assistant, the faculty declined the request, not on the basis of the congregation's theological position, but out of the need to maintain "synodical loyalty."[26] The irony is that this response of the faculty, including some who had criticized Lenski, was akin to what Lenski himself had argued regarding the NLC's granting of financial aid to meet the needs in postwar Europe: while the immediate participants in the program might not have presented a problem, there should have been an awareness of the overtones of larger ties. If there was a potential problem, it was better to find another way to meet the needs. The answer was not to let people suffer, but to create some other channel for dispensing aid. The issue seemed to be how to weigh the needs for relief against the synod's reputation and identity. Lenski was more concerned about the latter, a position that certainly should be respected. His critics should have been pressed to answer why alternative methods and channels could not have been found for the overseas work. But his tone made it hard for some to appreciate his stance.

After all was said and done, Lenski remained the editor of the *Kirchenzeitung;* by the time he stepped down, he had held the post for twenty years (1904–24). While the brouhaha over the NLC editorials got much attention, it should not be stressed disproportionately, for Lenski produced much for the benefit of his church. Others were not pleased at the time, but had they thought his position a fatal error, someone else would have replaced Lenski immediately. Instead he stayed several more years.

Writings

Because it was natural for Lenski to turn to print to educate others, he had been a prolific writer since his days in the parish ministry. He began in 1895 with his *Biblische Frauenbilder,* a volume on women of the Bible; its articles had originally been talks to the Ladies' Society of Zion Lutheran, his congregation in Springfield. In 1898 he published in English for the first time: *His Footsteps* consisted of devotions based on the life of Christ. To the commonly used Eisenach lectionary series he contributed *Eisenach Gospel Selections* (1910) and *Eisenach Epistle Selections* (1914). *St. Paul* (1916) was followed by *New Gospel Selections Made Ready for Pulpit Work* (1919) and *The Active Church Member* (1922). He returned to the Eisenach series with *Eisenach Old Testament Selections* in 1925. In 1927 he published both *Kings and Priests: The Universal Priesthood of Believers,* his book most oriented toward dogmatics, and *The Sermon: Its Homiletical Construction.* The latter grew out of one of his chief teaching areas. Lenski's string of monographs

---

26. Huber, *Educating Lutheran Pastors,* 198.

continued with *St. John* in 1929 and *The Epistle Selections of the Ancient Church* in 1935. Finally, *The Gospel Selections of the Ancient Church* came off the press the very week of his death in 1936.

Given the teaching expectations and the work involved in editing the synod's *Lutherische Kirchenzeitung*, Lenski's output is astounding. But our list is far from complete. During the 1920s, while busy on other titles, Lenski did the spadework on what would become his New Testament commentaries. Released between 1931 and 1938, the eleven volumes were grouped in a series as *The Interpretation of the New Testament*. Though many other commentaries have come in the decades since, Lenski's remain on the worktables of many Evangelical Lutheran pastors.

Lenski's commentaries evoke interesting reactions. He made much of language and vocabulary. Rather than speculate about what passages might mean, he focused on grammar and particular words in a pericope. His tendency was to argue for an interpretation on the basis of a particular word or grammatical construction. For the most part this can produce fruitful results. After all, words and grammar are there to help define and express meaning. The problem comes when a point is pressed beyond what it can bear. Thus he might say that something is *always* the case when it is only *mostly* the case. Or he might draw a conclusion on the basis of an overly subtle semantic distinction.[27] There is a danger in narrowly fixing on a word or phrase that, while it deserves attention, ought to be seen also in the wider sweep. Looking at words in isolation should be accompanied by examining them in their wider textual and cultural context. As Lenski extracts dogmatic lessons, Romans, Galatians, and Corinthians begin to look more like each other than they otherwise might.

In addition, Lenski sometimes argues in circles. He will contend that a certain grammatical construction leads to a theological conclusion; then, in expounding the basis of his view of the grammatical construction, he points to that very theological conclusion. The saving grace here is that he comes out in the right place theologically. That is because he reads the New Testament with an evangelical outlook and from deep Lutheran roots. To take just one example, his exposition of Romans 5 builds on the categories of objective and subjective justification even though those terms do not explicitly appear,

27. E.g., R. C. H. Lenski, *The Interpretation of St. Paul's Epistles to the Galatians, to the Ephesians and to the Philippians* (Columbus: Lutheran Book Concern, 1937), 35–36. In commenting on the use of *heteron* and *allo* in Gal. 1:6–7 and the distinct meanings of difference of kind and numerical nonidentity, he states: "This gospel is 'different' because it is '*not* another.' A gospel might be 'different' only because it is 'another,' is couched only in 'other' words but leaves the substance the same. But when it is 'different' because it is '*not* another,' the very substance is changed; such a gospel is a fake, a mere pretense or sham." Moisés Silva, *Explorations in Exegetical Method: Galatians as a Test Case* (Grand Rapids: Baker, 1996), 55 n. 10, argues that in the process of "exploit[ing] this supposed semantic distinction . . . Lenski's logic has gone awry. . . . But even if the point could be sustained, how likely is it that any author would depend on such subtleties to get the point across?" Space does not permit citing other examples that are better read in context; see D. A. Carson, *Exegetical Fallacies*, 2d ed. (Grand Rapids: Baker, 1996), 56, 70, 90.

being familiar to students of Lutheran dogmatics.[28] That is just the sort of discussion one would expect to find. In general, when it comes to understanding the doctrinal import of passages, Lenski does well. How he arrives at that point has bothered some later exegetes, though they still appreciate the theology that Lenski finds there.[29]

This is not to dismiss Lenski's commentaries, but to note reservations about individual exegetical examples and to be aware of some of his tendencies. In fact, the undertaking was titanic and succeeded admirably at understanding the New Testament in an evangelical way. Lenski clearly thought in terms of law and gospel; thus a doctrinal coherence shines through as he explains the varied New Testament texts. His results, his conclusions are solidly Lutheran. (A colleague sums up Lenski's achievements this way: Seminary professors would like all students to be linguistic geniuses, but many will struggle with exegesis. Then they ought to have Lenski, for he will keep them focused and help them think through the text in evangelical terms.)

Lenski was fortunate to have accomplished much in the 1920s toward preparing his commentaries for publication in the next decade. For in the 1930s his health took a turn for the worse.[30] Students knew him for his tall, erect stature and piercing gray eyes, but diabetes began to take its toll. He continued with his commentaries even as his strength waned. After a leave of absence in 1929–30 he returned to his duties, but it was largely his will that carried him through. In 1935 he gave up his administrative duties and cut back his teaching to five hours a week. The end came early Friday morning, August 14, 1936. He left behind his wife, the former Helen Gruner, and five children, including Gerhard, a pastor in Washington, D.C.

Lenski had planned his own funeral service. A. C. Schiff of Columbus was the officiant, and Glen Seamon, Lenski's pastor at St. Peter's, preached. He was buried in Green Lawn Cemetery, where other Capital faculty had been laid to rest. He wanted everything done simply with no fanfare. That extended even to his obituary. G. C. Gast, who was then editing *Church News* (*Kirchenzeitung* in its English format), felt obliged to write an explanation for those readers who would expect more than one column: "Repeatedly and very urgently Dr. Lenski requested the editor of this department to limit the account of his death in these columns to an unadorned record of a few objective facts of his life and his work. Very reluctantly we consented, and are hereby endeavoring to redeem the pledge made to our departed colleague."

28. R. C. H. Lenski, *The Interpretation of St. Paul's Epistle to the Romans* (Columbus: Lutheran Book Concern, 1936), 330–86.
29. A number of exegetes echo Silva's observation (*Explorations in Exegetical Method*, 29) that "the popular Lutheran commentator Lenski . . . routinely overinterprets the significance of the language." It is important to note that Silva does not say that Lenski is off line, but simply that he presses a bit beyond where it might have been better to stop. While there is nothing doctrinally wrong with the theology, and there are certainly passages that will justify the conclusions, the conclusions just do not rest all that comfortably on the particular verse under discussion at the moment. For more examples of Lenski's overreaching see Silva, *Explorations in Exegetical Method*, 75 n. 23.
30. Owens, *These Hundred Years*, 200–201; Huber, *Educating Lutheran Pastors*, 202.

Others followed suit so that it is difficult to lay hold of information on Lenski, especially on his private life. But his work survives in abundance, and his influence lives on as his writings continue to produce fruit. Lenski would be pleased.

Richard Lenski was a dominant figure in Lutheranism in the first third of the twentieth century. He stood tall for "old Lutheranism." To be sure, he could be controversial, but he was most certainly not without principle. His convictions and his commitment and love of classic Lutheran confessional theology drove him. It seems clear that there were times when he pressed farther than he ought, times he loosed public polemics that may not have helped matters. But his confrontations have to be balanced against his years of faithful service in many avenues. His manner could be irritating and infuriating, but he also received tremendous love and respect from those around him at the seminary, the kind of admiration that has to be earned, not commanded. In his memory students donated to the seminary library four art-glass windows depicting the four Evangelists,[31] and part of the building is named in his honor. It is a fitting memorial, given all that Lenski wrote. He left behind twenty-three volumes and a host of editorials, some fifteen thousand pages devoted to building up the body of Christ. An author, an editor, a pastor who served in parishes, and a professor who helped educate pastors—Lenski's is a rich legacy that continues to enliven evangelical circles.[32]

Primary Sources

Lenski, Richard C. H. *The Active Church Member.* Columbus: Lutheran Book Concern, 1922.

———. *Eisenach Epistle Selections.* Columbus: Lutheran Book Concern, 1914.

———. *Eisenach Gospel Selections.* Columbus: Lutheran Book Concern, 1910.

———. *Eisenach Old Testament Selections.* Columbus: Lutheran Book Concern, 1925.

———. *The Epistle Selections of the Ancient Church.* Columbus: Lutheran Book Concern, 1935.

———. *The Gospel Selections of the Ancient Church.* Columbus: Lutheran Book Concern, 1936.

———. *His Footsteps: Studies for Edification from the Life of Christ.* Columbus: Lutheran Book Concern, 1898.

———. *The Interpretation of St. John's Gospel.* Columbus: Lutheran Book Concern, 1931.

31. Owens, *These Hundred Years,* 184.
32. A number of people have provided information for this article. My thanks to Robert Roethemeyer and his research assistants at the library of Concordia Seminary, St. Louis, and to William Schmelder of the faculty for some bibliographical suggestions. Thanks are also due to Linda Fry of the library and Donald Huber of the faculty at Trinity Lutheran Seminary for checking on sources and offering advice. And finally, many thanks to Connie Conrad for providing from the archives of the Evangelical Lutheran Church in America, Region 6, material that afforded insight into Lenski's character and confirmed his scholarship.

———. *The Interpretation of St. John's Revelation.* Columbus: Lutheran Book Concern, 1935.

———. *The Interpretation of St. Mark's and St. Luke's Gospels.* Columbus: Lutheran Book Concern, 1934.

———. *The Interpretation of St. Matthew's Gospel.* Columbus: Lutheran Book Concern, 1932.

———. *The Interpretation of St. Paul's Epistles to the Colossians, to the Thessalonians, to Timothy, to Titus and to Philemon.* Columbus: Lutheran Book Concern, 1937.

———. *The Interpretation of St. Paul's Epistles to the Galatians, to the Ephesians and to the Philippians.* Columbus: Lutheran Book Concern, 1937.

———. *The Interpretation of St. Paul's Epistle to the Romans.* Columbus: Lutheran Book Concern, 1936.

———. *The Interpretation of St. Paul's First and Second Epistle to the Corinthians.* Columbus: Lutheran Book Concern, 1935.

———. *The Interpretation of the Acts of the Apostles.* Columbus: Lutheran Book Concern, 1934.

———. *The Interpretation of the Epistles of St. Peter, St. John, and St. Jude.* Columbus: Lutheran Book Concern, 1938.

———. *The Interpretation of the Epistle to the Hebrews and of the Epistle of James.* Columbus: Lutheran Book Concern, 1938.

———. *Kings and Priests: The Universal Priesthood of Believers.* Columbus: Lutheran Book Concern, 1927.

———. *New Gospel Selections Made Ready for Pulpit Work.* Columbus: Lutheran Book Concern, 1919.

———. *The Sermon: Its Homiletical Construction.* Columbus: Lutheran Book Concern, 1927.

———. *St. John.* Columbus: Lutheran Book Concern, 1929.

———. *St. Paul.* Columbus: Lutheran Book Concern, 1916.

Oswald T. Allis

John H. Skilton

Educator, clergyman, author, and editor, Oswald Thompson Allis was an influential defender of the Christian faith in the twentieth century. His specialty was the Old Testament, and he was an accomplished counterpart to his long-term colleague at Princeton and Westminister Seminaries, J. Gresham Machen, whose chief field of emphasis was the New Testament.

Allis was born on September 9, 1880, in Wallingford, Pennsylvania, where his family was staying temporarily. Their home was in downtown Philadelphia, where Oswald grew up. His father, Oscar Huntington Allis, was a physician of distinction with recognized teaching skills. Not only was he a teacher of medical subjects in hospitals, but he had earlier been a schoolteacher. In fact, Oswald's mother, Julia Waterbury Thompson, had taken special work in German language and literature under Oscar Allis before they were married. Her father was Oswald Thompson, president judge in the court of common pleas in Philadelphia.

The Allis line in the United States went back to William Allis, who came to Massachusetts in 1630. Galbraith Hall Todd reports in his biography of Oswald Allis that "the hereditary background of Dr. Allis has deep roots in colonial America, especially Puritan New England, and includes many ministers and persons of cultivation, with prestige in the political and educational fields."[1]

Education

Oswald benefited from his father's competence as a teacher, for he was home-taught until he was twelve years old. His parents' interest in German language and literature undoubtedly prepared him for his scholarly use of German in his doctoral studies in Berlin and beyond.

Philadelphia provided a very stimulating background for Allis's early years. Its variety of historical, cultural, and natural attractions must have nurtured and delighted his mind and spirit. From his home it was an easy

---

1. Galbraith Hall Todd, "Oswald Thompson Allis," in *The Law and the Prophets: Old Testament Studies Prepared in Honor of Oswald Thompson Allis,* ed. John H. Skilton (Nutley, N.J.: Presbyterian and Reformed, 1974), 9.

walk to Independence Hall and historic Philadelphia; to the Academy of Music, which was quite near; to the University of Pennsylvania and other centers of art, literature, and science; to City Hall and the palatial Wanamaker store; to commercial and manufacturing establishments; to the seemingly endless Fairmount Park, which brought the country right into the city.

Oswald must have been deeply influenced also by the religious environment in which he was brought up. He was reared in a Christian home in a city of churches in a day when churches were well attended. He was baptized and later made profession of faith in Christ in the Presbyterian church. His lifelong concern for Sabbath observance must have been encouraged by the fact that in Philadelphia there was little commercial or public recreational activity on the Lord's Day.

When Oswald was twelve, he attended the Penn Charter School, and then the following year he went to the Delancey School. In 1897 he entered the University of Pennsylvania, where he gave his chief attention to scientific studies.

The year 1902 brought a dramatic new development in Allis's life. In that year he entered Princeton Theological Seminary, and came under the influence of some of the great scholars who had brought distinction to that school. In the preface to his last work, *The Old Testament: Its Claims and Its Critics*, he expresses his indebtedness to the Old Princeton: "It was the privilege of the writer to study at Princeton Seminary under men who held firmly to the great tradition on which that institution was founded, men who not merely believed but gloried in that pervasive supernaturalism which alone can be called truly biblical. And he has felt that in striving to defend the heritage of unfeigned faith in the Holy Scriptures which dwelt in that noble succession of teachers, among whom Joseph Addison Alexander, William Henry Green and Robert Dick Wilson were so eminent, he was repaying in some measure the debt which he owed these mighty men of God."[2]

The speaker at the opening exercises in 1902 was Robert Dick Wilson, who had studied in Berlin and took as his subject an issue that was being discussed there at the time. The address was entitled "Babylon and Israel: A Comparison of Their Leading Ideas Based upon Their Vocabularies."[3] This was an effective response to a lecture which Friedrich Delitzsch had given in Berlin in January of 1902. In this lecture, "Babel und Bibel," Delitzsch had attempted to show that a large number of the beliefs of Israel were derived from Babylon and that the law of Moses was greatly indebted to the code of Hammurabi. Such theories were part of the comparative religions movement that impinged upon the authority of the biblical revelation. They were to cause Allis concern till the end of his life. From his first article to his last book he expresses his

---

2. Oswald T. Allis, *The Old Testament: Its Claims and Its Critics* (Nutley, N.J.: Presbyterian and Reformed, 1972), viii.

3. For Allis's report of Wilson's address see Allis, *Old Testament*, 346–47.

heartfelt conviction on the uniqueness and transcendence of the Hebrew and Christian God.

Allis's career at Princeton seemed to foreshadow his future. Two of the students who entered with him were J. Gresham Machen and Clarence Edward Macartney, who with Allis were to be closely identified with the battle for historic Christianity against the antisupernaturalism which was attacking the Christian world. His close association with Wilson would also continue. Another significant influence was his study of philosophy at nearby Princeton University, which awarded him the master of arts degree in 1907.

Well instructed and prepared to defend the Christian position, Allis went to Berlin, where he was exposed in that renowned center of Semitic studies to viewpoints quite different from his own. He learned firsthand the presuppositions and methods of those with whom he would be contending. His efforts culminated in his receiving the Ph.D. degree in 1913. Paul Woolley has commented on Allis's success in Germany: "Like many brilliant Americans of the period he pursued his graduate studies in Germany, in Berlin in this instance. Unlike many Americans, he pursued them long enough and diligently enough to receive his doctor's degree."[4]

Teaching Career

From 1910 on, Allis served in the Old Testament department of Princeton Seminary, assisting first John D. Davis and later Wilson. In 1914 he was ordained a Presbyterian minister. In 1922 he became an assistant professor of Semitic philology. As a teacher he was respected and admired, as Woolley has testified: "The writer had the high privilege of studying under Allis in Princeton Seminary. He was one of the most effective teachers in that famous faculty of the early twentieth century. Possessed of a piercing mind and of a well-nigh perfect memory, he was ideal for the teaching of Semitic languages. He was also of superb ability in penetrating the weak defenses of much of the higher critical opinion of the day. Even the opposition respected him."[5] R. Laird Harris similarly afforded high praise to his former mentor: "As a teacher you were not only interested in heads but in hearts. Your earnest personal faith was an encouragement to us all, and your kindly interest in us and your helpfulness on all occasions give us warm recollections of happy days under your tutelage."[6]

During Allis's professional years, doctrinal disagreement was sweeping through the Presbyterian Church in the U.S.A. This phase of the widespread fundamentalist-modernist controversy claimed the attention of Allis, Machen, and their friends. A group of conservatives met frequently in the Princeton home of Samuel G. Craig, editor of the *Presbyterian* and a trustee

4. Paul Woolley, "A Tribute," in *Law and the Prophets*, ed. Skilton, 5–6.
5. Ibid., 6.
6. R. Laird Harris, "A Salutation," in *Law and the Prophets*, ed. Skilton, 3.

of Princeton Seminary, to discuss issues and develop strategies. Craig's son Charles reported that Allis was one of the more influential members of the group. He likened his father to the quarterback or perhaps the coach, Machen to a brilliant halfback, and Allis to a line coach "who was not only a specialist in his field, but one whose overall wisdom played an important role in the team's success."[7]

Brilliant and worthy though Craig's team was, it was unable to save Princeton Seminary. In 1929 the seminary was reorganized in the interests of a more liberal doctrinal policy. Allis saw clearly that another seminary should be formed to keep the cherished witness of Old Princeton alive. Even before Machen, who was considering another possible move, he was persuaded that positive action should be taken to establish a successor to Old Princeton right away. With Machen's well-considered concurrence and that of others, strenuous efforts were undertaken that resulted in the establishment of Westminster Theological Seminary in Philadelphia in September of that very year. Allis worked assiduously toward this end. So great was his devotion to the cause that he gave not only of himself but of his resources for its success. At personal loss, he rented to the new seminary a building in downtown Philadelphia for the token sum of one dollar a year.

Regrettably, after serving till 1936 in the new seminary, Allis felt constrained to resign. Disagreements over ecclesiastical strategy and vision caused a separation between men who had worked together valiantly up to this point. They were friends and conscientious warriors, and one wishes that they had been able to continue to battle side by side against unbelief.[8]

Writings

However sad the division was, it did free Allis to continue his notable work of writing and editing. His productivity was enormous, and he exerted a powerful influence for the faith at home and abroad. His bibliography lists ten full-length books (including his dissertation in German and an unpublished manuscript on dispensationalism).[9] Prominent among these volumes is *The Five Books of Moses,* a classic vindication of the Mosaic authorship of the Pentateuch. It was published in 1943, and it was still in print more than fifty years later, continuing to expose the errors of the negative, divisive criticism concerning the books of Moses. R. Laird Harris testified in his tribute to Allis: "I have used your *Five Books of Moses* with many classes as textbook and resource book and have found that students have been satisfied, as I have been, with the correctness of your conclusions and the value of your defense of Scripture."[10] Similarly, W. J. Grier of Northern Ireland noted that

7. Charles Craig, publisher's note in *Law and the Prophets,* ed. Skilton, xii.

8. For an appraisal of the situation see Ned B. Stonehouse, *J. Gresham Machen: A Biographical Memoir* (Grand Rapids: Eerdmans, 1954), 497–99.

9. Arthur W. Kuschke, Jr., "A Bibliography," in *Law and the Prophets,* ed. Skilton, 20–28.

10. Harris, "Salutation," in *Law and the Prophets,* ed. Skilton, 3.

the book "met the needs of students in British theological colleges who were contending against prevailing critical views."[11]

Not everyone, however, had unqualified praise for the volume. William F. Albright reviewed it not without some appreciation, but with strictures.[12] Allis, although respectful of Albright, had taken issue in *The Five Books of Moses* with a number of his views. It would have been helpful if these two front-ranking scholars could have confronted one another directly. Also to be noted is that despite the great usefulness of *The Five Books of Moses* for many, it of course has not eliminated all the entrenched allegiance to the viewpoint that it opposes.

God Spake by Moses (1958) is designedly a more popular type of work than *The Five Books of Moses*. It is a brief running exposition of the Pentateuch. The author's condensed comments on the text and on some of its problems of interpretation give readers the benefit of his long years of study.

In *The Unity of Isaiah* (1950) Allis brings his learning and sharpness of intellect to bear on the allegations that the Book of Isaiah is the work of more than one author writing at different times. A major dividing point between Allis and liberal critics is his frank acceptance of the supernatural. He firmly believes that prophecy could be truly predictive.[13] He accepts the references to Cyrus by name in 44:28 and 45:1 as true prophecy written by Isaiah himself. They are not to be explained as written after Cyrus's birth. In this book Allis endeavors to speak in Isaiah's behalf as *The Five Books of Moses* did for Moses.

Prophecy and the Church (1945) describes itself on its title page as "an examination of the claim of dispensationalists that the Christian church is a mystery parenthesis which interrupts the fulfilment to Israel of the kingdom prophecies in the Old Testament." Allis, well aware of the gravity of the critics' attack on the Bible, recognized how important it is for Christians to stand together against destructive forces from without. He feared that the dispensationalism of his day was separating Christians and weakening their power to fight unitedly against their real enemies. In an irenic spirit Allis seeks to show from Scriptures that the dispensationalist construction as summarized on his title page is wrong because it does not recognize the typical and preparatory character of the Old Testament dispensation. The reaction to the book was divided. In some quarters it was well received and influential; in others the response was negative. This divided reception convinced Allis all the more of the vital importance of the subject.

Another area in which Allis drew on his vast learning was the evaluation of modern versions of the Bible. Ever since 1881, the year in which the New

---

11. W. J. Grier, "A Testimonial," in *Law and the Prophets*, ed. Skilton, 34.

12. William F. Albright, review of *The Five Books of Moses*, by Oswald T. Allis, *Journal of Biblical Literature* 62 (1943): 357–61.

13. On this point see R. K. Harrison, *Introduction to the Old Testament* (Grand Rapids: Eerdmans, 1969), 793–94.

Testament portion of the Revised Version appeared, there had been a cease-less flow of new translations of the New Testament. Throughout Allis's life-time at least one new English version or revision of a previous version of the New Testament (or much of it) appeared on the average every year. (New translations of the whole Bible were also issued, but less frequently.) This un-ceasing parade of versions so concerned him that he published various arti-cles and three full-length critiques. He was greatly desirous that Christians who could not read the Bible in its original languages have a dependable, ac-curate version in their own language. He concluded that "some of the new translations, especially those which are described as 'modern speech' ver-sions, are paraphrase rather than translation; and with a view to clarifying or simplifying the meaning of the text, they at times introduce into it mean-ings which are at least questionable. Sometimes they even change the text to bring out of it a meaning which is not clearly there."[14]

The Revised Standard Version of the New Testament is given a mixed re-view: "Considered as a 'modern speech' version, the RSV has this in its favor, that it is in general more conservative than its principal competitors. But it does not differ essentially from them. It shares their virtues and their defects. By dealing freely with the text, and substituting interpretive paraphrase for accurate translation, it is able at times to throw light on difficult passages and to produce a more 'understandable' and 'pleasurable' rendering than AV [the Authorized or King James Version] or RV [the Revised Version]."[15] In addi-tion, Allis declares that it is erroneous to call the Revised Standard Version a revision: "For in RSV the work of revision has been carried to such an extreme that the result is much more a new translation than a revision, and *A New Translation* is what the *Revised Standard Version* should be called."[16]

The Revised Standard Version of the Old Testament is regarded as even less trustworthy than the New Testament. It differs radically in diction and style from the Authorized Version. Indeed, it "is not merely a 'modern speech' but a 'modernist' or 'higher critical' revision of the version of 1611. . . . It makes many changes in the text of the Bible, either on the authority of the an-cient versions or simply on the basis of conjecture. And its marginal notes are at times inaccurate, inadequate, and misleading; and they tend quite definitely to undermine confidence in the authority and trustworthiness of the Bible."[17]

Finally, as for the New Testament portion of the New English Bible, Allis concluded that it is so paraphrastic and interpretative that it is not a faithful translation of the text.

In his valedictory volume, *The Old Testament: Its Claims and Its Critics* (1972), Allis expresses the convictions, the conclusions, and the loyalties of

14. Allis, *Old Testament*, 2.

15. Oswald T. Allis, *Revision or New Translation? "The Revised Standard Version of 1946"* (Phil-adelphia: Presbyterian and Reformed, 1948), 155.

16. Ibid., 156.

17. Oswald T. Allis, *Revised Version or Revised Bible? A Critique of the Revised Standard Version of the Old Testament (1952)* (Philadelphia: Presbyterian and Reformed, 1953), iii–iv.

a lifetime of distinguished service. It is the witness of a faithful believer to the all-glorious, transcendent God of the Bible. It is basically made up of the Payton Lectures that Allis delivered at Fuller Theological Seminary in 1952, but with substantial enlargement, including the addition of a whole new chapter on chronology. The chapter headings provide a handy outline of the book: "The Old Testament from Within—Its Facts and Its Doctrines"; "The Old Testament from Within—Its Literary Form"; "The Old Testament from Without" (i.e., its historical setting and background); "The Old Testament and Its Critics"; "Comparing the Incomparable"; and "Chronology." In this book we are reminded of Allis's Princeton heritage, of Wilson's address in the opening exercises of 1902, and of the glory of the biblical supernaturalism in which Allis rejoiced. Here we have a Christian manifesto exalting the perfections of the one, living, and true God of the Bible.

Allis's literary productivity was not limited to the writing of books. The bibliographical list of his articles, reviews, and pamphlets covers almost eight pages in small print.[18] And some of its titles represent a series of articles rather than just one article. Even in the stressful years when the battle for Princeton Seminary was producing much concern and claiming much time, Allis continued to write on various subjects. In 1925 he published seven articles, six reviews, and one pamphlet; in 1926, three articles and five reviews; in 1927, two articles and eleven reviews; in 1928, two articles and nine reviews; in 1929, the year of the departure from Princeton and the establishment of Westminster Seminary, three articles and eight reviews.

Covering a variety of subjects, the articles, reviews, and pamphlets are a tribute to the breadth of the author's competence. The first article that Allis published was "The Transcendence of Jehovah, God of Israel: Isaiah 44:24–28." His bibliographer comments: "It may not be amiss for the bibliographer to note Dr. Allis's own judgment that this, his first contribution to biblical studies, was his most important."[19] And Wilbur Smith was highly appreciative of a review that required exceptional knowledge of the Bible: "As an illustration of his loyalty to the great basic truths of the Christian faith, one need only call attention to his review some years ago of the second edition (1926) of the *Standard Bible Dictionary,* extending to over 30,000 words, probably the most important examination of any Bible dictionary in our language published in the last fifty years. . . . Not only was Dr. Allis scholastically equipped for this kind of work, but he also was convinced that he had a responsibility to use this knowledge, and his faith in the Word of God, in warning his generation of the danger of liberal tendencies in Biblical interpretation which result in the undermining of the faith of many."[20]

Allis's contribution to Christian literature may already seem overwhelming, but there is more to report. He served as editor of the *Princeton Theo-*

18. Kuschke, "Bibliography," in *Law and the Prophets,* ed. Skilton, 20–28.
19. Ibid., 21.
20. Wilbur M. Smith, "An Appreciation," in *Law and the Prophets,* ed. Skilton, 29.

logical Review from 1918 to 1929. Paul Woolley, who spent many years as the editor of a similar journal, the *Westminster Theological Journal,* has much praise for and understanding of Allis's achievement as an editor:

> A virtue which often goes unsung among the more flashy achievements of life is the quality of long and constant application to an unexciting but vital task. For many years, amidst very unsatisfactory degrees of support from some of his colleagues, Allis edited for the Princeton faculty the *Princeton Theological Review.* It carried on the work that Charles Hodge had begun with the *Biblical Repertory* in 1825. The *Review* did not cater to the cheap and easy conclusions which might be tempting, but represented solid, effective scholarship. A product of this character demands a great amount of slogging attention to detail. No one demonstrates his thanks, but without this painful work the results of more dashing forays into the problems of the field are weakened and, sometimes, nullified. This is the type of effort upon which Allis spent countless hours. The brilliant books which he produced have been appreciated on all sides. But who thinks of the hours devoted to the *Review*?[21]

And in addition to serving as editor of the *Review,* Allis was also a contributing editor of the original *Christianity Today* (1938–48) and an associate editor of the *Evangelical Quarterly* (1929–73).

One further comment about Allis's work as a writer. Charles Craig of the Presbyterian and Reformed Publishing Company, which produced Allis's books, reports that the manuscripts submitted by Allis were in virtually impeccable condition: "Editing was superfluous. Misplaced commas or misspelled words were absent, and even typographical errors were practically non-existent. Doubtless his years as the distinguished editor of the *Princeton Theological Review* sharpened this achievement, but the condition of his manuscripts as well as their content reflected his zeal for perfection."[22] Craig also suggests that Allis's wife might have helped in this achievement. In 1927 Allis had married the talented Ruth Robinson of Princeton. They were given to hospitality and made delightful hosts, as seminary students could attest. Two daughters came from their union, Julia Thompson, who became the wife of Walter Olof Seaborg, and Constance Ruth, who married J. Milton Neale II.

Allis died on January 12, 1973, a prince and a great man in Israel. A volume of Old Testament studies to be dedicated to him was in its final stages of preparation at the time. In God's good providence Allis had been shown a copy of the tentative table of contents and the first installment of the galley proofs shortly before he left us for the presence of the Lord. This volume, *The Law and the Prophets,* as he surely would have approved, was then dedicated and presented to one who had supported him through the years and who had contributed inexpressibly much to his long and fruitful life—Mrs. Oswald

---

21. Woolley, "Tribute," in *Law and the Prophets,* ed. Skilton, 6.
22. Craig, publisher's note in *Law and the Prophets,* ed. Skilton, xiv.

Thompson Allis. Although the tribute intended for Allis was regrettably late, Hampden-Sydney College as far back as 1927 had appropriately recognized his Christian character and service by bestowing on him a degree that he truly merited, the honorary degree of doctor of divinity.

Primary Sources

Allis, Oswald T. *The Five Books of Moses*. Philadelphia: Presbyterian and Reformed, 1943.

―――. *God Spake by Moses: An Exposition of the Pentateuch*. Nutley, N.J.: Presbyterian and Reformed, 1958.

―――. *The New English Bible, the New Testament of 1961: A Comparative Study*. Philadelphia: Presbyterian and Reformed, 1963.

―――. *The Old Testament: Its Claims and Its Critics*. Nutley, N.J.: Presbyterian and Reformed, 1972.

―――. *Prophecy and the Church*. Philadelphia: Presbyterian and Reformed, 1945.

―――. *Revised Version or Revised Bible? A Critique of the Revised Standard Version of the Old Testament (1952)*. Philadelphia: Presbyterian and Reformed, 1953.

―――. *Revision or New Translation? "The Revised Standard Version of 1946": A Comparative Study*. Philadelphia: Presbyterian and Reformed, 1948.

―――. *The Unity of Isaiah*. Philadelphia: Presbyterian and Reformed, 1950.

Secondary Source

The Law and the Prophets: Old Testament Studies Prepared in Honor of Oswald Thompson Allis. Edited by John H. Skilton. Nutley, N.J.: Presbyterian and Reformed, 1974.

Arthur W. Pink

Richard P. Belcher

The life of a man as he lives it is often deceiving. He may live in the limelight of popularity and acclaim all of his days with every indication that he and his works will be remembered for years to follow. Yet such a man can be forgotten almost immediately at his death or shortly thereafter. Another man may live and die in obscurity with no indication that he will have any influence after his earthly days, yet his works may be resurrected and elevated to prominence within a few years of his passing. Such a man was Arthur W. Pink. He lived to a great extent in obscurity, and died in the same manner with few knowing of the event or place. Yet this virtually unknown man's writings were resurrected within a few years following his death to influence multitudes. His life is truly a unique and fascinating testimony of God's grace and providence, the doctrines he so faithfully proclaimed.

Arthur Walkington Pink was born of godly parents in Nottingham, England, on April 1, 1886.[1] He was reared in the way of the Lord with strict discipline, including rigorous observance of the Sabbath.[2] He appears to have had a strong education, including musical studies; indeed, his skill as a baritone soloist prompted suggestions that he consider an operatic career.[3] Instead he went into business, and was very successful by his late teens and early twenties.[4]

However, during these years Pink had not experienced the grace of God's salvation in his life. Thus it is understandable that he drifted into a life of sin and rebellion. This was not so much a morally corrupt life as a deep religious rebellion. He became so enamored of the cult of theosophy that he was one of the movement's rising stars, marked for eventual promotion to leadership.[5]

---

1. Iain Murray, "Arthur W. Pink: A Voice in the Wilderness," *Banner of Truth* 203–4 (Aug.-Sept. 1980): 7.
2. Arthur W. Pink, "Caring for Children," *Studies in the Scriptures* 10 (June 1931): 138.
3. Murray, "Arthur W. Pink," 10–11.
4. Pink to Lowell Green, 3 June 1934, *Letters of A. W. Pink* (Edinburgh: Banner of Truth Trust, 1978), 38.
5. Arthur W. Pink, *Gleanings in the Godhead* (Chicago: Moody, 1975), 61; idem, *An Exposition of Hebrews* (Grand Rapids: Baker, 1954), 1014; idem, *Gleanings in Exodus* (Chicago: Moody, 1962), 18–19; Murray, "Arthur W. Pink," 10–11.

Pink's conversion came in 1908 in Nottingham during a series of meetings of the Theosophical Society.[6] Though only twenty-two years of age, he was one of the featured speakers for the week. But when he came home one night after a meeting, his father quoted to him Proverbs 14:12, "There is a way which seemeth right unto a man, but the end thereof are the ways of death." Smitten by this verse, Arthur spent several days in his room. He emerged converted to Christ and went to the society meeting to preach the gospel. One can only imagine the stir this bold young convert created at that gathering!

Pink himself was reluctant to talk of his conversion experience, considering it to be a private matter. Talking about it could mislead others to think that they had to have a similar experience.[7] He did say of this moment some years later, "This writer sought not the Lord, but hated, opposed, and endeavored to banish Him from his thoughts; but the Lord sought him, smote him to the ground (like Saul of Tarsus), subdued his vile rebellion, and made him willing in the day of His power. *That* is Grace indeed—sovereign, amazing, triumphant grace."[8]

Commitment to Independent Study

For the next two years (1908–10) Pink studied diligently on his own, meditating on and memorizing the Bible.[9] When his friends urged him to go to school, he refused because he felt that unbelief characterized most institutions of higher learning.[10] Finally, in 1910 he came to the United States to enrol at Moody Bible Institute for a summer course. He left in the middle of the term, however, perhaps because the level of study was of no great challenge.[11] This episode speaks more of Pink's personal characteristics, such as his ability to pursue his studies independently, than it does of any shortcomings in the courses at Moody.

We must not conclude that Pink had no use for schools, nor that he felt that no one under any circumstance should enrol. He admitted that God had used Bible schools to help many.[12] On the other hand, he argued that they were not an imperative necessity. God may use human instruments to instruct and enlighten us, but he may also give us the far greater privilege of teaching us directly. Each individual must ascertain God's will for one's own life.

Other reasons for Pink's advocacy of independent study included the belief that theological training had become an idol for many,[13] and that much of such training was misdirected, centering not on the pure Word of God, but

6. Arthur W. Pink, *Exposition of the Gospel of John*, 3 vols. (Grand Rapids: Zondervan, 1968), 1:177.

7. Ibid., 1:172.

8. Arthur W. Pink, *The Doctrines of Election and Justification* (Grand Rapids: Baker, 1974), 173.

9. Pink to Green, 18 Dec. 1933, *Letters*, 24.

10. Arthur W. Pink, *Gleanings from Elisha* (Chicago: Moody, 1972), 24.

11. Murray, "Arthur W. Pink," 14.

12. Pink, *John*, 1:386.

13. Arthur W. Pink, *Gleanings in Joshua* (Chicago: Moody, 1964), 159.

on the polluted streams of higher criticism[14] and matters which tended to foster intellectual conceit.[15] We must point out, however, that Pink suffered
some academic deficiencies because of his strong commitment to independent study—deficiencies which training could have alleviated. For example,
he trusted *Bagster's Interlinear* implicitly and strongly recommended it to
those with a desire to get into the Word of God in depth.[16] This literal word-
for-word translation he viewed as the best translation available.[17] He also
had a conviction that the word order of the Greek must be carried over into
English as one translates.[18] In one instance he seems to argue that a Greek
verb must be taken as an imperative simply because another text uses that
verb in the imperative mood.[19] He felt that lexicons were overrated[20] and
that textual criticism was not of much importance; indeed, he believed it
fruitless.[21] A final result of his commitment to independence was the loss of
the intellectual give-and-take of an academic setting, which does not necessarily temper one in his convictions, but surely tempers one's attitude toward
others who disagree—something Pink may never have learned.

Pink openly admitted that his Bible study and writing were dependent on
the works of others. He saw his task as arranging in a simple form the material
he had gleaned from many places, much like the work of a flower arranger
(note the number of his book titles that use the word *gleanings*).[22] He would
conduct his own in-depth study of a book or passage, and then extensively
read the commentaries of others, sometimes as many as forty.[23] Regardless of
what the commentaries said, however, he did not hesitate to follow wherever
he felt the Scriptures led him.[24] A deep student of the Word of God and an
extensive reader of commentaries, he took the material gleaned and skillfully
synthesized it into a form which laypeople could read and understand. Thus
he was a link between Puritan theology and the twentieth century.

Disappointments and Isolation

Withdrawing from Moody Bible Institute, Pink moved from place to place
between 1910 and 1920. He pastored several small churches, first in Silver-
ton, Colorado;[25] then in Garden Grove, California; two churches in Burkes-

---

14. Pink, *Exodus,* 186.
15. Arthur W. Pink, *An Exposition of the Sermon on the Mount* (Grand Rapids: Baker, 1950), 403.
16. Pink, *Hebrews,* 275, 344, 470; see also *Letters,* 26; and *John,* 1:385.
17. Pink, *Hebrews,* 197.
18. Arthur W. Pink, *Gleanings from Paul: Studies in the Prayers of the Apostle* (Chicago: Moody, 1967), 173, 292; see also *Hebrews,* 195; *John,* 1:211, 2:407, and 3:20; and *Studies in the Scriptures* 10 (April 1931): 88, and 15 (May 1936): 145.
19. Pink, *John,* 2:9.
20. Arthur W. Pink, *Interpretation of the Scriptures* (Grand Rapids: Baker, 1972), 115.
21. Pink, *John,* 2:9.
22. Arthur W. Pink, *The Redeemer's Return* (Ashland, Ky.: Calvary Baptist Book Store, n.d.), 8.
23. Pink, *Elisha,* 191; *Interpretation,* 25; *John,* 3:334; and *Hebrews,* 9.
24. Pink, *Hebrews,* 272.
25. Ibid., 1173.

ville, Kentucky;[26] and finally the Northside Baptist Church of Spartanburg, South Carolina.[27] While in Kentucky he married Vera Russell on November 16, 1916. He was thirty years of age and she was twenty-three. She proved to be a very faithful wife and helpmate in the years that followed.[28]

The ministry at Spartanburg was a very unhappy time; during this period Pink suffered his first nervous breakdown and also published his best-known book, *The Sovereignty of God*.[29] Several factors contributed to the nervous breakdown. First, as he preached on the sovereignty of God, some in the church rejected the message and the messenger.[30] Second, the book on sovereignty encountered some strong negative reactions; his friend Arno Gaebelein suggested that he had made a serious mistake in publishing it.[31] Third, through all of the criticism, Pink continued his stringent work schedule and study habits, toiling early and late, even to the point of exhaustion.[32] Included in this labor was an intensive reading schedule. He wrote in early 1919 that he had read forty-five books in the last three months, and still had forty unread books on his shelf (evidently books he intended to read).[33] A little later he wrote that he would complete Thomas Manton's twenty-two volumes in the next week, and then expected to study carefully Thomas Goodwin's twelve large volumes.[34]

Pink became so discouraged that he asked Gaebelein and William Pettingill to help him find another place of service, but no doors would open.[35] He began to ponder the possibility that the Lord wanted him to spend all of his time in writing rather than continuing in public ministry.[36] In 1920 he left the church in Spartanburg to live near his publisher and friend, I. C. Herendeen, in Swengel, Pennsylvania.[37] He hoped to spend more time in writing and some time in itinerant ministry. The writing, however, again was crowded out by public ministry, this time for a period of several years in churches in California. He also spent an extended number of weeks in tent meetings in Oakland, where he was accepted enthusiastically by crowds of over a thousand.[38] Pink was not the one who originally drew and won the

26. Alan McKerrell, "The Early Life of A. W. Pink," *Reformation Today* 11 (Aug.-Oct. 1972): 4.
27. Arthur W. Pink, *Letters from Spartanburg—1917–1920*, ed. Richard P. Belcher (Columbia, S.C.: Richbarry, 1991). This volume is a series of letters to I. C. Herendeen.
28. See Richard P. Belcher, *A. W. Pink—Born to Write* (Columbia, S.C.: Richbarry, 1980).
29. For Pink's breakdowns see Belcher, *Born to Write*, 61–68; and Pink, *Letters from Spartanburg*, 22 June 1919 and 23 June 1919.
30. Pink, *Letters from Spartanburg*, 5 Nov. 1918; 25 Nov. 1918; 27 Jan. 1919; and 31 Jan. 1919.
31. Ibid., 19 June 1919.
32. Ibid., 23 April 1918; 30 April 1918; and 30 July 1918.
33. Ibid., 13 Jan. 1919.
34. Ibid., 15 May 1919.
35. Ibid., 14 Jan. 1919; 21 Jan. 1919; 28 Jan. 1919; 4 June 1919; 13 June 1919; 22 June 1919; 23 June 1919; 28 June 1919; and 29 June 1919.
36. Ibid., 9 Jan. 1919; 23 June 1919; 26 July 1919; and 6 Nov. 1919.
37. Ibid., 17 Jan. 1920.
38. Arthur W. Pink, *Letters of an Itinerant Preacher—1920–1921*, ed. Richard P. Belcher (Columbia, S.C.: Richbarry, 1994). For the tent ministry in Oakland see esp. 17–24 and 38–53.

crowds, but came in after a Brother Thompson had spent a number of weeks doing evangelistic work in the tent. He brought Pink in to help establish the new believers in the Christian life and faith. Though it is not certain the plans materialized, Pink expected to follow Brother Thompson to Seattle for a similar ministry.

The meetings which have just been described were probably the primary reason Pink was willing to stay in itinerant ministry. Yet his heart was still burdened to write. When this period of traveling and preaching began, he had realized that the many demands of the people would make writing difficult.[39] Several months into the itinerant ministry his goal became to spend at least a third of his time in study and writing.[40] And in the final days of his tent ministry in 1921, he said that the writing of books was more important than his oral ministry.[41] Yet, seeking to be submissive to God's will, he declared regarding his writing ministry, "I *hope* to, I *want* to, but what is God's will in the matter I know not."[42]

Perhaps the conviction that he must write led Pink in 1922 to begin what eventually would become his primary ministry and tie to the future generations—his periodical titled *Studies in the Scriptures*.[43] This publication from the beginning was a work of faith,[44] and disappointments in its early years plunged Pink once again into deep depression and possibly another nervous breakdown. The purpose of the periodical was twofold: first, that God might be glorified in its pages, and second, that the people of God who were starving for spiritual nourishment might be fed through sound exposition of the Word.[45] The periodical lasted until 1953 (one year after his death) and had a small but faithful worldwide mailing list of about a thousand. Pink and his wife's dogged determination is evidenced in this aspect of their ministry, as the periodical continued to be produced and mailed as they moved all around the world. No one could begin to imagine that the articles written so faithfully for so few for so many years under such difficult circumstances would eventually be lifted from the pages of the periodical to be printed in book form to bless and influence hundreds of thousands of hearts.

The Pinks left the States on March 23, 1925, for ministry in Australia.[46] He was immediately accepted by the Baptist Union churches of Australia and drew great crowds till opposition to his emphasis on the sovereignty of God arose.[47] He was invited to address the Baptist pastors on the subject of human will; following his presentation they censured him for not believing

39. Pink, *Letters of an Itinerant Preacher*, 28 July 1920.
40. Ibid., 22 Sept. 1920 and 8 Oct. 1920.
41. Ibid., 7 April 1921.
42. Ibid., 21 April 1921.
43. Arthur W. Pink, "Our Semi-Jubilee Letter," *Studies in the Scriptures* 25 (Dec. 1946): 283.
44. Arthur W. Pink, "Welcome Tidings," *Studies in the Scriptures* 16 (July 1937): 220–21.
45. Arthur W. Pink, "Our Annual Letter," *Studies in the Scriptures* 23 (Dec. 1944): 285; and "Our Semi-Jubilee Letter," 282–83.
46. McKerrell, "Early Life," 5.
47. Ibid., 5, 7; and Pink, *Studies in the Scriptures* 5 (Dec. 1926): 5.

in free will.[48] He then took the pastorate of the Belvoir Street Particular Baptist Church in Sydney, from which he resigned when, ironically, he was accused of believing in free will. The basis of the accusation was his teaching a universal offer of the gospel and the responsibility of the lost to believe.[49] He started a new church, but soon resigned saying that it had been wrong to begin the new work.[50]

The date of July 20, 1928, found the Pinks on the move once again as they left for Britain with the deep sorrow of rejection.[51] He was forty-two years old now, and hoped for a renewal of his ministry in Britain. But again, nothing materialized.[52] Some bitterness began to show as he started making some strong statements against the churches, accusing them of worldliness, improper financial practices, questionable worship, and false preaching.

Finding no local churches open to his ministry, Pink left for the States once again on May 2, 1929, after less than a year in Britain.[53] Though he was hopeful of finding a ministry in the States, he was disappointed once again. Doors were closed, and former friends no longer so cordial.[54] He urged believers to come out of the corrupt churches. He pled for a small group that would hear him and embrace his ministry. But he found no open door or welcome in Kentucky or California. When an invitation finally did come, he was hesitant to accept it because of the worldliness he expected to face.[55] Not only did he speak negatively of the churches, but he also was now very critical of preachers and other periodicals.[56]

Following five very disappointing years in the States, Pink left for Britain once again in September of 1934.[57] Now forty-eight, it is clear that he was frustrated at this point of his life.[58] He knew the truth of God. He was a capable expositor of the Word of God. Yet his public ministry was at a dead end. Although he was still hopeful of a place of public ministry,[59] yet again the doors were closed.[60] He lived at Cheltenham, then Glasgow, and then in the Hove-Brighton area of England, till his house was strafed by German

48. McKerrell, "Early Life," 6–7.

49. Pink, *Studies in the Scriptures* 7 (Jan. 1928): 1.

50. McKerrell, "Early Life," 9.

51. Arthur W. Pink, "Get Thee Out," *Studies in the Scriptures* 7 (Sept. 1928): 215; idem, "Our Semi-Jubilee Letter," 283–84; idem, "A Gracious Meeting," *Studies in the Scriptures* 7 (Dec. 1928): 287.

52. Arthur W. Pink, "A Personal Word," *Studies in the Scriptures* 8 (Jan. 1929): 23; (March 1929): 71; and (June 1929): 143.

53. Arthur W. Pink, "A Personal Word," *Studies in the Scriptures* 8 (May 1929): 119; and (July 1929): 163.

54. Pink, "Our Semi-Jubilee Letter," 284.

55. Arthur W. Pink, "A Personal Word," *Studies in the Scriptures* 8 (Dec. 1929): 284.

56. Arthur W. Pink, "Dangerous Dainties," *Studies in the Scriptures* 12 (Sept. 1933): 213; idem, "A Word of Warning," *Studies in the Scriptures* 13 (Aug. 1934): 190; Pink to Green, 19 Aug. 1934, *Letters of A. W. Pink*, 37–38.

57. Pink to Green, 9 Sept. 1934, *Letters of A. W. Pink*, 49.

58. Pink to Green, 19 Aug. 1934, *Letters of A. W. Pink*, 44–45.

59. Pink to Green, 2 Sept. 1934, *Letters of A. W. Pink*, 48; and Pink, "Following the Cloud," *Studies in the Scriptures* 14 (Feb. 1935): 62.

60. Arthur W. Pink, "Our Annual Letter," *Studies in the Scriptures* 14 (Dec. 1935): 382.

planes during the Second World War.[61] This convinced him to move to the Outer Hebrides to the town of Stornoway on the Isle of Lewis. The date was September 1940, and Pink was now fifty-four years of age.

The Failure in Public Ministry

Some questions concerning Pink's public ministry seem in order at this point. Why the failure and the many closed doors, when he seemed to want to succeed so badly? First, he was not a sociable person. He did not seem to enjoy being with people. Serious in nature, he seldom smiled and was not much of a conversationalist. Finding it difficult to meet strangers, he was comfortable only around a few close friends. His shy and reserved nature prevented him from talking about himself. After he preached, he would retire to his study to pray rather than greet the people at the door.[62] He even recommended this practice to others.[63] It would certainly be easy for people to misunderstand him as aloof or unfriendly or unconcerned.

Second, Pink was very blunt of speech.[64] This did not endear him to the hearts of others.

Third, Pink preached for extended periods of time, not seeming to care about the length of his sermons. He writes of having once preached for two hours in one hundred–degree heat, and in other contexts he writes of occupying the pulpit for over an hour.[65]

Fourth, and probably the most important, Pink was a very sensitive soul who had experienced much rejection. His first three pastorates lasted only seven years. His fourth pastorate in South Carolina ended in rejection. Some of the members loved and accepted him, while a strong majority rejected him and his message. He was rejected in Australia by the Baptist pastors' conference, then by a church he pastored. It was here that an isolationist attitude seems to have begun to develop. He was rejected in Britain in 1928–29. He was rejected on his final sojourn in the States in 1929–34. He was rejected again upon returning to Britain. Finally he moved to Stornoway to live in isolation.

There is no doubt that Pink contributed to his unhappy circumstances. This sensitive soul slowly drifted into isolation as a result of the many rejections and the critical attitude he developed towards the established church.[66]

61. Arthur W. Pink, "A Personal Word," *Studies in the Scriptures* 14 (June 1935): 191; Pink to John C. Blackburn, 25 Aug. 1935, *Letters of A. W. Pink*, 72–73; and idem, "Our Semi-Jubilee Letter," 285.

62. Arthur W. Pink, *The Life of David*, 2 vols. in 1 (Grand Rapids: Baker, 1981), 1:43.

63. Arthur W. Pink, "A Personal Word," *Studies in the Scriptures* 8 (June 1929): 143.

64. Pink, *Election*, 12; and idem, *Hebrews*, 955.

65. Pink, *Hebrews*, 711; see also idem, *John*, 3:192; and "The Way of the Wicked," *Studies in the Scriptures* 7 (Oct. 1928): 231.

66. Arthur W. Pink, "A Call to Separation," *Studies in the Scriptures* 7 (March 1928): 72; idem, "Worship," *Studies in the Scriptures* 7 (Nov. 1928): 254; idem, "A Personal Word," *Studies in the Scriptures* 8 (Dec. 1929): 284, and 9 (June 1930): 143; idem, "Sound the Alarm," *Studies in the Scriptures* 10 (Feb. 1931): 45, and 11 (March 1932): 69; idem, "Dangerous Dainties," *Studies in the Scriptures* 12 (Sept. 1933): 213; idem, "A Word of Warning," *Studies in the Scriptures* 13 (Aug. 1934): 190; and idem, *Hebrews*, 435.

Could a pastor, even though he may have considered Pink to be doctrinally sound, invite him to preach, given the possibility of his making critical statements against the church and even pastors?

At times as Pink was healing from a rejection, he tried to emerge for further public ministry, only to be rejected again. With each rejection he seemed to go further back into an attitude of isolation and criticism until he finally was settled in that frame of mind and lifestyle. He was caught in a vicious circle of events that he himself had helped in part to create and that eventually shut him off from public ministry.

It must be admitted that God blessed Pink in spite of the uniqueness of his personality. Some of the greatest people of God have personality flaws. God sees the heart and at times even uses the uniqueness of the personality to bring an individual to his will. In Pink's case, the unique personality closed doors and shut him up with his pen, which made him a prolific and influential writer. So he stated in 1936, "We do not expect to engage again in any oral ministry, but we are devoting the energies of our remaining days to the Magazine and the correspondence it entails."[67] Though the cessation of public ministry was a bitter sorrow for Pink, he bowed to the sovereignty of God in the matter.[68]

The Years of Writing

From 1940 on, the periodical became Pink's life as he committed himself to the ministry God had for him—a life of writing. He labored faithfully for his remaining twelve years of life, writing and producing the periodical while he lived in virtual isolation, not even attending a local church. He justified this behavior by explaining that the admonition not to neglect the assembling of ourselves together does not mean that the sheep of Christ should attend a place where the goats predominate or where their attendance would sanction that which is dishonoring to Christ.[69] On Sundays he spent his time pastoring his flock of faithful readers by writing letters answering their questions concerning the Bible and theology. Would-be visitors who had traveled great distances to Stornoway were discouraged as they were usually turned away, not being allowed to see him.[70] The townspeople knew little about him, except that each day at a certain hour he took a walk through the town.

In May of 1952 Pink's health began to fail, but he continued his work in spite of signs of exhaustion and loss of energy.[71] In the next two months he was like a man planning a journey. He prepared further material for the periodical. A few days before his death he stopped his work as he was unable

67. Arthur W. Pink, "Our Annual Letter," *Studies in the Scriptures* 15 (Dec. 1936): 382.
68. Arthur W. Pink, "Our Annual Letter," *Studies in the Scriptures* 16 (Dec. 1937): 383.
69. Pink, *Elisha*, 106.
70. Arthur W. Pink, "Our Annual Letter," *Studies in the Scriptures* 27 (Dec. 1948): 262, and 30 (Dec. 1951): 285–86.
71. Vera Pink, "The Late Editor's Last Days," *Studies in the Scriptures* 31 (Sept. 1952): 214–16.

to push himself any further. He died on July 15, 1952, at the age of sixty-six. He was buried in an unmarked grave in a cemetery on a windswept hill outside of Stornoway. The magazine outlived him for more than a year, as Vera published it until December 1953.[72] She died on July 17, 1962, almost ten years to the day of her husband's death. She was sixty-nine years old, and her body lies at rest next to the body of her husband.

When Pink died, it appeared he would never be remembered or recognized by the Christian community, except for those faithful few who received and cherished his periodical. He had lived in obscurity and died in obscurity. Yet God in his providence chose to uncover the products of his pen as his works began to be published about a decade after his death. It is true, he had produced a few books in his lifetime, but most of his writing had been restricted to his periodical. These articles were finally taken and put into book form by various publishing houses, and began to sell over the following decades into the hundreds of thousands of copies.

Theology

Turning now to consider Pink's theology, we note that he was committed strongly to the Word of God and its faithful proclamation. From the time of his conversion until his death he was convinced of the verbal inspiration and full authority of Scripture. That his writings upheld this high view of the Bible is evident in *The Divine Inspiration of the Bible* (published in 1917), *The Doctrine of Revelation* (appearing in *Studies in the Scriptures* from 1947 to 1949), and *The Inspiration of Scripture* (appearing in *Studies* from 1950 to 1952). For the most part he was a solid exegete of the Scriptures, yet in a few places he produced some fanciful interpretations, though nothing heretical on the major doctrines.

There is no question that Pink was a Calvinist—a five-point Calvinist. He was also a balanced Calvinist, in that he held to human responsibility (the sinner is responsible to believe the gospel, and the church is responsible to spread the gospel). He also held to the necessity of a universal offer of the gospel. This was the point of disagreement with the Belvoir Street Particular Baptist Church in Australia.

In his early ministry Pink was a dispensationalist, but he repudiated dispensationalism in his later years. Numerous writings in his early ministry indicate a dispensational conviction. His rejection of dispensationalism was a progressive matter. During the decade of the twenties he was reading the Puritans extensively. His writings in the late twenties reflect a changing view in that he is critical of some dispensational ideas. By 1933–34 his rejection of dispensationalism is clear in a series of articles in *Studies in the Scriptures*. His embracing of an amillennial position is clear in his articles on "The Divine Covenants" appearing in the 1934–38 *Studies*. Also, a letter to Lowell

---

72. Vera Pink, "A Personal Word," *Studies in the Scriptures* 32 (July 1953): 168.

Green in 1934 states that "with few exceptions, all the notes and comments in the Scofield Bible are unreliable and unsound."[73] Despite a claim that Pink was close to repudiating his repudiation of dispensationalism at the time of his death,[74] there is not a single line of supporting evidence.

Few subjects are dealt with in Pink's writings as often and as sharply as the subject of modern evangelism and its methods.[75] His Calvinism definitely influenced his convictions in the area of evangelism. He was convinced that evangelism was no longer God-centered but human-centered. He rejected human-centered sermons, human-centered invitations to the lost, high-pressure tactics, worldly-looking and worldly-sounding musicians, schemes and programs smacking of big-business techniques. Instead of depending on God's power, God's methods, God's Spirit, and God's ways, it was all human-powered. Evangelism even had the wrong primary motivation: the conversion of sinners instead of the glory of God. He leveled other accusations against modern evangelism: the way of salvation is almost entirely ignored or misrepresented; thousands are assured they are bound for heaven while they are hastening toward hell; humans are no longer seen as totally depraved, but only partly depraved and thus capable of becoming Christians and loving God through their own powers; the law of God is neglected and bypassed; the evangelistic message is one of "easy believism," rejecting repentance and surrender to the lordship of Christ; and evangelistic preaching has sold out to anecdotal preaching, rhetorical embellishment, logic and human wisdom, entertaining and sensational experiences, jokes to amuse the audience, and the self-advancement of the minister instead of dynamic exposition of the Word by the power of the Holy Spirit bringing sinners face to face with a holy God.

Pink also believed in, practiced, and preached holiness of life, including sacrificial living for his Lord. He longed to do the will of God, whatever it might be. He searched and searched, prayed and prayed, waited and waited to learn the will of God, and finally surrendered to do what was unmistakably God's will—the use of his pen. His sacrificial life is seen in his existing on almost nothing till his parents died and left him a small inheritance. Even then he was extremely frugal. He desired nothing besides the necessities. Whenever he had more money than he needed, he either returned it to the donors or sent it to missions. Committed to others, he labored ardently for them in the study and ministry of the Word, intense activities that may have been the reason for his two nervous breakdowns.

73. Pink to Green, 3 June 1934, *Letters of A. W. Pink*, 38.

74. Milburn Cockrell, preface to *Redeemer's Return*, by Pink, 5.

75. For some of Pink's numerous statements on evangelism see *Studies on Saving Faith* (Swengel, Pa.: Reiner, 1974), 5, 7, 10, 13, 14, 137–38; *The Doctrine of Sanctification* (Grand Rapids: Baker, 1955), 30; *The Holy Spirit* (Grand Rapids: Baker, 1970), 45; *Gleanings from Paul*, 307; *Hebrews*, 668; "Preaching the Law," *Studies in the Scriptures* 13 (March 1934): 69; "Signs of the Times," *Studies in the Scriptures* 16 (Dec. 1937): 370; "Strange Fire," *Studies in the Scriptures* 19 (June 1940): 141; and Pink to Green, 3 Sept. 1933, *Letters of A. W. Pink*, 16–17.

Some of Pink's convictions were part of the reason for his lack of popularity and rejection in some circles. Calvinism was not popular in the first
half of the twentieth century. Accordingly, his book *The Sovereignty of God*
met with a strong negative response. On the other hand, dispensationalism
was very popular in the first half of the twentieth century. When Pink left dispensationalism, he was going against the grain of many. And as he began to
write against it, he no doubt offended many more. Both his embracing of
Calvinism and his rejecting dispensationalism created conflict.

Yet in God's divine providence this frail and sensitive soul who stood
boldly for his convictions through rejection after rejection has had an undeniable influence on multitudes through writings that have outlived him far
beyond his own or anyone's expectations. In fact, the revival of Calvinism in
Baptist and independent churches that took place in the 1960s and afterward
is in part due to Pink's writings. In spite of his problems, he is to be recognized as a man of God who can instruct us through his pen as well as through
his life. All the circumstances of his life, even the negative ones he could not
explain, propelled him to fulfil his God-ordained purpose: impacting the
twentieth-century church by his pen (whether one agrees or disagrees with
his total system of theology).

Primary Sources

Pink, Arthur W. *The Antichrist*. Grand Rapids: Kregel, 1988.
———. *The Application of the Scriptures: A Biblical Refutation of Dispensational-
ism*. Canton, Ga.: Word of Truth, 1977.
———. *The Atonement*. Swengel, Pa.: Reiner, n.d.
———. *The Attributes of God*. Grand Rapids: Baker, 1975.
———. *The Divine Covenants*. Grand Rapids: Baker, 1973.
———. *The Divine Inspiration of the Bible*. Rev. ed. Grand Rapids: Baker, 1976.
———. *The Doctrine of Revelation*. Grand Rapids: Baker, 1975.
———. *The Doctrine of Salvation*. Grand Rapids: Baker, 1975.
———. *The Doctrine of Sanctification*. Grand Rapids: Baker, 1955.
———. *The Doctrines of Election and Justification*. Grand Rapids: Baker, 1974.
———. *Eternal Punishment*. Swengel, Pa.: Reiner, n.d.
———. *Eternal Security*. Grand Rapids: Baker, 1974.
———. *An Exposition of Hebrews*. Grand Rapids: Baker, 1954.
———. *Exposition of the Gospel of John*. 3 vols. Grand Rapids: Zondervan, 1968.
———. *An Exposition of the Sermon on the Mount*. Grand Rapids: Baker, 1950.
———. *Gleanings from Elisha*. Chicago: Moody, 1972.
———. *Gleanings from Paul: Studies in the Prayers of the Apostle*. Chicago: Moody,
1967.
———. *Gleanings from the Scriptures—Man's Total Depravity*. Chicago: Moody,
1969.
———. *Gleanings in Exodus*. Chicago: Moody, 1962.
———. *Gleanings in Genesis*. 2 vols. in 1. Chicago: Moody, 1922.

———. *Gleanings in Joshua*. Chicago: Moody, 1964.

———. *Gleanings in the Godhead*. Chicago: Moody, 1975.

———. *The Holy Spirit*. Grand Rapids: Baker, 1970.

———. *Interpretation of the Scriptures*. Grand Rapids: Baker, 1972.

———. *The Life of David*. 2 vols. in 1. Grand Rapids: Baker, 1981.

———. *The Life of Elijah*. London: Banner of Truth Trust, 1963.

———. *Objections to God's Sovereignty Answered*. Ashland, Ky.: Calvary Baptist Church, n.d.

———. *Practical Christianity*. Grand Rapids: Baker, 1974.

———. *Profiting from the Word*. London: Banner of Truth Trust.

———. *The Redeemer's Return*. Ashland, Ky.: Calvary Baptist Book Store, n.d.

———. *Regeneration, or, the New Birth*. Swengel, Pa.: Bible Truth Depot, n.d.

———. *Repentance*. Swengel, Pa.: Reiner, n.d.

———. *Satan and His Gospel*. Swengel, Pa.: Bible Truth Depot, 1917.

———. *The Seven Sayings of the Saviour on the Cross*. Grand Rapids: Baker, 1958.

———. *The Sovereignty of God*. Grand Rapids: Baker, 1975 reprint.

———. *Spiritual Growth*. Grand Rapids: Baker, 1971.

———. *Spiritual Union and Communion*. Grand Rapids: Baker, 1971.

———. *Studies in the Scriptures* 1–32 (1922–53).

———. *Studies on Saving Faith*. Swengel, Pa.: Reiner, 1974.

———. *The Ten Commandments*. Rev. ed. Grand Rapids: Baker, 1976.

Secondary Sources

Belcher, Richard P. *Arthur W. Pink—Born to Write*. Columbia, S.C.: Richbarry, 1980.

———. *Arthur W. Pink—Predestination*. Columbia, S.C.: Richbarry, 1983.

Levick, Ray. "The Life of A. W. Pink." *Reformation Today* 36 (March-April 1977): 19–22; 38 (July-Aug. 1977): 29–34; 40 (Nov.-Dec. 1977): 9–14; 46 (Nov.-Dec. 1978): 19–25.

McKerrell, Alan. "The Early Life of A. W. Pink." *Reformation Today* 11 (Aug.-Oct. 1972): 4–9.

Murray, Iain. *The Life of Arthur W. Pink*. Edinburgh: Banner of Truth Trust, 1981.

Pink, Arthur W. *Letters from Spartanburg—1917–1920*. Edited by Richard P. Belcher. Columbia, S.C.: Richbarry, 1991.

———. *Letters of an Itinerant Preacher—1920–1921*. Edited by Richard P. Belcher. Columbia, S.C.: Richbarry, 1994.

———. *Letters of A. W. Pink*. Edinburgh: Banner of Truth Trust, 1978.

William Hendriksen

Simon J. Kistemaker

William Hendriksen was the youngest of the eight sons and one daughter of Bernardus Antonie Hendriksen and Jannetje van Ravestijn. He was born on November 18, 1900, in the city of Tiel, in the province of Gelderland, the Netherlands, where his father worked as a carpenter, woodcarver, and handyman. Both his father and mother were people who loved the Lord, faithfully read the Scriptures, and lived an exemplary Christian life. His father wrote Dutch poetry, and his mother committed poetry to memory, which she often recited while doing housework.

Already at the age of six, young William when asked what he wanted to be in life answered that he desired to be a minister of the gospel. His pastor and a Sunday school teacher were influential in his developing a close relationship to the Lord and a desire to proclaim the Word of God.

In 1911 the family moved from the Netherlands to the United States and settled in Kalamazoo, Michigan. There William attended a Christian elementary school and completed the eighth grade. His wish to enter high school did not materialize because of the poor economic conditions of that time. His parents wanted him to find gainful employment to help support the family. And so William worked at various jobs: selling vegetables, cutting wood, delivering groceries, and folding pages in a print shop. During the summer of 1916 his mother died. Some weeks later, father Bernardus decided to go to the Netherlands for a lengthy visit and took William along. World War I prevented them from returning to America until the following summer.

Education and Early Career

Hendriksen's desire to become a minister intensified to the point that he eventually asked his father for permission to go back to school. His father replied that he was unable to help financially. But William was undeterred and enrolled in a high school correspondence course. He worked during the day and diligently studied in the evening. He completed the course work in a remarkably short time. For two years he served as a teacher in an elementary school and during that time took examinations to receive the necessary teaching certificates.

Having his mind set on preparing for the ministry, William read widely and studied Reformed theology, archeology, Latin, and other appropriate subjects. He applied for admission to Calvin College in Grand Rapids in 1921; his request for financial assistance was granted on the basis of an essay that he had written on creation. Hendriksen passed his examinations with flying colors, finishing the four-year bachelor of arts program in three years. Then in 1924 he enrolled at Calvin Theological Seminary, from which he received the bachelor of theology degree in 1927.

Hendriksen entered the pastoral ministry of the Christian Reformed Church immediately upon graduation from the seminary. Throughout his pastorates in churches in Zeeland and Muskegon, Michigan, he took courses at Calvin Seminary that enabled him to graduate with the master of theology degree in 1934, for which he wrote an unpublished thesis on "The Premillennialistic Conception concerning Israel and the Church." This interest in eschatology developed further as he pastored a church in Grand Rapids. Although the workload in this large congregation was taxing, he nevertheless found time to write his book *More than Conquerors*. This volume on Revelation was privately printed in 1939 and was reviewed favorably in a few periodicals. It served as a doctoral dissertation submitted to Pike's Peak Bible Seminary, which awarded him the S.T.D. degree in 1939. The following year, Baker Book House decided to publish the book.

In 1942 the General Synod of the Christian Reformed Church appointed Hendriksen as professor of New Testament theology at Calvin Theological Seminary. He served this institution for a decade. But at the outset of his seminary career, Hendriksen asked for and was granted a year's leave of absence to enrol in a Th.D. program at Princeton Theological Seminary. While teaching a heavy load at Calvin Seminary, he wrote his doctoral dissertation "The Meaning of the Preposition *anti* in the New Testament." The New Testament use of this preposition, he contended, is evidence of the doctrine of the substitutionary atonement of Christ. On the basis of this unpublished dissertation Hendriksen received his doctorate from Princeton in 1948.

Author

The word *prolific* describes Hendriksen as a writer. He began his authorial profession in 1930 by supplying church news to his denominational magazine. Then year after year he wrote numerous articles on biblical topics, doctrinal issues, current religious trends, and Christian education. These articles were published in a variety of religious journals, magazines, and papers (e.g., the *Banner, Calvin Forum, Church Herald, Missionary Monthly,* and *Young Calvinist*).

Hendriksen also reviewed books that covered religious subjects in such diverse areas as Old and New Testament studies, theology, history, archeology, science, ecumenism, and missions. At times it was not uncommon for him to write reviews on twenty to thirty books per year. He read voraciously and was able to quickly analyze and critique the content of a volume.

In addition to writing reviews, Hendriksen himself penned several books. Sequentially, they include *The Covenant of Grace* (1932), *The Sermon on the Mount* (1934), and *Faith of Our Fathers* (1936). His book *More than Conquerors* (1939) has been reprinted more than thirty times. There followed *Preaching Prophecy in a World of War* (1940), *And So All Israel Shall Be Saved* (1945), *Bible Survey* (1947; a fourth revised edition retitled *Survey of the Bible* was issued in 1976), *Three Lectures on the Book of Revelation* (1949), and *Lectures on the Last Things* (1951).

Recognizing the enormous contribution of Herman Bavinck's four-volume set *Gereformeerde dogmatiek,* Hendriksen turned translator. He not only translated but also edited and provided annotations for volume 2, which was published under the title *The Doctrine of God* (1951).

In keeping with his lifelong interest in eschatology, Hendriksen in 1959 composed his work *The Bible on the Life Hereafter,* which has been reprinted seven times. In 1968 Hendriksen wrote *Israel and the Bible,* which Baker published but in that same year reprinted under the title *Israel in Prophecy.* This volume has been reprinted six times. And in 1978 he composed a *Beginner's Book of Doctrine,* meant for young Christians.

Hendriksen is best known, however, for the New Testament Commentary series published by Baker. The first work in this series was his *Exposition of the Gospel according to John,* which at first appeared in two volumes (1954), but in reprints as one volume. The author's *Exposition of I and II Thessalonians* was published in 1955 and has likewise been reprinted several times. Hendriksen wrote these commentaries while he was a busy pastor in a large congregation. Four years before his retirement he accepted a pastoral call to a smaller church. With less demands on his time as a minister of the gospel, he devoted more time to the writing of his commentaries. He worked indefatigably with the purpose of writing as many volumes as he could during the remaining years of his earthly life. Somewhere he wrote these memorable words: "In the kingdom of God is no room for drones, only for working bees." He certainly proved to be a living demonstration of his adage, for every two or three years an additional volume rolled off the printing presses.

The Pauline Epistles having captured Hendriksen's interest, at regular intervals he would present a new commentary to his readers. His *Exposition of I and II Timothy and Titus* appeared in 1957, the *Exposition of Philippians* in 1962, the *Exposition of Colossians and Philemon* in 1965, and the *Exposition of Ephesians* in 1967. Reprints of these works have been numerous.

Hendriksen served the Christian Reformed Church as a pastor from 1927 to 1965 with a ten-year interval as a professor (1942–52). But in 1965 he retired from these duties to devote himself full-time to his goal of writing commentaries on all the books of the New Testament. Within a year after his commentary on Paul's Epistle to the Ephesians appeared, his *Exposition of Galatians* came off the press (1968). Then a number of years went by with-

out any sign of another volume in the Hendriksen series. But the author had
not been idle, for a massive volume of more than a thousand pages surfaced
in 1973: the *Exposition of the Gospel according to Matthew*. Bypassing
Paul's epistles to the Romans and the Corinthians, Hendriksen had undertaken commentaries on the three Synoptic Gospels. Within two years (1975)
his volume on Mark appeared, and three years afterward (1978) he published his *Exposition of the Gospel according to Luke*.

When the author finally began his labors on Paul's Epistle to the Romans,
he knew that cancer was undermining his health. Having submitted to surgery
for the removal of a malignancy, he was severely weakened. He asked Baker
Book House to publish his commentary on the first eight chapters in case the
illness prevented him from completing the work. Baker granted his request.
Nonetheless, Hendriksen trusted God to grant him sufficient time to finish the
Exposition of Paul's Epistle to the Romans. Indeed, in the volume on Romans
1–8 are telltale marks of confidence of bringing the second volume (Rom. 9–
16) to completion. This occurred in 1981, and Baker combined both works in
one publication. Even though Hendriksen's physical body was ravaged by
cancer, he began preliminary work on a commentary on 1 Corinthians.

Impact

Hendriksen was a modest man who refused to accept royalties from translations of his books into other languages. Besides Dutch, Spanish, and Afri-
kaans, his writing has appeared in Japanese, Korean, Tamil, and Chinese. He
was gratified to know that his biblical studies were a blessing to countless
people around the globe. In fact, as of 1993 Baker Book House had printed
more than 600,000 copies of Hendriksen's works. In particular, his *More
than Conquerors* topped the 100,000 mark, and *The Bible on the Life Hereafter* was nearing the 90,000 mark.

As a speaker at Bible conferences, Hendriksen was in great demand. Despite his weak voice he was an excellent communicator. He frequently employed the personal pronoun *you* in addressing his listeners. He knew how
to keep his audience spellbound as he masterfully expounded Scripture and
summarized its message. Repeatedly he turned down invitations to lecture
abroad, because he felt that his writing schedule did not permit extended periods away from his desk. Near the end of his life, however, he accepted the
invitation of the Tabernacle School of Theology in London to lecture at the
site made famous by Charles Haddon Spurgeon. There in October 1979 he
presented four lectures on the heavenly Jerusalem, pointing out the symbol-
ism of Revelation. He called attention to the dimensions of the New Jerusalem, which measures 1,500 miles (2,500 kms.) wide, long, and high—a perfect cube (Rev. 21:16). His main point was that what deserves full attention
in the New Jerusalem is the object at its center—the throne of God.[1]

1. *Sword and Trowel* 26.1 (Jan. 1994): 25.

The Basic Design of the Commentaries

In the world of religious publishing there are three kinds of Bible commentaries. First, some authors compose technical works based on research into the original Hebrew or Greek of the text; they interact with the latest scholarly books and articles; and they address fellow scholars and astute theological students. Second, other writers make full use of the original languages and are abreast of the current debates in their field. However, they address preachers, teachers, and serious lay students of the Bible. Third, still other commentators are preachers who publish insightful sermonic material for fellow preachers.

Hendriksen's commentaries fall into the second category. As a communicator of God's truth, he always sought to combine scholarship and simplicity. His aim was to write so clearly that laypeople, for example, Sunday school teachers, could understand and benefit from his exposition. In other words, he cast the net for his audience as widely as possible but never at the expense of scholarship.

For Hendriksen, the Scriptures were verbally inspired and infallibly revealed to us by God himself. To illustrate, he notes that the last book in the New Testament, the Revelation of John, pointedly states that it is the revelation of Jesus Christ, the revelation that God gave to his Son, who made it known to his servants (Rev. 1:1).[2] In his writings Hendriksen always gives Jesus Christ the preeminence. He upholds the cardinal doctrines of the Christian faith, including the deity and humanity of Christ, the virgin birth, the Holy Spirit's work of convicting humans of sin, repentance, salvation by grace, justification, sanctification, the resurrection of the body, and glorification.

Seeing that the church benefited from his book *More than Conquerors*, as an ever-widening circulation indicated, Hendriksen began to think of writing a commentary on the Gospel of John. In the introduction to this volume, he has set out the objectives that govern this commentary in particular and the series in general. First, he aimed at a translation in "present-day, idiomatic English [that is] true to the original." Second, in the introductory survey of the problems of a given book, the matter of authorship must be thoroughly discussed. Third, a brief analysis of the text, including its concepts and relationships, should be offered. Central passages (e.g., John 3:16) are to receive more emphasis than do others. Fourth, at the conclusion of the discussion on a certain text a synthesis should summarize its main ideas. Analysis must always be followed by synthesis. Fifth, Hendriksen purposed always to give a defense of the conservative position. Sixth, the exegete must present current New Testament scholarship from articles, books, and doctoral dissertations. And last, an explanation of some grammatical constructions should be included. Hendriksen modestly notes that these objectives have not been fully

2. William Hendriksen, *More than Conquerors*, rev. ed. (Grand Rapids: Baker, 1982), 51.

met.[3] Nevertheless, his commentaries display the earmarks of careful exegesis based on the principles he adopted.

All of Hendriksen's commentaries have as their basis his own translation of the Greek text. His expertise as a translator was affirmed when he was asked to translate Revelation for the New International Version. Further, he initially served on editorial committees on the Old Testament and the New Testament, because he had shown himself equally adept in Hebrew and Greek. His translations are true to the original intent of the text; they are free from being pedantic; and they avoid being paraphrases. A striking illustration is found in Hendriksen's translation of Ephesians 3:14–15, where Paul has a play on the words *patera* and *patria*. Hendriksen captures the essence of the Greek in his version: "For this reason I bend my knees to the Father [*patera*] from whom the whole family [*patria*] in heaven and on earth derives its name: the Father's Family." Typically he also eloquently defends his translation by pointing out weaknesses and flaws in both older and other current versions.[4]

After explaining Ephesians 3:14–15, Hendriksen immediately draws the conclusion that the church in heaven and the church on earth are one. And he epitomizes this truth by quoting from William Wordsworth's poem "We Are Seven." This poem pictures a little girl who maintains that, although two of her siblings have died, they are still seven—two in heaven and five on earth.

> "How many are you, then," said I,
> "If they two are in heaven?"
> Quick was the little Maid's reply,
> "O master! we are seven."
>
> "But they are dead; those two are dead!
> Their spirits are in heaven!"
> 'Twas throwing words away; for still
> The little Maid would have her will,
> And said, "Nay, we are seven!"

Practical application of a profound spiritual truth is one of the hallmarks of the New Testament Commentary series. Doctrinal discussions frequently conclude with lessons applicable to everyday life. This combination, both unique and priceless, distinguishes the New Testament Commentary series.

Special Skills

Hendriksen had the uncanny ability to put together both useful outlines of Scripture passages and numbered lists of arguments supporting his interpretations. His material is well organized to help the busy pastor in constructing a

---

3. William Hendriksen, *Exposition of the Gospel according to John*, 2 vols. (Grand Rapids: Baker, 1954), 1:vii–viii.
4. William Hendriksen, *Exposition of Ephesians* (Grand Rapids: Baker, 1967), 167–68.

lucid sermon. His discussions are logical, to the point, and convincing. And his mnemonic devices, although not appreciated by all, are intended to facilitate fast recall. A noteworthy example of these various skills is to be found in the commentary on Philippians, where he champions the hypothesis that Paul wrote this epistle while in prison in Rome rather than Caesarea or Ephesus. Hendriksen arranges a list of twelve arguments in both logical and memorizable groupings that exhibit a certain degree of alliteration.[5] Clarity in writing is the key to good communication, and Hendriksen proved to be an expert.

Writers know that not all scholarly material can be presented in simple terms. So whenever Hendriksen had to write extensive technical material, he placed it in a footnote, often at the end of the chapter. He wisely refrained from making his discussion a stumbling block for the reader who is unacquainted with intricate details. Yet he had to interact with his peers on pertinent textual and grammatical issues. Thus, with respect to the textual reading of the personal pronoun *you* in Colossians 1:21–22a, Hendriksen writes a page and a half in small print as he ably invalidates opposing arguments, graciously proves his view with sound reasoning, and cautiously draws a conclusion. Similarly he formulates a technical argument on Colossians 1:24b in a lengthy footnote at the end of his discussion of that chapter. There he conclusively establishes his position with the help of his Princeton Seminary doctoral dissertation on the Greek preposition *anti*.[6]

Classic is Hendriksen's refutation of the theory that Paul teaches a trichotomy (spirit, soul, body) in 1 Thessalonians 5:23. Here the author relegates his technical discussion to a footnote that covers four-and-a-half pages in small print. The material is organized in such a manner that any serious student is able to follow the discourse and profit from it. Hendriksen asks whether Paul was a trichotomist and then lists six theories that address the question. He interacts with every one of these theories and then firmly establishes his dichotomistic view. Accordingly, he renders his own translation of the verse:

> And without flaw may be your spirit,
> And your soul-and-body . . .
> May it be kept.[7]

Equally classic is Hendriksen's thirty-page examination of the available evidence on the authorship of the Pastoral Epistles. He concludes that the burden of proof rests squarely on the shoulders of those who deny Pauline authorship. The evidence of the epistles themselves indicates that only Paul could have written them. Hendriksen proves that elements which supposedly undermine apostolic authorship actually favor it.[8]

---

5. William Hendriksen, *Exposition of Philippians* (Grand Rapids: Baker, 1962), 23–30.
6. See William Hendriksen, *Exposition of Colossians and Philemon* (Grand Rapids: Baker, 1965), 96–98 (nn. 60, 66).
7. William Hendriksen, *Exposition of I and II Thessalonians* (Grand Rapids: Baker, 1955), 146–50.
8. William Hendriksen, *Exposition of I and II Timothy and Titus* (Grand Rapids: Baker, 1957), 4–33.

Recognizing that the reading of commentaries can be a trifle monotonous, Hendriksen often attempts to put some spirit into his books. Basic to his approach is sound exegesis of the text, but as we saw earlier, he enlivens his study with practical applications incorporated into the discussion of the Scripture passage. At other times he supplies charts, drawings, or maps to clarify his commentary. His poetic ability, inherited from his father, is evident in the commentary on Romans, where Hendriksen versifies chapters 5 and 8. To illustrate, here is his versification of Romans 8:1–2:

> For those who in Jesus their refuge have found
> There's no condemnation. Their blessings abound.
> For through what Christ Jesus has done within me
> The Spirit from sin and from death set me free.

In the body of his commentaries, Hendriksen also shows himself a formidable debater who has all the pertinent facts at his fingertips. At times he even takes the reader into the arena of a public debate. He records, for example, a hypothetical debate on the resolution that the genealogy of Jesus as presented by Luke traces the line of Joseph. The affirmative and negative sides are presented in turn. In the footnotes Hendriksen identifies eminent scholars and commentators who take one side or the other. He continues his report with rebuttals presented by each side and then concludes that the debate has been won by the negative. He asserts, "It is *not* true that the genealogy presented by Luke (3:23–38) is necessarily that of Joseph. On the contrary, it is probably that of Mary."[9]

At other times Hendriksen uses his gifts as a logician. In discussing the account of the man born blind (John 9), for instance, he effectively analyzes the reasoning of the Pharisees by reducing it to syllogisms (major premise, minor premise, and conclusion).[10]

Another skill Hendriksen displays in his commentaries is the ability to synthesize. In addition to his outstanding knowledge of Scripture's content, he displays exceptional skill in bringing together seemingly unconnected truths that emerge from his analyses. At the conclusion of most chapters, the author customarily presents his summary in the form of a synthesis that is neatly outlined point by point.

Stance

When Hendriksen decided to write commentaries on the Synoptic Gospels, he was determined to prepare and write them from a conservative point of view. His commentary on Matthew with its introduction of ninety-nine pages is a first-rate example of contemporary scholarship by a conservative

---

9. William Hendriksen, *Exposition of the Gospel according to Luke* (Grand Rapids: Baker, 1978), 222–25.

10. Hendriksen, *John*, 2:81–84.

scholar. Hendriksen thoroughly discusses, describes, and evaluates the liberalism of Adolf von Harnack, the skepticism of William Wrede, the pessimism of Albert Schweitzer, and the radicalism of Rudolf Bultmann. He concludes that none of these positions is able to endure. "It is not surprising, therefore, that the various systems of skepticism and unbelief have vanished one by one. The facts defy the theories."[11] How, then, does Hendriksen deal with "discrepancies"? He suggests that harmonization can be an acceptable procedure if it is done without force in a natural manner and with due respect for the contexts of individual passages. And he is not afraid to admit that in some instances we lack sufficient information to solve a given problem.

The priority of Mark's Gospel is a topic that Hendriksen carefully researches, defends, and explains. He maintains that the arguments leveled against Markan priority are not strong enough to overpower the evidence that supports it. In his opinion the composition date of this Gospel is somewhere between the years 40 and 65, "with the balance of evidence now favoring the earlier part of this period."[12]

In his discussion of the Synoptic Problem, Hendriksen opines that the Q theory offers no solution. The Gospel writers, guided by the Holy Spirit, gained their material, whether oral or written, from eyewitnesses. "All the evidence, including the character of the language that is used, the customs that are described or implied, the places that are named, the vividness of the presentation, points to the fact that we are dealing here with very early material. In fact, we can go one step farther: via these earliest witnesses all the evidence points back to the Living Lord, Jesus Christ, himself. It is to him and his Spirit that these writings owe their origin."[13] Because numerous scholars writing on the Synoptic Problem overlook the role of the Holy Spirit, Hendriksen pointedly notes that the Gospel belongs to Jesus and that the Holy Spirit is Scripture's primary author. He takes a conservative stance in the arena of current scholarly debate on the origin of the four Gospels and thus upholds the integrity of God's Word.

The commentaries of Hendriksen reveal that their author is consistently Reformed in his doctrinal approach. Avoiding the use of labels, he graciously explains the Scriptures from a covenantal perspective, as is evident from his discussion of Galatians 4:24. He teaches that election is from eternity for all those whom God has chosen in Christ Jesus as their representative and surety (Eph. 1:4–6; Rom. 8:38–39). He notes that true believers are being guarded by God's power; they cling to God to the very end of their earthly life and are eternally secure. This is a recurring message of the Bible (see his commentary on John 6:39; 10:27–28). In discussing Romans 9:13 the author carefully an-

11. William Hendriksen, *Exposition of the Gospel according to Matthew* (Grand Rapids: Baker, 1973), 75.
12. William Hendriksen, *Exposition of the Gospel according to Mark* (Grand Rapids: Baker, 1975), 15.
13. Hendriksen, *Matthew*, 53.

alyzes the objections to the doctrine of election and reprobation, and proves that this tenet is the teaching of Scripture. Hendriksen also explains that the person described in Romans 7:14–25 is neither unconverted nor an immature believer; rather, the passage speaks of Paul himself and, by extension, of any believer, including the most mature.[14]

Eschatologically, Hendriksen is an amillennialist, but does not describe himself as such. In commenting on passages that teach about the last things, he abstains from criticizing other millennial views. Instead, Hendriksen takes a positive approach, stating his own views on the basis of his interpretation of the text. His interpretation of Revelation 20 is an example of his millennial convictions. He explains that the thousand years (20:2–7) refers to "this present gospel age" during which Satan's "influence [is] curtailed with respect to one definite sphere of activity: 'that he should deceive the nations no more.'"[15] Hendriksen alerts his readers, however, that the period during which the church can actively spread the gospel will not last forever, for Satan will be released from his prison for a short time (20:3b, 7). Hendriksen knows of only one general resurrection of the dead, for he writes: "Nowhere in the entire Bible do we read of a resurrection of the bodies of believers, followed, after a thousand years, by a resurrection of the bodies of the unbelievers."[16] Even though Hendriksen held firm convictions, he always accorded great respect to those who differed. His purpose was never to generate heat but always to spread the light of Scripture. He purposed to transmit God's light and thus testified with the psalmist: "For with you is the fountain of life; in your light we see light" (Ps. 36:9 NIV).

As a result of his lifelong work with Scripture, God's Word became an integral part of Hendriksen's life. At an interview, he testified to the joy and satisfaction of studying the Bible: "You know, when I work on any book of Scripture, that book always in my mind becomes more dear and beautiful. When you are working on the Scripture, how your appreciation grows and a tear comes to the eye! The Bible is so marvellous. How can one study, for example, the love of God shown as in Luke 15 and be unmoved?"[17]

The major step in this lifelong process of study was taken when Hendriksen's first wife, Rena Baker, encouraged him to borrow the necessary funds to publish privately his manuscript of *More than Conquerors*. Having married Hendriksen in 1925, she was a courageous wife and a wonderful mother of their three children. She died of cancer in 1960. The following year, Hendriksen married Reta De Boer, who assisted him in typing his manuscripts, performing editorial work, and reading the page proofs. Appropriately, he

14. William Hendriksen, *Exposition of Paul's Epistle to the Romans* (Grand Rapids: Baker, 1981), 222–39.

15. Hendriksen, *More than Conquerors*, 190.

16. Ibid., 196.

17. "An Interview with Dr. William Hendriksen," *Banner of Truth* 223 (April 1982): 10.

dedicated his commentary on Luke to his wife Reta, "who typed the entire final draft of the manuscript and without whose constant help in ever so many ways I could not have written it."

Healthy throughout most of his life, Hendriksen succumbed to cancer in his eighty-first year. On Tuesday, January 12, 1982, he departed from this life and entered the life hereafter about which he had often spoken and written. He himself had translated these words in the New International Version: "Blessed are the dead who die in the Lord from now on. 'Yes,' says the Spirit, 'they will rest from their labor, for their deeds will follow them'" (Rev. 14:13).

The Evangelical Christian Publishers Association in annual convention on July 12, 1982, awarded Hendriksen, posthumously, the Gold Medallion Book Award for his commentary on Romans. The award is a crown of well-deserved praise for the author who with his pen has blessed countless people throughout the world.

Primary Sources

Hendriksen, William. *And So All Israel Shall Be Saved*. Grand Rapids: Baker, 1945.

———. *The Bible on the Life Hereafter*. Grand Rapids: Baker, 1959.

———. *Bible Survey*. Grand Rapids: Baker, 1947.

———. *The Covenant of Grace*. Grand Rapids: Eerdmans, 1932. Rev. ed., Grand Rapids: Baker, 1978.

———. *Faith of Our Fathers*. 3 vols. Grand Rapids: Zondervan, 1936.

———. *Lectures on the Last Things*. Grand Rapids: Baker, 1951.

———. *More than Conquerors*. Grand Rapids: Baker, 1940. Rev. ed., 1982.

———. New Testament Commentary series. Grand Rapids: Baker. *Exposition of the Gospel according to John*, 2 vols., 1954; *Exposition of I and II Thessalonians*, 1955; *Exposition of I and II Timothy and Titus*,1957; *Exposition of Philippians*, 1962; *Exposition of Colossians and Philemon*, 1965; *Exposition of Ephesians*, 1967; *Exposition of Galatians*, 1968; *Exposition of the Gospel according to Matthew*, 1973; *Exposition of the Gospel according to Mark*, 1975; *Exposition of the Gospel according to Luke*, 1978; *Exposition of Paul's Epistle to the Romans*, 1981.

———. *Preaching Prophecy in a World of War*. Grand Rapids: Baker, 1940.

———. *The Sermon on the Mount*. Grand Rapids: Eerdmans, 1934.

———. *Three Lectures on the Book of Revelation*. Grand Rapids: Zondervan, 1949.

Ned Bernard Stonehouse

Dan G. McCartney

Life

Ned Bernard Stonehouse was born in 1902 in Grand Rapids, Michigan, to a Dutch immigrant family (the original family name was Steenhuysen), and was raised in the staunchly Calvinistic Christian Reformed Church. After attending Calvin College he went to Princeton Theological Seminary for his ministerial training, where he came under the influence of J. Gresham Machen and Geerhardus Vos. Machen made an especially deep impression which lasted throughout Stonehouse's life.

At Princeton Stonehouse flourished intellectually. He took extra hours each term, so that by the time he finished his B.D. he had also accrued the twenty extra hours necessary for an M.A. Even with the overload, Stonehouse wrote a prize-winning paper which gave him encouragement, and some financial help, to pursue advanced study in New Testament. Machen and others supported him in this pursuit, so Stonehouse elected to attend the Free University in Amsterdam.

First, however, Stonehouse married Winigrace Bylsma, whom he had been courting for seven years. Winigrace and Ned were eventually blessed with three children: Marilyn Helen, Elsie Mae, and Bernard John Stonehouse. Winigrace died in 1958.

Soon after Ned and Winigrace were married in 1927 they set out for Amsterdam. His doctoral supervisor at the Free University was F. W. Grosheide, with whom he developed a lifelong friendship. While working on his doctorate, Stonehouse managed to find a few months to spend in Tübingen, where he came in contact with the conservative Swiss theologian and exegete Adolf Schlatter. In 1929 he completed his dissertation on the acceptance and use of the Book of Revelation in the early church and was awarded a Th.D.

Machen knew a bright fellow when he saw one, and immediately invited Stonehouse to serve as instructor of New Testament at Westminster Seminary, which had been newly formed as an alternative to Princeton Seminary. Princeton's theological commitments had been compromised by the reorganization of its board. So it was that Stonehouse at age twenty-seven became a charter member of the faculty of Westminster. He taught New Testament from 1929 until his untimely demise in 1962; in 1955 he also began to serve as dean of the faculty.

In his early years Stonehouse taught courses on the ancient church as well as the New Testament, but by 1933 he was concentrating on his special areas of interest, including Gospels history, New Testament canon, the Book of Revelation, and Romans 9–11. In 1937 Machen died, and later that year the board appointed Stonehouse to replace him as professor of New Testament at Westminster. His inaugural address, given in April of 1938, was on Rudolf Bultmann's views of Jesus. In this lecture Stonehouse traced the developments leading up to the new view of Jesus advocated by Bultmann, demonstrated some of the questionableness of Bultmann's historical method, and showed how Bultmann's concept of Jesus is quite remote from the biblical portrayal and the historical person. Already in this address Stonehouse evinced some awareness of the character of the Gospels, a theme he would later develop in his books on the Synoptics.

Throughout the rest of his life, Stonehouse pursued vigorous involvement with New Testament scholars of various stripes. He was heavily involved in the formation and early development of the Evangelical Theological Society, and was also an active member of the Society of Biblical Literature, Studiorum Novi Testamenti Societas, and the Society for Calvinistic Philosophy (Vereniging voor Calvinistische wijsbegeerte). In 1949 he was special lecturer at the Free Church College in Edinburgh, and in 1959–60 he received a Fulbright sponsorship to lecture in New Testament at the Free University of Amsterdam. In 1962 he gave the Payton Lectures at Fuller Seminary, which became the basis for his last book, *The Origins of the Synoptic Gospels.*

In his youth Stonehouse had a bout with rheumatic fever which weakened his heart. In spite of this he often participated in sports, but by the late 1950s his heart was taking its toll on his health, and in the summer of 1962 he began to show signs of serious weakness. On November 18, 1962, after attending church in the morning, he lay down for an afternoon nap and passed peacefully into the presence of his Savior.

Teaching Ministry

Known as "Stoney" to his colleagues and students, Ned Bernard Stonehouse is remembered both for his considerate but incisive criticism of modernism's approaches to the New Testament, and his fearless pursuit of the theological message of the New Testament documents by exact and thorough exegesis. In addition to his courses in Gospels history, apostolic history, New Testament canon, and New Testament biblical theology, which were required of all students for most of his years on the faculty, Stonehouse at one time or another gave graduate courses and electives in the Book of Revelation, Romans 9–11, Jesus' messianic consciousness, the apostolic fathers, the passion narratives, Hebrews, Matthew, John, Luke, and the parables of Jesus.

Perhaps Stonehouse's most distinctive characteristic was the carefulness of his scholarship. His students remember him as being exceedingly exact and painstaking. As a critic of the critics, he was an eminent practitioner of the rule that one should not criticize opponents until one has thoroughly understood them. In all his works he is also careful to present the viewpoints of the critics as fairly and accurately as possible, even when he passionately believes them to be wrong.

Stonehouse was convinced that one reason liberalism had crept into the old Presbyterian church in the late nineteenth century was that so many of its ministers lacked any awareness of the implicit assumptions of certain forms of critical investigation. His required course in Gospels history therefore was largely dedicated to a minute examination of the history of Gospel investigation by critical scholars; he traced in great detail the history of criticism of the life of Jesus from Hermann Samuel Reimarus through Bultmann. Stonehouse showed that it was not just the radical critics like David Friedrich Strauss whose views undercut the integrity of the Gospels, but also those of liberal persuasion. The old liberalism generally had a positive view of the historical reliability of the Gospels, particularly Mark. But since the liberals adopted certain philosophical assumptions of modernity (which cut straight across biblical assumptions), their effort was just as destructive as that of the radicals, and their picture of Jesus was perhaps even more skewed than that of Bultmann and Albert Schweitzer.

Stonehouse himself never published the material from his course in Gospels history, though he did address form criticism in particular in his syllabus "Form Criticism and Gospel Reconstruction," which bears witness to his careful analysis. Recently, however, much of his analysis of the material on the life of Jesus has been re-presented in a book by one of his students.[1]

In his course on New Testament theology Stonehouse introduced his students to the approach originally developed by Geerhardus Vos at Princeton, who was only beginning to be appreciated among conservative scholars. This approach assumes the integrity and internal coherence of the biblical witnesses, but also recognizes a development and unfolding of revelation. The proclamation of the arrival of God's kingdom was a development that tied together the teaching of Paul and of Jesus. It seems unfortunate that Stonehouse wrote very little on this subject, though to some extent Vos's influence can be seen in his *Witness of Matthew and Mark to Christ* and *Witness of Luke to Christ.*

Ecclesiastical Involvement

Though Stonehouse had been raised in the Christian Reformed Church, his time at Princeton and his joining the faculty at Westminster thrust him into

---

1. Robert Strimple, *The Modern Search for the Real Jesus* (Phillipsburg, N.J.: Presbyterian and Reformed, 1995).

the thick of controversy in the Presbyterian church. When he was ordained in 1932, the Presbyterian church was already in great turmoil; and when separation became inevitable in 1935–36, Stonehouse sided with those who chose to form the new denomination, originally called the Presbyterian Church of America, the name later being changed to the Orthodox Presbyterian Church. From that time on he staunchly identified himself with historic Presbyterianism and was one of the most ecclesiastically active members of the faculty.

Not only was Stonehouse involved in the development of the Orthodox Presbyterian Church from its beginning, he also continued to have a formative influence in the church and his local presbytery until his death. He was heavily involved in the production of the new denomination's form of government and directory of worship, and he served for some time as president of the home missions committee.

Further, Storehouse maintained an interest in bringing sound theology and biblical instruction to the person in the pew. He wrote scores of articles on a popular level for the denominational magazine *Presbyterian Guardian;* these articles covered a huge range of subjects of concern to the church. He also edited the magazine in 1936–37, in 1945–48, and again in 1956–59. Reflecting his particular interest in Christian education, the article "Calvinism and the Christian University," which appeared in 1947, is a classic.

In spite of his deep commitment to the separatism and purity of his own denomination, Stonehouse was not at all narrowly sectarian. He maintained a wide involvement with nonevangelical and non-Reformed scholars. His gracious relations with theological opponents often gave him unique opportunities. For example, the liberal periodical *Christian Century* invited him to write an article on the subject of miracles, which was to have been answered by a liberal scholar. Stonehouse pointed out that orthodox Christians do not "believe the impossible"; rather, they believe that "with God all things are possible."[2] Curiously, the liberal answer never appeared!

Stonehouse was also a mover toward greater involvement of Reformed scholars with other evangelicals. In addition to being an active participant in the founding of the Evangelical Theological Society, he was three times (1949, 1953, and 1958) his denomination's delegate to the Reformed Ecumenical Synod, and a vigorous proponent of greater unity between the Christian Reformed Church, the Reformed Presbyterian Church (Evangelical Synod), and his own denomination. He also was the first editor of the New International Commentary on the New Testament, a series intended to incorporate the best evangelical scholarship from around the world. From 1951 until 1962 Stonehouse oversaw the production of seven of its volumes.

---

2. Ned B. Stonehouse, "Miracle Re-evaluated," *Christian Century* 78 (Nov. 1, 1961): 1295–97.

Publications

The Witness of Matthew and Mark to Christ

Stonehouse's first major scholarly publication was probably also his most significant, at least in terms of breaking new ground. *The Witness of Matthew and Mark to Christ* appeared in 1944 and met with a great deal of positive response not only among conservatives, but even among critics who did not at all share Stonehouse's theological convictions. His extremely thorough attention to details, and his inherent passion for understanding what a text actually says, led him to challenge both the liberal and the traditional understanding of the Gospels as biographical documents, and to focus on the Gospels as gospels, that is, as presentations of Jesus as the Lord and the Savior. The Gospels, Stonehouse says over and over, are not biographies. They do not intend to provide a life of Jesus or even material for one, and hence they are not concerned with chronological sequence, background and influences in Jesus' life, a psychological understanding of Jesus' self-consciousness, or any other usual feature of biographies. Thus in some ways Stonehouse sided more with the then-new radical approach than with the old liberal viewpoint.

But Stonehouse was equally concerned to demonstrate that the theological character of the Gospels does not at all vitiate their historical character. In fact, recognition of the true nature of the Gospels may very well be the only way to preserve their historical integrity. It seems undeniable, for example, that Matthew arranged material nonchronologically, molding it to suit his message and audience. But neither he nor the early church invented the traditions about Jesus—they adapted and re-presented those traditions in such a way as to bring out their true theological meaning[3] and to address the genuine needs of the Christian community. Stonehouse did give some place to harmonization, if for no other reason than to show that the shaping of a story does not mean a loss of its historicity. But such harmonization must never suppress what the text actually says—each Gospel has its own particular concerns and is addressed to its own particular setting. Thus *The Witness of Matthew and Mark to Christ* in many ways anticipated the more useful features of redaction criticism, as Moisés Silva has demonstrated.[4] Stonehouse inquired into the theological intent of the Evangelist, and he envisioned something of the church situation that gave rise to the Evangelist's special emphases.

Stonehouse even anticipated certain features of the literary-critical approaches of the late twentieth century. For example, while accepting B. W.

---

3. Note, e.g., Ned B. Stonehouse, *The Witness of Matthew and Mark to Christ* (Philadelphia: Presbyterian Guardian, 1944), 152: "The proclamation of the glad tidings of Jesus Christ did not require anything like an exhaustive account of his travels and activity, but only such an account of his history as would adequately display the *meaning* of his coming" (italics added).

4. Moisés Silva, "Ned Stonehouse and Redaction Criticism," *Westminster Theological Journal* 40.1 (Fall 1977): 77–88, and 40.2 (Spring 1978): 281–303.

Bacon's suggestion of the topical ordering of Matthew's teaching material in the five discourses, Stonehouse also noted that the phrase "from that time on, Jesus began to . . ." (4:17 and 16:21) serves as a marker which divides Matthew literally into three main parts: an introduction, a development section involving Jesus' self-presentation to Israel, and a culmination in Jesus' journey to Jerusalem, his death, and resurrection. This anticipated the literary analysis of Jack Kingsbury by forty-two years.[5]

Further, Stonehouse bravely challenged the authenticity of the longer ending of Mark. In a time when almost all Christians still used the King James Version, such a challenge was difficult for many to accept; and indeed, at least one of Stonehouse's theological allies was unhappy with this conclusion.[6] Of the potentially more disturbing difficulties inherent in Stonehouse's contention that the Gospel writers exercised considerable editorial freedom, evangelical reviewers seem to have been somewhat unaware.

Critical scholars likewise seem to have misunderstood much of what Stonehouse was saying, but were appreciative of his painstaking exegetical integrity. Paul Minear commended him for allegedly departing from the narrowness of his predecessor Machen, and even wondered whether Stonehouse had abandoned the doctrine of biblical infallibility, though of course Stonehouse saw himself as doing no such thing.[7] Rather, he was pursuing the lines of study which Machen himself pursued: strict attention to the text of the New Testament, both in its details and in its overall consistency, with an underlying commitment to its truthfulness. Otto Piper lauded the fact that Stonehouse "proceeds in his work irrespective of the traditional views concerning the Gospels, and unimpeded by the categories of a preconceived theological system," and suggested that Stonehouse spend less time refuting the more eccentric critical viewpoints.[8] Amos Wilder took Stonehouse to task for not paying more attention to the literary relationship of the Gospels and the history of the tradition (that is to say, contemporary-source- and form-critical hypotheses), but was greatly appreciative of Stonehouse's close examination of the theological purpose of the Evangelists.[9] With such a broad awareness

5. Jack Dean Kingsbury, *Matthew as Story* (Philadelphia: Fortress, 1986), 40.

6. Though Frank D. Frazer, review of *The Witness of Matthew and Mark to Christ,* by Ned B. Stonehouse, *Christian Opinion* 2.1 (Oct. 1944): 18–20, is positive towards Stonehouse's work, his review is dominated by an argument against Stonehouse's rejection of the longer ending of Mark.

7. Paul S. Minear, review of *The Witness of Matthew and Mark to Christ,* by Ned B. Stonehouse, *Christian Century* 61 (Sept. 27, 1944): 1104–5.

8. Otto A. Piper, review of *The Witness of Matthew and Mark to Christ,* by Ned B. Stonehouse, *Princeton Seminary Bulletin* 38.4 (March 1945): 34–35. It is noteworthy that Frank Frazer (see n. 6), writing from a very conservative point of view, says something very similar in complaining that Stonehouse "seems to take the critics too seriously" (p. 18).

9. Amos N. Wilder, review of *The Witness of Matthew and Mark to Christ,* by Ned B. Stonehouse, *Journal of Biblical Literature* 64 (1945): 408–10. Though such interest in the special theological purposes of the Gospel writers may today seem common, we must remember that Stonehouse was writing in 1944, four years before Günther Bornkamm's seminal article on the stilling of the storm in Matthew ("Die Sturmstillung im Matthäusevangelium," *Wort und Dienst,* n.s., 1 [1948]: 49–54), generally regarded as the first redaction-critical study.

and positive reception of his work, it is somewhat surprising and dismaying that later students of redaction criticism have ignored Stonehouse.

The Infallible Word

In 1946 Stonehouse edited with Paul Woolley a faculty symposium on *The Infallible Word*. Stonehouse himself contributed an article on the authority of the New Testament, which carefully outlined what is involved in the idea of a New Testament canon, reckoned with its historical character, and also showed its clear connection to genuine Christian supernaturalistic theism. A proper view of God as both transcendent and sovereign in history is integral to a proper view of the divine authority of a (unitary yet diverse) revelatory Scripture. Some think that this discussion of the nature of the New Testament canon has never been surpassed. It provided the grounding for Stonehouse's adventuresome examination of several books of the New Testament. His confidence in the self-attesting veracity of the books gave him the freedom to hear whatever the text was saying and the boldness to go wherever the text led.

The Witness of Luke to Christ

Though Stonehouse never finished his project of describing the testimony of all four Gospels to Christ, he did publish *The Witness of Luke to Christ* in 1951. As with *The Witness of Matthew and Mark to Christ,* Stonehouse is concerned to see Luke as an evangelist, not a biographer. Of particular note is his contention that by paying attention to the distinctives of Luke, we can gain a greater appreciation for the mighty person to whom all four Gospels bear witness. The way to grasp the unity of their testimony is not to artificially smooth over the differences between them (harmonization), but to understand those differences:

> It has seemed to me that Christians who are assured as to the unity of the witness of the Gospels should take greater pains to do justice to the diversity of expression of that witness. It is a thrilling experience to observe this unity, to be overwhelmed at the contemplation of the *one* Christ proclaimed by the four evangelists. But that experience is far richer and more satisfying if one has been absorbed and captured by each portrait in turn and has conscientiously been concerned with the minutest differentiating details as well as with the total impact of the evangelical witness.[10]

This is hardly a denial of the historicity of Luke. Indeed, Stonehouse's first major chapter is devoted to the immediacy of the historical tradition and the concern for accuracy, both of which are attested in Luke's prologue. Stonehouse then proceeds to attribute whatever peculiarities there might be in Luke to his special concerns, such as his interest in the fulfilment of a divine

---

10. Ned B. Stonehouse, *The Witness of Luke to Christ* (Grand Rapids: Eerdmans, 1951), 6.

plan. And this was written three years before Hans Conzelmann in his *Die Mitte der Zeit* "discovered" Luke's *Heilsgeschichte*.

J. Gresham Machen: A Biographical Memoir

In 1954, seventeen years after Machen's death, Stonehouse honored his teacher, mentor, and colleague by producing the first major biography of Machen. Though this work has been criticized as being too adulatory, it is certainly thorough and evidences countless hours spent in interviewing, in sifting through reams of personal correspondence, and even in digging up obscure references in college yearbooks.

Paul before the Areopagus, and Other New Testament Studies

The Tyndale Lecture in New Testament which Stonehouse gave in Edinburgh in 1949 dealt with the speech of Paul before the Areopagus. Here again Stonehouse's convictions that the text is both historical and theological are evident in his close examination of the address in Acts 17. Critical discussion had typically argued that this speech takes a positive view of and "natural law" approach to pagan religion as the efforts of humankind to get to God. Critics regarded the speech as the work of someone trying to show pagans that Christianity is simply the answer to good pagan religious affections. It was argued that because the sermon lacks Paul's uncompromisingly confrontational attitude toward paganism, the real Paul could not have spoken it. Stonehouse, by careful historical and textual analysis, demonstrates that, although in Acts 17 a point of contact is indeed made with the non-Christian's natural awareness of God (as may also be seen in Rom. 1), the antithesis of Christianity with paganism is just as sharp here as it is in Paul's Epistles. The speech of Acts 17 is not Luke's invention. On the other hand, Stonehouse also acknowledges Luke's intentions in recording this address—he is aware that Acts 17 is not a mere verbatim transcription of Paul's words, but involves Luke's adaptation and use of that speech to suit his own theological purpose. This is not one whit a denial of the historicity or accuracy of Luke's account—quite the opposite—but it is a recognition that Acts 17 is no bare record which Luke is disinterestedly reporting.

The "other studies" are mostly excerpted from the *Westminster Theological Journal,* and probably represent what Stonehouse himself thought to be his most significant articles. "Who Crucified Jesus?" is a response to Solomon Zeitlin's theory that it was not the Jewish people generally, but only a few traitorous scoundrels who were protecting their own interests with the Romans. Stonehouse shows that, though the Romans and the Jewish political machinery were indeed culpable, there is no escaping the fact that Jesus generated a great deal of antipathy among the Jewish religious establishment as well, and that his message often met resistance and hostility from many Jewish people throughout Palestine. The article on "Repentance, Baptism and the Gift of the Holy Spirit" deals carefully with what these biblical teachings entail and how they are related.[11] In "The Elders and the Living Beings in the Apocalypse" Stonehouse argues that the twenty-four elders and the living creatures refer to angelic beings, not to Israel or the church. "Rudolf Bultmann's Jesus" was, as we have seen, Stonehouse's inaugural address as professor of New Testament. "Martin Dibelius and the Relation of History and Faith" is an extensive critique of Dibelius's concept of "supra-history" as the plane of Christian revelation. Stonehouse also points out Dibelius's abiding liberalism, which was evident in his distaste for the christological character of Jesus' eschatological message as it appears in the Gospels. Finally, "Luther and the New Testament Canon" (an address to the Evangelical Theological Society in 1953) demonstrates that Luther did indeed regard at least James and Revelation as noncanonical. But Luther's artificial external criterion ("was Christum treibet"), while understandable within his historical context, is certainly insufficient.

The Origins of the Synoptic Gospels

Stonehouse's last published work was *The Origins of the Synoptic Gospels,* which comprised the Payton Lectures he gave at Fuller Seminary in 1962. Though Stonehouse was earlier very reluctant to side with any particular theory of Synoptic dependence, he here, with very cautious and thorough argumentation, comes out in favor of Markan priority. His main concern, however, is not source criticism, but the historical reliability and theological integrity of the apostolic tradition contained in the Gospels. In some ways Stonehouse's last book displays substantial awareness of the difference between modern historical expectations and the history in the Gospels. But, unlike many New Testament scholars, Stonehouse was always insistent that the theological purpose of the authors be defined on the basis of what is actually observable in the text.

In this regard it is interesting to note Stonehouse's critique of the thesis of Harald Riesenfeld. Riesenfeld had argued that the material of the Gospels is "the words and deeds of Jesus," and that these words and deeds, like those of other Jewish rabbis, were preserved in a fixed oral tradition. This would seem to support the notion of a historically reliable tradition. Stonehouse argues, however, that Riesenfeld's thesis simply does not fit with the Gospels as we have them. Considerable freedom, not fixity, characterizes the transmission of material; and the Gospels are not simply "the words and deeds of Jesus," but proclamations of the coming of God's reign, as inaugurated not just by Jesus' "words and deeds," but by his very presence, and especially by his passion and resurrection.[12]

11. The ensuing disagreement on this subject led to Stonehouse's involvement in the "Peniel" controversy over the place of Spirit baptism and the "sign" gifts in the present-day church, a debate that in somewhat different form is still going on today.

12. Stonehouse, *Witness of Luke,* twice refers positively to Martin Kähler's characterization of the Gospels as "passion narratives with extensive introductions" (pp. 72, 144).

Reviews

Among the many reviews Stonehouse wrote over the course of his teaching career, especially revealing are his reactions to the new developments in redaction criticism and the renewed interest that German circles showed in the historical Jesus. In 1961 he reviewed for the *Westminster Theological Journal* both Günther Bornkamm's *Jesus of Nazareth* and Hans Conzelmann's groundbreaking work *The Theology of St. Luke.*[13]

Bornkamm, Stonehouse observed, was trying desperately to restore some kind of connection between the Christ of faith and the Jesus of history, but was singularly unsuccessful because he still held to Bultmann's assumption that most of the material about Jesus is the creation of the church. Stonehouse summed up the problem well: "If so little as the emphasis upon the creative work of the community allows can be said concerning Jesus, how can so much [as Bornkamm wants to say] be said? And if so much, why not much more? These questions seem to be unanswerable for one like Bornkamm, and the ultimate reason why this is so is that his theological presuppositions are so much at variance with those of the history he is seeking to understand."

Since Stonehouse himself had identified Luke as an evangelist, not a biographer, one might expect more common ground with Conzelmann. And indeed, Stonehouse begins his review with a commendation of Conzelmann for his fresh examination of the text of Luke as we have it, as over against the piecemeal form-critical analysis that was de rigueur in the mid-twentieth century, and for his interest in Luke as a theologian. But in fact the presuppositions and operating framework of Conzelmann are, like those of Bornkamm, so far removed from those of the text itself that most of Stonehouse's review is sharply critical. In particular Stonehouse shows by several examples that Conzelmann's central thesis, that Luke modified the eschatological expectation of the early church to accommodate the delay of the parousia, is simply unsupportable from the text, unless one presupposes that the early church expected an almost immediate end of the world following Christ's resurrection, and that the church after A.D. 70 was in fact disturbed by the delay. Neither of these assumptions can be demonstrated from early sources, inside or outside the canon. Thus, although in his own *Witness of Luke to Christ* Stonehouse is quite conscious of Luke's interest in redemptive history, he is compelled to firmly reject Conzelmann's construction of how Luke developed that interest.

No glance at Stonehouse's life and work would be even marginally adequate if it failed to mention one other passion of Stonehouse—baseball. Stoney was both a fan and an active participant. Some thirty times a summer he would take his children and friends to the old Connie Mack Stadium in

13. Ned B. Stonehouse, review of *Jesus of Nazareth*, by Günther Bornkamm, *Westminster Theological Journal* 23.2 (May 1961): 181–87; idem, review of *The Theology of St. Luke*, by Hans Conzelmann, *Westminster Theological Journal* 24.1 (Nov. 1961): 65–70.

North Philadelphia to watch the Phillies. He was quick to take the children of his friends to the local ballpark for some batting and catching practice. And until his heart began to weaken him severely, the seminary's annual softball game pitting faculty against students could always count on Stoney being there to lead the faculty to victory.

But Stonehouse is best remembered as an evangelical scholar who always remained deeply committed to the Reformed confessions, yet also pursued with enormous integrity every question regarding the text of the New Testament. It was precisely his vigorous confidence in God's sovereignty and the integrity of the Bible as the very Word of God that made possible a rigorous and fearless pursuit of understanding what the Bible actually says. Stonehouse was always fully abreast of developments in New Testament, and was willing both to learn from and to intellectually engage the most critical scholars, yet he never did so with rancor or obloquy. As a result, he made progress when other evangelical scholars were either in denial or floundering. Few scholars would be better able to say with Paul, "Be imitators of me, as I am of Christ" (1 Cor. 11:1 RSV).

Primary Sources

Stonehouse, Ned B. *The Apocalypse in the Ancient Church.* Goes, The Netherlands: Oosterbaan and Le Cointre, 1929.

———. *J. Gresham Machen: A Biographical Memoir.* Grand Rapids: Eerdmans, 1954.

———. *The Origins of the Synoptic Gospels: Some Basic Questions.* Grand Rapids: Eerdmans, 1963.

———. *Paul before the Areopagus, and Other New Testament Studies.* Grand Rapids: Eerdmans, 1957.

———. *The Witness of Luke to Christ.* Grand Rapids: Eerdmans, 1951.

———. *The Witness of Matthew and Mark to Christ.* Philadelphia: Presbyterian Guardian, 1944.

Secondary Sources

Lane, William L. Foreword to *The Origins of the Synoptic Gospels: Some Basic Questions,* by Ned B. Stonehouse, v–vii. Grand Rapids: Baker, 1979 reprint.

———. Foreword to *The Witness of the Synoptic Gospels to Christ,* by Ned B. Stonehouse, v–viii. Grand Rapids: Baker, 1979 reprint.

"Ned Bernard Stonehouse." *Presbyterian Guardian* 31.11 (Dec. 1962): 167–68.

Silva, Moisés. "Ned Stonehouse and Redaction Criticism." *Westminster Theological Journal* 40.1 (Fall 1977): 77–88, and 40.2 (Spring 1978): 281–303.

Edward Musgrave Blaiklock

David G. Stewart

Life

The Early Years (1903–19)

Most people, having largely forgotten their childhood, are unconscious of
its deep influences upon their later development. Not so with Ted Blaiklock.
In autobiographical works he shares vivid memories of leaving his Birming-
ham (England) birthplace at the age of five for the beckoning land of promise
on the other side of the globe, of the wearisome two months of travel by
steamer (including desperate seasickness during the last few days across the
Tasman Sea from Sydney to Auckland), and the struggles of his parents to
establish a new life in the valley just under Titirangi, which is on the outskirts
of Auckland.[1]

It was a romantic but lonely boyhood for young Ted on the thirty acres
of unproductive clay which his father Edward, with visions of a great estate
and a self-supporting farm, bought in October 1910. The elder Blaiklock
built a house with second-hand timber and other materials brought out from
demolition sites by horse and cart every weekend and holiday. The father
was intrepid, always brimming over with optimism, and skilful with his
hands (an attribute young Ted did not share). The scrub, the trees, the few
farm animals enthralled the solitary child (his only brother Jack was born
when Ted was fourteen). Of special fascination was the creek that sprang
out of swampland and gurgled through the gully. He explored it to its
source, where he discovered to his delight that it divided around a small
wooded knoll. On this knoll he built a wigwam—a secret hideaway which
he never revealed to anyone, but to which he retired whenever he suffered
disappointment or hurt. It was destroyed, together with five acres of the
farm, by a fire early in 1914.

A prized possession the elder Blaiklock had brought from England was an
oak bookcase, with a small but select library of English classics from which
he would read aloud to his family every evening. This developed in young Ted

---

1. E. M. Blaiklock, *Ten Pounds an Acre* (Wellington: Reed, 1965); idem, *Between the Valley and
the Sea* (N.p.: Dunmore, 1979).

a love for reading and a delight in language, which were fostered through his primary school days and at Auckland Grammar School, which he entered on a national junior scholarship. Here he threw himself into his studies, his special delight being English language and literature. He also learned French and Latin, and decided to study Greek for himself. Here also he began to read the Bible, not for its spiritual meaning, but as a sample of great literature. Early in his three years at Auckland Grammar, he decided to become a doctor, but increasing family financial difficulties forced him to leave school a year early, and become a "pupil-teacher" in training for primary school teaching. In the same year, 1919, his parents in despair sold the farm they had all loved so much, and went to live in a rented cottage.

The Awakening Years (1920–32)

After a year as a pupil-teacher, Blaiklock was accepted at a teachers college. During his training period he heard an evangelistic message of Joseph Kemp, the recently appointed minister of Auckland Baptist Tabernacle, and sensed for the first time that God is more than an abstract intelligence behind creation. The next day he committed his life to God in a simple prayer. His conviction brought contentment and deepened throughout the rest of his life. Long after, he wrote of that experience, "That year I found Christ."[2]

After his teacher training, Blaiklock continued study in Latin, hoping eventually to earn an M.A. and an appointment at his old school, Auckland Grammar. To that end he studied for a year with his parents in England. In 1925 he was appointed teacher of senior French and Latin at Mount Albert Grammar School; while in that post he continued with his university studies part-time, winning first-class honors in both Latin and French in 1925, and a second master's degree in Latin in 1926.

At the end of 1926, encouraged by his close friend and mentor, Professor A. C. Paterson, Blaiklock applied for a position as lecturer in classics at Auckland University. This appointment changed the shape of his career. Blaiklock left secondary school teaching and became, for the rest of his life, university don par excellence.

In the mid-1920s two other people played vital roles in forming Blaiklock's future. First was Kathleen Mitchell, younger sister of his close chum Cliff. Kathleen and Ted were drawn to each other as early as 1923, and in December 1925 Ted made the most expensive single purchase of his life—an engagement ring with three large diamonds. However, it was not until November 13, 1928, that they were married in the Baptist Tabernacle. In Ted's view the ideal woman lived to support and care for husband and home. And Kath, a very capable, discerning, thoughtful woman, gave herself totally to that role. She slipped into the background throughout their life together. Though often unnoticed, she was always the loving, caring confidante with

2. E. M. Blaiklock, *Why I Am Still a Christian* (Grand Rapids: Zondervan, 1971), 12.

whom Ted would share every hurt and every distress, especially in the turbulent years of the thirties and forties. She held the home and family (which included two sons, Peter and David) together. When she died of a brain tumor
after forty-nine years of a beautiful marriage, Ted was inconsolable.[3]

The second major influence in the mid-1920s was Joseph Kemp. Blaiklock
joined the Baptist Tabernacle, and drank deeply from the strong, clear teaching of his spiritual mentor. On occasion Kemp asked the young university
lecturer to preach in his place; and when Kemp was on leave in 1932, it was
Blaiklock who occupied his pulpit. Blaiklock delighted in these opportunities
for preaching, passing on to others what he was finding for himself in the integration of faith and knowledge. Kemp also asked Blaiklock to teach New
Testament Greek at the Bible Training Institute, the college which Kemp had
founded in 1922. Blaiklock valued immensely his connection with this
school, which would later be called the Bible College of New Zealand. He
lectured on John's Gospel for more than thirty years, and also served on the
board of the Bible college from 1939 on, including ten years as its president
(1965–75).

Professor Paterson gave young Blaiklock every opportunity and encouragement during the six years they worked together. When the university
council refused Paterson's request for an additional instructor during his sabbatical year (1931), Blaiklock offered to cover all of the professor's classes as
well as his own; the offer was gratefully accepted. Blaiklock worked exceedingly hard as head of the department that year, and both he and Paterson
were delighted that at its end their students won the nationwide scholarship
competition in both Greek and Latin.

It was no secret that Paterson was grooming Blaiklock to succeed him
when he retired. As a preliminary step, in November 1932 he urged the university council to elevate Blaiklock to associate professor, with special responsibility for Greek. Tragically, while a committee of four was deliberating
the request, Paterson collapsed; he died on February 13, 1933. Blaiklock was
asked to direct the department for a year, until the council could make a permanent appointment. When the chair was advertised, Blaiklock was a confident applicant. But owing to the convolutions of university politics, the chair
was instead awarded to a Scotsman, Charles Cooper, a man a few months
younger than Blaiklock, with very similar credentials, and considerably less
experience. It was a bitter pill for Blaiklock to swallow.

To compound the distressing situation, in 1933 Blaiklock lost not only his
academic mentor, but his spiritual mentor as well. In February, the very
month in which Paterson died, Kemp suffered a complete breakdown; he lay
helpless for six months until he died. The remaining fifty years of Blaiklock's
life would prove to be an eminent realization of the convictions of those two
men, the one academic and the other theological.

---

3. For Blaiklock's poignant memories and awful sense of loss see his *Kathleen: A Record of a Sorrow* (London: Hodder and Stoughton, 1979).

The Dark Years (1933–47)

One may say that the fourteen years that followed Cooper's appointment were a black period in Blaiklock's life. In the university that certainly was true. The two men could not stand each other, and it is clear that both could be petty and malicious in their animosity. The department as a whole was an unhappy place until Cooper resigned and Blaiklock was appointed to the chairmanship in 1948, a position which he graced for twenty-one years. And yet those dark years, when Blaiklock could never rise above his bitter disappointment, proved to be years which God used to develop the classics lecturer and direct him into new paths.

With his lightened load of responsibility, Blaiklock was able to pursue his own interests much more. In 1934 he studied with great appreciation the five volumes of *The Expositor's Greek Testament.* He also gave time to his personal study of all thirty-five surviving tragedies in classical Greek, seeking to discover a unity and development leading up to the last of the three great Attic tragedians, Euripides. He produced an outstanding thesis, "The Male Characters of Euripides," which earned him a doctorate in literature (Litt.D.) in September 1945. In the meantime the university council had become so concerned over the differences between Cooper and Blaiklock that in 1938 they made Blaiklock directly responsible to them for the Greek program, and Cooper for the Latin. In 1941 the council officially separated the classics department into two sections, reintegrating them again only after Blaiklock's appointment to the chairmanship. Between 1940 and 1946, four of Blaiklock's students became Rhodes scholars.

An absorbing discovery of Blaiklock in the late 1930s was Arnold Toynbee's *Study of History.* He reveled in Toynbee's volumes, and accepted totally his thesis that history consists essentially in the rise and fall of independent societies and civilizations. Toynbee was to influence Blaiklock's approach to history the rest of his life.

To complement his love of ancient history, Blaiklock also developed an avid interest in archeology. Though he himself was never involved directly in on-site digs, he read everything he could lay his hands on about the discoveries of archeologists, particularly those which related to the Scriptures. The fruit of this lifelong interest is shared in many of his books, and specifically in *The Archaeology of the New Testament* and *The New International Dictionary of Biblical Archaeology.* In addition Blaiklock served as the archeology editor for Zondervan's five-volume *Pictorial Encyclopedia of the Bible.*

These were also the years when Blaiklock discovered and used his talent in journalism. In 1933 he began to write reviews of new books on classical subjects for the *New Zealand Herald.* Soon after that, he was asked to write regular editorials for the Saturday newspaper. In 1941 the editor of the *Weekly News* asked him to write a regular column "on whatever a classical scholar may have in mind"! Choosing the pen name Grammaticus, Blaiklock published weekly articles for the *News* and, after the *News* ceased publication, for the *New Zealand Herald* for over forty years without ever missing a week. His articles covered a wide range of subjects. Sometimes they were historical, sometimes topical. Often they would touch on biblical material, and his personal faith would shine through. At times his articles were whimsical, sometimes irascible. But whatever the theme, they were always written in impeccable English.[4]

Another benefit of those dark years was the development of family life. Blaiklock had time to give to his two boys, Peter and David, and many weekends would see the family travel out by train to New Lynn Station, and walk up the valley past the farm where Ted had grown up. On the ridge of Mount Atkinson they would enjoy a picnic lunch together and the view at their feet of both harbors that wash the isthmus on which Auckland is built. In October 1945 the Blaiklocks made their home in the area, at 47 Koromiko Road, Titirangi. The house was built on a steep slope a little below Mount Atkinson. It had a large window at which one could lounge of an evening and look down on the twinkling lights of the city. Ted loved the house, and grew to love the Waitakere Range spreading out to the west past Huia and down to the blacksand Whatipu Beach on the Tasman. Ted and the boys, now in their teenage years, explored the bypaths and the bush, sometimes staying overnight in the old Whatipu Fishing Lodge. Ted became an expert on the trees of the area, as is reflected in many of his Grammaticus articles, and especially in *Hills of Home* and *A Love of Trees*.[5]

Professor of Classics (1948–68)

Blaiklock's twenty-one years in the chairmanship were the happiest and most fulfilling in his life. Under him the classics department was a united, hard-working, harmonious place. Students revered their professor, but were never familiar with him. Blaiklock was, in fact, an austere figure, thoughtful, positive and encouraging to students, and yet somewhat aloof and distant. This was illustrated at the morning teas which he scheduled every Thursday at 10 A.M. in Room 004 for senior students and staff. The students would prepare tea and biscuits, then one by one the staff would arrive, the professor usually last. He would take his place in the impressive chair at the head of the table. He was always served first, and spoiled with the sweet iced biscuits that were his favorites. Yet Blaiklock cared deeply for his students, and a number of them were invited to tea at his Titirangi home. In his final year of teaching, the eight honor students formed a closed society called the Augustani. They continued to meet for a meal with the professor every year as near as possible to September 23, the birthday of the Roman Emperor Augustus. Their final meeting occurred only weeks before Blaiklock's death.

---

4. After his death a book of sixty of these articles was published under the title *The Best of Grammaticus* (Auckland: Wilson and Horton, 1984).

5. E. M. Blaiklock, *Hills of Home* (Wellington: Reed, 1966); idem, *A Love of Trees* (N.p.: Dunmore, 1982).

These were years when Blaiklock became known internationally as a biblical scholar and teacher. On his very first sabbatical, in 1951, when he went to England, he was invited to speak at the Keswick Convention, and here he made the acquaintance of Donald Grey Barnhouse and Harold Ockenga, who invited him to teach and preach in the United States. He also became known to some of the great publishing houses, such as Marshall, Morgan and Scott; Eerdmans; InterVarsity; Paternoster; Zondervan; Moody; Oliphants; and Pickering and Inglis. He never lacked a publisher for anything he wrote. And in those busy twenty-one years, he published no fewer than thirty-two books on a wide variety of topics, wrote "Daily Notes" for the worldwide Scripture Union (from 1959 to 1963), and continued to produce each week without fail an editorial for the *New Zealand Herald* and a Grammaticus article for the *Weekly News*.

The Last Phase (1969–83)

In retirement Blaiklock gave himself more and more to writing, mostly on biblical subjects, producing at least forty titles in the fifteen years left to him. He also planned occasional visits overseas, and accepted gladly invitations to lead Christian tours to the Middle East, Europe, and the United States. He and Kathleen led four such tours. After her death on February 8, 1978, Blaiklock led another three, taking his son David as tour manager.

Blaiklock's final years never abated in the constant round of preaching, teaching, traveling, and writing, even up to within a month of his death. One of his last ventures was to be *A Mind behind It All,* a series of six videos on the prologue of John's Gospel. The first was filmed in his study on Koromiko Road. Entitled "Why I Believe in God," it was vintage Blaiklock, as he developed his conviction that the Logos is the Reason which one can see behind the world. Three days later he entered the hospital for an operation on bowel cancer. The tumor was removed, but the cancer had spread into the liver, and he knew he had only a few months to live. He decided not to limit himself to John's prologue, but to range over the Gospel. The second video, "Why I Am Not Afraid to Die," was of like standard, with added poignancy because for him death was near. He struggled on to film three more, but it has to be admitted that they were not up to the standard of the first two. On October 26, 1983, lying in Kathleen's bed and lovingly cared for by family members, he breathed his last.

Blaiklock's Legacy

Edward Musgrave Blaiklock was a unique man and scholar. It is fair to say he was the foremost Christian scholar that the little country of New Zealand has produced. What were the areas of strength of the man?

First and foremost, he was a master of Latin and Greek. His Greek ranged through classical Attic literature, the Septuagint Old Testament, and the Greek New Testament. This expertise was called upon in his service as revising editor for both the New International Version and the New King James Version of the Bible. In his later years he translated three devotional Christian classics that to him were particularly meaningful—Thomas à Kempis's *Imitation of Christ* (1979), Brother Lawrence's *Practice of the Presence of God* (1981), and *The Confessions of Saint Augustine* (1983).

While detailed understanding of the Greek underlies the many commentaries Blaiklock wrote, none of them goes into the detailed analysis one would expect in a thorough Greek-based commentary. They were not written for the precise study of New Testament scholars, not even his volume on 1 Peter, which was stimulated by a small senior class in Greek exegesis at the Bible College of New Zealand. Rather, his many books on the Bible were designed to interest and inform the general Christian reader, and to stimulate study of the Bible text.

A prime example is *Blaiklock's Handbook to the Bible*. It offers for each of the sixty-six books, which are treated in the order of the English Bible, some comment on author or date or theme or authenticity, but mainly a description of the contents, and usually a section on the personalities of the book (Blaiklock reveled in concise pen-portraits of people). The limited scope of the book is commented on in his preface: "The Oxford English Dictionary defines 'handbook' as . . . 'A small book or treatise such as may be held in the hand' . . .'a book containing precise information'—originally for tourists and first used thus in 1836."[6] The introduction affirms the Bible as a book inspired by God and dependable. Blaiklock also gives a geographical background and a survey of English translations. He takes a conservative but reasonable position on the authorship of individual books. For example, he dismisses as absurd the postulate that different authors wrote Genesis, a postulate built on different names for God or on variant metaphors. "Such literary surgery murders to dissect," he writes graphically.[7] Instead, Blaiklock holds that Moses collected and edited various ancient documents. Ezra is accepted as the probable author of 1 and 2 Chronicles. The large number of psalms where David's name is mentioned in the rabbinic headings that were added at least by the time of the Septuagint translation are attributed to David. The Book of Proverbs, or at least chapters 1–29, is the product of King Solomon's work of "originating, compiling and editing"; and Solomon is the unquestioned author of Ecclesiastes. Blaiklock argues that Isaiah the son of Amoz wrote the whole Book of Isaiah, chapters 40–66 during the evil reign of Manasseh. Blaiklock's presentation of issues of authorship is, perhaps, evidence not so much of traditionalism or fundamentalism, but of his teaching style: having skimmed over any possible variants, he opts for the one particular understanding which he thinks will give his reader the most precise background to help elucidate the meaning of the text.

6. E. M. Blaiklock, *Blaiklock's Handbook to the Bible* (London: Hodder and Stoughton, 1980), 7.
7. Ibid., 29.

Blaiklock's earlier work, *Commentary on the New Testament,* goes through the New Testament chapter by chapter. Mostly this is an outline of the material, frequently illuminated by brief classical, historical, or geographical illustrations. The volume would certainly help a new Christian who wants to read through the New Testament with understanding.

Some of Blaiklock's best biblical writings were short pieces that he wrote for Scripture Union. The most memorable appeared in sixteen quarterly booklets that provided a four-year course of daily readings on Bible characters and doctrines. Different writers each quarter covered a wide range of doctrines, but Blaiklock wrote all the character studies, half drawing from the Old Testament and half from the New. In 1979 Blaiklock's 736 readings were collected in one volume, *Handbook of Bible People.* While most of the readings focus on separate individuals, some deal with groups of people, such as "The Galatians" or "The Children of Light." Five discuss character types described in the Book of Proverbs. Some individuals are the topic of many readings (e.g., David is the subject of twenty-six). All the readings are skillfully arranged so that if followed consecutively, they give a chronological overview of the whole Bible.

Two particular gifts which Blaiklock possessed to a remarkable degree colored all his writing. The first was a prodigious memory. If a poem (usually in English, but occasionally Latin, Greek, French, Italian, Spanish, or German) particularly impressed him, he could, after a couple of readings, recite it perfectly (even years later). His memory of historical events, dates, and people was extraordinary. Like William Barclay's *Daily Study Bible,* Blaiklock's writings are peppered with historical illustrations. All he ever read, it seemed, was grist for his mill. When he preached or lectured, he would frequently have no script, not even brief notes. Many in the audience would think his speech was completely spontaneous, brilliantly off the cuff. In fact, it was seldom so. In the privacy of his study Blaiklock would write out his script, polish it where needed, read it over, then leave his script behind, and speak it word for word. He had, in fact, little patience with slipshod extempore preaching and teaching.

The second gift was his use of the English language. Blaiklock had the knack of choosing exactly the right word. His written and spoken language was clear, concise, polished, expressive. Regarding his periodic *Faith for Today* broadcasts, a Radio New Zealand commentator wrote: "You are the undisputed champion among our contributors at using words. Style, approach, vocabulary—each is very much your own. . . . Listeners are introduced to ideas, writings and philosophies which are new to them; but the underlying message never fails to come through." It is no surprise that in 1965 Blaiklock was appointed the University of Auckland's first public orator.

The Apologist

In the 1960s a heated controversy arose within the Presbyterian Church of New Zealand. A "new theology" was being promoted in the United States

and Great Britain. Purporting to be a faith for "man come of age," it questioned many of the basic doctrines of Christianity, particularly the deity of
Christ, his virgin birth, his miracles, and his resurrection. Professor Lloyd
Geering, the principal of the Presbyterian theological college in New
Zealand, espoused these views, and made public utterances denying the
bodily resurrection of Christ. In 1967 a group within the Presbyterian church
brought a charge of heresy against Professor Geering at their annual assembly. The charge was dismissed, but only after prolonged and heated discussion, and a large group officially dissociated themselves from Geering's
views. In the following year Geering resigned, accepting an appointment as
professor of religious studies at Victoria University in Wellington. In early
1968 Geering produced a book developing his ideas.[8] The premise of *God in
the New World* is that much of the Bible is written in mythological, pre-
scientific language, and records the thoughts and aspirations of human
minds. Science leaves no room for any objective revelation given by God.

The book spread the controversy far beyond the confines of the Presbyterian church. Hodder and Stoughton, Geering's publisher, asked Blaiklock to
write a book presenting the other side. The task being thought urgent, he was
allowed only six weeks to complete it. Accordingly, *Layman's Answer* is not
a detailed rebuttal of each of Geering's arguments. Some have thought that
it does not grapple adequately with the basic philosophical premises that
underlie Geering's thought; and indeed other authors, notably Robert
Blaikie in *"Secular Christianity" and God Who Acts*, undertook to do that
in a more leisurely way.[9] It should be kept in mind that Blaiklock's book
does not have that aim. He wanted simply to reassure ordinary Christian
people on the reasonableness of their faith, to prevent their beliefs from
being shaken by the pressures of a pseudoscientific attack.

Accomplishing its simple yet crucial purpose, *Layman's Answer* has been
a help to many people. Blaiklock's method is to focus on a number of basic
questions that Geering's book raises:

1. Is there a new world radically different from the previous world?
2. Can the "facts" of history that are presented in the Gospels be separated from the "accretions of interpretation"?
3. Is the record of the Gospels myth or history?
4. What is the nature of faith in God?
5. Do the Gospels portray the real Jesus?
6. Is prayer merely a religious exercise?
7. What is the nature of humankind and their ultimate destiny?

For each question Blaiklock cites a few quotations from *God in the New
World,* and in many cases expresses the contempt and repugnance they

8. Lloyd Geering, *God in the New World* (London: Hodder and Stoughton, 1968).
9. Robert J. Blaikie, *"Secular Christianity" and God Who Acts* (Grand Rapids: Eerdmans, 1970).

arouse in him. Then, drawing widely from many sources, he seeks to build for each question the reasoned conviction of an intelligent conservative Christian. Perhaps *Layman's Answer* is not the book to convince a total skeptic, but it is certainly a book to reassure wavering Christians that their faith in God and trust in the biblical record are rationally sustainable.

Perhaps a better sample of Blaiklock as apologist is the book he wrote with his son David, *Is It, or Isn't It? Why We Believe in the Existence of God.* The authors do not seek to prove God's existence, but to show the reasonable nature of the choice of faith. Much of the material covered is the same as that of *Layman's Answer,* but without its polemic. While the Blaiklocks do not regard the classic proofs of God's existence as logically convincing, they introduce similar concepts to show how faith can align itself with our observations of the world around us. The authors argue that faith need not abandon reason. A sound theology is like a bridge built on three piers: reason, revelation, and experience (or natural, dogmatic, and mystical theology), which jointly carry the inquiring spirit to the assurance of faith.

The authors develop in particular the classic cosmological, teleological, and anthropological arguments. The magnificent order and pattern which we observe in the world around us, and which is increasingly revealed by scientific discoveries, argues strongly for an Intelligence that began it all, and a plan behind its design. Furthermore, human society is made possible by a sense of right and wrong behind the universe, a fundamental moral law which must flow from the nature of the Creator. The plan and moral nature of the Creator are seen progressively in the pages of the Bible, and supremely in the perfection of character and the stupendous claims of Jesus Christ, claims certified by his resurrection and the remarkable development of the early church.

Another very effective little book of an apologetic type is *Jesus Christ: Man or Myth?* Here Blaiklock writes on what was for him solid ground and a lifelong emphasis. The New Testament record of the historical Jesus is shown to be unparalleled in ancient literature, especially when seen against the scant writing we have from the first century. Rudolf Bultmann's attempts to see the Gospels as clad in the language of myth, which today's reader must seek to demythologize in order to discover the truth of history, are futile. The stories of the Gospels fall into none of the categories of myth recognized by classical scholars. Rather, all four Gospels must be accepted as authentic history. As Blaiklock says, "There is only one ready explanation. Four men, under the dire compulsion of a truth which made them free, wrote of what they saw, or of what immediate and reliable eyewitnesses reported to them." Blaiklock then moves on to consider the personality of Jesus, and the implications and personal challenge of that unique historical figure.

A Positive Affirmation of Faith

Unlike some learned scholars, Blaiklock was never an academician of minutiae. His instrument was not the microscope but the telescope. He needed a broad canvas on which to paint his vivid colors. And his strength was that he could communicate the essential Christian message to ordinary people. When he was nearly eighty, he participated in a weeklong Easter mission at Trinity Grammar School in Sydney. He achieved excellent rapport with the many groups of boys to whom he spoke. On the same visit, he addressed a large gathering of senior citizens on coming to terms with old age. There were two essential words of testimony that his entire life spoke without equivocation:

1. Jesus is a wonderful Savior to whom to entrust your life. Blaiklock's lifelong commitment to Christ is clearly depicted in his personal contribution to *Why I Am Still a Christian,* a book he edited. In this symposium Blaiklock joins eleven other academics from various disciplines. He relates his encounter with Christ when he was a student, emphasizing how as a youth he made a deliberate choice: "That choice is still the core of my experience after a lifetime in scholarship, authorship, journalism, travel and public life."[10] Far from cramping his style, this choice enlarged his vision. He urges his audience to make, and then reconfirm, a similar choice. Blaiklock goes into greater detail in *Still a Christian,* where he tells of his deepening conviction throughout a long life, relating it to some of his favorite New Testament passages and, inevitably, bringing in illustrations from history and poetry.

2. The Bible is an utterly dependable, God-given guide for life. When making this statement, Blaiklock vehemently rejected the tag of "fundamentalist," just as he did "liberal." He always described himself as an informed conservative. *The Bible and I* amplifies his view of Scripture: his lifetime of discovery of the Bible led to the conclusion that the Word of God, made alive by the living Christ, is the one book which makes life, in Emile Cailliet's phrase, a "journey into light."[11] The Bible was, for Blaiklock, a practical guidebook, and he sought to share from it simple and honest answers to life's most perplexing problems.[12]

Primary Sources

Blaiklock, E. M. *Acts: The Birth of the Church.* Old Tappan, N.J.: Revell, 1980.

———. *The Answer's in the Bible.* London: Hodder and Stoughton, 1978.

———. *The Archaeology of the New Testament.* Grand Rapids: Zondervan, 1970.

———. *The Bible and I.* London: Marshall, Morgan and Scott, 1983.

———. *Blaiklock's Handbook to the Bible.* London: Hodder and Stoughton, 1980.

———. *The Century of the New Testament.* Downers Grove, Ill.: InterVarsity, 1965.

———. *Cities of the New Testament.* Westwood, N.J.: Revell, 1966.

———. *Commentary on the New Testament.* London: Hodder and Stoughton, 1977.

10. Blaiklock, *Why I Am Still a Christian,* 12.
11. E. M. Blaiklock, *The Bible and I* (London: Marshall, Morgan and Scott, 1983).
12. For Blaiklock's responses to 101 questions that thoughtful Christians ask, see *The Answer's in the Bible* (London: Hodder and Stoughton, 1978).

————. *Commentary on the Psalms*. 2 vols. London: Scripture Union, 1977.

————. *The Epistles of John*. Carlisle, Eng.: Paternoster, 1959.

————. *First Peter*. Waco: Word, 1977.

————. *From Prison in Rome: Letters to the Philippians and Philemon*. Grand Rapids: Zondervan, 1964.

————. *Handbook of Bible People*. London: Scripture Union, 1979.

————. *Jesus Christ: Man or Myth?* Nashville: Nelson, 1984.

————. *Layman's Answer*. London: Hodder and Stoughton, 1968.

————. *Mark: The Man and His Message*. Chicago: Moody, 1967.

————. *Out of the Earth: The Witness of Archaeology to the New Testament*. 2d ed. Grand Rapids: Eerdmans, 1961.

————. *The Pastoral Epistles*. Grand Rapids: Zondervan, 1972.

————. *Still a Christian*. London: Hodder and Stoughton, 1980.

————. *Understanding the New Testament: Luke and Romans*. Scripture Union Bible Study Books. Grand Rapids: Eerdmans, 1971.

————. *The Way of Excellence*. Grand Rapids: Zondervan, 1968.

————, ed. *Why I Am Still a Christian*. Grand Rapids: Zondervan, 1971.

————, ed. *Zondervan Pictorial Bible Atlas*. Grand Rapids: Zondervan, 1969.

Blaiklock, E. M., and D. A. Blaiklock. *Is It, or Isn't It? Why We Believe in the Existence of God*. Grand Rapids: Zondervan, 1968.

Blaiklock, E. M., and R. K. Harrison, eds. *New International Dictionary of Biblical Archaeology*. Grand Rapids: Zondervan, 1983.

Blaiklock, E. M.; John Stafford Wright; and Geoffrey Grogan. *Bible Characters and Doctrines*. London: Scripture Union, 1973.

Secondary Source

Shaw, Trevor. *E. M. Blaiklock: A Christian Scholar*. London: Hodder and Stoughton, 1986.

Merrill Chapin Tenney

Walter A. Elwell

Merrill Chapin Tenney was born into a Christian family on April 16, 1904, in Chelsea, Massachusetts, a suburb of Boston. From his earliest days he was taken to church, taught the Scriptures, and trained in conservative Christian theology. His father, Wallace Fay Tenney, expected great things from young Merrill and required the very best of him. The elder Tenney was manager of the religious book department at Goodspeed's Bookstore in Boston and sometimes virtually buried young Merrill in books; it was great fun, but it also had the desired effect. Merrill grew up loving books; indeed, the passion he had for the learning they represented was as deep as the passion so many of his contemporaries had for sports. His love of books very soon included a love of languages, and the pattern of his life was set.

Tenney dated his conversion to a youthful experience in a tent revival meeting. It took deep root, and subsequently he never doubted its reality or the reality of the call of God into his service. Throughout his life Tenney never showed much emotion, adopting a rather formal and somewhat distant stance; he even addressed his wife as Mrs. Tenney and everyone else by surname. But when conversion or calling was under discussion, or a personal testimony was being given, his deepest feelings surfaced; here lay the core of his being.

An early interest in the mission field, in particular, Africa, caused Tenney to enrol in the Missionary Training Institute in Nyack, New York, upon graduation from Needham High School in 1922. He received his diploma in 1924 and enrolled in Gordon College of Theology and Missions back in Boston, where he received a Th.B. in 1927.

Those Gordon College years were important for Tenney. Young as he was, he accepted a pastorate at Storrs Avenue Baptist Church in Braintree, Massachusetts (where he served from 1926 to 1928). At the same time he distinguished himself in Greek to the extent that when the Greek professor became ill, Tenney taught the Greek classes, even though he was still a senior student. This combination of pastoral ministering to laypeople and academic thinking became the essence of the man. He would never venture too far into the world of technical scholarship; that was too far removed from people and their needs. He would always seek a way to translate the complexities of academic thought into terms that anyone could understand.

In 1928 Tenney began teaching at Gordon College as an instructor in Greek, was ordained in June at the First Baptist Church of Needham, and started graduate work at Boston University under Edgar Sheffield Brightman. He received his M.A. in 1930, his thesis being entitled "Plato as a Theist." The first half of the thesis was a careful literary and historical analysis that set the stage for the complicated question of Plato's definition of God. Tenney drew twelve conclusions, two of which should be mentioned. First, Plato's idea of God was ambiguous (not exactly henotheistic nor monotheistic; not quite equivalent to the Idea of the Good, but not unrelated to it; not explicitly personal, but not impersonal). Second, "this belief in theism made Nature a revelation of God, regarded the ultimate reality as good, and opened the way for personalism."[1] Tenney never embraced Brightman's brand of personalism, but he did see the need that gave it rise, and thus he never tired of stressing the need for a personal relationship with God in Christ.

In 1930 Tenney was advanced to assistant professor at Gordon College (a position he held until 1936), and that year married his former Greek professor's daughter, Helen Jaderquist. Helen was herself a graduate of Gordon College (B.A., B.D.), as well as of Wheaton College, Illinois (B.A.), and Northwestern University (M.A.). She was an immensely talented individual and collaborated with her husband on some of his major projects, notably *The Zondervan Pictorial Encyclopedia of the Bible.* On August 18, 1933, a son was born to the Tenneys and named John after his grandfather, the Greek professor at Gordon. On July 19, 1935, just a month short of his second birthday young John was killed in an auto accident at the Rumney Campgrounds, where he was buried. Tenney's faith was not shaken by this tragedy, but he always held himself responsible for what happened. The Tenneys had no more children, but adopted two sons later on.

In 1935 Tenney enrolled at Harvard University, where he studied under Henry J. Cadbury. He combined his studies with both his teaching chores at Gordon, where in 1936 he was made full professor of New Testament and Greek, and an interim pastorate at the Blaney Memorial Baptist Church in Dorchester, Massachusetts (1938–39). He took classes between 1935 and 1940, and received his Ph.D. in biblical and patristic Greek in 1944. His dissertation was on the text of Tertullian.

Tenney accepted a visiting professorship of Bible and theology at Wheaton College in the summers of 1941 and 1942, and was persuaded to take a full-time position there as associate professor in the fall of 1943. In keeping with his desire to combine pastoral and academic work, he accepted the pastorate of the United Gospel Tabernacle in Wheaton (1943–49). In 1945 he was made a full professor at the college.

Tenney always looked back upon his Gordon years with great fondness. It was there that he matured into an excellent teacher and scholar. But he had

---

1. Merrill C. Tenney, "Plato as a Theist" (M.A. thesis, Boston University, 1930), 82–83.

also weathered the storms of graduate training and early married life and made those fundamental decisions as to what one should become. He wanted to serve the people of God by combining academic work with practical application suited to the needs of inquiring laity. He wanted to give scholarship a human face, and it was this that he brought to Wheaton College in 1943.

Early Writings and a Methodical Approach

By 1945 Tenney had embarked on his writing career with the publication of his first book, *Resurrection Realities*. The chief reason for writing the book was "the general neglect of [the] subject even among evangelical believers."[2] He proceeds in vigorous fashion to expound the fundamental doctrine of the "Resurrection Fact" (ch. 1). Though he is well aware of the discrepancies in the Gospel accounts, he argues that they do not invalidate the fact itself.[3] To bolster his argument, he tangentially includes scholarly sources, such as F. J. Foakes-Jackson, an ultraliberal New Testament scholar.[4] But the purpose of the book is not a detailed analysis of the New Testament documents, nor a scholarly study of current opinion, but a challenge to the church to live its life in resurrection reality. The interests of the average person were ever before Tenney's eyes.

The next three years were spent writing *John: The Gospel of Belief*, subtitled *An Analytic Study of the Text*. Tenney had been struggling in his own mind as to how best to move biblical studies away from opinions about the Bible—scholars' theories—back to the Bible itself. He went so far as to say that the study of scholarly opinions constituted a "real peril."[5] This comment reveals one of Tenney's distinctive features. Although a scholar himself, he never paraded that fact and, indeed, seemed to mistrust scholars as a whole. Thus he only rarely quoted other writers and often brushed off their concerns in the interest of the average person. Typical was his approach in the writing of *John*: "Critical questions of authorship, integrity, genuineness, sequence of text, historical value of the narrative, etc., will not be treated extensively in this volume, since the casual reader is not usually interested in technical minutiae. . . . The chief purpose of this book is to treat analytically the existing structure of *John* rather than produce a critical introduction to it."[6] Tenney was convinced that the text will interpret itself, that the average person can understand it, that the distance from the past is not so great as to create any insuperable problems, that our current English translations adequately convey the meaning of the original, and that technical scholarship often stands in the way of finding that "key to self-interpretation which

2. Merrill C. Tenney, *Resurrection Realities* (Los Angeles: Bible House of Los Angeles, 1945), 7.
3. Ibid., 14–16.
4. Ibid., 21.
5. Merrill C. Tenney, *John: The Gospel of Belief. An Analytic Study of the Text* (Grand Rapids: Eerdmans, 1948), 21.
6. Ibid., 23–24.

would enable the casual recipient to benefit by its truth."[7] That golden key to understanding will not come from endless hours of academic study, but from the *text itself;* it lies buried in the literary structure of the book, and an "analytic study based on the natural structure of the book is most likely to reveal the author's intention in writing."[8] So the author's stated purpose in writing the book (as found, e.g., in John 20:31), an analysis of the literary structure that embodies that purpose, and a consecutive examination of the component parts of the book will best explain what the book is all about. Tenney declares that "this method is applicable to almost any book of the Bible; and if the reader will master and use it, he will be able to uncover new and startling treasures in the Book of God."[9]

Tenney refined this approach to Scripture rather dramatically in his *Galatians: The Charter of Christian Liberty* (1950), where he made use of ten methods, namely, the synthetic, the critical, the biographical, the historical, the theological, the rhetorical, the topical, the analytical, the comparative, and the devotional. By 1955 Tenney had begun backing off this overly elaborate scheme. In *Philippians: The Gospel at Work* he was simply trying "to translate the teaching of Philippians into the terms of the Pauline gospel as that gospel was applied to the contemporary world."[10] And then in *Interpreting Revelation* (1957) and *The Book of Revelation* (1963) Tenney, who was a "premillenarian and moderate futurist,"[11] attempted to adapt and bring his "methodical" approach to bear on the most difficult book of the New Testament, the Apocalypse. He was able to develop a "chronological approach" and an "eschatological method,"[12] but reverted to more traditional topical, linguistic, and hermeneutical analyses for most of Revelation. After that, he never used his methodical approach again, in all probability because it was not as adaptable as he originally thought it was, but also because his interests had turned elsewhere, to meet what he perceived to be more pressing needs in the evangelical world.

A Foray into Critical Scholarship

In the midst of all this literary activity, Tenney, upon the retirement of Henry C. Thiessen, was given the additional responsibility of being the dean of Wheaton College Graduate School. In those days deans were expected to maintain a full teaching schedule along with their administrative work; shouldering those duties in addition to preaching and writing reminds us of Genesis 6:4 about the giants who were on the earth. He held this post for

7. Ibid., 22.
8. Ibid., 23.
9. Ibid.
10. Merrill C. Tenney, *Philippians: The Gospel at Work* (Grand Rapids: Eerdmans, 1955), 7.
11. Merrill C. Tenney, *Interpreting Revelation* (Grand Rapids: Eerdmans, 1957), vii–viii.
12. Ibid., 135–67 (chs. 13–14).

twenty-four years, from 1947 until 1971, when he returned full-time to the classroom that he loved.

In 1951 Tenney was elected the second president of the fledgling Evangelical Theological Society and delivered the fifth annual midyear lectures at Western Conservative Baptist Theological Seminary (Portland, Ore.). He chose to speak on "The Genius of the Gospels," and the lectures were published that same year. These lectures represented Tenney's first (and virtually only) foray into the world of critical scholarship. He had hoped to bring some of his academic work to bear on the practical homiletical needs of the church by resolving some of the "mechanical problems of the Gospels without ignoring the spiritual dynamic which makes them unique."[13] He nowhere explicitly says so, but he based his ideas primarily upon the form criticism of Martin Dibelius's *From Tradition to Gospel* (although Tenney himself never became a form critic).[14] He argued that the Gospels represent the basic preaching of the early Christians. He little realized that an unfortunate controversy would arise because of a misunderstanding of what he was trying to do, but the consequence was that he would never again stray very far from views easily identified as conservative.

A little background will be helpful. In 1950 conservative New Testament scholarship was very limited in America, and what did exist was typically quite insular. Those whose names were to dominate the evangelical scene—George Eldon Ladd, E. Earle Ellis, Everett Harrison, Robert H. Mounce, John Walvoord, A. Berkeley Mickelsen, and William Hendriksen, to name just a few—had not even begun (or had just barely begun) their writing careers; Ned Stonehouse had written only *The Witness of Matthew and Mark to Christ* (1944); Fuller Seminary was a scant three years old, Gordon-Conwell Seminary did not yet exist, and Dallas Theological Seminary, Westminster Seminary, and even Tenney's own Wheaton College Graduate School of Theology were barely twenty-five years old or less. Carl F. H. Henry's *Uneasy Conscience of Modern Fundamentalism* was newly stirring up the waters of conservative theology, and Harold John Ockenga had recently proclaimed the need for a "new evangelicalism," hoping to revitalize what he perceived to be a moribund fundamentalism. The unfortunate and sometimes acrimonious fundamentalist-neoevangelical squabble was just beginning.

Wheaton College itself at that time was quite fundamentalistic, and even John R. Rice was on good terms with it. In fact, he had moved to Wheaton so his daughters could go to school there while he published his *Sword of the Lord* magazine and pastored the Calvary Baptist Church. V. Raymond Edman, president of Wheaton College at the time, worked closely with Rice, serving on one of his boards and writing for his magazine, and there was mutual esteem between them.

13. Merrill C. Tenney, *The Genius of the Gospels* (Grand Rapids: Eerdmans, 1951), 10.
14. Ibid., 39 n. 21.

It was into this situation that *The Genius of the Gospels* landed. Rice wrote and hastily sent to Edman a massive forty-eight-page review demanding that Tenney retract what he said and stop the book's publication (Rice had seen an advance copy). A three-hour meeting involving Rice, Tenney, and William Eerdmans, the publisher, failed to resolve the issue to Rice's satisfaction, so he determined to go public with it in the *Sword of the Lord* and later in a book entitled *Our God-Breathed Book—The Bible* (1969). At the meeting Tenney did agree, should a second edition appear (it did not), to rewrite the preface to state more forcefully his commitment to the full inspiration of Scripture.

Rice's criticisms were basically five. First, he felt the book was too one-sided, giving almost all its attention to the human element, while neglecting the divine side of Scripture. Rice does acknowledge that on page 41 Tenney affirms his faith in plenary inspiration, but the overemphasis on the human authors gives the wrong impression. Second, "the book teaches that the Gospels grew out of conscious human need, and that the materials were used regularly as evangelistic preaching material before they were written down in the Gospels." Rice continues with the essence of his complaint: "I do not believe, as Dr. Tenney thinks, that the Gospels 'codify the "tradition" which was uniformly believed.' I do not believe that they were drawn from 'the testimony of eyewitnesses.' I believe that is very seriously wrong. The Bible does not claim to be written by men who made investigation, who talked to witnesses, who searched for documentary proof. Rather, the Bible claims to be written by men who spoke as they were moved by the Holy Ghost. The Bible does not claim to be simply nor primarily the report of eyewitnesses, but it claims to be breathed of God."[15] Third, Tenney believes that the Gospel writers selected, copied, edited, and organized their material according to their own designs, whereas in reality "the Spirit of God selected the material."[16] Fourth, Tenney (and virtually everyone else) mistranslates the *anōthen* of Luke 1:3 as "from the very first." It really means "from above." Hence Luke is saying that the source of his material is God himself, who gave it "from above," not earthly people who guarded the traditions from the beginning and passed them on to Luke.[17] Fifth, Tenney, along with others, is the victim of the trend in Christian colleges and seminaries of uncritically accepting liberal theories, such as the two-document theory (Matthew and Luke had two sources: Mark and Q). The verbal similarities that exist among the Synoptics are not the result of their copying one another, but come from God himself. "Could not God give his own very words through the three men and follow the same correct outline?"[18]

15. John R. Rice, *Sword of the Lord* 14.9 (Feb. 15, 1952): 2.
16. Ibid.
17. Ibid., 4; Rice would later return to this criticism in *Our God-Breathed Book—The Bible* (Murfreesboro, Tenn.: Sword of the Lord, 1969), 161–63.
18. Rice, *Our God-Breathed Book*, 138.

The heart of this conflict was over the nature of the Bible's inspiration. For Rice, who was virtually a "dictationist," the matter was a simple either/or. Either God wrote the Bible or human beings did; it could not be both. Anyone who disagreed was either naively or purposely adopting a modernistic view. Tenney saw the issue otherwise. There was no reason why God could not have made use of human instruments, allowing them their full freedom as writers, and at the same time so guided them that they would be preserved from error. It was not a question of either/or, but of both/and. Those who approached the Scripture this way were not being modernistic, but were being true to the Scripture itself, which is God's word in human language.

In retrospect, this conflict had several ramifications. First, it was the beginning of what was later to flare up in much more vitriolic fashion when Harold Lindsell, a Wheaton College trustee, wrote his *Battle for the Bible* (1976). In it he singles out for condemnation many of those who followed in Tenney's footsteps (but not Tenney himself) as having gone too far with their critical studies and ending up by denying the full inspiration of the Bible. Second, it became part of a larger separation between the more fundamentalistic and the more neoevangelical conservatives. Their differences centered on the nature of the Bible, but went far beyond that, including matters of lifestyle, relation to the world, and cooperation with those whose views differed. Third, it raised the issue of to what degree evangelicals could or should use the methods of critical biblical scholarship. Should it be rejected entirely, or could some of it be made use of while one continued to hold on to Christian belief? Here it must be said that some of Rice's concerns turned out to be prophetic. Over the course of the next generation many who started out as believing critics would end up simply as critics. An original faith in the verbal inspiration of the Bible would gradually be eroded by the relentless pressures of negative criticism.

For Tenney personally it was most disheartening that his orthodoxy and commitment to verbal inspiration should be questioned. They had never been in doubt even during his Boston University and Harvard days, and to ensure that they would never be questioned again, he turned away from attempts to bring essentially secular methods of Bible study into his evangelical endeavors. He renewed his commitment to the students and laypeople of the church and began writing specifically for them again. He did speak one final word on the subject seven years later in an essay entitled "Reversals of New Testament Criticism." The essay itself is a survey of some of the changes in thinking that had occurred in critical studies relating to the Synoptic Problem, the date of Acts, the date and authorship of the fourth Gospel, the Pastoral Epistles, and textual criticism. In most cases Tenney finds cause for encouragement in that some of the liberal thinkers were beginning to reverse themselves somewhat and move toward a more traditional position. He concludes rather optimistically: "Two things become increasingly apparent as the critical process of developing hypotheses and the consequent verification or contradiction of them continues: speculative theories and attacks upon the veracity and authenticity of the Scriptures tend to lose their support as the field of knowledge broadens, and fuller research increases the tenability of a conservative attitude in Biblical studies. Time is on the side of the believer who has confidence in the eternal truth of God revealed in the Scriptures."[19] Tenney could maintain this optimism only by selecting from the evidence. It is noteworthy that in a survey of contemporary New Testament scholarship Frederick C. Grant, Rudolf Bultmann, C. H. Dodd, Ernst Käsemann, Günther Bornkamm, and Oscar Cullmann, to name just a few, go unnoticed. New Testament scholarship was, in fact, moving in a decidedly leftward direction, and to this day critical scholarship is largely unrepentant of its negative and minimalist approach to the Scriptures.

Whatever the fashion of the day, however, Tenney's faith in Scripture was not dependent upon it. Ten years later he would write that in an era of relativism and skepticism "the divine origin and authority of the Holy Scriptures as the Word of God to men, revealed to and through His prophets and apostles," must be the source of evangelical confidence.[20] Tenney's confidence that modern critical scholarship would sooner or later move closer to the traditional view gradually disappeared, and before his death he acknowledged that what he had hoped had never really happened. Yet he continued to declare that we must build upon the solid foundation of Scripture, not upon the shifting sands of current opinion. Whether humans see it or not, the truth of God remains.

Textbooks and Reference Works

After the conflict of 1951, Tenney rethought how he wanted to invest his time and settled upon providing basic textbooks and reference works that embodied the evangelical perspective. This was no hasty decision. As a teacher he knew the power that textbooks and reference works have in the development and continuing education of people. That the evangelical point of view was underrepresented struck him with great force.

Providing those textbooks took concrete shape in 1953 with the publication of *The New Testament: An Historical and Analytical Survey*, followed in 1965 by *New Testament Times*. Tenney's immensely popular New Testament survey had as its sole aim "a general integrated approach which will increase understanding of the New Testament and a love for it."[21] As was true of almost all of his writings, "technical problems of introduction and of theology are not treated here at any length."[22] Full play is given instead to background matters—geography, history, Jewish sectarian religion. As these

19. Merrill C. Tenney, "Reversals of New Testament Criticism," in *Revelation and the Bible*, ed. Carl F. H. Henry (Grand Rapids: Baker, 1958), 367.

20. Merrill C. Tenney, preface to *The Bible—The Living Word of Revelation*, ed. Merrill C. Tenney (Grand Rapids: Zondervan, 1968), 5.

21. Merrill C. Tenney, *New Testament Survey*, rev. ed. (Grand Rapids: Eerdmans, 1961), viii.

22. Ibid.

background matters come to be understood, the message of the New Testament will become increasingly clear, but Tenney emphasized that they are only the context for the revelation of God in Christ. The revelation itself is there for anyone to see, with or without that context. As Tenney put it, "The vitality of the word of God is not dependent upon the chance similarity of two eras. Its eternal quality transcends local conditions of space, time, and society. Once the meaning of the words of Scripture is correctly understood, the words are as true today as they ever were, and they cannot be discarded as the obsolete sentiments of a vanished civilization. They still convey the living gospel of the eternal God to the thirsty souls of sinning men."[23] Tenney included a chapter on "The Gospels as Literary Works" and continued to emphasize the human element of the Gospels, although he argued from a very conservative platform. He rejected the existence of a Q document and postulated a possible personal interaction between the Synoptic writers, whom he took to be Matthew, Mark, and Luke; he also maintained the formative nature of early Christian preaching. He summarized the relationship of the Synoptics in this way: "The very differences between the writers speak of independence; the similarities reflect a common background of information, a common subject of writing, and the common inspiration of God."[24] This last point was to remove any doubt as to where Tenney stood with respect to verbal inspiration: it must be a vital part of our understanding of everything about the Bible, even its human dimension.

Two major reference works were edited by Tenney, *The Zondervan Pictorial Bible Dictionary* and the five-volume *Zondervan Pictorial Bible Encyclopedia;* they represented the beginning of a new generation of evangelical reference books. The authoritative multivolume evangelical work, *The International Standard Bible Encyclopedia* (published in 1915 and revised in 1929), was obsolescent. John D. Davis's *Dictionary of the Bible* (1898) had been revised and rewritten in a more liberal direction by Henry Snyder Gehman (1944); and *Unger's Bible Dictionary* (1957) was basically an updating of Charles Randall Barnes's *Bible Encyclopedia* (1900). All this pointed to an obvious need for a whole new generation of biblical and theological reference works for evangelicals; the meeting of this need would occupy Tenney for the remainder of his days.

The first of the new reference works was *Baker's Dictionary of Theology* (1960), to which Tenney contributed five articles ("Docetism," "Pentecost," "Persecution," "Sanhedrin," "Zealot"). J. D. Douglas's *New Bible Dictionary* (1962), published in Great Britain, was the first of the Bible dictionaries. It was followed in 1963 by the first American Bible dictionary, Tenney's own *Zondervan Pictorial Bible Dictionary*. Characteristically, Tenney started from scratch and aimed the dictionary at the "pastors, Sunday-school teachers, Bible class leaders and students who desire concise and accurate infor-

23. Ibid.
24. Ibid., 139.

mation on questions raised by ordinary reading."[25] He explains that "the function of a Bible dictionary is to render accessible a body of information which will enable [the average reader] to comprehend the meaning of the text he is reading, and to obtain ready and complete data concerning any related subject."[26] Tenney's one-volume dictionary fulfilled its stated purpose admirably. Zondervan followed in 1969 with a pictorial Bible atlas to which Tenney contributed the section entitled "The Expansion of the Church."[27]

The publication in 1962 of the multivolume *Interpreter's Dictionary of the Bible*, which came at the subject from a liberal perspective, and the inherent limitations of Tenney's one-volume work, successful though it was, pointed up "the need for a more extensive work that would deal in greater detail with the technical aspects of Biblical backgrounds and interpretation . . . for scholarly study."[28] To that end *The Zondervan Pictorial Encyclopedia of the Bible* was undertaken, a work that would occupy Tenney for over eight years, taxing his energies to the utmost. As an alternative to *The Interpreter's Dictionary of the Bible*, "the critical and theological position of this work is conservative. . . . The emphasis is that of historic Christianity. . . . [Its] conclusions are founded on a fundamental conviction of the veracity of the Biblical record."[29] Tenney's multivolume reference work quickly established itself as the premier evangelical Bible encyclopedia, soon to be joined by the equally useful revision of the *International Standard Bible Encyclopedia* (1979–88).

In 1975, the year in which the *Pictorial Encyclopedia* was published, two other notable events occurred in Tenney's life. He formally retired from teaching at Wheaton College Graduate School (although he filled in for several years after that), and he was honored by a festschrift written primarily by his former students.[30] He continued to play a vital, though diminishing role at Wheaton College until he passed away on March 18, 1985, after a long illness. He wrote during that time, but at a devotional rather than a scholastic level.[31]

In Tenney's long career as a New Testament scholar, three characteristics stood out as of most consequence. The first was his personal embodiment of those many qualities that constitute spirituality and academic attainment. He was the perfect blend of pastor and teacher. He regularly said to both colleagues and students, "I pray for you every day," but could with equal sin-

25. Merrill C. Tenney, preface to *Zondervan Pictorial Bible Dictionary,* ed. Merrill C. Tenney (Grand Rapids: Zondervan, 1963), vi.
26. Ibid., v.
27. Merrill C. Tenney, "The Expansion of the Church," in *Zondervan Pictorial Bible Atlas,* ed. E. M. Blaiklock (Grand Rapids: Zondervan, 1969), 321–49.
28. Merrill C. Tenney, preface to *Zondervan Pictorial Encyclopedia of the Bible,* ed. Merrill C. Tenney, 5 vols. (Grand Rapids: Zondervan, 1975), 1:xxiii.
29. Ibid.
30. *Current Issues in Biblical and Patristic Interpretation,* ed. Gerald F. Hawthorne (Grand Rapids: Eerdmans, 1975).
31. Merrill C. Tenney, *Roads a Christian Must Travel* (Wheaton, Ill.: Tyndale, 1979).

cerity demand better work from everyone, down to Greek accents and correct punctuation in term papers. For over forty years at Gordon and Wheaton, he encouraged and rebuked his students into being better people as well as better scholars. The worldwide service of those students is the fruit of his efforts.

Second, Tenney was unwavering in his commitment to what is really fundamental in Christianity. He was too wise to follow the latest fads; he had lived through too many of them. To him the authority of Scripture and of Christ was paramount, with the resurrection being the absolute foundation of what Christians believe. Significantly, this the deepest affirmation of his life was explicitly expressed in his first publication: "From the empty grave in Joseph's garden, the most stupendous and best-attested fact of history, comes the dynamic faith in Christ risen, which is the vital heart of Christianity and the everlasting hope of a death-ridden world."[32]

Third was Tenney's commitment to scholarship for the sake of the people. He could have written for other scholars, but he chose to feed the sheep rather than other shepherds. Many of his books are still in print and in numerous languages, still speaking the sure word of truth to yet another generation. There is a certain gentle irony in the fact that Tenney, who never sought to make a mark in this world, did so by finding a place of service rather than eminence. His service in the academic world, whether we are thinking of his books, the students whom he nurtured along the way, or his steadfastness in administrative work, *was* his eminence, and that was enough for him. F. F. Bruce summed it up nicely in the 1975 festschrift to Tenney, "To bear consistent witness to [the] Christian fact, in teaching and in writing, for so many years is a noble achievement for any man, a valuable service to render in any age. Because I appreciate so highly what Dr. Tenney has accomplished through his witness, I am glad to be associated with his pupils in paying this tribute of esteem and gratitude to him."[33]

Primary Sources

Tenney, Merrill C. *The Book of Revelation*. Proclaiming the New Testament. Grand Rapids: Baker, 1963.

———. *Galatians: The Charter of Christian Liberty*. Grand Rapids: Eerdmans, 1950.

———. *The Genius of the Gospels*. Grand Rapids: Eerdmans, 1951.

———. *Interpreting Revelation*. Grand Rapids: Eerdmans, 1957.

———. *John: The Gospel of Belief. An Analytic Study of the Text*. Grand Rapids: Eerdmans, 1948.

———. *The New Testament: An Historical and Analytical Survey*. Grand Rapids: Eerdmans, 1953; rev. ed., 1961 *(New Testament Survey)*.

———. *New Testament Times*. Grand Rapids: Eerdmans, 1965.

32. Tenney, *Resurrection Realities*, 24.
33. F. F. Bruce, introduction in *Current Issues*, ed. Hawthorne, 11.

———. *Philippians: The Gospel at Work*. Grand Rapids: Eerdmans, 1955.

———. *Resurrection Realities*. Los Angeles: Bible House of Los Angeles, 1945.

———. "Reversals of New Testament Criticism." In *Revelation and the Bible*, edited by Carl F. H. Henry, 353–67. Grand Rapids: Baker, 1958.

———, ed. *The Bible—The Living Word of Revelation*. Grand Rapids: Zondervan, 1968.

———, ed. *Zondervan Pictorial Bible Dictionary*. Grand Rapids: Zondervan, 1963.

———, ed. *Zondervan Pictorial Encyclopedia of the Bible*. 5 vols. Grand Rapids: Zondervan, 1975.

Edward Joseph Young

Allan Harmon

Though E. J. Young came from the West Coast, his theological study and teaching were to center at Westminster Theological Seminary in Philadelphia. The son of an architect, he was born in San Francisco on November 29, 1907. He came from a family with strong Christian convictions, and at the age of fifteen made a decision to study for the Presbyterian ministry. Accordingly, after taking Greek at school, he planned his college career to include Hebrew and other Semitic languages so he could specialize in Old Testament studies. As a ministerial candidate he came under the care of a presbytery during his college career and spent a fruitful summer of ministry in Nevada. After graduating cum laude from Stanford University in 1929, he traveled and studied in Europe and the Far East for two years.

On return to the United States, Young spent a year at San Francisco Seminary, but then transferred to Westminster Theological Seminary as he shared the theological standpoint of J. Gresham Machen and other faculty members there. On completion of his theological course and following his marriage in July 1935, he returned to California for examination for ordination by the California Presbytery of the Presbyterian Church in the U.S.A. He was denied ordination because of the orthodoxy of his views. He and his wife then left for Leipzig, where he studied on a fellowship, and the following spring he received an invitation to return to Westminster to teach. He responded affirmatively to this invitation and began teaching at Westminster in September 1936, and continued there until his sudden death at the age of sixty on February 14, 1968.

The impact of Young's teachers and later colleagues was clearly considerable. He recognized that his views on the Old Testament were deeply influenced by his former teacher Oswald T. Allis, but he also acknowledged the debt he owed to others, including Allan A. MacRae, Albrecht Alt, Joachim Begrich, and Karl Elliger. The reference to his teachers in Germany is apt, because he held German scholarship in high regard and believed that "the serious student cannot afford to neglect what is written in German."[1] He maintained contact by correspondence with a wide range of scholars, and had a

---

1. E. J. Young, *An Introduction to the Old Testament,* rev. ed. (Grand Rapids: Eerdmans, 1964), 13.

special friendship with H. H. Rowley of Manchester. His relationship to scholars of quite different theological convictions was exemplary. Repeatedly he commended them for their work, interacted with their positions, and, while differing fundamentally from them, treated them with courtesy and respect. It is also easy to see the influence of John Murray and Cornelius Van Til on his thought; indeed, there are many passages in his writings where he skillfully restates their positions. Moreover, because the early faculty of Westminster Theological Seminary was small and cohesive, the influence was not just one way. Young's thinking and work clearly had an influence on his colleagues as well. He stood in the Princeton/Westminster tradition; and the influence of Joseph Addison Alexander, William Henry Green,[2] B. B. Warfield, Robert Dick Wilson,[3] and Geerhardus Vos is clearly discernible in his writings. Of the Continental scholars it was probably E. W. Hengstenberg who had the greatest impact on him.

Young was ordained in the newly formed Orthodox Presbyterian Church, and was active on many of its committees. He served as moderator of the denomination's general assembly in 1956. An amateur cellist and a student of hymnody, he took a prominent part in the work which led to the publication of the Trinity Hymnal in 1961. In addition, he helped to found the Philadelphia-Montgomery Christian Academy, and was active in the work of the Evangelical Theological Society.

While most of Young's work focused on Westminster Seminary and the Orthodox Presbyterian Church, he frequently lectured in other circles. In the year before his death he spoke at a Lutheran conference in Minnesota, at Toronto Baptist Seminary, and at L'Abri Fellowship in Switzerland. He wrote popular articles on Christian subjects, many of them for the *Presbyterian Guardian*. In addition to being a prominent Old Testament scholar, he was a popularizer who wrote with cultivated simplicity.

Linguistic Studies

Young had amazing gifts as a linguist, which he developed for biblical research and teaching. Learning languages was a hobby for him; he had a knowledge of thirty and spoke seven of them. In many ways he resembled Robert Dick Wilson of Princeton and Westminster, and it was altogether fitting that he revised Wilson's *Scientific Investigation of the Old Testament*.[4] While the main text was left intact, Young added an introduction, some additional footnotes, appendices, and a glossary.

2. Young commented that "Green had been a chosen associate of Joseph Addison Alexander, and was well equipped to carry on the Old Princeton tradition of intelligent loyalty to the Bible" (ibid., 139).
3. Young referred to Wilson as "a hero of the Faith" (*Psalm 139* [London: Banner of Truth, 1965], 42).
4. Robert Dick Wilson, *A Scientific Investigation of the Old Testament*, revised by E. J. Young (Chicago: Moody, 1959).

Young's immense knowledge of ancient and, in particular, Semitic languages was displayed in his scholarly work. The footnotes to his commentary on Isaiah, for example, contain references to over twenty languages. He taught Arabic, publishing a grammar of it in 1949,[5] and maintaining a deep interest to the end of his life.[6] After years of developing his teaching of biblical Hebrew, he published privately his *Old Testament Hebrew for Beginners* (1960). His Hebrew vowel chart is testimony to his understanding of Hebrew vocalization.[7] But while he was interested in Semitic languages and their grammar in general,[8] his major concern was the elucidation of the Hebrew text of the Old Testament.

Biblical Commentaries

Subjects relating to Old Testament prophecy were clearly of great interest to Young from an early period. His first published work was entitled *Study Your Bible: A Self Study Course for Bible Believing Christians;*[9] he also wrote a workbook entitled *Old Testament Prophecy: A Course Designed for Individual Home Study.*[10]

Two major Old Testament prophetic books occupied most of Young's efforts. In 1949 his commentary on Daniel was published,[11] and he also contributed the commentary on Daniel in the *New Bible Commentary.*[12] As with his other commentaries, Young wrote on Daniel with the express intention of helping ministers and other trained Bible students, but also the average educated reader of the Scriptures. His commentary set out to give a clear exposition of the book, but also to come to grips with two viewpoints to which he was opposed. On the one hand, he dealt with the critical position which maintained that the Book of Daniel stems from the Maccabean age. To hold this position, argued Young, is to deny that Daniel is a work of predictive prophecy. On the other hand, he also contended with the dispensational position that the fulfilment of many of the prophecies of Daniel is to be found in the seven-year period after the return of Christ.

Young expressly disclaimed the intention to write on textual and philological matters, acknowledging his own indebtedness to James A. Montgomery and to H. H. Rowley. Writing on Daniel 9:24–27, he noted that his aim was

5. E. J. Young, *Arabic for Beginners* (Grand Rapids: Eerdmans, 1949).

6. See, e.g., E. J. Young, review of *A Reader in Modern Literary Arabic,* by Farhat J. Ziadeh, *Westminster Theological Journal* 27.2 (May 1965): 164–66.

7. The chart appears in E. J. Young, *The Book of Isaiah,* 3 vols. (Grand Rapids: Eerdmans, 1965–72), 1:482–83.

8. See, e.g., E. J. Young, "Adverbial *-u* in Semitic," *Westminster Theological Journal* 13.2 (May 1951): 151–54.

9. E. J. Young, *Study Your Bible: A Self Study Course for Bible Believing Christians* (Grand Rapids: Eerdmans, 1934).

10. E. J. Young, *Old Testament Prophecy: A Course Designed for Individual Home Study* (Phillipsburg, N.J.: Committee on Christian Education of the Orthodox Presbyterian Church, 1948).

11. E. J. Young, *The Prophecy of Daniel: A Commentary* (Grand Rapids: Eerdmans, 1949).

12. *New Bible Commentary,* ed. F. Davidson (Grand Rapids: Eerdmans, 1953).

to do what C. F. Keil had done during the nineteenth century: "first of all to ascertain the meaning of the words of each clause and verse, and then, after determining exegetically the import of the words, [to] take into consideration the historical references and calculations of the periods of time named."[13] What he said about his method in that passage applies to the whole of his commentary. He discussed difficulties without introducing Hebrew and Aramaic, explaining the text in simple language so that his intended audience would understand.

Young discusses parts of Daniel 7 even more fully in his Tyndale Lecture, *The Son of Man in Daniel.*[14] In this study he considers the context of Daniel 7:13–14 and concludes that the writer is speaking of an individual, the Messiah. Jesus took over this teaching and rightly applied it to himself, because he believed that he himself was the Messiah. It is noteworthy that Young makes use of both Vos's and Hengstenberg's discussions of this chapter.[15]

Towards the end of his life Young managed to complete his magnum opus, a three-volume work on *The Book of Isaiah.* This was the first publication in the New International Commentary on the Old Testament series, of which Young was the first general editor (since then, John Oswalt's commentary has replaced Young's in the NICOT series, while R. K. Harrison succeeded him as general editor). As with his commentary on Daniel, Young disclaimed any desire to devote himself primarily to textual questions and problems. Rather, he wanted to translate and comment on the Masoretic Hebrew text itself, trying to keep in mind the needs of ministers and Sunday school teachers (presumably he had in mind teachers of adult Bible classes). In the main, discussions of Hebrew words and technical points on archeology are placed in the footnotes. However, for detailed study of Isaiah these notes are important as they contain Young's references to other Semitic literature, to the views of other scholars, and to detailed points of exegesis. It is in these notes that Young's mastery of his field is displayed. They contain references to the whole range of Semitic languages and literature, and draw upon scholarly discussion in at least nine modern European languages. They also deal with the history of the exegesis of Isaiah from pre-Christian to modern times.[16]

There can be little doubt that Young modeled his own exegetical work on Isaiah after that of Joseph Addison Alexander of Princeton. Young lists Alexander's qualifications to write on Isaiah. He was a linguist and a philologist, but he had "certain other qualifications which are indispensable for one

13. Young, *Prophecy of Daniel,* 195.

14. E. J. Young, *The Son of Man in Daniel* (London: Tyndale, 1958). This study was reprinted in *The Law and the Prophets,* ed. John H. Skilton (Nutley, N.J.: Presbyterian and Reformed, 1974), 425–51.

15. See the comments in Young, *Son of Man,* 6–7, 18–20, 28.

16. For Young's discussion of Isaianic studies from the time of Joseph Addison Alexander to his own day, see *Studies in Isaiah* (Grand Rapids: Eerdmans, 1954), 1–126.

who would expound the Scriptures. He had . . . a sincere and humble piety coupled with firm faith in the Bible and reverence for the Bible as the Word of God."[17] Had Alexander followed his own preferences, he would have written a popular commentary, but he decided to write for the ministry. There are clear links between Alexander and Young in qualifications, attitude toward the biblical text, intention, and exegetical approach.

Young's style of approach to Isaiah had manifested itself in several earlier writings on the subject.[18] For example, he had pointed out that a legitimate response to Bernhard Duhm's views on the composition of Isaiah would "be found [only] in a sober exegesis of the text," and then he proceeded with an exegetical discussion demonstrating the weakness of Duhm's position.[19] Young was familiar with a very broad range of literature on Isaiah, and disagreed with other writers on the basis of his own exegetical understanding of the text. Because he had treated the question of the authorship of Isaiah elsewhere, the commentary does not deal with it at any great length.[20] Unfortunately, because of the size of the volumes and their immensely detailed nature, the commentary on Isaiah has not been as influential as have many of his other writings.

Young's interest in the messianic prophecy of Isaiah is shown by his repeated return to the Servant Songs, and especially to the fourth song (Isa. 52:13–53:12). In articles in the *Westminster Theological Journal* he considered the subject of the Servant Songs[21] and also the origin of the idea of the Suffering Servant, especially against the background of Ugaritic material.[22] In 1952 he published a study devoted entirely to the fourth Servant Song.[23] He begins this discussion by quoting J. Gresham Machen in reference to Isaiah 53, and then raises the question whether the time-honored belief that this chapter refers to the atonement of Jesus Christ is justified. To show that this belief is valid, Young comments verse by verse on the song. His discussion is a popular presentation, but he does not avoid difficulties of Hebrew grammar or of interpretation. After we have come to God's Word like little children, says Young, we can then think God's thoughts after him. This means that we can know that Isaiah 53 is "what it claims to be and what the New Testament says it is, a prophecy concerning God's Servant who was to deliver mankind from the guilt and pollution of sin."[24]

17. Young, *Studies in Isaiah*, 10.

18. See especially his articles from the *Westminster Theological Journal* that were reprinted in *Studies in Isaiah*, 127–98.

19. Young, *Studies in Isaiah*, 39–61.

20. See in particular E. J. Young, *Who Wrote Isaiah?* (Grand Rapids: Eerdmans, 1958); and the summary in idem, *Introduction to the Old Testament*, 202–11.

21. E. J. Young, "Of Whom Speaketh the Prophet This?" *Westminster Theological Journal* 11.2 (May 1949): 133–55.

22. E. J. Young, "The Origin of the Suffering Servant Idea," *Westminster Theological Journal* 13.1 (Nov. 1950): 19–33.

23. E. J. Young, *Isaiah Fifty-Three* (Grand Rapids: Eerdmans, 1952).

24. Ibid., 91.

Shortly after the publication of this study, Young devoted attention to H. S. Nyberg's interpretation of Isaiah 53.[25] In 1958 he returned to this the last of the Servant Songs when he gave the annual lecture of the Evangelical Library in London ("Jesus Christ the Servant of the Lord"). He again considered aspects of it when he gave a series of lectures on "Old Testament Prophecy" at Toronto Baptist Seminary in March 1965.

Briefer studies appeared from Young's pen on Psalm 139, Genesis 1–3,[26] and Genesis 3.[27] These are of a popular nature, showing Young's ability to simplify matters and communicate with those who have no knowledge of Hebrew. For example, in his work on Psalm 139 he explains chiastic structures, parallelism, the various Hebrew names for God, Aramaisms in the Old Testament, the Tell el-Amarna tablets, the nature of the covenant, and Hebrew word order. The apologetic element appears as he speaks of "the infinite distinction between man the creature and God the Creator."[28] Dealing with the question of hating sinners gives him the opportunity to state his own position on the relationship of believers to unbelievers: "It is by serving and loving God and keeping His commandments that we are manifesting our hatred of the wicked. . . . All we can do is to oppose evil wherever we find it, and to deal in love with those individuals who are doing wrong and apparently opposing God."[29]

General Works on the Old Testament

During 1947–48 Young contributed a series of articles to the *Southern Presbyterian Journal*. He drew upon these articles and revised them as he wrote his *Introduction to the Old Testament*. In the preface he sets out the general lines of his approach to the Old Testament. He explains that he omits topics not germane to his purpose of writing a basic introduction to each of the various books. Moreover, recognizing the Old Testament to be holy ground, he repudiates the viewpoint that "assumes that man can approach the facts of the universe, including the Bible, with a neutral mind, and pronounce judgment upon them. [This viewpoint] is not scientific, for it does not take into consideration all the facts, and the basic fact it overlooks is that of God and His relation to the world which He has created. Unless we first think rightly about God we shall be in basic error about everything else."[30] While he acknowledges the debt he owes to many scholars, including those of quite different persuasions, Young insists that we must approach the text of Scripture

25. E. J. Young, "Professor Nyberg on Isaiah 53" (paper read at the Seventh Annual Meeting of the Evangelical Theological Society, Ringwood, N.J., 29–30 Dec. 1954).

26. E. J. Young, *In the Beginning: Genesis Chapters 1–3 and the Authority of Scripture* (London: Banner of Truth, 1976).

27. E. J. Young, *Genesis 3: A Devotional and Expository Study* (London: Banner of Truth Trust, 1966).

28. Young, *Psalm 139*, 50.

29. Ibid., 107.

30. Young, *Introduction to the Old Testament*, 10.

with "humble hearts, ready to hear what the Lord God says."[31] The same point comes out emphatically a little later on, when he answers the question, "How shall we regard the Old Testament?" He rejects the so-called neutral attitude towards the Bible, which he insists substitutes "the mind of man as ultimate judge and reference point in place of God Himself."[32] This neatly summarizes what Young himself had written at fuller length in the volume entitled *The Infallible Word*.[33]

The *Introduction* itself follows conventional lines, giving attention to the name, the purpose, an analysis of, and special literature on each book. The one unconventional feature is a long section on "The Literary Criticism of the Pentateuch."[34] This evidences Young's longtime interest in the historical development of biblical studies. His doctoral thesis had been on "Biblical Criticism to the End of the Second Christian Century," and his interest in the history of Isaianic studies is also patent. In the main, the positions which Young adopts are general conservative views on the authorship, composition, and date of the various Old Testament books. The one surprising position is the acceptance of a non-Solomonic authorship for Ecclesiastes. Listing factors which point to an author other than Solomon, he believes that the background and language of the book suggest a time probably around that of Malachi.

In a series of three articles in the *Westminster Theological Journal* during 1959–62 Young presented his views on the nature of Genesis 1.[35] He argued strongly that Genesis 1:1 is a broad comprehensive statement of the fact of creation, which is immediately followed by a description of the state of the earth (v. 2) just prior to the declaration "Let there be light" (v. 3). Young then proceeded to discuss the nature of the days in Genesis 1, and in particular dealt with the so-called framework hypothesis, which holds that the presentation of events is nonchronological. While he related his discussion to a range of scholars (including Arie Noordtzij, N. H. Ridderbos, and Anton Deimel), it is interesting that he referred specifically, on several occasions, to a discussion by Meredith Kline. Kline was, at the time of Young's writings of these articles, his colleague in the Old Testament department at Westminster, and clearly held to a nonliteral approach to Genesis 1.[36] While admitting that

31. Ibid., 11.
32. Ibid., 27.
33. E. J. Young, "The Authority of the Old Testament," in *The Infallible Word: A Symposium by the Members of the Faculty of Westminster Theological Seminary* (Philadelphia: Presbyterian Guardian, 1946), 53–87. When republished by Presbyterian and Reformed (1967), the articles by Young, John Murray, and John H. Skilton had undergone thorough revision.
34. Young, *Introduction to the Old Testament*, 107–54; cf. the summary in E. J. Young, "History of the Literary Criticism of the Pentateuch," in *New Bible Commentary,* rev. ed., ed. D. Guthrie and J. A. Motyer (Grand Rapids: Eerdmans, 1970), 34–40.
35. These articles were later published in book form—E. J. Young, *Studies in Genesis One* (Philadelphia: Presbyterian and Reformed, 1964).
36. Meredith G. Kline, "Because It Had Not Rained," *Westminster Theological Journal* 20.2 (May 1958): 146–57.

the material in Genesis 1 is arranged schematically, Young was not prepared to admit that the arrangement is other than chronological. He did concede, however, that chapter 2 is not intended as a chronological account; rather, the order there is for emphasis as a prelude to the account of the fall of humankind in chapter 3. While Young admitted the force of Kline's arguments in relation to Genesis 2:5–6, he strongly opposed the idea that these verses can be used "to establish the thesis that the present *modus operandi* of divine providence [with regard to God's watering of the earth] *prevailed* during the third day. At most it shows that such a mode may have been present."[37] Nor would he concede that there is strict parallelism between the first three days of creation and the second three days. The content of the two trios is different; moreover, he denied that the first trio set forth the realms of creation while the second trio designate the ruler over those realms.

Time and again Young came back to his basic assertions concerning the early chapters of Genesis. He regarded the material as being Mosaic in origin (though allowing that Moses may have used previously existing sources), and saw it as a case of divine revelation shedding its light on the origins of the universe. He held Genesis 1 to be "a special revelation from God in the sense that it is a communication of information to man from God concerning the subjects of which it treats."[38] The events of Genesis 1 are historical events, and even when the facts are not discernible through scientific investigation, they are to be accepted because they come through the inscripturated revelation of God.

The influence of Young's colleague at Westminster, Cornelius Van Til, is clearly discernible. In discussing Karl Barth's position on creation, and specifically whether he viewed the creation account as historical, Young referred readers to Van Til's *New Modernism*.[39] And when Young asserted that general revelation is to be interpreted by special revelation, and therefore scientific discovery is not to be given precedence over biblical revelation, Young again referred readers to Van Til, on this occasion to his *Defense of the Faith*.[40] The apologetic method of Van Til was clearly espoused by his early colleagues at Westminster; just as he depended upon his colleagues in the biblical field for exegetical detail, so they depended upon him for broader apologetic presentation.

Young's general views on prophecy as an institution were crystalized in his book *My Servants the Prophets*.[41] He began with the foundational passage Deuteronomy 18:9–22, contending that prophecy was not simply religious genius exerting itself. It was God's gracious gift to Israel, and any resemblances to ostensibly similar movements outside of Israel were coincidental.

37. Young, *Studies in Genesis One*, 64.
38. Ibid., 48.
39. Ibid., 23 n. 18.
40. Ibid., 53 n. 31.
41. E. J. Young, *My Servants the Prophets* (Grand Rapids: Eerdmans, 1952).

Prophecy was not of Canaanitish origin but a means which God instituted to reveal his will. (An appendix discussed more fully the question of extrabiblical prophecy in the ancient world.)[42] Young went on to survey the work of the prophets in general (there was no treatment of individual prophetic books). In the conclusion he stated his apologetic position that Christianity is based on revelation in history. All attempts to place it in a supratemporal and suprahistorical realm have to be resisted. The work of the prophets is to be seen in relation to the coming of Jesus, for God sent them into a sinful world to proclaim the coming of the Redeemer.

The Doctrine of Scripture

Young's personal Christian experience brought him to a high appreciation of Scripture as the Word of God. Seeking throughout his life to encourage Bible-believing Christians, he defended the orthodox view of the inspiration and authority of the Scriptures. His first major discussion in this area was "The Authority of the Old Testament," which appeared in the volume *The Infallible Word*, a symposium by the members of the faculty of Westminster Theological Seminary. Young began by noting the way in which Jesus viewed the Old Testament as an organic whole, and how he set his seal of approval on the canon that was accepted by the Jews of his day. Young then took up the question of canonicity, maintaining that the criterion of canonicity is inspiration, with the work of the Holy Spirit also being required to convince and persuade us that the Scriptures are the Word of God. Like his colleague John Murray in the preceding chapter of *The Infallible Word*, he quoted the Westminster Confession 1.5 and enlarged on its treatment of the internal testimony of the Holy Spirit. He then defended the traditional threefold division of the Old Testament canon, though admitting that there is little evidence to show how the Prophets and the Writings were incorporated into the canon. Once an inspired book appeared, it was immediately recognized by God's people. At the time of its revision, Young's presentation could have been strengthened by incorporating the approach taken by his former colleague Meredith Kline, which is orientated more towards biblical theology, and which also brings in relevant material from extrabiblical treaties.[43]

Young's longest discussion of the doctrine of Scripture is *Thy Word Is Truth*. In the preface he disclaims any intention to write "a technical theological treatise." What he aims at is "a popular book, designed to acquaint the intelligent layman with the Biblical doctrine of inspiration and to convince him of its importance."[44] He sets his own presentation over against a viewpoint which uses the terminology of the Bible and the church, yet puts into it content which is antithetical to historic Christianity. Clearly he has the

42. Ibid., 193–205.
43. See Meredith G. Kline, *The Structure of Biblical Authority* (Grand Rapids: Eerdmans, 1972), 21–93.
44. E. J. Young, *Thy Word Is Truth* (Grand Rapids: Eerdmans, 1957), 7.

neoorthodox movement in mind.[45] Once again the apologetic element enters quickly into his presentation. Christian theism and the presupposition that the Scriptures are from God form his starting point: "If God is the Creator of all things, then all things are His and must bear His impress upon them. There can be no neutral position. We believe that either God is our Creator and the One who alone gives meaning to all aspects of life, or that we are faced with the dismal gloom of relying upon the human mind as the ultimate point of reference and predication."[46]

While Young does not follow slavishly the order of chapter 1 of the Westminster Confession, yet the view of inspiration he expounds is clearly the Westminster position (chapter 1 of the confession is printed as an appendix). *Thy Word Is Truth* is a popular presentation of the approach to inspiration adopted earlier by Charles Hodge, Archibald Alexander Hodge, and B. B. Warfield; indeed, Young declares that "no one has written quite as deeply and profoundly on the subject" as has Warfield.[47] By placing the doctrine of Scripture within the framework of coming to saving faith in Jesus Christ, Young not only instructs, but also points again to the message of salvation. Proclaiming that message "is the most beautiful task on earth today."[48]

Young's third discussion of Scripture focuses on the canon of the Old Testament, but he also reasserts the position on inspiration that he set forth in his earlier writings.[49] The views of Herbert Edward Ryle, W. O. E. Oesterley and Theodore H. Robinson, and Robert H. Pfeiffer are analyzed briefly, with the criticism that they consider canonization to be a human process and nothing more. From Young's standpoint, canonicity was Israel's recognition of the divinely inspired books. While we may not be able fully to understand or explain how the conviction was wrought in the hearts of God's people, regeneration by the Spirit of God brought with it a recognition that the Scriptures are from God.

Young' final discussion on Scripture (published after his death) related to the question of inerrancy.[50] His position on this issue was an outworking of his basic viewpoint. He held that the assertion that the Bible is inerrant does not depend on demonstration by human ability. "One does not believe that Scripture is God's Word on the basis of [one's] ability to demonstrate that it does not contain errors. The Bible is the Word of God because God has himself so declared."[51]

---

45. Ibid., 96.
46. Ibid., 32.
47. Ibid., 115.
48. Ibid., 267.
49. E. J. Young, "The Canon of the Old Testament," in *Revelation and the Bible,* ed. Carl F. H. Henry (Grand Rapids: Baker, 1958), 153–68.
50. E. J. Young, "Are the Scriptures Inerrant?" in *The Bible: The Living Word of Revelation,* ed. Merrill C. Tenney (Grand Rapids: Zondervan, 1968), 101–19.
51. Ibid., 118.

Biblical Theology

Very little of Young's writing deals directly with the subject of Old Testament theology. While a foundation of biblical theology underlies his other work, it is only in *The Study of Old Testament Theology Today* that he spells out the framework of thinking which is implicit in all his writing. The book consists of four lectures which he gave at the opening of new premises for London Bible College in May 1958. He considered first of all the relationship between Old Testament theology and history, and then proceeded to discuss the nature, content, and influence of Old Testament theology.

Two things stand out concerning *The Study of Old Testament Theology Today*. One is the impact that Young's apologetic position has on his presentation. He asserts that "the religion of the Bible is a religion that is founded squarely upon certain things that God did in history."[52] After discussing the historical setting of the Old Testament and dealing with the distinction between *Historie* and *Geschichte,* Young goes on to speak of the need for Christian-theistic presuppositions.[53] He asserts that the Old Testament is word-revelation from God by which we can interpret the workings of God in history. Those who hold this position, admits Young, are indeed arguing in a circle: "If Christian theism undergirds a person's thinking, he will reason in a circle. He will see all truth in the light of God's truth. He will see light in God's light. Our final persuasion that the Scriptures are the Word of God is the inward testimony of the Holy Spirit, and, being persuaded of the Divine origin of Scripture, we accept what the Scriptures say as the very Word of God."[54]

The second noteworthy aspect is that while Young makes almost no mention of Geerhardus Vos (he does so only in reference to the messianic consciousness of Jesus),[55] his presentation closely follows Vos's delineation of biblical theology.[56] It must be remembered that Young studied and taught with at least five men who had studied under Vos at Princeton (Oswald T. Allis, John Murray, Ned B. Stonehouse, Cornelius Van Til, and Paul Woolley). Elsewhere he does ask the question, "Who has done more to bring Old Testament Theology to its rights than Geerhardus Vos?"[57] Further, he notes approvingly Vos's recognition of the epochal nature of Old Testament reve-

---

52. E. J. Young, *The Study of Old Testament Theology Today* (London: James Clarke, 1958), 13.
53. Ibid., 24–31.
54. Ibid., 26.
55. Ibid., 89–92.
56. For Vos's understanding of biblical theology see his *Biblical Theology: Old and New Testaments* (London: Banner of Truth, 1975), 3–18; and *Redemptive History and Biblical Interpretation: The Shorter Writings of Geerhardus Vos,* edited by Richard B. Gaffin, Jr. (Phillipsburg, N.J.: Presbyterian and Reformed, 1980), 3–24. Young clearly was very familiar with all of Vos's writings. In a popular lecture on "Old Testament Prophecy" which Young near the end of his life delivered at Toronto Baptist Seminary, he referred to Vos's *Pauline Eschatology* and commented on his use of the term *semi-eschatological* to describe the present age.
57. E. J. Young, comment on a review by H. L. Ellison of *The Study of Old Testament Theology Today,* in *Evangelical Quarterly* 31.1 (Jan.-March 1959): 52.

lation.[58] In similar fashion Young speaks about "the progressive nature of Old Testament revelation," and the fact that the Old Testament itself "divides the history of the chosen race into what we may term epochs or periods of revelation," epochs that are recognized by Old Testament theology.[59]

As we sum up Young's career in biblical studies, three features stand out. First, he held unswervingly to a high view of Scripture and never deviated from it. The position he held was basically the same as that of B. B. Warfield, J. Gresham Machen, and John Murray, but expressed in a simpler style. As Murray himself put it: "The Bible, he believed, was revelation from God, always relevant and by the Holy Spirit sealed in our hearts to be what it intrinsically is, the inerrant Word of God. That this was the controlling factor in Dr. Young's thinking is evident in all of his writings. . . . He knew nothing of the antithesis between devotion to the Lord and devotion to the Bible."[60] Second, he was deeply read in the literature of his chosen field, and he was always concerned to interact with viewpoints at variance with his own. Third, he had set out from adolescence to prepare himself for the Christian ministry and to use his talents in the service of his Lord. This he did as preacher, teacher, writer, and churchman, all the while holding strongly yet graciously to the Westminster Confession as his doctrinal standard, and enjoying the friendship and respect of a wide cross-section of Christian people in many countries. He was a humble Christian who dedicated his outstanding gifts to the service of Christ's church and kingdom. That so many of his books are still in print is itself a testimony to the usefulness of his labors for the Christian community.

Primary Sources

Young, E. J. *Arabic for Beginners*. Grand Rapids: Eerdmans, 1949.

———. "The Authority of the Old Testament." In *The Infallible Word: A Symposium by the Members of the Faculty of Westminster Theological Seminary*, 53–87. Philadelphia: Presbyterian Guardian, 1946. Rev. ed., Nutley, N.J.: Presbyterian and Reformed, 1967.

———. *The Book of Isaiah*. 3 vols. Grand Rapids: Eerdmans, 1965–72.

———. *Genesis 3: A Devotional and Expository Study*. London: Banner of Truth Trust, 1966.

———. *In the Beginning: Genesis Chapters 1 to 3 and the Authority of Scripture*. London: Banner of Truth, 1976.

58. E. J. Young, "What Is Old Testament Biblical Theology?" *Evangelical Quarterly* 31.3 (July-Sept. 1959): 140.
59. Young, *Study of Old Testament Theology Today*, 38. Another clear influence on Young is that of Benne Holwerda. A professor at Kampen from 1946 to 1952, Holwerda is best known for his *Historia revelationis Veteris Testamenti* and his unfinished commentary on Deuteronomy. Young says that in the field of biblical theology few scholars "have written more penetratingly" than Holwerda (*Evangelical Quarterly* 31.1 [Jan.-March 1959]: 52).
60. "Edward J. Young," *Banner of Truth* 54 (March 1968): 2.

————. *An Introduction to the Old Testament.* Grand Rapids: Eerdmans, 1949. Rev. ed., 1964.

————. *Isaiah Fifty-Three: A Devotional and Expository Study.* Grand Rapids: Eerdmans, 1952.

————. *My Servants the Prophets.* Grand Rapids: Eerdmans, 1952.

————. *Old Testament Hebrew for Beginners.* Philadelphia: E. J. Young, 1960.

————. *The Prophecy of Daniel: A Commentary.* Grand Rapids: Eerdmans, 1949.

————. *Psalm 139: A Study in the Omniscience of God.* London: Banner of Truth, 1965.

————. *Studies in Genesis One.* Philadelphia: Presbyterian and Reformed, 1964.

————. *Studies in Isaiah.* Grand Rapids: Eerdmans, 1954.

————. *The Study of Old Testament Theology Today.* London: James Clarke, 1958.

————. *Thy Word Is Truth.* Grand Rapids: Eerdmans, 1957.

————. *Who Wrote Isaiah?* Grand Rapids: Eerdmans, 1958.

Secondary Sources

"Edward Joseph Young." *Presbyterian Guardian* 37.2 (Feb. 1968): 18.

"Edward J. Young." *Banner of Truth* 54 (March 1968): 1–6.

Gaffin, R. B. "Young, Edward Joseph (1907–1968)." In *Dictionary of Christianity in America,* edited by Daniel G. Reid et al., 1298–99. Downers Grove, Ill.: Inter-Varsity, 1990.

Merrill Frederick Unger

John Hannah

Life

Merrill Frederick Unger was born on July 16, 1909,[1] at English Consul Estates,[2] Lansdowne, Maryland, into the upper-middle-class family of Conrad and Katherine Leister Unger; he was one of five children.[3] His father was a civilian employee of the United States military, serving as the chief purchasing clerk for the Third Army Corps. The sparse record of Merrill's early upbringing indicates that the Ungers provided both a stimulating educational environment for their children and a conservative evangelical heritage. The Ungers were active members of the Scott Street United Brethren Church in Baltimore. An insight into the Unger family heritage comes from Ralph E. Boyer, their pastor, who stated in a letter of reference supporting Merrill's application to the Evangelical Theological College, now Dallas Theological Seminary, that his "parents are the kind America needs—Bible students and filled with the Holy Spirit."[4] At the age of fifteen, Merrill experienced an evangelical conversion and became increasingly prominent in the youth activities of his church; at one point, he was elected president of the young people's society, a position which offered him a platform to express his faith at church and to his peers.[5]

1. Unger's birth certificate incorrectly lists July 15, 1909, as his birth date. In his personal diaries he consistently notes that he was born on the sixteenth. For example, in the entry for July 16, 1934, he notes, "Spent this my twenty-fifth birthday in prayer and study."

2. English Consul Estates was a colonial home that the family owned; in the early 1800s it had been occupied by the British foreign ministry.

3. Published biographical sources are very limited, often contain errors, and lack critical perspective. See Wilbur M. Smith, "Introducing This Book and Its Author," in Merrill F. Unger, *Biblical Demonology: A Study of the Spiritual Forces behind the Present World Unrest* (Wheaton, Ill.: Van Kampen, 1953), xi–xv; and Mark I. Bubeck, foreword to *What Demons Can Do to Saints*, by Merrill F. Unger (Chicago: Moody, 1977), 7–9. Also, several of Unger's hardbound works have a brief biographical statement on the dust jacket. The most important source of information on the life and activities of Unger is his private diaries, which he dutifully maintained from 1933 to 1967. They are in the possession of his daughter, Shelley Lamplough, in Severna Park, Maryland.

4. Letter, Ralph E. Boyer to Rollin T. Chafer, 10 March 1931, Registrar's Records, Dallas Theological Seminary.

5. Some of these biographical details come from the archives of Dallas Seminary; e.g., Merrill F. Unger, "Application for Admission to the Evangelical Theological College," 23 Feb. 1931, and "Application for Admission to the Dallas Theological Seminary," 15 Dec. 1940, Registrar's Records, Dallas Theological Seminary.

From his earliest years, Unger's bent was toward the realm of academics; he showed little, if any, interest in such boyhood preoccupations as athletics, finding, instead, delight in the world of books. Though possessing an outgoing, buoyant personality, the young Unger did not appear to possess the talents of a public communicator; his mental accomplishments and interests outshone his oral abilities. Those that knew him perceived him as "an exceptionally brilliant student," "a very hard and conscientious student . . . with a liking to study."[6] During his high school years in Catonsville, a suburb of Baltimore, he pursued language study with an emphasis on French and Latin. Having finished Catonsville High School in 1927, he matriculated at the prestigious Johns Hopkins University, where he majored in English, but also took several years of German and French. A member of the Tudor and Stuart Literary Club during his undergraduate career, he was granted the A.B. degree with honors in June of 1930, having completed the four-year program in three years.

At his parents' insistence, Unger then enrolled in the Peabody Conservatory of Music in Baltimore, where he studied piano for over a year. As the winter of 1930–31 approached, however, he became convinced that he should enter the ministry. He described his calling against the background of the modernist-fundamentalist controversies that had fragmented and fractured the churches in the 1920s: "In these days of darkness when men are attacking God's word, the Holy Spirit had laid on my heart the crying need for preachers who will defend and preach the whole gospel." And so he applied to the Evangelical Theological College for the following autumn. His "paramount reasons" for wishing to study there were "the foundation of the institution on faith and prayer, its vigorous defense of the truth as it is in God's Word, and its high standards of training."[7] Although he was accepted on March 13, 1931, Unger reversed his decision and did not enter the seminary as planned.

For unknown reasons, Unger in January 1932 matriculated at Southern Theological Seminary, a Southern Baptist institution in Louisville. He completed two years of course work in three semesters, but chose not to return in the fall of 1933.[8] Instead, he entered the Missionary Training Institute of the Christian and Missionary Alliance (Nyack, N.Y.). It is evident that exposure to the Christian and Missionary Alliance doctrine of the spiritual life had wrought a transformation. At the Alliance campground in Mahaffey, Pennsylvania, he had received the Holy Spirit as an experience subsequent to

6. Letter, Albert F. Zimmerman to Rollin T. Chafer, 9 March 1931; and letter, Floyd W. Cullen to John F. Walvoord, 14 Dec. 1940, Registrar's Records, Dallas Theological Seminary.
7. Letter, Merrill F. Unger to Rollin T. Chafer, 6 Feb. 1931; and Unger, "Application for Admission to the Evangelical Theological College," Merrill F. Unger Archives, Dallas Theological Seminary (hereafter Unger Archives).
8. After reading the life and writings of George Müller, particularly in regard to his emphasis on the life of faith and his view of debt, Unger determined that borrowing money is unbiblical. To return to Southern would have entailed borrowing, so when a tuition-free invitation to attend the Missionary Training Institute presented itself, he felt that it was the Lord's leading (personal diary, 22 Aug. 1933).

conversion.[9] This experience during the summer of 1933 was life-changing: "By faith I shall have a fruitful ministry from now on."[10]

Unger began his studies at Nyack in the fall of 1933 and completed his degree in one year. He found the rigor of devotional activities and opportunities for ministry exhilarating, though he confided privately that "the scholastic standards are nothing like they are at the Southern Baptist Seminary."[11] After graduation, he accepted a call to Buffalo to direct the William Street Gospel Mission, an embryonic work with loose Alliance affiliation;[12] the emerging congregation would be the locus of his labors through the decade. In 1935, the mission became a church, the Lafayette Avenue Gospel Tabernacle,[13] and he was ordained in the Alliance though the church itself remained unaffiliated.[14] Two years later, in 1937, property was purchased and the church renamed the West Ferry Full Gospel Tabernacle.[15] In addition to his pastoral duties, Unger was indefatigable in speaking at prayer meetings, conducting Bible studies, filling in as pulpit supply, and occasionally preaching at evangelistic tent meetings. He believed that "many souls found Christ" through his gospel-preaching ministry.[16]

Events in the closing years of the decade are particularly instructive in light of Unger's subsequent education, ministry, and doctrinal beliefs. As a Christian and Missionary Alliance cleric, he was committed to the Holiness (Keswick) understanding of the spiritual life, an understanding quite parallel to his own Mahaffey experience in 1933. Though he embraced a belief in faith healing and exuberance in worship, he seemed determined to maintain neither a condemnatory nor an affirmative attitude toward Pentecostal influences in his church; his position on the issue of the second baptism was that there is no single sign of it.[17] It was not that he denied the follow-up experience or tongues; he simply did not feel that tongues are the exclusive evidence of the second baptism.[18] Yet he was under some strain because he felt that he

---

9. Unger, personal diary, 1 Aug. 1933. In the weeks to follow, Unger several times referred to this experience as a surrender of his life to God: "I thank God for the decision I made at Mahaffey to follow Jesus all the way" (Aug. 1); "I made a complete surrender" (Aug. 2); "it was an experience subsequent to conversion" (Aug. 20).

10. Unger, personal diary, 2 Aug. 1933.

11. Ibid., 6 Oct. 1933. While at the school Unger was extremely energetic in activities such as preaching, directing the World Prayer Band, playing the piano in evangelistic campaigns, and teaching classes. Taking his surrender to Jesus seriously, he was rigorous in cultivating his private spiritual life.

12. Ibid., 15 April 1934, and 9–10 July 1934.

13. Ibid., 22 Feb. 1935.

14. Ibid., 10 Nov. 1935. The entry for Oct. 14, 1938, identifies Unger as the "founder of the work."

15. Ibid., 14 Dec. 1937.

16. Unger's pastoral and preaching ministry is known to some degree through notations on hundreds of unpublished sermon manuscripts that are located in the Unger Archives, and through his "Application for Admission to the Dallas Theological Seminary."

17. Unger, personal diary, 15 Feb. 1938: "I can see the Pentecostal people in our Tabernacle are going to cause us trouble on the Tongues Question. . . . [It is] not the one and only sign."

18. Ibid., 4 Jan. 1938: "One outstanding feature of the condition of the church here is its Pentecostal drift. . . . My heart is open to the *truth*. Is tongues the evidence? Is baptism in Jesus' name the apostolic way? . . . I am determined by the grace of God to remain Independent, Non-sectarian and Full Gospel."

was laboring without the Holy Spirit ("One of the severest crosses I have had to bear here is laboring on without the Gift of the Holy Spirit in my own life."[19] His resolve of neutrality was brief; he received the Holy Spirit with tongues at the Greater Bethlehem Temple of Detroit,[20] and subsequently withdrew from the Alliance to join the Pentecostal Assemblies of Jesus Christ, a Jesus Only group.[21] He noted, "The Holy Ghost in one's heart makes a vast difference."[22] Though he spoke of preaching in tongues,[23] he became disillusioned with the teaching and withdrew from the Jesus Only movement in 1939.[24] He was subsequently ordained by a nonaffiliated group of pastors[25] and joined the Independent Fundamental Churches of America.[26]

By 1940 the strain of constant sermon preparation and pastoral duties had convinced Unger that his ministerial training was inadequate.[27] At first he considered reentering Southern Theological Seminary because he could earn his degree there in one year. However, about this time Unger met Herbert E. Kann, the pastor of Buffalo Gospel Center and an alumnus of Dallas, who challenged him to study there rather than Southern. Kann wrote, "I talked with him and persuaded him to yield, and grasp after not merely a good education but the best that could be had."[28]

19. Ibid., 28 June 1938.

20. Ibid., 13 April 1938: "I am becoming convinced that tongues is the evidence of the Baptism." It became an experiential reality that summer: "Tonight, July 4. I received the H[oly] G[host]. . . . The H.G. is a reality. Tongues is a reality."

21. Ibid., 28 July 1938: "I am in Pentecost and in the Jesus' Name group." He had previously written, "Since I am returned from Detroit, I have started in boldly and uncompromisingly for Acts 2:38, and the truth of Jesus' name" (July 15). Notice of his ordination in the Apostolic Gospel Church of Columbus, Ohio, appears in his diary entry for August 16. Following a merger with another Jesus Only group, the denomination is now the United Pentecostal Church, International. For more information see *Dictionary of Pentecostal and Charismatic Movements,* ed. Stanley M. Burgess et al. (Grand Rapids: Zondervan, 1988), 860–65; and Vinson Synan, *The Holiness-Pentecostal Movement in the United States* (Grand Rapids: Eerdmans, 1971), 158–59.

22. Unger, personal diary, 23 Aug. 1938.

23. Ibid., 6 Feb. 1939: "I gave a message in tongues in our tabernacle from the pulpit."

24. Ibid., 27 Sept. 1939. On Oct. 30 he recorded in his diary: "I see conversion as forgiveness of sins (receiving Christ) means receiving the H[oly] S[pirit]. I see the baptism of the Spirit was for the church. The great need today is to preach to believers 'Be ye filled with Him.'"

25. Ibid., 3 Oct. 1939.

26. Ibid., 5 June and 16 June 1940. He regained ordination in the Christian and Missionary Alliance when he joined this separatist umbrella group.

27. As early as 1937 Unger had been having second thoughts about his education: "I gave up my Seminary Degree (ThM), and I have been surrendering scholastic attainment ever since" (personal diary, 17 April 1937).

28. Letter, Herbert E. Kann to John F. Walvoord, 12 Dec. 1940, Unger Archives. Other sources here include Unger, personal diary, 2 Dec. 1940; and letter, Merrill F. Unger to John F. Walvoord, 18 Nov. 1940, Unger Archives. Though founded in 1924 to provide conservative clergymen for the theologically diverse mainline churches, Dallas Seminary had become in its third decade a major source of professionally trained ministers for the independent and separatist splinter movements. The eclectic heritage of the school combined the Bible conference movement's distinctives of the Keswick sanctification scheme, Darbyite dispensationalism, and modern premillennialism with the Princetonian emphasis on the inerrancy of the Bible. By embracing a modified or Saumurian Calvinism (i.e., hypothetical universalism), a stress on world missions and evangelism, and study of the entire English Bible, Dallas created a syncretistic substructure (see John D. Hannah, "The Social and Intellectual Origins of the Evangelical Theological College" [Ph.D. diss., University of Texas at Dallas, 1988], 164–70, 189–93, and 201–9).

Unger reapplied to Dallas Seminary, was accepted on December 30, 1940, and began his studies there on January 28, 1941. With two years of transferable credit, most from Southern Seminary, but some from the Missionary Training Institute as well, he was able to complete the Th.M. degree in four semesters, graduating magna cum laude in 1943. He had indicated on his application that he planned to finance his studies at the seminary through either filling in as pulpit supply or waiting tables. The former seems to have been the method he used to finance this phase of graduate studies; he did interim preaching at the Spring Branch Community Church of Houston in the summer of 1941,[29] pastored two churches in Washington State in the summer of 1942,[30] and accepted a pastorate at the Winnetka Congregational Church of Dallas in the autumn of the same year.[31]

In his two years of study at Dallas Seminary, Unger not only earned the Th.M. degree, but also completed the course work for the Th.D. degree, receiving it magna cum laude in 1945. His teachers at the seminary regarded his scholarship highly: "Unger . . . established an enviable record as to scholarship and character"; "Unger has manifested unusual ability as a student, not only doing far more than is normally expected of students in the way of preparation and study, but he achieved distinction in his scholarship while carrying an unusually heavy schedule of study"; and "Unger . . . stood first in a class of eleven in his graduation with the Master of Theology degree."[32]

With the conclusion of his course work at Dallas Seminary, Unger entered the Ph.D. program of the Department of Semitics and Biblical Archeology at Johns Hopkins University, whose Oriental Seminary of Higher Studies was under the direction of the renowned scholar William F. Albright. Unger completed his degree there in 1947; his dissertation, which has been recognized as his most serious contribution to scholarship, was revised and published in 1957 under the title *Israel and the Aramaeans of Damascus.*[33] While doing graduate work in the Baltimore area, he pastored two churches: the Relay Presbyterian Church (1944–45)[34] and the Bible Presbyterian Church (1945–47).[35] At this point, his formal academic training was completed.

29. Unger, personal diary, 21 May 1941 through 31 Aug. 1941.
30. Ibid., 20 May 1942. He pastored the Community Presbyterian Church of Toledo, Washington, and the First Presbyterian Church of Castle Rock, Washington. On July 24 he requested to be put under the care of the Columbia Presbytery of the Synod of Washington; he was licensed by the presbytery on Jan. 26, 1943.
31. Letter, Merrill F. Unger to Lewis Sperry Chafer, 21 Aug. 1943, Unger Archives. He served at the church from March 2, 1943, to Jan. 1, 1944 (Unger, personal diary, 8 Feb. 1943 and 13 Nov. 1944).
32. Letter, Lewis Sperry Chafer to Isaiah Bowman, 30 Aug. 1943; letter, John F. Walvoord to Isaiah Bowman, 24 Aug. 1943; and letter, A. H. D. Duncan to Isaiah Bowman, 23 Aug. 1943, Unger Archives.
33. Merrill F. Unger, *Israel and the Aramaeans of Damascus* (Grand Rapids: Zondervan, 1957; Grand Rapids: Baker, 1980).
34. He served as interim pastor in this church from June 1944 to March 1945 (Unger, personal diary, 28 June 1944 and 22 March 1945). The Baltimore Presbytery would not accept his ordination from the Columbia Presbytery because he had been pastoring a non-Presbyterian church in Dallas (personal diary, 25 Feb. and 4 June 1945).
35. Unger obtained certification in the Bible Presbyterian Church and was elevated from the post of stated supply to pastor (personal diary, 29 April, 4 June, 10 July, and 23 Aug. 1945).

In the autumn of 1947, Unger moved to Boston, where, though the stay was brief, he experienced several significant changes in his life. First, he entered a profession for which he was well suited when he joined the faculty of Gordon College of Theology and Missions (a school founded in 1889 by Baptist pastor Adoniram Judson Gordon as part of the Bible institute movement) and of the Gordon Divinity School. Before hiring Unger, the dean at Gordon, Burton L. Goddard, had written to Charles A. Nash, the registrar of Dallas Seminary, to inquire concerning Unger's personality and theological views. The importance which Goddard placed upon the character of a prospective teacher is evident from his letter: "We would be interested in anything you might have to say about his personal qualities since it is our conviction that a good teacher should have something in the way of a personality gift."[36] Nash responded: "I would not say that Dr. Unger has a strong or striking personality, nor do I desire to indicate at all that there is any particular weakness in that regard. Perhaps . . . *average* would be the term to use in designating Dr. Unger."[37] Nash attempted to qualify this statement by noting that Unger's personality had probably "developed" during his doctoral work at Johns Hopkins. In regard to theology, Nash confirmed that Unger did not hold to extreme positions which would be out of harmony with the interdenominational character of Gordon College. Surprisingly, the college offered a teaching position to Unger despite this unimpressive letter of reference. Unger seemed to flourish in his new academic vocation as a professor of archeology in the graduate school and Greek in the college. He later commented, "My work here at Gordon College and in the Divinity School has been most happy in every respect."[38] Yet, as a portent of a future redirection of his life, he confided in his diary: "Often as I have prayed I have been conscious that God doesn't want me in Boston permanently. As much as I am enjoying my work, it is obvious I am not in my field. This experience is evidently a stepping stone to something else."[39]

Second, it was during his time in Boston that Unger met his future wife, Elsie Aileen Dawson. Aileen, who would later be described as a person who "dressed well, [was] attractive, with a Boston air about her,"[40] was working as a secretary in the business office of the college when he began courting her. The relationship grew, and the forty-year-old scholar was married in the summer of 1949. Unable to have children of their own, they would adopt two children, Clark and Shelley.

Third, on February 6, 1948, Unger received a letter which would alter the course of his professional life; Lewis Sperry Chafer wrote that the chairmanship of the Department of Semitics and Old Testament was vacant

---

36. Letter, Burton L. Goddard to Charles A. Nash, 4 Aug. 1947, Unger Archives.
37. Letter, Nash to Goddard, 11 Aug. 1947, Unger Archives.
38. Letter, Merrill F. Unger to Lewis Sperry Chafer, 1 June 1948, Unger Archives.
39. Unger, personal diary, 6 Feb. 1948.
40. Geraldine Walvoord, "Questions concerning Merrill F. Unger," 26 Aug. 1994, Unger Archives.

(Charles L. Feinberg having joined the faculty of the Talbot Theological Seminary in La Mirada, California); in his typically declarative style, Chafer announced that he had "no one in mind but" Unger.[41] A little over a month later John F. Walvoord, the seminary's vice president, echoed Chafer's sentiments: "It is Dr. Chafer's mind, as well as the rest of us who have been consulted, that you are the one whom God has prepared to undertake the work beginning next fall. . . . It seems apparent that God has divinely prepared you by way of education for the work here."[42] Although the president of Gordon College strongly urged Unger to remain at the Boston school, he decided "to respond to God's evident leading" and joined the faculty of Dallas Seminary.[43]

After preaching, studying, and writing in New England during the summer, Unger arrived in Dallas in the early part of September to assume the chairmanship of the Old Testament department and undertake teaching duties. He remained in that position until his retirement in 1967, nearly twenty years later. During his time at Dallas, he became well known within American evangelicalism, especially within the narrow segment of evangelicalism that was heavily influenced by the seminary. His fame as an evangelical scholar escalated quickly at his new post as he became a regular at Bible conferences; in addition, he undertook a writing and publishing ministry which aimed at general audiences rather than the scholarly community.[44]

Following the death of his wife Aileen, which coincided with his retirement from Dallas Seminary in 1967 to devote himself full-time to writing, Unger and his two children, Clark and Shelley, returned to the Baltimore area and settled in Severna Park, Maryland, where he resided for nearly thirteen years. He continued his rigorous writing and conference ministries throughout the late 1960s and into the 1970s. In the winter of 1968, he married Pearl C. Stoffers of San Francisco. Though formally retired, he continued his close relations with Dallas Seminary. In addition to supporting the seminary financially, he spoke at conferences that it hosted. In 1974, he was invited to deliver an address at the school's fiftieth anniversary. And it was quite fitting that one of his last letters was addressed to the seminary; in part it was a request for prayer: "I face surgery at Johns Hopkins Hospital for a brain tumor on September 29. Pray that God will use the skill of the two famous surgeons. . . . Pray for ability to complete Unger's Bible Commentary."[45] He did not recover from the surgery, dying on October 14, 1980.

41. Letter, Lewis Sperry Chafer to Merrill F. Unger, 6 Feb. 1948, Unger Archives.

42. Letter, John F. Walvoord to Merrill F. Unger, 18 March 1948, Unger Archives.

43. Letter, Unger to Walvoord, 3 April 1948, Unger Archives.

44. Unger's literary ministry was described in grandiose terms by Bubeck (foreword to *What Demons Can Do*, 7): "All of Christendom has benefited from the scholarly pen of Merrill Unger. Evangelical Christians have gladly owned him as one of their most able spokesmen for the Christian faith. . . . His contribution of scholarly assistance in numerous fields of biblical study is almost legendary." In spite of the gratuitous laudation, Bubeck is correct that Unger's works were accepted beyond the realm of his subgroup within evangelicalism.

45. Letter, Merrill F. Unger to Dallas Theological Seminary, n.d., Unger Archives.

Scholarly Contribution: Biblical Studies

Assuming teaching duties at Dallas in 1948 also marks the beginning of what would primarily consume Unger's time into the 1970s—writing. Clearly evident in his diaries and letters are, first, his eminent godliness in devotional exercises both in private and in the classroom and, second, an equally compelling passion to write. The impetus for such a ministry came, apparently, from Chafer. Two comments to this effect appear in Unger's diary: "Dr. Chafer also recommended me on my talent of writing urging me to cultivate it";[46] and, several months later, "A very encouraging meeting with Dr. Chafer. He spoke very favorably of my written work. And told me I must continue to write."[47]

Although Unger published excerpts from his master's thesis in *Bibliotheca Sacra* in 1944, he did not contribute significantly to periodical literature until he joined the faculty at Dallas in 1948. At that point Unger's literary work, which ranged from popular to technical, began appearing regularly in Christian periodicals such as the *Alliance Weekly, Biblical Archeologist, Bible Expositor and Illuminator, Christian Victory (Grace and Truth), Christianity Today, Eternity, Evangelical Christian, Journal of Biblical Literature, King's Business, Moody Monthly,* and *Our Hope.* The bulk of Unger's periodical writings, however, were published in Dallas Seminary's journal, *Bibliotheca Sacra.* During his twenty years at Dallas, Unger in fact contributed over forty articles to the school's periodical. While a majority of these pieces related to biblical studies, some were devoted to practical or theological themes.

As an author of book-length works, Unger rapidly rose to a place of prominence within the evangelical community. In 1951 his *Introductory Guide to the Old Testament* won the first prize in Zondervan's contest for Christian textbooks. In 1953, Van Kampen Press (later Scripture Press) published revised versions of both his doctoral dissertation from Dallas *(Biblical Demonology: A Study of the Spiritual Forces behind the Present World Unrest)* and his master's thesis *(The Baptizing Work of the Holy Spirit).* Also in 1953 Zondervan issued *Pathways to Power,* a compilation of several previously published articles on the spiritual life. The same year Unger won another Zondervan textbook competition for his *Archaeology and the Old Testament.* The combination of the two award-winning texts was a major factor in Unger's emergence at the forefront of the Christian publishing scene.

After his early successes, Unger went on to write another nineteen books and edited two others. His most significant contribution to American evangelicalism was in the area of biblical studies. Most of his books on Bible survey or backgrounds were popular in nature, designed for the serious layperson or inquiring Bible student. His works in this area can be categorized into four groupings: (1) archeological background; (2) reference works for

---

46. Unger, personal diary, 11 May 1944.
47. Ibid., 17 Dec. 1944.

biblical studies; (3) study companions to the biblical text; and (4) commentaries on the biblical text.

First, Unger produced a number of works which elucidate the historical and cultural background of biblical texts on the basis of archeological evidence. In addition to his survey texts, such as *Archaeology and the Old Testament*, there is his only full-length technical work, *Israel and the Aramaeans of Damascus*. One-third of this work, which is a revision of his Ph.D. dissertation, is taken up by notes. It has been broadly recognized for its scholarly achievement, even in periodicals generally critical of his conservative perspective on biblical studies.[48]

Second, Unger either wrote or edited several reference works in the field of biblical studies. For example, *Unger's Bible Dictionary* is an extensive one-volume Bible dictionary which revises and combines *Barnes's Bible Encyclopedia* of 1900 and *The People's Bible Encyclopedia* of 1913. Unger's revisions tend to be polemical in nature and conservative in bias, reflecting the historical and archeological methods, and sometimes the views, of his mentor William F. Albright.[49] In addition, Unger served as a co-editor with William White, Jr., on *Nelson's Expository Dictionary of the Old Testament*, an expositional dictionary of Hebrew words that is designed for English readers.[50]

Third, Unger produced three survey texts, one dealing with the Old Testament and two encompassing the entire Protestant Bible. His award-winning *Introductory Guide to the Old Testament* was intended as a textbook for "Bible institutes, Christian colleges, and theological seminaries." Unger hoped that this volume would provide a "conservative, evangelical" alternative to the overly technical material and destructive critical bias of the majority of works then available.[51] The design of *Unger's Bible Handbook*

48. E.g., Horace D. Hummel, review of *Israel and the Aramaeans of Damascus*, by Merrill F. Unger, *Concordia Theological Monthly* 29 (Aug. 1958): 620–21; and Arnold Anderson, review of *Israel and the Aramaeans of Damascus*, by Merrill F. Unger, *Scottish Journal of Theology* 12 (1959): 309, were positive about Unger's contribution and scholarship. See also Kenneth L. Barker's commendation of the "careful scholarship" of this "classic" (introduction to *Israel and the Aramaeans* [1980 ed.], v–vi). Concerning a later work, Raymond F. Surburg, review of *Unger's Commentary on the Old Testament*, by Merrill F. Unger, *Concordia Theological Quarterly* 48 (Jan. 1984): 75–76, cautions against the "aberrant hermeneutic" used in the exposition of biblical texts. Similarly, Ernest Best, review of *New Testament Teaching on Tongues*, by Merrill F. Unger, *Scottish Journal of Theology* 29 (1976): 194–95, offers harsh criticism: "It is difficult to recommend this book without considerable reservation." The implication is that as a result of *Israel and the Aramaeans* the scholarly value of Unger's work had achieved recognition outside his narrow segment of evangelicalism.

49. For an analysis that critically compares the relative merits and deficiencies of several one-volume Bible dictionaries, including *Unger's Bible Dictionary* (Chicago: Moody, 1957, 1961, 1966), see James C. Moyer and Victor H. Matthews, "The Use and Abuse of Archeology in Current One-Volume Bible Dictionaries," *Biblical Archaeologist* 48 (Dec. 1985): 228, 233, 235–36.

50. *Nelson's Expository Dictionary of the Old Testament,* ed. Merrill F. Unger and William White, Jr. (Nashville: Nelson, 1980). This volume was later combined with *Vine's Expository Dictionary of New Testament Words* and published as *Vine's Expository Dictionary of Biblical Words* (Nashville: Nelson, 1985).

51. Merrill F. Unger, *Introductory Guide to the Old Testament* (Grand Rapids: Zondervan, 1951), 7.

was to provide entry-level information for accessing the content of the Bible. In addition to brief introductory essays, the work contains a summary of each book of the Bible.[52] *Unger's Guide to the Bible* attempts to be an all-in-one companion for Bible study. It includes an introduction to and survey of each book of the Bible, a Bible dictionary containing brief articles on historical and cultural subjects, a concordance of biblical terms, and a series of maps.[53]

Fourth, Unger composed commentaries on the books of the Old Testament. In 1963, Zondervan published his most thorough commentary, *Unger's Bible Commentary: Zechariah*. While the title suggests that other volumes might follow, it was the only one to appear. In 1973, Unger began a project which would occupy him for the rest of his life, writing a commentary on every book of the Bible. In 1975, he sought to have the first section of the commentary, the Pentateuch, released, but his publisher insisted that the work be issued in its entirety.[54] This decision was later reversed, and the Old Testament portion was published posthumously in 1981 under the title *Unger's Commentary on the Old Testament*. It was both praised and criticized, largely along the lines of the reviewers' theological perspectives.[55] Within the substratum of evangelicalism to which Unger belonged, the commentary was widely acclaimed for its attempt to demonstrate that premillennial dispensationalism is compatible with the data of Scripture.[56]

Theological Contributions

Though Unger should be remembered primarily for his work in biblical and archeological studies, his writing and speaking ministries demonstrated a significant contribution to evangelical thinking relative to various theological issues. His theological contributions were not innovative or particularly creative; he studied, taught, and wrote within the tradition of his own religious training, principally, if not exclusively, from the insights and grids he learned at Dallas Seminary. To access his theological emphases, it is best to reflect on

52. *Unger's Bible Handbook* (Chicago: Moody, 1966) has appeared in a number of revised editions: e.g., *The Parallel New Testament and Unger's Bible Handbook* (New York: Iversen-Norman, 1975); *The Hodder Bible Handbook* (London: Hodder and Stoughton, 1984); and *The New Unger's Bible Handbook*, revised by Gary N. Larson (Chicago: Moody, 1984).

53. There have been two abridged editions of *Unger's Guide to the Bible* (Wheaton, Ill.: Tyndale, 1974). The Bible dictionary and concordance appear in *Unger's Concise Bible Dictionary* (Grand Rapids: Baker, 1985); and the Bible survey appears in *Unger's Survey of the Bible* (Eugene, Oreg.: Harvest House, 1981).

54. Letter, Leslie H. Stobbe to Merrill F. Unger, 27 Oct. 1975, Unger Archives.

55. See, e.g., Surburg, review of *Unger's Commentary on the Old Testament;* and F. D. Lindsey, review of *Unger's Commentary on the Old Testament,* by Merrill F. Unger, *Bibliotheca Sacra* 140 (April-June 1983): 182–83.

56. For recent discussions of the rise of premillennial dispensationalism see Hannah, "Social and Intellectual Origins," 187–88; Ernest R. Sandeen, *The Roots of Fundamentalism: British and American Millenarianism, 1800–1930* (Chicago: University of Chicago Press, 1970); and Timothy P. Weber, *Living in the Shadow of the Second Coming: American Premillennialism, 1875–1982* (Grand Rapids: Zondervan, 1983).

the several areas of his graduate research; these areas of study were lifelong sources for his academic and popular writings.

Unger's interest in various aspects of pneumatology emerged during his studies at Dallas Seminary (and out of his pastoral experience), where he wrote his master's thesis on the baptism of the Holy Spirit, a relevant, often controverted point in the 1940s (we do not mention here his own intriguing religious sojourn in this area). Although some of his views are evident in his unpublished sermons prior to his studies at Dallas, Unger stated that his perspectives on the doctrine of the person and work of the Holy Spirit crystalized under Lewis Sperry Chafer, the school's president, and John F. Walvoord.[57] Both of them wrote on the theme of the Holy Spirit: the former in the area of sanctification, *He That Is Spiritual*;[58] the latter, *The Doctrine of the Holy Spirit*.[59] Like his mentors, Unger understood the spiritual life through a two-step rubric, that is, a dual division of Christians into carnal and spiritual, and salvation by grace through faith followed by sanctification through surrender (a single baptism of the Spirit and a later experience of dedication commencing a progressive spirituality). His thought in this area extended the mildly Keswickian two-step methodology taught by Chafer, which was quite commonly held within premillennial dispensationalism.[60] In contrast to the increasingly influential Pentecostal movement, which shared with Unger not only a common theological heritage, but a historical one as well, he believed that the so-called sign gifts, such as tongues, prophecy, and the word of knowledge, had ceased.[61]

While Unger did not write extensively on the subject of premillennialism or dispensationalism, his scholarly pursuits and intellectual assumptions were framed and controlled by those positions. Thus his work in Old Testament studies is a defense of the hermeneutical and eschatological views embraced by the school he served for nearly twenty years. He accepted the theological structure that premillennial dispensationalism imposes upon the Bible: a literal or plain (as opposed to the more finely nuanced literary) interpretation of the language of the Bible; progressive revelation, with the church understood in the Old Testament as a mystery; discontinuity between the old and new covenants in relation to the function of the law; and a sharp division

57. Merrill F. Unger, *The Baptizing Work of the Holy Spirit* (Chicago: Scripture, 1953), 3.
58. Lewis Sperry Chafer, *He That Is Spiritual* (Wheaton, Ill.: Van Kampen, 1918), 23–38; see also idem, *Systematic Theology*, 8 vols. (Dallas: Dallas Theological Seminary Press, 1947–48), 6:24–26; Merrill F. Unger, *The Baptism and Gifts of the Holy Spirit* (Chicago: Moody, 1974), 21–34; idem, *Baptizing Work*, 8–24.
59. Walvoord's only full-length publication at this time was *The Doctrine of the Holy Spirit: A Study in Pneumatology* (Dallas: Dallas Theological Seminary Press, 1943), esp. 114–78.
60. See Merrill F. Unger, *Pathways to Power* (Grand Rapids: Zondervan, 1953), 103–28. For a discussion of the influence of the Keswick movement on this segment of evangelicalism see George M. Marsden, *Fundamentalism and American Culture* (New York: Oxford University Press, 1980), 72–80; and Douglas W. Frank, *Less than Conquerors: How Evangelicals Entered the Twentieth Century* (Grand Rapids: Eerdmans, 1986), 103–66.
61. Merrill F. Unger, *New Testament Teaching on Tongues* (Grand Rapids: Kregel, 1971); idem, *Baptism and Gifts*, 135–42.

between Israel and the church into two separate peoples of God with distinct programs and destinies. In *Great Neglected Bible Prophecies* Unger argues that the integrity of the Scriptures is best sustained by a literal interpretation of the prophetic texts, which he understands to support the ethnic restoration of Israel in the end times.[62] To him, premillennial dispensationalism was a nonnegotiable aspect of correct biblical interpretation ("a correct and workable system of interpretation that harmonizes many difficult and seemingly conflicting passages is needed as a vital part of the apologetic for the truth of full scriptural authority").[63] The view of premillennial dispensationalism as a hermeneutical and apologetic issue, rather than an eschatological position, was well established in Unger's substratum of evangelicalism and was bolstered by his scholarship.[64]

With his retirement from Dallas Seminary in 1967, Unger became more intensely interested in the study of demonology and the occult. Revival of the topic of his dissertation, which had been published as *Biblical Demonology*, led to *Demons in the World Today* (1971), *The Haunting of Bishop Pike* (1971), *Beyond the Crystal Ball* (1973), and *What Demons Can Do to Saints* (1977). His attention was drawn to the subject again, at least in part, because of its growing popularity in the youth culture. Unger realized that many Americans, in rejecting and abandoning the supernatural God of the Scriptures, had not abandoned supernaturalism, but were embracing the real, powerful, dark spirit-world of fallen angelic beings.[65] As a result of his work in this area, he received a large amount of correspondence from both religious and nonreligious people seeking his guidance in regard to demonic oppression. He viewed the increase of such activity as evidence of the nearness of the end of the age and the great tribulation, when such phenomena would increase unrestrained.[66] Between the publication of his doctoral dissertation in 1953 and the flurry of books in the 1970s, Unger had changed his view of demonic activity in at least one important respect; he had come to the conclusion that Christians can be demon-possessed, not simply oppressed.[67] He challenged the church of his day not to relinquish its charismatic ministry and power, which includes healing and exorcism; indeed, he argued that an unwillingness by many in the church to believe in the exist-

62. Merrill F. Unger, *Great Neglected Bible Prophecies* (Chicago: Scripture, 1955).
63. See Merrill F. Unger, *Principles of Expository Preaching* (Grand Rapids: Zondervan, 1955), 19–23.
64. See Chafer, *Systematic Theology*, 1:xi–xiii; and Charles C. Ryrie, *Dispensationalism Today* (Chicago: Moody, 1965), 86–109.
65. Merrill F. Unger, *Demons in the World Today* (Wheaton, Ill.: Tyndale, 1971), 7; idem, *The Haunting of Bishop Pike* (Wheaton, Ill.: Tyndale, 1971), 43–45.
66. Merrill F. Unger, *Beyond the Crystal Ball* (Chicago: Moody, 1973), 7–28; idem, *Demons*, 179–83; and Smith, "Introducing This Book," in *Biblical Demonology*, xiv–xv.
67. For the earlier position see Unger, *Biblical Demonology*, 100. In *Demons*, 185–86, he states: "Believers can be hindered, bound, and oppressed by Satan and even indwelt by one or more [demons]. . . . That many regenerated people need to claim deliverance from evil spirits indwelling them is a fact that we would prefer to think is not true, but which is all too true."

ence of the demonic had caused them to regard certain gifts of the Spirit as merely first-century realities and thus to lose their supernatural power.[68]

The contribution of Merrill F. Unger to the evangelical movement in America, and beyond, has been primarily as a scholar-writer. Unger's thinking emerged from his educational inheritance that combined the distinctive ideology of the Bible conference movement (which had been embodied in a number of Bible institutes as well as Dallas Theological Seminary) with Semitic, archeological, and biblical studies under the tutelage of the internationally acclaimed William F. Albright. Unger was able to translate his biblical and theological views into a lucid style and clear format which challenge inquiring Bible students and assist biblical scholars. While his writings at times evidence a broad scholarly perspective, they continually reveal his alignment with a more narrow premillennial-dispensational interpretation of the biblical texts. However, this should not eclipse the fact that many of Unger's works have enjoyed an ongoing usefulness beyond the bounds of his segment of evangelicalism.

Primary Sources

Unger, Merrill F. *Archaeology and the New Testament*. Grand Rapids: Zondervan, 1962.

———. *Archaeology and the Old Testament*. Grand Rapids: Zondervan, 1954.

———. *The Baptism and Gifts of the Holy Spirit*. Chicago: Moody, 1974.

———. *The Baptizing Work of the Holy Spirit*. Chicago: Scripture, 1953.

———. *Beyond the Crystal Ball*. Chicago: Moody, 1973.

———. *Biblical Demonology: A Study of the Spiritual Forces behind the Present World Unrest*. Wheaton, Ill.: Van Kampen, 1953.

———. *Demons in the World Today: A Study of Occultism in the Light of God's Word*. Wheaton, Ill.: Tyndale, 1971.

———. *Famous Archaeological Discoveries*. Grand Rapids: Zondervan, 1963.

———. *Great Neglected Bible Prophecies*. Chicago: Scripture, 1955.

———. *The Haunting of Bishop Pike: A Christian View of the Other Side*. Wheaton, Ill.: Tyndale, 1971.

———. *Introductory Guide to the Old Testament*. Grand Rapids: Zondervan, 1951.

———. *Israel and the Aramaeans of Damascus*. Grand Rapids: Zondervan, 1957; Grand Rapids: Baker, 1980.

———. *New Testament Teaching on Tongues*. Grand Rapids: Kregel, 1971.

———. *Pathways to Power*. Grand Rapids: Zondervan, 1953.

———. *Principles of Expository Preaching*. Grand Rapids: Zondervan, 1955.

68. Unger maintained that only three of the nine spiritual gifts listed in 1 Corinthians 12:7–11 are temporary; the other six are permanent. With regard to the gift of healing as it relates to exorcism he wrote: "When we remind the Church of its obligation to use its charismatic gifts of healing to deliver those chained by satanic powers, we need to point out that this gift is not included in the temporary list" (*Demons*, 189; see also 188–92).

————. *Unger's Bible Commentary: Zechariah.* Grand Rapids: Zondervan, 1963.

————. *Unger's Bible Dictionary.* Chicago: Moody, 1957, 1961, 1966, 1988.

————. *Unger's Bible Handbook: An Essential Guide to Understanding the Bible.* Chicago: Moody, 1966.

————. *Unger's Commentary on the Old Testament.* 2 vols. Chicago: Moody, 1981.

————. *Unger's Guide to the Bible.* Wheaton, Ill.: Tyndale, 1974.

————. *What Demons Can Do to Saints.* Chicago: Moody, 1977.

————, and William White, Jr., eds. *Nelson's Expository Dictionary of the Old Testament.* Nashville: Nelson, 1980.

Frederick Fyvie Bruce

Murray J. Harris

Life

Born in Elgin, Morayshire, in the north of Scotland on October 12, 1910, Frederick Fyvie Bruce gave evidence of remarkable academic abilities from his earliest days. Consider, for example, the poem that he wrote at the age of thirteen to celebrate the Latin motto of Elgin Academy, which he attended from 1923 to 1928:

> **Sic itur ad astra**
> When Volscia's chieftain fell by Julus' hand,
> And "Thus it is that men to Heav'n aspire!"
> Exclaimèd was by Phoebus of the lyre,
> Did he, whose kinsman ruled our happy land
> When Britain's shores were peopled by a band
> of Trojans, did young Julus or his sire
> Ænéas, or Apollo of the lyre,
> Know that some day on a far-distant strand
> A school would rise, and for its motto claim
> Those words called forth by Julus' deed of fame?
> Or did they think that for its badge and sign
> 'Twould have the words of Virgil's famous line?
> Yet Fate ordained, that when millenniums three
> Had passed away, this school and badge should be.[1]

The dux medalist (valedictorian) of his class, Bruce was the only Elgin pupil ever to win first place (*facile princeps*, "easily first" according to the examiners) in the Aberdeen University Bursary Competition. Commenting on Bruce's achievement in winning this "blue ribbon of Northern scholarship," a reporter for the academy's magazine issued a challenge: "As this success gained a holiday for the school, we would recommend Bruce's example as one to be followed by all school captains or other members of Class VI in the future, if they wish their memories to be treasured long after their departure!"[2]

---

1. Frederick Fyvie Bruce, *Elgin Academy Magazine,* December 1923, p. 11.
2. *Elgin Academy Magazine,* December 1928, p. 12.

At Aberdeen University, Bruce earned an M.A. with first-class honors in classics (Greek and Latin) in 1932, securing many awards en route.[3] In 1933 he was honored as the Ferguson Scholar in Classics, the examiner that year being the eminent Oxford classicist Sir Cyril Bailey.[4] This scholarship took him to Gonville and Caius College at Cambridge University, where he was college prizeman in Greek verse composition and Greek New Testament and the Sandys student, earning a B.A. in 1934 (M.A., 1945) with a first-class classical tripos. From Cambridge he went to Vienna to pursue doctoral studies on Roman slave names under Paul Kretschmer, professor of Indo-European philology. But after a year in Vienna (1934–35) he heard of a vacancy for an assistant lecturer in Greek at Edinburgh University, and knowing that such openings did not occur frequently, he applied for the post, was appointed, and served there for three years (1935–38) under the genial direction of Professor W. M. Calder, a distinguished classical archeologist. On August 19, 1936, Bruce married Annie Bertha (Betty) Davidson, a teacher who had earned an M.A. in classics from Aberdeen in 1932. The couple was blessed with two children—a son Iain and a daughter Sheila—and seven grandchildren.

The period in Edinburgh was followed by nine years (1938–47) south of the border at the University of Leeds as lecturer in Greek. During this period in Leeds Bruce found that his academic interests were moving more and more in the direction of biblical studies. Needing some additional finances, he became a candidate for and won the Crombie Scholarship in Biblical Criticism, which forced him to study the biblical text at a deeper academic level than previously. Three other factors that accounted for the change of focus were an invitation to give lectures on the Greek New Testament to theological students at the university, his study for a diploma in Hebrew at the university, and the formation in 1938 of the Inter-Varsity Fellowship Biblical Research Committee. To advance the cause of British evangelicalism, this committee sponsored summer schools in Cambridge beginning in 1941, with Bruce as the New Testament specialist and W. J. Martin of Liverpool University as the Old Testament specialist.[5] The committee also invited Bruce to write a technical commentary on the Greek text of Acts, a volume that appeared in 1951. In addition, while teaching at the University of Leeds, Bruce wrote what was to become his most widely circulated book, *Are the New Testament Documents Reliable?* (now entitled *The New Testament Documents: Are They*

---

3. Viz., the Earl of Buchan's Silver Pen in Greek, 1929; Baroness de Gurbs Prizeman in Greek, 1929; Jenkyns Prizeman in Classical Philology, 1931; Liddell Prizeman in Greek Verse Composition, 1931; Simpson Prizeman and Robbie Gold Medallist in Greek, 1932; Seafield Gold Medallist in Latin, 1932; Fullerton, Moir and Gray Scholar in Classics, 1932.

4. It is of interest that Bruce's predecessor in the Rylands Chair at the University of Manchester, T. W. Manson, had been a Ferguson Scholar in Philosophy in 1919.

5. On this situation Bruce observes wryly: "It is a commentary on the situation of biblical scholarship in the IVF thirty years ago that a predominantly Anglican committee should have had to enlist in this way the services of two of the people called Brethren, who moreover were not professional theologians but teachers in the Arts Faculties of two secular universities" (*In Retrospect* [Grand Rapids: Eerdmans, 1980; rev. ed., Grand Rapids: Baker, 1993], 111).

Reliable?), a robust defense of the authenticity of the New Testament. This work has proved helpful and reassuring to multitudes.

In 1947 Bruce was appointed senior lecturer and head of the newly created Department of Biblical History and Literature at the University of Sheffield. Under his leadership the department so flourished that in 1955 he was promoted to a professorship. Sheffield was the first university in the British Isles to institute a chair of biblical studies in the faculty of arts (as opposed to the faculty of divinity). Bruce's Sheffield years (1947–59) saw the publication of two major commentaries on Acts (on the Greek text, 1951; on the English text, 1954); a commentary on Colossians; a history of the rise and progress of Christianity from its beginnings to the conversion of the English (*The Spreading Flame*—incorporating three earlier works, this volume was a response to E. W. Barnes's liberal views regarding the rise of Christianity); a handbook on *The Books and the Parchments: Some Chapters on the Transmission of the Bible,* which was the product of lectures delivered at Sheffield; and *Second Thoughts on the Dead Sea Scrolls.* It came as no surprise, then, that his alma mater, Aberdeen University, awarded him an honorary doctor of divinity degree in 1957 in recognition of his distinctive contribution to scholarship. What is fascinating about this award is that Bruce was a layman and had no formal academic training in biblical studies or theology apart from his Leeds diploma in Hebrew!

In May 1959 Bruce accepted an invitation to become the fourth occupant of the prestigious Rylands Chair at the University of Manchester. His predecessors in this post were A. S. Peake (1904–29), C. H. Dodd (1929–35), and T. W. Manson (1935–58). The two finalists for this appointment in 1959 were Bruce and J. A. T. Robinson, then dean of Clare College, Cambridge, and later the bishop of Woolwich and author of *Honest to God.* In all probability one of the considerations that finally tipped the scales in favor of Elgin's famous son in the estimation of the selection committee was his superior competence in the field of Old Testament studies, the official title of the position being Rylands Professor of Biblical Criticism and Exegesis, and not simply of New Testament studies. Bruce held this position until his retirement in 1978, whereupon he was elected professor emeritus of the university.

During his nineteen years (1959–78) as the Rylands professor, Bruce maintained a full teaching load of nine hours a week. Administrative responsibilities and committee work also consumed a large portion of his time, but his literary output continued unabated. Most notable were commentaries on Romans, Hebrews, and 1 and 2 Corinthians, and more general works such as *The English Bible: A History of Translations; Israel and the Nations from the Exodus to the Fall of the Second Temple; An Expanded Paraphrase of the Epistles of Paul; This Is That: The New Testament Development of Some Old Testament Themes; New Testament History; Tradition Old and New; Jesus and Christian Origins outside the New Testament;* and *Paul: Apostle of the Heart Set Free.* This last book gave him the most satisfaction to write. Of its subject he said, "I have learned to regard Paul as the greatest man who ever wrote in Greek. If anyone should call him the greatest writer of all time, I would not dispute the claim."[6]

Bruce's retirement was spent in Buxton, which lies some twenty-five miles from Manchester. A town in the High Peak district of Derbyshire, Buxton is renowned for its spa waters. The Crossways had been the family home there for over thirty years when Professor Bruce was called to his heavenly home on September 11, 1990, a month short of his eightieth birthday. Though battling against inoperable cancer, he was active in literary tasks until the day before his death. Among the many works that appeared during his retirement years we might mention commentaries on Galatians, 1 and 2 Thessalonians, Philippians, Ephesians, and Habakkuk as well as revisions of his two commentaries on Acts, a study of *The Real Jesus,* and a comprehensive treatment of *The Canon of Scripture.*[7]

The Person

Among the personal characteristics that Bruce's friends, students, and acquaintances are most likely to recall is his generous, kindly disposition. For example, Professor C. F. D. Moule noted in a celebratory volume dedicated to Bruce that "to think of Fred Bruce is to be assured that the Psalmist's vision can come true: 'Mercy and truth are met together; Righteousness and peace have kissed each other [Ps. 85:10].' I know no better example of uncompromising truthfulness wedded to that most excellent gift of charity: Fred Bruce always speaks the truth in love."[8] Like Barnabas (Acts 11:23), he was glad at any display of the grace of God. While he was relentlessly demanding of himself, he was invariably gentle with others' failings or inadequacies. This was particularly evident when he described or reviewed the work of others. His book reviews are literary models of the Golden Rule. But his generosity and scrupulous evenhandedness did not prevent forthright evaluation. Thus in reviewing "Commentaries on Acts" he once wrote: "Even scholars of the eminence of Haenchen and Conzelmann are not immune from the temptation of failing to verify their data: both, for example, reproduce Kirsopp Lake's erroneous statement that in Acts 16:6 'Phrygia' must be a noun and cannot be an adjective (as the rendering 'the Phrygian and Galatian region' implies)."[9]

---

6. "A Man of Unchanging Faith: An Interview with F. F. Bruce," by J. D. Douglas, *Christianity Today* 24.17 (Oct. 10, 1980): 17.

7. Bibliographies of Bruce's writings (books, articles, and reviews) until 1980 may be found in *Apostolic History and the Gospel: Biblical and Historical Essays Presented to F. F. Bruce on His 60th Birthday,* ed. W. Ward Gasque and Ralph P. Martin (Grand Rapids: Eerdmans, 1970), 21–33; *Journal of the Christian Brethren Research Fellowship* 22 (1971): 21–47; and *Pauline Studies: Essays Presented to Professor F. F. Bruce on His 70th Birthday,* ed. Donald A. Hagner and Murray J. Harris (Grand Rapids: Eerdmans, 1980), xxii–xxxvi. All of these bibliographies were compiled by W. Ward Gasque.

8. C. F. D. Moule, "Frederick Fyvie Bruce," in *Pauline Studies,* ed. Hagner and Harris, xviii.

9. F. F. Bruce, "Commentaries on Acts," *Bible Translator* 40.3 (July 1989): 317.

Akin to the kindly disposition were a spontaneous humor and dry wit. As a fourteen-year-old he concluded an article on "The Antiquity of the Scottish Race": "It has been shown that the Scots are descended from the Egyptian Queen Scota and the Assyrian King Sheshonk. Sheshonk's ancestors came to Egypt from Mesopotamia, the cradle of the human race, where man was never uncivilized! Thus people should think twice before saying that our progenitors were barbarians in the time of Tut-ankh-amen. They may say it of the English with perfect truth."[10] Or again, when a Manchester colleague who was an expert on Luther came to a faculty meeting directly after attending Vatican II as an observer and dumped a large attaché case on the table, Bruce's immediate comment was, "Here comes Gordon, bearing with him a parcel of pardons from the Pope!"[11]

Yet there was also a remarkable discipline in thought and in use of time. Very aptly, the collection of Bruce's essays that was intended to mark his eightieth birthday was entitled *A Mind for What Matters*. But as well as always giving attention to the larger picture and to what mattered, he remained preoccupied with accuracy in detail. The present writer recalls Bruce's disquiet at being unable to remember the precise length of his new grandchild at birth; he remedied the situation immediately by fetching his daughter's letter and checking the facts. As for his management of time, it is widely known that he completed the monumental task of proofreading the nine volumes of the *Theological Dictionary of the New Testament* while commuting by train between Buxton and Manchester during the decade 1963–73. What is more, the translator of these volumes from the German, Geoffrey W. Bromiley, commented that "if some errors still slip through the net . . . there is the consolation that Dr. Bruce in particular has been able to correct not a few errors in the original German."[12]

Bruce's discipline in thought was well served by his prodigious knowledge and memory. On one occasion he was serving as examiner for a Ph.D. student who had been researching aspects of French Protestantism in the nineteenth century. The candidate bears testimony that during the oral examination he discovered—to his amazement and chagrin—that Bruce, as the result of his own study of the original sources, already possessed certain items of information that the candidate imagined to be his alone. Or what a surprise to chance upon a review in which Bruce points out various spelling errors in a volume in Dutch on early church history, or to have him recall with ease and accuracy the names of various streets along which he passed during a visit to Auckland, New Zealand![13]

Despite his prodigious knowledge Bruce always exhibited a love of children and young people. He seemed to be as much at home in playing on the

10. F. F. Bruce, *Elgin Academy Magazine,* June 1925, p. 8.
11. An episode recounted by Moule, "Frederick Fyvie Bruce," xviii.
12. Geoffrey W. Bromiley, editor's preface in *Theological Dictionary of the New Testament,* ed. Gerhard Kittel and Gerhard Friedrich, 10 vols. (Grand Rapids: Eerdmans, 1964–76), 5:ix.
13. These examples are drawn from "Frederick Fyvie Bruce," in *Pauline Studies,* ed. Hagner and Harris, xx–xxi.

floor with the children of his research students as in chairing the seminars the fathers would attend. And although he was aware of the weaknesses of the Living Bible, he endorsed this paraphrase in advertisements found in a range of periodicals: "The strength of the Living Bible lies particularly in its ability to communicate to young people. They are a class for which I have a special concern, and I am glad it has met their needs so effectively."

Complementing this love of young people were a simple yet deep faith and an unpretentious manner. As one who sought to live in straightforward obedience to Christ, Bruce viewed vital faith not as the intellectual apprehension of truth but as absolute reliance on Christ. In the final chapter ("The Bible and the Faith") of *A Mind for What Matters,* he writes: "Christianity ceases to be Christianity if it does not remain founded on the person, the teaching and the saving work of this Christ, crucified Savior and risen Lord; and to his person, teaching and saving work the New Testament writings constitute our unique source of testimony. To sit loose to Scripture is thus to sit loose to the Christ to whom it bears witness, and to sit loose to him is to relax our Christian faith and life."[14] When asked about the principles he himself followed in determining God's will for his life, he replied: "Very simply: First I do what I am paid to do; then I do what I have to do; and then I do what I would like to do."

There is always the danger that an academic may lose touch with the common person. This may have been true of Bruce in his later years; he seemed, for example, to be unaware of the consternation caused among rank-and-file Christians by the bishop of Durham's (David Jenkins) statements in the early 1980s about the virgin birth and the resurrection. Yet Bruce moved easily among uneducated people, reflecting his favorite author's admonition, "Do not be haughty, but associate with the lowly" (Rom. 12:16 RSV). A delightful story is told of a workman who began attending Brinnington Chapel (near Stockport in Manchester), the church Bruce attended during his Manchester days. This recent convert so impressed his workmates with his convincing answers to their probing questions that they asked him, "Where did you learn all this?" "O well," came the answer, "there's an old fellow in our church called Fred. He seems to know all about these things."[15]

Finally, we must mention Bruce's commitment to the local church. Throughout his life he worshiped and served among the Christian (or Plymouth) Brethren. When asked what he found attractive about the particular pattern of the Brethren churches, he was accustomed to mention two points: the lack of any denominational principles that might restrict the full exercise of Christian unity ("I should find it intolerable to belong to a church which would not receive all whom Christ has received"); and an atmosphere of spiritual and intellectual freedom that he described as "so congenial and indeed

14. F. F. Bruce, *A Mind for What Matters* (Grand Rapids: Eerdmans, 1990), 279.
15. This story is related by I. Howard Marshall, "Frederick Fyvie Bruce, 1910–1990," *Proceedings of the British Academy* 80 (1991): 260.

exhilarating that I doubt if it could be matched elsewhere."[16] In various local churches over the years Bruce served as an elder, living up to his own description of the ideal elder as one who tries "to guide by example rather than rule by decree."[17] He endeared himself to all, whether he was welcoming worshipers as they entered church or dedicating an infant to God or expounding Scripture or leading the congregation in prayer or chairing a meeting of the elders or counseling young people who were about to enter a university.

The Scholar

F. F. Bruce was representative of a long—but unfortunately passing—tradition of British scholars, including other notable figures such as C. H. Dodd, C. F. D. Moule, and C. K. Barrett, who studied Greek and Latin before turning to specialization in the New Testament. Theirs was the distinct advantage of reading the documents of the New Testament against the wider background of Greek literature. This broad perspective gave them an impressive command of the grammar of New Testament Greek, as well as a sane and salutary attitude towards such issues as the historical reliability of the New Testament and the applicability of modern literary techniques to New Testament study. Bruce always had a well-founded skepticism of trendy theories propounded by those who had read no Greek other than the New Testament and the Septuagint. Yet he himself used and appreciated the full range of tried and proven literary techniques available to the modern investigator. Thus he states in a review of Helmut Merkel's *Die Widersprüche zwischen den Evangelien* (The contradictions between the Gospels) that such a study "makes the NT student the more grateful for the critical tools which enable him to solve with ease historical and theological problems with which the greatest Christian minds of the early centuries A.D. grappled so unsuccessfully."[18]

Bruce was superbly competent in both the Old and New Testaments. Although most of his commentaries are on New Testament books, he was among the swiftly diminishing number of scholars who are at home in either Testament. He was one of only two persons (Matthew Black was the other) ever to be elected to the presidency of both the Society for Old Testament Study (1965) and the Society for New Testament Study (1975); he held, as we noted earlier, the Rylands Chair of *Biblical* Criticism and Exegesis; he wrote three short monographs on the Dead Sea Scrolls,[19] documents which are at

---

16. F. F. Bruce, "Why I Have Stayed with the Brethren," *Journal of the Christian Brethren Research Fellowship* 10 (1965): 5.

17. Bruce, *In Retrospect*, 317.

18. F. F. Bruce, review of *Die Widersprüche zwischen den Evangelien: Ihre polemische und apologetische Behandlung in der alten Kirche bis zu Augustin*, by Helmut Merkel, *Erasmus* 25 (1973): 18.

19. F. F. Bruce, *Second Thoughts on the Dead Sea Scrolls* (Grand Rapids: Eerdmans, 1956); idem, *The Teacher of Righteousness in the Qumran Texts* (London: Tyndale, 1957); idem, *Biblical Exegesis in the Qumran Texts* (The Hague: van Keulen, 1959; rev. ed., Grand Rapids: Eerdmans, 1959). Bruce served as departmental editor for the Dead Sea Scrolls in the *Encyclopaedia Judaica*, ed. Cecil Roth and Geoffrey Wigoder, 16 vols. (Jerusalem: Macmillan, 1971–72).

the intersection of the Testaments; he delivered Tyndale Lectures on both the Old Testament (1947)[20] and the New (1941, 1968);[21] he authored what amounts to an introduction to the Bible, *The Books and the Parchments,* and a comprehensive investigation of *The Canon of Scripture;* and he was editor of the *Palestine Exploration Quarterly* for fourteen years (1957–71).

Did Bruce regard himself as a historian or a theologian, an exegete or a theoretician? The former in each case. If one is puzzled by a technical exegetical point in Scripture, one almost invariably finds in a commentary by Bruce the relevant technical information, whether historical or grammatical. On the other hand, if the point at issue is theological, one does not always find the desired help. In addition, Bruce preferred engaging in the exegetical task to discussing the principles of interpretation: playing the game was much more satisfying to him than discussing the rules.

That Bruce was not a scintillating lecturer comes as a surprise to those who did not have the opportunity to hear him speak. Where he shone—indeed dazzled—was in his writing, his answering of questions, and his extempore comments.[22] One of his research students at Manchester recalls it this way: "With his mild Scots brogue, Bruce usually lectured from a carefully prepared manuscript which was more often than not destined for publication. Unfailingly precise, he would now and then pencil in a correction without breaking stride. But awaited above all were the not infrequent interruptions when he would tug at the lapels of his gown, glance out the windows at the Mancunian skyline, and extemporize on this or that detail, often leaving his listeners breathless at his sheer mastery of the pertinent material and his penetrating, common-sense wisdom."[23]

What comes as no surprise, however, is that the author of nearly fifty books and over two thousand articles and reviews achieved an immaculate, pellucid English style. He could cut to the heart of an issue and sum it up with consummate aphoristic skill. Consider the following:

On Romans 14:1–12: "So completely was he [Paul] emancipated from spiritual bondage that he was not even in bondage to his emancipation."[24]

On Paul's opponents: "The earlier form of judaizing activity in Paul's mission field, which invoked the name of James and insisted on circumcision, gave way to a later form, which invoked rather the name of Peter and did not insist on circumcision. The former is reflected in Galatians, the latter in the Corinthian correspondence."[25]

20. F. F. Bruce, *The Hittites and the Old Testament* (London: Tyndale, 1948).
21. F. F. Bruce, *The Speeches in the Acts of the Apostles* (London: Tyndale, 1943); idem, "Paul and Jerusalem," *Tyndale Bulletin* 19 (1968): 3–25.
22. For twenty years Bruce answered readers' questions in *The Harvester,* a monthly magazine. For a selection see F. F. Bruce, *Answers to Questions* (Grand Rapids: Zondervan, 1973).
23. From "Frederick Fyvie Bruce," in *Pauline Studies,* ed. Hagner and Harris, xx.
24. F. F. Bruce, *The Epistle of Paul to the Romans* (Grand Rapids: Eerdmans, 1963), 243.
25. Bruce, "Paul and Jerusalem," 12–13.

On Romans 11:13–14: "So far as the offer of the gospel was concerned, the order might be 'to the Jew first and also to the Greek'; so far as its acceptance was concerned, the order was to be 'by the Greek first and also by the Jew.'"[26]

Contribution

Formal recognition of Bruce's distinction as a biblical scholar came from many quarters, but most notably from Aberdeen University (D.D., 1957—the award he treasured most), the British Academy (Fellow, 1973; Burkitt Medal for Biblical Studies, 1979), and the University of Sheffield (D.Litt., 1988).[27] His greatest pride, however, was in his students: "As I look back over forty-three years of teaching, there are few things that give me such undiluted joy as the contemplation of my pupils. . . . I shall be well content to have the quality of my teaching assessed by the quality of my students."[28] These students, women and men, are now scattered worldwide, serving as pastors and missionaries, seminary professors and university teachers. At Manchester, Bruce supervised more Ph.D. students in biblical studies than has any other professor in a British university.

Unlike many eminent biblical scholars, Professor Bruce is not celebrated for propounding and championing some revolutionary or distinctive thesis. He epitomized nonfaddishness, and was mildly impatient with those current trends that he instinctively recognized as temporary fads, and with those scholars who were given "merely to parroting the Germans," as he once put it. There is no Manchester School that owes its genesis to F. F. Bruce. Yet his name is rightly associated with specific opinions or critical positions of which he was a chief or prominent exponent—positions such as the historical value of Acts in the reconstruction of early Christianity, and especially of the chronology of Paul's life;[29] the equation of Galatians 2:1 with Acts 11:30; an early date for Galatians; Ephesians as "the quintessence of Paulinism"; and the view that Paul's main legacy is his law-free gospel that creates equality.

It is sometimes said of Erasmus that he "laid the egg that Luther hatched." Of Bruce it could be said that he laid the egg which evangelical scholarship worldwide has now hatched. Fifty years ago first-rate evangelical biblical scholarship was scarcely visible in any part of the globe; today it is flourishing throughout the English-speaking world. We cannot account for this mon-

26. Ibid., 22.
27. For assessments of Bruce's contribution to biblical studies see I. Howard Marshall, "Frederick Fyvie Bruce," 245–60; idem, "F. F. Bruce as a Biblical Scholar," *Journal of the Christian Brethren Research Fellowship* 22 (1971): 5–12; A. R. Millard, "Frederick Fyvie Bruce, 1910–1990," *Journal of Semitic Studies* 36 (1991): 1–6. I am grateful to Professor Millard for reading the present article and making useful suggestions for its improvement.
28. Bruce, *In Retrospect,* 228–29.
29. Significantly, Bruce was invited to contribute the article "The Acts of the Apostles: Historical Record or Theological Reconstruction?" to the influential and prestigious *Aufstieg und Niedergang der römischen Welt* (II.25.3, 2569–2603).

umental reversal without recognizing the worldwide influence of British evangelicalism and in particular the pioneering leadership of F. F. Bruce. He was intimately involved in the discussions and plans which led to the establishment of a residential library for biblical research (Tyndale House) in Cambridge (1944) and the creation of the Tyndale Fellowship for Biblical Research (1945), both actions being aimed at removing the stigma of unscholarliness and obscurantism from evangelicalism by fostering biblical research in a spirit of loyalty to the historic Christian faith.[30] Bruce served on the Tyndale Fellowship committee from 1941 to 1974, acting as chairman from 1942 to 1951. From Tyndale House and the Tyndale Fellowship have come a myriad of scholarly and popular works over the last half-century, works such as the Tyndale Old and New Testament Commentaries, the *Tyndale Bulletin*, the *New Bible Commentary*, the *New Bible Dictionary*, the six-volume Gospel Perspectives series, and now the projected six-volume series on *The Book of Acts in Its First-Century Setting*, not to mention the dozens of Ph.D. theses and monographs produced by individual members of the fellowship and readers at the library of Tyndale House.

For over thirty years (1949–80) Bruce captained the flagship of British evangelicalism as editor of the *Evangelical Quarterly*. But while known and esteemed as an evangelical,[31] he was also a gentleman of broad interests and sympathies and maintained a wide circle of friends. Witness the facts that he was president of the Yorkshire Society for Celtic Studies from 1948 to 1950, and editor of its journal *Yorkshire Celtic Studies* from 1945 to 1957; the editor of the *Journal of the Transactions of the Victoria Institute* from 1949 to 1957, a periodical dealing particularly with the relation between science and religion; a contributor to the Catholic Layman's Library;[32] and an active member of the advisory committee of the *Journal of Semitic Studies* from 1959 to 1978 (vol. 23.2 was dedicated to him).

Professor Bruce's most technical work is his commentary on the Greek text of Acts, now in its third edition. But most of his books are more popular, designed for a wider audience than those who have enjoyed the privilege of a college or university education. He never forgot that he had been gifted "for the common good" (1 Cor. 12:7). Along with his friends A. M. Hunter and William Barclay he formed what we might call "that Scottish triumvirate of brilliant popularizers."

---

30. For a fascinating account of these events see F. F. Bruce, "The Tyndale Fellowship for Biblical Research," *Evangelical Quarterly* 19 (1947): 52–61.

31. Bruce himself preferred to be known simply as an evangelical—not a conservative evangelical, but an "unhyphenated" evangelical: "Conservatism is not the essence of my position. If many of my critical conclusions, for example, are described as being conservative, they are so not because they are conservative, nor because I am conservative, but because I believe them to be the conclusions to which the evidence points. If they are conservative, then none the worse for that" ("F. F. Bruce: A Mind for What Matters. A Conversation with a Pioneer of Evangelical Biblical Scholarship," by W. Ward Gasque and Laurel Gasque, *Christianity Today* 33.6 [April 7, 1989]: 24).

32. F. F. Bruce, "Exiles in an Alien World," in *Understanding the Bible*, ed. John P. Bradley and John Quinlan, 2 vols. (Gastonia, N.C.: Good Will, 1970), 2:265–301.

F. F. Bruce is evangelicalism's Erasmus, a man of phenomenal knowledge and prodigious literary output, the main stimulus in a revival of biblical scholarship, and one of the most renowned biblical scholars of his time. But for all these and other fascinating similarities,[33] Bruce of Buxton differs from Erasmus of Rotterdam in one important respect: whereas Erasmus ended his days suspect in the eyes of both Roman Catholics and Protestants, Bruce is recognized on all sides—Protestant, Catholic, and Jewish—as one of the twentieth century's foremost evangelical biblical scholars.

Primary Sources

Bruce, F. F. *The Acts of the Apostles: The Greek Text with Introduction and Commentary.* Grand Rapids: Eerdmans, 1951; 3d ed., 1990.

———. *Are the New Testament Documents Reliable?* London: Inter-Varsity, 1943; 5th ed. *(The New Testament Documents: Are They Reliable?)*, Grand Rapids: Eerdmans, 1960.

———. *The Books and the Parchments: Some Chapters on the Transmission of the Bible.* London: Pickering and Inglis, 1950; 5th ed., London: Marshall Pickering, 1991.

———. *The Canon of Scripture.* Downers Grove, Ill.: InterVarsity, 1988.

———. "Colossians." In E. K. Simpson and F. F. Bruce, *Commentary on the Epistles to the Ephesians and the Colossians.* New International Commentary on the New Testament. Grand Rapids: Eerdmans, 1957.

———. *Commentary on the Book of the Acts: The English Text with Introduction, Exposition, and Notes.* New International Commentary on the New Testament. Grand Rapids: Eerdmans, 1954; rev. ed., 1988.

———. *The English Bible: A History of Translations.* London: Lutterworth, 1961.

———. *The Epistle of Paul to the Romans: An Introduction and Commentary.* Tyndale New Testament Commentaries. Grand Rapids: Eerdmans, 1963.

———. *The Epistles to the Colossians, to Philemon, and to the Ephesians.* New International Commentary on the New Testament. Grand Rapids: Eerdmans, 1984.

———. *The Epistle to the Galatians: A Commentary on the Greek Text.* New International Greek Testament Commentary. Grand Rapids: Eerdmans, 1981.

———. *The Epistle to the Hebrews: The English Text with Introduction, Exposition, and Notes.* New International Commentary on the New Testament. Grand Rapids: Eerdmans, 1964.

———. *An Expanded Paraphrase of the Epistles of Paul.* Exeter: Paternoster, 1965.

———. *1 and 2 Corinthians.* London: Oliphants, 1971.

———. *1 and 2 Thessalonians.* Word Biblical Commentary. Waco: Word, 1982.

33. Both men were distinguished classicists whose principal love was the Greek New Testament; both cherished independence (although Bruce was never averse to routine); both moved with ease in international settings; both pioneered the teaching of a new subject at a British university (Erasmus, Greek at Cambridge; Bruce, biblical studies at Sheffield); both published paraphrases of New Testament books that enjoyed wide popular appeal; both regularly laid out both sides of an argument and showed that each contained an element of truth; the opinions of both were sought by correspondents from many nations.

————. "Habakkuk." In *The Minor Prophets*, edited by Thomas E. McComiskey, 2:831–96. Grand Rapids: Baker, 1993.

————. *Israel and the Nations from the Exodus to the Fall of the Second Temple.* Grand Rapids: Eerdmans, 1963.

————. *Jesus and Christian Origins outside the New Testament.* Grand Rapids: Eerdmans, 1974.

————. *A Mind for What Matters: Collected Essays of F. F. Bruce.* Grand Rapids: Eerdmans, 1990.

————. *New Testament History.* London: Nelson, 1969.

————. *Paul: Apostle of the Heart Set Free.* Grand Rapids: Eerdmans, 1977.

————. *Philippians.* San Francisco: Harper and Row, 1983.

————. *The Real Jesus.* Downers Grove, Ill.: InterVarsity, 1985.

————. *Second Thoughts on the Dead Sea Scrolls.* Grand Rapids: Eerdmans, 1956.

————. *The Spreading Flame.* Grand Rapids: Eerdmans, 1953.

————. *This Is That: The New Testament Development of Some Old Testament Themes.* Exeter: Paternoster, 1968.

————. *Tradition Old and New.* Grand Rapids: Zondervan, 1970.

Secondary Source

Bruce, F. F. *In Retrospect: Remembrance of Things Past.* Grand Rapids: Eerdmans, 1980; rev. ed., Grand Rapids: Baker, 1993.

George Eldon Ladd

Donald A. Hagner

As soon as George Ladd became a Christian at the age of eighteen, he knew that he wanted to devote his life to serving Christ. The way in which he was to be employed in the service of the kingdom of God he could not yet know.

Born in Alberta, Canada, on July 31, 1911, Ladd was raised in New England. His father, who was a country doctor in New Hampshire, had become a Christian shortly before George's birth. As a boy George had wondered about the meaning of a phrase written in his father's Bible: "Born again, August 10, 1910." George realized for himself the meaning of those words in 1929, when, as a young woman graduate of Moody Bible Institute preached in a small Methodist church in Maine, he was moved to respond to the gospel.

George became an undergraduate student at Gordon College in Massachusetts, from which he graduated in 1933 with a bachelor of theology degree. Already in his college years he began his service of Christ as a student pastor at a small Baptist church in Gilford, New Hampshire. In the year of his graduation he was ordained as a minister in the Northern Baptist (American Baptist) denomination. He immediately began further theological education at Gordon Divinity School, from which he was eventually to graduate with his bachelor of divinity degree in 1941. He remained as pastor of the Gilford church, married a young woman named Winifred Webber, whom he had met when a freshman at Gordon College, and traveled to Boston twice a week for his classes at Gordon. In 1936 he became the pastor of the First Baptist Church of Montpelier, Vermont, where he remained for six years.

Ladd had been captivated by his theological studies (especially of the Greek New Testament) at Gordon and was now longing to do advanced work. A move in 1942 to become pastor of the Blaney Memorial Church in Boston provided the opportunity for which he was waiting. He enrolled in the classics department at Boston University. His appetite now fully whetted, he applied to the graduate program of Harvard University. Ladd's acceptance there in 1943 signaled a turn in his career that moved him from the church to academia. (Actually, the move had begun a little earlier, for he served as instructor of Greek at Gordon College from 1942 to 1945.) And yet it must be said that he never weakened in his concern for and commitment to the church or, more accurately, to his initial call to the service of

Christ. It was obedience to Christ that provided the fundamental motivation for his intense scholarly work throughout his entire career. But never did he lose his pastor's heart.

After somewhat over a year in the classics department of Boston University, Ladd moved with alacrity to the classics department at Harvard, where he specialized in biblical and patristic Greek. At Harvard he studied not only Greek, but also related subjects such as the history and literature of the intertestamental period, the Hellenistic background of the New Testament, and the Septuagint. He was able to supplement his studies with work at the Episcopal Theological Seminary in Cambridge. And in 1946, while he worked away on his doctoral studies, he became head of the New Testament department at Gordon Divinity School. The experience at Harvard brought Ladd into direct contact with scholarship of the highest caliber and provided him with a personal standard throughout his career. He is reported to have said, "Harvard didn't change what I believed, but it certainly did change the way I held my belief."[1]

Ladd passed his comprehensive exams in 1947 and, on the basis of his dissertation "The Eschatology of the Didache," was awarded the Ph.D. in 1949. In his very first book, which was published three years later, Ladd wrote: "In the course of graduate studies, I determined to go as deeply as possible into the backgrounds of biblical eschatology."[2] In the same book, Wilbur M. Smith, Ladd's colleague at Fuller Seminary, noted, "Dr. Ladd is contemplating a much larger work, covering the whole field of New Testament eschatology."[3] Thus from virtually the beginning of his advanced studies and his scholarly career, Ladd had oriented himself to what would become a lifetime study of eschatology.

In 1950 George Ladd embarked upon a new adventure: he crossed the continent to the West Coast to join the faculty of Fuller Seminary in the fourth year of its existence, a fledgling seminary in comparison with the venerable academic establishments of the East. His motivation is clear. Fuller had exciting dreams of establishing a new standard of excellence in evangelical scholarship, and with that in mind had advantaged its faculty members with light teaching loads, small classes (the school was not large), abundant secretarial help, and exceptionally generous sabbatical allowances. Fuller, in short, offered just what Ladd craved: a context of openness to critical scholarship and the luxury of time for research and writing.

Ladd knew at least one of the faculty members he would join, namely Edward John Carnell, who had been a fellow student at Harvard. He also knew the president of the seminary, Harold John Ockenga, who tried to run the

1. Reported in Rudolph Nelson, *The Making and Unmaking of an Evangelical Mind: The Case of Edward Carnell* (New York: Cambridge University Press, 1987), 69, 235 n. 22.
2. George Eldon Ladd, *Crucial Questions about the Kingdom of God* (Grand Rapids: Eerdmans, 1952), 13.
3. Ibid., 11.

school from Boston, where he continued as pastor of the Park Street Church. In his new position Ladd became the colleague of New Testament scholar Everett F. Harrison, who had left the faculty of Dallas Theological Seminary in 1947 to become one of the four original faculty members at Fuller. It was fortunate for Ladd that Harrison had experienced difficulties with the dispensational system of Lewis Sperry Chafer.

The Fuller faculty was clearly in the process of breaking away from certain aspects of fundamentalism, notably its ecclesiastical separatism, its dispensational system of eschatology, and its closed-minded attitude to the theological scholarship of the wider Christian world. Ladd fit particularly well into this innovative context and eventually became one of the key figures in developing the seminary's direction. At the same time, as we shall see, Ladd never departed in any significant way from his conservative roots.

The Early Works on Eschatology

With his thorough knowledge of Jewish and Christian eschatology, Ladd was in a position to make an important contribution to evangelical New Testament scholarship. Not surprisingly, more than half of the books that he would write are directly on eschatological themes, including his first, *Crucial Questions about the Kingdom of God* (1952), and his last, *The Last Things* (1978).

In the middle of the twentieth century, the system of dispensational eschatology promoted by Lewis Sperry Chafer at Dallas Seminary was enjoying a very wide acceptance in the United States thanks to the great popularity of the Scofield Bible. Ladd had great trouble with much in this system, especially with its understanding of the Old Testament, the bifurcation of Israel and the church into two groups with two separate destinies, and the notion of a secret pretribulation rapture. It was predictable that Ladd's first book would deal with the eschatology of the dispensationalists.

Apparently to soften the impact of *Crucial Questions about the Kingdom of God,* Wilbur Smith was careful to point out that Ladd was "a thoroughgoing premillennialist, a believer in a Messianic Kingdom and in the millennium to come."[4] This remained true of Ladd throughout his career, although he was never very demonstrative about it. He defended historic premillennialism in a 1977 essay,[5] but in the same volume he could say in response to the essay of Anthony Hoekema representing amillennialism, "I am in agreement with practically all that Hoekema has written with the exception of his exegesis of Revelation 20."[6] In his own essay Ladd frankly admitted that there are "serious theological problems with the doctrine of a

4. Ibid.
5. George Eldon Ladd, "Historic Premillennialism," in *The Meaning of the Millennium: Four Views,* ed. Robert G. Clouse (Downers Grove, Ill.: InterVarsity, 1977), 17–40.
6. George Eldon Ladd, "An Historic Premillennial Response," in *Meaning of the Millennium,* ed. Clouse, 189.

millennium," and that the millennium is "found in only one passage of Scripture."[7] This latter fact, however, is "no reason for rejecting it."[8] In his final book, *The Last Things,* it is significant that although Ladd admits to being premillennialist,[9] no main section or chapter is devoted to the millennium. A pertinent *obiter dictum* in Ladd's lectures was that he would give no more emphasis to an element of theology than Scripture itself did. In *The Last Things* Ladd refers to amillennialists as "godly, evangelical Christians" and defends them against the dispensationalist claims that theirs is a liberal hermeneutic.[10] Instead, they hold their view "because they feel the Word of God demands it."[11]

On the other hand, *Crucial Questions* does present a devastating critique of dispensational eschatology. Ladd notes that he has been led "to espouse positions which do not coincide with those with which many American Evangelicals are familiar and to differ with many students of the Word with whom I would prefer to agree."[12] His study has led him, indeed, to turn against his own earlier dispensational background. The book consists of lectures given at Western Conservative Baptist Seminary in Portland, Oregon, a dispensationally oriented school, as can be seen in a remark in President Earl S. Kalland's foreword, "Though one's opinions differ, the material here presented should be carefully evaluated."[13] After a skillful presentation of the history of the problem of how to understand the kingdom of God, Ladd provides strong evidence for the conclusion that the kingdom is to be understood as a present spiritual reign as well as a future reign on earth. Turning to the so-called postponed-kingdom theory, he demonstrates that Jesus did not offer the earthly Davidic kingdom to the Jewish people, but a kingdom that can be experienced in the present. Finally, Ladd turns to exegesis of Revelation 20 and a consideration of the objections to millennial interpretation.[14]

Ladd was aware that his book was only a beginning. Indeed, he already had in mind a more thorough treatment of the subject of New Testament eschatology, for no one had as yet written "a comprehensive study of the kingdom of God in the New Testament from a conservative, premillennial position which takes into account the critical literature."[15] This gap would be

7. Ladd, "Historic Premillennialism," 40, 38.
8. Ladd, "Response," 190.
9. George Eldon Ladd, *The Last Things* (Grand Rapids: Eerdmans, 1978), 109; see also idem, *A Theology of the New Testament,* rev. ed., ed. Donald A. Hagner (Grand Rapids: Eerdmans, 1993), 680–81.
10. Ladd, *Last Things,* 110.
11. Ibid., 111.
12. Ladd, *Crucial Questions,* 13.
13. Earl S. Kalland, foreword to Ladd, *Crucial Questions,* 7.
14. Ladd's views in this book have had considerable impact on the so-called revised dispensationalists, who accept his main conclusions. See Craig A. Blaising and Darrell L. Bock, *Progressive Dispensationalism* (Wheaton, Ill.: Scripture, 1993), 39.
15. Ladd, *Crucial Questions,* 59.

filled more than ten years later by *Jesus and the Kingdom* (1964), which is Ladd's most significant book, at least from the standpoint of technical New Testament scholarship.

Ladd's second book, *The Blessed Hope* (1956), was also devoted to correcting what he considered to be the errors of dispensational eschatology, this time the notion of the pretribulation rapture of the church. The thesis of the book is that "the Blessed Hope is the second coming of Jesus Christ and not a pre-tribulation rapture";[16] what Christians await is not a secret rapture, but "the glorious appearing of our great God and Savior, Jesus Christ" (Titus 2:13). Although Ladd insists that the book should "not be interpreted primarily as an attack on pretribulationists or pretribulationism,"[17] it is hard to see it as anything other than a painstaking demolition of that viewpoint. He is concerned, however, to be irenic and to preserve for both sides "the right to differ 'in the Lord.'"[18] The book is popularly written, but obviously rests on careful and thorough research. Arguing that his view has been the historic hope of the church, Ladd documents the rise of pretribulationism, examines the scriptural data, and shows that the rapture is at best a questionable inference. In *The Last Things* Ladd notes that John Walvoord, the longtime president of Dallas Theological Seminary (who over the years reviewed in *Bibliotheca Sacra* every book of Ladd's on eschatology), in his 1957 book *The Rapture Question* had written the following words: "The fact is that neither posttribulationism nor pretribulationism is an explicit teaching of Scripture. The Bible does not in so many words state either."[19] Ladd adds that lamentably these words were deleted from later printings of the book.[20]

Three years after *The Blessed Hope*, Ladd's third book appeared under the title *The Gospel of the Kingdom: Scriptural Studies in the Kingdom of God* (1959). This was in many senses the precursor to the technical treatment of the same subject that appeared in 1964, *Jesus and the Kingdom. The Gospel of the Kingdom,* dedicated to Charles E. Fuller, consisted of popular expositions that had been given at various churches and Bible conferences. They are, as Ladd indicates in his foreword, edifying "proclamation" appealing "to the heart and the will." This is the best example we have of Ladd the preacher-scholar, combining his scholarly expertise in eschatology with the burden of the preacher for his congregation. The foreword also sums up the fundamental orientation of his entire teaching career: "Serious students of the Bible sometimes lose sight of the fact that the study and interpretation of Scripture should never be an end in itself. . . . When a gulf exists between the lecture-room and the pulpit, sterility in the class-room and superficiality in the pulpit often result."[21]

16. George Eldon Ladd, *The Blessed Hope* (Grand Rapids: Eerdmans, 1956), 11.
17. Ibid., 12.
18. Ibid., 13.
19. John F. Walvoord, *The Rapture Question* (Findlay, Ohio: Dunham, 1957), 148.
20. Ladd, *Last Things*, 64.
21. George Eldon Ladd, *The Gospel of the Kingdom* (Grand Rapids: Eerdmans, 1959), 7.

Works on the Problem of History

Having studied the writings of European (especially German) scholars, Ladd took up the opportunity to become personally acquainted with Continental scholarship by spending sabbatical leaves in Heidelberg (1958 and 1964) and Basel (1961). The influence of Rudolf Bultmann was at its zenith in that era, and an evangelical scholar like Ladd simply had to address the issue of the possibility of the supernatural in history, as well as other issues raised by Bultmann. These concerns typify the second of Ladd's great interests, namely the problem of history. Ladd published a number of articles on the subject and produced two quite short, but nevertheless helpful books, *Jesus Christ and History* (1963) and *Rudolf Bultmann* (1964). Then in 1967 came his extremely influential *The New Testament and Criticism*.

In *Jesus Christ and History,* Ladd affirms the second coming of Christ and the establishment of the kingdom of God on earth as the final goal of history; they are realities that will involve a literal historicity. The biblical narrative causes us to conclude that "what we call the 'natural' and the 'supernatural' in the Bible are nothing other than two different modes of the divine activity in the world."[22] The two comings of Christ "involve nothing less than an inbreaking of the world of God into human history."[23] At the same time, however, "there is not nor can there be any natural 'historical' explanation or analogy of the resurrection [of Christ]. It is suprahistorical. It is a direct unmediated act of God."[24]

The book on Bultmann presents a lucid exposition of Bultmann's views followed by a brief critique. Here too we find Ladd's insistence that "the Bible's message includes real futurity."[25] And here Ladd also stresses that the redemptive acts of God occur in *history,* and concludes therefrom that history is essential to revelation. In responding to Bultmann's strict historicism, Ladd notes that "the scientific historical method, valid as it is for most historical study, has its limitations and is incapable by virtue of its very presuppositions of understanding redemptive history."[26] Of the acts of God in history "the historian as historian cannot speak, for to him, history can be understood only as an unbroken flow of causes and effects."[27] Ladd concludes that "what God has done for me in the past can be understood only by the eye of faith. It occurred in history, but it transcends history."[28]

Although it is not Ladd's most important book, *The New Testament and Criticism* is to be reckoned among his most influential. The reason for this

22. George Eldon Ladd, *Jesus Christ and History* (Chicago: InterVarsity, 1963), 17.
23. Ibid., 53.
24. Ibid., 54.
25. George Eldon Ladd, *Rudolf Bultmann* (Chicago: InterVarsity, 1964), 41.
26. Ibid., 46.
27. Ibid.
28. Ibid., 50. For an extended discussion of Ladd's treatment of Bultmann, see John A. D'Elia, "The Mediatorial Character of the New Evangelical Movement in the Life and Work of George Eldon Ladd" (Th.M. thesis, Fuller Theological Seminary, 1992), 29–48.

statement is that this small book opened the door to a positive affirmation of biblical criticism for countless conservative, Bible-believing Christians who wanted to study their Bibles seriously, but who had been taught that criticism is the Bible's deadly enemy. Written with great conviction, *The New Testament and Criticism* has an undeniable autobiographical aspect to it. It can be considered an apology for Ladd's own scholarly work, for he had himself traveled the road from naive believer to critical scholar, but without abandoning the evangelical faith. Thus, not surprisingly, one of the dedicatees of the book was Henry J. Cadbury, Ladd's mentor at Harvard, who was almost certainly also in view when Ladd wrote: "A sincere tribute should be paid to university teachers in the critical tradition who are truly liberal in spirit, and who may feel that their evangelical students are very slow to learn, but who, recognizing an earnestness in searching for facts, are therefore tolerant of critical conclusions different from their own."[29]

Ladd's central thesis, that "the Bible is the Word of God given in the words of men in history,"[30] placed him between the liberals, who denied the full meaning of "the Word of God," and the fundamentalists, who denied the full implications of "the words of men in history." The historical rootedness of these human words mandates use of the critical method. Ladd was well aware, however, of the mistaken and unfounded presuppositions of most practitioners of that method, and thus advocated what he called "a historical-theological methodology"[31]—a method that would not exclude a priori the possibility of God's directly acting in history: "Because it is history, the Bible must be studied critically and historically; but because it is *revelatory* history, the critical method must make room for this supra-historical dimension of the divine activity in revelation and redemption."[32] Later in the book Ladd writes: "Faith can never contradict established facts. But faith means accepting the witness of the biblical authors to events which transcend the strict historical method."[33]

Ladd carefully defines biblical criticism not as *criticizing* the Bible, but as making informed judgments about a host of historical questions that of necessity attach to the ancient documents. He then proceeds to describe different types of biblical criticism: textual, linguistic, literary, form, historical, and comparative religions. The final paragraph of his conclusion is worth quoting in full:

> Here is perhaps the greatest miracle of the Bible: that in the contingencies and relativities of history God has given to men His saving self-revelation in Jesus of Nazareth, recorded and interpreted in the New Testament; and that in the

29. George Eldon Ladd, *The New Testament and Criticism* (Grand Rapids: Eerdmans, 1967), 13 n. 4.
30. Ibid., 12.
31. Ibid., 14, 16.
32. Ibid., 33.
33. Ibid., 187.

New Testament itself, which is the words of men written within specific historical situations, and therefore subject to the theories and hypotheses of historical and critical investigation, we have the saving, edifying, sure Word of God.
In hearing and obeying the Word of God, the scholar must take the same stance
as the layman: a humble response which falls to its knees with the prayer,
Speak, Lord, for thy servant heareth.[34]

Although Ladd affirms the inspiration of Scripture,[35] he rather scrupu-
lously avoids the word *inerrancy* in *The New Testament and Criticism.* By
contrast, in the foreword to his first book he had been described as "a true
evangelical believer in an inerrant Bible."[36] Indeed, when Ladd came to
Fuller in 1950, the seminary's statement of faith included reference to the inerrancy of the Bible. Very much depends, naturally, on how the word *inerrancy* is understood. Although we may assume that Ladd signed this statement in good faith, over the years he, like a number of his colleagues, began
to feel increasingly that the word was an ill-chosen one and could not do justice to the actual phenomena of Scripture. In the conclusion to *The New Testament and Criticism,* Ladd quotes his colleague Everett F. Harrison, who in
a path-breaking article had written: "We may have our own ideas as to how
God should have inspired the Word, but it is more profitable to learn, if we
can, how He has actually inspired it."[37] Ladd agreed fully with Harrison that
the doctrine of the nature of inspiration must be framed on inductive rather
than deductive grounds. Already in a faculty meeting in 1960 Ladd had
"frankly stated his own opinions about inerrancy [namely, that discrepancies
in the Gospels rule out the notion], prefacing them with the remark that he
realized that his views could cost him his job."[38] In December of 1962, when
the dispute among faculty members came to a head, Ladd readily lined up
with those who were against describing inspiration with the word *inerrant.*

Ladd preferred, however, not to be polemical on this point. Some years
earlier, in the controversy over Carnell's inauguration address as president of
the seminary, Ladd had sided with his old friend against a number of his colleagues. Carnell's address had championed tolerance and love in the realm of
theological debate, an attitude that was close to Ladd's heart.

Jesus and the Kingdom

In 1964 Ladd published three books. In addition to the work on Bultmann,
he published a brief introduction to Acts, *The Young Church,* which appeared in the Bible Guides series edited by William Barclay and F. F. Bruce.
Ladd's view of Acts is conservative. Frankly admitting the difficulties to

34. Ibid., 218.
35. Ibid., 21, 110, 118.
36. Kalland, foreword to Ladd, *Crucial Questions,* 7.
37. Ladd, *New Testament and Criticism,* 217, quoting Everett F. Harrison, "The Phenomena of
Scripture," in *Revelation and the Bible,* ed. Carl F. H. Henry (Grand Rapids: Baker, 1958), 249.
38. George M. Marsden, *Reforming Fundamentalism* (Grand Rapids: Eerdmans, 1987), 213.

which scholars have long pointed, he concludes: "In spite of such difficult historical problems, it is clear that Acts intends to be an historical record; yet it is not a record of history for its own sake but history with a purpose, history that tells a story. If this purpose includes a theological viewpoint, it need be no less historical."[39] This little book is exceptionally rich in its theological analysis, as one might indeed expect given Ladd's interests.

The big book of 1964, however, was Ladd's most technical book, *Jesus and the Kingdom,* dedicated to his wife Winnie. It was here above all that Ladd hoped to make a major and lasting contribution to the world of New Testament scholarship. The book is subtitled *The Eschatology of Biblical Realism,* signifying that Ladd was making "the effort to understand the New Testament [eschatology] from within the mind of the authors, to stand where the biblical writers stood, rather than to force the biblical message into modern thought forms."[40] His treatment of the main subject attempts to "make use of the dynamic concept of the rule of God as the integrating center for Jesus' message and mission."[41] The direction of the book is set by the initial chapter, which provides an extensive review of "The Debate over Eschatology." The questions that emerge concern the definition of the kingdom and the way in which its presence is to be conceived, as well as the role of apocalyptic in all of this. The main sections of the book are "The Promise of the Kingdom," which reviews the Old Testament promise and the apocalyptic interpretation thereof; "The Fulfillment of the Promise," which constitutes the heart of the book and explains the nature of the present kingdom as being "Fulfillment without Consummation" (and includes discussions of the church and ethics); and, finally, "The Consummation of the Kingdom," which is followed by a concluding chapter on "The Abiding Values for Theology."[42]

The book reveals a wide acquaintance with the pertinent literature, both European and American. The analytical power of the author's mind is apparent throughout. The lucid writing typical of Ladd is also evident here. Ladd superbly marshals the evidence for his conclusions. *Jesus and the Kingdom* is, in brief, a very fine book that makes a most persuasive case for the author's position.

Unfortunately, not everyone shared this evaluation. And even more unfortunately, Norman Perrin, an influential New Testament scholar who had just published his own book on the kingdom, wrote a very negative review of Ladd's book for the widely read journal *Interpretation.*[43] Everyone in academia who teaches New Testament knows the story. No other word is appropriate: Ladd was simply *devastated* by this review. Perrin was troubled

---

39. George Eldon Ladd, *The Young Church* (Nashville: Abingdon, 1964), 17.

40. George Eldon Ladd, *Jesus and the Kingdom* (New York: Harper and Row, 1964), xiii.

41. Ibid., xi.

42. For a thorough evaluation of Ladd's contribution on this subject, see Bradley J. Harper, "The Kingdom of God in the Theology of George Eldon Ladd" (Ph.D. diss., St. Louis University, 1994).

43. Norman Perrin, "Against the Current," *Interpretation* 19.2 (April 1965): 228–31; idem, *The Kingdom of God in the Teaching of Jesus* (Philadelphia: Westminster, 1963).

by "the author's approach and methodology, his understanding of contemporary critical scholarship, and his attitude to its findings." More specifically, Ladd assumes "an uncritical view of the Gospels as historical sources"; his exegesis of the texts is arbitrary in that he "simply extracts from them what he needs . . . ignoring everything else"; in the quest to find support for his views in the writings of critical scholars Ladd "is quite capable of misunderstanding the scholar concerned," and has "an equal passion for dismissing contemptuously aspects of their work which do not support him." The penultimate sentence in the review is scathing: "Ladd thus takes his stand squarely in midstream of the contemporary concern about eschatology—with his face turned resolutely upstream, whence we all came some considerable time ago."

Negative reviews of a book are, of course, painful for any author. But why did Ladd take this particular review so hard? One must of course point to the fact that this was not just another book for Ladd. He was very highly invested in it, not only in that he had put so much time and work into it, but in that it was a major statement in the area of his specialization and expertise. It was in a sense his life's work. But the review was painful for another reason. The criticisms made by Perrin in effect called into question Ladd's claim (and deep desire) to be considered a critical scholar. It was as though Ladd were being excluded from a club in which he felt he deserved membership. Perrin's review was virtually an attack on Ladd's self-perceived identity.

One might have hoped that Ladd would have been able to take the review with objectivity, considering the position of its author, whose own book on the kingdom could not hold if Ladd were right. The author of the present article remembers the apropos comment of F. F. Bruce about the whole matter: "What else could he have expected from someone with the orientation of a Norman Perrin?" All the same, Ladd, who never had a strong self-image, remained deeply hurt by the review. When Perrin heard about Ladd's painful reaction to the review and was informed of Ladd's fundamentalist background, he regretted having written such a sharply critical review. Some years afterwards at a professional conference, Ladd and Perrin happened to sit at the same table. Ladd, it is reported, shook throughout the meal and was unable to speak. After the others had left the table, Perrin to his credit was gentlemanly enough to apologize to Ladd for the hurt he had caused him. A little later at the same conference, Ladd burst into tears when he told Robert Guelich what had happened.[44]

Others on the left also attacked the book. Oddly enough, Ladd never spoke of any pain caused by other negative reviews, such as the blistering one of Erich Grässer,[45] or the thoughtful, but strongly critical one of M. E. Boring, who concluded that Ladd's "failure to admit the presence of problems

44. D'Elia, "Mediatorial Character," 26–27.
45. Erich Grässer, review of *Jesus and the Kingdom*, by George Eldon Ladd, *Theologische Literaturzeitung* 92.9 (Sept. 1967): 665–67.

[especially concerning the reliability of the Jesus tradition] nullifies much of the effect that his work might have had in answering them, and we must look elsewhere for help."[46] Nor was Ladd particularly bothered by criticism from the right, for example, Walvoord's comment that "readers who want a clear path through the jungle will not find it in this volume."[47]

When Ladd reissued his book ten years after the first edition, this time under the title *The Presence of the Future,* he felt constrained to make only a few changes. In the reworked preface he introduced a new paragraph in which, with an eye on Perrin's review, he notes that the first edition of the book "raised critical questions which the author had not intended, particularly the degree to which the Gospels accurately embody the teachings of Jesus."[48] His purpose, rather, had been to expound the theology of the kingdom of God. He concedes that we do not have the *ipsissima verba* of Jesus, but also notes his conviction "that the Gospels embody a substantially accurate report of the teachings of Jesus."[49] At the end of the preface he thanks those reviewers of the first edition, "particularly in Britain and on the Continent," who understood his purpose and wrote favorable reviews. In the updated first chapter Ladd takes up Perrin's 1967 book, *Rediscovering the Teaching of Jesus.*[50] Describing Perrin's methodology as "surely an exercise in historical implausibility," Ladd concludes that Perrin was in error "at three important points": his rejection of all the "Son of man" sayings on the grounds that they were creations of the church; his locating the present kingdom in individual experience; and his denial of the literal futurity of the kingdom.[51]

Ladd's assessment of the earlier book of Perrin, *The Kingdom of God in the Teaching of Jesus,* is to be found in *The Pattern of New Testament Truth,* which comprises lectures given at North Park Seminary. Here he explicitly mentions the painful review,[52] and criticizes Perrin for his attempt "to demythologize the eschatology of the Kingdom of God" and for his total lack of clarity concerning the nature of the future consummation. Ladd's book was devoted to illuminating the unity and diversity of the New Testament, treating the Synoptics, John, and Paul within a *Heilsgeschichte* framework.

The Prime Years

By the year 1970 Ladd's stature as a New Testament scholar had become increasingly recognized, and his alma mater, Gordon Divinity School, awarded

46. M. E. Boring, review of *Jesus and the Kingdom,* by George Eldon Ladd, *Encounter* 29.2 (Spring 1968): 232.
47. John F. Walvoord, review of *Jesus and the Kingdom,* by George Eldon Ladd, *Bibliotheca Sacra* 122.1 (Jan.-March 1965): 75.
48. George Eldon Ladd, *The Presence of the Future* (Grand Rapids: Eerdmans, 1974), xii.
49. Ibid.
50. Norman Perrin, *Rediscovering the Teaching of Jesus* (New York: Harper and Row, 1967).
51. Ladd, *Presence of the Future,* 37–38.
52. George Eldon Ladd, *The Pattern of New Testament Truth* (Grand Rapids: Eerdmans, 1968), 57–63.

him an honorary doctorate in divinity. Now in his twentieth year at Fuller, Ladd had reached his prime. One indication of the stature he enjoyed was the invitation to be a contributor to the twenty-fifth-anniversary edition of *Interpretation,* with the likes of James Barr and James M. Robinson. Ladd wrote a fine piece entitled "The Search for Perspective," in which he unabashedly admits his fundamentalist background and defends his unmodish *Heilsgeschichte* approach to New Testament theology.[53] Ladd here presents one of his most powerful and personal statements of his theological perspective and Christian faith. In a way the article serves as a distillation of his work on the problem of theology, history, and criticism.

In 1972 Ladd published his only full-length commentary (he had earlier produced very brief commentaries on Matthew [1960] and Acts [1962]), *A Commentary on the Revelation of John.* Although this is a full commentary, it is written not so much for scholars as for lay students of the Bible. Again Ladd's gift for clarity is evident throughout. Ladd the exegete focuses on the significance of the book for the original readers, but at the same time understands much of the material as a foreshadowing of events that will involve the church of the last times: "We conclude that the correct method of interpreting the Revelation is a blending of the preterist and the futurist methods."[54] Thus he maintains that the beast refers both to Rome and to the eschatological Antichrist; similarly, the great tribulation refers primarily to the future eschatological event, but also to the tribulation of the first century and subsequent eras. In his discussion of chapter 20, Ladd rejects the dispensational understanding of the millennium as involving fulfilment of the theocratic promises to Israel; he affirms his own view in these words: "The form of premillennialism which sees the Revelation as a prophecy of the destiny of the church is not widely held today but it is the theology expounded in the present commentary."[55]

In 1974 Ladd published *A Theology of the New Testament.* This book should be considered his magnum opus, not because it is his most creative or original work, but because of its scope, its scholarly excellence, and its synthetic character. The influence of the book among evangelicals has been considerable. Indeed, in Mark Noll's 1984 poll of evangelical biblical and theological scholars, Ladd's *Theology* ranked as the second most influential book, second only to Calvin's *Institutes!*[56] The work had a long history, since years earlier Ladd had begun to build up a series of chapters on key subjects in the form of mimeographed pages made available to his students. All students who took New Testament theology at Fuller with Ladd, from the 1950s to the appearance of the book, were familiar with one form or another

53. George Eldon Ladd, "The Search for Perspective," *Interpretation* 25.1 (Jan. 1971): 41–62.

54. George Eldon Ladd, *A Commentary on the Revelation of John* (Grand Rapids: Eerdmans, 1972), 14.

55. Ibid., 261.

56. Mark A. Noll, *Between Faith and Criticism: Evangelicals, Scholarship, and the Bible in America* (San Francisco: Harper and Row, 1986), 212.

of this growing collection of essays. Avowedly a textbook, *A Theology of the New Testament* was written "to give a survey of the discipline, to state its problems, and to offer positive solutions as the author sees them."[57] A superb introduction to New Testament theology, it shows that the framework of salvation history illumines how the New Testament coheres and how its teaching developed in the decades following the ministry of Jesus. As one would guess, Ladd is particularly strong in his discussion of Jesus and the kingdom according to the Synoptics! Equally strong, however, is his treatment of Paul's theology. Ladd's discussion of the fourth Gospel and Acts shows how cautious and conservative he remained, despite his affirmation and use of the critical method. If the book has any weakness, it is that the discussion of Hebrews and the General Epistles is too brief and does not meet the high standard set by the other material.

Reviews of the *Theology* quite consistently criticized it for failure to discuss the theologies of the Synoptic writers individually and for insufficient treatment of the issue of unity and diversity. Ladd himself planned to deal with these matters in a new edition of the book, but was unable to accomplish this before the stroke that incapacitated him in 1980. A revised edition issued in 1993 does fulfil Ladd's plan.[58]

In 1975 Ladd published *I Believe in the Resurrection of Jesus*. Here Ladd returned to his interest in historical method and the question of how a genuinely critical method can be compatible with evangelical faith. Now, however, the discussion moved from the abstract plane to the consideration of a particular issue, the resurrection of Jesus. Again Ladd insists that the historian qua historian has no direct access to events whose causation lies outside the normal chain of cause and effect. Miracles are God's intervention into that familiar process; there can be no historical proof of such matters. Nevertheless there are historical facts related to the resurrection that must be explained—in particular the bedrock fact of the belief of the disciples in the resurrection. Ladd argues that "the bodily resurrection of Christ is the only adequate explanation to account for the resurrection faith and the admitted 'historical' facts."[59]

The book, however, is not only a rational defense of the resurrection of Jesus, but a brilliant treatment of the theology of the resurrection. Among the topics covered are the centrality of the resurrection, the Old Testament and Judaic background, the relation of the Messiah and the resurrection, and then the witness of the Gospels and Paul. In his discussion of the data of the Gospels, Ladd includes an attempted harmonization of the resurrection accounts which he had some years earlier done for his own amusement.[60] At

57. George Eldon Ladd, *A Theology of the New Testament* (Grand Rapids: Eerdmans, 1974), xi.
58. George Eldon Ladd, *A Theology of the New Testament*, rev. ed., ed. Donald A. Hagner (Grand Rapids: Eerdmans, 1993).
59. George Eldon Ladd, *I Believe in the Resurrection of Jesus* (Grand Rapids: Eerdmans, 1975), 27.
60. Ibid., 91–93.

the same time, discussing the nature of the Gospels, Ladd observes that "we may expect to find variation in unimportant details, but a sound memory as to the major events." This point is followed by one of the very few personal allusions in Ladd's writings. He tells of getting a detail wrong as he recounted an experience he and his wife had had: "My wife said to me, 'George, why don't you get your dates straight? It was on a Friday night, not Sunday.' Friday or Sunday—that was unimportant to the purpose for which I told the story. I was wrong in the date, but I was in no way wrong about the fact."[61]

The sudden and totally unexpected death of Winnie in 1977 was a tragedy from which Ladd never recovered. It was in a real way the beginning of the end for Ladd himself. Without the stability she had provided he became prey to his deep-seated insecurity and lingering feelings of inferiority, conditions for which he had received counseling for quite a number of years. He publicly spoke of the real help that psychological counseling can afford the Christian. But with Winnie gone, Ladd began to decline both physically and psychologically.

At a special dinner at Fuller in 1978, Ladd was presented with a festschrift in his honor, *Unity and Diversity in New Testament Theology*, edited by his star pupil, Robert Guelich. Among the contributors were world-class New Testament scholars, colleagues, and former students. The large number of individuals offering their congratulations in the list at the end of the volume testifies to the widespread appreciation for Ladd.

It is only fitting that in the last book he published Ladd returned to the subject of his first books. *The Last Things* (1978) is a lay-level account of the main themes of eschatology. It is a poignant thought that in a mere four years Ladd would know for himself what he had written in this little volume: "The one fact that is taught by both the Gospels and Paul is that the righteous dead—believers—are with Christ in the presence of God, awaiting the resurrection."[62] In 1980 Ladd suffered a stroke that left him unable to read or write. Although he was in a pitiable state, his faith did not weaken. Two years later he went to the reward he awaited with such eager expectation.

Legacy

There is no little irony in the fact that Ladd was disappointed in what he had been able to accomplish for Christ through his scholarship. He had little sense of what he had achieved. But David Allan Hubbard, president of Fuller Seminary, pointed to Ladd's "incredible ability to stimulate graduate students."[63] His teaching and his conviction of the importance of scholarship for the church inspired many of his students to go on to more advanced study of the New Testament. He also had a tremendous influence on those who

61. Ibid., 77.
62. Ladd, *Last Things*, 39.
63. David Allan Hubbard, "Biographical Sketch and Appreciation," in *Unity and Diversity in New Testament Theology*, ed. Robert A. Guelich (Grand Rapids: Eerdmans, 1978), xiii.

knew him only through his writings. Noll's 1984 poll showed Ladd to be "the most widely influential figure on the current generation of evangelical Bible scholars."[64] Already in 1979 James D. Smart, discussing the uncertain future of biblical theology, had singled out Ladd's *Theology* as exemplary of a trend among evangelicals that "has great promise for the future," namely, the ability "to combine a thoroughgoing historical scholarship with . . . deeply rooted devotion to a biblical faith."[65] Yet the so-called neoevangelicals did have problems: "Fundamentalists and conservatives did not trust them . . . , and the mainline academic community refused to take them seriously."[66] Accordingly, Ladd did not have as much impact on the large world of critical scholarship as he desired, but through his remarkable impact on the current generation of evangelical scholars his ultimate dream may perhaps yet begin to be realized.

Ladd himself went as far as his fundamental background and the climate of the times allowed. Hubbard catches the very essence of the man in referring to his creating an effective bridge between evangelical faith and contemporary scholarship: "He has refused to compromise either his commitment to the basic doctrines of the Christian church or to sound technical study. Devout and critical, critical because of the devoutness and devout because of what he had learned from biblical criticism—these are the measured adjectives in George Ladd's life and witness."[67]

In 1992, thanks to a generous donor, the first endowed chair in the biblical and theological divisions at Fuller Seminary came into being, the George Eldon Ladd Chair in New Testament, and in an inauguration in 1993 the writer of the present article was installed as its first incumbent. In this manner the name of Ladd has been memorialized at Fuller Seminary, but more importantly, the seminary has thus indicated its continuing support for the vision that so motivated Ladd in his service for Christ and his kingdom.

Primary Sources

Ladd, George Eldon. "The Acts of the Apostles." In *Wycliffe Bible Commentary,* edited by Charles F. Pfeiffer and Everett F. Harrison, 1123–78. Chicago: Moody, 1962.

———. *The Blessed Hope.* Grand Rapids: Eerdmans, 1956.

———. *A Commentary on the Revelation of John.* Grand Rapids: Eerdmans, 1972.

———. *Crucial Questions about the Kingdom of God.* Grand Rapids: Eerdmans, 1952.

64. Noll, *Between Faith and Criticism,* 112; see also the statistics on pp. 209–14. For members of the Institute for Biblical Research, which represents evangelical biblical scholars in the United States, Ladd is far and away the most influential theologian.
65. James D. Smart, *The Past, Present, and Future of Biblical Theology* (Philadelphia: Westminster, 1979), 155.
66. Marsden, *Reforming Fundamentalism,* 250.
67. Hubbard, "Biographical Sketch," xiii.

————. *The Gospel of the Kingdom: Scriptural Studies in the Kingdom of God.* Grand Rapids: Eerdmans, 1959.

————. *I Believe in the Resurrection of Jesus.* Grand Rapids: Eerdmans, 1975.

————. *Jesus and the Kingdom: The Eschatology of Biblical Realism.* New York: Harper and Row, 1964.

————. *Jesus Christ and History.* Chicago: InterVarsity, 1963.

————. *The Last Things.* Grand Rapids: Eerdmans, 1978.

————. "Matthew." In *The Biblical Expositor,* edited by Carl F. H. Henry, 3:23–72. Philadelphia: Holman, 1960.

————. *The New Testament and Criticism.* Grand Rapids: Eerdmans, 1967.

————. *The Pattern of New Testament Truth.* Grand Rapids: Eerdmans, 1968.

————. *The Presence of the Future: The Eschatology of Biblical Realism.* Grand Rapids: Eerdmans, 1974.

————. *Rudolf Bultmann.* Chicago: InterVarsity, 1964.

————. "The Search for Perspective." *Interpretation* 25.1 (Jan. 1971): 41–62.

————. *A Theology of the New Testament.* Grand Rapids: Eerdmans, 1974; rev. ed., edited by Donald A. Hagner, 1993.

————. *The Young Church: Acts of the Apostles.* Nashville: Abingdon, 1964.

Secondary Sources

D'Elia, John A. "The Mediatorial Character of the New Evangelical Movement in the Life and Work of George Eldon Ladd." Th.M. thesis, Fuller Theological Seminary, 1992.

Harper, Bradley J. "The Kingdom of God in the Theology of George Eldon Ladd: A Reflection of 20th Century American Evangelicalism." Ph.D. diss., St. Louis University, 1994.

Hubbard, David Allan. "Biographical Sketch and Appreciation." In *Unity and Diversity in New Testament Theology,* edited by Robert A. Guelich, xi–xv. Grand Rapids: Eerdmans, 1978.

Marsden, George M. *Reforming Fundamentalism: Fuller Seminary and the New Evangelicalism.* Grand Rapids: Eerdmans, 1987.

Unity and Diversity in New Testament Theology: Essays in Honor of George E. Ladd. Edited by Robert A. Guelich. Grand Rapids: Eerdmans, 1978. (For a full bibliography of Ladd's writings see pp. 214–17.)

William Sanford LaSor

David Allan Hubbard

Born in 1911 to a father who was a Presbyterian elder and a mother who was a loyal daughter of the Scottish church, William Sanford LaSor exhibited two of his chief characteristics at an early age: a penchant for academic scholarship and a passion for Christian service. He was just fifteen when he graduated from high school in Philadelphia. At nineteen, after earning a B.A. degree in chemistry from the University of Pennsylvania, he matriculated at Princeton Theological Seminary. His prodigious appetite for learning showed itself dramatically in his Princeton years: he completed simultaneously a bachelor of theology degree with honors from the seminary and a master of arts program in comparative religion at the university.

LaSor's later academic achievements included a master of theology degree from Princeton Seminary (1943), a Ph.D. from Dropsie College for Hebrew and Cognate Learning (1949), and a Th.D. from the University of Southern California (1956). Amazingly, each of these advanced degrees was garnered while LaSor was engaged in full-time ministries of preaching or teaching.

LaSor's pastorates were in Presbyterian congregations in Ocean City, New Jersey (1934–38), and Scranton, Pennsylvania (1938–43). World War II found him serving as a chaplain in the United States Navy (1943–46). A tour of duty took him through central China, including the Gobi Desert, as he ministered to the personnel at weather stations during one of the truly unusual chapters in American naval history. His formal teaching career began in 1946 when he was called to Lafayette College as professor of religion and chair of the department.

Fuller Theological Seminary was in only its third year of existence (1949) when LaSor accepted the invitation to join the faculty as an associate professor of Old Testament, thus teaming with Gleason Archer, who had moved to Fuller a year earlier. LaSor's years at Fuller consumed the rest of his career. Soon promoted to full professor, he taught Old Testament, Hebrew, and a range of Semitic languages including epigraphic South Arabic, Akkadian, Aramaic, Syriac, Ugaritic, and Ethiopic. Following his retirement in 1977, he continued to teach on a restricted schedule as senior professor until 1980, when he was awarded emeritus status, which he held until his death in 1991.

Principal Interests

Biblical and Related Languages

Of the many and varied subjects that seized LaSor's interest during his decades of labor at Fuller, only a handful can be touched on here. Language teaching may well warrant first mention. His Hebrew students in the fall of 1949 would never forget the sheaves of notes that he prepared for virtually every class session. The inductive method of learning a language was more than his practice, it was his passion. He yearned for students to be plunged into the language like newborn babies and to learn to swim quickly and in time feel as at home in it as possible. His mentor at Dropsie had been Cyrus Gordon, a master of Semitic philology and expert in both Akkadian texts from Nuzi and the huge corpus of Ugaritic tablets. From Gordon, LaSor had absorbed the inductive method and then adapted it and transplanted it into his students with the dogged persistence of a Johnny Appleseed.

LaSor's *Handbook of Biblical Hebrew* was the written expression of his superb ability to stimulate language learning. Its subtitle clarifies its method: *An Inductive Approach Based on the Hebrew Text of Esther*. Published privately in 1951, the work was finally made available to the general public in 1978. LaSor's choice of the Book of Esther was a happy one: (1) it contains virtually all the basic vocabulary of the Old Testament; (2) it is rich in feminine words not readily apparent in the more masculine narratives; and (3) the relative absence of specific theological statements frees students to concentrate on vocabulary and grammar.

Convinced that New Testament Greek could also be taught inductively, LaSor developed a similar handbook keyed to the Book of Acts. It was first used at Fuller in 1964 and was later published in an enlarged, revised form. In addition to these teaching aids for language students we should mention syllabi on biblical Aramaic (1968) and Old Babylonian (1970).[1]

Underlying most of LaSor's scholarly endeavors and never far from his consciousness was his rich knowledge of Semitic philology. Grammatical structures and lexicography, especially the pursuit of cognate words among the branch languages of the Semitic tree, were important to him. Closest to his heart were the patterns of sound shifts in the alphabets and syllabaries of the languages. His Dropsie dissertation, "Semitic Phonemes, with Special Reference to Ugaritic and in Light of Egyptian Evidence" (1949), put him among the leaders in this field internationally. He published surprising little of his research, but it undergirded all his exegetical and linguistic teaching and writing.[2]

---

1. For a summary of his approach to teaching biblical and related languages, his analysis of a number of introductions to Greek and Hebrew, and a list of auxiliary works see William Sanford LaSor, "Learning Biblical Languages," *Biblical Archaeology Review* 13.6 (1987): 50–55.
2. For a couple of samples of the quality of his work see William Sanford LaSor, "Secondary Opening of Syllables Originally Closed with Gutturals (in Hebrew)," *Journal of Near Eastern Studies* 15 (1956): 246–50; idem, "The Sibilants in Old South Arabic," *Jewish Quarterly Review* 48.2 (Oct. 1957): 161–73.

He drilled into his students the patterns in which the sounds of the Semitic languages were either retained or regularly modified as they appeared in sister languages. Stern were his warnings about confusion between ʾaleph and ʿayin or a random mixing of the sibilants in Ugaritic, Hebrew, Akkadian, and Arabic—shibbōleth (Judg. 12:6) was indeed a watchword for him!

These linguistic niceties were not a game but a guard against inaccurate etymologies which could skew the meaning of biblical words and muddle the sense of the inspired text. LaSor's career-long focus on the interrelationship of the Semitic languages was given vent in his last published article.[3] In it he argued for the existence of a proto-Semitic language, an *Ursprache* from which developed the tongues now extant in textual or spoken form. The bases of his argument were the common grammatical constructions, the common vocabulary for domestic and cultural elements, and, above all, the phonemic relationships of the most basic words in the various languages.

The Dead Sea Scrolls

A second passion was the Dead Sea Scrolls. Their discovery in 1947 was shaking the scholarly world with Richter-scale intensity about the time LaSor moved to Fuller (1949). Not having access to the texts themselves in those early years, LaSor chose to make his contribution in two significant ways. First, he became one of the early bibliographers of publications related to Qumran. The firstfruits of this work was his *Bibliography of the Dead Sea Scrolls, 1948–1957*. Immediately thereafter the French scholarly journal *Revue de Qumran* appointed him contributing editor of bibliography, a post he held for a half dozen years. From 1960 to 1965 he published in that journal eleven lists of books, articles, and reviews. Anyone who chooses to study the early history of work on the Dead Sea Scrolls will be LaSor's debtor.

LaSor's second contribution in the field was to interpret for evangelical Christians the significance of the scrolls. At a time when opinions of the scrolls were running the gamut from almost idolatrous veneration to deep suspicion, LaSor's evenhanded evaluations were a boon. His Th.D. thesis had drawn him into investigating the importance of the scrolls for both intertestamental Judaism and the Johannine writings of the New Testament. Thus prepared, he published two books, *Amazing Dead Sea Scrolls and the Christian Faith* and *The Dead Sea Scrolls and the New Testament*, along with a cluster of articles and reviews in magazines, festschrifts, and learned journals.

Biblical Geography

Another virtually career-long preoccupation was biblical geography. One of LaSor's early hopes had been to write a historical geography that would

---

3. William Sanford LaSor, "Proto-Semitic: Is the Concept No Longer Valid?" *Maarav* 5.6 (1990): 189–205.

be a modern counterpart to George Adam Smith's classic *Historical Geography of the Holy Land*. Instead, he made his contribution to the field in the revision of *The International Standard Bible Encyclopedia*. The first volume (1979) lists him as associate editor for archeology. The later volumes (1982, 1986, 1988) expand his portfolio to biblical geography and archeology. He authored, edited, or revised approximately two thousand articles. Especially noteworthy are his magisterial presentations on Egypt and Jerusalem. To all these labors for the encyclopedia which spanned more than two decades, LaSor brought firsthand experience of the terrain as well as an eagle eye for accuracy of detail. His biographical summary lists twenty-three trips to the Near East, some on his own, some as a popular and effective tour guide. His records and reports of his geographical explorations were greatly enhanced by his skill as a photographer. Scores of his photos grace the pages of the encyclopedia. Others are found in the *Old Testament Survey,* which he co-authored with David Allan Hubbard and Frederic Bush. Another testimony to his love of Bible sites and his eye for texture and color is the ambiance of the McAlister Library on Fuller's Pasadena campus.

Biblical Interpretation

Interpreting Scripture for students, laypeople, and pastors was certainly among LaSor's most cherished activities. Indeed it formed the core of his sense of mission. His earliest listed publication (1935) was a privately published booklet of *Six Sermons on the Person and Work of Jesus*. The project in his computer when he died fifty-five years later was his revision of the *Old Testament Survey*. In between there hatched from his typewriter a clutch of books on biblical characters (*Great Personalities of the Old Testament* and *Great Personalities of the New Testament;* revised forms appeared as *Men Who Knew God* and *Men Who Knew Christ*) whose faith, feats, and foibles were set in the contexts of their times and places. His eagerness to help readers understand biblical backgrounds issued in *Daily Life in Bible Times*. His love of geography, chronology, and history beams from his comments on 1 and 2 Kings in the third edition of *The New Bible Commentary*. The diversity of his interests is attested in the fact that his largest volume of biblical interpretation is *Church Alive!* an exposition of Acts. In addition, dozens of timely articles along with reviews of significant books or new versions of the Bible appeared in a host of journals and periodicals from 1937 to 1987. Virtually all were geared to enrich the reader's understanding of Scripture and Christian theology.

Biblical Eschatology

It is no surprise that LaSor's last full-scale book deals with biblical eschatology—*The Truth about Armageddon: What the Bible Says about the End Times*. For from beginning to end there is in his writing and teaching a strand of interest in such matters:

1. His two master's degrees delved into eschatology—Zoroastrianism (Princeton University, 1934) and premillennialism (Princeton Seminary, 1943).
2. The role of the Messiah had been the focus of his attention in several studies.[4]
3. The future role of the Jews in God's plan was another ongoing subject of his study.[5]
4. Interpretation of biblical prophecy was his central hermeneutical concern. He wrote of the potential fullness of biblical prophecies, a meaning beyond the meaning for the prophet's own times—a *sensus plenior*, LaSor called it, borrowing a term from Roman Catholic exegesis.[6] Though such meanings lie outside the watch of historical-grammatical exegesis, they are to be understood as part of redemptive history and as controlled by the message of Scripture as a whole, the canon inspired and preserved by the Holy Spirit.

The Truth about Armageddon is the overdramatic title given the book that distills a lot of LaSor's thinking on biblical theology and its application to Christian life. The president of the United States was using the term in the early 1980s; "Armageddon" had become the buzzword for pending calamity in the Middle East. LaSor's scope of interest was much wider, as a summarization of the book's chapters makes clear:

1. In the biblical understanding the "end" is not the cessation of existence, but the achievement of God's redemptive plan that has been under way since the fall of humanity.
2. The present age is both a satanic age and a redemptive age in which the saving love of God in Christ will ultimately triumph.
3. The one God, the Lord of Abraham and of Jesus Christ, is forming one people—Jews and Gentiles (Paul's picture in Rom. 11 has *one* tree, not two)—through one redemptive plan and one covenant of grace.
4. The suffering that God has called his servant people and his servant Son to endure in a fallen world touches God himself, as Hosea's painful story illustrates.

---

4. E.g., William Sanford LaSor, "The Messiahs of Aaron and Israel," *Vetus Testamentum* 6 (1956): 425–29; idem, "The Messianic Idea in Qumran," in *Studies and Essays in Honor of Abraham A. Neuman,* ed. Meir Ben-Horin, Bernard D. Weinryb, and Solomon Zeitlin (Philadelphia: Dropsie College for Hebrew and Cognate Learning, 1962), 343–64; and idem, "The Messiah: An Evangelical Christian View" (paper presented at the Conference of Jews and Evangelical Christians, New York, 8 Dec. 1975).

5. E.g., William Sanford LaSor, "Have the 'Times of the Gentiles' Been Fulfilled?" *Eternity* 18.8 (Aug. 1967): 32–34; and idem, "The Conversion of the Jews," *Reformed Journal* 26.9 (Nov. 1976): 12–14. The gist of LaSor's thinking on this subject is compressed in *Israel: A Biblical View* (Grand Rapids: Eerdmans, 1976).

6. See, e.g., William Sanford LaSor, "Interpretation of Prophecy," in *Baker's Dictionary of Practical Theology,* ed. Ralph G. Turnbull (Grand Rapids: Baker, 1967), 128–35.

5. A satanic spirit, powerful but finite, seeks to frustrate God's program, deceive God's people, and control human governments. These efforts will intensify sharply toward the end, but are ultimately doomed.
6. The picture of the Messiah, painted in the intertestamental centuries with the use of Old Testament materials, is fulfilled and embellished in Jesus the Christ. The messianic age is both material and spiritual. To describe it as only spiritual is to sever it from its Old Testament roots.
7. The Lord Jesus Christ, risen from the dead, will return to earth to raise the dead, establish his kingdom, execute the last judgment, and destroy Satan and his hosts.
8. Antichrist, a pervasive spirit executing Satan's work in present political, economic, and religious power structures, will, toward the end, be embodied in a person with great force of deception against which God's elect must be on guard.
9. The end times will see an unprecedented outburst of satanic oppression from which the church also may suffer and yet be preserved.
10. Simplistic interpretations of Armageddon itself are to be rejected. The biblical emphasis is on conflict between the forces of Satan and the people of God, not on the location, specific participants, and timing.
11. There will be a millennium, a long-lasting period of Christ's earthly rule of righteousness and prosperity following the second coming. The purposes of the millennium are to vindicate God's creative activity and triumph over Satan and to fulfil God's promises of an earthly kingdom to Abraham and his posterity.
12. The return of Christ will trigger the resurrection of all the dead. Those dead in Christ will be raised at the return; the others will be raised and be judged after the millennial kingdom has run its course.
13. The final judgment brings the age of God's forbearance to a close; it marks a clear distinction between those who trust God in Christ and those who do not, though the exact nature and duration of God's punishment are not made clear in Scripture.
14. God will make new our sin-cursed, Satan-dominated planet. God will be the supreme and unchallenged ruler of the universe, whose people will not only serve him but rule with him in an eternity of unsullied righteousness and unfettered praise.

This final book shows where LaSor stood as Christian believer and biblical interpreter. His upbringing with the Scofield Bible was reshaped but not entirely shed by his further study. Neither truly dispensationalist nor fully Reformed, LaSor imbibed from the springs of both traditions. His emphases on Israel's future role and Christ's earthly reign were dispensational in nature. His view of God's people, Christians and Jews, as one and not two was more Reformed; so was his view that there is a continuity rather than discontinuity between the two Testaments. He resisted almost equally the detailed eschatological scheduling of dispensationalism (leaning as he did toward a posttribulation timing of Christ's coming) and the minimizing of human free-will that is characteristic of much Calvinism.

A Classical Evangelical

To call LaSor a typical, classical evangelical would not miss the mark by much. He was a classical evangelical in the mold of B. F. Westcott, J. B. Lightfoot, and F. J. A. Hort, as well as B. B. Warfield, James Orr, Robert Dick Wilson, and J. Gresham Machen—intellectuals all, but without a drop of obscurantism in their veins. LaSor, like them, not only eschewed but despised the anti-intellectualism, the suspicion of higher education, that is characteristic of a substantial stream of American fundamentalism. His choice of Dropsie for his doctoral studies was a deliberate attempt to equip himself to deal with the extremes of higher criticism practiced in virtually all the graduate universities in the 1930s and 1940s.

LaSor's evangelical commitment was unwavering from start to finish in his ministry. It showed itself academically in his love for and trust in the biblical text, which he tried fervently to hear on its own terms. It was demonstrated also in his encouragement and support of evangelical missions around the world. Christ's Great Commission weighed on his shoulders with an urgency akin to that of many missionary leaders. Much of his extensive foreign travel was in fact part of an effort to understand and then explain to Christians in North America the task of cross-cultural evangelism.

LaSor did not lend his weight to separation from the old-line denominations. Here his path diverged from Machen's and Wilson's. He chose Princeton not Westminster as his theological alma mater. Under Otto Piper he was heavily influenced by a Reformed biblical theology with a European flavor that left a large mark also on the work of George Eldon Ladd, who for a quarter of a century toiled in a study next door to LaSor's.

LaSor's loyalty to his Presbyterian denomination was sorely tested during his first years at Fuller. In opposition to the school, the Los Angeles presbytery contended that the four Presbyterian members of the early faculty—Wilbur M. Smith, Everett F. Harrison, Gleason Archer, and LaSor—should not be granted permission to labor "outside the bounds of Presbytery." This contention was based on statements and actions of Charles E. Fuller, Harold John Ockenga, and Smith that were branded "divisive." Also, Fuller's founding was seen as an incursion on Presbyterian turf that had theretofore been assigned to San Francisco Theological Seminary. The conflict was finally settled (1953) by the General Assembly of the Presbyterian Church in the U.S.A. in favor of the presbytery. The four Fuller Presbyterians had to transfer their ordinations to other ecclesiastical bodies. LaSor chose the Reformed Episcopal Church. In 1965 the Los Angeles presbytery reversed its decision and recognized Fuller as a suitable place for Presbyterians to be trained and, therefore, for Presbyterians to serve as faculty members. LaSor immediately applied for reacceptance and with great delight in 1967 was restored to full standing in his cherished denomination.

In addition to denominational loyalty LaSor had a flexibility which kept his staunchly conservative theology from turning harsh or brittle. In the rounds of debates that marked Fuller's early history he was virtually always on the progressive side. He preferred "infallibility" to "inerrancy" as the basic term to describe the nature of biblical authority, though he lived with the latter word during the two decades that it was included in Fuller's doctrinal statement (1950–72). He wrote and spoke openly in favor of the Revised Standard Version, whose translation of Isaiah 7:14 and other passages sparked controversy among fundamentalists and evangelicals in 1952. Along with Harrison, Ladd, Daniel P. Fuller, Paul King Jewett, and Clarence Roddy, he was supportive of David Allan Hubbard's call to Fuller's presidency in 1963 over the misgivings of Archer, Smith, and Harold Lindsell.

LaSor's flexibility together with his inductive method of studying Scripture and its languages endeared him to graduate students. During his thirty years of active teaching, he mentored more Th.M. students and encouraged a greater number into Ph.D. studies than did any other Fuller faculty member. Literally dozens of his disciples serve in academic posts and have produced hundreds of learned articles and scores of useful books. This team of teachers along with the crew of military chaplains that he nurtured throughout his academic tenure may be his greatest legacy.

A year before he died LaSor looked glum as he strolled into my office. "No projects to tackle" was his summation of his depression. "Let's get on with the revision of the *Old Testament Survey*" was my eager answer. His whole demeanor brightened. The bell of a call to duty had rung, and the elderly scholar, like a seasoned firehorse, was ready for the harness and the pull. He enjoyed hard work as much as anybody I have ever known and had the rare capacity of infecting others with that joy.

At LaSor's memorial on January 23, 1991, the theme was "The Good Shepherd," the text John 10:11–18. The homily focused on the qualities of shepherding that Bill LaSor had learned and adopted from Jesus' description of himself: (1) intimacy in caring for the sheep—LaSor knew his students by name, shared himself with them, affirmed their worth and potential; (2) an inclusive view of the flock—a concern for students that ranged far beyond his own campus (hence his textbooks), a burden for the larger church beyond the evangelical movement, a desire for closer relations between Christians and Jews; and (3) personal investment in rescuing the sheep—immense voluntary sacrifice graced his labors as pastor, chaplain, teacher, scholar. His was a lifetime of all-out effort for the sake of the Master's sheep.

Primary Sources

LaSor, William Sanford. *Amazing Dead Sea Scrolls and the Christian Faith*. Chicago: Moody, 1956; rev. ed., 1962.

————. *Bibliography of the Dead Sea Scrolls, 1948–1957*. Pasadena: Fuller Theological Seminary Library, 1958.

————. *Church Alive!* Glendale, Calif.: Regal, 1972.

————. *Daily Life in Bible Times*. Cincinnati: Standard, 1966.

————. *The Dead Sea Scrolls and the New Testament*. Grand Rapids: Eerdmans, 1972.

————. "1 and 2 Kings." In *New Bible Commentary*, 3d ed., 320–68. Grand Rapids: Eerdmans, 1970.

————. *Great Personalities of the New Testament*. Westwood, N.J.: Revell, 1961.

————. *Great Personalities of the Old Testament*. Westwood, N.J.: Revell, 1959.

————. *Handbook of Biblical Hebrew: An Inductive Approach Based on the Hebrew Text of Esther*. 2 vols. Grand Rapids: Eerdmans, 1978.

————. *Handbook of New Testament Greek: An Inductive Approach Based on the Greek Text of Acts*. 2 vols. Grand Rapids: Eerdmans, 1973.

————. *Men Who Knew Christ*. Glendale, Calif.: Regal, 1971.

————. *Men Who Knew God*. Glendale, Calif.: Regal, 1970.

————. *The Truth about Armageddon: What the Bible Says about the End Times*. San Francisco: Harper and Row, 1982.

LaSor, William Sanford, David Allan Hubbard, and Frederic W. Bush. *Old Testament Survey: The Message, Form, and Background of the Old Testament*. Grand Rapids: Eerdmans, 1982; rev. ed., 1996.

Secondary Sources

Marsden, George M. *Reforming Fundamentalism: Fuller Seminary and the New Evangelicalism*. Grand Rapids: Eerdmans, 1987.

Tuttle, Gary A., ed. *Biblical and Near Eastern Studies: Essays in Honor of William Sanford LaSor*. Grand Rapids: Eerdmans, 1987. (Especially helpful is Dawn Waring's bibliography of LaSor's work, 1935–78.)

John Wenham

Roger Beckwith

John William Wenham was born at Sanderstead, Surrey, on December 9, 1913, one of four children of a chartered accountant.[1] Educated at Uppingham School and Pembroke College, Cambridge, he trained at Ridley Hall, Cambridge, for ordination in the Church of England just before the Second World War. While at Uppingham he had been won to a living faith in Christ through a Varsity and Public Schools house party in Switzerland, and was thereafter a keen soul-winner and a convinced member of the evangelical school of thought in the Church of England, though always open-minded towards others.

A visionary, Wenham was ever convinced of the necessity of true theology and ready with plans for its promotion, plans to which he gave boundless energy and dedication. He was, for example, closely associated with Douglas Johnson in the founding of the Inter-Varsity Fellowship (now Universities and Colleges Christian Fellowship), which fostered and united evangelical student groups in universities and colleges. The aims of the organization were to encourage concentration on Protestant essentials and avoidance of denominational distinctives, to oppose theological liberalism, and to present to other students a clear evangelistic message based upon the authority of the Bible. Wenham served as the theological students' representative on the executive committee and then as its chairman. Later, when Inter-Varsity founded Tyndale House, Cambridge, for advanced biblical study, he took a great interest in the project, and successfully resisted a plan to close it down. It has flourished ever since.

After ordination in 1938, Wenham taught for three years at St. John's College, Highbury (now St. John's College, Nottingham), a Church of England theological college. In 1942 he married. His wife Grace was the embodiment of her name and a wonderful helpmate. To her husband's sterling

---

1. Many of the facts in the following essay are drawn from Wenham's as yet unpublished autobiography, which has the rather ambiguous provisional title *Facing Hell*. Other details come from the firsthand knowledge of the writer, who first made Wenham's acquaintance more than forty years ago, and who has been more or less closely associated with him ever since. How much the writer owes to Wenham's thinking, teaching, and example needs to be acknowledged here in a summary way in order to avoid repeated references to it later.

qualities she added the element of human sympathy. She was to bear him four sons, all of whom would share their parents' Christian faith, and two of whom, Gordon and David, would like their father become distinguished biblical scholars.

During the Second World War Wenham joined up as a Royal Air Force chaplain, and in the course of his service spent an extended period in Jerusalem, an experience on which he drew richly in his future studies. After the war he was for five years vicar of St. Nicholas's Church, Durham, where he had the opportunity to commend the faith in a university city.

The Years at Tyndale Hall, Bristol

In 1953 Wenham succeeded Philip Edgcumbe Hughes as vice-principal of Tyndale Hall, Bristol (another theological college of the Church of England). He continued in this post for seventeen years. There were in 1953 eight evangelical colleges training ordinands for the Church of England, but only three of them were conservative evangelical (i.e., committed to the infallibility of Scripture), and of these three Tyndale Hall was the most seriously concerned for the study of theology. It taught the Bible and the theology of the Bible, the theories of biblical criticism and answers to them. It also had a firmer Anglican churchmanship than did most of the other evangelical colleges. Thus Bishop Frederick Cockin of Bristol (certainly an unprejudiced witness) once defended the college against a critic by saying that it "taught its students not only to love the Bible, but also to love the Book of Common Prayer—which was more than could be said for some colleges of other persuasions!" To the staff of this college John Wenham, with his inquiring mind, his concern for biblical principles, and his parochial experience, made a valuable contribution.

One of Wenham's tasks at the college was to teach New Testament Greek, and out of these labors came one of his most famous publications. *The Elements of New Testament Greek* is a simplified manual, the usefulness of which is attested by its frequent reprints and its translation into other languages.

Another of Wenham's achievements at the college was a strengthening of its practical training. His efficient organization of instruction in preaching, involving both the planning and delivery of sermons (with the congregation augmented for the occasion by a critical group of fellow students), soon became a model for other colleges to follow.

At this period of his life Wenham was for five years a proctor in convocation—an elected representative of the clergy in the central governing body of the Church of England. It was at his suggestion that Archbishop Arthur Ramsey included an exposition of Scripture in its program, a practice that has continued ever since.

While teaching at Bristol, Wenham also formulated a plan for uniting the evangelical colleges in Bristol, of which there were three, into a much larger college that would enable the staff to specialize and have time for writing. This was a period when evangelical students were growing in numbers, owing to the combined influence of the Billy Graham crusades and the university Christian Unions affiliated with the Inter-Varsity Fellowship. Men of ability were coming forward in greater numbers, not only as students but as teachers. Liberal evangelicalism was in decline, and conservative evangelicalism seemed to have a promising future, even though the most influential positions in the ecclesiastical and academic worlds were still held by people of other persuasions. A united college at Bristol did eventually come into being, but only after much conflict and a decline from the theological ideals of its original proposer.

The Work at Oxford

Another project of this period was a theological research center for conservative evangelicals in the Church of England. The aims were to address the current needs of the church and to produce literature that would argue theologically for all fields of church life to follow biblical and Reformation principles. John Wenham was one of the originators of this project; as its first secretary he contacted countless potential supporters and raised the funds that brought it into being. A house was bought in Oxford and given the name of Latimer after the martyred Reformation bishop. From its opening in 1960, a succession of scholars from Tyndale Hall, including the renowned J. I. Packer, have served there as warden or librarian. From 1970 to 1973 Wenham served as its third warden. One of his writings during this period was the small book *The Renewal and Unity of the Church of England*. Most noteworthy from those days were the regular meetings that Wenham arranged for conversation, for prayer with friends, and for the dispensing of advice to theological students struggling with the liberal regime in the university.

At that time it was becoming increasingly difficult to hold the conservative evangelical constituency together. Owing to theological waywardness, untheological thoughtlessness, and love or hatred of change, the period of transition in the church was becoming a period of polarization between the more traditional and the less traditional members of the constituency. Wenham attempted to keep evangelicals united on biblical principles; when it became clear, however, that some were treating those principles with increasing indifference, he called them back to their roots. A prime example is the lecture given at Cambridge and later published under the title "Fifty Years of Evangelical Scholarship: Retrospect and Prospect."

In 1973 Wenham returned part-time to parish work for two years, and then decided to take early retirement in order to give himself to writing. He lived in the vicinity of Salisbury until his wife's death in a tragic road accident, an irreparable loss that he bore with Christian resignation and without recrimination. He then returned to Oxford and made his home with one of his sons. Though still zealous in the work of personal evangelism and always ready to make time, as before, to help students of theology at the university, his main energies were now devoted to writing.

Magnum Opus: *The Christian View of the Bible*

At an early stage in his Christian life, Wenham conceived the plan of a large work to be called *The Christian View of the Bible*. The full text, which exists in draft, consists of six parts:

1. The Authority of Christ and the Truth of Scripture
2. The Reliability of the Bible Text
3. The Truth of Old Testament History
4. The Truth of New Testament History
5. The Extent of the Canon
6. The Moral Difficulties of the Bible

These titles reflect a work of exposition and apologetics requiring an expertise in both Old Testament and New Testament studies, in doctrine, ethics, and philosophy. Though the author is always modest about his acquirements, such wide-ranging interests and so ambitious a project give evidence of a remarkably comprehensive mind that does not shrink from difficult problems and cherishes an ambition to give people help with their intellectual problems and to settle them in a firm, consistent, biblical faith. As he says in his autobiography, "we have access to an infinity of facts which we cannot hope to make sense of unless we have revelation to tell us which are the significant facts. . . . My passion has been to try to find ways of making the Christian faith intelligible to ordinary people."

For a number of reasons the author abandoned the plan of publishing *The Christian View of the Bible* as a single book. Instead, he decided to publish it in portions, and in a different order. All his major works, apart from *The Elements of New Testament Greek*, are revisions and expansions of portions of his great project.

The first work to appear was *Our Lord's View of the Old Testament*, a chapter from part 1. Delivered at Cambridge as the Tyndale New Testament Lecture for 1953, this most telling exposition of Christ's own attitude to Scripture, as recorded and reflected in the Gospels, argues that absolute deference to the divine authority of Scripture is the Christian way. Many readers have been strengthened by this lecture and led to recognize that, if we know anything at all of Jesus Christ's teaching, we know that he taught the inspiration and complete reliability of the Old Testament Scriptures.

Next to appear was "Large Numbers in the Old Testament" (1967). This thought-provoking discussion is the only chapter of part 3 ever to have been published.

In 1972 the whole of part 1, together with the briefer parts 2 and 5, appeared as a book under the title *Christ and the Bible*. The lecture on our

Lord's view of the Old Testament reappeared with much additional matter. The authority of Jesus as a teacher and objections to his claims were also seriously handled. The third edition of *Christ and the Bible* (1994) includes a new preface and outlines the scheme of *The Christian View of the Bible* as a whole. Moreover, in revisions of the sections on the canon and the text Wenham declares himself a convert to belief in the substantial originality of the Byzantine or traditional text of the New Testament (like most textual critics, he had previously favored an eclectic form of text).

The next part of the magnum opus to appear was part 6, which was published in 1974 under the title *The Goodness of God*. This too has now been issued in a third edition (1994), but under the revised title *The Enigma of Evil*. In this work Wenham impressively restates Bishop Joseph Butler's contention that the moral difficulties that one finds in the Bible are paralleled by difficulties found in nature, and that, if the God of creation is the author of Scripture, this is what one should expect. Wenham goes on to categorize the various difficulties and to consider the categories separately; he ends up by reminding us that the Christian God is just and terrible as well as loving and merciful. It is only on this basis that the biblical teaching on hell, to which a chapter is devoted, can be understood. In the third edition, the author has rewritten this chapter, declaring himself a believer in conditional immortality. Although many evangelical scholars of his generation have adopted this belief, in a book on moral difficulties it is bound to strike many readers as simply explaining a problem away. Nevertheless, the book is so much better than most others on its subject as to deserve the widest readership.

Up to this stage, no portion of part 4, "The Truth of New Testament History," had seen the light. In 1984, however, there appeared the now famous book called *Easter Enigma: Are the Resurrection Accounts in Conflict?* This is an exercise in harmonization directed towards one of the most crucial facts of the faith, a fact that is the climax of each of the Gospels, but is narrated by them in quite distinctive ways. How the accounts fit together, if they do, has been a long-standing puzzle, and John Wenham's solution has convinced many by its simplicity and by his personal knowledge of the topography of Jerusalem. Though some specialists have criticized him for not distinguishing between ancient and modern sites sufficiently, the broad lines of his thesis are unaffected.

Wenham's work of harmonization, which he rightly recognizes is necessarily required by a belief in the infallibility and historicity of Scripture, leads into related discussions. For instance, *Easter Enigma* deals with the various passages referring to Mary Magdalene (ch. 2 and app. 2) as well as with the identity of the women at the tomb (chs. 6–8 and app. 1) and Jesus' human relatives (ch. 3 and app. 3).[2]

2. For similar discussions see John W. Wenham, "The Relatives of Jesus," *Evangelical Quarterly* 47 (Jan. 1975): 6–15; and idem, *Modern Evangelical Views of the Virgin Mary*, a booklet published by the Ecumenical Society of the Blessed Virgin Mary.

A second major portion of part 4 of the magnum opus followed in 1991. *Redating Matthew, Mark and Luke: A Fresh Assault on the Synoptic Problem* is Wenham's largest and most ambitious book, but in some ways his least successful. This is not because of lack of thoroughness or thought, for it is both thorough and thoughtful, and has drawn very respectful reviews. Its weakness is that it attempts too much. Having realized that the case for the historicity of the Gospels would be strengthened if they were dated earlier than is customary, Wenham develops an elaborate argument for early dates (from A.D. 40 onwards) based partly upon internal and partly upon external evidence. Pointing out both that modern scholars are uncertain about the older solutions of the Synoptic Problem and that earlier dates would afford a greater degree of independence to the individual Gospels, he develops some novel arguments to support this hypothesis. Yet he ends up by having shown the possibility, rather than the probability or certainty, of early dates.

An apparent weakness in Wenham's argument is that, if the Synoptic Gospels are as early and independent as he thinks, their selecting so much of the same material is surprising. Another weakness is that some of the earliest external evidence is against his thesis. Irenaeus (despite the author's attempt to show the contrary) dates the earliest of the Gospels about A.D. 60, and Clement of Alexandria dates Luke earlier than Mark. These traditions of Irenaeus and Clement are older than others on which the author lays great weight.

Wenham does not hesitate to champion disputable opinions or (as in this case) to pioneer them. One admires his courage. Yet it cannot but conflict with his apologetic aim since, unless the opinion in question is a necessary implication of the truth of the Bible, it reduces automatically the number of people whom he is likely to convince. This matters less if the disputable opinion is confined to a small portion of a book (like his argument for the traditional text in the new edition of *Christ and the Bible* or for conditional immortality in the new edition of *The Enigma of Evil*), but in *Redating Matthew, Mark and Luke* the disputable opinion is the thesis of the book. If he had contented himself with arguing that the Synoptic Gospels, according to early tradition, date from the 60s, rather than later; that the internal evidence is consistent with this position, which places the date of composition only thirty years after the events, well within the lifetime of eyewitnesses; and that the Gospels would then be reckoned early and reliable evidence rather than late and dubious, his case would have been hard to dispute and would have carried widespread conviction. Unfortunately, by attempting more he seems to have achieved less.

Whether the remaining portions of part 4 of Wenham's great work, on the Gospel of John and on residual problems of Gospel harmony, will yet be published in some form, and whether the bulk of part 3, "The Truth of Old Testament History," will likewise be published, one does not know. One can only hope that they will. At John Wenham's advanced years, and with his health much impaired since 1994, he would need considerable editorial assistance. If he gets it, from sufficiently able and faithful hands, we may yet see *The Christian View of the Bible* published in all its parts, and the unique apologetic work which has been the controlling vision of his life will be able to achieve its full potential for the instruction and persuasion and encouragement of readers in the twenty-first century.

Primary Sources

Wenham, John W. *Christ and the Bible*. Downers Grove, Ill.: InterVarsity, 1972; 3d ed., Grand Rapids: Baker, 1994.

———. *Easter Enigma: Are the Resurrection Accounts in Conflict?* Grand Rapids: Zondervan, 1984; 2d ed., Grand Rapids: Baker, 1992.

———. *The Elements of New Testament Greek*. New York: Cambridge University Press, 1965.

———. *The Enigma of Evil*. 3d ed. Guildford, Eng.: Eagle, 1994.

———. "Fifty Years of Evangelical Scholarship: Retrospect and Prospect." *Churchman* 103.3 (1989): 209–18.

———. *The Goodness of God*. Downers Grove, Ill.: InterVarsity, 1974.

———. "Large Numbers in the Old Testament." *Tyndale Bulletin* 18 (1967): 19–53.

———. *Our Lord's View of the Old Testament*. London: Tyndale, 1953.

———. *Redating Matthew, Mark and Luke: A Fresh Assault on the Synoptic Problem*. Downers Grove, Ill.: InterVarsity, 1991.

———. "The Relatives of Jesus." *Evangelical Quarterly* 47 (Jan. 1975): 6–15.

———. *The Renewal and Unity of the Church of England*. London: S.P.C.K., 1972.

Bruce M. Metzger

James A. Brooks

Bruce Manning Metzger was born in Middletown, Pennsylvania, on February 9, 1914. In the middle of the eighteenth century his great-great-great-grandfather Jacob Metzger had emigrated from where the Rhine valley enters the Netherlands and settled near Middletown as a farmer. Thus the family was Pennsylvania Dutch in background. Bruce's maternal great-great-grandfather George Manning had emigrated from England late in the eighteenth century and also became a farmer. Bruce's father forsook life on the farm, earned a college degree, and became an attorney in Harrisburg and Middletown.

Bruce in turn decided not to pursue his father's profession but an academic and ministerial career. In 1935 he graduated from nearby Lebanon Valley College, which was then affiliated with the United Brethren Church, but now with the United Methodist Church. During his last year or two in college he decided that he could best turn his interest in Greek into a Christian vocation by becoming a teacher of New Testament Greek. He had originally planned to study with A. T. Robertson at Southern Baptist Theological Seminary, but Robertson died in 1934 and as a result Metzger enrolled instead at Princeton Seminary.

At Princeton, Metzger studied under such greats as Henry S. Gehman, William Park Armstrong, Otto Piper, and even Emil Brunner. He earned the seminary's Th.B. degree in 1938 and its Th.M. in 1939. Having turned Presbyterian during his third year there, he was ordained as a Presbyterian minister in 1939.[1] Then, instead of pursuing a Th.D. degree at the seminary, he earned A.M. and Ph.D. degrees in classics and patristics at Princeton University in 1940 and 1942 respectively. He became a member of the faculty at Princeton Seminary in 1940 and continued to teach there for forty-four years—forty-six if one includes two earlier years as a teaching fellow. In 1944 he married Isobel Mackay, the daughter of the president of the seminary. Metzger's many honors include the presidency of the Society of Biblical Literature (1971), the presidency of the Studiorum Novi Testamenti Societas

---

1. While Jacob Metzger and his descendants were Mennonites, Bruce's mother was reared in the Churches of God in North America (General Eldership), a small denomination that his father also joined when the couple married.

(1970–71), five honorary doctorates, three festschriften,[2] a corresponding fellowship in the British Academy (it is most unusual for an American to be so honored), and the British Academy's Burkitt Medal in Biblical Studies.

Bruce Metzger is a scholar of many different interests and abilities. A perusal of his bibliography will find works on Bible translation, exegesis, the Old Testament Apocrypha, Qumran, New Testament introduction, New Testament canon, New Testament Greek, ancient versions, New Testament bibliography, New Testament apocrypha, patristics, early Christian history, ancient mystery religions, and even modern cults. His greatest contribution, however, has been in the area of New Testament textual criticism.

New Testament Textual Criticism

Metzger's first exposure to textual criticism came in college during a third-year Greek course that required him to read a portion of James Hardy Rope's *Text of Acts.* His interest having been aroused, he proceeded to read also A. T. Robertson's *Introduction to the Textual Criticism of the New Testament,* volume two of B. F. Westcott and F. J. A. Hort's *New Testament in the Original Greek,* and Eugène Jacquier's *Le Texte du Nouveau Testament.* He was well prepared for an academic career in general and textual criticism in particular by his extensive language study: four years of Latin in high school; three years of Latin, four of Greek, three of German, and two of French in college; and in seminary three of Greek, three of Hebrew, one of Aramaic, and one of Syriac. In graduate school he spent three years reading Greek and Latin texts. Subsequently he studied Coptic, Armenian, and Ethiopic privately.

Major Publications on Textual Criticism

Commitment to textual criticism is already evident in Metzger's doctoral dissertation, a portion of which was revised and published in 1944 under the title *The Saturday and Sunday Lessons from Luke in the Greek Gospel Lectionary.* In it he examines fourteen lectionaries and finds that the New Testament text as reconstructed from them is most closely related to the Caesarean type of text, especially the pre-Caesarean type. This conclusion differs from the traditional view that lectionary texts are predominantly Byzantine. The Byzantine elements that are present he explains as being the result of a gradual attempt to conform the original lectionary text to the type of text which prevailed later. Not only did the dissertation lead to Metzger's first book, but research for it required him to spend several summers at the University of Chicago, where he gained the respect of Ernest C. Colwell, one of

---

2. *New Testament Textual Criticism: Its Significance for Exegesis,* ed. Eldon J. Epp and Gordon D. Fee (New York: Oxford University Press, 1981); *A South African Perspective on the New Testament,* ed. J. H. Petzer and P. J. Hartin (Leiden: Brill, 1986); and *The Text of the New Testament in Contemporary Research: Essays on the* Status Quaestionis, ed. Bart D. Ehrman and Michael W. Holmes (Grand Rapids: Eerdmans, 1995).

the leading textual critics of the day. The relationship with Colwell opened the door to participation in the International Greek New Testament Project on Luke and eventually to the chairmanship of its American committee on versions.

In 1945 Metzger published his first major article, "The Caesarean Text of the Gospels."[3] In it he surveys the research on the Caesarean type of text after the discovery of Family 13 and concludes that the Caesarean text is disintegrating in scholarly estimation. It is interesting to note, however, that he continued to write of a Caesarean text and to enumerate Caesarean witnesses in the three editions of his *Text of the New Testament* and in the first edition of *A Textual Commentary on the Greek New Testament*. In the second edition of the latter, however, the Caesarean type of text is no longer recognized.

In 1955 there appeared the *Annotated Bibliography of the Textual Criticism of the New Testament*. It was the first comprehensive bibliography on the subject.

Another major article appeared in 1961, namely "Lucian and the Lucianic Recension of the Greek Bible."[4] Most of it deals with the history, influence, critical value, and problems of what has come to be known as the Lucianic or Antiochian (i.e., the Byzantine) text of the Septuagint and the New Testament. Although the article gives a thorough survey of ancient testimonies to Lucian, there is probably not enough extant material to determine his exact role in the origin of this text. One value of the article is that it treats together both divisions of the Greek Bible.

In addition to the publication of *Chapters in the History of New Testament Textual Criticism*, which contains revised versions of seven earlier articles, the year 1963 brought another significant article: "Explicit References in the Works of Origen to Variant Readings in New Testament Manuscripts." It sets forth and discusses about twenty-five passages in which Origen shows an awareness of variant readings. Metzger's conclusion is that Origen "was an acute observer of textual phenomena but was quite uncritical in his evaluation of their significance."[5] A companion article was published in 1979, "St. Jerome's Explicit References to Variant Readings in Manuscripts of the New Testament."[6] It reviews twenty-seven places where Jerome comments on variations. Metzger concludes that Jerome was an able textual critic who employed both external and internal evidence. An adden-

3. Bruce M. Metzger, "The Caesarean Text of the Gospels," *Journal of Biblical Literature* 64 (1945): 457–89—reprinted in idem, *Chapters in the History of New Testament Textual Criticism* (Grand Rapids: Eerdmans, 1963), 42–72.

4. Bruce M. Metzger, "Lucian and the Lucianic Recension of the Greek Bible," *New Testament Studies* 8 (1961–62): 189–203—reprinted in idem, *Chapters in the History*, 1–41.

5. Bruce M. Metzger, "Explicit References in the Works of Origen to Variant Readings in New Testament Manuscripts," in *Biblical and Patristic Studies in Memory of Robert Pierce Casey*, ed. J. Neville Birdsall and Robert W. Thomson (New York: Herder, 1963), 93.

6. Bruce M. Metzger, "St. Jerome's Explicit References to Variant Readings in Manuscripts of the New Testament," in *Text and Interpretation: Studies in the New Testament Presented to Matthew Black*, ed. Ernest Best and R. McL. Wilson (New York: Cambridge University Press, 1979), 179–90.

dum lists references where forty-seven other Fathers show awareness of variant readings and calls upon the scholarly world to compile a complete list—something which has not been done.

In 1964 Metzger published the first edition of *The Text of the New Testament,* which is probably his best-known and most influential work. The second and third editions (1968 and 1992 respectively) are not rewritings but contain additional notes and bibliography and, in the case of the third edition, an appendix which brings up-to-date most of the subjects treated in the first edition. In 1964 there was no satisfactory handbook on the subject in English. The volumes by A. T. Robertson, Leon Vaganay, and Frederic G. Kenyon were out-of-date, and those by Alexander Souter (as revised by C. S. C. Williams) and Vincent Taylor were very brief. (J. Harold Greenlee's helpful but also somewhat brief *Introduction to New Testament Textual Criticism* was published the same year as Metzger's first edition.) Metzger's *Text* became the standard handbook and had no serious rival until the publication of the English edition of Kurt and Barbara Aland's *Text of the New Testament* in 1987 (2d ed., 1989). Even then it was not displaced but has continued to be used widely. Probably the most helpful part of the book is the thorough treatment of the history of the printed text. A possible weakness is the lack of a section on the history of the handwritten text, although such topics as paleography, manuscript witnesses to the New Testament text, the kinds of errors found in manuscripts, and types of text are related.

Metzger was one of the five editors of the United Bible Societies' Greek text that appears in both *The Greek New Testament* (1966)[7] and the Nestle-Aland *Novum Testamentum Graece.*[8] This has become the most widely used Greek text. The critical apparatus of *The Greek New Testament* gives variant readings for only 1,437 passages, but includes the evidence from a comparatively large number of Greek manuscripts, ancient versions, and church fathers in each case. The apparatus is unquestionably the most usable of all those available. Another helpful feature is an indication of the degree of probability of the reading that the editors finally selected. Of course neither the text nor the apparatus is the work of Metzger alone, but that he made a major contribution, especially to the text, is unquestioned.

A Textual Commentary on the Greek New Testament followed in 1971. For every passage for which the critical apparatus of *The Greek New Testament* offers variant readings (and for some other passages as well), this volume sets forth the editors' reasons for their choice of the reading printed in the text. There is no other volume devoted to evaluation of variant readings in the Greek New Testament.

Certainly one of Metzger's more important works is *The Early Versions of the New Testament* (1977). In addition to a consideration of the origin, history, characteristics, manuscripts, editions, and textual affinities of the

---

7. *Greek New Testament* (Stuttgart: Deutsche Bibelgesellschaft, 1966; 4th ed., 1993).
8. *Novum Testamentum Graece,* 27th ed. (Stuttgart: Deutsche Bibelgesellschaft, 1993).

early versions of the New Testament, a unique feature in most chapters is a discussion of the limitations of the particular version in reconstructing the original text of the Greek New Testament. These discussions are written by experts in the individual languages. This volume quickly replaced Arthur Vööbus's 1954 survey *(Early Versions of the New Testament)* as the standard work on the subject, and today it has no rival.

The Manuscripts of the Greek Bible: An Introduction to Paleography was published in 1981. It treats Septuagint as well as New Testament manuscripts. Probably the most valuable feature is the section containing descriptions and facsimiles of forty-five manuscripts.

Also in 1981 Metzger published as a centenary celebration "The Westcott and Hort Greek New Testament—Yesterday and Today."[9] After reviewing the lives of these Cambridge scholars, their twenty-eight years of work on the project, and their textual theory, Metzger affirmed the continuing value of their work: "The international committee that produced the United Bible Societies' Greek New Testament not only adopted the Westcott and Hort edition as its basic text, but followed their methodology in giving attention to both external evidence and internal considerations."

Textual Theory

There is nothing unique about Metzger's theory of textual criticism. It is simply a refinement of Westcott and Hort's theory in *The New Testament in the Original Greek* (1881). Called rational or moderate or general eclecticism (as opposed to the thoroughgoing or consistent or special eclecticism of G. D. Kilpatrick and J. K. Elliott), this theory is dominant today in part because of Metzger's great influence. It was the theory employed in producing the United Bible Societies' Greek text. It is the theory lying behind the Greek text used by most recent versions: the Revised Standard, the New Revised Standard, the New English Bible, the Revised English Bible, the New American Bible, the New American Standard, the Good News Bible, the New International Version, and, to a slightly lesser extent, also the Jerusalem Bible and the New Jerusalem Bible. Metzger describes the theory in both his *Text of the New Testament* and *Textual Commentary on the Greek New Testament*, but he neither names nor defends it at length.

The basic principle of rational eclecticism is that equal weight should be given to external evidence and internal evidence. Beyond that no principle, manuscript, or group of manuscripts is determinative. A rational explanation is required for each textual choice—an explanation which will commend itself to most capable and objective scholars and even to informed laypersons. Metzger himself, on behalf of the committee which produced the United Bible Societies' Greek text, provides such explanations in his *Textual Commentary*, although in many instances somewhat briefly.

9. Bruce M. Metzger, "The Westcott and Hort Greek New Testament—Yesterday and Today," *Cambridge Review* 20 (1981): 71–76.

In considering the external evidence—the Greek manuscripts, the ancient versions, and patristic quotations of the New Testament—preference is given to the reading having the earliest attestation, the most geographically diverse attestation, and the attestation of witnesses with the Alexandrian type of text (especially if combined with some witnesses of the Western type). The consideration of internal evidence includes both transcriptional probabilities, that is, what scribes likely did in copying, and intrinsic probabilities, that is, what the author likely wrote. In regard to transcriptional probabilities preference is usually given to (1) a shorter reading, on the assumption that scribes more often added than deleted; (2) a reading which differs from a parallel passage, on the assumption that scribes often assimilated similar passages; (3) a more difficult reading, on the assumption that scribes attempted to alleviate difficulties; and (4) a reading which can best explain the origin of other readings. In regard to intrinsic probabilities preference is given to the reading which is most in accord with the author's language and theology and with the context. Of course, not all of these criteria will always point to the same reading; in such cases it is necessary to formulate a rational explanation for the choice that is made.[10]

Additional insight into Metzger's practice of rational eclecticism may be gleaned from his dissenting notes in the *Textual Commentary*. There are only thirty-two dissenting notes to the editors' decisions that are explained in the first edition of the *Textual Commentary*, and Metzger signed twenty-five of those notes—far more than the eleven of Allen Wikgren, who has the second largest number of dissensions. In fourteen cases Metzger appeals only to internal evidence to support the reading he prefers. In ten he employs both external and internal evidence in his argument. Only once does he employ external evidence alone. It would appear that he gives more weight to internal evidence than do the other members of the committee.

New Testament Canon

Text and canon are often treated together, so it is not surprising that Metzger has dealt with the latter. In fact, one of his most important books is *The Canon of the New Testament* (1987). Often described as the third volume of a trilogy consisting also of his *Text of the New Testament* and *Early Versions of the New Testament*, it is certainly one of the most comprehensive books ever written on the subject. Part 1 surveys and briefly evaluates previous

---

10. Two other theories of textual criticism are also maintained today. Thoroughgoing eclecticism makes all of its decisions on the basis of internal evidence alone—and mostly on the basis of intrinsic probabilities. The majority-text theory makes all of its decisions on the basis of external evidence alone—but not on the basis of the three principles mentioned above. It always chooses the reading that is supported by the majority of Greek manuscripts. There is still another Greek text, the textus receptus, which was edited by the sixteenth-century scholar Erasmus and used for the King James and New King James Versions. The textus receptus does not reflect a theory of textual criticism as such and thus can be defended only by dogmatic assertion. It is, however, closely related to the majority text, which has some support from rational argument.

works. Thus the reader is made aware of the various theories about the canon and also has some basis for evaluating Metzger's work. Part 2, the heart of the book, consists of a historical survey—again with some critical analysis—of the ancient testimonies about the canon and the individual books which constitute it. The survey treats the development of the canon and the attempts at closing it in the East and in the West. Included is a chapter on factors that may have influenced the development of the canon: Gnosticism, Marcionism, Montanism, and persecution. Here Metzger gives less place to the influence of heresy than do some recent studies. Another chapter discusses "Books of Temporary and Local Canonicity: Apocryphal Literature." Part 3 deals with canon-related historical and theological problems both in the early church and in the scholarly world today. The book concludes with four helpful appendixes: the history of the word *canon;* variations in the order of the books in manuscripts and canon lists; the titles of the books of the New Testament; and early lists of New Testament books.

Metzger stresses a number of points in regard to the canon:

1. The canon is the result of a long, involved, uneven historical process rather than a theological necessity. It emerged in response to the needs of the churches. It was not the product of ecclesiastical decree.

2. The books which eventually came to be received as canonical are vastly superior to those which eventually came to be treated as apocryphal. For example, "even the *Gospel of Peter* and the *Gospel of Thomas*, both of which may preserve scraps of independent tradition, are obviously inferior theologically and historically to the four accounts that eventually came to be regarded as the only canonical Gospels."[11] Similarly, "the apocryphal Acts cannot be put on a level with the Lucan work."[12] Metzger is, then, firmly committed to the legitimacy of the canon. In this he differs sharply with such scholars as Helmut Koester, who speak only of "early Christian literature" with no distinction between canonical and apocryphal.

3. Metzger has no doubts about a second-century date for the Muratorian Canon, thus showing that the idea of a canon was firmly in place in orthodox circles as early as 180.[13]

4. The three criteria used by the early church to determine canonicity were conformity to the "rule of faith," apostolicity, and continuous acceptance and usage by most churches. Inspiration was not a criterion. Certainly the early church looked upon apostolic writings as inspired, but many other documents were as well. Therefore the Scrip-

11. Bruce M. Metzger, *The Canon of the New Testament* (New York: Oxford University Press, 1987), 173–74.
12. Ibid., 180.
13. Ibid., 193: "The arguments used recently by [A. C.] Sundberg to prove the list to be of eastern provenance . . . and from the mid-fourth century have been sufficiently refuted (not to say demolished!) by [Everett] Ferguson and need not be rehearsed here."

tures "are authoritative, and hence canonical," not because they are inspired, but "because they are the extant literary deposit of the direct and indirect apostolic witness on which the later witness of the Church depends."[14]

5. No particular form of text should be considered canonical: "The question of canonicity pertains to the document *qua* document, and not to one particular form or version of that document. Translated into modern terms, Churches today accept a wide variety of contemporary versions as the canonical New Testament, though the versions differ not only as to rendering but also with respect to the presence or absence of certain verses."[15]

6. The canon should be considered closed. Although the "canon should, from a theoretical point of view, be regarded as open in principle for either the addition or the deletion of one or more books, from a practical point of view such a modification can scarcely be contemplated as either possible or desirable. . . . The several parts have all been cemented together by usage and by general acceptance in the Church, which has recognized, and recognizes, that God has spoken and is speaking to her in and through this body of early Christian literature. As regards this social fact, nothing can be changed. . . . The canon cannot be remade—for the simple reason that history cannot be remade."[16]

7. The concept of a "canon within the canon" is not helpful. "To trim the dimensions of the canon in accord with an arbitrarily chosen 'canon within the canon' would result only in muting certain voices in the choir of witnesses that the Church has long found to be normative." Further, "as long as the chief doctrines and patterns of Christian life and thought . . . point in the same direction, and not away from one another, they can coexist in the same canon. The homogeneity of the canon is not jeopardized even in the face of tensions that exist within the New Testament. These tensions, however, must not be exaggerated into contradictions."[17]

Some of the reviews of *The Canon of the New Testament* criticized it for being too traditional, for not breaking new ground, for not setting forth new theories about the origin or present role of the canon. The book's traditional methodology and conclusions, however, constitute part of its significance. An outstanding scholar who is as objective as it is possible to be, and who is not associated with fundamentalism, has demonstrated again the validity of the canon and its component parts.

14. Ibid., 256.
15. Ibid., 270.
16. Ibid., 275.
17. Ibid., 280.

Bible Translation

Metzger's first venture into Bible translation was as a member of the committee which translated the Apocrypha for the Revised Standard Version (1952–57). From 1964 to 1970 he was chairman of the Committee on Translations of the American Bible Society. In 1971 he was appointed chairman of the New Testament section of the Revised Standard Version committee and in 1976 chairman of the entire committee. Most important, from 1977 to 1990 he was the chairman of the committee which translated the New Revised Standard Version. He is also a coauthor of *The Making of the New Revised Standard Version of the Bible* (1991).

This is not the place to review or evaluate the New Revised Standard Version, but several points should be noted. First, with few exceptions its New Testament is a translation of the United Bible Societies' Greek text, which Metzger had such a large part in editing. Second, its New Testament has more textual notes (about five hundred) than does any other English translation, with the possible exception of the Jerusalem Bible and the New Jerusalem Bible, whose notes of various kinds constitute a minicommentary. Here one strongly suspects the influence of Metzger the textual critic. And third, the New Revised Standard has taken a moderate stand on male-oriented language. It has eliminated such language that is unnecessary and inappropriate, but, unlike the *Inclusive Language Lectionary*, it does not call God "Mother." Again one suspects Metzger's influence here.

Indirectly related to Bible translation is Metzger's editorship of *The Reader's Digest Bible* (1982). It was he who selected the passages from the Revised Standard Version that were included.

New Testament Introduction

The New Testament: Its Background, Growth and Content appeared in 1965. Because it is written for high school students and college freshmen, many would not consider it to be a significant book. It is, however, one of Metzger's most frequently reprinted books,[18] meeting as it does the need of a group that otherwise has been neglected (at least the high school group has). Although it is sometimes difficult to distinguish Metzger's personal views from his objective description of theories, this book is the only source for his views on various critical issues.

A few examples will suffice. Moderate form criticism and redaction criticism have done much to enlighten understanding of the Gospels. Matthew was more likely the collector of the sayings of Jesus than the final author of the Gospel which bears his name. John may have had some involvement in the composition of the Gospel attributed to him, but it is clear that others were also involved. The dates of the Gospels and Acts cannot be established with

---

18. Metzger's best-selling book is actually his *Lexical Aids for Students of New Testament Greek.*

confidence. No questions are raised about the authenticity of Ephesians (the view that the epistle is pseudonymous is in fact described as "improbable"), Colossians, and 2 Thessalonians, but it is difficult to attribute the Pastoral Epistles in their present form to Paul. (Metzger seems to lean toward the fragment theory: these letters are mostly the work of a later admirer of Paul, but some fragments of genuine Pauline correspondence are included.) Second Corinthians is probably a composite. The author of Hebrews cannot be determined, but was not Paul. The tract was probably written before A.D. 70 to Jewish Christians who were in danger of drifting back to their ancestral religion. James contains a compilation of Jewish-Christian teachings, some of which may go back to the Lord's brother. First Peter may well be by the apostle, but 2 Peter was written after A.D. 100 by an admirer of Peter. No position is taken on the authorship of the Johannine Epistles or the Revelation. Jude was probably written by the brother of Jesus. We can conclude that Metzger is a moderate on most of the issues raised by modern New Testament criticism.

Bible Commentary

Metzger has done comparatively little in the area of biblical commentary. His one commentary as such is a brief popular book entitled *Breaking the Code: Understanding the Book of Revelation* (1993). It is a nonmillenarian interpretation which is suitable for use in Bible discussion groups.

It would not be inappropriate also to mention here Metzger's annotations to several books in *The Oxford Annotated Apocrypha*,[19] to 4 Ezra,[20] and to several books of the Apocrypha and the New Testament in *The New Oxford Annotated Bible*.[21]

Personal Characteristics

It is fitting to conclude with a list of some of the more noteworthy characteristics of Bruce Manning Metzger and his work as a biblical scholar:

1. The magnitude of his output has been surpassed by few in his field. And even more important than the quantity of his work is its quality. It is consistently careful, accurate, thorough, and fair. One needs to realize that he did all this while teaching large classes, conducting graduate seminars, directing doctoral dissertations, serving on seminary and church committees, lecturing far and wide, and preaching in the churches.

19. *Oxford Annotated Apocrypha of the Old Testament: Revised Standard Version* (New York: Oxford University Press, 1965; 2d ed., 1977).

20. "The Fourth Book of Ezra," in *Old Testament Pseudepigrapha*, ed. James H. Charlesworth (Garden City, N.Y.: Doubleday, 1983), 1:517–59.

21. *New Oxford Annotated Bible: Revised Standard Version* (New York: Oxford University Press, 1977); *New Oxford Annotated Bible: New Revised Standard Version* (New York: Oxford University Press, 1991).

2. He has dealt with many different aspects of biblical studies as well as some issues on the periphery of his chosen field. It would be difficult to name anyone in the history of the discipline who has written on a broader range of topics with corresponding depth than has Bruce Metzger.
3. He appreciates the work of and cooperates with other scholars. Consider, for example, his role on the committee which produced the United Bible Societies' text, his chairmanship of the New Revised Standard committee, and his invitation to other scholars to contribute to his volume on early versions.
4. He has maintained a noncontroversial, irenic spirit. As a result he has won the respect of scholars and churchmen of different persuasions.
5. His scholarship has been accompanied by practical application. This is especially evident in his editorship of *The Reader's Digest Bible* and his work on the New Revised Standard.
6. He is a man of the church who has exhibited reverence and reserve in technical studies which are often controversial.
7. Despite his great ability, prolific publications, many honors, and widespread acclaim, he is a man of deep humility.
8. He has taken a personal interest in and inspired a number of his students to follow him in textual criticism and related disciplines.

Clearly, the scholarly community and the church have benefited much from the work of Bruce Metzger.

Primary Sources

Metzger, Bruce M. *Annotated Bibliography of the Textual Criticism of the New Testament*. Studies and Documents 16. Copenhagen: Munksgaard, 1955.
————. *Breaking the Code: Understanding the Book of Revelation*. Nashville: Abingdon, 1993.
————. *The Canon of the New Testament: Its Origin, Development, and Significance*. New York: Oxford University Press, 1987.
————. *Chapters in the History of New Testament Textual Criticism*. New Testament Tools and Studies 4. Grand Rapids: Eerdmans, 1963.
————. *The Early Versions of the New Testament: Their Origin, Transmission, and Limitations*. New York: Oxford University Press, 1977.
————. *Historical and Literary Studies: Pagan, Jewish, and Christian*. New Testament Tools and Studies 8. Grand Rapids: Eerdmans, 1968.
————. *Lexical Aids for Students of New Testament Greek*. 3d ed. Naperville, Ill.: Allenson, 1969.
————. *The Manuscripts of the Greek Bible: An Introduction to Paleography*. New York: Oxford University Press, 1981.
————. *The New Testament: Its Background, Growth and Content*. Nashville: Abingdon, 1965; 2d ed., 1983.

————. *New Testament Studies: Philological, Versional, and Patristic.* New Testament Tools and Studies 10. Leiden: Brill, 1980.

————. *The Saturday and Sunday Lessons from Luke in the Greek Gospel Lectionary.* Studies in the Lectionary Text of the Greek New Testament 2.3. Chicago: University of Chicago Press, 1944.

————. *The Text of the New Testament: Its Transmission, Corruption, and Restoration.* New York: Oxford University Press, 1964; 3d ed., 1992.

————. *A Textual Commentary on the Greek New Testament: A Companion Volume to the United Bible Societies' Greek New Testament.* New York: United Bible Societies, 1971; 2d ed., 1994.

Metzger, Bruce M., Robert C. Dentan, and Walter J. Harrelson. *The Making of the New Revised Standard Version of the Bible.* Grand Rapids: Eerdmans, 1991.

Leon Lamb Morris

David John Williams

Leon Lamb Morris was born at Lithgow in New South Wales, Australia, on March 15, 1914. His parents were Christians of the formal churchgoing kind. He had an older half brother, Philip, but was the eldest child of his father's second marriage. Three other children were born to that marriage, two boys, John and Max, and a sister Jean.

At the age of seventeen years, in 1931, Leon went up to the University of Sydney to study science. This was a momentous year in the young man's life. It was his first experience away from home for any length of time, but, more significantly, it saw him respond to God's call to put his trust in Christ as Savior and Lord. The greatest influences in his making this decision were R. B. Robinson, the rector of his parish church, All Souls, Leichhardt,[1] and two other members of that congregation, Reg Langshaw and Eric Norgate.

Morris graduated as a bachelor of science in 1934 (his major was in mathematics) and followed with a year at the Sydney Teachers' College. His first appointment was to Warren, in central New South Wales, as a primary school teacher (1935), although his training had been for high schools. From there he was transferred to North Newtown, an inner district of Sydney, where for two years he did serve as a high school teacher (1936–37). At the Katoomba Convention of 1932,[2] shortly after his conversion, he had felt the call to serve God in the ordained ministry. Subsequently, that call became more specific to serve God through the Bush Church Aid Society, an agency of the Church of England committed to bringing Christian ministry to the people of outback Australia. With this in view, during his three years of teaching Morris taught himself New Testament Greek and then proceeded to the licentiate of theology, the standard prerequisite at that time for ordination. Most people worked toward the degree as full-time students at a theological college, but Morris did so as a full-time teacher and a part-time (private) student. Nevertheless, not only did he complete the degree in the

---

1. Morris lived in digs at Leichhardt throughout his student days, walking approximately two miles to the university each day. Later, he stayed with the same family when he was posted to a school in North Newtown.

2. An annual interdenominational gathering of Christians at Katoomba, in the Blue Mountains west of Sydney.

normal time of two years, but he gained first-class honors to boot and won the Hey-Sharp Prize as the top graduating student.

A Pastor and a Preacher

Ordination followed. Morris was made a deacon in the Church of England in 1938 and a priest in 1939. During those two years he was the assistant curate at Campsie (another Sydney district). Then came five years with the Bush Church Aid Society as priest in charge of Minnipa, in the diocese of Willochra, South Australia. There he held services in more than twenty centers which were scattered across a parish of largely semiarid sheep country, with a little mixed farming on its southern fringes.[3] While at Minnipa, Morris continued his courtship of Mildred Dann (largely at a distance by correspondence) and married her in January 1941. He had known Mildred from his schooldays in Lithgow, but it was only when she came to Sydney to continue her training as a nurse, while Leon was at Campsie, that their relationship had blossomed. Mildred had become a Christian in 1937. She was an accomplished musician and, by the time she went to Minnipa, a triple-certificated nurse who was able in her own right to exercise a most effective ministry as a medic, a musician, and a woman alongside her husband.

The years in South Australia also saw the continuation of Morris's theological studies. Often Mildred drove the car between the various outposts at which they ministered while Leon read in preparation for the University of London's bachelor of divinity examinations, in which (as an external student) he achieved first-class honors in 1943.[4] With this accomplishment under his belt his next objective was the master of theology degree.

Thanks to a recommendation by Tom Jones, the general secretary of the Bush Church Aid Society, Morris was invited by Donald Baker, sometime bishop of Bendigo in Victoria, Australia, but then principal of Ridley College in Melbourne, to become vice-principal of that college. Baker was a convinced evangelical and was looking for a colleague of like mind. Morris took up this appointment in August 1945.[5] With this it might be said that he was now launched on his career as an academic theologian.[6] But the cure of souls still remained a priority for him, with a special concern always for the people of the outback. This led him in 1952–53 to accept the position of acting sec-

---

3. During Morris's time at Minnipa, the mission district was at first confined to the farming area along the Port Lincoln to Ceduna railway line. But with the wartime decline in the population during the early 1940s, the mission district was extended to cover the station (ranch) country to the north, so that in the end Morris was ministering to about the same number of people as when he first went to Minnipa, but over a much larger area. The final extent of his parish has been estimated at forty thousand square miles. For Morris's own story of these years see his *Bush Parson* (Brunswick East, Victoria, Australia: Acorn, 1995).

4. Morris, *Bush Parson*, 62.

5. Ibid., 81–82.

6. Morris never consciously made academics his goal. His degrees from the University of London were intended simply to give a focus to his private study while he ministered at Minnipa.

retary of the Victoria chapter of the Bush Church Aid Society and, forty years later, to write *Bush Parson* as a tribute to "the bighearted people" he had met in the outback. "I want to acknowledge my debt," he says in the conclusion of the book, "to so many battlers in their very difficult situations."[7]

Leon Morris was never only an academic, but brought to that life the wide and enriching experience of ministry in a variety of parishes. While vice-principal of Ridley College (albeit at that time a much smaller and less demanding college than it is today), he also served as assistant curate in the parishes of Holy Trinity, Coburg (1948–49, 1953–55); St. John's, Bentleigh (1957–58); and St. George's, Bentleigh (1958–59). Although responsibility for the Sunday services at the college and periods of absence overseas made it impossible in later years to continue this parish ministry on a regular basis, he was often called on as a visiting preacher, and his pastoral concern for and love of preaching to ordinary people never diminished.

Morris's preaching is best described as expository, relevant, and evangelical. His general rule was to let the church's lectionary set the agenda; he would then open up the message of that reading, whatever it might be, to his hearers. When a visiting preacher failed to turn up, he would amaze (and inadvertently intimidate) his students by preaching an extempore sermon on the set passage, the likes of which they would have been hard pressed to emulate with ample notice and hours of preparation. His preaching, of course, was a product of and at one with his scholarship. J. Davis McCaughey (then master of Ormond College, University of Melbourne, and later governor of the state of Victoria) once said of him, "It has been one of Dr. Leon Morris's great virtues as a scholar that he has again and again sought to expose his readers to the text, even if it brings them to an alien world."[8] This has been no less a goal of his preaching.

Added to the authority which his scholarship gives to his preaching is Morris's considerable gift as a communicator, honed by his years as a teacher. He preaches as he writes, with simplicity, clarity, and relevance. Few preachers are better able than Leon Morris to translate the message of the Bible into the language and setting of the audience—here his quite remarkable ability to tune into a local culture is evident. At Minnipa, despite having no previous experience in farming, he became something of an authority on pigs by talking to farmers, reading the agricultural notes in the local papers, and, on one occasion, attending a lecture by an expert. In fact, he was eventually consulted on the subject by the farmers themselves.[9] Many years later, David Hubbard, the president of Fuller Theological Seminary, said of Morris, "I have never met anyone from overseas who learned so quickly and followed so avidly American sports. . . . He knows not only the names of the

7. Morris, *Bush Parson*, 82.
8. J. Davis McCaughey, "The Death of Death," in *Reconciliation and Hope: New Testament Essays on Atonement and Eschatology*, ed. Robert Banks (Grand Rapids: Eerdmans, 1975), 255.
9. Morris, *Bush Parson*, 32.

star players but the intricacies of the rules. Some of my finest memories," Hubbard continued, "are recollections of hours passed at athletic events discussing theology and sports with Dr. Morris."[10] His study gives him a rare insight into the original context of the biblical message, and his perception and intuition give him a perhaps even rarer consciousness of the needs of his hearers and the ability to sheet the message home by translating it into their setting. And at the heart of his preaching is a concern for the gospel, that it be heard and understood, and that his listeners be challenged to respond to it with decision. Again Hubbard says of him, "It is the person and work of Jesus Christ on which his studies have centered. This focus has made Morris's work (and we include in this his preaching) evangelical to the core."[11]

But gospel ministry is of necessity more than preaching. It is giving. Leon Morris has always given of himself without reservation to his parishioners, his students, his colleagues, his friends, although by nature he is reserved and not a man who easily opens up to others.[12] In his days as vice-principal and later as principal of Ridley College, his accessibility was symbolized by the open door—his study door was deliberately kept wide open as a sign that people were his priority no matter how urgent the task which occupied him within. "Hundreds of students," says Hubbard, "in Great Britain, the United States, as well as Australia have been nurtured by his personal interest in them. Discussions over coffee have blended scholarly acumen, pastoral experience, innate common sense, keen concern for persons. Individual counseling sessions have helped scores of students to find a way through their problems. At heart, administration is the service of people—not the shuffling of paper. At such service Leon Morris excels."[13]

It is as much in recognition of Morris's pastoral and preaching ministry as of his scholarship that invitations to teach, to preach, and to preside have come to him in a steady stream from both within Australia and overseas. These invitations have taken him to many countries and in his own have led to his chairing the Billy Graham Melbourne Crusade of 1968, the Inter-Varsity Fellowship of Australia, and the Evangelical Alliance of Victoria. As president of the Evangelical Alliance, he was instrumental in establishing The Evangelical Alliance Relief (TEAR) Fund in Australia, which he himself regards as one of his great achievements. Mention should also be made here of the Tyndale Fellowship, although it was of a more specifically academic focus. When he cofounded it with a handful of others, there was hardly any forum in Australia where evangelicals could air their insights with any hope of a sympathetic hearing. In time, the need for the fellowship diminished as

10. David A. Hubbard, "Leon Lamb Morris: An Appreciation," in *Reconciliation and Hope*, ed. Banks, 13–14.

11. Ibid., 13.

12. In *Bush Parson* there is an understated reference to the Morrises' taking into their home at Minnipa for two years two teenage girls whose mother Leon had buried and whose father could not adequately provide for them on his farm (p. 63).

13. Hubbard, "Morris: An Appreciation," 12.

other avenues of expression opened for evangelicals (thanks in large part to the credibility gained for their cause by Leon Morris and like-minded individuals). But in its day the Tyndale Fellowship did much to promote the study and application of Scripture, and throughout its twenty-five years of existence Leon Morris was its leading light.

Within his own denomination (the Church of England, now called the Anglican Church of Australia) an appreciation of Morris's ministry led to his election in 1964 as a canon of St. Paul's Cathedral, Melbourne, and to his nomination in 1966 for the archbishopric of Sydney (which he lost in the final ballot to Bishop Marcus Loane). For many years he served as secretary to the Doctrine Commission, a body set up by the General Synod of the Anglican Church. This position gave unique opportunity for expression of both his pastoral sensitivity and his great learning.

An Academic

From 1945 to 1960 Leon Morris was vice-principal of Ridley College. In these years he earned his master of theology degree from the University of London (he began this program while at Minnipa) and his doctor of philosophy degree from Cambridge University, the latter culminating the work of several years capped by two years of residence in Cambridge while on leave of absence from Ridley. His doctoral work (which in the end is reputed to have prompted the introduction of a new regulation governing the length of dissertations) entailed an examination of the language describing the atonement. The degree was awarded in Cambridge on Australia Day, January 26, 1952.

With the retirement of Bishop Baker as principal of Ridley College, Morris was passed over as his replacement in favor of Stuart Barton Babbage (principal of Ridley, 1953–63). Morris was already embarked on a career of writing and had no great ambition for the office of principal. There was no rancor, therefore, and the two men worked well together, their respective gifts complementing each other. Babbage was a man of big ideas, the supreme publicist, but not always practical in what he proposed. Morris was the realist and better equipped temperamentally to give attention to details. The college prospered under this duumvirate. In 1960 Morris was again given leave from Ridley and spent it largely in the United States as a visiting professor at Columbia (Decatur, Ga.) and Westminster. These were the first of a number of such appointments, which took him to Fuller (more than once), Gordon-Conwell, Trinity Evangelical Divinity School (several times), Westminster (twice), and the Western Conservative Baptist Seminary in Portland, Oregon. During one brief period in 1966 he also lent a hand to the editorial staff of *Christianity Today* in Washington, D.C.; and in this same year he took part in interdenominational discussions on biblical authority (Wenham, Mass.) and on world evangelism (Berlin). While he was at Columbia in 1960, the invitation was extended to be warden of Tyndale House, Cambridge.

After fifteen years at Ridley, the time seemed ripe for a move, and so began three idyllic years (1961–63) in a center (if not *the* center) of biblical scholarship rather than on its fringes in Australia. The new setting gave Morris almost untrammeled freedom to pursue his research and to get on with his writing. Meanwhile, however, Ridley College had fallen on difficult times with the departure of Babbage, strained relationships with the diocese, and a generally low morale among students and staff.[14] Someone was needed to head the college who could work with the local Anglican hierarchy (Ridley is an independent college, but does its job best when it can work in harmony with the bishops and other church leaders), attract students, and raise the college's profile in both the academic and ecclesiastical world. Leon Morris was an obvious candidate and, in its need, the college turned to him. He has never spoken publicly of what it cost him to go back, but it was one of the most difficult decisions that he ever had to make to leave Tyndale House (as near to heaven on earth as a biblical scholar can find) and return to Melbourne as principal of Ridley. He made the decision in the belief that it was God's will and out of a deep sense of loyalty to the college.

Morris's principalship ran from 1964 to 1979. In those years, under his leadership, the college underwent enormous change. It should be explained that Ridley is, in a sense, two colleges. On the one hand, it is a university college in the Oxford-Cambridge tradition—a hall of residence for university students, providing them with tutorials and pastoral care. On the other hand, it is a theological college, a teaching institution in its own right, offering theological degrees and diplomas (not its own, but those of the Australian College of Theology, an external examining and accrediting body set up by the General Synod of the Anglican Church), and concerned primarily with preparing men and (now) women for ordained ministry. There is some overlap between the two sides of the college, chiefly in their use of common facilities. But, for the most part, they go their separate ways; and this means that the principal, who presides over both, must wear two very different hats. The task is a difficult one. Morris's achievements in each of the two areas of responsibility must be acknowledged.

The very fact that Ridley is a university college is due largely to Morris. From its inception in 1910, the college had always included some nontheological students (for many years known as seculars), but their position was always an anomalous one—they were not really students of the college, and the college was not really (in the university sense) a hall of residence. All this changed in 1965 when the University of Melbourne accepted Ridley officially within its fold. There were financial benefits for the college in making this move, so that it was not entirely altruistic, but there was also a real con-

---

14. Morris recalls that, soon after his return as principal, he overheard a student complain, "This is a lousy college." He determined to make Ridley a college of which its students could be proud. Few would dispute that he succeeded.

cern on the part of the principal that the seculars have a better status within the college and that more be done for them.

In 1972 Morris chalked up a first not only for Ridley, but for the university, in making the college, that is, its residential and (largely) university dimension, coeducational. There had been the occasional female theological student, but to have female students living on campus was a new and, at that time, a brave departure. Again, there was an element of expediency in this decision. There were empty rooms. But the fact remains that Leon Morris was prepared to "give it a go," and it went well. The nine women (eight students and one tutor) whom Morris admitted brought such a change of tone to the college that there was never any thought of reverting to the all-male institution that Ridley had been.

The university side of the college was always important to Morris; and, in time, the university came to recognize his importance to it. By the time of his retirement, the heads of the colleges (the twelve residential halls associated with the University of Melbourne) looked upon him as an elder statesman whose counsel they often sought and always respected. The university itself paid tribute by granting him an honorary degree in science and, in 1977, inviting him to become a member of its council.

On the theological side of the college, Morris's achievement was no less impressive. Here change was more difficult because the traditions of the past were more deeply rooted, but the times were changing, and Morris saw that the college must change with them if it was to go on serving the church. The outcome was that in 1979, when he retired, Ridley was a vastly different place from what it had been in 1964 (and certainly in 1945, when he first came to the college). For one thing, the growth in student numbers, in large measure due to the drawing power of Morris's name, exceeded the wildest dreams of those earlier days. From an average of about thirty theological students in any one year, the number had grown to more than two hundred. Nor were all of them ordinands. The college had moved, partly by accident, partly by design of the principal, to a role in Christian education, that is, in educating the Christian public as well as prospective ministers. And there were many more women taking courses than there had ever been in the past (until the 1960s there had been an occasional deaconess in training, and that had been about all). But the theological student population had aged. There were many more married students and even people who had taken early retirement. Consequently, fewer were living on campus. In the years of Morris's principalship, the (theological) college had moved from being an almost monastic, all-male institution to one that was open, largely nonresidential, and coeducational.

Matching this growth and the changing needs of the student body, the number of courses multiplied during these years. From the time of its foundation, the standard course at the college had led to the licentiate of theology, an award of the Australian College of Theology. By the late 1970s the college was presenting candidates not only for the Th.L. and the kindred Th.Dip., but also for the diploma in ministry and the bachelor, master, and, on occasion, doctor of theology degrees (all awarded by the Australian College of Theology). With this came other developments. The faculty (never large) quadrupled from the two full-time members in the 1940s, supported by a number of visiting lecturers, to eight in the later 1970s, still with help from ancillary staff. New buildings began to appear. Under Morris's leadership, two public appeals for funds were launched, which, with some government help because of the university connection, resulted in the construction of additional single-student accommodation, apartments for faculty and married students—another first within the University of Melbourne—a dining hall, and common rooms for faculty and students.

After years of making do with inadequate and hired premises, the college now had, thanks to the drive and the reputation of its principal, buildings that went a long way towards meeting its needs. Morris involved himself not only in raising the money for these buildings, but in planning the details of their design. And nowhere more so than in the crowning achievement of his building program, the chapel. The Ridley College chapel is round (actually, octagonal), with the Lord's Table at the center overhung by a plain wooden cross. Standing behind and higher than the table is the pulpit/lectern. This arrangement encapsulates the theology which has informed the whole of Morris's Christian life: the centrality of the cross (i.e., the saving grace of God in the person and work of Christ) and the authority of the Scriptures.

An Author

The theology expressed in the architecture of the chapel has a fuller embodiment in Morris's writing. Leon Morris is a prolific author. Almost as soon as he became vice-principal of Ridley College, articles began to appear under his name in both popular and learned Christian journals. Once his doctoral work was out of the way, the trickle became a flood and began to include monographs of major importance. Even after his return to Ridley College in 1964, when there were so many more demands on his time and energy than at Tyndale House, by dint of an extraordinary discipline the writing continued. E. M. B. Green, reviewing Morris's commentary on John, expressed amazement that he "should have succeeded in writing so much . . . in the years when his time has been fully engaged in reviving the luster of Ridley College, Melbourne."[15] But it became more and more difficult to write as the administration of the college became increasingly complex. The regimen he had set himself was wearing him out, and the milestone of reaching the age of sixty-five and compulsory retirement came as a tremendous relief. It released him to do again what he had done at Tyndale House and liked above all: to read and to write, without the care of the college weighing upon him.

15. E. M. B. Green, review of *The Gospel according to John,* by Leon Morris, *Churchman* 87.4 (Winter 1973): 296.

To this day the stream of books and articles flows undiminished from his home in the outer suburbs of Melbourne.

This remarkable output exhibits an equally remarkable range and variety within the boundaries of biblical and especially New Testament scholarship. The general Christian reader probably knows Morris best through his commentaries. Hubbard divides these between what he calls the weightier commentaries and the more popular works,[16] although where to draw the line between the two categories is not always easy to decide. When Hubbard wrote, he classified the commentaries on 1 and 2 Thessalonians (1959) and on John (1971) as the weightier, but to that list must now be added the commentaries on Romans (1988) and Matthew (1992). There is no question, however, that people most readily associate the name of Leon Morris with his commentary on John. Understandably so. It has been around for a long time and is now accepted as a standard work of reference on that Gospel. It is a classic example of Morris's work. The text is clear, lucid, capable of being read and understood by the layperson no less than the scholar and of giving benefit to both. Those who are in the know are well aware of the depth of the scholarship expressed in the text, but it does not obtrude. The scholarship is demonstrated more explicitly in the footnotes and the occasional excursus. "The bulk of the commentary," writes David Wenham, "is given over to exegesis of the text. . . . Discussion of the Greek text which presupposes a knowledge of Greek on the part of the reader is limited to the footnotes; and this means that the commentary will be of use to the non-specialist, not just the trained theologian."[17] But the trained theologian, or the theologian in training, is certainly not neglected. Generations of students credit a large part of their education in Johannine studies to their reading of the footnotes of this book.

Morris's interest in the fourth Gospel produced a number of other works along the way: *The Dead Sea Scrolls* (1960), *The New Testament and the Jewish Lectionaries* (1964),[18] and, most importantly, preceding the publication of the commentary by two years and now regarded as a companion volume to it, *Studies in the Fourth Gospel* (1969). This collection of essays, which stems from lectures and material published elsewhere in the form of articles, deals with a number of the critical issues associated with the Gospel. The conclusions of the *Studies,* like those of the commentary, "are predictably conservative. [Morris] comes out strongly in favor of the 'new look' on the Fourth Gospel, and finds that Johannine tradition is independent of the Synoptic tradition although parallel and complementary to it, and that it has a high claim to reliability as a result. Dr. Morris is also prepared to argue for

16. Hubbard, "Morris: An Appreciation," 13.
    17. David Wenham, review of *The Gospel according to John,* by Leon Morris, *Evangelical Quarterly* 45.1 (Jan.-March 1973): 54.
    18. More recent is Leon Morris, "The Gospels and the Jewish Lectionaries," in *Studies in Midrash and Historiography,* ed. R. T. France and David Wenham (Sheffield: JSOT, 1983), 129–56.

eye-witness authorship . . . and to ascribe that authorship to John himself."[19] In sum, both the *Studies* and the subsequent commentary itself make a positive contribution to Johannine studies, to which may now be added *Jesus Is the Christ: Studies in the Theology of John* (1989). I. Howard Marshall describes this latest book on the Gospel (the belated publication of lectures given in 1976 at Trinity Evangelical Divinity School) as "a straightforward exposition of John's teaching without too much side-glancing at scholars who interpret the texts differently."[20]

This could, indeed, be a judgment passed on many of Morris's later works. The same careful attention to philological and grammatical detail is there as in the earlier works, the same encyclopedic knowledge of what has been said in the major commentaries of the last one hundred years, the same clarity of expression. But there is less and less engagement with the scholarly issues of the day. A reviewer of the commentary on Romans commends the "meticulous research and careful thinking" that went into the work, but laments that "Morris nowhere shows familiarity with the re-examination of ancient Jewish soteriology which has taken place." This would not be that serious, the reviewer adds, "if he defended his statements against the well-articulated and well-known works of . . . ," and here are listed a number of contemporary scholars who currently hold the floor in the Romans debate, "but he nowhere interacts with these scholars."[21] Morris himself readily concedes the point. His critics are mistaken, however, in assuming that he is unfamiliar with the work of recent scholars. Conversation with him reveals, rather, that he has read them or is at least familiar with their position, but he simply has lost patience with what he regards as matters peripheral to the understanding of the text.

In the case of Romans, although his work subsequently became the prototype of the Pillar series published by Eerdmans, Morris simply wrote, as he

19. Stephen Smalley, review of *Studies in the Fourth Gospel*, by Leon Morris, *Evangelical Quarterly* 43.1 (Jan.-March 1971): 52. Similarly, Wenham, review of *The Gospel*, 55, observes that the commentary "gives a sensible conservative view on numerous critical questions."

20. I. Howard Marshall, review of *Jesus Is the Christ*, by Leon Morris, *Evangelical Quarterly* 63.3 (July 1991): 276.

21. Frank Thielman, review of *The Epistle to the Romans*, by Leon Morris, *Journal of Biblical Literature* 108.4 (Winter 1989): 742. See also the reviews by John Paul Heil, *Catholic Biblical Quarterly* 51.4 (Oct. 1989): 750–52; and Ronald L. Tyler, *Interpretation* 44.3 (July 1990): 315–16. Similar complaints were leveled at some of the earlier commentaries, most notably that on John. "Those familiar with the extensive literature on the subject may be surprised," wrote E. M. B. Green (review of *The Gospel*, 296), "at Dr. Morris's predilection on the whole for older writers . . . and the rarity of his allusions to some of the contemporary writers on the Gospel." See also Wenham, review of *The Gospel*, 55; and D. M. Smith, review of *The Gospel according to John*, by Leon Morris, *Journal of Biblical Literature* 91.3 (Sept. 1972): 422. Here the point is valid that silence should not be taken as ignorance. Further, critics often overlook the considerable span of time between the completion of a large work and its publication. In the case of Morris's commentary on John it was four years, and some of the books that he was accused of overlooking were not available or even published at the time of his writing. Perhaps the last word on this matter should be given to the wife of a Canadian minister; she wrote Morris that his commentary on John had led to her giving her life to Christ. Being of help to ordinary people is what concerns Morris most as he writes.

puts it, "the kind of commentary I like to write. What do these words mean? I asked. I wrote simply to express what the biblical writer had to say so that the ordinary reader could understand. Modern critical scholarship does not interest the ordinary reader."[22] But even the most critical reviewer must concede, in this particular case, that "Morris has produced a valuable exposition of Romans. It offers several fresh approaches to difficult passages, relates old but helpful positions with eloquence, and provides a feast of philological and grammatical information on Romans that no serious student of the epistle can afford to neglect."[23] Others more in sympathy with Morris's position go further in their commendation. In this commentary, writes Graham Houston, "we have all that could reasonably be asked of a modern conservative treatment of Romans. It will prove to be the standard work to which we will refer for many years to come."[24] Whatever may be deemed to be the shortcomings of Morris's recent writing, they are offset by the riches of the insights which a life steeped in the Scriptures brings to the text—insights applied with compassion and made relevant by perception.

We have spoken of what Hubbard called Morris's weightier commentaries, but all of the virtues of these works are found no less in those designed for the more popular market, which differ from the others chiefly in the virtual absence of footnotes. In this category Morris has written on Ruth (for the Tyndale Old Testament series), chapters 26 to 28 of Matthew *(The Story of the Cross)*, John *(Reflections on the Gospel of John)*, 1 and 2 Thessalonians (for the Word Biblical Themes series), Hebrews, and the Johannine Epistles (in the *New Bible Commentary*). Four commentaries were written for the Tyndale New Testament series: Luke, 1 Corinthians,[25] 1 and 2 Thessalonians, and Revelation. This series was completed by Morris's volume on Luke, which many scholars regard as the most notable of all the Tyndale commentaries. (Not surprisingly, then, Morris served as editor when the series was revised.) It is considerably longer than the other volumes in the series; and, in light of the criticisms that have been leveled at its author in other connections, it is noteworthy that a number of reviewers remarked on its sensitivity "to currents of modern criticism."[26] R. T. France knew of "no better guide [within the limitations of the series format] to an intelligent grasp of Luke's Gospel, both in its details and in its 'profoundly theological purpose.'"[27] And Hub-

22. Leon Morris, conversation with the author, 3 March 1995.

23. Thielman, review of *The Epistle*, 740.

24. Graham Houston, review of *The Epistle to the Romans*, by Leon Morris, *Evangelical Quarterly* 62.3 (July 1990): 273.

25. This volume in the Tyndale Commentary series is Morris's biggest seller. At last count the sales were approaching 240,000.

26. R. T. France, review of *The Gospel according to St. Luke*, by Leon Morris, *Churchman* 89.2 (April-June 1975): 136; I. Howard Marshall, review of *The Gospel according to St. Luke*, by Leon Morris, *Evangelical Quarterly* 47.1 (Jan.-March 1975): 46; and Marcus Ward, review of *The Gospel according to St. Luke*, by Leon Morris, *Expository Times* 86.9 (June 1975): 280. None of these reviewers, however, is entirely uncritical of the work.

27. France, review of *The Gospel*, 136.

bard declared that Morris's popular commentaries in general are "exemplary in their field, models of deep learning clearly and simply expressed."[28]

We have already referred to Hubbard's description of Morris's work as "evangelical to the core." Nowhere is this more evident than in his thematic studies—his works of biblical theology. Here, repeatedly, he focuses attention on the cross of Christ. He first made his name by writing on this theme in *The Apostolic Preaching of the Cross* (1955), which is based on his doctoral dissertation. J. I. Packer, reviewing it in the *Evangelical Quarterly,* greeted it as "a book of the first importance" to which, he was sure, "[James] Denney would have given . . . an alpha, perhaps an alpha plus. . . . It is a delight," Packer says, "to follow Dr. Morris as time and time again he shifts the emphasis back to that which the New Testament is concerned to emphasize above all—that Christ saved God's people from wrath and ruin by dying for their sins in their place."[29] Subsequent editions included some minor alterations and rearrangements of the material and two major additions: a chapter on "The Lamb of God" and, in the chapter entitled "Propitiation (2)," a new section dealing with the word *hilastērion.* Some ten years later, I. Howard Marshall referred with approval to Morris's work on *hilastērion* as having been confirmed by the work of other scholars. "Similarly," he adds, Morris's "interpretation of the terminology of redemption, though open to some correction, is essentially sound, and there is not much more to be said on the matter." In short, "his careful linguistic scholarship provides the exegetical foundation for a systematic statement of the meaning of the death of Christ."[30]

Posterity may well reckon that *The Apostolic Preaching of the Cross* is Morris's most important contribution to New Testament scholarship. With this book in mind Hubbard said, "The Savior and the good news he has brought are [Morris's] chief interests. While appreciating all aspects of the academic task, he has personally chosen to test some of the main currents of biblical scholarship, rather than to paddle in the backwaters. . . . A legion of Bible students," Hubbard goes on to say, "have been convinced of the truth and the power of the gospel by Morris's scholarship."[31] This is so largely because Morris, not being prepared to leave the matter to one book, teased it out in one book after another. Thus *The Cross in the New Testament* (1965), based on the John A. McElwain Lectures delivered at Gordon Divinity School in 1960, builds on the foundation laid in the earlier work. Whereas *The Apostolic Preaching of the Cross* was organized on a lexical basis, *The Cross in the New Testament* approaches the subject in terms of the principal divisions of the New Testament—the Gospels of Matthew and Mark, the Lucan writ-

28. Hubbard, "Morris: An Appreciation," 13.

29. J. I. Packer, review of *The Apostolic Preaching of the Cross,* by Leon Morris, *Evangelical Quarterly* 28.2 (April-June 1956): 113–14.

30. I. Howard Marshall, "The Development of the Concept of Redemption in the New Testament," in *Reconciliation and Hope,* ed. Banks, 153.

31. Hubbard, "Morris: An Appreciation," 13.

ings, the fourth Gospel, the Pauline Epistles, and so on, much as Denney had done in *The Death of Christ.* F. F. Bruce saw *The Cross in the New Testament* as "a great book. It deals worthily," he said, "with a great subject. Without anything that smacks of special pleading, it shows that the evangelical understanding of the cross of Christ is the biblical understanding."[32]

In 1986 Morris published his *New Testament Theology,* which must be numbered among his most important works. Its purpose is "to provide a compact introduction to the theology of the New Testament." Descriptive rather than interpretative, the book makes no attempt to trace the history of the development of doctrine. Summing up the work as "clear, very readable, and not too lengthy," Marshall observes that "Morris limits his task to describing what the authors say."[33] It is striking that in a theology of such comparative brevity, detailed attention is given to the centrality of the cross in the New Testament and, in particular, to the propitiation effected thereby. No one, on reading this book, could be left in any doubt as to where Leon Morris's interest lies.

Some of the criticism directed at Morris's commentaries is also leveled against his work in biblical theology, namely, that he is out of touch with the latest currents of scholarship. Be that as it may, he has never lost touch with ordinary people and their pastoral needs. This point is borne out by *The Cross of Jesus.* Here Morris explores aspects of the work of Christ which evangelicals have often tended to underrate, such as (to summarize some of the chapters) the cross as the answer to futility, to ignorance, to loneliness, and to selfishness. The biblical tradition, the author claims, has much to say precisely in these areas. And to the end that people might hear what it says, Morris "is willing to descend from the high ground of objective atonement doctrine onto the softer terrain of the subjective, confident that no one would ever dare to accuse him of liberalism."[34] To correct even further the mistaken idea that Morris thinks only in terms of God's wrath and of the need for propitiation, we should also take note of another of his major works, *Testaments of Love: A Study of Love in the Bible.*[35]

Besides the commentaries and major works on biblical theology, there have also issued from Morris's pen (and more recently from his computer) a string of smaller thematic works, many with a popular appeal, some more esoteric in nature. These include *The Wages of Sin, The Biblical Doctrine of*

---

32. F. F. Bruce, review of *The Cross in the New Testament,* by Leon Morris, *Evangelical Quarterly* 38.1 (Jan.-March 1966): 63.

33. I. Howard Marshall, review of *New Testament Theology,* by Leon Morris, *Expository Times* 98.11 (Aug. 1987): 349.

34. John Muddiman, review of *The Cross of Jesus,* by Leon Morris, *Expository Times* 100.2 (Nov. 1988): 67.

35. Morris has always felt uncomfortable with this title, which was not his own, and with the editing that the book received. On the same theme he has also written *Love, Christian Style* (Portland, Oreg.: Western Conservative Baptist Seminary, 1976); and "Love in the Johannine Epistles," in *Through Christ's Word,* ed. W. Robert Godfrey and Jesse L. Boyd III (Phillipsburg, N.J.: Presbyterian and Reformed, 1985), 23–37.

Judgment, Glory in the Cross, and *The Atonement: Its Meaning and Significance,* all of which bear on Morris's great theme of the work of Christ; *The
Lord from Heaven* and *Jesus* (his first book for an Australian publisher) on
the person of Christ; *Spirit of the Living God, Ministers of God,* and *I Believe
in Revelation,* all self-explanatory as to their theme. Other topics covered include evangelism, the ministry of women, and apocalyptic literature; there is
also, in association with D. A. Carson and Douglas Moo, a magisterial introduction to the literature of the New Testament *(An Introduction to the New
Testament).* Finally, in this overview of Leon Morris's literary activity, mention should be made both of his work as a translator of the New International Version of the Bible[36] and of the almost countless articles that he has
for more than forty years contributed not only to learned journals, but to
popular church papers and magazines. These are of first importance in understanding the man, for they show that with Morris scholarship is not an
end in itself, but a means to the end that as many people as possible "grasp
how wide and long and high and deep is the love of Christ," and "know this
love that surpasses knowledge" (Eph. 3:18–19).

Primary Sources

Morris, Leon. *The Apostolic Preaching of the Cross.* Grand Rapids: Eerdmans,
1955; 2d ed., 1960.

———. *The Atonement: Its Meaning and Significance.* Downers Grove, Ill.: Inter-
Varsity, 1983.

———. *The Biblical Doctrine of Judgment.* Grand Rapids: Eerdmans, 1960.

———. *The Cross in the New Testament.* Grand Rapids: Eerdmans, 1965.

———. *The Cross of Jesus.* Grand Rapids: Eerdmans, 1988.

———. "The Epistles of John." In *New Bible Commentary,* 3d ed., edited by
Donald Guthrie and J. A. Motyer, 1259–73. Grand Rapids: Eerdmans, 1970.

———. *The Epistles of Paul to the Thessalonians.* Tyndale New Testament Commentaries. Grand Rapids: Eerdmans, 1957; rev. ed., 1984.

———. *The Epistle to the Romans.* Grand Rapids: Eerdmans, 1988.

———. *The First and Second Epistles to the Thessalonians.* New International
Commentary on the New Testament. Grand Rapids: Eerdmans, 1959; rev. ed.,
1991.

———. *First and Second Thessalonians.* Word Biblical Themes. Waco: Word, 1989.

———. *The First Epistle of Paul to the Corinthians.* Tyndale New Testament Commentaries. Grand Rapids: Eerdmans, 1958; rev. ed., 1986.

———. *Glory in the Cross.* London: Hodder and Stoughton, 1966.

———. *The Gospel according to John.* New International Commentary on the New
Testament. Grand Rapids: Eerdmans, 1971.

———. *The Gospel according to Matthew.* Pillar New Testament Commentary.
Grand Rapids: Eerdmans, 1992.

36. Morris headed a group based in Melbourne whose other members were Francis Foulkes and
David John Williams. They worked on 1 and 2 Corinthians.

———. *The Gospel according to St. Luke.* Tyndale New Testament Commentaries. Grand Rapids: Eerdmans, 1974; rev. ed., 1988.

———. *Hebrews: Bible Study Commentary.* Grand Rapids: Zondervan, 1983.

———. *I Believe in Revelation.* Grand Rapids: Eerdmans, 1976.

———. *Jesus Is the Christ: Studies in the Theology of John.* Grand Rapids: Eerdmans, 1989.

———. *The Lord from Heaven.* Grand Rapids: Eerdmans, 1958.

———. *Ministers of God.* Chicago: InterVarsity, 1964.

———. *The New Testament and the Jewish Lectionaries.* London: Tyndale, 1964.

———. *New Testament Theology.* Grand Rapids: Zondervan, 1986.

———. *Reflections on the Gospel of John.* 4 vols. Grand Rapids: Baker, 1986–88.

———. *The Revelation of St. John.* Tyndale New Testament Commentaries. Grand Rapids: Eerdmans, 1969; rev. ed., 1987.

———. "Ruth." In Arthur Ernest Cundall and Leon Morris, *Judges [and] Ruth.* Tyndale Old Testament Commentaries. Chicago: InterVarsity, 1968.

———. *Spirit of the Living God.* Chicago: InterVarsity, 1960.

———. *The Story of the Cross.* Grand Rapids: Eerdmans, 1957.

———. *Studies in the Fourth Gospel.* Grand Rapids: Eerdmans, 1969.

———. *Testaments of Love: A Study of Love in the Bible.* Grand Rapids: Eerdmans, 1981.

———, D. A. Carson, and Douglas J. Moo. *An Introduction to the New Testament.* Grand Rapids: Zondervan, 1992.

Secondary Sources

Morris, Leon. *Bush Parson.* Brunswick East, Victoria, Australia: Acorn, 1995.

Reconciliation and Hope: New Testament Essays on Atonement and Eschatology. Edited by Robert Banks. Grand Rapids: Eerdmans, 1975.

Donald Guthrie

Steve Motyer

Donald Guthrie, for thirty-three years lecturer in New Testament at London Bible College, was himself amazed by the worldwide success and influence of his two major works—his *New Testament Introduction,* which was published in three volumes in the early 1960s and then issued as a single volume in 1970, and his *New Testament Theology* (1981). By 1995, worldwide sales of his *Introduction* totaled approximately 145,000, and of his *Theology* 35,000. Research conducted by Mark Noll in 1984 amongst the leading evangelical professional societies in North America revealed that 10 percent of the members of the Institute for Biblical Research regarded Guthrie as the single most dominant influence on their scholarly work, ranking alongside Rudolf Bultmann and only slightly behind Joachim Jeremias and Oscar Cullmann. No less than 14 percent of the scholars holding joint membership in the Institute for Biblical Research and the Evangelical Theological Society accorded Guthrie this position, ranking ahead of John Calvin and C. H. Dodd.[1]

Since Guthrie undertook only two brief teaching visits to the United States, the extent of his influence there can be ascribed wholly to his *New Testament Introduction* and *New Testament Theology.*[2] Along with F. F. Bruce (a personal friend), Donald Guthrie was the mouthpiece of British evangelical biblical scholarship in North America, and this British influence played a crucial formative role in the resurrection of biblical scholarship in evangelical seminaries in the United States.[3] In Britain Guthrie's position was not so unique, for there were other conservative evangelical scholars equally influential in the 1960s and 1970s, some even in university posts. But his impact was still singular, for his *New Testament Introduction* had (and in its revised edition continues to have) a unique usefulness for evangelical students. In fact it could be argued that his influence was wider in Britain, for while he was largely ignored by nonevangelical scholarship in the United

---

1. Mark A. Noll, *Between Faith and Criticism: Evangelicals, Scholarship, and the Bible in America* (New York: Harper and Row, 1986), 209–10.
2. In 1964 and 1968 Guthrie taught at the Winona Lake Summer School of Theology. That the American edition accounts for 68 percent of the total sales of the *New Testament Introduction* underscores his influence in the United States.
3. Noll, *Between Faith and Criticism,* 91, 101, 105–6, 120, 134.

States, in Britain his work was featured in general university courses, and scholars felt obliged to interact with his arguments.

Personal History

The personal and the professional interact for all scholars, of course, often in quite unrecognized ways. In Donald Guthrie's case this interaction was clear, and had some most unusual features. In his early years he struggled to overcome a severe speech impediment, and the means he discovered to combat it intersected significantly with his whole scholarly approach and method, as we shall see.

Donald Guthrie and his twin brother Raymond were born in Ipswich, Suffolk, on February 21, 1916, to Malcolm and Maude Guthrie. The family was of Scottish ancestry, and in later life Donald took particular delight in the Guthrie clan motto, *Sto pro veritate* (I stand for truth). He wrote, "I recognized its aptness for summing up what I felt the overriding purpose of my life to be."[4] His affection for his Scottish roots came to poignant prominence in the last years of his life, when he took to wearing a kilt because of the debilitating lymphatic cancer against which he fought a losing battle.

Donald was not the only academic in the family. He and Raymond had an older brother Malcolm, thirteen years their senior, who became a professor of Bantu at the School of Oriental and African Studies in London. Their father was an engineer and a quiet man of simple faith. Both Donald and Malcolm inherited their academic gifts from their mother, who imparted to young Donald a thirst for theological understanding and a taste for Bible teaching. She would debate doctrine with the pastor of the Bethesda Strict Baptist Church, which they attended; she would also expound Scripture to her family as well as speak at other local churches. Donald later recalled, "Her grasp of Scripture was phenomenal and I never ceased to marvel at the insight she seemed to have with so little formal education."[5] Guthrie was not the first, nor will be the last, biblical scholar whose work is a tribute to the foundations laid by a godly parent.

But his mother died when Donald was nineteen. Her death affected him deeply: "I felt I was losing the only person who really understood me."[6] Then began a period which he described as the most traumatic of his life. Having left school he eventually found a dead-end clerical job in which the next ten years slowly slipped past.

Fundamental to Donald's problems at this time was his stammer. His school years had been blighted by it. Convinced that it was incurable, he felt, as he said, "destined to remain a prisoner within my own world. . . . I was like a person in a tunnel with hardly a speck of light to beckon me on."[7] At

4. Donald Guthrie, "I Stand for Truth" (autobiography), 1985, typescript, 5.
5. Ibid., 10.
6. Ibid., 12.
7. Ibid., 21, 23.

school he had retreated into academic study, and was always one of the highest achievers in his class, but this success simply underlined the difference between Donald and his twin brother Raymond.

Raymond was boisterous and assertive, talkative, good at sports and full of self-confidence. But Donald seemed very different: academic, nonathletic, and marked by a sensitive femininity that in childhood made him feel more at home playing with his younger sister Doris than with Raymond. But inevitably he also felt intense pressure to compete with his brother and to be as self-assertive. Later on, he identified this tension as the fundamental reason for his handicap. But during his late teens and twenties, it was simply a terrible burden to be borne.

Various cures were tried, but since the cause had not been diagnosed as emotional, none of them worked. Remarkably, Donald was able, through this period, to follow his mother's example in developing an extensive ministry as a local preacher in the many village chapels near Ipswich. Though his stammer inevitably affected his fluency, he was able to preach with a confidence which he lacked in ordinary conversation. A turning point was reached when he discovered that he could sing without stammering. This revealed that the problem was not physical, but one of attitude. He did not take decisive steps towards overcoming it, however, until his life had moved in a different direction.

The first and most important factor in changing Guthrie's life was his marriage to Mary. Within six months of their wedding in March 1946, Donald had enrolled as one of the first full-time students at London Bible College, which had started by offering evening classes in central London during the war, and then opened its doors to full-time students in January 1946.[8] He notes in his autobiography that Mary "encouraged me to proceed when both her parents and my own father had grave doubts about the venture."[9] She gave him the confidence to respond to God's prompting, a prompting which was quickly recognized by Ernest Kevan, the first principal. Thus began an association with the college that continued unbroken for the rest of Guthrie's life.

Married to Mary, and settling into theological studies, Donald began to accept his personality. He began to learn not to deny the feminine side of his nature through an ill-suited competitive self-assertiveness. One day a staff member surprised him by commenting on the elegance of his physical movements, and connected it with the obvious elegance of his handwriting. Donald began to cultivate this side of his personality, in turn surprising the college by appearing one day in a light green corduroy jacket with dark green corduroy trousers and a bright yellow pullover, instead of the regulation somber postwar suit!

---

8. The early history of the college is recounted in Harold H. Rowdon, *London Bible College: The First Twenty-five Years* (Worthing: J. W. Walter, 1968). I am very grateful to Mary Guthrie for her help in the preparation of this article.
9. Guthrie, "I Stand for Truth," 36.

To his delight Guthrie discovered that if he worked at cultivating a similar natural elegance in his speech, using a higher tone and thinking of sentences as if they were musical phrases, he was able to speak with much greater fluency: "I began to realise that my stammer sprang from an ill-conceived assertiveness, whereas I should have allowed myself to adopt a more passive approach and let my words flow with as much elegance as my other movements would suggest."[10] The problem never left him entirely (for many years he hated using the telephone), but it receded as he took a new delight simply in being the person God had made him.

Guthrie's pleasure in handwriting was intense. A meticulously crafted page gave him great satisfaction: "It did not matter to me that possibly no one except a typist would see the finished product. As I looked at it I saw a reflection of myself."[11] So most of his books and lectures were handwritten. The Guthrie archive at London Bible College contains the handwritten first draft of his *New Testament Theology*, meticulously revised and emended in the margins, as well as thousands of pages of lecture notes, all beautifully executed, and often supplemented by neat and colorful acetates for the overhead projector.

On the other hand, there was also a boisterous, outgoing element in Donald's character; in fact, the tensions and misery he had experienced in his twenties resulted in part from his not recognizing and expressing his natural capacity for self-advertisement. But with growing confidence he was able to do so, both through his writing and in personal relationships. Generations of students remember his warmth and concern, particularly for those with special needs, his infectious sense of fun, and his extraordinary pleasure in organizing the faculty contribution to college concerts. Often Donald would be the star, appearing in female costume amid gales of laughter. In retirement he amazed his family and friends by taking up Scottish country dancing, which appealed greatly to his love of elegant dress, music, and movement. He gave himself to learning this new skill with the same single-minded concentration that had enabled him to write major works of scholarship while rearing the family of six children born to him and Mary.

More than a year before he graduated in 1949, Guthrie was offered a job as a lecturer at London Bible College. From 1964 he also served as registrar for advanced studies, and from 1978 as vice-principal. When the college moved to its present site in Northwood in 1970, Guthrie played a prominent role in designing the new buildings, and was delighted with the result. On his retirement in 1982 he was presented with a festschrift written by colleagues, friends, and former students.[12] As much as his progressive illness would allow, he used his ten remaining years for further lecturing and writing. From

10. Ibid., 31.
11. Ibid.
12. *Christ the Lord: Studies in Christology Presented to Donald Guthrie*, ed. Harold H. Rowdon (Downers Grove, Ill.: InterVarsity, 1982).

1989 until his death on September 8, 1992, he served London Bible College further in the honorary position of president. He remained active and alert until the end, presenting degrees to the graduating students two months before his death, and managing with great difficulty to complete his last projects.[13]

Throughout his life Guthrie was also involved in local church ministry, continuing the pattern of his early years in preferring ministry in small country churches. For over forty years, for instance, he preached regularly at the small Strict Baptist church in King's Langley, Hertfordshire (not far from London). For many years, too, he served on the board of the Scripture Gift Mission.

Approach to Biblical Scholarship

Guthrie's students were constantly impressed by the courtesy with which he would describe and critique the views of other scholars, especially those who had no time for a conservative evangelical approach to the Bible. Inevitably, some students were exasperated by his readiness to give ample lecture-time to the views of liberal scholars. Others were exasperated by the detailed attention he gave to issues of introduction—authorship, composition, date. But both teaching emphases were consciously conceived commitments on Guthrie's part, and go back to his early years at London Bible College when he was both engaging initially with biblical scholarship, and also finding the self-understanding to overcome his stammer.

From the earliest days of his biblical studies Guthrie rejected what he called the polemical approach, which simply charged liberal scholarship with unfaithfulness and error. Instead, he resolved to engage in open dialogue, which meant "the exclusion of any arguments based on dogmatic considerations. It seemed to me that such arguments were invalid in the debate with scholars devoted to the historical-critical method. My view was that if the biblical text was the authoritative word of God, it would establish its own truth. My quest was therefore for the truth. It was for this reason that the Guthrie motto, *Sto pro veritate* . . . seemed so relevant to me. It sums up my whole academic policy."[14]

Many of Guthrie's fellow evangelicals felt that the right response to liberal views of the Bible and theology was to reject them wholesale and preach the gospel instead. And this was undoubtedly the style of the Strict Baptist tradition in which he had been raised. But he moved away from this approach. He

---

13. Donald Guthrie, "The Pastoral Letters," in *New Bible Commentary: 21st Century Edition*, ed. G. J. Wenham et al. (Downers Grove, Ill.: InterVarsity, 1994), 1292–1315; idem, "God," in *Dictionary of Paul and His Letters*, ed. Gerald F. Hawthorne et al. (Downers Grove, Ill.: InterVarsity, 1993), 354–69; idem, "The Christology of Revelation," in *Jesus of Nazareth: Lord and Christ*, ed. Joel B. Green and Max Turner (Grand Rapids: Eerdmans, 1994), 397–409. The latter two were completed with the help of his long-standing colleague Max Turner.

14. Guthrie, "I Stand for Truth," 55.

later wrote, "Whatever sympathy I might have felt for this point of view was overshadowed by the importance of understanding the total theological climate in which the modern Christian church is obliged to operate." [15]

Guthrie's approach can be traced to several influences. He found himself at an interdenominational institution where it was natural to feel related to the whole Christian church, rather than to just one part of it. His mother's godly combination of inquiry and faithfulness was living on in her son, but had now been transposed into the world of professional biblical studies. And in his personal life he was rejecting the polemical approach as he sought to overcome his speech impediment.

Probably the last factor is the most important. The new Donald had stopped trying to be self-assertive and combative, and was cultivating a gentler, more passive persona. This new style in his personal relations came to be mirrored in the style of his biblical studies and led to a conscious hermeneutical theory. He endorsed the historical-critical method, which meant engaging in open and courteous debate with scholars of all theological persuasions. His delight in elegance was deeply contributory here. Both his lectures and his writing revealed his pleasure in beautifully crafted arguments that carefully presented the evidence, explained and evaluated rival theories, and reached a judicious conclusion. Scholars swirled elegantly across the text and footnotes like dancers in a Scottish reel, interweaving in an argument neatly divided into points and subpoints, and building a massive defense of a conservative view of the Bible and theology.

Though he rejected the polemical approach and endorsed historical criticism, Guthrie never broke faith with his evangelical background and heritage. That was unthinkable to him. He was convinced that if the evangelical view of Scripture is true, then it has nothing to fear from open and honest study. So from his earliest years as a lecturer he was a member of the Tyndale Fellowship for Biblical Research, and later also a member of the Society for New Testament Study.

But Guthrie's friendly debate with nonevangelical scholarship could be misunderstood. Because in the course of the debate he would exclude all "arguments based on dogmatic considerations," it was sometimes overlooked that his own approach to Scripture rested on a firm doctrinal foundation. And so when James Barr published his book *Fundamentalism*, a sustained and hostile assault on conservatism both popular and scholarly, Guthrie found himself being praised by the devil. Friends and fellow New Testament scholars like Michael Green and John Wenham, and Old Testament colleagues like R. K. Harrison and Kenneth Kitchen, were roundly condemned for blinkered dogmatism and inconsistency, and for imposing conservative presuppositions on the Bible. And the Inter-Varsity Press, which had published much of Guthrie's work, including his *New Testament Introduction*,

---

15. Ibid.

was censured for bolstering the evangelical subculture with comforting literature at the cost of truth.[16]

But Guthrie's *Introduction* was praised by Barr: "Guthrie's work, while conservative, is irenic and understanding throughout. . . . At no point does he sweep these [Bultmannian and form-critical] approaches away by asserting that they are built upon non-Christian presuppositions, denials of the supernatural and so on. It is evident that Guthrie belongs in the same world with critical New Testament scholars and accepts his membership of that one world."[17] Barr pressed home his attack with a challenge: "Are Harrison and Kitchen going to turn their violence on to Guthrie? And if not, are they not admitting that their own anti-critical vehemence is no more than pure partisanship?"[18]

Guthrie contemplated a response for some time. In 1981 an article was announced as forthcoming. But it was not until 1985 that he replied, in the Laing Lecture at London Bible College.[19] By then, Barr had published further attacks, including some barbs which—for all his kind words in *Fundamentalism*—seemed directed at Guthrie personally.[20] Some of his friends felt that Guthrie's usual scrupulous fairness was missing from his response, for he roundly criticized Barr both for his derogatory style and for his inaccurate content. But, typically, he set his response within a broad discussion of the nature of biblical authority, which he discerned as the "real battleground" in the debate.[21] And here he revealed the theological basis of his own work. Starting from John Calvin's view that the Spirit confirms the authority of Scripture directly to the church and the believer, he went on to affirm (a) the necessity for biblical scholarship to resist any conclusions about the Bible which conflict with its divine authority, and (b) the indispensability of biblical scholarship for elucidating the meaning of the Bible.[22]

Thus, for Guthrie, biblical authority was not just a general presupposition, but a doctrinal fact confirmed by the Spirit. He recognized that Barr, too, was prepared to affirm the authority of the Bible. The vital point of disagreement, the real battleground, was the different perceptions of the implications of affirming biblical authority as a presupposition of scholarly work.

16. See James Barr, *Fundamentalism* (Philadelphia: Westminster, 1978), 76–80 (attacking Wenham), 126–30 (Green), 130–32 (Kitchen), 141 (Harrison), and 120–24 (attacking Inter-Varsity Press along with other conservative publishing houses).

17. Ibid., 140–41.

18. Ibid., 143.

19. Donald Guthrie, "Biblical Authority and New Testament Scholarship," *Vox Evangelica* 16 (1986): 7–23.

20. E.g., James Barr, "The Problem of Fundamentalism Today," in *The Scope and Authority of the Bible* (Philadelphia: Westminster, 1980), 65–90; idem, *Holy Scripture: Canon, Authority, Criticism* (Philadelphia: Westminster, 1983), 31–32. Barr accused conservative biblical scholarship of being obsessed with issues of authorship and date (Guthrie's first publication, based on his first attempt at a Ph.D. dissertation, had been devoted to the authorship of the Pastoral Epistles), and of being "stodgy, dull, uninspiring, and lacking in fervour" ("Problem of Fundamentalism," 87).

21. Guthrie, "Biblical Authority," 17.

22. Ibid., 11–12.

Guthrie was not happy with the word *inerrancy*, but only because he thought it was unclear and defensive in tone.[23] He believed firmly that many widely held critical opinions on issues of authorship, composition, date, historical background, and theological coherence were incompatible with biblical authority. Hence his deep interest in these matters of introduction: he wanted to show that the evidence, objectively weighed, does not require a questioning of this fundamental authority.

This straightforward approach was also foundational in Guthrie's second magnum opus, his *New Testament Theology*. In contrast to other New Testament theologies, Guthrie's work is built on an "approach which sees the NT teaching as an abiding revelation from God, which therefore concentrates on what God has to say to man rather than on man's various religious experiences in his search for God. If divine truth of an authoritative kind is conveyed in the NT, the interpreter is circumscribed in his task. He is not at liberty to pick and choose. He must take all or nothing. . . . He is committed to discover the unifying factors because he knows that revelation cannot be contradictory."[24] From this principle Guthrie constructed the whole work, arranging it on the basis of themes rather than individual writers, because the latter approach would inevitably highlight differences rather than the message common to all.

But Guthrie was aware that he was treading a tightrope, for at the same time he insisted on a *historical* study of each writer. As he puts it in his lecture on biblical authority, "All we can learn about the writers, their times, their purposes, their relations with their readers, can only illuminate our understanding of the text."[25] Each must be allowed to speak with his own authentic voice, but the unique personalities of the authors must not be so understood that they end up in competition with each other.[26] Though he never directly criticized fellow evangelical George Eldon Ladd's *Theology of the New Testament*, which was published as Guthrie started work on his volume, it is clear that he saw dangers in Ladd's analytical approach that treated each New Testament author separately.[27]

The reviews of Guthrie's *Theology* were predictable. His enormous erudition was universally admired. At one end of the theological spectrum, evangelical reviewers were highly enthusiastic.[28] But some fellow evangelicals found his approach conservative even for evangelical New Testament scholarship,[29]

23. Ibid., 10–11.

24. Donald Guthrie, *New Testament Theology* (Downers Grove, Ill.: InterVarsity, 1981), 29–30.

25. Guthrie, "Biblical Authority," 12.

26. Guthrie, *New Testament Theology*, 37–40.

27. George Eldon Ladd, *A Theology of the New Testament* (Grand Rapids: Eerdmans, 1974).

28. E.g., Drew Trotter, review of *New Testament Theology*, by Donald Guthrie, *Journal of the Evangelical Theological Society* 25.2 (June 1982): 248–52.

29. Gordon D. Fee, review of *New Testament Theology*, by Donald Guthrie, *Catholic Biblical Quarterly* 44.3 (July 1982): 507–9; Stephen S. Smalley, review of *New Testament Theology*, by Donald Guthrie, *Journal for the Study of the New Testament* 20 (Feb. 1984): 110–11 ("nevertheless, this book represents conservative scholarship at its very best").

and nonevangelical scholars were dismissive about the way in which the shape and outcome of the study had been determined in advance by his presuppositions.[30] Of course, Guthrie's work will always challenge those who want to affirm biblical authority, but yet allow the presence of error and contradiction in the Bible.[31]

Writings

In addition to the two major volumes already mentioned, his *Introduction* and his *Theology*, Guthrie produced a stream of other works throughout his career. There was never a period when he was not writing, alongside his lecturing at London Bible College. The sheer volume of his writing is truly astounding, especially for a man with six children. Within two years of his appointment he was awarded an M.Th. by the University of London (1951). Three years later he submitted a Ph.D. thesis on the authorship and background of the Pastoral Letters. But for all its meticulous attention to detail, "A Critical Examination of the Fragment Theory of the Pastoral Epistles in Relation to the Hypothesis of Paul's Ephesian Imprisonments" shows evidence of hasty production, and in fact was not accepted. Guthrie was eventually awarded a Ph.D. in 1961 for an entirely different thesis, "Early Christian Pseudepigraphy and Its Antecedents," a work of massive erudition and careful scholarship.

Neither thesis was ever published, although the substance of both contributed indirectly to other publications. The first thesis bore direct fruit in 1955 when Guthrie gave the Tyndale New Testament Lecture on "The Pastoral Epistles and the Mind of Paul." This became his first publication (1956). By then the lecture had already led to an invitation to contribute a volume on the Pastorals to the new Tyndale Commentary series. Such was the speed of Guthrie's work that this was published in 1957. The next three years saw him writing not only his Ph.D. thesis on pseudepigraphy, but also the first volume of his *New Testament Introduction;* this volume on the Pauline Epistles was published in 1961. The second volume, on Hebrews to Revelation, followed in 1962. Remarkably, in this period Guthrie also wrote his commentary on Galatians for the New Century Bible series (although it was not published until 1969), and found time to contribute articles to the *New Bible Dictionary*.[32] The third volume of his *New Testament Introduction,* on the Gospels and Acts, was published in 1965. In the meantime he contributed

---

30. E.g., Heikki Räisänen, review of *New Testament Theology,* by Donald Guthrie, *Theologische Literaturzeitung* 110.12 (Dec. 1985): 889–90; George B. Caird, review of *New Testament Theology,* by Donald Guthrie, *Journal of Theological Studies* 33.1 (April 1982): 253–56.

31. In his autobiography Guthrie expresses concern that the new generation of evangelical scholars is too ready to accept critical conclusions about the Bible. He fears "a situation in which scholars who claim to maintain Biblical authority are actually denying it in the position being adopted" ("I Stand for Truth," 65).

32. *New Bible Dictionary,* ed. J. D. Douglas (Grand Rapids: Eerdmans, 1962); Guthrie wrote the articles on Romans, Hebrews, Timothy and Titus, pseudepigrapha, and pseudonymity.

Epistles from Prison to the Bible Guides series, then being edited by William Barclay and F. F. Bruce.

During the next few years Guthrie undertook more-popular writing. He felt deeply committed to using his writing skills in the service of the wider church, and not just for scholarship. So he wrote some long articles for *The Zondervan Pictorial Encyclopedia of the Bible,* one of which was published as a separate book entitled *A Shorter Life of Christ* (1970). Further products for the same market followed—a life of Christ entitled *Jesus the Messiah* (1972) and a companion volume on the apostles (1975), both of them works of four hundred pages. Guthrie successfully avoided technical theological jargon when writing for a general readership, but his style was never lively or sparkling.

During this same period an editorial mantle fell upon Guthrie's shoulders: in 1965 he became editor of *Vox Evangelica,* the journal of London Bible College, and he also served as New Testament editor of the *New Bible Commentary Revised* (1970), to which he contributed the introductory article on the Pauline Letters and the commentaries on John, Colossians, and Philemon.

In 1974 Guthrie began work on his *New Testament Theology,* a project in which he invested very considerable labor over a six-year period. It was published in 1981, a year before his retirement. Its 982 pages of text are eloquent testimony to the maturity of his evangelical scholarship, and its 1,100-item bibliography to the breadth of his research and engagement. But working on this project did not preclude all else. During this time he also served as consulting editor for Inter-Varsity's *Illustrated Bible Dictionary* (1980) and for the revision of the *New Bible Dictionary* (1982), to which he also contributed long articles. He also wrote an important article on "The Historical and Literary Criticism of the New Testament" for *The Expositor's Bible Commentary.*[33]

There was no pause in Guthrie's productivity. The end of the *Theology* project merged seamlessly with the next, the writing of the Tyndale commentary on Hebrews, published in 1983. This was very well received by reviewers in scholarly journals: it compares favorably with all recent middle-sized commentaries in English, French, and German;[34] shows both scholarly insight and sensitivity to contemporary relevance;[35] and is "undoubtedly the best . . . medium-sized commentary on Hebrews."[36] It is certainly one of the best in the Tyndale series.

33. Donald Guthrie, "The Historical and Literary Criticism of the New Testament," in *Expositor's Bible Commentary,* ed. Frank E. Gaebelein, vol. 1 (Grand Rapids: Zondervan, 1979), 437–56.

34. Paul Ellingworth, review of *The Epistle to the Hebrews,* by Donald Guthrie, *Evangelical Quarterly* 57.1 (Jan. 1985): 79.

35. Carol L. Stockhausen, review of *The Epistle to the Hebrews,* by Donald Guthrie, *Biblical Theology Bulletin* 16.4 (Oct. 1986): 153.

36. Ronald Williamson, review of *The Epistle to the Hebrews,* by Donald Guthrie, *Expository Times* 95.5 (Feb. 1984): 186.

In retirement Guthrie worked on some popular Bible guides under the over-all title *Exploring God's Word,* and turned his 1985 Didsbury Lectures into a study of *The Relevance of John's Apocalypse.* Much of his time was then taken up with the revision of his *New Testament Introduction* and also of his Tyndale commentary on *The Pastoral Epistles.* The work on the Tyndale commentary served as a launching pad for one of his last publications, the article on the Pastoral Epistles for the 1994 edition of the *New Bible Commentary.*

This broad summary of what Guthrie called his "literary adventures" takes no account of the numerous articles and reviews which constantly appeared, often in small evangelical publications. Nor does it take account of his role in the writing undertaken by others. He piloted several students successfully through research degrees, although only one of the theses written under his supervision has been published.[37]

"I was a firm believer in the principle that everyone must develop and use the particular gifts that God has given, and I could not deny where my gifts lay," Guthrie wrote in his autobiography.[38] Having discovered his niche in biblical studies after those early years in a personal wilderness, he stuck single-mindedly to the calling to teach and write, and his legacy is a testament to his dedication and faithfulness—and to the woman who made it possible. At his last public appearance, the July 1992 graduation ceremony of London Bible College, Donald was presented with an honorary doctorate by the vice-chancellor of the British Council for National Academic Awards, and then made a moving speech of acceptance in which he paid glowing tribute to his wife Mary. Without her, he would undoubtedly never have entered theological study, nor discovered the confidence to overcome his stammer. Though she never features in his writings, her hand is visible on every page.

In 1991 London Bible College launched a campaign to mark its golden jubilee by founding an Islamic studies center and a research institute. A building was planned to house these new projects, and donations invited. It was clear that this was an opportunity to commemorate the name of the scholar who, more than any other, had established the reputation of the college during its first fifty years. And so in November 1995 the Guthrie Center was opened as a home for the biblical research which will take forward the tradition of the scholar whose name adorns it. The closing words of his 1985 lecture summarize its vision, which was his before: "The word of God will vindicate itself!"[39]

Primary Sources

Guthrie, Donald. *The Apostles.* Grand Rapids: Zondervan, 1975.

---

37. Mary J. Evans, *Woman in the Bible: An Overview of All the Crucial Passages on Women's Roles* (Downers Grove, Ill.: InterVarsity, 1984).
38. Guthrie, "I Stand for Truth," 57.
39. Guthrie, "Biblical Authority," 20.

————. *Epistles from Prison: Philippians, Ephesians, Colossians, Philemon*. Bible Guides 19. New York: Abingdon, 1964.

————. *The Epistle to the Hebrews: An Introduction and Commentary*. Tyndale New Testament Commentaries. Grand Rapids: Eerdmans, 1983.

————. *Exploring God's Word: A Guide to Ephesians, Philippians, and Colossians*. Grand Rapids: Eerdmans, 1985.

————. *Exploring God's Word: A Guide to John's Gospel*. Grand Rapids: Eerdmans, 1986.

————. *Galatians*. New Century Bible Commentary. London: Nelson, 1969; Grand Rapids: Eerdmans, 1981.

————. *Jesus the Messiah*. Grand Rapids: Zondervan, 1972.

————. *New Testament Introduction*. Downers Grove, Ill.: InterVarsity, 1970; rev. ed., 1990.

————. *New Testament Theology*. Downers Grove, Ill.: InterVarsity, 1981.

————. *The Pastoral Epistles: An Introduction and Commentary*. Tyndale New Testament Commentaries. Grand Rapids: Eerdmans, 1957; rev. ed., 1990.

————. *The Relevance of John's Apocalypse*. Grand Rapids: Eerdmans, 1987.

————. *A Shorter Life of Christ*. Grand Rapids: Zondervan, 1970.

Donald J. Wiseman

Martin J. Selman

When the full history of British evangelicalism in the latter half of the twentieth century comes to be written, the contribution of Donald Wiseman to biblical scholarship will emerge as one of the most significant factors. That this has not always been recognized is due partly to the nature of the man and of his achievements. Donald Wiseman is modest by nature and by Christian conviction and would be genuinely surprised by such an assessment of his life and career. It is entirely consistent with his character that he was both reluctant to consent to the writing of this article, but generous in providing unstinting help to the author.

Since much of Wiseman's activity has been carried out behind the scenes, an assessment of his contribution cannot be limited to his published work, though this is extensive and gives evidence of a lively, broad-ranging, and fertile mind. Equally important, and perhaps with ultimately more far-reaching consequences, has been his personal influence on others. He has been constantly active both in private conversation and in committee work, and though few details have ever reached public notice, many people are grateful for his quiet encouragement. Typical is an expression of appreciation for his various activities in behalf of the British School of Archaeology in Iraq: "It is perhaps for Donald's devoted work behind the scenes that we should be most grateful to him. He has presided over our Council and Executive Committee meetings with a kindly—sometimes perhaps too tolerant—hand, but few realize the day-to-day complexities of the School's affairs, the negotiations with and the preparation of reports for the British Academy, the resolution of difficulties in Baghdad which require immediate action and the Chairman's authority. Still less known is the support he has constantly given to young scholars, Assyriologists and archaeologists alike. We are deeply in his debt on many counts."[1]

Early Influences and Education

Despite his many achievements, the most important aspect of Donald Wiseman's life is that he is first and foremost an evangelical Christian. The origins of his Christian faith can be traced back to his early years. Though he was born

---

1. D. Oates, *Iraq* 50 (1988): v–vi.

in the pretty Hampshire village of Emsworth in 1918, his family soon moved to what was in the 1920s the pleasant south London suburb of Upper Norwood. Here Donald came under the influence of the Crusaders, an inter-denominational evangelical organization active among young people. He had been encouraged to attend their meetings by his parents, who belonged to the Plymouth Brethren. The Crusader group was led by Neville Russell, whose name is still associated with the London accounting firm he founded, but the young Donald was particularly impressed by J. B. Tupman. Tupman lectured at All Nations Bible College, a missionary training school then based in Beulah Hill, Upper Norwood, but he also led a Bible class before church on Sunday mornings. As a result of Tupman's influence, Donald learned to enjoy studying the Bible and, when only nine years old, responded eagerly to a challenge to have a faith of his own rather than rely on that of his parents. An important seed had been sown, and his early interest in the Bible eventually became the chief motivation of his life and his career. A somewhat unusual sign of things to come was Donald's teaching himself the Hebrew alphabet from the headings in Psalm 119 (KJV) when he became bored with the Brethren meetings!

Donald Wiseman was educated at nearby Dulwich College, one of Britain's leading public schools, and in 1936 began undergraduate studies at King's College, London. His initial course was in general arts, but this clearly did not satisfy him; so he inquired about the possibility of studying ancient Semitic languages as a way of pursuing his interest in the world of the Bible. This brought him into contact with a number of distinguished scholars at King's, including Sidney Smith, a prominent Assyriologist who was then at the British Museum, and S. H. Hooke, well known in the 1930s for his controversial views on Hebrew myth and ritual. (Fellow students at that time included both Lady Stansgate, mother of Anthony Wedgwood Benn, M.P., and Ulrich Simon, who later wrote an important commentary on Isa. 40–66.) However, it was with the encouragement of a lesser-known King's scholar, S. L. Brown, that in 1939 Wiseman obtained a grant to study at Wadham College, Oxford, having shown signs of promise by winning the McCaul Hebrew Prize at the University of London. At this point, Wiseman's academic career was interrupted by war, though this gave him opportunity to demonstrate his leadership gifts and linguistic skills. Serving in North Africa and Italy with the Mediterranean Allied Tactical Air Forces, he became a chief intelligence officer with the rank of group captain. His intelligence work was awarded both the Order of the British Empire in 1943 and the Bronze Star (U.S.) in 1944.

Academic study was resumed as soon as the war ended, and Wiseman finally took his place at Oxford in order to read Oriental studies, specializing in Hebrew and Akkadian. As in his prewar studies in London, he came under the tutelage of several noted scholars, including L. H. Brockington, who specialized in Aramaic; Chaim Rabin, a leading Jewish authority on rabbinics and the Hebrew language; Oliver Gurney, who was to become the leading authority on the Hittites; and Herbert Danby, who produced the standard edition of the Mishnah. The most important influence, however, was proba-

bly Godfrey Driver, who enjoyed a leading role in Old Testament and Semitic
language studies and was already working on the New English Bible. Driver
was an outstanding teacher, and he had a more than capable pupil. Wiseman
took the Hebrew prize at Oxford as he had done at London, and as soon as
he had completed his M.A. degree, was invited by Sidney Smith to work in
the Department of Egyptian and Assyrian Antiquities at the British Museum.

Work at the British Museum

Here, however, Wiseman was thrown in at the deep end: without having previously read an actual clay tablet (he had learned entirely from copies), he
was asked to publish some important cuneiform texts from the ancient Syrian city of Alalakh on the Orontes River. It is one thing to read cuneiform
(wedge-shaped) signs that have been painstakingly copied, and quite another
to handle a tablet on which the signs are indented at various angles into the
clay and the surface shows the wear and tear of three or four millennia. In
this instance, the texts had to be returned to Turkey at the end of eighteen
months, so Wiseman had to learn quickly. That he did so was no mean feat.

The relatively speedy publication of *The Alalakh Tablets* (that the volume
did not appear until 1953 was mainly due to the rapid increase of other responsibilities placed on his shoulders) provides evidence of one of Donald
Wiseman's distinctive qualities, namely his willingness to publish primary
evidence quickly without enjoying the luxury of a leisurely assessment as to
whether every single detail has been fully considered. Such boldness and generosity, which were not exercised at the cost of accurate and careful scholarship, have been greatly appreciated by other scholars. Using a catalogue
method for the publication of the 457 inscribed tablets from Alalakh, Wiseman presents basic information about all the texts found in the two major
occupation levels at the site as well as provides a transliteration and translation of the most important texts. *The Alalakh Tablets* has in fact stood the
test of time and has been recognized as an important contribution to our understanding of Syrian history and culture in the mid-second millennium B.C.

Wiseman stayed at the British Museum until 1961, during which time he
was able to publish a number of important cuneiform inscriptions which he
discovered in his own researches in the museum archives. Two volumes have
proved to be of considerable significance for both ancient Near Eastern and
biblical studies. The first is the *Chronicles of Chaldaean Kings (626–556
B.C.)*. These chronicles are typical of a distinctive type of document which recorded on an annual basis the most important events in the history of Babylon over two thousand years. Their value lies not just in their contents but in
their impersonal and objective style of writing. Those published by Wiseman
deal with the rise of the New Babylonian Empire under Nabopolassar (626–
605 B.C.) and Nebuchadnezzar (605–561 B.C.), and include a great deal of
new data about a vital period of ancient Near Eastern history which had previously been known only through brief scattered details.

One important new piece of information is that the date of Nebuchadnez-zar's first capture of Jerusalem can be established as the second day of the month Adar (March 15/16), 597 B.C. The chronicles also put into perspective a number of important details about the battle of Carchemish (605 B.C.) in which the Babylonians led by their crown prince Nebuchadnezzar achieved a crucial victory over the Egyptian army. Scholars had previously been aware of this battle only through short comments in Josephus and the Old Testa-ment (Jer. 46:2), but now both the course and significance of events can be much better appreciated.[2] According to Wiseman, the chronicles even help to explain the biblical reference to a siege of Jerusalem by Nebuchadnezzar which resulted in Daniel's exile to Babylon (Dan. 1:1–7). The statement in the chronicles that after Carchemish Nebuchadnezzar "conquered the whole area of Hatti-land" suggests that the Babylonian army, probably without its commander in chief, who had returned home as king on the news of his fa-ther's death, may have followed up the victory at Carchemish with an attack on Jerusalem. The objection that "Hatti-land" in the Babylonian Chronicles probably refers to northern Syria[3] is unconvincing, since this is a rather loose Akkadian term for the whole of Syria-Palestine, and the chronicles show no evidence of a more restricted sense. Wiseman further suggests that the after-math of Carchemish may explain the statement in 2 Kings 24:7 that the king of Egypt did not march out of his country again,[4] though this point is perhaps more debatable since the context in 2 Kings mentions no date and another major confrontation took place between Nebuchadnezzar and Egypt in 601–600 B.C. Nevertheless, Wiseman's interpretation of the evidence must be taken seriously, despite the preference of many scholars to associate the bib-lical passages in question with either the Babylonian campaign against Ash-kelon in 604 or the stalemate with Egypt in the winter of 601/600.

The second text of note is *The Vassal-Treaties of Esarhaddon* (1958). Its publication was a considerable undertaking since it is a large text comprising 674 lines discovered in several fragments in excavations at the Assyrian city of Nimrud. The comments of Max Mallowan, director of the Nimrud exca-vations, are worth quoting: "We are indeed indebted to Mr. Wiseman, who has thrice accompanied expeditions to Nimrud, both for his courage in deal-ing with so difficult a document and for publishing it within three years of discovery although fully occupied with his official duties."[5] The largest As-syrian treaty yet known, it had been made by Esarhaddon, king of Assyria

---

2. See, e.g., Siegfried Herrmann, *A History of Israel in Old Testament Times*, trans. John Bowden (Philadelphia: Fortress, 1975), 275–79, for discussion of how these chronicles have clarified the last years of Judah's history.

3. Herrmann, *History of Israel*, 276.

4. Donald J. Wiseman, *Chronicles of Chaldaean Kings (626–556 B.C.) in the British Museum* (London: Trustees of the British Museum, 1956), 23–26; see also Donald J. Wiseman, ed., *Notes on Some Problems in the Book of Daniel* (London: Tyndale, 1965), 16–18.

5. M. E. L. Mallowan, introduction to Donald J. Wiseman, *The Vassal-Treaties of Esarhaddon* (London: British School of Archaeology in Iraq, 1958), ii.

from 681 to 669 B.C., with nine of his vassals in order to ensure the succession of his son Ashurbanipal to the throne of Assyria and of another son Sha-mashshumukin to the throne of Babylon. Wiseman quickly recognized the significance of this text not just in relation to Mesopotamian history, but also for Old Testament interpretation.[6] The relationship between the political treaties of the ancient Near East and Israel's covenants was one of Wiseman's major interests. As early as January 1948, he had presented to the Society for Old Testament Study a paper on the relationship between Old Testament treaties and those of the Assyrians and Hittites,[7] anticipating by some years an influential article by George Mendenhall, who is usually credited with es-tablishing such a connection.[8] In his 1958 publication Wiseman argued that the Old Testament was fully aware of and participated in the basic treaty tra-dition of ancient Near Eastern law and contract: "the form of treaties was already 'standardised' by the Hittite empire and this text [i.e., Esarhaddon's treaty] shows that it remained basically unchanged through Neo-Assyrian times."[9] This was a more cautious approach than that of Mendenhall, who saw a development from fixed forms in the second millennium to more fluid arrangements in first-millennium texts like the Esarhaddon treaties.[10] Wise-man's caution is all the more notable in that other evangelical scholars used the supposed formal differences between the earlier and later treaties to argue for the antiquity of the Sinai covenant; his view remained consistent even in later work.[11]

Wiseman continued to publish frequently while he remained at the British Museum. With A. J. Sachs he jointly published an important late example of a king list,[12] and he worked with Sidney Smith on *Cuneiform Texts from Cappadocian Tablets*.[13] His only major work on material from the third mil-lennium B.C. was the *Catalogue of Western Asiatic Seals in the British Mu-seum*.[14] At the same time, he was publishing inscriptions from excavations at Nimrud and continued his work on the texts from Alalakh. He also found time to produce some more popular works: a beautifully illustrated edition

6. Wiseman, *Vassal-Treaties*, 3.
7. Ibid., 26. Wiseman returned to the same theme in his 1980 presidential address to the Society for Old Testament Study, "'Is It Peace?' Covenant and Diplomacy," *Vetus Testamentum* 32 (1982): 311–26.
8. George E. Mendenhall, "Covenant Forms in Israelite Tradition," *Biblical Archaeologist* 17.3 (Sept. 1954): 50–76.
9. Wiseman, *Vassal-Treaties*, 28.
10. Mendenhall, "Covenant Forms," esp. 56–57.
11. See, e.g., Kenneth A. Kitchen, *The Bible in Its World* (Downers Grove, Ill.: InterVarsity, 1978), 79–85; idem, "The Fall and Rise of Covenant, Law and Treaty," *Tyndale Bulletin* 40 (1989): 118–35; Meredith G. Kline, *Treaty of the Great King* (Grand Rapids: Eerdmans, 1963). Cf. Donald J. Wiseman and Edwin M. Yamauchi, *Archaeology and the Bible* (Grand Rapids: Zondervan, 1979), 23–24, 48.
12. A. J. Sachs and Donald J. Wiseman, "A Babylonian King List of the Hellenistic Period," *Iraq* 16 (1954): 202–11.
13. Sidney Smith and Donald J. Wiseman, *Cuneiform Texts from Cappadocian Tablets,* vol. 5 (London: British Museum, 1960).
14. Donald J. Wiseman, *Catalogue of Western Asiatic Seals in the British Museum* (London: Brit-ish Museum, 1962).

of *Cylinder Seals of Western Asia;*[15] *Fifty Masterpieces of Ancient Near Eastern Art,* which was jointly published with R. D. Barnett;[16] and *Illustrations
from Biblical Archaeology,* a brief but extremely helpful introduction to the
benefits of archeology for biblical study.[17]

After Wiseman moved across the road from the British Museum to the
School of Oriental and African Studies to become professor of Assyriology
at the University of London (1961), the steady flow of publications slowed
only slightly as a result of the increasing administrative responsibilities which
are part and parcel of university life. A new dimension of his work is indicated in the title of his inaugural lecture to the School of Oriental and African
Studies: "The Expansion of Assyrian Studies." This was followed in 1967 by
a report on the state of Assyriological studies throughout Europe.[18] It is typical of Wiseman's approach that a significant part of the report's recommendations concentrated on providing fresh opportunities for young scholars,
including the setting up of research fellowships for postgraduate students
outside their own country and a scheme involving a greater interchange of
students among European universities.

Publications on the Bible

From 1961 onwards, Wiseman began to publish much more on the Bible,
though it was perhaps a little unusual that his first major contribution in the
biblical field was as a consulting editor for *The New Bible Dictionary*
(1962).[19] This was a major new venture by the Inter-Varsity Fellowship, a
conservative evangelical organization that worked among students and was
concerned to produce good-quality Bible reference material. Unfortunately,
there were few evangelicals in the United Kingdom at that time qualified to
write such material; so in addition to editing the Old Testament contributions, Wiseman himself wrote no fewer than 152 articles for the project.

Wiseman's first book in the Old Testament field also required his editorial
skills, though he was involved as a contributor as well. *Notes on Some Problems in the Book of Daniel* (1965) is a slim volume with an unprepossessing
title, but for Wiseman it represented an important evangelical contribution
to scholarly debate. It began to bring to fruition his vision that, in view of the
small number of evangelical biblical scholars, corporate efforts by members

15. Donald J. Wiseman, *Cylinder Seals of Western Asia* (London: Batchworth, 1958).
16. Donald J. Wiseman and R. D. Barnett, *Fifty Masterpieces of Ancient Near Eastern Art* (London: British Museum, 1960).
17. Donald J. Wiseman, *Illustrations from Biblical Archaeology* (Grand Rapids: Eerdmans, 1958).
18. Donald J. Wiseman, *Assyriology in Europe* (Strasbourg: Council for Cultural Co-operation,
Council of Europe, 1967).
19. *New Bible Dictionary,* ed. J. D. Douglas (Grand Rapids: Eerdmans, 1962). A revised edition
appeared both with illustrations (*Illustrated Bible Dictionary,* 3 vols. [Wheaton, Ill.: Tyndale, 1980])
and without (Downers Grove, Ill.: InterVarsity, 1982). Wiseman also acted as consulting editor for the
Old Testament portion of the third and fourth editions of *The New Bible Commentary* (Grand Rapids:
Eerdmans, 1970; Downers Grove, Ill.: InterVarsity, 1994), and for *The New Bible Atlas* (Wheaton,
Ill.: Tyndale, 1985).

of the Tyndale Fellowship for Biblical Research would produce results more quickly than would hard-pressed individuals. The Book of Daniel could hardly have represented a greater challenge for evangelicals, since at that period Old Testament scholarship had little time for those who did not accept the consensus view that Daniel had originated in the context of the Maccabean revolt. Like the documentary hypothesis of the Pentateuch and a multiple authorship for Isaiah, a second-century B.C. date for Daniel was one of the so-called assured results of higher criticism which scholars rarely questioned, but Wiseman encouraged some of his evangelical colleagues to write contributions which would "present a challenge to commonly held views." The aim of the volume was to provide a basis for further discussion of, rather than a prepackaged set of answers to, some of the historical and linguistic issues regarding Daniel. Wiseman was encouraged that, in spite of the book's modest appearance, it continued to be quoted in later discussion on Daniel. His own particular contribution included a proposal for solving the most intractable historical problem in Daniel: the problematic Darius the Mede should be regarded as another name for the well-known Persian emperor Cyrus.

Wiseman's corporate approach is also evident in two projects on the Book of Genesis. With Alan Millard he edited a volume on Genesis 12–50 exploring the evidence for the traditional dating of the patriarchs in the early- and mid-second millennium B.C.[20] This was in response to a recently advocated view that they were the literary creations of later Israelite writers.[21] Wiseman himself suggested that Abraham be viewed primarily as a prince (Gen. 23:5–6) or local governor rather than a seminomad, a proposal which provided further testimony to Wiseman's ability to approach a long-standing problem in a creative manner. He was also instrumental in setting up a different kind of cooperative project on Genesis 1–11, which resulted in a number of separate volumes on the ancient Near Eastern context of these crucial chapters of the Bible.[22] An indication of his own interest in Genesis is his combining under the title *Clues to Creation in Genesis* two of his father's works in this area.[23] Though his father had no specialist knowledge of ancient Near Eastern languages and culture and did not directly influence Donald's choice of

20. A. R. Millard and Donald J. Wiseman, eds., *Essays on the Patriarchal Narratives* (Leicester: Inter-Varsity, 1980).

21. Thomas L. Thompson, *The Historicity of the Patriarchal Narratives*, Beiheft zur Zeitschrift für die alttestamentliche Wissenschaft 133 (New York: De Gruyter, 1974); John Van Seters, *Abraham in History and Tradition* (New Haven: Yale University Press, 1975).

22. David Toshio Tsumura, *The Earth and the Waters in Genesis 1 and 2: A Linguistic Investigation*, Journal for the Study of the Old Testament, supplement 83 (Sheffield: JSOT, 1989); Richard S. Hess, *Personal Names in Genesis 1–11*, Alter Orient und Altes Testament 234 (Neukirchen-Vluyn: Neukirchener, 1993); Richard S. Hess and David Toshio Tsumura, eds., *"I Studied Inscriptions from before the Flood": Ancient Near Eastern, Literary, and Linguistic Approaches to Genesis 1–11*, Sources for Biblical and Theological Study 4 (Winona Lake, Ind.: Eisenbrauns, 1994).

23. P. J. Wiseman, *Clues to Creation in Genesis* (London: Marshall, Morgan and Scott, 1977). The two original works were *New Discoveries in Babylonia about Genesis* (1936) and *Creation Revealed in Six Days* (1948).

career, his enthusiasm for the Bible and archeology did encourage his son to study these subjects in depth.

Another of Donald Wiseman's major activities in the biblical sphere was his general editorship of the Tyndale Old Testament Commentaries series. This was yet another means of encouraging evangelical scholars to cooperate in getting material published; indeed, he personally nominated every author who contributed to the series. A particularly successful enterprise, the series has maintained its appeal at both the serious and more popular levels since the first volume was published in 1964.[24] The editor's own contribution was *1 and 2 Kings*, which appeared in 1993. It reflects Wiseman's basic thesis with regard to the study of Old Testament texts: the Bible makes most sense when it is interpreted in the light of its own ancient Near Eastern cultural context. The commentary includes a survey of the archeological evidence relevant to the history of the Israelite monarchy, as well as a helpful listing of people and places in Kings that are also mentioned outside the Bible. Moreover, it gives some insight into Wiseman's approach to theological and literary issues. Though he is very much concerned with the message of the Bible, he is not an instinctive theologian; instead, his approach to the theology of Kings is closely tied up with his historical interests. In his view, the theological element emerges as comments on the continuing historical story of God at work rather than as an overarching theme. His approach to literary issues is equally restrained, though the commentary does provide a useful discussion of the possible relationship between Kings and the so-called deuteronomistic history. In Wiseman's view, however, "literary analysis is insufficiently exact and often subjective,"[25] and its results are much less useful than those produced by the hard evidence of archeology. He shows little sympathy for modern literary approaches to biblical study, whether source criticism or the newer narrative analysis, and devotes little space to them in his published work.

On the other hand, Wiseman's archeological interests continued to play a major part in his writings, which were increasingly reflecting the regard in which he was held. The Society for Old Testament Study asked him to edit a volume by various distinguished scholars on the culture and history of Israel's neighbors. Appearing in 1973, *Peoples of Old Testament Times* took its place alongside the society's other important publications on the cultural background of the Old Testament. Wiseman was also invited to contribute to the third edition of the *Cambridge Ancient History*,[26] but the greatest honor was an invitation from the British Academy to deliver the prestigious Schweich Lectures for 1983. His chosen subject was "Nebuchadrezzar and Babylon," which marked a return to the topic on which he had first made his

24. Derek Kidner, *The Proverbs: An Introduction and Commentary*, Tyndale Old Testament Commentaries (Chicago: InterVarsity, 1964).

25. Donald J. Wiseman, *1 and 2 Kings: An Introduction and Commentary*, Tyndale Old Testament Commentaries (Downers Grove, Ill.: InterVarsity, 1993), 48.

26. Donald J. Wiseman, "Assyria and Babylonia, c. 1200–1000 B.C.," in *Cambridge Ancient History*, ed. I. E. S. Edwards et al., 3d ed. (Cambridge: Cambridge University Press, 1975), 2.2.443–81.

reputation.[27] His aim on this occasion was a mature reevaluation of this New Babylonian monarch on the basis of all the primary data about him, including the extensive material in the Old Testament. This was no easy task since, "remarkably, less is known from Mesopotamian sources of Nebuchadnezzar than about the reign of almost any other king of the Chaldean period."[28] Nevertheless, Wiseman succeeded in bringing together a detailed and authoritative presentation of the current state of knowledge about Nebuchadnezzar, and incorporated new proposals about the location of the Hanging Gardens and the architecture of the ziggurat of Babylon.

Wiseman's approach to archeology is most evident in the volume he wrote with Edwin Yamauchi, *Archaeology and the Bible.* In the Old Testament section Wiseman summarizes the archeological discoveries he believes to be the most important for biblical interpretation. Archeology in his view supplies "abundant documentary evidence" for illustrating and explaining many features of the biblical text as well as for correcting erroneous interpretations. He is aware of its limitations, however, and advises appropriate caution in making use of its findings: "Such studies must not be expected to elucidate all problems, especially those of a nonmaterial nature." For "archaeology is not an exact science," and "its results may undergo subjective selection and interpretation."[29] Nevertheless, archeology does have a considerable advantage over literary criticism in that it provides primary evidence against which the claims of the Bible can be checked.

Wiseman's preferred approach is to allow the archeological evidence to speak for itself, and by this process to demonstrate the intrinsic reasonableness of the biblical data. This procedure, however, leads him to adopt different kinds of positions. On some issues he can be quite cautious or agnostic, as in the case of the date of the exodus or the implications of the parallels between Israelite covenants and ancient Near Eastern treaties. Even when defending the historical reliability of the Book of Daniel, he does not commit himself to any particular date;[30] thus he differs from the conservative scholars of previous generations, many of whom assigned the writing of Daniel to the sixth century B.C. On other occasions, however, he is unafraid to take up unfashionable interpretations, as when defending the historicity of the Philistines of Genesis, identifying Darius the Mede in Daniel with the Persian emperor Cyrus, and even advocating the possibility of Davidic authorship of the Psalms. These differences of approach arise from his insistence on specific detail establishing a meaningful relationship between the biblical text and extra-

27. The lectures were published as *Nebuchadrezzar and Babylon* (New York: Oxford University Press, 1985). The spelling "Nebuchadrezzar," which is used in Jeremiah, more closely reflects the Babylonian form Nabu-kudurri-usur than does the familiar "Nebuchadnezzar" known from the rest of the Old Testament.

28. Ronald Herbert Sack, *Images of Nebuchadnezzar* (Selinsgrove, Pa.: Susquehanna University Press, 1991), 21.

29. Wiseman and Yamauchi, *Archaeology and the Bible*, 4.

30. E.g., Wiseman, *Nebuchadrezzar and Babylon*, 81–115.

biblical evidence. On many of the broader issues he is content for others to draw their own conclusions on the basis of the evidence he has assembled.

Participation in Organizations

No account of Donald Wiseman's scholarship would be complete without some mention of his participation in various organizations, since this has been a very influential part of his scholarly activities. As a student at Oxford in 1948, he was invited to join the Biblical Research Committee. This committee, established by the Inter-Varsity Fellowship (IVF) to develop evangelical biblical research, had in 1944 purchased Tyndale House in Cambridge as a residential library dedicated to that purpose. The committee included evangelical leaders such as F. F. Bruce, Martyn Lloyd-Jones, and W. J. Martin; Wiseman, who had already been president of the Christian Union at Oxford, was welcomed into this distinguished company and very soon became secretary of the committee. He was also instrumental in suggesting and implementing the proposal that the increasing number of scholars involved should divide into groups; with Martin he took immediate responsibility for the Old Testament group.

So began an association with Tyndale House that lasted for almost fifty years. Wiseman remained secretary of the Biblical Research Committee (later the Tyndale House Council) until 1957, served as chairman from 1957 to 1986, and regularly attended meetings until 1996. He was chairman of the Old Testament study group from its inception in 1948 until he retired in 1981, and for most of that time also chaired the biblical archeology group, which he had also established. In addition, he played a large part in wider IVF (later, the Universities and Colleges Christian Fellowship [UCCF]) activities, being chairman of the international committee from 1951 to 1957, and of the literature committee from 1961 to 1967, and twice president of IVF itself (1965–66 and 1973–74). His international interests are also indicated by his having been a member of the founding committee of the International Fellowship of Evangelical Students, which met at Harvard in 1947. But statistics like these do not tell the real story of his involvement. This can be recounted only by people such as Douglas Johnson, general secretary of IVF, who worked with him for many years: "No account of Tyndale House and its projects will be accurate which does not pay adequate tribute to the vast expenditure of time and energy by Donald Wiseman."[31] Similar testimony comes from Johnson's successor Oliver Barclay: "From his student days, Donald has been a friend and counsellor of the senior staff of UCCF, and he was just as effective behind the scenes as he was in a more public role."[32]

---

31. Douglas Johnson, supplement to "The Origin and History of Tyndale House" (unpublished), 20 January 1987.

32. Oliver Barclay, communication with author, 4 July 1994.

As if this were not enough on top of all his academic responsibilities, Wiseman was equally committed to his work with the British School of Archaeology in Iraq. An invitation in 1953 to become assistant editor of the school's journal led to a twenty-five-year association with *Iraq*. He began by working under Max Mallowan, and continued as joint editor first with Mallowan (1961–71) and then with David Hawkins (1971–78). He was also joint director of the school from 1961 to 1965, chairman from 1970 to 1988, and president on the death of Lady Mallowan in 1993. In earlier years, he had acted as epigraphist on excavations at Nimrud, Haran, and Tell al-Rimah; various issues of *Iraq* provide eloquent testimony to his willingness to publish the results of these excavations as quickly as possible.

Throughout his career Wiseman also maintained a close interest in several Christian organizations, including the Scripture Gift Mission, the Gideons, and the Crusaders. (An incidental claim to fame is that he was the leader of the Crusader class at Finchley which had some early influence on Cliff Richard.) His special interest in the Bible led to a particularly close association with the Scripture Gift Mission, which he served as a council member from 1961 and as chairman from 1978 until 1992. He was notably active on the translations committee, where his insistence that biblical translations be linguistically accurate and culturally acceptable made a significant contribution to the quality of Bible publication in many languages. Wiseman also became heavily involved in the production of the New International Version *(NIV)* of the Bible. Part of the international team of translators since 1965, he was later invited to chair a small committee which would prepare suggestions for an anglicized version of the text. This group had just six weeks in which to work, but Wiseman capably steered the whole enterprise through in time for publication (1979).[33] He continued to be involved thereafter. In 1983 he joined the committee for Bible translation, which had ongoing responsibility for the NIV, and he also chaired the related anglicization committee from its inception in 1984 until the rules required him to retire from both groups in 1993.

Colleagues in all these enterprises have referred constantly to Wiseman's personal warmth and graciousness as well as his wisdom. He has always been ready to give encouragement, whether representing the British School of Archaeology in Iraq within the hallowed confines of the British Academy or guiding individuals at various points in their lives. His conscientious and concerned approach to teaching has been much appreciated, and in his own inimitable diplomatic style he has often been able to steer meetings through awkward patches. No one has been too insignificant for him to talk to; in fact, when he was first appointed to his professorship, he would stop people in the corridors of the School of Oriental and African Studies just to introduce himself. At that time he also jointly hosted a fortnightly Bible study with Norman Anderson for members of the academic and administrative staff of

33. For details see Donald J. Wiseman, "Anglicizing the NIV," in *The NIV: The Making of a Contemporary Translation*, ed. Kenneth L. Barker (Grand Rapids: Academie, 1986), 137–41.

the University of London. Alan Millard, now Rankin Professor of Hebrew and Semitic Languages at the University of Liverpool, recalls that at the tender age of twelve he learned from Wiseman about the rewards of a career in biblical scholarship; many others are similarly grateful for Wiseman's advice in the development of their careers.

It is no surprise that many honors have come Donald Wiseman's way. He was awarded the doctor of letters degree from the University of London for his published work. In 1966 he became one of the very few evangelicals ever to be elected a fellow of the British Academy, the most distinguished group of humanities scholars in Britain. In 1980 he was elected president of the Society for Old Testament Study. Two volumes have been dedicated to him, a special edition of *Iraq* on his seventieth birthday and a collection of essays on Genesis 12–50 presented by the members of the Tyndale Fellowship on his seventy-fifth birthday.[34] But he has never been one to rest on his laurels. He has continued to publish: the year 1996 saw the appearance of major works in the fields of both Mesopotamian archeology and the Bible.[35]

The qualities of boldness and vision for the future have always characterized Wiseman. Not surprisingly, then, in a 1995 assessment of Tyndale House's future role he urges current evangelical scholars to take up the torch of the "founder" generation and suggests innovative ways in which they might do so. Wiseman's own vision is based on a deep Christian conviction about the Bible's reliability and relevance, and he has constantly stimulated and encouraged others to be equally committed to such a vision. His own contribution, based on a distinctive blend of wholehearted faith, genuine personal warmth, and outstanding intellectual skills, has certainly provided an excellent model for others to follow.

Primary Sources

Wiseman, Donald J. *The Alalakh Tablets.* London: British Institute of Archaeology at Ankara, 1953.

———. *Chronicles of Chaldaean Kings (626–556 B.C.) in the British Museum.* London: Trustees of the British Museum, 1956.

———. *1 and 2 Kings: An Introduction and Commentary.* Tyndale Old Testament Commentaries. Downers Grove, Ill.: InterVarsity, 1993.

———. *Illustrations from Biblical Archaeology.* Grand Rapids: Eerdmans, 1958.

———. *Nebuchadrezzar and Babylon.* New York: Oxford University Press, 1985.

———. *The Vassal-Treaties of Esarhaddon.* London: British School of Archaeology in Iraq, 1958 (=*Iraq* 20 [1958], part 1).

---

34. *Iraq* 50 (1988); *He Swore an Oath: Biblical Themes from Genesis 12–50,* ed. Richard S. Hess et al., 2d ed. (Grand Rapids: Baker, 1994).

35. Donald J. Wiseman and J. Black, *Literary Tablets from the Nabu Temple,* Cuneiform Tablets from Nimrud 4 (London: British School of Archaeology in Iraq, 1996); *The NIV Thematic Study Bible* (London: Hodder and Stoughton, 1996) (consulting editor).

Wiseman, Donald J., ed. *Notes on Some Problems in the Book of Daniel.* London: Tyndale, 1965.

———. *Peoples of Old Testament Times.* Oxford: Clarendon, 1973.

Wiseman, Donald J., and Edwin M. Yamauchi. *Archaeology and the Bible.* Grand Rapids: Zondervan, 1979.

Wiseman, Donald J., and A. R. Millard, eds. *Essays on the Patriarchal Narratives.* Leicester: Inter-Varsity, 1980.

R. K. Harrison

J. Glen Taylor

Roland Kenneth Harrison, a prominent Old Testament scholar in the conservative evangelical tradition, taught and wrote extensively from 1950 until the time of his death in 1993. He is perhaps best known for his massive *Introduction to the Old Testament* (1969), which combines an encyclopedic knowledge of the discipline with an unrelenting critique of the Graf-Wellhausen hypothesis. He is also well known as a commentator on several Old Testament books, the author of a number of books on archeology, and an editor of conservative reference works on the Bible and biblical archeology.[1]

Harrison was born in Lancaster, England, on August 4, 1920. His parents, William and Hilda Mary Harrison (née Marsden), farmed in the north of England. Both came from devout families with ties to the Church of England. Roland was one of three children. His sister died of scarlet fever in her youth. Raymond, a younger brother by eight years, proved to be no less brilliant than Roland and went on to Cambridge, and thereafter to a truly outstanding career in the civil service. As a boy Roland sang in the choir at the evangelical Anglican church where his father served as people's warden. Always dedicate of frame, Roland nearly died of rheumatic fever at age twelve and was weak for a considerable time thereafter. Nevertheless his strong personal drive and sense of Christian calling led him toward theological studies, which he undertook during the dark period of World War II. In 1943 he earned a B.D. with honors from the University of London.[2] The same year he was awarded an associate diploma in theology (again with

---

1. Regarding R. K. Harrison and his contribution to biblical studies see Peter C. Craigie, foreword to *Israel's Apostasy and Restoration: Essays in Honor of Roland K. Harrison,* ed. Avraham Gileadi (Grand Rapids: Baker, 1988), vii–xi.

2. At the time Harrison began his theological education, the study of the Old Testament at the University of London (including King's College, where Anglican ordinands studied) was under the influence of several members of the myth and ritual school: S. H. Hooke (who was of retirement age when Harrison arrived), F. J. Hollis, and E. O. James. The chair of New Testament exegesis at King's College was held by the evangelical textual critic R. V. G. Tasker, who later became editor of the Tyndale New Testament Commentaries series (1954) and a consulting editor of the popular and influential *New Bible Dictionary* (ed. J. D. Douglas [Grand Rapids: Eerdmans, 1962]), to which Harrison contributed.

honors) by the London College of Divinity and was ordained in the Church of England.

Although there was vitality within the church, these were not easy times for evangelicals in the Church of England. Harrison grew up in an environment in which, although nothing like the fundamentalist-modernist controversy in America, there were tensions between conservative and more liberal elements. The 1930s in particular had left many evangelicals within the Church of England feeling marginalized. As late as 1944, Max Warren, then secretary of the Church Missionary Society, observed: "All too commonly to-day, an Evangelical in the Church of England is a person labouring under a sense of frustration and discouragement often so deep as to engender . . . an inferiority complex."[3] Nor was the situation any brighter in the field of conservative biblical scholarship.[4] The twentieth century had failed to produce first-rate conservative biblical scholars and works of scholarship in Britain, leaving Harrison with only a few mentors such as G. T. Manley and, from the turn of the previous century, A. H. Sayce.[5] The situation was no doubt especially trying for evangelical students of the Old Testament, for the higher-critical scholarship of Julius Wellhausen and others appeared to have struck a substantial blow to many traditional views.[6]

At the time Harrison entered theological study, however, the situation was beginning to reverse. Newly formed bodies such as the Theological Students Fellowship (1938) and the Anglican-led Biblical Research Committee (1939) represented a strong movement towards placing evangelical biblical scholarship on a more secure footing in Britain. Part of the strategy included encouraging postgraduate students to undertake research from a conservative point of view.[7] Whether specifically targeted or not, Harrison clearly rose to the occasion, as is demonstrated by an impressive number of articles written in the 1950s,[8] and also by contributions to the *New Bible Dictionary*

3. Cited in David Bebbington, "Evangelicalism in Its Settings: The British and American Movements since 1940," in *Evangelicalism: Comparative Studies of Popular Protestantism in North America, the British Isles, and Beyond, 1700–1990*, ed. Mark A. Noll, David Bebbington, and George Rawlyk (New York: Oxford University Press, 1994), 367.

4. On the state of evangelical biblical scholarship at the time see Mark A. Noll, *Between Faith and Criticism*, 2d ed. (Grand Rapids: Baker, 1991), 62–90; David Bebbington, *Evangelicalism in Modern Britain* (Grand Rapids: Baker, 1992), 181–228.

5. On Harrison's regard for Sayce see R. K. Harrison, *Introduction to the Old Testament* (Grand Rapids: Eerdmans, 1969), 29–30.

6. In his Griffith Thomas Lectures at Dallas Theological Seminary (1988) Harrison told of a fellow conservative seminarian whose "whole theology had been ruined by his study of the documentary hypothesis and similar liberal teachings" (R. K. Harrison, "Credibility and Enthusiasm in Preaching the Old Testament," *Bibliotheca Sacra* 146 [1989]: 124–25).

7. Douglas Johnson, *Contending for the Faith: A History of the Evangelical Movement in the Universities and Colleges* (Leicester: Inter-Varsity, 1979), 210. (Before 1945 the Theological Students Fellowship was called the Theological Students' Prayer Union.)

8. In the 1950s Harrison wrote several articles for the *Evangelical Quarterly* and the *St. Raphael Quarterly*. Articles also appeared in the journals *Philosophy, Biblical Archaeologist, Church Quarterly Review, Modern Churchman, Churchman,* and the *Canadian Association of Medical Students and Internes Journal.*

(1962), the *New Bible Commentary Revised* (1970), and the Tyndale Old Testament Commentaries series (1973, 1980), all three of which were fruits of this fresh conservative initiative.[9]

After being ordained in 1943, Harrison assumed a curacy. Two years later, on October 18, 1945, he married Kathleen Beattie. His four years of required curacy were interrupted when after three years the principal of Clifton (later Trinity) College in Bristol invited Harrison, a former pupil of his, to become chaplain and to teach biblical studies. The same year he began teaching at Clifton (1947) Roland earned an M.Th. from the University of London, the institution that would later award him the Ph.D. (1952).

While attending the Lambeth Conference in 1948 in place of the ailing principal of Clifton, Harrison met a bishop from London, Ontario, who invited him to teach at Huron College, an Anglican college associated with the University of Western Ontario. He accepted the invitation and, after two years of service at Clifton (1947–49), emigrated to Canada. He was initially responsible for instruction in Greek and New Testament studies, but in 1952, the same year he successfully defended his doctoral dissertation on "The Problem of Evil with Special Reference to Disease," he was appointed Hellmuth Professor of Old Testament Studies. At the same time he was appointed chairman of the small Department of Hebrew at the University of Western Ontario. It was during this period that Roland established his reputation as a learned and prolific scholar. Also during this period twin girls, Felicity and Judith, were born to the Harrisons (1956); a son, Graham, followed in 1959.

After eleven years of teaching and administration at Huron College (which in 1963 awarded him an honorary D.D.), Harrison accepted an invitation from Principal Leslie Hunt of Wycliffe College, University of Toronto, to become professor of Old Testament studies. He occupied this position for twenty-six years until his retirement in 1986.

During his time at Wycliffe, Harrison assumed various administrative and teaching duties, and wrote extensively. In the theologically dark mid-sixties he played a pivotal role in founding a college-based Lay School of Theology, a teaching initiative undertaken long before lay education was popular in theological institutions. From 1966 to 1968 Harrison was chairman of the Toronto Graduate School of Theology (which later became the Toronto School of Theology). In the 1960s the faculty of Wycliffe College were poorly paid, overworked, and awarded no sabbaticals. Harrison, who was

---

9. In 1988 Harrison reflected on this transition period: "On the conservative side the overall situation has changed gradually during the last century from one where those who proclaimed scriptural inspiration and authority were either derided as obscurantists, or assailed by the opprobrious epithet 'fundamentalist,' to the point where erudite conservative scholars are producing standard theological works that rank in scholarship with the best that liberalism can produce. This is a very gratifying situation" (R. K. Harrison, "The Critical Use of the Old Testament," *Bibliotheca Sacra* 146 [1989]: 12–13).

highly prolific despite these limitations, remained there because of what he later described as a "concern for the survival of Wycliffe College as an evangelical witness in the church and the world."[10] Throughout his time at Wycliffe, Harrison maintained an unwavering sense of duty to Christian scholarship[11] and to the institution's evangelical Anglican heritage. For Harrison this heritage had been embodied most notably in W. H. Griffith Thomas, who had taught Old Testament at Wycliffe some fifty years earlier and whose *Principles of Theology* Harrison was fond of citing.[12] Richard Longenecker, a colleague at Wycliffe for many years, recalls Harrison himself as being

> gregarious, welcoming, witty and generous, yet he was by nature a very private person. He seemed never to be in a hurry, yet he worked very hard and for long hours—almost always being at his office before breakfast and often continuing until late at night. . . . He had an obvious interest in everything philological, historical and archaeological, yet he also prided himself on his understanding of the medical sciences and psychology. He was an active priest in the Anglican Church of Canada. . . . But he seldom assumed any clerical airs and was often a critic of the ecclesiastical establishment. He had a great interest in politics, frequently lending support to various national and Tory candidates and arguing for certain key issues of the day. . . . He was also an able and meticulous administrator, serving in all sorts of capacities . . . and as interim principal. . . . He even fancied himself to be astute in business and knowledgeable about the stock market. . . . In the setting of a lectureship, where he worked from a carefully prepared text, he was superb. . . . In the classroom, where he often illustrated his lectures anecdotally, he was a joy to his devotees and a bane to those who thought him too opinionated.[13]

In the months prior to his retirement in 1986, Harrison suffered from an illness and appeared to be near death. Once properly diagnosed, however, the malady was easily cured. From 1987 until his sudden death on May 2, 1993, of congestive heart failure, Harrison enjoyed relatively good health and continued to write extensively.

Harrison was a prolific writer. His entries in Bible dictionaries and other reference works would be difficult to count. He was the author (or coauthor) of sixteen books on various biblical and archeological subjects, and the editor of three symposia. In addition he served as the general editor for the New International Commentary on the Old Testament series, an as-

10. R. K. Harrison, "The Turbulent Years: The Principalship of Leslie Hunt, 1959–1975," in *The Enduring Word: A Centennial History of Wycliffe College,* ed. Arnold Edinborough (Toronto: University of Toronto Press, 1978), 95.

11. Shortly after arriving at Wycliffe in the early 1970s, a colleague was informed by Harrison that unswerving duty to the task of Christian scholarship would preclude any lengthy socialization between them.

12. E.g., Harrison, *Introduction,* 3, 472.

13. Richard N. Longenecker, "In Remembrance of R. K. Harrison" (article submitted to the journal *Archaeology in the Biblical World,* 1993; manuscript courtesy of R. N. Longenecker).

sociate editor for *The International Standard Bible Encyclopedia*, and either a consulting or revising editor for at least five other reference works on the Bible. He served as an editor of academic books for Thomas Nelson Publishers (1984–86) and as editorial consultant on Old Testament books for Baker Book House (1988–93). His books range from entries in the Teach Yourself series—*Biblical Hebrew, The Dead Sea Scrolls, The Archaeology of the Old Testament, The Archaeology of the New Testament*—to more substantive works such as *Introduction to the Old Testament* and *Old Testament Times*. There are commentaries on several Old Testament books, including Leviticus, Numbers, Deuteronomy, Ruth, Chronicles (not yet available), Proverbs, Jeremiah and Lamentations, and Amos. His interest in archeology is reflected in his coeditorship (with E. M. Blaiklock) of *The New International Dictionary of Biblical Archaeology* and in his authoring of *Major Cities of the Biblical World*. Finally, Harrison played a key role in translating several of the Minor Prophets for the New International Version of the Bible, and he was a member of the executive review committee which oversaw translation work on the Old Testament for the New King James Version. Harrison's productivity may be attributed to, among other factors, his highly retentive memory, his ability to produce an acceptable written product in the first attempt, his unusually strong sense of duty towards the ministry of scholarly writing, and his discipline and tireless energy.[14]

Medicine and the Bible

A relevant subject that may be examined somewhat independently of Harrison's other interests in biblical studies is the relationship of the Bible to medicine. Harrison wrote extensively on this subject, and with knowledge one expects from a physician or biologist.[15] Significantly, thirteen of the eighteen articles Harrison elected to mention by name in his curriculum vitae are on medical topics, including the treatment of neuroses, healing herbs of the Bible (the topic of a book published in 1966), and, a particular favorite, the relation of Christianity to disease and mental health. That all thirteen of these articles, as well as a small book entitled *Health and Personality*, were published

14. Harrison's breadth as well as his capacity for writing and editing is well illustrated by his editorship of *The Encyclopedia of Biblical and Christian Ethics* (Nashville: Nelson, 1987). In addition to writing hundreds of letters to the individual contributors on an old typewriter, he authored over three hundred of the articles himself, dealing with topics such as surrogate motherhood, skyjacking, abortion, shoplifting, capital punishment (a favorite topic), and apartheid. Many of these articles were written because the scheduled contributors were unable to complete their assignments.

15. E.g., R. K. Harrison, "Heal," in *International Standard Bible Encyclopedia*, ed. Geoffrey W. Bromiley et al., 4 vols. (Grand Rapids: Eerdmans, 1979–88), 2:646: "The sick man of Bethzatha (Jn. 5:2) had a disease that produced progressive muscular atrophy, perhaps amyotrophic lateral sclerosis." For some of Harrison's more important early writings on medicine and the Bible see "A Christian Interpretation of Disease," *Churchman* 67.4 (Oct.-Dec. 1953): 220–27; "The Problem of Suffering and the Book of Job," *Evangelical Quarterly* 25 (1953): 18–27; and "New Horizons for Medicine and Christianity," *Modern Churchman* 46.1 (March 1956): 42–51.

in the 1950s reflects the wake of his doctoral dissertation. Harrison's scholarly interest in the subject nonetheless lasted throughout his career, as is witnessed by articles written on medical topics for Bible encyclopedias[16] as well as for local newspapers.[17]

Harrison contended that the ancient Hebrews' understanding of the relationship between spiritual and physical well-being differed from that of their contemporaries:

> Whereas contemporary civilization uniformly regarded the incidence of disease as the result of demonic activity, the ancient Hebrews held that everything, good and evil alike, ultimately proceeded from the omnipotent Lord of the universe. By establishing Yahweh's moral supremacy they . . . placed the entire disease situation on a spiritual footing whereby the personal relationship which existed between the individual and his God was the determinative factor.
>
> This did not exempt the righteous from sickness any more than it condemned the wicked to lifelong affliction. What it did, however, was to make clear that disease was conditioned largely by factors of a moral and spiritual, rather than a primarily physical, nature.[18]

Expounding on this unique Israelite perspective, Harrison argued that the moral concepts of holiness found in the Mosaic law reflect a new approach to the problems of sickness and disease, namely a preventative approach:

> If a man pursued a life of spiritual fellowship with God, he was entertaining the most valuable safeguard possible against sickness. But if, when disease arose, he attempted to cure it, he was trespassing upon the prerogatives of the Great Physician and interfering with functions which lay solely within the operation of divine discretion. Thus the primary emphasis of the law in this respect was prophylaxis, and because of this unique therapeutic emphasis Moses may well be spoken of as the father of preventative medicine. In the medical enactments of the Pentateuch, social hygiene was elevated to the level of a science, and the precepts of the Mosaic era survive to the present as a model of sanitary and hygienic insight.[19]

Not surprisingly, reviewers of the commentary he would later write on Leviticus (1980) noted Harrison's preference for hygienic explanations in his

---

16. E.g., R. K. Harrison, "Disease," and "Heal," in *International Standard Bible Encyclopedia,* 1:953–60; 2:640–47.

17. In one such article Harrison wrote of a man whose symptoms of abdominal cancer had miraculously disappeared. After being converted to Christ, the man forgave another against whom he had harbored a serious grudge for many years. While Harrison was careful in the article not to associate all cancer with personal failings such as hatred, he nonetheless affirmed an association in general between spiritual well-being and good health, and concluded with a reference to John 10:10 ("The Bible Gives Sound Advice about Health, Professor Says," *Toronto Star,* 5 May 1973).

18. R. K. Harrison, "Healing, Health," in *Interpreter's Dictionary of the Bible,* ed. George A. Buttrick et al., 4 vols. (Nashville: Abingdon, 1962), 2:542.

19. Ibid.

treatment of laws and his fastidious attention to medical matters.[20] Harrison's earlier research on the relationship between holistic health and spiritual communion with God found its way into the commentary in other ways as well, including a new interpretation of the peace offering, which Harrison calls the "sacrifice of well-being."[21]

According to Harrison, Jesus advanced the Old Testament concept of disease as predominantly penal. Jesus saw a close relationship between sickness and the effect of evil on the personality because he recognized the mind and body to be an integer. To Harrison, Jesus' healing ministry was thus characterized by a kind of holistic therapy consistent with modern-day principles of psychiatry and psychotherapy.[22] Moreover, on the basis of terms for healing that are used in the Servant passages of Isaiah, Harrison argued that on Calvary "the incarnate Lord dealt also with disease as well as with human sin— i.e., his atonement avails for the whole personality, body as well as soul. On this basis, therefore, it is theoretically justifiable to appeal to the finished work of Jesus for healing as well as for spiritual restoration."[23]

A Critical Anti-critical Approach

Mark Noll's distinction between two types of evangelical Bible scholars— critical anti-critics and believing critics—offers us help in understanding Harrison's approach. After describing what distinguishes these two groups, Noll elaborates on the former category:

> The major division lies between those who tie the belief in biblical inspiration tightly to traditional interpretations and those for whom this bond is somewhat less secure. For the first, more traditionalist scholars, research is primarily

20. E.g., Horace D. Hummel, review of *Leviticus: An Introduction and Commentary,* by R. K. Harrison, *Concordia Journal* 8 (1982): 72, comments, "Occasionally one almost needs to have a medical dictionary at hand" (the same could be said about many of Harrison's articles on disease and healing that appear in various Bible dictionaries and encyclopedias). Robert P. Gordon, review of *Leviticus,* by R. K. Harrison, *Evangelical Quarterly* 54 (1982): 190, declares, "Never has a commentary made the reviewer itch and scratch as this one has!"

21. R. K. Harrison, *Leviticus: An Introduction and Commentary* (Downers Grove, Ill.: InterVarsity, 1980), 56. He observes that the word *shalom* can include the notion of good health and apply to the human personality (which he in turn equates with the "living soul" of Gen. 2:7). "The *sacrifice* (*zebah*) of well-being indicates conscious social communion, in which what is deficient in the offerer will be remedied as he comes in faith and penitence to God, the healer and restorer (cf. Ex. 15:26; Ps. 103:3)."

22. E.g., Harrison comments that Jesus' interview with the woman at the well (John 4) is "a superb example of nondirective counseling, and could serve as a model for psychotherapists" (Harrison, "Healing, Health," 546). In a similar vein, Harrison believed that Paul anticipated Freud, for in Romans 7 "the willful, rebellious aspect of human personality ('*id*'), the self, and the 'super-ego' are described in terms of psychological conflict bearing an uncomfortably modern sound" (Harrison, "Medicine and Christianity," 45).

23. Harrison, "Healing, Health," 547. In light of his understanding of the relationship between the gospel and holistic health, Harrison believed that clergy who rely on divine power can play a unique role in the ministry of healing by administering a kind of Christian psychotherapy. In a rare autobiographical moment he comments, "I myself have witnessed the rational application of Divine Power at work on many occasions in the relief of mental tension, bringing about an almost miraculous restoration from a variety of ailments" (Harrison, "Medicine and Christianity," 51).

useful as a way of protecting Scripture. It is necessary to carry on academic work because erroneous critical opinions must be rebutted and correct views of Scripture reinforced. This stance may be called "critical anti-criticism." . . . Critical anti-critics make a commitment to scholarship, they sometimes achieve widespread recognition for linguistic or historical competence, and they are concerned about professional certification.[24]

Noll's description of the critical anti-critic matches Harrison almost perfectly.[25]

Presuppositions

Harrison brought to his scholarship certain presuppositions. First and most obviously, Harrison believed in the divine inspiration of the Bible.[26] In this respect he was no different from many other scholars. Where the difference lay was in Harrison's firm belief that this doctrine was at stake if traditional views concerning such matters as the date and authorship of various books of the Old Testament were compromised. It is little wonder, then, that Harrison's scholarly defense of traditional views was characterized by vigor and tenacity.

A second presupposition had to do with epistemology. Harrison believed that although complete objectivity is an impossibility for humans, a worthwhile close approximation can nonetheless be attained through the application of proper scientific methods that take an inductive, a posteriori approach as opposed to a deductive, a priori approach.[27] Harrison's careful attention to a truly scientific method often proved effective and useful. At the same time, however, it is somewhat ironic that his scientific intellectual framework had many points in common with the nineteenth-century positiv-

24. Noll, *Between Faith and Criticism,* 156 (see pp. 154–61 for further discussion of this distinction, including important nuances and variations not elaborated upon here). Noll describes believing critics as affirming "that historical, textual, literary, and other forms of research (if they are not predicated on the denial of the supernatural) may legitimately produce conclusions that overturn traditional beliefs about the Bible. Moreover, such reversals need not necessarily undermine beliefs in the inspired or inerrant character of Scripture's revelatory truthfulness" (p. 158).

25. Also helpful is Noll's further distinction within the category of critical anti-critics between, on the one hand, those who address only their conservative constituencies because the task of refuting the entire critical enterprise appears too daunting or tiresome, and, on the other, those "who find their convictions a goad to active participation in the broader world of biblical scholarship." The latter group, which would include Harrison, believe that "the inappropriate or prejudicial use of scholarship needs to be refuted, and so it is necessary to engage wholeheartedly in professional biblical work where so many false conclusions have been drawn on the basis of insubstantial or tainted evidence" (Noll, *Between Faith and Criticism,* 156).

26. For Harrison's views on inspiration see his *Introduction,* 467–75. Although Harrison was reluctant to tie the notion of inspiration with inerrancy (and with other terms such as "plenary" and "verbal"), that he nonetheless believed in biblical inerrancy is suggested by his involvement with the New King James Version, a prerequisite of which was belief in inerrancy, and by several passages in his writings.

27. See especially R. K. Harrison, "Perspective on Old Testament Study," in *Toward a Theology for the Future,* ed. David F. Wells and Clark H. Pinnock (Carol Stream, Ill.: Creation House, 1971), 11–39.

ism of the higher critics whom he opposed.[28] Although Harrison was quite forthright in stating his belief in the inspiration (and the consequent historical veracity) of Scripture, it is less clear that he was similarly aware of the philosophical underpinnings of his modern scientific approach. Harrison was, regardless, quite familiar with philosophy in general.

Harrison's commitments to (1) the historical veracity of the Bible as a necessary corollary to its authority and inspiration and (2) scientific scholarship existed at times in creative tension. When Harrison dealt with an instance where valid critical research proved to be ambiguous or problematic for belief in the historical veracity of Scripture, he would in more technical works suggest various possible reasons for the discrepancy; in the more popular works he would mention the issue only briefly or not at all.[29] In dealing with problematic data, he would often express confidence that with further knowledge the problem would be resolved in a manner supportive of the biblical witness.[30] Although Harrison's confidence was rooted in his understanding of the nature of the Bible, such optimism did little to win him a hearing outside his constituency; such optimism was considered unwarranted on academic grounds or, at the very least, premature.

Method

A good sense of Harrison's general approach to Old Testament study may be gained from his own statements regarding his method. One such statement, reflecting his thought at an early period, is found in his *Introduction to the Old Testament* (1969):

> Considerable emphasis has been placed upon methodology in an endeavor to permit the Hebrew Scriptures to speak for themselves against their ancient Near Eastern background. Much of what has passed for critical study in this field has in fact consisted largely of the application of *a priori* literary-critical theories, often in apparent isolation from methodological approaches involving archaeology, comparative religion, sociology, history, linguistics, and aspects of the biological and physical sciences. All of these have a part to play in the proper understanding of the Scriptural record, and must now take their

28. Several terms used by Harrison, e.g., "a priori" and "inductive," reflect developments in positivist thinking made by figures like Francis Bacon and John Stuart Mill. An obvious difference between Harrison and many higher critics lies in the fact that some of these scholars were, at least in practice if not in theory, completely rationalistic in outlook.

29. E.g., R. K. Harrison, "Tell es-Sultan" (i.e., ancient Jericho), in *New International Dictionary of Biblical Archaeology,* ed. E. M. Blaiklock and R. K. Harrison (Grand Rapids: Zondervan, 1983), 440, provides no clue concerning a problem posed by archeology. Referring evidently only to the biblical material, Harrison writes: "Until its conquest by the Israelites after 1240 b.c. [Jericho] was inhabited continuously. . . . By the period of the Hebrew conquest Jericho served as a fortress to block the approach to Canaan." In the same volume J. A. Thompson's article on "Jericho" (p. 260) comments on the evidence that the site was not occupied at this time.

30. E.g., R. K. Harrison, "The Historical and Literary Criticism of the Old Testament," in R. K. Harrison et al., *Biblical Criticism: Historical, Literary, and Textual* (Grand Rapids: Zondervan, 1978), 8: "If the excavation of the Cave of Machpelah ever becomes a possibility, there is little doubt that the historical criticism of the patriarchal narratives would be marked by immediate and significant advances."

place beside literary [i.e. source] and textual criticism as valid means to this end. The methodology adopted in this book is inductive. . . . The conclusions that appear in the book are tentative and amenable to modification in the light of whatever relevant factual information may emerge in the future.[31]

Later statements about method are offered in the Griffith Thomas Lectures (1988) and the commentary on Numbers (1990):

This writer has adopted a process of criticism which he has dubbed "eclectic criticism." It involves applying all the foregoing principles of study [i.e., the various critical methods] to each book of the Old Testament, so that against a background of textual, cultural, historical, and whatever other form of criticism may seem to be relevant and objective, a proper knowledge of the particular book in its original setting might be expected. . . . One great merit of eclectic criticism is that it frees the investigator from the bonds of a schema such as J, E, D, and P, and encourages independent research. It must conform rigidly to fact, however, and anything that is speculative must be controlled carefully.[32]

The present study of Numbers repudiates the theorizing of Wellhausen and his followers and instead prefers to employ eclectic criticism, based upon the scribal traditions of antiquity, archaeological insights, firm linguistic evidence, and as accurate a Hebrew text as can be devised, in an attempt to comprehend the meaning of God's revealed Word.[33]

From these and other passages in his writings it is clear that Harrison's basic approach changed only slightly during his career. Particularly notable for its constancy is the restatement of vehement opposition to the Graf-Wellhausen hypothesis despite its waning influence and its previous adaptations to reckon with many of the types of objections rehearsed by Harrison in his *Introduction*.[34] Equally consistent is a commitment to gain as wide a knowledge as possible concerning ancient Near Eastern life in order to appreciate more fully the context and message of the Old Testament.

Although the dominant impression left by an analysis of Harrison's method is that it remained the same, there are some subtle differences. At some point in the 1980s Harrison began to use the term "eclectic criticism" to describe his method. Further, in his commentary on Numbers, Harrison wrote of the "canonical form" of the book, evidently a mild concession to the views of Brevard Childs.[35] Finally, Harrison's reference to "as accurate a Hebrew text as can be

---

31. Harrison, *Introduction*, vii.
32. Harrison, "Critical Use of the Old Testament," 19–20.
33. R. K. Harrison, *Numbers* (Chicago: Moody, 1990), 11.
34. Lloyd R. Bailey, review of *Introduction to the Old Testament*, by R. K. Harrison, *Journal of Biblical Literature* 89 (1970): 227, comments: "Perhaps the greatest limitation of the book is the amount of space consumed with needless reiteration of the faults of Julius Wellhausen and his followers, e.g., that they applied the evolutionary schema of Hegel and Darwin to the biblical materials (pp. 19, 303, 352, 381, 426, 506, etc.) and that they ignored the results of archaeology (which is repeated to the point of tedium). These faults are now everywhere admitted, as Harrison himself realized (p. 381), thus rendering gratuitous the vast majority of his polemic."
35. Harrison, *Numbers*, xiv.

devised"[36] suggests that, in the light of the evidence from Qumran for varying forms of biblical books such as Jeremiah, Harrison was no longer hopeful that scholars might someday recover the wording of the original autographs.[37] Only in this last case does the change appear to be more than cosmetic.

The continuity in Harrison's approach over time is all the more striking when compared with recent changes within contemporary evangelical biblical scholarship. Whereas Harrison began and remained a critical anti-critic, over this same period other evangelicals were joining the ranks of believing critics in ever-increasing numbers. As a result, Harrison's writings in the latter half of his career were often reviewed far more negatively in evangelical journals than they were in mainline scholarly publications.[38] For better or worse, both in his writings and in his attitude towards biblical criticism Harrison found himself out of step not only with liberals (a situation he expected) but, more and more, with other evangelicals.

Literary and Historical Criticism

A further aspect of Harrison's method has to do with his view of various types of biblical criticism, a view which through his numerous articles in conservative Bible dictionaries and encyclopedias has had considerable influence on the way evangelicals think about the scholarly methods of higher criticism. His schema for understanding the relationship between the various methods of biblical criticism is rather elaborate; in general, however, Harrison follows the conventional distinction drawn between textual (lower) criticism and literary (higher) criticism.[39] To this Harrison adds a third type of criticism, namely historical criticism.

Concerning textual criticism, Harrison differed little from mainline scholars in his understanding of its canons, value, and necessity.[40] He also saw value in literary criticism in its more limited sense of a quest for sources un-

36. Ibid., 11.
37. Harrison probably concedes this point when he writes, "Scholars were once hopeful that textual criticism could restore the OT text to what had been written originally. With the discovery that several Hebrew textual types circulated during the 1st century AD, that hope is now considered unrealistic" (R. K. Harrison, "Biblical Criticism, Old Testament," in *Baker Encyclopedia of the Bible*, ed. Walter A. Elwell, 2 vols. [Grand Rapids: Baker, 1988], 1:328).
38. Compare, e.g., Robert P. Gordon, review of *Leviticus*, by R. K. Harrison, *Evangelical Quarterly* 54 (1982): 190–91, with the review by Baruch Levine, *Journal of Biblical Literature* 102 (1983): 130–33.
39. For the sake of clarity we will not distinguish the various types of criticism in the way Harrison did. Under the category of higher (or literary) criticism he often spoke of (1) genre criticism, (2) literary (i.e., source) criticism, and (3) historical criticism. Emanating from class (2) were form, redaction, and traditio-historical criticism, etc.
40. Although the New King James Version, with which Harrison was heavily involved, was criticized by reviewers for following the majority text for the New Testament, we should keep in view that Harrison's involvement was limited to the Old Testament, where standard text-critical methods were followed. Thus, whereas the King James had followed the ben Chayyim tradition, the New King James followed the ben Asher text (the Leningrad codex) and also made use of the Septuagint, the Vulgate, the Dead Sea Scrolls, and the Bomberg edition of 1524–25. Craigie, foreword to *Israel's Apostasy*, ix, is probably right that "there is nothing obscurantist or fundamentalist about Harrison's love for the KJV, both old and new; it is rather an appreciation for fine language, balanced by the recognition that the use of scripture in public worship calls for particular and unusual sensitivity on the part of the translator."

derlying the finished composition. However, when the quest becomes tied up with elaborate theories and speculation, it becomes, in Harrison's words, "increasingly negative in character" and "in some instances . . . hostile to the concepts of inspiration and revelation."[41]

When Harrison referred to "source criticism," he usually had in view the theory that different documentary sources lay behind the Pentateuch, a theory that eventually led to the well-known and highly influential Graf-Wellhausen hypothesis, which posited four sources, labeled J, E, D, and P. Harrison often rehearsed his objections to this hypothesis: it had so many variations as to call its validity into question; it was devised without reference to archeological data known even at the time; it read into the Old Testament the prevailing Hegelian philosophy of the day; it accepted uncritically the view that the P source was late; its early adherents did not recognize that writing, monotheism, priestly writers, and high culture were early developments; its modus operandi was unscientific despite boastful claims to the contrary.[42] Although Harrison was gentlemanly towards Wellhausen himself (and others with whom he disagreed), his writings often oozed with disdain for the hypothesis and its effects.[43]

Concerning form criticism, Harrison was positive about its focus on the actual life setting of ancient Israel. However, he was critical of Old Testament scholars such as Hermann Gunkel for assuming the primacy of oral tradition over written transmission. Citing the work of Kenneth Kitchen, Harrison argued that oral transmission in the ancient Near East (as in the case of a family history being passed on for posterity) was shortly followed by a written record.[44] Hence he warned others to be wary of claims for late dating of biblical books.[45]

Harrison's favorite theory, concerning the structure of the Book of Genesis,[46] illustrates what he regarded to be a positive application of form criticism:

This writer understands תּוֹלְדֹת [generations], which occurs in a stereotyped formula 11 times in Genesis, to be a distinctive and technical "marker" for linguistic purposes that indicates the end of a section of source material, resembling the colophons of ancient Mesopotamian tablets. . . . By seeing this "marker" form critically as indicating the end of a literary section, one is able to divide Genesis into 11 units of material, to which were added the Joseph narratives, making 12 literary units in all.[47]

41. Harrison, "Biblical Criticism, Old Testament," 329.
42. For his full discussion see Harrison, *Introduction*, 19–82.
43. For Harrison's remarks about Wellhausen see ibid., 21, 24–26.
44. E.g., Harrison, "Critical Use of the Old Testament," 14; idem, "Perspective on Old Testament Study," 26–28; see also Kenneth A. Kitchen, *Ancient Orient and Old Testament* (London: Tyndale, 1966), 135–37.
45. Harrison, "Critical Use of the Old Testament," 14.
46. Harrison's inaugural address when he assumed the Bishops Frederick and Heber Wilkinson Chair at Wycliffe was on the structure of Genesis.
47. Harrison, "Critical Use of the Old Testament," 16; see also idem, *Introduction*, 543–47; and "Genesis," in *International Standard Bible Encyclopedia*, 2:436–37.

Harrison believed this "tablet theory," original with P. J. Wiseman,[48] to be extremely helpful for understanding the structure of Genesis. In his judgment, it destroyed "the Graf-Wellhausen source theory of Genesis, and therefore of the Pentateuch completely."[49] Unfortunately, the tablet theory suffers from a number of major difficulties and has consequently not been widely accepted.[50]

The predominant view of Harrison towards form and related types of criticisms was clearly negative, however. He regarded these types of criticism variously either as reactions to the Graf-Wellhausen hypothesis[51] or as derivations from it.[52] Whether reactionary or derivational, the very existence of these criticisms calls into question the parent source-critical hypothesis. Using a biological analogy, and thinking of the various criticisms in the derivational sense, he writes:

> All these [i.e., redaction criticism, form criticism, genre criticism, rhetorical criticism, and others] are mutations, to use a biological term, of the original literary-critical processes initiated in the 18th and 19th centuries. Those approaches work as mutations do, namely, by weakening the basic stock because of their divergence from it. Many people think and act as though a mutation were an improvement of the original that leads to a new and grander species, but biologists have discovered that mutations normally harm rather than benefit the stock from which they come.[53]

Over against the potentially destructive nature of literary (or higher) criticism Harrison pits historical criticism, by which he means the discipline that endeavors to establish the historicity of events such as the Noachian flood, the exodus, and the conquest of Canaan.[54] Its purpose is "to give the readers of Scripture as accredited an historical picture of ancient Hebrew life as possible."[55] Historical criticism as Harrison defined it clearly lay at the heart of his method; it played an important role both as an apologetic of Scripture and as a vital foundation for historical-grammatical exegesis and interpreta-

---

48. While Harrison was serving as an editor of academic books for Thomas Nelson, a reprint of P. J. Wiseman's 1936 work on this topic appeared under the title *Ancient Records and the Structure of Genesis* (Nashville: Nelson, 1985). Harrison wrote in the preface (p. 18), "After studying [Wiseman's] contention that this great work was written for the most part on clay tablets . . . it is difficult to resist the conclusion that there could possibly be any other credible way in which the book was compiled."

49. Harrison, "Critical Use of the Old Testament," 16.

50. For a discussion of the theory and its problems see Victor P. Hamilton, *The Book of Genesis: Chapters 1–17* (Grand Rapids: Eerdmans, 1990), 8–10. One difficulty is the unlikely implication that Ishmael preserved the family history of Abraham, Isaac the family history of Ishmael, and Esau the family history of Jacob.

51. Harrison, *Introduction,* 33–61; idem, "Biblical Criticism, Old Testament," 330.

52. Harrison, "Critical Use of the Old Testament," 15.

53. Ibid. For further insight into Harrison's understanding of form criticism, redaction criticism, and tradition criticism, including his objections to each, see his "Biblical Criticism, Old Testament," 330–31.

54. See, e.g., Harrison, "Credibility and Enthusiasm," 125; idem, "Biblical Criticism, Old Testament," 329.

55. Harrison et al., *Biblical Criticism,* 4. Despite its positive contribution, Harrison saw a difficulty in historical criticism, namely "the *a priori* notion that nothing in the Old Testament should be accepted as historical fact until it can be demonstrated as such by extrabiblical evidence," a view he found unacceptable on both theoretical and practical grounds (pp. 5–6).

tion. Indeed, apart from his book on Hebrew grammar and works on medicine, all of Harrison's major volumes were to some extent written in the interests of either apologetics or grammatical-historical exegesis. Harrison was
nonetheless careful to clarify that historical criticism (including its mainstay,
archeology) cannot prove the Bible, for no human activity can confirm theology or disclose the realm of faith.[56]

Although Harrison's historical-critical agenda was often transparent, it
should not be judged therefrom that his writings lacked substance or that they
failed to make a solid contribution to Old Testament scholarship. On the contrary, Harrison's capacity for both depth and independence of judgment made
his 1,300-page *Introduction* a first-rate proof that scholarship and traditional
conservative views regarding the Old Testament can exist in harmony.[57]

Archeology

Harrison also wrote and taught extensively on the topic of archeology. (In-
cidentally, his students often referred to his courses in this field as "R. K.ol-
ogy"!) Despite his vast knowledge of the subject, he made no pretense of
being a professional archeologist, nor did he ever participate in a dig. As a
result, his writings on archeological topics have proved to be of far more use
to nonspecialists than to specialists.[58] Indeed, Harrison was passionate about
archeology not so much for its own sake but for the important roles it plays
in Old Testament studies. Harrison saw these roles as (1) furnishing the
background necessary for understanding Scripture and its theological message[59] to the people it addressed (his commentaries thus often focus on his-

56. See, e.g., Harrison, *Introduction,* 93.
57. The substantive nature of Harrison's brand of historical criticism as presented in his *Introduction* is well illustrated by his discussion of Jonah (pp. 904–18). Here he summarizes the story, considers
rabbinic and critical views on the prophet's identity, treats in detail all relevant compositional issues, and
examines three possible interpretations—historical, allegorical, and parabolic. This last discussion illustrates his thoroughness. Under historical interpretation he offers possible explanations for various problems: the swallowing of a human by a great fish; the conversion and seemingly exaggerated size of Nin-
eveh; the identity and rapid growth of the "gourd" (Jonah 4:10); and even the alleged problem of
whether seaweed could grow in the belly of the great fish. Harrison's discussion also illustrates his capacity for judgment independent of traditional conservative opinions in that he does not rule out interpreting
the book parabolically, even though Christ interpreted it historically (pp. 906, 910, 914). Nor does he
rule out the possibility that the rapid growth of the plant may not be literal but hyperbolic (p. 910). Here
was no lightweight fundamentalist parroting old views, but a learned evangelical scholar wrestling seriously and openly with various options, some of them quite daring for an evangelical scholar at that time.
58. Scholarly reviews of Harrison's works on archeology typically commend his works for offering a useful and readable survey, but often note points where his discussions are out of date. Almost
inevitably his conservative stance is also noted. See, e.g., the following reviews of *The New International Dictionary of Biblical Archaeology,* edited by E. M. Blaiklock and R. K. Harrison: Joel F.
Drinkard, Jr., in *Review and Expositor* 81 (1984): 496–97; Judith M. Hadley, in *Vetus Testamentum*
36 (1986): 372–73; and Eugene H. Merrill, in *Bibliotheca Sacra* 142 (1985): 274–75.
59. In Harrison's view the purpose of biblical archeology is "to awaken a sense of the vitality of
the Hebrew past in the student of Old Testament life and times. This is of great importance for the
simple, though frequently unappreciated, reason that the essential message of the Old Testament cannot be fully comprehended without a knowledge of the cultural, religious, historical, and social background of the people to whom the revelation of God was given" (*Introduction,* 93).

torical background and detail); (2) repudiating the Graf-Wellhausen hypothesis; and (3) doing most of the spadework for the apologetic aspect of historical criticism. This role of archeology as an apologetic tool accounts almost entirely for what critics have called his predilection for emphasizing the positive contribution which archeology has made in confirming various events or customs mentioned in the Bible.[60] (We should note here that Harrison's book on *The Dead Sea Scrolls*, where no matter of biblical reference is directly at stake, testifies clearly to his ability to discuss complex and hotly debated issues in an entirely evenhanded manner.[61])

Influence

Although Harrison's work has been influential primarily within conservative evangelical circles, there are at least two cases in which his influence has been felt within a broader sphere. First, before his *Introduction* appeared in the late 1960s, Harrison wrote articles and books for nonevangelical as well as for evangelical constituencies.[62] And second, in addition to his Tyndale commentaries, his articles in *The International Standard Bible Encyclopedia* circulate among a fairly wide readership in the field of biblical studies.

Undoubtedly, however, it is within conservative evangelical circles that the influence of R. K. Harrison has been felt most widely. In particular, in addition to serving as a standard resource in conservative seminaries,[63] his *Introduction* has had considerable influence on evangelicals studying in other schools. Peter Craigie put it very well:

But perhaps one of the most significant roles Harrison played has been the encouragement he has given to a whole generation of theological students in

60. L. H. Brockington, review of *A History of Old Testament Times*, by R. K. Harrison, *Journal of Theological Studies* 9 (1958): 416, remarked that Harrison wrote "in such a way as to suggest that the Old Testament, as traditionally interpreted, is confirmed by every new find." Harrison, *Introduction*, 94–95, responded, "The purpose of the work [*History*] was to show the extent to which the Biblical self-estimate had been vindicated and supported by the discoveries of the Near Eastern archaeologists." He justified the positive approach taken in both his *History* and *Introduction* as a corrective to certain scholarly circles that focused on the difficulties, ignoring the points of correspondence between the Old Testament and archeological discoveries. (In fairness to Brockington, it should be noted that Harrison did not make this purpose clear in the preface to his *History.*)

61. See, e.g., B. J. Roberts, review of *The Dead Sea Scrolls*, by R. K. Harrison, *Expository Times* 72 (1961): 328; and John C. Trevor, review of *The Dead Sea Scrolls*, by R. K. Harrison, *Journal of Biblical Literature* 81 (1962): 320.

62. After this period only a few of Harrison's works were published by nonevangelical presses. These rare cases include his contribution to *The Enduring Word* (University of Toronto Press); his book *Teach Yourself the Ancient World* (London: English Universities Press, 1971); and his article "Philistine Origins: A Reappraisal," in *Ascribe to the Lord: Biblical and Other Studies in Memory of Peter C. Craigie*, ed. J. Glen Taylor and Lyle Eslinger (Sheffield: Sheffield Academic, 1988), 11–19.

63. This role was diminished somewhat by Gleason Archer's shorter and more conservative *Survey of Old Testament Introduction* (Chicago: Moody, 1964; rev. ed., 1974), and, later on, by William S. LaSor, David A. Hubbard, and Frederic W. Bush, *Old Testament Survey* (Grand Rapids: Eerdmans, 1981). Prior to his death Harrison completed a revision of his *Introduction*. If it is published, Harrison's *Introduction* may yet again become a textbook in traditional evangelical seminaries.

the conservative tradition. Swamped by a mass of scholarly tomes whose methods they found both disturbing and difficult, students found that Harrison's books provided a new perspective. It was clear that one did not have to abandon scholarship if one wished to remain faithful to scripture. And simply knowing that there was someone "out there" who had thought through the difficulties of scholarship from a conservative perspective was a source of strength to many young students.[64]

Moreover, the commentaries Harrison wrote and the various reference works on the Bible and archeology which he edited or authored frequently find a place on the bookshelves of pastors, teachers, and others interested in the Bible and biblical archeology. Further, several of Harrison's books have appeared in foreign languages in the interests of serving evangelical communities abroad.

In other respects, however, Harrison's influence has been quite limited, even within evangelical biblical scholarship. During his long career he played virtually no role as a supervisor of doctoral students. (This may in part be due to the fact that Harrison was a private person who rarely left Toronto.) Moreover, the more than three hundred respondents to Mark Noll's 1984 survey of evangelical Bible scholars did not list Harrison as a person who had influenced them.[65] (Because of his *Introduction,* however, a number of respondents, and believing critics in particular, did list Harrison as an author who had influenced them.)[66] Another consideration here is that within evangelicalism in North America there has been a general decline in interest in the works of British evangelicals and in the more technical kinds of contributions which scholars like Harrison have made.[67]

There are of course many reasons why Harrison's writings have not been more influential within mainline scholarly circles, among them the deep and long-standing chasm between liberal and conservative (especially in Old Testament studies),[68] and a distaste within postmodernity for the positivist thinking of a former era. And yet, as Noll writes, "the best of [the biblical] scholarship [of the critical anti-critics], as indeed much of scholarship before

64. Craigie, foreword to *Israel's Apostasy,* x.

65. Noll, *Between Faith and Criticism,* 211–26.

66. Ibid., 224–26. It was basically through his writings that Harrison was known within scholarly communities. Harrison's *Introduction* was cited about as frequently as John Bright's *History of Israel* (note that the respondents were asked to state only what book had been most influential on them, not whether the influence had been positive or negative). One might expect Harrison to have been more influential among the critical anti-critics, but, as Noll observes (pp. 158–59), they tended to cite conservative theologians, whereas the believing critics tended to list the works of other biblical scholars.

67. David F. Wells, "On Being Evangelical: Some Theological Differences and Similarities," in *Evangelicalism,* ed. Noll, Bebbington, and Rawlyk, 398.

68. Peter C. Craigie, "Narrowing the Scholar-Preacher Gap in Old Testament Studies," *Christianity Today* 27.5 (March 4, 1983): 105, makes an observation that applies to Harrison: "The great debates of Old Testament scholarship during the last century were so loaded with theological overtones that conservatives have usually been on the defensive. For the most part, their writings have defended traditionalist views in a polemical tone. As a consequence, they have not been influential and they have not been widely read outside the conservative camp."

the rise of criticism, deserves a recognition it rarely receives."[69] For four-and-a-half decades R. K. Harrison strove with great energy and discipline to represent the best of this type of scholarship. Harrison's scholarship was never for its own sake, but rather with a view to a need within both the church and the academy for a better appreciation and understanding of the Old Testament. For this we can be truly grateful, and from it we may take example.

Primary Sources

Harrison, R. K. "Amos." In *Evangelical Commentary on the Bible*, edited by Walter A. Elwell, 625–37. Grand Rapids: Baker, 1989.

———. *The Archaeology of the New Testament*. New York: Association, 1964.

———. *The Archaeology of the Old Testament*. New York: Harper, 1963.

———. *The Dead Sea Scrolls*. New York: Harper, 1961.

———. "Deuteronomy." In *New Bible Commentary Revised*, edited by Donald Guthrie et al., 201–29. Grand Rapids: Eerdmans, 1970.

———. *Healing Herbs of the Bible*. Leiden: Brill, 1966.

———. *Introduction to the Old Testament*. Grand Rapids: Eerdmans, 1969.

———. *Jeremiah and Lamentations: An Introduction and Commentary*. Tyndale Old Testament Commentaries. Downers Grove, Ill.: InterVarsity, 1973.

———. *Leviticus: An Introduction and Commentary*. Tyndale Old Testament Commentaries. Downers Grove, Ill.: InterVarsity, 1980.

———. *Major Cities of the Biblical World*. Nashville: Nelson, 1985.

———. *Numbers*. Chicago: Moody, 1990.

———. *Old Testament Times*. Grand Rapids: Eerdmans, 1970.

———. "Proverbs." In *Evangelical Commentary on the Bible*, edited by Walter A. Elwell, 399–431. Grand Rapids: Baker, 1989.

———. "Ruth." In *Evangelical Commentary on the Bible*, edited by Walter A. Elwell, 179–87. Grand Rapids: Baker, 1989.

———, et al. *Biblical Criticism: Historical, Literary, and Textual*. Grand Rapids: Zondervan, 1978.

Harrison, R. K., and E. M. Blaiklock, eds. *New International Dictionary of Biblical Archaeology*. Grand Rapids: Zondervan, 1983.

69. Noll, *Between Faith and Criticism*, 158.

Joyce Baldwin-Caine

Valerie Griffiths

Joyce Baldwin was born in Essex County in 1921, and grew up in a Christian home reinforced by school and church. The family moved to Nottingham in 1937. In her first weeks at Mundella School, Joyce was invited to a mission to the city, and there she committed her life to Christ. Two years of spiritual growth followed as she was introduced to evangelical leaders through the school's Christian Union; a local young man named John Caine was among them.

World War II broke out in 1939 as Joyce finished school. She began university studies in Nottingham toward a degree in French with German as a subsidiary. The next three years were dominated by austerity, air raids, blackout regulations, clothing coupons, and food- and petrol-rationing. As a teacher trainee, Joyce was in a reserved occupation and exempted from national service, but she took part-time training as an auxiliary nurse in the Civil Defense Force.

During her student years at Nottingham, the university's Christian Union played a formative role in Joyce's life; and at the 1941 conference of the Inter-Varsity Fellowship she signed a pledge to do her utmost to serve God overseas. China was on her mind, but in 1941 there was no possibility in the foreseeable future. So she earned an honors degree in French and German in 1942 and a Cambridge postgraduate certificate in education in 1943.

From China to Dalton House

For the next four years Joyce taught French, German, and religious studies at two grammar schools in Lancashire.[1] When World War II came to an end in 1945, the call to mission surfaced again. She applied to the China Inland Mission (CIM), and was accepted for training in 1947. Sensing increasingly that her future ministry lay in Bible teaching, she augmented her CIM train-

---

1. The 1944 Education Act in Britain required that religious studies be taught at all levels in the state schools, and that the teachers have an appropriate academic degree. Accordingly, increasing numbers of women took undergraduate theological degrees at secular universities. The situation in North America was very different: women were often excluded from theological studies, and there were no career prospects even if they were qualified.

ing with evening classes given by the London Bible College, which had been established at the end of the war to provide an evangelical center for theological study. She found these courses so valuable that she asked for permission to acquire a diploma in theology from the University of London before going to China. Though this step postponed her departure to China for a year, it ultimately proved to be very significant.

Some of the other CIM trainees found Joyce's delay hard to understand. In Britain, academic theological credentials could be gained only through the universities set up by royal charter, and all the teaching was liberal. Many evangelicals had misgivings with regard to the value of such study. Moreover, female missionaries usually worked among rural women, so less was expected of them than of male missionaries.[2] Fortunately, Fred Mitchell, the home director of CIM, was aware that China's young women needed higher education at the college and university levels, and that a diploma in theology in addition to Joyce's degree in modern languages would be invaluable. It was a heavy program for Joyce, combining the two-year theological studies with her CIM commitments, but she succeeded. During that period she became aware of the dearth of academic books written from an evangelical perspective. The war had resulted in a long hiatus for biblical research. Throughout the United Kingdom, F. F. Bruce was probably the only evangelical serving in a university department of biblical studies.

Joyce sailed for China in September 1949, expecting an initial seven-year term of service. The Communist armies were already on the march when she joined the "forty-niners" at the CIM Language School at Chongqing. (There were forty-nine recruits in 1949.) Four weeks later the People's Liberation Army took charge. She enjoyed the international community at the school as they studied Chinese together, but restrictions steadily increased, and their presence became an embarrassment to the Chinese church. Most of the group never left the grounds of the language school. Just over a year later, the CIM made the decision to withdraw, but the Chinese authorities were in no hurry to move them out. When Joyce finally left China in August 1951, she was seriously debilitated by dysentery and needed months to recover. Her health had been permanently damaged.

When well enough, Joyce took another teaching post in French, German, and religious studies. Three years later she approached the China Inland Mission again (now the Overseas Missionary Fellowship) about serving the Chinese population in Malaya. The medical advisor felt her health would be at risk in the tropics and suggested the more temperate climate in Japan. But Joyce had studied Chinese for two years, and felt that if she could not handle Malaya, she would not cope with the pressures of beginning Japanese lan-

2. As late as 1951, a committee reviewing candidates suggested that female missionaries primarily needed an ability to tell Bible stories in an interesting way and a knowledge of cooking, housekeeping, and nursing.

guage study either. The door overseas had apparently closed for her, and she so informed her friends in a circular letter.

Ernest Kevan, the principal of London Bible College, had just received Joyce's letter when the principal of Dalton House in Bristol approached him for suggestions for a new lecturer. As a result, in September 1956 Joyce found herself lecturing at Dalton House, which trained female missionaries, parish workers, and deaconesses for work in the Anglican church. A variety of one-, two-, and three-year courses were offered, but there was a strong emphasis on pastoral studies, which covered the main sphere of service for parish workers. In order to teach Old Testament, philosophy, and ethics as well as coach women for the University of London's diploma in theology, Joyce had to revive the work she had done seven years earlier for her own diploma. Those students taking the university's bachelor of divinity exams gained further help from the tutors at two nearby theological colleges for men (Clifton Theological College and Tyndale Hall).

Joyce sensed that teaching at Dalton House would be her lifework, and in consequence she herself earned the London bachelor of divinity degree as an external student. In spite of her degree in modern languages and her diploma in theology, she was not allowed to study for a master's degree in theology until she had studied the subject first at the undergraduate level. As a graduate, she was allowed to take the degree in two instead of the usual three years, but this created additional pressure *and* she had begun lecturing full-time. Her previous work for the diploma had covered a wide area and provided a good foundation, but earning the bachelor's degree was nevertheless a formidable task. That lectures are less important in the British system than is private study only added to the difficulty. Though not strong physically, Joyce obtained her degree in 1958, and subsequently became vice-principal of the college.

The students of Dalton House in the 1950s and 1960s remember the strict regime under Miss Weeks, the principal. It was run like a girls' boarding school, but so were most of the Bible colleges in that period. Joyce relaxed the rules when she became principal, but she had experienced a rigorous missionary training herself and also, for months on end in China as the Communists took over, the pressures under which missionaries live. She expected a high degree of discipline and self-control as part of the training for people who were probably going to work in unstructured situations, but these were unfamiliar virtues to the postwar generation of the 1960s and 1970s, and both staff and students lived uneasily with the tensions. A colleague said that the only issue on which Joyce was negative was student indiscipline. On the other hand, the students were encouraged to take degrees and stretch themselves academically, and they did. At least one student with no previous degree achieved a bachelor of divinity with first-class honors.

Over the following years Baldwin took every opportunity to meet with other Old Testament scholars, and attended the summer Old Testament study groups held at Tyndale House, a newly established evangelical study center at Cambridge. In 1962, on the invitation of Donald Wiseman she presented a paper entitled "*Ṣemaḥ* as a Technical Term in the Prophets." She was urged to expand and submit the article to *Vetus Testamentum*, which to her enormous encouragement published it. Through careful exegesis of five texts in Isaiah, Jeremiah, and Zechariah, she argued that the word *shoot* has messianic implications and represents someone whom "Yahweh will cause to rise from obscurity to become . . . a king and a priest."[3] In making this argument, she was not afraid to challenge some commonly held interpretations.

The First Commentary

At Tyndale House, Donald Wiseman, who was the general editor for the Tyndale Old Testament Commentaries series, had recognized Baldwin's gift for exegesis. In 1966, she received a request from Tyndale Press in Britain (now Inter-Varsity Press) not only to contribute three articles to the revision of the *New Bible Commentary* ("The History of Israel," "Ruth," and "Esther"), but also to produce a Tyndale commentary on Haggai, Zechariah, and Malachi. She was "astonished to be entrusted with such a commitment on the slender evidence of my writing to that date, but I accepted the challenge." Her degree in modern languages enabled her to access literature in French and German, and this proved to be very significant. She set aside her free day each week and her vacations for the next five years. She had no previous training in research, but set out to master it. She had acquired some Hebrew in evening classes, and learned more as she went along. The resulting commentary surprised and delighted her colleagues and publishers and fully justified Wiseman's discernment of her gifts.

The Tyndale commentaries had been launched "to provide the student of the Bible with a handy, up-to-date commentary on each book, with the primary emphasis on exegesis." The authors were expected to discuss major critical questions in the introduction and additional notes, but without becoming too technical. The ultimate goal was to illuminate the overall meaning and message of the Old Testament. In bridging the gap between biblical scholarship and the exposition of the message, the commentaries were intended as a tool for pastors, Christian lay leaders, and students. Alec Motyer, principal of Trinity College and a well-known preacher, commented that he found Baldwin's careful exegesis raised innumerable points from the text which the preacher could explore with profit.

For many decades, scholars had analyzed the Book of Zechariah, searching for its date and origins. The suggested dates varied from the fourth to the second century B.C., and the analyses of possible sources fragmented the book, until P. R. Ackroyd could wonder whether "the attempt to date is the

---

3. Joyce Baldwin, "*Ṣemaḥ* as a Technical Term in the Prophets," *Vetus Testamentum* 14.1 (1964): 97.

most useful approach to the material."[4] Baldwin herself commented, "Scholars now admit that too little information is available for linguistic evidence to provide any sure basis for the date of the book."[5] She found the key to a different approach when reading Paul Lamarche's *Zacharie ix–xiv: Structure littéraire et messianisme.*[6] In searching for structure in the second half of the book, he had discovered a chiastic pattern: the subject matter moves forward and then backward in the order *abccba.* By its nature a chiastic structure reinforces the message by stating it and then repeating the themes in reverse order. This scheme unites chapters 9–14, revealing the oneness of the material without rearranging the text, as had been so common before.

Such an approach was new to Baldwin, and when she consulted a colleague, he knew nothing about it. But after years of source criticism which lacked objective verification and left the text fragmented, Baldwin leaped at the possibility of handling the Book of Zechariah as a whole. Lamarche had found the pattern in the later chapters. Baldwin began searching for a similar pattern in chapters 1–8. It was clear in the visions. Finding chiastic structure in some of the prophecies as well convinced her that their final arrangement must have come, if not from the prophet himself, at least from an editor closely associated with him. This challenged the prevailing theories of multiple authorship and widely spread dating, and also had a bearing on the date and origins of early apocalyptic literature. Clearly, the Hebrew writers were familiar with chiastic structure, but Western scholars had been so preoccupied with questions of date and source that they had failed to look at the book as a whole and to realize that the biblical writers expressed their message not only in words, but also in the very forms and structures which they used.

Baldwin's unique approach won praise. Typical is Brevard Childs's evaluation of *Haggai, Zechariah, Malachi:* "In my opinion the best all-around commentary on these three prophets for the pastor is Joyce G. Baldwin's recent commentary. The approach of Baldwin is far more thorough and balanced than is the comparable volume by Douglas R. Jones. Baldwin's judgments are usually cautious, but she handles the critical questions in an honest fashion. I appreciate her attempt to distinguish between the question of the unity of original authorship and the integrity of the book in its canonical shape."[7]

In a similar vein Frank Entwistle, her editor, recalls a paper Baldwin presented in this period to the Evangelical Fellowship for Mission Studies.[8] With meticulous attention to scholarly detail, she examined some thirty-five au-

4. P. R. Ackroyd, "Zechariah," in *Peake's Commentary on the Bible,* rev. ed., ed. Matthew Black and H. H. Rowley (New York: Nelson, 1962), 651, quoted in Joyce Baldwin, *Haggai, Zechariah, Malachi: An Introduction and Commentary* (Downers Grove, Ill.: InterVarsity, 1972), 65.

5. Baldwin, *Haggai, Zechariah, Malachi,* 68.

6. Paul Lamarche, *Zacharie ix–xiv: Structure littéraire et messianisme* (Paris: Gabalda, 1961).

7. Brevard S. Childs, *Old Testament Books for Pastor and Teacher* (Philadelphia: Westminster, 1977), 87–88.

8. Joyce Baldwin, "Malachi 1:11 and the Worship of the Nations," *Tyndale Bulletin* 23 (1972): 117–24.

thorities to ascertain whether the main verb of Malachi 1:11, which determines the tense of the verbs that occur before and after, is present or future. She concluded that "incense is about to be offered" is the true reading, and all nations will worship not their own gods, but the God of Israel. Her careful scholarship was the foundation for a powerful message on world mission today. Entwistle has never forgotten it.

The Establishment of Trinity College

The decade of the 1960s brought turmoil and uncertainty for the three Bristol theological colleges: they had independent foundations, and the Anglican church paid student fees only at colleges which it officially "recognized." Without recognition the colleges could not survive. The 1960s were years of retrenchment and upgrading, and the bishops decided that Tyndale Hall should close, and Clifton Theological College merge with Wycliffe Hall in Oxford. This would have been a significant loss to the evangelical wing of the Anglican church, which was growing in strength.

At this point Dalton House came into the picture. It had been founded in 1930 by the Bible Churchmen's Missionary Society (now Crosslinks) to train women missionaries and parish workers, and was the only evangelical Anglican college still doing so! In the 1960s the status of women in the Anglican church was in some confusion. The order of deaconesses had been introduced in 1862, but the Lambeth Conference of 1930 insisted that they were "distinct from the historic threefold male order of deacons, priests and bishops," and kept them in the position of paid parish workers who "assisted the clergy, to whom all liturgical functions belonged."[9] The differentiation between deaconesses and clergy was jealously guarded, and women were kept in a subordinate and secondary role. There had been a call for a new training center for women in 1944, but no money was available.[10]

In the early 1950s licensed lay-workers and deaconesses were permitted to take part in services for the first time, with the exception of the communion service. In 1968 the functions of the laywomen and deaconesses were broadened to include preparing children and adults for baptism and confirmation, and conducting courses, missions, baptisms and funerals (if the relatives did not object). By this stage, in the vicar's absence women were sometimes doing the same work as a curate (deacon), including preaching, but they remained second-class citizens, with much lower salaries and pensions, and with the scope of their ministry dependent on the views of the particular vicars under whom they worked. In a world where ever-greater numbers of women were university graduates and professionals, it was increasingly unacceptable for the churches to so treat women called to full-time service.[11] In

9. Sean Gill, *Women and the Church of England* (London: S.P.C.K., 1994), 219.
10. Ibid., 217.
11. Ibid., 263.

consequence there was growing pressure in the Anglican church for women to be given the same dignity and freedom in ministry as were given to men.

In the light of this history it is perhaps not surprising that when the bishops considered the future of the theological colleges for ordinands, Dalton House "was not under the scope of the bishops' inquiry."[12] It is surprising, however, that the faculty whose lectures and tutorials at Tyndale Hall and Clifton College were attended by women who were taking bachelor's degrees did not seem to realize that the discussions had great bearing on the women. They had never been accorded the same status as the students at the men's colleges and were in consequence marginalized. But financial constraints meant that Dalton House could not survive on its own. If the men's colleges went, Dalton House would also fold, with serious results for the training of women. Although they had never been consulted, the axe hung over the women's heads too.

The decision went back to the drawing board. Dalton House wanted to merge with the two men's colleges and in the end was instrumental in bringing that about.[13] Miss Weeks was approaching retirement, so Joyce Baldwin was closely involved in several years of discussion prior to the union. She finished her commentary *Haggai, Zechariah, Malachi* just before she took over as principal of Dalton House for its final term before the merger took place.

The year 1972 marked a new era. The fledgling Trinity College had ninety students, one third of whom were women, and the four women lecturers from Dalton House made up one third of the faculty. It would be over a decade before the Council for National Academic Awards allowed the college to grant its own bachelor's degrees, but the greater size of the faculty allowed specialization and improved standards. The task of blending the three groups together fell to the new principal, Alec Motyer. He disliked the word *student* for mature adults, believing that if adults are treated as children, they will respond as such. He insisted on treating them as mature adults, with as much freedom as possible—a contrast to the earlier approach at Dalton House. At the same time, an increasing number of the students had been converted in adult life; they arrived with less Christian background than had previous students, and also belonged to a generation that tended to throw tradition to the winds.

A dean was appointed from each of the former colleges. Technically, in this position J. I. Packer and Joyce Baldwin retained their status as principals, but everyone had to be ready for the necessary adjustments. As dean of women, responsible for the selection, processing, and supervision of all the women students, Baldwin experienced unexpected moments of truth when her decisions concerning the women were overruled by male colleagues. She

12. Personal conversation with Alec Motyer.
13. Similarly, in 1971 All Nations Bible College for men amalgamated with Ridgelands and Mount Hermon Bible Colleges for women to become the interdenominational All Nations Christian College, which concentrated on cross-cultural missionary training.

did not encroach on their responsibilities, but they could encroach on hers without realizing the implications. She had suffered an unanticipated loss of authority within her designated sphere. The amalgamation of colleges inevitably creates problems, but they are magnified when competent women find themselves alongside men who have trained and worked solely at single-sex theological colleges, served in an entirely male-led church, and had limited experience of working with women professionally. This was a difficult and painful situation for some of the women who pioneered in such circumstances, and some did not survive. It says much for Baldwin's character that she was able to live with it, and her male colleagues had nothing but praise for her quiet and gracious spirit.

"Doing Something for the Church": The Issue of the Ordination of Women

With new opportunities ahead, Baldwin sought advice about tackling a doctorate. She was fifty-one and had just finished her first commentary. Graduate education was limited to a small percentage of the population. In consequence a first degree was still highly regarded in Britain, and people were judged by their work rather than their diplomas. Donald Wiseman advised her instead to "do something for the church," something that had always been close to her heart. At that stage of her life, spending three years on a doctorate was neither a priority nor a necessity.[14]

And so Joyce produced a booklet designed to inform women of their opportunities for serving full-time in the churches. The Anglican church had 17,000 ordained men, but only 500 full-time women, and 160 part-time. Most of the part-timers were located in the three dioceses of London, Southwark, and Chelmsford, where they worked in teams with the clergy.[15] The majority of women called to full-time work found better opportunities overseas.

Baldwin led her readers through their various options and gave examples of the ministries in which women were then engaged. She went on to address the confusion many women felt about their ministry in the light of various biblical passages. In 1984 she covered the same material in greater depth for a nondenominational book on *The Role of Women*, in which a team of writers presented the traditional and liberated views in an effort to persuade readers at least to listen to the other side. Warning against lifting texts out of context, she showed that on occasion apparently simple rules have to be interpreted by more important precepts, as in the case of plucking corn on the Sabbath (Matt. 12:1–8).[16] Quoting verses is not enough. She then focused on the principle of male headship, leadership, and authority, so often described as a "creation ordinance" and used to restrict women's ministry in the churches. Her careful exegesis of the Hebrew text and examination of the

---

14. F. F. Bruce never acquired a doctorate.

15. Joyce Baldwin, *Women Likewise* (London: Falcon, 1973), 4.

16. Joyce Baldwin, "Women's Ministry: A New Look at the Biblical Texts," in *The Role of Women*, ed. Shirley Lees (Leicester: Inter-Varsity, 1984), 160–62.

standard commentaries demonstrated that Genesis 1 describes the partnership of men and women together sharing dominion over creation, but not
over each other. Genesis 2 describes a "mutually satisfying partnership [in
marriage] in which each delights to serve the other."[17] The rule of the man
over the woman is not found until *after* the fall in Genesis 3 and is the result
of sin. We must bear in mind that "Christ died to reverse the deadly effects
of Adam's fall, and in Christ there is to be mutual submission (Eph. 5:21)."[18]
Are the churches called to institutionalize the results of the fall by giving dominion and rule to men alone, or are they called to withstand the results of
the fall and work for a restoration of the original partnership of men and
women exercising dominion together over creation?

J. I. Packer commented that Baldwin carried the torch quietly for women's
ordination to the presbyterate. She was a member of the Movement for the
Ordination of Women and organized two conferences in Bristol on the subject until others could take over. She was neither strident nor militant, but
she could not ignore the situation the women students would face in the
churches. In China she had seen what women, both national and missionary,
can do when they are given freedom to use their spiritual gifts and abilities.
She had also spent some years in secular teaching, where men and women did
exactly the same work. The church's position, then, seemed both unjust and
unbiblical. Within her own field of exegesis she was prepared to expound the
relevant Scriptures and remind the church that

> authority has been accorded an importance out of all proportion to Scripture's
> teaching on the subject. . . . Our squabbles are reminiscent of the disciples' pre-
> occupation with working out who was the greatest in the Kingdom when Jesus
> was about to submit to crucifixion. The great commission of Jesus (Mt. 28:18–
> 20) involves all believers and demands priority. . . . There are occasions when
> the church has pioneered social change, [but] it has more frequently been reac-
> tionary. . . . With hindsight it is possible to see the damage done to the Christian
> cause, and we need to beware lest yet another example be added to the list of
> mistaken attitudes from Scripture.[19]

In her earlier booklet for prospective parish workers *(You and the Ministry)* Baldwin had insisted that the Great Commission given by Jesus to proclaim his gospel to the ends of the earth means that both men and women are
called to ministry in the church. She covered the problematic New Testament
passages, pointing out that the Greek word for "head" simply does not include the metaphorical sense of "rule." She ended by mentioning the growing
recognition that spiritual gifts are not limited to the ordained clergy, but are
found throughout the church, and in the future the use of the spiritual gifts
of the whole congregation will be vital if the churches are to grow as they

17. Ibid., 167.
18. Ibid., 165.
19. Ibid., 175–76.

should. Characteristically, she was objective and clear in her reasoning on what was becoming an increasingly volatile issue in the churches, with bishops, clergy, and laity taking their stands on both sides.

Trinity College could not avoid the burning issue within the Anglican church over women's ordination. The women students soon showed that they were in no way inferior to the men academically or spiritually. They all now received the same training (the women were not excluded from any courses), and it became increasingly illogical to many that although all were called and gifted for Christian service, the women, purely on the grounds of their gender, were confined to a subordinate form of service in the churches, with lower salaries and status, even when shortage of personnel meant that some were doing the same work as the men. Both faculty and students held deep convictions on biblical teaching and church order and found themselves split on the issue of women's ordination. George Carey, who succeeded Baldwin as principal, would one day as archbishop of Canterbury see the first women come forward for ordination to the presbyterate.[20]

But that was still far off. The topic of the ordination of women would dominate the Anglican synods for the next twenty years. The college with its coeducational foundation could scarcely avoid the issue. For ten years Baldwin faced a steady stream of young evangelical men (and a few women, usually fiancées trying to define their role) questioning the right of women to teach. Her teaching did not stop with lectures, but continued informally over meals as, without anger or bitterness, she quietly and patiently talked over the biblical principles with individuals. Demonstrating in class that women who are called and gifted to teach do so on the authority of Scripture, she felt that "God's providential ordering of events had taken over and was pointing the way ahead. The publication of my first Tyndale commentary in May 1972 seemed to me God's endorsement. It would go far beyond the walls of Trinity College. If it was permissible to teach through a book, why not by word of mouth?"

Teaching and Writing at Trinity

In 1976 Joyce took a sabbatical, enabling her to accept an invitation to teach Old Testament for a term at the Discipleship Training Centre in Singapore, which offered the University of London's diploma in theology to Asian university graduates who needed theological training. Delighted to be back in an Asian environment after twenty-five years and contribute something to future church leaders, she was able to teach at two other Bible colleges. In Singapore she also gave eight well-attended public lectures on "Archaeology and the Old Testament," which were liberally illustrated with her own slides from a previous sabbatical in Israel. It was typical of her generosity that she allowed a missionary colleague to copy her personal collection of slides. If

20. Gill, *Women and the Church*, 260.

they had been misplaced or damaged in the process, her loss would have been incalculable. She found the whole experience "mind-broadening" as she met students from many countries round the Pacific rim, some of whom would at a later date study at Trinity College.

In 1978 Baldwin produced her second Tyndale commentary, *Daniel,* which some regard as her greatest achievement. With characteristic clarity she provided a masterly summary of the current views of scholars. And without submerging her readers in too much detail, she enabled them to explore further themselves before she gave her own conclusions. Once again she brought a rigorous and meticulous standard of scholarship to bear on the text, and while her conclusions tended to be conservative, she was not afraid to be radical in challenging the scholarly consensus.

In the introduction Baldwin covers the linguistic material, the date and unity of the book, the literary genre, structure, and interpretation. The linguistic evidence is inadequate for accurate dating of the text, but unity of authorship is now widely accepted, and there is a growing consensus that the canon of the Old Testament was closed by Maccabean times.[21] The authority accorded to the book at Qumran makes a Maccabean date unlikely. The internal indications of earlier material require that the book either is a composite put together in the second century B.C. or was produced in its entirety at an earlier date: "Prove that part of the book comes from an earlier period, and the Maccabean dating becomes untenable unless its unity is abandoned."[22] It is on these grounds that Baldwin argues for a fifth century B.C. dating of the Book of Daniel. Commenting on the literary genre, she asserts that "the book of Daniel is thoroughly integrated with the Old Testament as a whole, but at the same time presents its truth from a world standpoint to an extent that was never attempted by a prophet. . . . This is the significance of Old Testament apocalyptic . . . out-worked in the book of Daniel."[23]

Baldwin finds the unity of Daniel corroborated by the work of Cyrus Gordon and A. Lenglet on the chiastic structure.[24] The block of Aramaic in Daniel is not a random source from another hand, but a deliberate highlighting of a message relevant beyond Israel to the nations. Written in a language they could understand, this message is sandwiched on both sides by messages in Hebrew addressed to Judah, thus giving a chiastic pattern, *aba.* But the structure of the Aramaic central section (chs. 2–7) can be analyzed further as presenting a pattern of *abbccbba,* making it impossible to propose a simple division of the book into stories (chs. 1–6) and visions (chs. 7–12). Since the chiastic structure reinforces the unity of the book, it was written at one time,

---

21. Sid Z. Leiman, *The Canonization of Hebrew Scripture* (Hamden, Conn.: Archon, 1976), cited in Joyce Baldwin, *Daniel: An Introduction and Commentary* (Downers Grove, Ill.: InterVarsity, 1978), 72 n. 5.
22. Baldwin, *Daniel,* 40.
23. Ibid., 59.
24. Cyrus H. Gordon, *The World of the Old Testament* (Garden City, N.Y.: Doubleday, 1958), 83–84; A. Lenglet, "La Structure littéraire de Daniel 2–7," *Biblica* 53 (1972): 169–90.

probably the fifth century B.C. Further, if it is a unity, then the whole book is apocalyptic, a fact that impinges on the early roots of apocalyptic in Judah.

In addition to her teaching, Baldwin continued to write. She contributed to *The New International Dictionary of New Testament Theology* (1975–78) and was invited to give the Tyndale Lecture for 1978 ("Some Literary Affinities of the Book of Daniel"). She also contributed to *The Illustrated Bible Dictionary* (1980) and the following year gave the Laing Lecture at London Bible College ("The Role of the Ten Commandments").

In 1981 Alec Motyer retired as principal. Because George Carey could not take up the appointment for a year, Baldwin was asked to be acting principal for her final year before her own retirement. She suggested that the term *acting* was inappropriate since she and Packer had retained their status as principals after the college merger. The board agreed, the term was dropped, and she became the first woman principal. It was another quiet step taken not for herself, but for her sisters in Christ, who were still excluded from full freedom to minister in their church. For her year as principal she had no deputy, but continued her responsibilities as dean of women and, in addition, as an only daughter shouldered the increasing burden of caring for very elderly parents living in Bristol.

Baldwin's students at Dalton House remember her concern that women be stretched and work for diplomas and degrees at a time when many would have settled for much less. When church leadership was almost entirely male, Baldwin in her own life and work demonstrated the gifts and calling that come to women as well as men. She was known as a good and conscientious teacher, and as dean of women was a thorough and efficient administrator. Her supervision of external examinations taken by students at Trinity College was "worked to a fine art."[25] Throughout her career she had to battle fragile health—frequent migraines curtailed outside engagements and prevented the development of a preaching and teaching ministry beyond the college; but she won the respect and admiration of staff and students alike for her insistence on continuing her work, however much she was suffering.

As a scholar Joyce Baldwin was a British pioneer of the chiastic approach, which treated biblical books as a whole. She demonstrated that chiastic formats were not meaningless devices: in addition to throwing light on issues such as date and authorship, they were carefully constructed to enhance the message of the book. A major contribution to Old Testament scholarship, her approach was rigorous, meticulous, and of the highest scholastic standard. Her editors found her work well prepared to the last detail, and her publishers were pleased with what she produced. Packer described her as "tenacious for biblical truth—with a gift for analysing evidence with luminous clarity." He referred to her "computer mind" and "sober reason which con-

25. Personal conversation with Alec Motyer.

firms the reasonableness of accepting what is said." Other colleagues commented that she had Donald Guthrie's gift for analysis of evidence, Leon Morris's gift for thoroughness, and a temperament similar to that of Alan Stibbs. There are no evangelical women scholars with whom to compare her. Perhaps it is most fitting to describe her as the apotheosis of what James Barr has called the British contribution to the understanding of apocalyptic: "It has approached the complicated and obscure mixtures which form the apocalyptic books with rather clear and simple questions, to which in principle a yes-or-no may be obtained. . . . This reduction of the very enigmatic material to essentially simple questions seems to me to be a feature of our British tradition of scholarship in apocalyptic."[26]

The Years of Retirement

On Joyce's last day at college in 1982, as she cleared her study to make way for her successor, George Carey, a phone call came from John Caine, whom she had not seen since her time at Mundella School in Nottingham more than forty years earlier. He had overheard her name mentioned by faculty members of Trinity College who were visiting St. John's College in Nottingham. Normally she would never have had time to see anyone during the school year, but retirement began the next day, so they met. The following year they were married, and she had her own home after a lifetime in college accommodations.

Free from college commitments, Joyce was able to get on with writing. She completed the Tyndale commentary on Esther, having made use of the work of Yehuda Radday to tackle the overall structure of the book.[27] The commentary was enriched by the growing general awareness of the place of biblical narrative and by Baldwin's illumination of the background through her archeological studies. She astutely observed that "a study of the literary themes [of Esther] has done more to promote an understanding of the book than all the discussions about historicity, which so occupied scholars earlier this century." While a preoccupation with historicity can lock people into the past, "the predominant themes of a book and the way the author handles them take the reader close to the eternal dimension of Scripture."[28]

In 1988 Baldwin produced a commentary on 1 and 2 Samuel, building on the work of Brevard Childs and other scholars who used rhetorical criticism in treating the books as a unity rather than a composite of fragmented sources. This approach recognized not only the history recorded in the books of Samuel, but also the theology of the writers which unified that history and gave it a deeper and lasting significance. Other commentaries produced dur-

26. James Barr, "Jewish Apocalyptic in Recent Scholarly Study," *Bulletin of the John Rylands Library* 58 (1975): 32–33.

27. Yehuda T. Radday, "Chiasm in Joshua, Judges and Others," *Linguistica Biblica* 3 (1973): 9.

28. Joyce Baldwin, *Esther: An Introduction and Commentary* (Downers Grove, Ill.: InterVarsity, 1984), 29.

ing retirement include *Lamentations-Daniel* for Scripture Union and *The Message of Genesis 12–50* for The Bible Speaks Today series. In addition to writing the articles on Ruth and Esther for *The New Bible Commentary: 21st Century Edition* and articles on Daniel and Naboth for the third edition of *The New Bible Dictionary*, she authored the commentary on Jonah for an exegetical series on the Minor Prophets. Only Derek Kidner has contributed more to the Tyndale Old Testament Commentaries series than has Baldwin. Throughout these years her husband Jack loyally supported her in their retirement and enabled her to continue her work.

In 1987 the first women were ordained to the diaconate of the Anglican church, and Joyce Baldwin-Caine was ordained in Bristol Cathedral as a nonstipendiary minister at Redland Parish Church. However, feeling that her "calling to ministry had been adequately fulfilled," she did not go forward for ordination to the priesthood in 1994. She was still writing, and two of her commentaries (*Esther* and *1 and 2 Samuel*) were being translated into Chinese. As she turned her face homewards from China in 1951, she could never have anticipated what lay ahead for her in Britain, "but God meant it for good" (Gen. 50:20 RSV). She had never been ambitious for promotion or advance. She was content to serve God where he put her, whether it was in China for life, or with the women at Dalton House, or with the men and women at Trinity College. There her gifts as an Old Testament scholar had blossomed and, six years before women could be ordained as deacons in the Anglican church, she found herself principal of an Anglican theological college. But her greatest personal joy before her death on December 30, 1995, was probably the knowledge that forty years after the disappointment of having to leave China with her call to serve there apparently unfulfilled, her books were going where she could not. The fruits of her scholarship would be a resource for leaders and lay Christians in the rapidly expanding Chinese church.

Primary Sources

Baldwin, Joyce. *Daniel: An Introduction and Commentary.* Tyndale Old Testament Commentaries. Downers Grove, Ill.: InterVarsity, 1978.

———. *Esther: An Introduction and Commentary.* Tyndale Old Testament Commentaries. Downers Grove, Ill.: InterVarsity, 1984.

———. *1 and 2 Samuel: An Introduction and Commentary.* Tyndale Old Testament Commentaries. Downers Grove, Ill.: InterVarsity, 1988.

———. *Haggai, Zechariah, Malachi: An Introduction and Commentary.* Tyndale Old Testament Commentaries. Downers Grove, Ill.: InterVarsity, 1972.

———. "Jonah." In *The Minor Prophets: An Exegetical and Expository Commentary,* edited by Thomas E. McComiskey, 2:543–90. Grand Rapids: Baker, 1993.

———. *Lamentations–Daniel.* Bible Study Commentary. London: Scripture Union, 1984.

———. *The Message of Genesis 12–50: From Abraham to Joseph.* The Bible Speaks Today. Downers Grove, Ill.: InterVarsity, 1986.

———. "Ruth" and "Esther." In *New Bible Commentary: 21st Century Edition*, edited by D. A. Carson et al., 287–95, 442–52. Downers Grove, Ill.: InterVarsity, 1994.

———. "Ṣemaḥ as a Technical Term in the Prophets." *Vetus Testamentum* 14.1 (1964): 93–97.

———. *Women Likewise*. London: Falcon, 1973.

———. "Women's Ministry: A New Look at the Biblical Texts." In *The Role of Women*, edited by Shirley Lees, 158–76. Leicester: Inter-Varsity, 1984.

———. *You and the Ministry*. London: Church Pastoral Aid Society, 1979.

J. Barton Payne

Philip Barton Payne

John Barton Payne was a man of great energy, delight in life, and personal devotion that infused his contributions as a Hebraist, Bible translator, author, conference speaker, and teacher. He was born on September 12, 1922, in San Francisco, the only son of Philip F. Payne and Alice Mould Payne. His father had moved from Iowa to pastor a church in San Francisco. Shortly after Barton's birth his father was elected executive of the Synod of California, Presbyterian Church in the U.S.A., and then was appointed director of Oriental missions for the Presbyterian Board of National Missions. Later, as assistant secretary of the Board of National Missions, he continued to work with Chinese, Japanese, Korean, and Filipino churches throughout the West Coast. Barton's uncle, Paul C. Payne, served as general secretary of the Board of Christian Education of the Presbyterian Church in the U.S.A. His grandfather, William B. Payne, who died when Barton was ten, had been a pastor in the Midwest.

The Years of Formal Education

At the age of sixteen Barton graduated first in the January 1939 class of 350 at Fremont High School. He then commuted every day in a Model A roadster across the foothills to the campus of the University of California at Berkeley. He worked on the rally committee, setting up the card stunts for the football games. In the fall of 1939 he felt the call to Christian ministry, but providentially he continued his ancient history major, which provided a superb background for understanding the history of salvation as revealed in the Old Testament. Under the influence of the university's InterVarsity Christian Fellowship and his family, he came to realize the extent to which the Christian faith depends on the full inspiration and authority of the Bible.

When Barton was eighteen, in May of 1941, his father was struck with Guillain-Barré syndrome, a rapid paralysis, while he was preaching. After losing sensation in his legs he sat in a chair to finish his sermon. He died a few days later, shortly after hearing that Barton was one of fifteen in his junior class of three thousand to be elected to Phi Beta Kappa. The family emergency spurred Barton to finish college half a year early in June of 1942. The rush to complete his studies did not, however, keep him from being chairman of the campus law court in his senior year. He also was appointed cadet commander of the Berkeley R.O.T.C. At nineteen, after just thirty-three months at Berkeley, he earned the B.A. degree with highest honors, graduating second in his class. His solid foundation in ancient history would have a profound influence on his subsequent teaching and writing. Although Pearl Harbor had occurred just six months before, the army allowed him to enter seminary as a civilian, following in the steps of his father, uncle, and grandfather.

In his first Old Testament class at San Francisco Theological Seminary, Barton was shocked when the professor took the class into the parking lot, tossed his Bible on the pavement, put his car jack on the Bible, and then jacked up his car on top of it! The lesson the teacher intended to drive home was that the Bible should be given no more reverence than any other book. Similar attempts by his teachers to undermine the reliability of the Old Testament was a key factor in Barton's decision to specialize in Old Testament studies.

While a student, Barton had short-term pastorates in Oakland, Glennville, Davis, and San Diego, California. In the summers he worked for the forest service and served mission churches in California and Nevada. Despite his opposition to the destructive higher criticism of the seminary faculty, he was appointed to be a teaching assistant in Hebrew in 1944–45, and in 1945 he graduated with the B.D. degree summa cum laude, the first time San Francisco Theological Seminary had awarded this honor. He also won an alumni fellowship for graduate study, but postponed using it in order to be ordained to the gospel ministry by the San Francisco Presbytery in 1945. He was installed as pastor of Fulton Presbyterian Church in Fulton, California, where he ministered in 1945–46 and even led the scout troop.

The most important event of 1946 was Barton's marriage to his sweetheart, Dorothy Dean Dosker. The couple had met at the First Presbyterian Church in Berkeley. The daughter of former missionaries to Japan with the Presbyterian Church in the U.S.A., Dorothy was the student body president of the California College of Arts and Crafts in Oakland. Her father had worked at Byron Hot Springs, a secret camp near Tracy, California, where he interviewed Japanese prisoners of war for naval intelligence. Dorothy was also the granddaughter of the renowned church historian Henry E. Dosker of Louisville Presbyterian Seminary and of Edwin M. Ellis, a pioneer Presbyterian missionary in Montana.

While pastoring the Presbyterian church at Fulton, which is near Santa Rosa, Payne pursued studies in Semitic languages at Berkeley. In the summer of 1946 he earned an M.A. degree. His 325-page thesis, "The Historicity of Ezra-Nehemiah," laid the foundation for his later work, which is remarkable for its exacting analysis of data and its confidence in the reliability of the historical accounts in the Bible.

Payne then took up his fellowship at Princeton Theological Seminary, where he completed his Th.M. in biblical literature in 1948 and his Th.D. in Old Testament in 1949, after just nine months in the Th.D. program. Frustrated by Princeton's neoorthodoxy and the supposedly assured results of higher criticism, he was convinced of the futility of trying to preach Christ apart from a belief in the full truthfulness of the Bible. To balance Princeton's perspective, he also took courses at Westminster Theological Seminary, where he particularly appreciated those taught by John Murray. Payne was appointed a teaching fellow in Old Testament Hebrew at Princeton from 1947 to 1949. His Th.M. thesis, "The Relationship of the Chester Beatty Biblical Papyri of Ezekiel to Codex Vaticanus," set the pattern for his continuing sensitivity to the implications of the original form of the text. His Th.D. dissertation, "A Critical and Comparative Study of the Sahidic Coptic Texts of the First Book of Samuel," was completed in March 1949.[1] During this period of study at Princeton two boys were born to the Paynes, John Calvin Payne and Philip Barton Payne.

Payne's final requirement for the Th.D. was a theology paper in which he expressed his statement of faith. He based his paper on Scripture alone. The paper was returned ungraded with a demand that it be written without proof-texting from Scripture. He rewrote it, this time supporting his convictions from the Westminster Confession of Faith, which was the official theological basis of Princeton Seminary at that time. Again no grade was given, nor any sign that he would pass or get a degree. Only when his name was called at graduation and he looked at his diploma did he know that his degree had been granted in spite of his belief in the complete truth of the Bible as God's Word. At this time many of today's leading evangelical institutions— the Evangelical Theological Society, Tyndale Fellowship, Institute for Biblical Research, Fuller Theological Seminary, Trinity Evangelical Divinity School, Gordon-Conwell Theological Seminary, and *Christianity Today*— either did not exist or were not yet well established. Only a few institutions were supportive of faith in the complete trustworthiness of the Scriptures.

The Years at Bob Jones University (1949–54)

Although Payne had hoped to teach at a Presbyterian seminary, word had spread that he was strongly proinerrancy, so none of those seminaries responded positively to his applications. Barton and Dorothy retreated to the Payne family cabin in Mount Hermon, California. A week before the fall semester started, Bob Jones, Sr., called Barton and asked him to teach Old Testament in the School of Religion at Bob Jones University in Greenville, South Carolina. Although he had no prior knowledge of the school, its aim to prepare missionaries and ministers appealed to him, so he accepted. Hundreds of soldiers who had returned from World War II were eager to go back as Christian missionaries to the countries where they had served. Many of them flocked to schools like Bob Jones University and Wheaton College.

---

1. The dissertation provided the basis for the subsequent article "The Sahidic Coptic Text of I Samuel," *Journal of Biblical Literature* 72 (1953): 51–62.

In 1951 Payne was appointed chairman of the graduate division's Department of Old Testament at Bob Jones. One of his chapel sermons, "A Criticism of the Revised Standard Version of the Bible," was published as a pamphlet by the university and widely distributed. It was reprinted in various journals, including *Christian Observer* and *Sword of the Lord*. It analyzed the influence of higher criticism on the Revised Standard Version and argued for a theory of translation that viewed God as inspiring all of Scripture. Moreover, since God can use a passage of Scripture to elucidate his intention in another part of Scripture, faithful translation should avoid contradictions.

Payne taught at Bob Jones for five years and saw hundreds of his students go all over the world as missionaries. Early in this period the Paynes were blessed with two more sons, Peter Ellis Payne and James Richard Payne. In addition to teaching up to twenty-seven hours of classes a semester at Bob Jones, Barton served as interim pastor at Powell Memorial Presbyterian Church in Spartanburg, South Carolina, from 1950 to 1954. He also completed his *Outline of Hebrew History*, a chronological analysis of the events in biblical history. It shows how God's plan of salvation shaped the course of the history of Israel, climaxing in Christ's "new testament" (a rendering Payne preferred to "new covenant"). Even today many still turn to the paperback reprint for solutions to confusing historical interrelationships.

The Evangelical Theological Society

Although Bob Jones University was making a major contribution to evangelical outreach around the world, some there tended to isolate themselves from other evangelicals. This made Payne careful throughout his life to avoid personal criticism of others and to focus on the central issues of the faith. Determined to foster the unity of evangelicals, he was a founding member of the Evangelical Theological Society. In 1952 he was elected chairman of its southern section. From 1955 to 1962 he was the secretary of the society, then chairman of its nominating committee in 1964, vice-president in 1965, and president in 1966. His presidential address, *"Apeitheō:* Current Resistance to Biblical Inerrancy," focused on the implications of Jesus' view that the Scriptures are totally reliable. Payne also noted that older critics like William Sanday and liberals like Frederick C. Grant concurred that in the New Testament "it is everywhere taken for granted that Scripture is trustworthy, infallible, and inerrant."[2] He concluded that disbelief in what the Bible originally taught entails disbelief in what Jesus taught. Furthermore, to love Christ is to obey him and "to commit our lives to identification with both Him and His commitments," including his commitment to the Scriptures as God's Word.[3]

2. Frederick C. Grant, *Introduction to New Testament Thought* (New York: Abingdon-Cokesbury, 1950), 75.
3. J. Barton Payne, *"Apeitheō:* Current Resistance to Biblical Inerrancy," *Bulletin of the Evangelical Theological Society* 19 (1967): 14.

Dorothy, too, played a role in the society, using her artistic skills to create the logo that has appeared on the cover of each issue of the *Bulletin of the Evangelical Theological Society* and then the *Journal of the Evangelical Theological Society*. At the center of the logo is an empty cross representing the risen Christ. Superimposed on the cross is an open Bible. At the base of the cross lies a broken sword, representing the attacks of higher criticism. Around the logo are Jesus' words from John 10:35, ΟΥ ΔΥΝΑΤΑΙ ΛΥΘΗ-ΝΑΙ Η ΓΡΑΦΗ ("the Scripture cannot be broken"). The use of Greek points to the importance of understanding God's revelation in its original form.

Payne's devotion to the development of the Evangelical Theological Society is evident in the key papers he regularly read at its annual meetings.[4] And from the very first issue of the *Bulletin* of the society he provided articles on crucial issues: "The Uneasy Conscience of Modern Liberal Exegesis," "The Imminent Appearing of Christ," "Hermeneutics as a Cloak for the Denial of Scripture," "The Unity of Isaiah: Evidence from Chapters 36–39," "The Arrangement of Jeremiah's Prophecies," "Theistic Evolution and the Hebrew of Genesis 1–2," and "Faith and History in the Old Testament."[5] Serving as editor of the third volume in the society's symposium series, he contributed an article on "The B'rith of Yahweh," focusing on the continuity of God's testament as described in the Old and New Testaments.[6] Payne also continued to contribute to the successor to the *Bulletin*, the *Journal of the Evangelical Theological Society*.[7]

The Years at Trinity and Wheaton (1954–72)

Payne's first contact with Trinity Seminary and the Evangelical Free Church occurred in December 1953, when the national meeting of the Evangelical Theological Society was held at Trinity. In April of 1954 the Trinity board extended him a call to chair the Old Testament department, where he taught from 1954 to 1959 and again from 1970 to 1972. Transferring his ordination to the Evangelical Free Church, Payne became active as a Bible teacher, deacon, and then elder at the Wheaton Evangelical Free Church. In 1963 he helped to found the Naperville Evangelical Free Church, where he taught the adult Sunday school class and served as pulpit supply until Paul Cedar was called as pastor.

---

4. E.g., J. Barton Payne, "The Revised Standard Version of the Old Testament and Higher Criticism," *Papers Read at the Annual Meeting of the Evangelical Theological Society* 5 (1952): 6–10; idem, "So-Called Dual Fulfillment in Messianic Psalms," *Papers Read* 6 (1953): 62–71; idem, "Hosea's Family Prophecies and the Kingdom," *Papers Read* 7 (1954): 11–21; idem, "The Church and Zionism in the Predictive Cycles of Zechariah 9–14," *Papers Read* 9 (1956): 55–68.

5. See, respectively, *Bulletin of the Evangelical Theological Society* 1.1 (1958): 14–18; 2.3 (1959): 8–13; 3.4 (1960): 93–99; 6 (1963): 50–56; 7 (1964): 120–30; 8 (1965): 85–90; and 11 (1968): 111–20.

6. J. Barton Payne, "The B'rith of Yahweh," in *New Perspectives on the Old Testament*, ed. J. Barton Payne (Waco: Word, 1970), 240–64.

7. E.g., J. Barton Payne, "Partial Omniscience: Observations on Limited Inerrancy," *Journal of the Evangelical Theological Society* 18 (1975): 37–40.

Each summer Barton drove his family out to Mount Hermon, so his mother could read to the children and enjoy the family. While there he regularly taught the Anchor Class at the nearby Felton Evangelical Free Church. When away from his mother, he wrote her a long letter each week without fail until her death at age eighty-five.

Barton would eagerly accept as a challenge what others said was impossible. On the summer trip to California in 1957 he hiked with his three oldest boys from the South Rim to the North Rim of the Grand Canyon in one day, even though experienced hikers were advised to take two days. Two days later he climbed Mount Whitney with his oldest son. He succeeded in climbing Mount Olympus in Greece. He departed solo, but joined a climbing group he met on the way. His willingness to attempt what others said was impossible was also evident in the decades of study he devoted to resolving the complexities of biblical prophecy.

In 1958 the family was delighted by the birth of Paula Patience Payne. In that same year Barton accepted an invitation to become professor of Old Testament at Wheaton College Graduate School of Theology, where he taught for fourteen years. For the first year, 1958–59, and the last two years, 1970–72, he taught full-time at both Trinity and Wheaton. At both schools he was a beloved teacher. Wesley Pippert, a correspondent for United Press International, commented: "I loved him. He was the best teacher I ever had, unquestionably, and his courses did more to shape my adult life than almost anything." He put the rules of Hebrew grammar into a form resembling the lyrics of popular songs and had students memorize a key verse that encapsulated the message of each Old Testament book. He always returned his students' papers within twenty-four hours of their being handed in, even if that meant grading all night. This practice not only proved valuable to the students in that the material was fresh in their minds, but it also freed him to be more creative, since it cleared his desk and allowed him to focus on other projects. He was so dedicated to teaching that in his entire career he never missed a class, not even when he was afflicted with dysentery in Jordan.

During his early years in the Chicago area Payne published his *Hebrew Vocabularies,* lists of the most common words in the Hebrew Scriptures. Reprinted frequently, it has helped generations of students to learn Hebrew. He also translated 2 Samuel and 1 Chronicles for the Berkeley Version. He served as a translator for the New American Standard Bible as well.

Published in 1962, Payne's *Theology of the Older Testament* soon became a standard textbook for courses in Old Testament theology. This book is actually an adventure to read. The work focuses on the continuity of God's revelation of his testament with humankind, which was fully effected by the death of Christ, the New Testament not displacing the Old, but building on and fulfilling God's older testament. *Theology of the Older Testament* unfolds God's eternal plan for salvation in a way that has brought it to life for generations of students.

Also in 1962 Payne published his groundbreaking work *The Imminent Appearing of Christ*. In explaining the different views on the tribulation, he focused on three key propositions which many believe the Bible teaches. The problem here is that if any two of them are true, the third cannot be true.[8] First is the hope of the imminent coming of Christ. The Bible teaches that believers should live as though Christ might come at any time. Consequently, biblical eschatology should accommodate at least the possibility that Christ's return could be imminent. Second is the expectation of a unified appearing of Christ. That Christ's second coming will be visible to the world is suggested by the word "appearing" (ἐπιφάνεια) in 1 Timothy 6:14; Titus 2:13; and 2 Thessalonians 2:8. The last of these verses equates his "appearing" with his "coming," his παρουσία. This appearing is consistently described as one event, not as two separate events, for example, a secret rapture followed by a later appearing. The third commonly believed proposition is that some things must still occur before Christ's coming. If this is true, either imminency or the unified appearing of Christ must be jettisoned.

The first two propositions, imminency and the unified appearing of Christ, are affirmed by classical posttribulationism. This view fits all the biblical data if everything which the Bible predicts will occur prior to Christ's coming either could have already occurred or could occur so quickly that imminency would not be compromised. This view is reasonable since there is considerable difference of opinion both as to what must happen before Christ returns and whether it may already have been adequately fulfilled. However, some posttribulationists ("reacting posttribulationists") have jettisoned imminency because they believe that some events must still occur before Christ's coming. Dispensational pretribulationists likewise believe that some events must still occur before Christ's coming. To retain the hope of imminency they are forced to separate the final appearing of Christ from an earlier secret rapture.

Payne argued that it is preferable to acknowledge the ambiguity about what the Bible predicts will precede Christ's return and to be open to the possibility that these events may already have happened than either to jettison the hope of imminent union with Christ or to interpret as separate events what the Bible describes as the unified appearing of Christ. Since, however, it is possible, or even probable, that some predicted events have not yet happened, Barton preferred the designation "potentially-past-tribulationism." Both pretribulationism and midtribulationism, he noted, sacrifice the hope of Christ's unified appearing "immediately after the tribulation of those days" (Matt. 24:29–31; Mark 13:24–27 KJV) in order to preserve their expectation of prolonged future antecedents to his advent and possibly also to avoid the prospect of going through the tribulation. Midtribulationism in general also sacrifices the hope of Christ's imminent appearing.

8. J. Barton Payne, *The Imminent Appearing of Christ* (Grand Rapids: Eerdmans, 1962), 157.

Payne was invited to speak at many prophecy conferences, where his lectures proved refreshingly coherent and irenic. It was his policy in these lectures not to label or even identify his own view, but simply to highlight the key themes and practical implications of biblical prophecy. He was careful to point out the scriptural support for each of the major viewpoints, and stressed the practical impact that prophecy should have on our lives. Thus he played a key role in fostering mutual respect between proponents of differing eschatological viewpoints.

Payne was also a member of the Near East Archaeological Society. During his time at Wheaton he joined Joseph Free and others in archaeological expeditions at Dothan, at Tekoa, and on the Jerusalem wall. He was guest professor at the Near East School of Archaeological and Biblical Studies in Jordan in 1964. Dorothy and all five of the children had the privilege of being at Dothan for the spring term of 1964, the year Bob Cooley uncovered one of the most productive tombs ever found in Palestine, with over three thousand objects spanning the Early and Middle Bronze periods. The children were amazed at their father's grasp of Palestinian geography and history as he corrected errors made by tour guides and brought the historical significance of remains like Hezekiah's tunnel to life. After the excavation he took the family on a three-month-long camping exploration of virtually all the countries of Europe. His enthusiasm and careful preparation, his encyclopedic knowledge of European history and geography, and facility in French and German combined to open up whole new worlds to the family as they visited unforgettable museums, cities, and countrysides. In 1968 and 1971 Payne was the director of the Wheaton Summer Institute of Biblical Studies in Israel; in this capacity he arranged for and led insightful field trips of the excavation under Saint Peter's Basilica in Rome, the great pyramids, and sites from Dan to Mount Sinai.

When Kenneth Kantzer became dean of Trinity Evangelical Divinity School (formerly Trinity Seminary), he invited Payne back. So from 1970 to 1972 Barton again taught full-time at both Wheaton and Trinity. During this period he was instrumental in the International Council on Biblical Inerrancy and served on the committee that drafted "The Chicago Statement on Biblical Inerrancy." This statement affirms that the autographic text of Scripture "is of infallible divine authority in all matters upon which it touches: It is to be believed, as God's instruction, in all that it affirms; obeyed, as God's command, in all that it requires; embraced, as God's pledge, in all that it promises." It affirms progressive revelation, with later revelation fulfilling, but not contradicting, earlier revelation. It affirms that "God in His work of inspiration utilized [but did not override] the distinctive personalities and literary styles of the writers whom He had chosen and prepared." It affirms that it is improper "to evaluate Scripture according to standards of truth and error that are alien to its usage or purpose," such as modern technical precision. Consequently, "irregularities of grammar or spelling, observational descriptions of nature, the reporting of falsehoods, the use of hyperbole and round numbers, the topical arrangement of material, variant selections of material in parallel accounts, [and] the use of free citations" do not undermine inerrancy. The statement also affirms "grammatico-historical exegesis, taking account of [Scripture's] literary forms and devices."[9] James Boice later assessed Payne's contributions to the work of the International Council on Biblical Inerrancy as being "of great value." Indeed, the council's symposium on *Inerrancy: The Extent of Biblical Authority* was dedicated to him.[10]

The Years at Covenant Theological Seminary (1972–79)

After Wheaton dropped its B.D. program, Barton accepted an invitation to become professor of Old Testament at Covenant Theological Seminary because he wanted to focus his energies on training pastors and missionaries. Returning to his Presbyterian roots, he transferred his ordination to the Reformed Presbyterian Church, Evangelical Synod, and was appointed to its administrative committee in 1973–74. In 1973 he also began to serve as a member of the judicial committee and the fraternal relations committee, of which he was appointed secretary. In this position he fostered closer ties to other Presbyterian and Reformed denominations. In 1974 he was appointed a member of the magazine committee, and in 1975 he joined the North American Presbyterian and Reformed Council. He enjoyed the collegiality of the Covenant faculty and their mutual commitment to God-centered theology, firm grounding in the authority of Scripture, and focus on preparing men and women for church ministries at home and abroad. His *What Is a Reformed Presbyterian?* outlines the history and central beliefs of the denomination.

In 1973 Payne's magnum opus, *Encyclopedia of Biblical Prophecy: The Complete Guide to Scriptural Predictions and Their Fulfillment,* was published along with its companion, *Prophecy Map of World History.* The culmination of over twenty years of research and writing, this achievement was made possible by Barton's encyclopedic knowledge of the Bible, Hebrew, and history. The project was undertaken to help bring understanding and consensus to a topic that has been the basis for a great deal of division within the evangelical community. The whole area is arguably the most difficult and most misunderstood part of hermeneutics. Many people simply skip over predictive material because they do not understand the historical context and do not know whether the predictions have been fulfilled. A huge amount of Scripture is, as a consequence, inadequately understood. The comprehensive analysis of biblical prophecy that the *Encyclopedia* provides significantly reinforces confidence in the reliability of the Scriptures. The statistical appendix points out that 27 percent of the Bible contains predictive proph-

9. "The Chicago Statement on Biblical Inerrancy," *Journal of the Evangelical Theological Society* 21 (1978): 290–95.
10. *Inerrancy: The Extent of Biblical Authority,* ed. Norman L. Geisler (Grand Rapids: Zondervan, 1980).

ecy: 8,352 out of the total of 31,124 verses.[11] Even excluding types, 5,457 verses make 737 separate predictions. The major focus of prophecies throughout Scripture is on Christ. The life of Christ on earth is the subject of 127 predictions (82 nontypical and 45 typical) involving 3,348 verses (574 nontypical and 2,774 typical). Twenty-nine books of the Bible prophesy Christ's second coming, and twenty books prophesy his future rule over the earth.

Also during the Covenant years Payne translated parts of the Old Testament for the New International Version. As chairman of the general editorial committee he spent many summers in places like Saint Andrews University, Athens, and Salamanca, Spain, carefully going over every clause, phrase, and word of the Old Testament. Each word in the translation was argued and then voted on. His skills in interpersonal relations and communication were crucial in bridging the tens of thousands of differences of opinion that were expressed. His arguments and collegial spirit usually prevailed. Edwin Palmer, the executive secretary of the project, said of him, "I liked him, especially on those long editorial sessions. When I had some particularly knotty problems, I turned to Barton." It was with great joy that Barton saw the complete New International Version published in 1978. Its simplicity and clarity of language have helped millions of readers to understand the Scriptures. Its dignity has made it a widely used pulpit Bible.

An amazingly prolific writer, Payne's final major work was his commentary on 1 and 2 Chronicles for *The Expositor's Bible Commentary*. It provides satisfying solutions to many of the historical questions regarding these two books and highlights their theological content. This expository work capped a career in which he authored twelve books as well as scholarly contributions for upwards of thirty journals and twenty major reference volumes. In addition, Payne served as one of the editors of *The Encyclopedia of Christianity* and *The Zondervan Pictorial Bible Atlas*.[12]

Payne taught in public lectures that the Bible does not exclude women from any form of ministry. During his final missionary trip in 1979 to lecture at seminaries throughout Asia, he encouraged his wife Dorothy to teach the course on the Gospel of John at the Presbyterian Theological Seminary in Dera Dun, India. Following their time in India, Barton lectured in Taiwan, Hong Kong, Korea, and Japan, stressing the dual themes of biblical authority and communication of the gospel in word and deed. The lectures in Japan made such an impact that scores of students, faculty, pastors, and missionaries came to search for him when he failed to return from a solo climb up Mount Fuji. After his body was found in a dangerous part of the mountain,

11. J. Barton Payne, *Encyclopedia of Biblical Prophecy: The Complete Guide to Scriptural Predictions and Their Fulfillment* (New York: Harper and Row, 1973), 674–75.
12. *The Encyclopedia of Christianity*, ed. Edwin H. Palmer, 4 vols. (Wilmington, Del.: National Foundation for Christian Education, 1964–72); *The Zondervan Pictorial Bible Atlas*, ed. E. M. Blaiklock (Grand Rapids: Zondervan, 1969).

a professor told Dorothy, "We will never forget what your husband has taught us, especially after this experience."

On hearing of Payne's death Bruce Waltke wrote to Laird Harris, "We have lost a great man." Harris wrote, "It was a comfort to be able to turn to a capable colleague trained in the necessary languages, Sumerian, Akkadian, Egyptian, Arabic, as well as the biblical languages, to ask a question, test a theory or just to share some interesting observation. Barton had studied them all and with characteristic industry would look up every problem, follow out every lead and would have a helpful word, carefully considered and sure to be biblical in approach." The breadth of his collegiality was reflected in the letters of tribute sent from leaders of many of the evangelical seminaries in the United States. Robert Rayburn said, "I greatly admired his magnificent intellect and the wonderful gifts the Lord gave him. Moreover, I deeply appreciated his willingness always to help out when needed." Barton Payne was that rare combination of true genius with the humble spirit of a servant.

Payne's keen missionary spirit grew from his deep personal devotion and belief that faith in Christ is the only foundation for eternal salvation. Every day he would read and meditate on a chapter from the Hebrew Old Testament and a chapter from the Greek New Testament. The thoughts that God impressed on him during the day's reading were recorded in a notebook covering every chapter of the Bible. Following his reading and meditation he would kneel on a thin foam seat-cushion and pray. His children often found him kneeling in prayer. This personal devotional life overflowed to family devotions as well. The whole family ate breakfast and dinner together, beginning with a prayer of blessing. They read one chapter from the New Testament after breakfast and one from the Old Testament after dinner, each reading in turn around the table. Barton always gave an extemporaneous translation from the Greek or Hebrew text. When the children were old enough to study foreign languages, he encouraged them to try to translate their verses from a French, German, or Greek Bible. Questions were always welcome during these readings. After the reading the meal was closed with prayers of thanks. Both Barton and Dorothy were delighted to see their children grow up into dedicated Christians. Their missionary involvement has been diverse: John in medical missions in inner-city Chicago, Phil in France and Japan, Peter in Mexico and with InterVarsity's graduate-student ministry, and Patty in Russia and with InterVarsity's graduate-student ministry. This is a legacy every bit as rich as the writings Barton Payne left to the Christian world.

Primary Sources

J. Barton Payne. *Biblical Prophecy for Today*. Grand Rapids: Baker, 1978.

———. *Encyclopedia of Biblical Prophecy: The Complete Guide to Scriptural Predictions and Their Fulfillment*. New York: Harper and Row, 1973.

———. "1, 2 Chronicles." In *The Expositor's Bible Commentary,* ed. Frank E. Gaebelein, 4:303–562. Grand Rapids: Zondervan, 1988.

———. *Hebrew Vocabularies.* Grand Rapids: Baker, 1956.

———. *The Imminent Appearing of Christ.* Grand Rapids: Eerdmans, 1962.

———. *An Outline of Hebrew History.* Grand Rapids: Baker, 1954.

———. *Prophecy Map of World History.* New York: Harper and Row, 1973.

———. *Theology of the Older Testament.* Grand Rapids: Zondervan, 1962.

———, ed. *New Perspectives on the Old Testament.* Waco: Word, 1970.

Ralph Philip Martin

Michael J. Wilkins

Biblical scholars regularly pay lip service to the need not only to contribute to the academic community, but also to serve the church with their scholarship. But in practice the results of scholarly efforts often are deemed incomprehensible or irrelevant by clergy and laypersons. However, some biblical scholars not only intend to, but actually do serve both the academy and the church. Such an individual is Ralph P. Martin, whom students, fellow scholars, and clergy alike recognize as a scholar in service of the church. Typical is Gerald Hawthorne's festschrift characterization of Martin as "a beloved man who has devoted his life to the ministry of the church through his faith in God, his love and care for his family, his parish work, his writings, his teaching and his pastoral concern for his many students. . . . [His] very life incarnates the concept of ministry in and to the church."[1] Hawthorne's heartfelt words reflect a consensus of those who know the person and the work.

Ralph Philip Martin was born in Anfield, Liverpool, England, on August 4, 1925, to Philip and Ada Martin.[2] He received his early education at the Anfield Road School and then at the Liverpool Collegiate. When war broke out in 1939, Ralph was evacuated along with his classmates to Bangor, North Wales, for several months. A little over a year after returning to Liverpool, Martin left school at sixteen to work in an insurance office.

About this time two young women, Lily Nelson and her sister Eva, began attending the Anfield Methodist Church, which Ralph had attended since childhood. The young women invited Ralph to the monthly Saturday evening "squash meetings" of the Young Life Campaign. On February 6, 1943, after four months of exposure to the simple gospel message proclaimed at these meetings and through the guidance of an older man, W. J. Wilson, he made a public profession of faith in Jesus Christ as his Savior.

---

1. Gerald F. Hawthorne, "Faith: The Essential Ingredient of Effective Christian Ministry," in *Worship, Theology and Ministry in the Early Church: Essays in Honor of Ralph P. Martin*, ed. Michael J. Wilkins and Terence Paige, Journal for the Study of the New Testament Supplement 87 (Sheffield: JSOT, 1992), 249.

2. The biographical information in this article is based largely upon the curriculum vitae provided by Lynn A. Losie and other essays in *Worship, Theology and Ministry*. Among those supplying personal information were Losie, Martin's son-in-law; James Tootill, Martin's longtime friend; and Leslie C. Allen, Martin's colleague on both sides of the Atlantic.

Martin soon felt God's call to the ministry and began preparing to attend Manchester Methodist College. But a growing conviction concerning the doctrine of believers' baptism led him to consider affiliating with the Baptists. Called up to serve the war effort as a "Bevan boy" in the coal mines of Lancashire, Martin made his decision to join the Baptists and was baptized by the Rev. H. S. Phillips at the Aenon Baptist Church, Burnley.

The Early Years: Pastor and Professor

After three years of service in the mines, Ralph was released and began training for the pastorate at Manchester Baptist College, earning a degree in theology from the University of Manchester (with distinction). Because of an administrative oversight he was unaware that he had won a scholarship to Cambridge University, so he entered the Baptist ministry in 1949. He was ordained at the Kendal Road Baptist Church, Gloucester, inaugurating his ministry with a sermon on the "unswerving conviction," "unfailing communion," and "unshakable confidence" expressed in Psalm 16:8. It was also at this time that Martin married Lily Nelson, through whose influence he had come to a deeper spiritual commitment and who shared his desire for Christian service. In time the family expanded to four with the birth of two daughters, Patricia and Elizabeth. After four years in Gloucester, Martin moved to a pastorate at the West Street Baptist Church in Dunstable, Bedfordshire.

During ten years of pastoral work, Martin continued to pursue further academic training. Under the supervision of T. W. Manson he earned an M.A. from the University of Manchester. His M.A. thesis, "Eucharistic Teaching in 1 Corinthians," set him on a course to emphasize aspects of worship in the early church and to become one of the leading students of the apostle Paul's writings. During this time Martin completed a commentary on Paul's Epistle to the Philippians.[3]

These accomplishments did not go unnoticed. In 1959 Martin was invited to become a lecturer in theology at the London Bible College, a post he held from 1959 to 1965. Leslie Allen, one of his colleagues during those years of teaching at London Bible College, recalls this period:

Although his heart was in the New Testament, unfortunately there was no opportunity to teach it at that time. He taught Systematic Theology. It was rumored that he had mistaken his assignment for Historical Theology. Students groaned under the papers on Luther and Calvin they had to produce. The subject was a supposedly easier "college" course rather than part of the academic curriculum they had to take for their University of London degree, but it was difficult for them to spot the difference. However, they grudgingly acknowledged that Dr. Martin got to the root of the matter and that it was

3. Ralph P. Martin, *The Epistle of Paul to the Philippians: An Introduction and Commentary,* Tyndale New Testament Commentaries 11 (Grand Rapids: Eerdmans, 1959).

doing them good. If he has made heavy demands on his students, it is because he has always made such demands on himself as a perpetual student.[4]

And Martin indeed did not spare the demands on himself. While serving at London Bible College as lecturer in theology, and college librarian to boot, Martin finished his Ph.D. at King's College, University of London, under the supervision of D. E. Nineham. The focus of his research—Philippians 2:5–11—would eventually bring him international acclaim. Technical analysis had attempted to arrange this early Christian hymn into stanzas and strophes. Martin especially appreciated what he considered the revolutionary analysis carried out by Ernst Lohmeyer and later by Ernst Käsemann.[5] Following their lead in part, Martin delineated how early Christian hymnology grew out of an appreciation for the person of Christ and played a distinct role in shaping Christology, while giving a response to pressing pastoral needs in the early Christian communities. This research was finalized in his doctoral thesis, "Philippians ii:5–11 in Recent Interpretation and in the Setting of Early Christian Worship."

Martin eventually moved to the University of Manchester to teach at last New Testament in F. F. Bruce's department. During his years at Manchester (1965–69), Martin established himself firmly as one of the significant figures in New Testament studies. His doctoral thesis was one of the first volumes published in the Society for New Testament Studies monograph series. Even as the series was destined to become a prestigious voice for New Testament studies, so Martin's *Carmen Christi* would become a classic treatment of the Philippians passage and early Christian hymnology in general.[6]

A Pastor's Teacher

But Ralph Martin's pastoral heart was never far removed from the church. Even while he was providing leadership within the scholarly community with his research and writing, he was at the same time bringing his research to bear upon the life of the church, especially its liturgical life. He became a teacher for pastors who wanted sound scholarly insights into the world of the New Testament.

A series of Bible studies for the weekly British paper *The Life of Faith* was revised and expanded to produce the book *Worship in the Early Church*. Although he did not intend it as a practical guide to meet contemporary needs, Martin did offer it as an attempt to unfold the teaching of the New Testa-

---

4. Leslie C. Allen, "Personal Reminiscences," in *Worship, Theology and Ministry*, ed. Wilkins and Paige, 33.

5. Ernst Lohmeyer, *Kyrios Jesus: Eine Untersuchung zu Phil. 2,5–11* (Heidelberg: Carl Winters, 1928); Ernst Käsemann, "Kritische Analyse von Phil. 2. 5–11," *Zeitschrift für Theologie und Kirche* 47 (1950): 313–60.

6. Ralph P. Martin, *Carmen Christi: Philippians ii.5–11 in Recent Interpretation and in the Setting of Early Christian Worship*, Society for New Testament Studies Monograph 4 (Cambridge: Cambridge University Press, 1967).

ment so as "to quicken a practical concern in the life and worship of our Churches today."[7]

Martin early in his career set a high standard for his scholarly work, and that personal demand allowed him to bring the heart of the New Testament message to nonscholars. William Barclay insightfully observed, when reviewing Martin's commentary on Philippians in the Tyndale series, "We think that the warmth of this letter created a warmth in the heart of Mr. Martin as he worked on this book, for it is certainly written *con amore*. For the reader who cannot work from the Greek text there is no better commentary on Philippians than this volume, short as it is."[8]

The Fuller Years and Beyond

International acclaim for Martin's scholarship soon called him to leave Manchester to cross the Atlantic to take a position in the United States at Fuller Theological Seminary in Pasadena, California. Germany had been the leading center of New Testament studies for much of the twentieth century, but the center increasingly was shifting from Germany to Britain and to the United States. Martin's career is reflective of that shift.

Ralph Martin was professor of New Testament at Fuller from 1969 to 1988, the major part of his academic career. Fuller was just twenty years old, but it was rapidly gaining a reputation as a leader in theological education, research, and publication. Martin's tenure at Fuller contributed to that reputation, and he shared in its unfolding as an eminent evangelical institution.

Fuller had been founded with the purpose, at least in part, of countering an anti-intellectualism found in certain quarters of American fundamentalism.[9] The first generation of faculty members included some of the leading scholars in American evangelicalism: Carl Henry, Edward John Carnell, Wilbur M. Smith, Everett Harrison, Gleason Archer, Harold Lindsell, George Eldon Ladd, William LaSor, and Paul King Jewett. The second generation of faculty continued to expand the school's academic influence by drawing upon British scholarship: Ralph Martin, Geoffrey Bromiley, Colin Brown, Leslie Allen. The British scholars helped to take Fuller into an international leadership position in scholarly studies.

British evangelicalism had not been divided over some of the issues, such as inerrancy, that rocked American evangelicalism. The newer British faculty seemed somewhat immune to the controversies. For example, Geoffrey Bromiley, the first of the British connection to go to Fuller, benefited from a sort of diplomatic immunity even during the storm that broke out with the appointment of David Allan Hubbard as president. In George Marsden's

7. Ralph P. Martin, *Worship in the Early Church* (Westwood, N.J.: Revell, 1964), 4–5.
8. William Barclay, review of *The Epistle of Paul to the Philippians*, by Ralph P. Martin, *Expository Times* 71 (1960): 334–35.
9. George M. Marsden, *Understanding Fundamentalism and Evangelicalism* (Grand Rapids: Eerdmans, 1991), 72.

documentary of the early Fuller years and the doctrinal controversies of the sixties and seventies, no mention is made of the British faculty's being controversial. However, the second-generation American faculty members at Fuller (e.g., David Hubbard, Daniel Fuller, Robert Meye, Lewis Smedes, Donald Hagner, and Richard Muller) did include some who were at the heart of the controversy (e.g., Jack Rogers).[10]

In spite of the controversies that surrounded Fuller's unfolding as an institution, Martin came into full maturity as a New Testament scholar and played an increasingly significant role. In 1979 he was appointed director of Fuller's burgeoning graduate studies program. Martin's leadership in the graduate program came at a critical time. Built on a combination of British and American models, the program increasingly attracted doctoral students from all over the world. It also provided the opportunity to attract faculty members who would become the basis of Fuller's future.

Martin left Fuller in 1988 to return to England. He was in semiretirement, but served part-time in the Department of Biblical Studies at the University of Sheffield. He also served a pastoral role at Norwood Avenue Baptist Church, Southport, Lancashire. These were difficult personal years for Martin. Two of his grandchildren had suffered tragic accidents in the United States, and his beloved wife Lily had been in ill health for several years. The return to England allowed them to have her treated in their homeland, but in 1995 Lily passed away. Lily's ill health had weighed heavily upon Ralph, as had the tragic accidents of his two grandchildren. Yet out of his own personal suffering came some of the depth reflected in his scholarly work. His emphases upon the worship and centrality of Christ were not merely academic; they were basic realities in his own life.

"Doxological Theology"

On the occasion of his appointment to the faculty at Sheffield in 1988 Ralph Martin gave an inaugural lecture. In the opening section of that lecture he coined an expression that encapsulates his lifelong contributions: "doxological theology."[11] Since theology is the doctrine of God and doxology is the praise of God, doxological theology is the doctrine of God that emerged out of the worshiping life of the early church. The focus on doxological theology moved his New Testament research away from speculation, away from purely academic studies, to see how it relates to the ongoing life of the church and its worship. His initial interest in Philippians 2:6–11 and the way in which the Bible functions in the life of the church liturgically had carried him

10. George M. Marsden, *Reforming Fundamentalism: Fuller Seminary and the New Evangelicalism* (Grand Rapids: Eerdmans, 1987), 277–98. It is noteworthy that Martin's name does not appear in the index, even though he had been at Fuller for several years when Harold Lindsell's *Battle for the Bible* (Grand Rapids: Zondervan, 1976) initiated the "last battle with fundamentalism."

11. Ralph P. Martin, interview with Steven Felder, Feb. 1995, Talbot School of Theology, La Mirada, Calif.

into the whole area of early Christian hymnology and liturgical materials in the New Testament.

A related main endeavor throughout Martin's career has been to discover how Christology arose. The worshiping life of the early congregations gave definition to the person and work of Christ, because they appreciated who he was and what he had done, beliefs they expressed in their worship. This theory impacted Martin's understanding of New Testament Christology: hymns helped shape Christology.

The fact that Paul quoted hymns, and the way he did so, suggests that he was sharing familiar material with the early Christian communities; he was not introducing something new. Further, when Paul took over hymnic or traditional material, he did not always leave it as it was, but he edited it so that it became relevant to the needs of the particular congregations in mind. Martin sees an editorial process going on in, for example, Philippians 2:6–11; Colossians 1:15–20; and 1 Timothy 3:16.[12] Paul made the traditional truth relevant to his purposes and the needs of the community, sometimes by way of correction of their ideas about the person of Christ.

Martin's emphasis upon doxological theology has compelling significance for modern worship as well. Bruce Shelley observes that "Martin's aim is to help ministers and seminarians to think theologically about worship and to apply this thinking to their own situations."[13] While Martin emphasizes that there is no one prevailing form of worship in the New Testament, there are certain guidelines. These guidelines or features of early Christian worship are also to be seen in the second-century church, and offer a picture and paradigm to us today. Those features of early Christian worship are (1) the presence of the living Lord in the midst of his own (Matt. 18:20; 28:20); (2) the pervasive influence of the Holy Spirit (Phil. 3:3); and (3) a concern for upbuilding, which has three components—charismatic, didactic, and eucharistic. These features characterize communities that worship in unity to glorify God and seek the welfare of the whole fellowship of the church.[14]

So, Martin stresses, if we are looking for patterns of worship, we have nothing in the New Testament comparable with the services that developed in later church history. But we do have certain fundamental ideas that were emphasized in early synagogue practice: the holiness of God, the election of Israel, praise of God, the reading and expounding of Scripture, and care for the needy and poor. The very earliest Christians of whom we have knowledge were Jews who, when they became messianic believers, brought with them not only the cardinal doctrines of their faith—the oneness of God, the essentiality of the Word—but also their patterns of synagogue worship that

---

12. Ralph P. Martin, *Carmen Christi*, 297–311; idem, *New Testament Foundations: A Guide for Christian Students*, 2 vols. (Grand Rapids: Eerdmans, 1975, 1978), 2:251–75; idem, *Reconciliation: A Study of Paul's Theology* (Atlanta: John Knox, 1981), 71–89.

13. Bruce Shelley, review of *The Worship of God*, by Ralph P. Martin, *Leadership* 4.1 (Winter 1983): 55.

14. Martin, *Worship in the Early Church*, rev. ed. (Grand Rapids: Eerdmans, 1974), 130–40.

had been set by the ancestral faith, like reciting the creed and the *Shema* in each service, prayers and praise, the reading and exposition of Scripture.[15] Those elements are perennial; they are built into the legacy that has been bequeathed to us today.

Scholarship in the Service of the Church

A recurring theme echoes from those who have been acquainted with Ralph Martin during his career. I. Howard Marshall captured well the essence of this theme: Martin "has always seen his task as a scholar in terms of service to the gospel and the church."[16] This requires a balance between scholarship and service, between academic and spiritual growth. Martin himself would periodically refer to the need for such a balance: "A perennial question that is sure to surface in an institution of academic research and study such as Fuller (especially in the Graduate Studies Program) is one that runs like this: how does the student strike a balance between scholarship and spirituality? With a rightful concern with rigorously technical and academic pursuits, how may we attend to the needs of spiritual development and nurture?"[17] Colleagues, students, and friends all attest that Martin's remarkable synthesis of extraordinary scholarship, sincere devotion, and pastoral concern embodies the answer to his question. Even those outside of evangelical circles have been struck by this synthesis. Florence Gillman, for example, notes "three areas of broad interest that Martin has been concerned with synthesizing in his distinguished scholarship: the worship, theology, and ministry of early Christianity. These concerns mirror a merger between scholarship and spirituality in Martin's own life through his dedication to devotion, his wide-ranging, meticulous scholarship, and his continuous pastoral involvement."[18]

Scholar

As a scholar, Martin is exemplary in his attempt to be objective and to apply consistent methods of exegesis. His essay "Approaches to New Testament Exegesis" advocates a balanced, well-rounded approach to the text of the New Testament.[19] As my doctoral mentor, Professor Martin guided me through the intricacies of Gospel research. While he did not always agree fully with some of my methodological approaches and conclusions, he supported my work if I in turn solidly supported my case. I remember well one

15. Ibid., 18–27.
16. I. Howard Marshall, "The Parousia in the New Testament—and Today," in *Worship, Theology and Ministry*, ed. Wilkins and Paige, 194.
17. Ralph P. Martin, in *Occasional Bulletin of the Graduate Studies Program [Fuller Theological Seminary]* 7.2 (Jan. 1986): 1.
18. Florence M. Gillman, review of *Worship, Theology and Ministry in the Early Church*, edited by Michael J. Wilkins and Terence Paige, *Catholic Biblical Quarterly* 56 (1994): 626–27.
19. Ralph P. Martin, "Approaches to New Testament Exegesis," in *New Testament Interpretation: Essays on Principles and Methods*, ed. I. Howard Marshall (Grand Rapids: Eerdmans, 1977), 220–51.

doctoral seminar in which I rather simplistically made an assumption about a passage. In his quietly dignified manner he roundly scolded me for having assumed, not established, my point. But when I laid out my support in a later paper, Martin commended me, even though he did not take my position. His colleague Leslie Allen says, "He was—and is—never one to pursue a safe path because it was the right view for conservatives to hold, but would leave no stone unturned in his quest for exegetical truth and in his fair assessment of any proposal, regardless of its source."[20]

Martin is also remarkably well-rounded as a New Testament scholar, something which is increasingly rare in this age of specialization. In addition to being a leading authority on the range of New Testament topics and literature, he has expertise in Herodian Judaism, the Greco-Roman world, and patristics.

Service to the Church

A chord often struck in Martin's writings is the link between biblical studies and the living faith of the contemporary church. Perhaps because of his own involvement in the life of the church during much of his career, Martin has a sensitivity for ways in which biblical studies can be concretely applied to the church today. He is also acutely aware of the dangers of misapplication.

Another consistent note one finds in many of Martin's works is that he writes from a scholarly, yet a distinctly Christian confessional point of view. Thus when a reviewer objected that the first volume of *New Testament Foundations* stood between "the competing claims of scholarly objectivity and Christian commitment," Martin responded, "That no neutral stance was intended should have been clear. . . . My conviction remains that New Testament study is of special relevance to those who stand within the household of Christian faith. But this conviction is not to be interpreted in any narrow sectarian or exclusive fashion."[21]

Scholarly service to the church is not an easy balance to maintain, nor is it always appreciated. Thus though well-equipped to offer advice to pastors, teachers, and students on the selection of library resources, Martin has been criticized for allowing his "bias toward critical studies" to influence his recommendations.[22] Or consider the case of a reviewer of Martin's *Worship of God* who appreciated greatly his presenting "the biblical, theological, and historical rationale behind all the main constituents of worship, thus providing an excellent text book for those in training for the Ministry . . . it would make a splendid basis for discussion in many a ministers' fraternal. . . . It sets high standards for those who are called to lead God's people in their worship. Short shrift is given to cheap and superficial attitudes."[23] This same re-

20. Allen, "Personal Reminiscences," 33.
21. Martin, *New Testament Foundations,* 2:x.
22. Douglas J. Moo, review of *New Testament Books for Pastor and Teacher,* by Ralph P. Martin, *Journal of the Evangelical Theological Society* 28 (1985): 238–39.
23. John Wood, review of *The Worship of God,* by Ralph P. Martin, *Evangelical Quarterly* 57 (Oct. 1985): 80.

viewer, however, takes Martin to task: "Martin's denial that the early Church was anxious to preserve the words of the Lord as sacred *ipsissima verba,* requires some qualification." Martin himself qualifies this statement by contending that the church preserved not the *ipsissima verba,* but the *ipsissima vox.*[24] To appreciate Martin's balance requires a measure of theological sophistication not possessed by every Christian.

Another mark of Martin's service is that throughout his academic career in England and the United States he has ministered in local churches. He has frequently served as interim pastor and been constantly in demand as a teacher of adult Bible classes. Clearly, Martin has pursued a life truly characterized by "scholarship in the service of the church."[25]

Writings

While surveying the writings of Ralph Martin, one is struck by how consistently he has aimed at scholarship in service of the church. His familiarity with primary sources is profound, giving his descriptions of the first-century setting of Judaism, Hellenism, and Christianity an air of credibility not often found. Yet Martin consistently directs his penetrating research toward the church, not only the academy. Reviewing a commentary designed for teaching and preaching, Ernest Best notes, "Though Martin is a distinguished Pauline scholar, this is not an academic commentary and should not be judged as such; we can, however, be sure that all the academic questions have been carefully evaluated though treated only briefly in the introductions to each letter."[26] Martin's writings give evidence that he is a scholar's scholar, but that he is a pastor's teacher as well.

Carmen Christi

Pride of place among the writings of Ralph Martin must go to *Carmen Christi.* Graham Stanton states, "In my view none of Ralph Martin's many distinguished contributions to New Testament scholarship surpasses his . . . *Carmen Christi: Philippians 2:5–11 in Recent Interpretation and in the Setting of Early Christian Worship.*"[27] Published initially in 1967, *Carmen Christi* is called by Andrew Lincoln a "classic study of the hymn" which continues to generate discussion today.[28] In the 1983 revised edition Martin ad-

24. Ralph P. Martin, *The Worship of God: Some Theological, Pastoral, and Practical Reflections* (Grand Rapids: Eerdmans, 1982), 152–53.
25. Lynn A. Losie, "Curriculum Vitae," in *Worship, Theology and Ministry,* ed. Wilkins and Paige, 22.
26. Ernest Best, review of *Ephesians, Colossians, and Philemon,* by Ralph P. Martin, *Interpretation* 47 (July 1993): 315.
27. Graham Stanton, "Aspects of Early Christian and Jewish Worship," in *Worship, Theology and Ministry,* ed. Wilkins and Paige, 84.
28. Andrew T. Lincoln, review of *Carmen Christi,* rev. ed., by Ralph P. Martin, *Evangelical Quarterly* 57 (Oct. 1985): 372–73. *Carmen Christi* is given prominence in recent studies of the hymn and in recent commentaries on Philippians (e.g., those of Gerald Hawthorne, Moisés Silva, and Peter O'Brien).

dresses three of the issues most widely discussed: the purpose of Philippians 2:5–11, the descriptions of Jesus in the hymn, and the use of the hymn in context.[29] At the heart of the discussion is the distinction between ethical and soteriological (or kerygmatic) interpretations of the hymn. Martin continues to maintain that Paul does not use the hymn to give the fractious community an ethical example that presents Christ as a model to be followed. This had been the traditional view of the passage from the Reformers until the middle of the twentieth century. Rather, Martin insists that Paul's paraenetic appeal in the passage "consists in giving a kerygmatic dimension to [the Philippians'] life-in-Christ by anchoring what they understood as life under His lordly control in a 'theology of the cross.' The boundaries of Paul's understanding of Christ's achievement are set by His cross, which is not a station on the way to glory but of the *esse* of Christian experience, and by His humanity which is now elevated to share the throne of God."[30] Peter O'Brien declares that since the 1950s, primarily because of the influence of the work of Ernst Käsemann and Ralph Martin, this interpretation has become the majority scholarly opinion concerning Paul's use of the christological hymn.[31] That some commentators have, however, returned to the ethical interpretation is an indication that the hymn will continue to be discussed for years to come.[32]

Paul

Martin's interest in Paul was stimulated initially through exploring the hymnic setting of Philippians, but it has since traversed the Pauline landscape. He has written on virtually all of the Pauline Epistles and has sought to find a theological *centrum Paulinum*.

Significantly, Martin's first publications were a commentary on Philippians for the Tyndale New Testament Commentaries and an article on Philippians 2:6 for *Expository Times*. Both appeared in 1959, the year he concluded ten years of pastoral work and accepted a teaching position at London Bible College. They blended Martin's academic and pastoral interests, while setting him on a course to be a premier interpreter of Paul. He wrote a separate commentary on Philippians for the New Century Bible in 1976 (rev. ed., 1980) and then revised the original Tyndale commentary in 1987.

Martin's early Pauline commentaries included Ephesians,[33] Romans,[34]

---

29. Ralph P. Martin, *Carmen Christi*, rev. ed. (Grand Rapids: Eerdmans, 1983), xii–xxxix.

30. Ibid., xix.

31. Peter T. O'Brien, *The Epistle to the Philippians*, New International Greek Testament Commentary (Grand Rapids: Eerdmans, 1991), 256.

32. Not least among these commentators is O'Brien, *Philippians*, 262.

33. Ralph P. Martin, "Ephesians," in *New Bible Commentary, Revised*, ed. Donald Guthrie and J. A. Motyer (Grand Rapids: Eerdmans, 1970), 1105–24; idem, "Ephesians," in *2 Corinthians–Philemon*, ed. Clifton J. Allen et al., Broadman Bible Commentary 11 (Nashville: Broadman, 1971), 125–77.

34. Ralph P. Martin (with F. Davidson), "Romans," in *New Bible Commentary, Revised*, ed. Guthrie and Motyer, 1012–48.

and Colossians and Philemon,[35] which were written for both the pastoral reader as well as a more scholarly audience. A review of the expository commentary on Colossians notes that Martin "presents an expository commentary in the best sense of the term. Its purpose is to interpret for our day and situation the meaning and message of Colossians on the basis of an honest and thorough exegesis of its meaning for those to whom it originally was addressed. . . . It is this sane and serious approach to biblical interpretation and this basic conviction of 'timeless validity' that makes Martin's commentary an important contribution to the Church's ongoing task of rightly interpreting Scripture."[36]

In a later commentary on Ephesians, Colossians, and Philemon, Martin brought his discussion of these epistles up to date. Ernest Best describes Martin's position on general matters as "mildly conservative."[37] For example, Colossians and Philemon are Pauline, Ephesians is not, and Ephesians is dependent on Colossians; this approach has made unhappy both those to Martin's left[38] and those to his right.[39] Unlike Colossians, Ephesians is not directed to a particular congregation, but is an encyclical. Further, Martin believes that the heresy at Colossae had roots in the local religious tradition. This was not a pure form of Jewish belief (e.g., neither orthodox Judaism nor Essenism), but a syncretistic form. While Martin has been criticized for not linking the heresy to some recognizable form of Judaism, Colossians scholar Clinton Arnold says that Martin's understanding of the heresy reflects the syncretistic phenomenon found in that region of Asia Minor.[40]

Martin wrote a lay-oriented commentary on 1 and 2 Corinthians early in his career;[41] an extensive volume on 2 Corinthians appeared in the Word Biblical Commentary in 1986.[42] Although it arrived nearly contemporaneously with a slate of other distinguished commentaries on 2 Corinthians (those of Ernest Best, Victor Paul Furnish, Hans Dieter Betz, and Charles Talbert), one reviewer declares that "Martin's work is clearly the most valu-

---

35. Ralph P. Martin, *Colossians: The Church's Lord and the Christian's Liberty* (Grand Rapids: Zondervan, 1973); idem, *Colossians and Philemon,* New Century Bible (London: Oliphants, 1974); idem, "Reconciliation and Forgiveness in Colossians," in *Reconciliation and Hope: New Testament Essays on Atonement and Eschatology Presented to L. L. Morris on His 60th Birthday,* ed. Robert Banks (Grand Rapids: Eerdmans, 1974), 104–24; idem, "Colossians," in *Zondervan Pictorial Encyclopedia of the Bible,* ed. Merrill C. Tenney (Grand Rapids: Zondervan, 1975), 1:914–18.

36. Edmond L. Rowell, Jr., review of *Colossians: The Church's Lord and the Christian's Liberty,* by Ralph P. Martin, *Christianity Today* 18.5 (Dec. 7, 1973): 41–42.

37. Ernest Best, review of *Ephesians, Colossians, and Philemon,* 315.

38. E.g., Beverly Roberts Gaventa, review of *Reconciliation: A Study of Paul's Theology,* by Ralph P. Martin, *Journal of Biblical Literature* 102 (Oct. 1983): 509.

39. E.g., Darrell L. Bock, review of *Ephesians, Colossians, and Philemon,* by Ralph P. Martin, *Bibliotheca Sacra* 150 (Jan.-March 1993): 124.

40. Clinton E. Arnold, *The Colossian Syncretism: The Interface between Christianity and Folk Belief at Colossae* (Grand Rapids: Baker, 1996), passim.

41. Ralph P. Martin, *First Corinthians to Galatians,* Scripture Union Bible Study Books (Grand Rapids: Eerdmans, 1968).

42. Ralph P. Martin, *2 Corinthians,* Word Biblical Commentary 40 (Waco: Word, 1986).

able of the recent studies on 2 Corinthians."[43] Moisés Silva notes that the highly regarded commentaries on 2 Corinthians by Philip Hughes and C. K. Barrett had for several years needed to be supplemented by a more technical and up-to-date commentary, and that Martin's "admirably meets this need." His impressive control over the scholarly literature, "the magnificent bibliographies that head each section, coupled with his ability to formulate the *status quaestionis*, are sufficient reason to treasure the commentary."[44] Synthesizing his understanding of Paul's opponents at Corinth with his understanding of Paul's opponents elsewhere (e.g., Philippi), Martin sees as a major theme in 2 Corinthians and as a central concern of Paul's ministry the stark contrast between the *theologia gloriae* that characterized the false apostles and Paul's *theologia crucis*.[45] But confrontation is not the central theme of Paul's message to the Corinthians. Rather, Paul's thought moves in the direction of reconciliation.

Martin's emphasis on a *centrum Paulinum* stands apart from many Pauline scholars on the current scene. Relevant background here includes the so-called biblical theology movement, which was in its heyday when he was a theological student in the 1940s. A major focus of biblical theology was synthesis. Books such as A. M. Hunter's *Unity of the New Testament* attempted to show a synthesis between the biblical authors as they converged on the kerygma. Today the emphasis is much more on diversity, the large number and variety of biblical authors. While he does not advocate going back to the old simplistic synthetic point of view, Martin does suggest that we look for a theme which most effectively and comprehensively reflects Paul's understanding of the action of God toward the universe, and in turn Paul's own life and ministry (2 Cor. 5:18).

Harking back to a theme that he had first encountered as a student under Professor T. W. Manson at Manchester, Martin suggests in his book *Reconciliation* that the term *reconciliation* most effectively acts as a true *centrum Paulinum*.[46] God has taken the initiative to reclaim the universe from the cosmic predicament in which it finds itself. The apostolic community was a living demonstration of this reclamation (which is achieved by divine power, forgiveness, life in the Spirit of the resurrected Christ in this new age, and the ending of the separation both between God and humans and between humans themselves); and the church is the ongoing divine promise of this reconciliation. Paul's theology, which centers on the relational work of God for

43. David C. Baker, review of *2 Corinthians*, by Ralph P. Martin, *Grace Theological Journal* 9 (Fall 1988): 292–93.

44. Moisés Silva, review of *2 Corinthians*, by Ralph P. Martin, *Westminster Theological Journal* 49 (Fall 1987): 433–34.

45. Martin, *2 Corinthians*, lvi–lxi. Martin draws out this theme from both epistles in his *First and Second Corinthians*, Word Biblical Themes (Waco: Word, 1988).

46. Martin, *Reconciliation*, 3. Martin first explored this theme in "Reconciliation and Forgiveness in Colossians" and "New Testament Theology. A Proposal: The Theme of Reconciliation," *Expository Times* 91 (1980): 364–68.

the well-being of his people, finds its starting point and focus in the concept of reconciliation: soteriologically, ecclesiologically, and eschatologically.

Some scholars do not accept the suggestion that one can or should look for a *centrum Paulinum*. Others laud the effort but do not agree that reconciliation is the unifying theme. For example, Beverly Gaventa seems to welcome the attempt to discover an underlying unity in New Testament theology, but believes that Martin's focusing on the term *reconciliation* borders on being reductionistic: "In the end, the reader comes away with the impression that any form of religious language may be subsumed under the heading of reconciliation."[47]

In an appendix in the revised edition of *Reconciliation* Martin addresses the various concerns. He accepts the suggestion of one critic that reconciliation was not originally but became the theme in terms of which Paul formulated his gospel as he communicated it to the Gentiles. In other words, reconciliation was a developing theme in and "eventually came to stand at the apex of" Paul's thought.[48] Reviewers uniformly commend Martin's *Reconciliation* as an apex of this premier Pauline scholar. In this vein John Drane concludes his review with the statement that "Professor Martin has once more placed every student of Paul in his debt."[49]

Mark and the Gospels

Martin did not exclude the Gospels in his study of the New Testament. Indeed, one of his most influential works is his treatment of the Gospel of Mark. Most of the first half of the twentieth century had been dominated by a form-critical approach to the Gospels. Attention was given to the tradition prior to the Gospels rather than to the Gospels themselves. But with the advent of redaction criticism in the 1950s the focus shifted to the Evangelists' theology, purpose, and communities. The contributions of Willi Marxsen, Theodore Weeden, S. G. F. Brandon, and Ralph Martin were seminal in the attempt to understand Mark as a theologian.[50] They sought to identify the central characteristics of Mark's Gospel as clues to its purpose. Martin's influential study *Mark: Evangelist and Theologian* sees two general concerns in that Gospel—Christology and discipleship.[51] Attempting to discover "a suitable background in early Christianity for Mark's publication and to place it in an appropriate *Sitz im Leben*," Martin understands Mark as "a supplement to Paul's kerygma."[52] As Mark writes a dramatization of the life of

---

47. Gaventa, review of *Reconciliation*, 509.
48. William S. Campbell, review of *Reconciliation*, by Ralph P. Martin, *Theology* 86 (1983): 302. Martin accepts this suggestion in the revised edition of *Reconciliation* (p. 242).
49. John Drane, review of *Reconciliation*, by Ralph P. Martin, *Evangelical Quarterly* 56 (1984): 63.
50. D. A. Carson, Douglas J. Moo, and Leon Morris, *An Introduction to the New Testament* (Grand Rapids: Zondervan, 1992), 100–104.
51. Ralph P. Martin, *Mark: Evangelist and Theologian* (Grand Rapids: Zondervan, 1972), 156–62. Martin first suggested these Markan concerns in an earlier article, "A Gospel in Search of a Life-Setting," *Expository Times* 80 (1969): 361–64.
52. Martin, *Mark*, 156.

Jesus, focusing on the humiliation of the suffering Messiah, he gives encouragement to the persecuted church in Rome and summons it to faithful discipleship. In the interim between the resurrection and the parousia the exalted Christ will strengthen those who confess him under persecution.[53]

Martin has been criticized for being too conservative in that he argues that John Mark was the author of the Gospel,[54] while at the same time he has been criticized for describing Mark as a "creative" theologian. He did not pursue Markan studies into the era of sociological and literary criticism during the 1980s–90s, yet his study of Mark as evangelist and theologian prepared the way for such studies and still ought to be consulted today.[55]

Martin's popular commentary on the Gospel of Mark (Where the Action Is) was followed by a helpful volume on Mark in the Knox Preaching Guides, which has been described as providing "a wealth of ideas."[56] He also wrote several significant articles on other aspects of the Gospels.[57]

James

Two years after the release of Martin's extensive commentary on 2 Corinthians came the release of his substantial commentary on James, also in the Word Biblical Commentary series.[58] This volume came as a surprise to some in the scholarly community, because he was not known as a leading figure in the study of James.[59] However, Martin drew upon his strengths in understanding the early church and the later development of traditions to provide an outstanding contribution to the study of this epistle. Peter Davids, himself a leading figure in the study of James, has said that Martin's commentary is first-class and "in keeping with [Martin's] own usual standard of scholarship, for he is certainly one of the premier contemporary evangelical scholars." Further, Davids declares that "it is surely a 'must have' on the list of

53. Ibid., 70, 161.

54. See, e.g., Hugh Anderson, *The Gospel of Mark*, New Century Bible Commentary (Grand Rapids: Eerdmans, 1981), 31–32.

55. For appreciation of his approach see Robert A. Guelich, *Mark 1–8:26*, Word Biblical Commentary 34A (Waco: Word, 1989), xxxix–xl; Jack D. Kingsbury, *Conflict in Mark: Jesus, Authorities, Disciples* (Minneapolis: Fortress, 1989), 142.

56. Cyril S. Rodd, review of *Mark* (Knox Preaching Guides), by Ralph P. Martin, *Expository Times* 93 (1982): 289.

57. E.g., Ralph P. Martin, "The Kingdom of God in Recent Writing," *Christianity Today* 8.8 (Jan. 17, 1964): 5–7; idem, "The New Quest of the Historical Jesus," in *Jesus of Nazareth: Saviour and Lord*, ed. Carl F. H. Henry (Grand Rapids: Eerdmans, 1966), 25–45; idem, "St. Matthew's Gospel in Recent Study," *Expository Times* 80 (1969): 132–36; idem, "The Pericope of the Healing of the 'Centurion's' Servant/Son (Matt. 8:5–13 par. Luke 7:1–10): Some Exegetical Notes," in *Unity and Diversity in New Testament Theology: Essays in Honor of George Eldon Ladd*, ed. Robert A. Guelich (Grand Rapids: Eerdmans, 1978), 14–22; idem, "Gospel" and "Jesus Christ," in *International Standard Bible Encyclopedia*, ed. Geoffrey W. Bromiley (Grand Rapids: Eerdmans, 1982), 2:529–32, 1034–49.

58. Ralph P. Martin, *James*, Word Biblical Commentary 48 (Waco: Word, 1988).

59. Martin's primary earlier writing on James was "The Life-Setting of the Epistle of James in the Light of Jewish History," in *Biblical and Near Eastern Studies: Essays in Honor of William Sanford LaSor*, ed. Gary A. Tuttle (Grand Rapids: Eerdmans, 1978), 97–103.

everyone seriously interested in the study of the epistle of James, ranking as one of the three or four significant works on this epistle of the last fifty years."[60]

Martin is both commended and criticized for his distinctive views about the original setting for this epistle. He sees a two-stage composition (along with others, such as Peter Davids): first, the teaching of James the Just, the brother of the Lord, in Palestine in the early 60s; second, the teaching of James's disciples some decades later at Antioch of Syria.[61] Ruth Edwards commends Martin for this helpful suggestion about the epistle's *Sitz im Leben*, especially because he applies its implications to the main body of the text.[62] Others argue that it is unnecessary to hypothesize two levels of composition for which there is no textual or solid historical evidence.[63] Regardless, even some evangelicals who criticize him for his views on composition still commend Martin for the attempt to understand the epistle within a real historical setting, instead of treating it like a "general" epistle or an amalgam of essentially disconnected wisdom sayings.[64]

New Testament Foundations

The 1970s were a monumental decade for Ralph Martin. Not only did he occupy himself with writing seminal commentaries and background studies, but his two-volume *New Testament Foundations* was completed. To appreciate these volumes fully the reader needs to keep clearly in mind Martin's purpose in writing them: "The book which now appears [vol. 1] is offered as a handbook of introduction to the study of the Four Gospels. It is chiefly a student's book, but the author hopes that it will be of interest and service to a wider public. It aims at encouraging a serious and disciplined study of the background and contents of the Christian Gospels, and at laying a foundation on which readers will build."[65]

Arising out of Martin's experience in the classroom, *New Testament Foundations* is designed to help walk students through the basics of New Testament study, exposing them to current trends, leading authorities, and helpful summaries and conclusions. One reviewer castigates Martin for giving "authoritative guidance" instead of challenging students to discover conclusions for themselves,[66] but given the overwhelming amount of material

60. Peter H. Davids, review of *James*, by Ralph P. Martin, *Christian Scholar's Review* 19.3 (1990): 325–26.

61. Martin, *James*, lxix–lxxvii.

62. Ruth B. Edwards, review of *James*, by Ralph P. Martin, *Evangelical Quarterly* 64 (1992): 364–65.

63. Carson, Moo, and Morris, *Introduction*, 413. For an even more pointed criticism see Adrian Lane, review of *James*, by Ralph P. Martin, *Reformed Theological Review* 49 (1990): 104–5.

64. E.g., William R. Baker, review of *James*, by Ralph P. Martin, *Themelios* 16 (1991): 25–26. See also David R. Bauer, review of *James*, by Ralph P. Martin, *Catholic Biblical Quarterly* 53 (1991): 707–8.

65. Martin, *New Testament Foundations*, 1:7.

66. Frances M. Young, review of *New Testament Foundations*, vol. 1, by Ralph P. Martin, *Expository Times* 87 (1976): 247.

with which Martin deals, such criticism seems out of place. A general criticism is that Martin treats more fully the material on which he has written elsewhere (e.g., in volume 1 Mark is given by far the most space, and Paul receives the greatest attention in volume 2),[67] but most reviewers have profuse praise for these volumes as guides for students.

Stephen Smalley describes Martin's position as "neo-conservative," because, for example, his views on authorship and dating are at times unpredictable (e.g., 1 Peter was written by Peter early, 2 Peter was written by someone else at a late date). Smalley is among those who criticize the unevenness of the treatment of the various portions of the New Testament. But he notes five overall strengths: (1) The historical and contextual setting of the New Testament materials is given appropriate attention; a constant theme of *Foundations* is that these documents arose from and were addressed to *living* situations. (2) Martin's treatment of "special issues in the Pauline corpus" (including "authority" and "church and state") helps the student to understand the relevance of those issues today. (3) Martin is "pleasingly sensitive" to the unity as well as the diversity of the New Testament. (4) Martin demonstrates how his studies can be used as an aid to exegesis. (5) In the "sum of the matter" Martin offers a characteristically skillful exegesis of three passages from 1 Corinthians; in addition to demonstrating the how-to of exegesis, he leads the student to practical and personal applications. Smalley concludes: "Here now are two volumes which will be an indispensable guide to *all* students of the New Testament, and which will significantly help them in the difficult but essential task of relating scholarship to faith."[68]

Editor

Finally, Ralph Martin has through various editorial positions played an indispensable leadership role as a scholar in service to the church. He began as editor of *Vox Evangelica* from 1962 to 1964. In 1970 he co-edited with Ward Gasque a festschrift for F. F. Bruce[69] which is described by Richard Longenecker as "twenty-four articles by twenty-four leading constructive scholars . . . [the volume] is carefully planned to parallel Bruce's own interests and his type of critical, reverent, and expansive scholarship."[70] Martin was the advisory editor of *Studia Biblica et Theologica,* the scholarly journal of Fuller Theological Seminary, from 1972 to 1987. He was also con-

---

67. E.g., Stanley Riegel, review of *New Testament Foundations,* vol. 1, by Ralph P. Martin, *Christianity Today* 20.22 (Aug. 6, 1976): 33; Frances M. Young, review of *New Testament Foundations,* vol. 2, *Expository Times* 90 (1978): 94–95.
68. Stephen S. Smalley, review of *New Testament Foundations,* vol. 2, *Evangelical Quarterly* 51 (1979): 46–47.
69. Ralph P. Martin and W. Ward Gasque, eds., *Apostolic History and the Gospel: Biblical and Historical Essays Presented to F. F. Bruce on His 60th Birthday* (Grand Rapids: Eerdmans, 1970).
70. Richard N. Longenecker, review of *Apostolic History and the Gospel,* edited by Ralph P. Martin and W. Ward Gasque, *Christianity Today* 16.5 (Dec. 3, 1971): 18–19.

sultant editor of Marshalls Theological Library from 1978 to 1979, and consultant editor for the New Foundations Theological Library from 1979 to 1980.

In 1977 began one of Martin's most important roles, New Testament editor for the newly established Word Biblical Commentary series. To peruse the names of the contributors to the series is to read a who's who of basically evangelical New Testament scholars. The series offers not only up-to-date exegesis, but in many volumes seminal interpretative perspectives (e.g., the new perspective on Paul in James Dunn's Romans commentaries).

Martin has also served as co-editor on two reference volumes. He co-edited with Gerald Hawthorne and Daniel Reid the *Dictionary of Paul and His Letters*,[71] a companion volume to the *Dictionary of Jesus and the Gospels*. At the time of this writing he is co-editing with Peter Davids a third companion volume, the *Dictionary of the Latter New Testament and Its Developments*. The first two volumes have been received with tremendous enthusiasm, as should the third. Representative of the kind of work that Ralph Martin, a scholar in service to the church, has carried on throughout his career, they, together with all the other volumes he has written and edited, promise to have an impact on students, Christian workers, and scholars for years to come.

Primary Sources

Martin, Ralph P. *Acts*. Scripture Union Bible Study Books. Grand Rapids: Eerdmans, 1967.

———. "Approaches to New Testament Exegesis." In *New Testament Interpretation: Essays on Principles and Methods*, edited by I. Howard Marshall, 220–51. Grand Rapids: Eerdmans, 1977.

———. *Carmen Christi: Philippians ii.5–11 in Recent Interpretation and in the Setting of Early Christian Worship*. Society for New Testament Studies Monograph 4. Cambridge: Cambridge University Press, 1967. Rev. ed., Grand Rapids: Eerdmans, 1983.

———. *Colossians: The Church's Lord and the Christian's Liberty; An Expository Commentary with a Present-Day Application*. Grand Rapids: Zondervan, 1973.

———. *Colossians and Philemon*. New Century Bible. London: Oliphants, 1974; Grand Rapids: Eerdmans, 1981.

———. *Ephesians, Colossians, and Philemon*. Interpretation: A Bible Commentary for Preaching and Teaching. Louisville: Westminster/John Knox, 1992.

———. *The Epistle of Paul to the Philippians: An Introduction and Commentary*. Tyndale New Testament Commentaries. Grand Rapids: Eerdmans, 1959.

———. *The Family and the Fellowship: New Testament Images of the Church*. Grand Rapids: Eerdmans, 1979.

———. *First and Second Corinthians*. Word Biblical Themes. Waco: Word, 1988.

71. Gerald F. Hawthorne, Ralph P. Martin, and Daniel G. Reid, eds., *Dictionary of Paul and His Letters* (Downers Grove, Ill.: InterVarsity, 1993).

————. *First Corinthians to Galatians.* Scripture Union Bible Study Books. Grand Rapids: Eerdmans, 1968.

————. *James.* Word Biblical Commentary 48. Waco: Word, 1988.

————. "The Life-Setting of the Epistle of James in the Light of Jewish History." In *Biblical and Near Eastern Studies: Essays in Honor of William Sanford LaSor,* edited by Gary A. Tuttle, 97–103. Grand Rapids: Eerdmans, 1978.

————. *Mark.* Knox Preaching Guides. Atlanta: John Knox, 1982.

————. *Mark: Evangelist and Theologian.* Grand Rapids: Zondervan, 1972.

————. "The New Quest of the Historical Jesus." In *Jesus of Nazareth: Saviour and Lord,* edited by Carl F. H. Henry, 25–45. Grand Rapids: Eerdmans, 1966.

————. *New Testament Books for Pastor and Teacher.* Philadelphia: Westminster, 1984.

————. *New Testament Foundations: A Guide for Christian Students.* 2 vols. Grand Rapids: Eerdmans, 1975, 1978.

————. "New Testament Theology. A Proposal: The Theme of Reconciliation." *Expository Times* 91 (1980): 364–68.

————. "The Opponents of Paul in 2 Corinthians: An Old Issue Revisited." In *Tradition and Interpretation in the New Testament: Essays in Honor of E. Earle Ellis for His Sixtieth Birthday,* edited by Gerald F. Hawthorne and Otto Betz, 279–89. Grand Rapids: Eerdmans, 1987.

————. "The Pericope of the Healing of the 'Centurion's' Servant/Son (Matt. 8:5–13 par. Luke 7:1–10): Some Exegetical Notes." In *Unity and Diversity in New Testament Theology: Essays in Honor of George Eldon Ladd,* edited by Robert A. Guelich, 14–22. Grand Rapids: Eerdmans, 1978.

————. *Philippians.* New Century Bible. London: Oliphants, 1976. Rev. ed., Grand Rapids: Eerdmans, 1980.

————. *Reconciliation: A Study of Paul's Theology.* Atlanta: John Knox, 1981.

————. "Reconciliation and Forgiveness in Colossians." In *Reconciliation and Hope: New Testament Essays on Atonement and Eschatology Presented to L. L. Morris on His 60th Birthday,* edited by Robert Banks, 104–24. Grand Rapids: Eerdmans, 1974.

————. *2 Corinthians.* Word Biblical Commentary 40. Waco: Word, 1986.

————. "Some Reflections on New Testament Hymns." In *Christ the Lord: Studies in Christology Presented to Donald Guthrie,* edited by Harold H. Rowdon, 37–49. Downers Grove, Ill.: InterVarsity, 1982.

————. *The Spirit and the Congregation: Studies in 1 Corinthians 12–15.* Grand Rapids: Eerdmans, 1984.

————. "The Spirit in 2 Corinthians in Light of the 'Fellowship of the Holy Spirit.'" In *Eschatology and the New Testament: Essays in Honor of George Raymond Beasley-Murray,* edited by W. H. Gloer, 113–28. Peabody, Mass.: Hendrickson, 1988.

————. *Where the Action Is.* Glendale, Calif.: Regal, 1977.

————. *Worship in the Early Church.* Westwood, N.J.: Revell, 1964. Rev. ed., Grand Rapids: Eerdmans, 1974.

————. *The Worship of God: Some Theological, Pastoral, and Practical Reflections.* Grand Rapids: Eerdmans, 1982.

————, and Andrew Chester. *The Theology of the Letters of James, Peter and Jude.* New Testament Theology. New York: Cambridge University Press, 1994.

Secondary Sources

Martin, Ralph P., and W. Ward Gasque, eds. *Apostolic History and the Gospel: Biblical and Historical Essays Presented to F. F. Bruce on His 60th Birthday.* Grand Rapids: Eerdmans, 1970.

Wilkins, Michael J., and Terence Paige, eds. *Worship, Theology and Ministry in the Early Church: Essays in Honor of Ralph P. Martin.* Journal for the Study of the New Testament Supplement 87. Sheffield: JSOT, 1992.

Walter C. Kaiser, Jr.

John H. Sailhamer

Life and Times

Walter Christian Kaiser, Jr., was born into a German Baptist (now North American Baptist) home on April 11, 1933, in Folcroft, Pennsylvania. He was the oldest of the six children of Walter Christian Kaiser, Sr., a farmer and a godly Christian leader in the local church, and Estelle Jaworsky Kaiser. Feeling obliged to worship in the community where they lived and worked, the family attended an independent fundamental church in Folcroft. At that time Kaiser came under the influence of the Scofield Reference Bible and dispensational teaching. Later, during his seminary days, Kaiser would discover Willis J. Beecher's *Prophets and the Promise,* and a revolution would take place in his thinking that would carry with it a large portion of contemporary evangelical scholarship. Instead of casting his dispensational heritage aside, this revolution swept it back into the broader heritage of the nineteenth century whence it had come. This was to be an ongoing theme in the life and work of Kaiser—a linking of the burgeoning postwar evangelicalism of the twentieth century with its rich and nearly forgotten spiritual heritage from the past. In the end, Kaiser's approach to Scripture, which he calls promise theology, would prove to be an effective means of transcending the narrow walls that had built up around modern evangelicalism.

Kaiser entered Wheaton College in 1952. While at Wheaton he majored in Bible and minored in Greek and philosophy. He served as a teaching assistant to Arthur Holmes. Kaiser worked his way through both college and seminary, still finding time to sing in the chapel choir and to teach in Sunday schools on Chicago's South Side.

By his own reckoning, Kaiser's interest in the Old Testament was first sparked by a high school biology class in which the Genesis account was kindly, but firmly, debunked. When Kaiser dared to voice another opinion, he was challenged to do a report that would convince his teacher otherwise. Undaunted, Kaiser prepared a forty-page paper complete with anthropological drawings and bibliography. His interest in the Old Testament continued while at Wheaton College. Though most of his classmates were planning to go into New Testament studies or theology, Kaiser felt the call, from both his early experiences and a perceived need, to enter graduate studies in Old Testament. While pursing a B.D. degree at Wheaton Graduate School, he studied Hebrew for the first time. His Hebrew professor was Frank Neuberg, a pioneer in his own right, who had earned his doctorate under William F. Albright at Johns Hopkins. Kaiser's other professors at Wheaton Graduate School included Merrill Tenney, Kenneth Kantzer, and Berkeley Mickelson.

Kaiser was married just before his final year of study at Wheaton Graduate School. During that last year, in addition to teaching two senior apologetics courses at Wheaton College, Kaiser served as assistant pastor at the Geneva Baptist Church (General Conference), where his responsibilities included preparing the worship bulletins each week, pastoral calls, and teaching an adult Sunday school class.

After graduation from Wheaton Graduate School in 1958, Kaiser taught full-time at Wheaton College. During the summer months he pursued further graduate studies in Old Testament and ancient history at Brandeis University, where his mentors included Benjamin Mazar, Samuel Noah Kramer, Harry Orlinsky, and Cyrus H. Gordon. His course of study at Brandeis included Middle and Late Egyptian hieroglyphics, Ugaritic, Homeric Greek, biblical Hebrew, Old Babylonian cuneiform, Assyrian cuneiform, and the history and archeology of the ancient Near Eastern empires.

In the late fall of 1963, Kaiser was asked to teach a class at Trinity Evangelical Divinity School when the instructor, Wilbur Smith, suddenly took ill. In 1964 Kaiser began a two-year term of teaching at both Trinity and Wheaton. In the fall of 1966 he joined the Trinity faculty on a full-time basis. While pursuing graduate studies at Brandeis, Kaiser became professor and chairman of the Old Testament department at Trinity. He completed his Ph.D. dissertation in 1973.

In 1980 Kaiser assumed the responsibilities of vice president and academic dean of Trinity and continued in that office until June of 1992. In the fall of 1993 he accepted an invitation from Gordon-Conwell Theological Seminary to serve as the first Colman M. Mockler Distinguished Professor of Old Testament. He taught during the fall semester, and lived on his Wisconsin farm and spoke around the world the remaining eight months of the year. In the summer of 1997 Kaiser assumed the presidency of Gordon-Conwell while retaining the Mockler chair. In addition to being a Wheaton College trustee since 1982, Kaiser has served on various other boards.

Kaiser's Work in Historical Perspective

Nineteenth-Century Roots

It is not possible to understand Kaiser's work, nor to appreciate his importance, apart from the history of evangelical theology. More than almost any other contemporary theologian, Kaiser has come to embody the convictions and beliefs of a wide sector of past generations of evangelicals. Among the most characteristic features of his work is its success in preserving and appropriating nearly two centuries of Protestant orthodoxy. Here one encounters afresh and in contemporary form the central tenets of the once thriving evangelicalism of the nineteenth century.

Three names from the evangelical past stand out as essential for understanding Kaiser's work: the German evangelical Old Testament scholar Ernst Wilhelm Hengstenberg, Willis Judson Beecher, and Milton Terry. Hengstenberg (1802–69), a product of the evangelical revivals that swept through Europe in the wake of the Napoleonic wars, is best known for his relentless attack against the rise of biblical criticism, rationalism, and anti-supernaturalism. Most of his works were quickly translated into English, spreading his influence far beyond the narrow confines of Prussia and the German-speaking world. Many of his writings are, in fact, still in print today. In a foreword to Hengstenberg's *Christology of the Old Testament* Kaiser writes, "This man, more than many others of his day or ours, epitomized that wonderful combination of an earnest Christian experience and thorough Biblical scholarship. . . . [He] fearlessly asserted the neglected truths of orthodoxy to a modern age."[1] Kaiser's concluding remarks suggest his own theological debt to Hengstenberg: "May his spiritual descendants follow in his train to the Glory of our Great God and Savior Jesus Christ."

It is clear from Kaiser's comments, and from his work in general, that he saw in Hengstenberg a ready starting point for his own work of asserting the neglected truths of orthodoxy to a modern age, and particularly those rooted in the Old Testament. In deliberately choosing to drive his piton into the legacy of Hengstenberg, Kaiser was accepting the common evangelical view that Hengstenberg had successfully cleared the ground of destructive criticism and heterodoxy. He had adequately answered the Bible's critics. He had provided the believing community with the kind of thorough biblical scholarship that could address the needs and issues of the contemporary world. The prevalent view among evangelicals in the middle part of the twentieth century was that after Hengstenberg there was little left to contend against. The major battles had been won. Consequently, one does not find in Kaiser the kind of nervous preoccupation with attacks on the Bible which is so often a part of more recent evangelical Old Testament scholarship. Rather, Kaiser exhibits a calm confidence in the historical trustworthiness of the Bible, an assurance grounded in the belief that the best minds of the past have already fought and won the great territorial battles. What remains is to occupy the land.

Building on the ground cleared by Hengstenberg, Kaiser set out to construct his own theological vision, one that would speak to the particular needs of his own day. His plan, if one can judge by his works, was to revive the basic vision of nineteenth-century evangelicalism. In particular Kaiser returned to the work of Milton Terry and Willis Judson Beecher, both of whom

---

1. Walter C. Kaiser, Jr., foreword to *Christology of the Old Testament,* by Ernst Wilhelm Hengstenberg (Grand Rapids: Kregel, 1970), ix–x.

he had discovered while still a student in seminary. Terry's *Biblical Herme-neutics*, with its numerous examples of biblical interpretation, and the biblical theology of Beecher proved pivotal for Kaiser's developing ideas.

Kaiser saw in Terry's work a thorough guide to a grammatical-historical approach to the study of the Old Testament. If the Bible is true and historically accurate, as Kaiser believed Hengstenberg had shown, then one need fear nothing from applying the grammatical-historical method to the Bible. Particularly advantageous for Kaiser was the fact that Terry had already merged two of Kaiser's central concerns, the classical orthodox view of Scripture as the inspired Word of God and the increasingly popular concept of salvation history. For Terry, as for Kaiser, the meaning of the inspired Scriptures was directly tied to the meaning of the facts of history recorded in the Bible.

Kaiser recognized that if the Bible is to be studied historically, then the central themes of the Bible, and of the Old Testament in particular, should be understood within the context of their own historical development. Beecher's *Prophets and the Promise* developed the classical orthodox view of Scripture within the framework of its gradual revelation of salvation history.[2] Kaiser also found in Beecher expression of a future millennial hope for Israel, so necessary to his own brand of mid-twentieth-century evangelicalism. Conveniently for Kaiser, Beecher was a highly Anglicized version of the great German theologian J. C. Conrad von Hofmann's approach to salvation history. In Beecher Kaiser found Hofmann stripped of his complex theological and cultural heritage and already transplanted into the soil of a simple biblical realism. Like Hofmann and Beecher, Kaiser maintained that the central message of the Old Testament is embodied in the notion of a promise of redemption that God made to all humanity. The Bible is, in fact, a historical account of the vicissitudes of that promise. To understand the whole of the Old Testament, or any of its parts, one must view it in the context of the continuous and continuing outworking of God's promise. The Bible is a repository of historical facts waiting to be sorted and organized, along with evidence from ancient history, into a single, meaningful whole.

There are other, less conspicuous legacies bequeathed to Kaiser by the nineteenth century. We would do well to note them before surveying his central themes. Throughout his many and varied works Kaiser has remained faithful to the clarion call of nineteenth-century evangelicalism that history is the primary sphere of God's activities, both redemptive and revelatory. Though Kaiser never fully accepted the stringent nineteenth- and twentieth-century canons of historical criticism, he fully endorsed the notion that God's actions in history can be known, indeed must be known, through the normal channels of historical research. Time and again Kaiser returns to the thesis of Johann Ernesti that the Bible is a historical document and is to be read as such.

---

2. Willis Judson Beecher, *The Prophets and the Promise* (Grand Rapids: Baker, 1963 reprint).

Another general tenet of evangelical theology that lies at the heart of Kaiser's work is the belief that in the original manuscripts the Scriptures are the inspired Word of God. Perhaps this, more than any other single belief, is what has characterized the whole of Kaiser's work. In holding this view, Kaiser is quick to acknowledge that we do not now have the original manuscripts, and hence we cannot claim a final or ultimate authority for the texts of the Bible we possess. God in his providence, however, has not abandoned his church; and hence, Kaiser maintains, we can come to the Scriptures with the great confidence that our manuscript copies are early and accurate representations of the Bible's history.

A third common evangelical view held by Kaiser is the conviction that the historical-critical method is fundamentally flawed by an antisupernatural bias. The great scholars of the past, such as Hengstenberg and C. F. Keil, proved its logical inconsistencies. Contemporary historians and archeologists have, time and again, demonstrated its failure to take seriously the historical veracity of Scripture. Biblical criticism is thus a misdirected attempt to squeeze God out of both past history and the contemporary world. Kaiser maintains, to the contrary, that because the Bible is clear that the past, the present, and the future bear the unmistakable signature of the living God, we need only to read and study his Word, and to some extent his world, to know him and understand his actions.

Finally, Kaiser shares the common view of evangelical scholarship that the meaning of biblical statements lies in what they tell us about God and his actions in the past, present, and future. The Old Testament is a book about history. It is about real events. Those events are recorded just as they happened and are to be interpreted in the context of our ever-growing knowledge of the world of the Bible. Kaiser constantly gives evidence of his conviction that historical background garnered from archeology and ancient Near Eastern studies often provides a missing key to understanding the Bible.

Twentieth-Century Context

In addition to being rooted in nineteenth-century evangelicalism, Kaiser is, in many ways, the immediate product of three major trends within twentieth-century evangelicalism. The first trend is the almost wholesale adoption by American evangelicals of the views of the so-called Albright school of biblical archeology. During the first half of the twentieth century, William F. Albright, a brilliant biblical scholar and linguist, waged a remarkably successful attack against the historical skepticism of the scholarly world. Contrary to most biblical critics, Albright maintained that the biblical sources are reliable and accurate accounts of real events in Israel's ancient past. Using the newly developed tools of archeology and the study of ancient languages to confirm his theories, Albright argued that there are no scientifically compelling reasons to doubt the historical accuracy of the Old Testament narratives. By the middle of the century Albright's views were well represented in the faculties of many major universities. Evangelicals, who were attracted to Albright's conservative historical views, made up a significant portion of the students in the graduate departments of ancient Near Eastern history and archeology. The historical confidence engendered by Albright and his students pervades the work of Kaiser, as it does evangelical Old Testament scholarship in general. There is the unwavering conviction that the weight of history lies on the side of Scripture and little ground need be ceded to the voices of doubt.

Closely associated with this conservative turn of events in many American universities in the 1950s and 1960s was an awakening of interest in serious biblical scholarship. One can, in fact, speak of an evangelical renaissance in biblical studies. In increasing numbers evangelical biblical scholars felt the call to pursue advanced graduate studies. For most Old Testament scholars at mid-century this call meant pursuing a career in ancient Near Eastern history and archeology. Only in that way could one take up firsthand the tools of the trade and apply them to the defense and interpretation of the biblical narratives. Along with many other evangelical Old Testament students at that time, Kaiser followed that call and, taking a leave of absence from his teaching assignments at Wheaton College, began a course of study with Cyrus Gordon at Brandeis University. There was a singular difference in the direction taken by Kaiser, however. While like many young evangelical scholars he chose to study at Brandeis with Gordon, his goal was neither apologetic demonstration of the truthfulness of Scripture nor fuller explication of the Old Testament by use of historical background. Though Kaiser never shied away from such tasks, his ultimate goal was to construct a complete biblical and theological vision rooted in the past, but equipped to take evangelicalism a further step into the future.

Finally, after the Second World War evangelicalism began to take on the characteristics of a full-scale social movement, complete with its own institutions, schools, and publishing houses. The first wave of biblical scholars found themselves content to study reprints of the works of earlier conservative scholars. Increasingly their shelves were also being filled with the conservative, but nonetheless critical, works of the so-called biblical theology movement. Such works afforded evangelicals a degree of serious scholarship without having to accept the radical conclusions of classical literary criticism. By the early 1970s, however, the conservative biblical theology movement had begun to fragment in the face of a more radical approach to history and archeology. The scholarly ground beneath the feet of many evangelical Old Testament scholars was beginning to shift. At the same time a new generation of biblical archeologists was beginning to question many of the conclusions of the Albright school. Within the guild of Old Testament scholars interest was increasingly turning away from the classical studies of texts, history, and language toward various literary and theological approaches to the Scriptures. This was a time for evangelicalism to stake out its own identity within the scholarly world. Indeed, the scholarly world itself had begun to give it room. In pursuing such a goal, the choice was simple: evangelicalism could either revive its past glory or move in any number of new directions opened by the changes within the field of biblical studies.

If evangelical biblical scholarship was to preserve its identity in terms of its nineteenth-century heritage, someone had to step forward to show the way and to take the lead in forming a body of literature with which it could identify. Kaiser's work helped to fill that need. In it one can see the laying of a complete biblical, theological, and homiletical foundation, the casting of a new vision, one that both preserves intact the central concerns of the past and points the way for the building of the future.

Basic Foundations

The Inspiration and Inerrancy of Scripture

One does not have to read very far in Kaiser's work to note the presence of recurring themes and the basic foundations upon which those themes are built. A basic foundation that is never very far from the surface is the belief that the Bible is inspired and inerrant. Indeed, Kaiser's overriding thesis is that the Scriptures cannot be broken. Nowhere does he extensively discuss that thesis, however. For the most part, Kaiser appears content with past demonstrations of the Bible's inspiration and inerrancy, notably those of Hengstenberg, Keil, William Henry Green, A. A. Hodge, and B. B. Warfield, which have been greatly aided in the present by biblical archeologists like Albright working in the field of ancient history. Kaiser's concern is not so much that the Bible is inspired as what the inspiration and inerrancy of the Bible mean for its interpretation.

It is significant, however, that on at least one occasion Kaiser felt it necessary to take up and defend the notion of biblical inspiration as developed long ago by Warfield and Hodge: the doctrine of inspiration extends to the original texts rather than to copies of those originals. Kaiser's particularly evangelical concerns are evident in his argument that to give up the notion that only the original texts, the autographs, are inspired "could bring devastating results for the spiritual health of the Church in the next generation."[3] Even though we do not have the originals today, the science of textual criticism and the traditional notion of biblical authorship depend on the assumption that such texts once existed and that they can confidently be reconstructed from existing manuscripts. To give up the notion of inspired originals merely because we do not physically possess such texts today would be tantamount to giving up our faith in the laws of science merely because we do not actually see the rules of science in nature. "The presumption of the fact of the uniformitarianism of nature is exactly what makes all of scientific research in the natural realm possible";[4] in a similar way, the presumption

---

3. Walter C. Kaiser, Jr., "The Doctrine of Scripture and the Autographa" (paper presented to the Evangelical Theological Society, Northwest Region, 16 March 1991), 23.
4. Ibid., 14.

of the inerrancy of the original manuscripts makes possible the coherent study of Scripture.

"Positive" Historical Criticism

Another important assumption is that the historical-critical study of the Scriptures is not only fundamentally wrong, but also fundamentally wrong-headed. It has divorced meaning from the historical events it seeks to explain, and it excludes a transcendent God from any activity in history. Kaiser renders this assessment not only for such notoriously negative approaches as the documentary hypothesis and tradition criticism, but even for historical criticism and historiography whenever they offer a conclusion that appears to cast doubt on some aspect of the biblical record. Rather than assuming the biblical record is false until proven true by an accredited historical method, Kaiser insists on giving the Bible the benefit of the doubt unless it can clearly be shown to be in error.[5] He points out that the discovery of a new historical fact or a new understanding of an obscure biblical word has often shown the skepticism of critical biblical scholars to be ill founded. For Kaiser, the historical evidence consistently favors the biblical record.

Another aspect of Kaiser's positive historical criticism bears heavily on his approach to the meaning and theology of the Old Testament. There is no mistaking that Kaiser holds a firm confidence in the ability of the historical method to uncover the genuine meaning of discrete historical events. Thus he quotes with approval Wolfhart Pannenberg's affirmation that "every event has its original meaning within the context of occurrence and tradition in which it took place."[6] For Kaiser, though not for Pannenberg, to know that an event actually happened is tantamount to knowing the meaning of that event. There is thus a correlation between the factualness of a biblical event and the theological value which that historical event has for the life of faith.[7] The historical truthfulness of the Old Testament is therefore not merely a matter of whether the Bible has errors, but also a matter of what the biblical texts themselves actually mean.

It is not hard to find in Kaiser's view of history the recurring influence of the early evangelical concept of salvation history. In Kaiser's view historical events such as the exodus and the destruction of Jericho are caught up and find their meaning in the total web of sacred history. We know the meaning of historical events from the interpretation given them in Scripture. It is thus from the whole of biblical salvation-history that Kaiser essays to discover the meaning of the individual historical facts he finds in Scripture and elsewhere. It is, in other words, from the view of Israel's total history as offered by the text of Scripture itself that Kaiser discovers the meaning of individual events of history.

5. Walter C. Kaiser, Jr., *Toward Rediscovering the Old Testament* (Grand Rapids: Zondervan, 1991), 66.
6. Ibid., 64.
7. Ibid., 65.

Note that we are not saying that Kaiser does not also derive a historical and hence, for him, biblical meaning from actual events outside the text. The total of salvation history may well include information about Israel's past drawn from contemporary sources such as archeology and ancient Near Eastern history. In his discussion of the unconditionality of the Abrahamic and Davidic covenants, for example, Kaiser points to the unconditional nature of the "promissory land grant treaties of the Hittites and neo-Assyrians," which he takes to be analogous to the biblical covenants.[8] Thus ancient Near Eastern history and culture can become part of biblical salvation-history.

Ancient Near Eastern Studies

A related and final assumption in the work of Kaiser is the notion that archeology and ancient Near Eastern studies provide a valuable and necessary check on the largely theologically motivated conclusions of biblical criticism. When in doubt about the meaning of a biblical passage, we may look with confidence to the largely secular studies of ancient history. Kaiser's confidence in such studies is closely linked to his view that history is inherently meaningful and accessible to objective scholarship.

Recurring Themes

Single Intent of Scripture/Multiple Fulfilment

Having looked at the basic foundations undergirding Kaiser's work, we turn now to certain key themes built on them. His hermeneutics is firmly rooted in the grammatical-historical method, particularly as developed by Milton Terry in the late nineteenth century. Terry defined the grammatical-historical sense of a biblical writer as "an interpretation of his language as is required by the laws of grammar and the facts of history."[9] For Terry, "the fundamental principle in grammatico-historical exposition is that words and sentences can have but one signification in one and the same connection."[10] Like Terry, Kaiser puts great weight on the notion that the biblical authors wrote with only one meaning in mind. The meaning of Scripture is the simple, literal message of the historical author. Moreover, for Kaiser, as for Terry, the intention of the historical authors is one and the same with the divine meaning. One cannot assign a new meaning to words in the Old Testament, nor replace their historical meaning with a later interpretation, even if that later meaning should be derived from the New Testament. The grammatical-historical meaning of Scripture can be derived from the text only if it is properly understood within its original historical context.

8. Walter C. Kaiser, Jr., *Toward an Old Testament Theology* (Grand Rapids: Zondervan, 1978), 157.

9. Milton S. Terry, *Biblical Hermeneutics* (Grand Rapids: Zondervan, 1974 reprint), 203.

10. Ibid., 205.

But what if the historical sense appears to conflict with the meaning as-
signed to an Old Testament passage by the New Testament? What if the his-
torical sense of Isaiah 7:14, an Old Testament passage understood in the
New Testament as referring to Jesus' birth, involved a sign given to King
Ahaz in his own day? How could the New Testament writers see the birth of
Jesus as a fulfilment of that text? It is necessary, argues Kaiser, not to limit
Old Testament prophecies to a single fulfilment. There is, to be sure, only one
meaning, but there may also be many fulfilments of that intended meaning.
The one meaning is about the promised seed of David (2 Sam. 7:12–16) who
would be born to the house of David in Ahaz's day and whose birth would
be a sign of a future Seed of David, the Messiah.[11] In the birth of Hezekiah,
the son of Ahaz, there was a fulfilment of Isaiah's prophecy shortly after the
time it was delivered. There would also be a fulfilment of that same promise
at the time of the birth of Jesus. There could have been, in fact, many fulfilments of this same prophecy during the intervening time. One must see these
fulfilments as prior verifications, in actual historical events, of the certainty
of the ultimate intended meaning. All such prior historical fulfilments should
be understood as earnests serving "as encouragements for OT saints to believe that the total prediction would be realized in space and time in a climactic, total, and final way."[12] A single prophetic word can thus be understood
as fulfilled in installments. Each installment makes the ultimate fulfilment of
the promise that much more certain. Thus "there was a single meaning in the
mind of the author even though he might know of or experience multiple fulfilments of that single meaning!"[13]

Promise Theology

The single most important theme in Kaiser's work is that of promise theology, to which he devoted his most important book, *Toward an Old Testament Theology.* Simply put, promise theology is an attempt to discover the
central thematic structure of the Bible in the outworking of an ancient divine
promise of salvation to humanity. Promise theology begins by focusing on
the historical events and epochs recorded in Scripture. As varied and diverse
as that history may at times appear, Kaiser maintains that it represents a
"network of interlocking moments in history made significant because of
their content, free allusions to one another, and their organic unity."[14] The
content of biblical history, Kaiser argues, is "a divine 'blessing,' a 'given
word,' a 'declaration,' a 'pledge,' or 'oath' that God Himself would freely do
or be something for all men, nations, and nature."[15] This content is revealed
through a single salvation-history that shows God's ultimate intention to

11. Kaiser, *Toward an Old Testament Theology,* 208–9.
12. Kaiser, *Toward Rediscovering,* 104–5.
13. Kaiser, *Toward an Old Testament Theology,* 129.
14. Ibid., 34.
15. Ibid., 34–35.

deal with a fallen world, judge Satan, and send a Redeemer. That Redeemer is Jesus Christ, who was promised to Adam and Eve in the Garden and whose return Christians still await today. God has acted in "revelatory events" that offer a "promissory word" or "pledge" about the future. Such acts and words give significance "to man's present history and by this, simultaneously to future generations, also."[16]

As all historical events, the history of the promise follows a progressive development. There are growth and refinement in the unfolding of this history. Kaiser speaks of a progressive revelation of God's will in the history of the promise. Thus not all the features of the promise are known in the same way at every stage of history. The promise does not change, but the mode and clarity of its expression do. Its growth is like that of a tree or a vine. It begins with a simple seed. In that seed all the essential features of the promise are contained, but they have yet to be developed and brought to fruition. Over time, and in the course of history, aspects of the promise come into being and grow into maturity as fully formed ideas and concepts. It is only in the historical development that we can see the full realization of God's work. A messianic text in the Old Testament may contain only germinal features of the promise, such as a pledge to the nation Israel or a historical king at a crisis moment in his reign. Within such a passage, however, one can discover a word of promise whose fulfilment serves also as an earnest of a future work of God in history.

Kaiser maintains that to understand God's promise fully, it is necessary to view it along its natural course of development. Each stage of the history of the promise represents a cumulative stage of revelation. Each stage builds on the revelatory stages that precede it. Thus, within the course of the history of the promise there is a growing antecedent revelation which provides the proper context for each new stage. The prophets built their message of judgment and salvation on the revelation available to them in their own antecedent Scripture, that is, the Pentateuch. Kaiser sees his task as a biblical theologian "to provide the exegete with a set of accumulating technical, theological terms, identifications of the key interpretive moments in the history of God's plan for man, and an appreciation for the range of concepts grouped around a unifying core—all of these according to their historical progression in time."[17] Ultimately the Old Testament as a whole or, rather, the history recorded in the Old Testament provided the appropriate and proper context for understanding the New Testament. One fully understands the New Testament only when one views it as the fulfilment of the Old Testament.

Principlization

In suggesting that the Old Testament is fulfilled in the New, Kaiser does not mean to say that the Old Testament has no relevance today for the Chris-

16. Ibid., 35.
17. Ibid., 19.

tian. When properly understood and interpreted, the Old Testament remains divine revelation for the Christian church today. Given the nature of its progressive development, however, it would be a mistake to take a biblical text out of its historical past and apply it directly to situations today. A process is needed that will guide the interpreter in moving from the past to the present.

The first part of the process of applying the Old Testament consists in the recognition that today there are various kinds of laws and injunctions in Scripture. Some are expressed in general terms; others are written in culturally bound particulars. The contemporary meaning of direct principles like "Thou shalt not commit adultery" is not difficult to discover. Culturally bound laws are not as easy to apply in our contemporary world, for example, "You shall not boil a kid in its mother's milk" (Exod. 23:19 rsv). It is also the case, Kaiser argues, that many laws in the Old Testament were intended to be applicable only within the ceremonial rituals of ancient Israel. How then can they be applied today?

The second part of Kaiser's process of applying the Old Testament laws consists in recognizing that each and every culturally or ceremonially bound injunction is the embodiment of a general, or universal, ethical principle. Thus a process which Kaiser calls principlization is necessary. One must first identify the underlying principles behind biblical injunctions, and then one must apply those principles to the life of faith. When Scripture says, "You shall not muzzle an ox when it treads out the grain" (Deut. 24:4 rsv), it is not speaking only about proper feeding of and care for oxen. There is a deeper, more universal ethical principle behind that injunction. One must discover that principle and apply it to the contemporary context.

Biblical Exposition

Kaiser's belief in the continuing relevance of the Old Testament translates quite naturally into a firm commitment to expository preaching or, as he would phrase it, exegetical theology. Both in his busy schedule of preaching and in his writing, Kaiser has come to champion biblical preaching—the proclamation of the meaning and message of the biblical text.

Two central themes emerge from Kaiser's focus on expository preaching. The first is an emphasis on the prophetic role of the preacher. Today's expository preacher would do well to emulate Israel's prophets, who confronted God's people directly and honestly with the demands of the Word of God. The task of the preacher and the sermon is to call the church to repentance and revival.

The second theme is the necessity of proper biblical teaching. If the Bible is to be correctly and clearly expounded from the pulpit, pastors and teachers should be thoroughly trained and equipped in the biblical languages. But not only that—laypersons must have accurate and readable translations. Accordingly, Kaiser has devoted much attention to equipping future pastors with a knowledge of the biblical languages and providing the Christian public with new and accurate translations of the Scriptures. This work may well prove to be his most substantial legacy.

Primary Sources

Kaiser, Walter C., Jr. *Hard Sayings of the Old Testament*. Downers Grove, Ill.: Inter-Varsity, 1988.

————. *The Messiah in the Old Testament*. Grand Rapids: Zondervan, 1995.

————. *Micah-Malachi*. Mastering the Old Testament, vol. 21. Dallas: Word, 1992.

————. *More Hard Sayings of the Old Testament*. Downers Grove, Ill.: InterVarsity, 1992.

————. *Toward an Exegetical Theology*. Grand Rapids: Baker, 1981.

————. *Toward an Old Testament Theology*. Grand Rapids: Zondervan, 1978.

————. *Toward Rediscovering the Old Testament*. Grand Rapids: Zondervan, 1991.

————, and Moisés Silva. *An Introduction to Biblical Hermeneutics: The Search for Meaning*. Grand Rapids: Zondervan, 1994.

Gordon D. Fee

Patrick H. Alexander

Gordon Donald Fee emerged in the 1980s and 1990s as a prominent New Testament scholar with strong ties both to the academic community and to Protestant evangelicalism. His blending of a rigorous historical-critical method in his scholarly work with the passion that he displays in the classroom and the pulpit for life lived under the power and influence of the Holy Spirit has won him many an audience. Fee's Pentecostal heritage interfaces with who Fee is as a biblical scholar and a theologian and a human being; any effort to understand him theologically must take that heritage into account.

The Early Years

Born the son of an Assemblies of God minister in 1934 in Ashland, Oregon, Fee grew up Pentecostal before the charismatic renewal movement arose. Consequently, his early religious experiences occurred when Pentecostal expressions of piety and spirituality—speaking in tongues, the laying on of hands for healing, and the exercising of other gifts of the Spirit—were neither in fashion nor commonplace outside the walls of Pentecostal churches. Criticism of Pentecostalism as being anti-intellectual, antirational, or even cultic almost certainly colored Fee's image of himself and his faith, and ultimately shaped his person and career. If this portrait is accurate, we may assume that it is probably no accident that Fee the Pentecostal scholar came to represent sound reason, commonsense hermeneutics, and intellectual rigor. Nonetheless, his commitment to life in the Spirit—defined not by doctrinal truths or Pentecostal dogma but by traditionally Pentecostal expressions of faith—has never left him, even though Fee's ties to his denomination remain largely in name only.

Having earned an M.A. in biblical studies at Seattle Pacific University, an evangelical Free Methodist institution, Fee pastored a small congregation in Des Moines, Washington, from 1958 to 1962. Ordained an Assemblies of God minister in 1959, he also taught English part-time at nearby Northwest College. The year 1962 saw Fee move to California, where he entered a Ph.D. program at the University of Southern California. He completed his dissertation in 1966 under the noted textual critic Eldon J. Epp. He was then invited to become an assistant professor of religion at Southern California College in Costa Mesa, a liberal arts college affiliated with the Assemblies of God. He proved immensely popular with the students, but differences between his eschatology and that of the denomination contributed to a decision to leave the college in 1969 and to take an assistant professorship at Wheaton College.[1] Although he left on good terms, the episode in some ways augured a bumpy history with his denomination for at least the next twenty years and in some ways defines Fee. When it comes to choosing between denominational assertions and what he understands as a New Testament scholar, he sides with his scholarly instincts and training. At the same time, if forced to choose between following the status quo of scholarship's understanding of life in the Spirit and his own, Fee will choose his own understanding. In either case, it is Fee the scholar who makes the decision. This resolve, of course, has won him both friend and foe.

The Textual Critic

Fee's early academic career continued the trajectory begun during his doctoral studies. When his dissertation was published in 1968, Bruce Metzger, the patron saint of New Testament textual criticism, referred to it as "a definitive analysis of the text and characteristics of the Bodmer Papyrus of Jn."[2] Even before the dissertation was published, however, Fee had begun to make his mark in textual criticism. Holding to the text-critical methods of B. F. Westcott and F. J. A. Hort, Fee resisted the temptation to follow the scholarly trend toward "rigorous eclecticism," which tended to make textual choices on the basis of so-called internal evidence, that is, on the basis of the textual critic's understanding of a given author's style or of what seems theologically or exegetically most likely. Little value was accorded the manuscripts themselves. Fee resisted such methodology. His conviction of the essential rightness of the text-critical methods of Westcott and Hort, which afforded the external evidence an equal role in determining the likely original reading (a more "reasoned eclecticism"), was supported by a pen that vigorously argued his point well and often. Fee wrestled with the proponents of the rigorous eclectic method (as well as with the advocates of the majority-text method, who believed the sheer quantity of a manuscript reading to be determinative) and breathed new life into a discipline that some regarded as passé.[3] Furthermore, he applied textual criticism in other areas; he used it,

1. This was not the first time Fee's eschatology caused him difficulty. His early plans to become a missionary were frustrated by his denomination's dispensational doctrines. As a result his calling took another turn. His commitment to missions, however, has never waned. He has taught in numerous overseas contexts for his denomination, including the former Yugoslavia, Sweden, Africa, and the Far East.

2. Bruce M. Metzger, review of *Papyrus Bodmer II (P66)*, by Gordon D. Fee, *Catholic Biblical Quarterly* 32.3 (1970): 450–51.

3. Jerry Camery-Hoggatt, "At Issue: On the Life and Work of Gordon Fee" (unpublished paper), 8–9, notes the timeliness of Fee's appearance on the scene of textual criticism. Since the Greek text that was standard in the 1970s so closely resembled that of Westcott and Hort, some scholars, including Kurt Aland and the great Joachim Jeremias, had imagined the end of the discipline.

for example, in his examination of the Synoptic Problem[4] and his explanation of the inferiority of the so-called textus receptus, the text behind the King James Version.[5] Such sorties outside the narrow field of textual criticism gave him exposure among a wider, mainly evangelical, audience.

At Wheaton College Fee continued to hone his academic reputation as a textual critic. The year 1970 was most notable. He wrote relentlessly. He became a member of the American Executive Committee of the International Greek New Testament Project, and was elected to both the prestigious Studiorum Novi Testamenti Societas and the Chicago Society of Biblical Research. He was also one of the original members of the Institute for Biblical Research. By this time his work on patristic citations was establishing him internationally as one of the leading authorities in textual criticism.[6] And in the Wheaton classroom Fee's passionate style of teaching and thoroughgoing dedication to biblical exegesis had earned him the admiration and respect of students. Here he established enduring friendships and ties that would later give him entrée to a wide variety of denominational forums.

Throughout the early track of his career as a textual critic, Fee's Pentecostal roots remained buried. Only as he established himself as a scholar did he address issues that touched upon his Pentecostal birthright. Besides being the place where his professional career blossomed, Wheaton became the site of Fee's first academic foray as a Pentecostal. Though he had written a few pieces in the 1960s for denominational publications, Pentecostalism was a subject he scarcely broached in the academic arena until 1972, when he reviewed James Dunn's classic *Baptism in the Holy Spirit* and Frederick Dale Bruner's *Theology of the Holy Spirit* for the most prominent journal on biblical studies.[7] However, Fee's writings for the most part continued to avoid issues relating to the Holy Spirit.

At Wheaton Fee's enthusiasm at the podium resulted in full classrooms. Though by no means a gauge of Fee's influence and impact, it is not insignificant that for the academic year 1972–73 he was elected senior teacher

---

4. Gordon D. Fee, "A Text-Critical Look at the Synoptic Problem," *Novum Testamentum* 22 (1980): 12–28.

5. Gordon D. Fee, "Modern Textual Criticism and the Revival of the *Textus Receptus,*" *Journal of the Evangelical Theological Society* 21 (1978): 19–34; idem, "Modern Textual Criticism and the Majority Text: A Rejoinder," *Journal of the Evangelical Theological Society* 21 (1978): 157–60; idem, "The Majority Text and the Original Text of the New Testament," *Bible Translator* 31 (1980): 107–18. He even wrote an article applying methods of textual criticism to a passage from Qumran: "Some Dissenting Notes on 7Q5 = Mark 6:52–53," *Journal of Biblical Literature* 92 (1973): 109–12. Most of Fee's major text-critical articles are collected in Eldon J. Epp and Gordon D. Fee, *Studies in the Theory and Method of New Testament Textual Criticism,* Studies and Documents 45 (Grand Rapids: Eerdmans, 1993).

6. E.g., Gordon D. Fee, "Patristic Citations—Their Recovery and Use for New Testament Textual Criticism" (paper read at the 1970 meeting of the Society of Biblical Literature); idem, "The Text of John in *The Jerusalem Bible*: A Critique of the Use of Patristic Citations in New Testament Textual Criticism," *Journal of Biblical Literature* 90 (1971): 357–94. Fee's work as a textual critic has been ongoing: in 1986 he was named the founding editor for the New Testament segment of the Greek Fathers Project (Scholars Press), and all of his subsequent exegetical works reflect meticulous attention to text-critical issues.

7. Gordon D. Fee, review of *Baptism in the Holy Spirit,* by James D. G. Dunn, and of *A Theology of the Holy Spirit,* by Frederick Dale Bruner, *Journal of Biblical Literature* 91 (1972): 128–29.

of the year at Wheaton College.[8] His rising star in the scholarly guild and his contagious style in the classroom eventually made him a logical choice for a post at Gordon-Conwell Theological Seminary in 1974. With the charismatic renewal movement in full swing, inviting a Pentecostal could only enhance this institution's interdenominational appeal. Fee drew students to Gordon-Conwell not only from the charismatic movement, but from his own Pentecostal tradition as well. With his denomination's own graduate school in its infancy, some wondered why Fee was never invited to be a professor there.[9] But at Gordon-Conwell he continued to work toward welding his scholarship with issues relevant to Pentecostal theology.

The Exegete

The move to Massachusetts and Gordon-Conwell paralleled a shift in Fee's interests. Textual criticism did not recede completely, but hermeneutics and then Paul became the chief subjects of his writing. Hermeneutics may long have been an interest, but one disclosed publicly, academically, only after careful testing and trial in the classroom. Fee's first two articles on hermeneutics (1976) were addressed to two audiences, one evangelical, the other Pentecostal.[10] Both articles reflected his insistence that interpretation must take seriously the genre of a biblical passage. This anthem resounds throughout all of Fee's subsequent hermeneutical compositions, including *How to Read the Bible for All Its Worth* (1982).

The two 1976 articles also signaled Fee's willingness to bring, albeit circumspectly, his Pentecostalism to the scholarly table.[11] This is not to say that Fee was a closet Pentecostal. Rather, when he wrote or spoke to Pentecostal audiences, he tended to do so as a New Testament scholar who happened to be Pentecostal. When he wrote for the guild, he did so as a New Testament scholar; his Pentecostalism rarely governed the direction of his scholarly pen. This quality of being first of all a New Testament scholar made Fee the target of denominational scrutiny, especially with the appearance of *How to Read the Bible for All Its Worth*. This volume brought Fee

---

8. Camery-Hoggatt, "At Issue," 2.

9. The school was originally called the Assemblies of God Graduate School because of the reluctance of denominational leaders to have a seminary. They often labeled seminaries "cemeteries," a reflection of the notion that intellect and education are inversely proportional to spirituality. In 1984, however, the school was renamed the Assemblies of God Theological Seminary. Fee serves as an adjunct faculty member in the seminary's extension program.

10. Gordon D. Fee, "The Genre of New Testament Literature and Biblical Hermeneutics," in *Interpreting the Word of God: Festschrift in Honor of Steven Barabas*, ed. Samuel J. Schultz and Morris A. Inch (Chicago: Moody, 1976), 105–27; idem, "Hermeneutics and Historical Precedent—A Major Problem in Pentecostal Hermeneutics," in *Perspectives on the New Pentecostalism*, ed. Russell P. Spittler (Grand Rapids: Baker, 1976), 119–32.

11. Undoubtedly Fee's Pentecostalism and his New Testament scholarship embraced on other occasions, such as a February 1975 lecture on the charismatic movement, which he gave at the Cornell Graduate Forum; but the scholarly writings suggest that Pentecostalism was not part of his scholarly persona. Almost certainly, though, Fee spoke as a Pentecostal scholar at various churches, retreats, charismatic conferences, and chaplain schools as well as in missionary settings.

a much broader audience than the classroom and academy had afforded. Chapter 6, which discusses the Book of Acts, caused denominational leaders not a little consternation. Here the implications of the writings of one of the few Pentecostal scholars with the ear of the academy[12] ran, if not contrary to, at least at odds with denominational dogma, particularly concerning the normative character of tongues as evidence of Spirit baptism. Eventually Fee adjusted chapter 6 to mollify the denomination, since his intent in the book had not been to criticize the denomination's position, but merely to address the issue of the role of historical precedent.[13]

New Testament Exegesis: A Handbook for Students and Pastors fleshed out Fee's passion for exegesis and for teaching others how to do it. This handbook walked students through the principles and practice of interpretation, from establishing genre and the original text, to translating and comprehending the flow of the Greek sentence, to researching the historical background of a passage. The citation of Karl Barth on the dedication page aptly depicts what drove Fee: "Exegesis, exegesis, and yet more exegesis!"

The second object of Fee's scholarly affection at Gordon-Conwell was Paul. A commentary on the Pastoral Epistles appeared first. Swimming against scholarly currents, Fee argued for Pauline authorship of the Pastorals. He was convinced that the best indication of the occasion for writing is the historical issue addressed in the writings themselves. Fee saw this issue as the overriding problem of false teachers (1 Tim. 1:3), and he proceeded to interpret the letters from that "singular point of view."[14] The reception was mixed but anticipated. Those who regarded Paul as the author welcomed Fee's position that in these letters Paul was battling the problem of false teachers; of those rejecting Fee's conclusions, some took him seriously, but remained unconvinced.[15]

More important for Fee's career was his study of Paul's first letter to Corinth. This study began with a course on 1 Corinthians which he taught at Wheaton in 1970, and continued to teach there and at other schools for the next seventeen years. Along the way he wrote a study guide (1979) for a college-level course offered through his denomination's International Correspondence Institute (Brussels). His passion for 1 Corinthians culminated

12. Certainly there were others, including Russell P. Spittler of Fuller Theological Seminary, but none were as visible as Fee in academic settings nor as popular among grassroots Pentecostals. In recent years more Pentecostal and charismatic scholars have become involved in serious academic inquiry.

13. That Fee did implicitly challenge denominational teachings can be deduced from some of his articles, notably, "Hermeneutics and Historical Precedent." This article later appeared in Gordon D. Fee, *Gospel and Spirit: Issues in New Testament Hermeneutics* (Peabody, Mass.: Hendrickson, 1991), 83–104, a collection of his articles on hermeneutics, including "Baptism in the Holy Spirit: The Issue of Separability and Subsequence," 105–19.

14. Gordon D. Fee, *1 and 2 Timothy, Titus,* New International Biblical Commentary (Peabody, Mass.: Hendrickson, 1989), xiii–xiv, 5–14.

15. J. A. Ziesler, "Which Is the Best Commentary? XII. The Pastoral Epistles," *Expository Times* 99.9 (1988): 264–65, calls Fee's effort "the best of the recent conservative commentaries, quite substantial in treatment." While Ziesler could have included it in his discussion of major commentaries, for some reason he relegated it to his discussion of commentaries for church groups and nonspecialist readers.

in 1987 with the publication of *The First Epistle to the Corinthians* in the celebrated New International Commentary on the New Testament series edited by F. F. Bruce.[16] Fee composed the greater part of the volume while at Gordon-Conwell and put the finishing touches on it after moving to Regent College (Vancouver) in 1986.

In the commentary Fee's rigorous hermeneutic seeks to discover precisely what Paul was saying in the original context. As in all of his exegesis, Fee takes seriously the genre of the document and establishes the occasion for its writing. He implores the reader to "see how everything fits into the historical/literary context both of the individual paragraphs and of the larger sections." He also pledges to "exegete the whole book from a consistent perspective as to the historical situation." Finally he notes his "own deep concern" that "the living Word of God be a living word for today."[17] This threefold aim resounds throughout virtually all of his exegetical writings and epitomizes his interests and zeal as an interpreter.

The reception of the 1 Corinthians commentary reveals something about both Fee's place in the academy and his place as a native son of Pentecostalism. At the grassroots level *The First Epistle to the Corinthians* is presently the best-selling commentary in the entire series. At the scholarly level, reviewers almost unanimously accorded the book a place alongside other notable commentaries on 1 Corinthians. This praise for the volume did seem tempered, however, by scholars outside evangelical traditions. For instance, one reviewer tagged it as "a bulky commentary of slightly evangelical flavor";[18] others faulted Fee for taking seriously the historicity of Acts and for accepting the deutero-Paulines as genuinely Pauline. Nonetheless the commentary was hailed as lucid, well-crafted, and significant, and has become a standard text in courses on 1 Corinthians. Its appearance landed Fee squarely in the middle of subsequent academic discussions on Paul and his Corinthian correspondence.

One of the most intriguing assessments of the work came from Fee's own tradition. John Christopher Thomas, now a professor of New Testament at the Church of God School of Theology in Cleveland, Tennessee, enthusiastically endorsed the volume. He especially praised Fee for his discussion of 1 Corinthians 12–14. Then he ever so gently chided Fee for his "failure to interact with or even cite many Pentecostal scholars who have published in this area. Most often he simply fails to cite the relevant literature."[19] Thomas's remarks are

16. Gordon D. Fee, *The First Epistle to the Corinthians* (Grand Rapids: Eerdmans, 1987). At the 1980 Toronto meeting of the Society of New Testament Studies, Bruce invited Fee to write this volume (p. ix).

17. Ibid., x.

18. Joseph Plevnik, review of *The First Epistle to the Corinthians,* by Gordon D. Fee, *Catholic Biblical Quarterly* 50.4 (1988): 715–17. Although the overall review is quite positive, the opening pitch seems suspicious as to whether Fee can really step up to the plate of scholarship.

19. John Christopher Thomas, review of *The First Epistle to the Corinthians,* by Gordon D. Fee, *Pneuma* 10.1 (1988): 73–74.

telling both as to how Fee's work is received in his tradition and as to how Fee regards himself in that tradition. Scholars within Fee's tradition respect his work as a New Testament academic, and they welcome his voice as having secured Pentecostalism an entrée to the guild. They seem frustrated, however, that Fee does not bear the banner of the Pentecostal intellectual tradition into the academy's camp. Fee, in turn, apparently does not see himself as a standard-bearer at all. First and foremost, he is from an academic standpoint a New Testament scholar; he is a Pentecostal by virtue of his experience and by virtue of his *own scholarly*—and not his tradition's confessional—understanding of life in the Spirit. That his scholarly understanding of the Spirit is at times at odds with his tradition's understanding suggests that the differences in presuppositions may preclude his engaging those within his tradition in academic dialog. One can only speculate. On the one hand, Fee's commitment to the Pentecostal experience has not kept him from engaging in academic debate and dialog. On the other hand, his commitment to New Testament scholarship does baffle Pentecostals.

After F. F. Bruce's death in 1990, Fee was invited to assume the editorship of the New International Commentary on the New Testament series, a post that Bruce had held since 1962. This honor solidified Fee's position in the evangelical community and further enhanced his overall academic standing. Five years later he contributed his second volume to the series, *Paul's Letter to the Philippians*. The use of the word *Letter* rather than *Epistle* probably reflects Fee's editorial hand:[20] Paul in a real time and place wrote a real letter (not an epistle) to real believers at Philippi. As is typical in Fee's exegesis, issues of genre and historical circumstance dominate his interpretation of the letter. Careful attention to detail and an ear to the ground of the letter's theology allow Fee to hear the text in a way that has modern readers in view—especially the "parish minister and teacher of Scripture."[21]

The Pentecostal Scholar

As we noted earlier, before the 1970s Fee only rarely addressed scholarly issues concerning the Holy Spirit. Even in the late 1970s and 1980s, his scholarly focus on the Spirit was minimal. The commentary on 1 Corinthians (1987) perhaps afforded him the most visible opportunity to speak as a scholar on issues germane to pneumatology (especially in his analysis of 1 Cor. 12–14), but even here his primary concern was to produce a commentary on 1 Corinthians. His approach was first and foremost that of a New Testament scholar.

But with an article on "Pauline Literature" in the *Dictionary of Pentecostal and Charismatic Movements* (1988) Fee's interests in Paul, hermeneutics,

20. Fee's volume replaced J. J. Müller, *The Epistles of Paul to the Philippians and Philemon*, New International Commentary on the New Testament (Grand Rapids: Eerdmans, 1955); cf. also Fee's *First Epistle to the Corinthians*.
21. Gordon D. Fee, *Paul's Letter to the Philippians* (Grand Rapids: Eerdmans, 1995), xi.

and the Spirit converged.[22] He wrote the piece for an audience largely comprising Pentecostals and charismatics, and he spoke explicitly on matters relating to the Spirit. Almost certainly Fee had undertaken such exposition before—at retreats, for ministers' conferences, or in preaching contexts—but this time he wrote for general readers on issues concerning the Spirit. The nearly twenty-page article set the stage not only for a more academic inquiry into issues surrounding the Holy Spirit, but for a volume that articulated fully his understanding of the Holy Spirit in the letters of Paul.

God's Empowering Presence: The Holy Spirit in the Letters of Paul examines exegetically every passage in the Pauline corpus (including the deutero-Paulines) that relates to the Spirit. There are nearly eight hundred pages of intense analysis of language, grammar, and context. Another two hundred pages synthesize Fee's findings and relate his theology of the Spirit. Fee sets out the Spirit's role under the rubric "salvation in Christ."[23] Here he sees as essential issues (1) the eschatological framework of Paul's existence and thinking, (2) his understanding of Christ, (3) his understanding of salvation itself, and (4) his understanding of the people of God, the sphere of God's eschatological salvation in Christ. Crucial for Fee is the coming of the Spirit as the eschatological fulfilment of the promises of the Jewish Scriptures and of Jesus, confirmed as Messiah by his resurrection and his sending of the Spirit. Seeing in the kingdom of God as proclaimed by Jesus the "already/not yet" quality of the eschatological age to come, Fee contends that the Spirit stands as the "guarantor"[24] that "*already* the future had begun, *not yet* had it been consummated. From the New Testament perspective the whole of Christian existence—and theology—has this eschatological 'tension' as its basic framework."[25]

Within this framework, and in sharp distinction to those who see the gifts of the Spirit as having ceased (e.g., B. B. Warfield), Fee envisions the ongoing activity of the Holy Spirit in the life of the people of God. The Spirit is "God's Empowering Presence" in the here and now. This means that tongues, prophecy, the working of miracles, and the exercising of the Spirit's gifts (which are not limited to any specific list, e.g., 1 Cor. 12–14; Rom. 12:7–8; 2 Cor. 12:12) have a place in the life of the people of God today. But lest one think Fee is grinding an axe solely on the basis of the church's failure to ex-

---

22. Gordon D. Fee, "Pauline Literature," in *Dictionary of Pentecostal and Charismatic Movements,* ed. Stanley M. Burgess, Gary B. McGee, and Patrick H. Alexander (Grand Rapids: Zondervan, 1988), 665–83.

23. Gordon D. Fee, *God's Empowering Presence: The Holy Spirit in the Letters of Paul* (Peabody, Mass.: Hendrickson, 1994), 801. In the introduction (pp. 11–13) Fee sets out what he means by "salvation in Christ." His categories echo Clark Pinnock, "The Concept of Spirit in the Epistles of Paul," Ph.D. diss., University of Manchester, 1963.

24. Scriptural promises of the coming of the Spirit include Jer. 31:31; Ezek. 36:36; and Joel 2:28. See the discussions of 2 Cor. 1:22; 5:5; and Eph. 1:14 in *God's Empowering Presence,* 293, 324–27, 671, and especially 806–7, where Fee sees ἀρραβών as one of Paul's most fitting metaphors for capturing the eschatological tension of "already/not yet."

25. Fee, *God's Empowering Presence,* 801.

ercise the Spirit's gifts, he is careful to insist that the fruits of the Spirit (Gal.
5:22–23) are to be equally in evidence. Both the gifts and the fruits come
from the Spirit's empowering God's people, and both have an eschatological
edge. The gifts attest to the certainty of the coming end; the fruits are evident
when God's people live their lives in full recognition of the coming end.[26]
God's dwelling in the midst of his people summons them to holy living and
gives them the power to accomplish it.

Fee also examines the contrast between life in the Spirit and the flesh[27]
and rejects the notion that believers live in a constant state of tension between the two. On the contrary, because the eschatological presence of the
Spirit is sufficient for our living in the present, Fee can state unequivocally,
"Nowhere does Paul describe life in the Spirit as one of constant struggle
with the flesh."[28]

Another urgent concern of Fee is the personhood of the Spirit. Fee contends that contemporary Christianity has tacitly ignored the Spirit as the
Third Person of the Godhead and instead "treats the Spirit as a matter of
creed and doctrine, but not as a vital experienced reality in believers' lives."[29]
Fee is particularly troubled that the church has lost sight of the Godhead by
referring to the Spirit as "it." Such disregard defines the Spirit in impersonal
terms (though the Bible itself uses such metaphors as fire, wind, and oil) and
relegates the Spirit to the margins of Christian experience. Instead of viewing
the Spirit as some unidentifiable abstract force, the church must, Fee argues,
recognize that Paul was trinitarian to the core and should take its lead therefrom. Thus *God's Empowering Presence* shows as fully as any of his writings
Fee the Pentecostal scholar, Fee the Pentecostal theologian.[30]

Fee's efforts to investigate the topic of the Holy Spirit in the letters of Paul
represent the culmination of thirty years of scholarly preparation and a lifetime of personal interest. His writings, whether on textual criticism, hermeneutics, Pauline literature, or the Spirit, consistently epitomize his concern to
investigate thoroughly the writings of the New Testament, including in particular their genre and occasion. Ultimately, all of Fee's writings witness to
his deepest passion that "the living Word of God be a living word for to-

26. Ibid., 843–45, 864–69.
27. Ibid., 816–26.
28. Ibid., 817.
29. Gordon D. Fee, *Paul, the Spirit, and the People of God* (Peabody, Mass.: Hendrickson, 1996),
37. In this popular-level sequel to *God's Empowering Presence*, Fee devotes two chapters to the personhood of the Spirit and the Trinity (pp. 24–35, 36–48).
30. The volume was generally well received in academic reviews across denominational lines:
"an outstanding contribution to the study of the Holy Spirit in the Pauline Corpus" (*Orientalia
christiana periodica* 61 [1995]: 2); "a veritable *tour de force*" (*Catholic Biblical Quarterly* 57.4
[1995]: 804–5); "magnificent scholarship" (*Southwestern Journal of Theology* 38.1 [1995]: 61).
Nonetheless, some questioned the method and thesis (e.g., *Restoration Quarterly* 37.3 [1995], 184).
Ironically, a denominational review was assigned not to another scholar, but to the head of Berean
College, the denomination's "distance education" (i.e., correspondence) school (*Advance*, May
1995, p. 37). More than half of this review consists of a caution that mainline Pentecostals will question Fee's conclusions.

day."[31] Fee's work as a scholar who happens to be Pentecostal—and vice versa—has not only opened the door for an entire generation of Pentecostal and charismatic scholars who want to take scholarship and their spirituality seriously. It has also opened the eyes of those not within a Pentecostal tradition to see that a faith that embraces the experiential dimension can also take seriously the role of scholarship.

Primary Sources

Fee, Gordon D. *1 and 2 Timothy, Titus.* Good News Commentary. San Francisco: Harper and Row, 1984. Also, New International Biblical Commentary. Peabody, Mass.: Hendrickson, 1989.

———. *The First Epistle to the Corinthians.* New International Commentary on the New Testament. Grand Rapids: Eerdmans, 1987.

———. *God's Empowering Presence: The Holy Spirit in the Letters of Paul.* Peabody, Mass.: Hendrickson, 1994.

———. *Gospel and Spirit: Issues in New Testament Hermeneutics.* Peabody, Mass.: Hendrickson, 1991.

———. *New Testament Exegesis: A Handbook for Students and Pastors.* Philadelphia: Westminster, 1983; 2d ed., Louisville: Westminster/John Knox, 1993.

———. *Papyrus Bodmer II (P66): Its Textual Relationships and Scribal Characteristics.* Salt Lake City: University of Utah Press, 1968.

———. *Paul's Letter to the Philippians.* New International Commentary on the New Testament. Grand Rapids: Eerdmans, 1995.

Fee, Gordon D., and Eldon J. Epp. *Studies in the Theory and Method of New Testament Textual Criticism.* Studies and Documents 45. Grand Rapids: Eerdmans, 1993.

Fee, Gordon D., and Douglas Stuart. *How to Read the Bible for All Its Worth.* Grand Rapids: Zondervan, 1982; 2d ed., 1993.

---

31. Fee, *First Epistle to the Corinthians,* x. *Christianity Today,* not noted for including Pentecostals in discussions of evangelicalism, invited Craig S. Keener, a charismatic from a Pentecostal tradition, to review *God's Empowering Presence* (39.3 [March 6, 1995]: 35–36). Subsequently, a cover story dealt with some of Fee's insights concerning the Holy Spirit—Wendy Murray Zoba, "Father, Son, and . . .," *Christianity Today* 40.7 (June 17, 1996): 18–24.

Edwin M. Yamauchi

Kenneth R. Calvert

Edwin Masao Yamauchi was born in the city of Hilo on the island of Hawaii in February of 1937. In his youth Edwin's father Shokyo died, leaving his mother Haruko to provide for his welfare and education. Though his father had been a devout Buddhist, Edwin received only a nominal understanding of this Eastern philosophy. In his early teens he attended an Episcopal boys' school where he obtained an equally nominal understanding of Christianity. His earliest exposure to an evangelical faith was through his classmate Richard Lum, who invited Yamauchi to attend the Kalihi Union Church where a visiting basketball player from Taylor University was presenting the gospel. In the autumn of 1952 Theodore Yeh, an Episcopal minister from China, introduced Edwin to Robert Hambrook, a retired British educator, who encouraged Yamauchi toward a final Christian commitment.[1]

In his late teens Edwin worked summers on a missionary farm in Wahiawa on the island of Oahu. Though Yamauchi had little aptitude for farming, the administrator Claude Curtis influenced Edwin's early faith and understanding of Scripture. Interests in fiction and math were replaced by a love for Greek and linguistics, which formed the foundation of Yamauchi's scholarship.[2] At Shelton College he polished his abilities while working on a B.A. in Hebrew and Hellenistics. There he held his first teaching post as an instructor of Greek (1960–61). From 1961 to 1964 Yamauchi swiftly completed his graduate work in Mediterranean studies at Brandeis University, while honing his linguistic and archeological skills through summer sessions at Brandeis, Oklahoma, and Harvard.

In the 1960s biblical studies were dominated by higher criticism. Few universities offered alternatives, making it difficult for scholars to enter into serious research without accepting Julius Wellhausen's documentary hypothesis and its broad influence. However, Cyrus Gordon of Brandeis University rejected critical theory that neglected evidence tending to corroborate biblical and classical accounts.[3] A group of evangelicals were drawn to Gordon; Yamauchi emerged as one of the most prolific.

---

1. Edwin M. Yamauchi, interview by author, 6–8 May 1994.
2. Edwin M. Yamauchi, "Imprisoned in Paradise," *Christianity Today* 36.13 (Nov. 9, 1992): 11; by 1994 he had studied twenty-one languages.
3. Cyrus H. Gordon, *Ugaritic Literature* (Rome: Pontificium Institutum Biblicum, 1949); idem, "Higher Critics and Forbidden Fruit," *Christianity Today* 4.4 (Nov. 23, 1959): 3–6; idem, *The Common*

Elements of Yamauchi's earliest scholarly contributions were also influenced by Kimie Honda, whom he married in August 1962. In fact, her studies at Wheaton College on ancient slavery served as a foundation for his first paper at a scholarly conference and an article for the *Bulletin of the Evangelical Theological Society.*[4] This article displays his command of ancient languages and his focus on the historical and cultural settings of the biblical accounts.

The Early Monographs

Yamauchi's first monographs foreshadowed the themes of nearly his entire corpus of work. In 1966 and 1967 he produced two texts dealing with the application of higher-critical analysis to classical and biblical documents. In *Composition and Corroboration in Classical and Biblical Studies* he reviewed critical treatments of Homer and Herodotus as well as of the texts of Genesis and Daniel.[5] He questioned why classicists, in light of the evidence, had retreated from extreme critical methodology while biblical scholars stubbornly retained theories not corroborated by the data. His second monograph, *Greece and Babylon: Early Contacts between the Aegean and the Near East,* focused primarily on the Book of Daniel.[6] Whereas S. R. Driver had asserted that the content and a few Greek words found in Daniel "demanded" a Hellenistic dating (c. 165 B.C.),[7] Yamauchi argued that Akkadian prototypes of the apocalyptic element in Daniel, etymological considerations, and, above all, the physical evidence of pre-Hellenistic contacts between the Aegean and the Near East all support an early date for this biblical text (sixth century B.C.). He postulated that the few Greek influences found in Daniel are better explained by centuries of cultural interaction than by the Hellenistic influx of Alexander and the Diadochoi (the lieutenants who succeeded him and split up his empire). These two works quickly placed Yamauchi among a number of evangelical scholars specifically questioning higher-critical theory.[8]

Background of Greek and Hebrew Civilizations (New York: Norton, 1965); idem, *The Ancient Near East* (New York: Norton, 1965). Gordon proposed deciphering Linear A as a Northwest Semitic dialect; see "Notes on Minoan Linear A," *Antiquity* 31 (1957): 124–30; "Toward a Grammar of Minoan," *Orientalia* 32 (1963): 292–97; "The Decipherment of Minoan," *Natural History* 72 (Nov. 1963): 22–31.

4. Edwin M. Yamauchi, "Slaves of God," *Bulletin of the Evangelical Theological Society* 9.1 (1966): 31–49 (esp. n. 41). Yamauchi regards Kimie, who earned a second degree from Columbia University, the most important influence on his faith. Their two children are Brian (b. 1966) and Gail (b. 1970).

5. Edwin M. Yamauchi, *Composition and Corroboration in Classical and Biblical Studies* (Philadelphia: Presbyterian and Reformed, 1966).

6. Edwin M. Yamauchi, *Greece and Babylon: Early Contacts between the Aegean and the Near East* (Grand Rapids: Baker, 1967); see also Bernard Goldman, review of *Greece and Babylon,* by Edwin M. Yamauchi, *Classical World* 61 (Jan. 1968): 181.

7. S. R. Driver, *An Introduction to the Literature of the Old Testament* (New York: Meridian, 1956 reprint), 508; cf. Edwin M. Yamauchi, "The Greek Words in Daniel in the Light of Greek Influence in the Near East," in *New Perspectives on the Old Testament,* ed. J. Barton Payne (Waco: Word, 1970), 170–200.

8. E.g., Kenneth A. Kitchen, *Ancient Orient and Old Testament* (Chicago: InterVarsity, 1966); see also Edwin M. Yamauchi, review of *Ancient Orient and Old Testament,* by Kenneth A. Kitchen, *Journal of the American Scientific Affiliation* 20 (1968): 94.

In 1967 Yamauchi published his dissertation, *Mandaic Incantation Texts.*[9] In 1970 he produced *Gnostic Ethics and Mandaean Origins.*[10] These two works marked his entrance into the field of Gnostic studies. Here again Yamauchi brought physical evidence to bear on critical theory. The German scholars Richard Reitzenstein, Rudolf Bultmann, and Kurt Rudolph had used the modern Mandaean Gnostics of Iraq and Iran as evidence that crucial elements of ancient Christian doctrine were rooted in a pre-Christian Gnosticism.[11] Yamauchi's treatments of the data concluded that the Mandaean sect was a synthesis of a Mesopotamian cultic tradition and Gnostic teaching (it is possible that they were Jewish-Christian Gnostic Elkesaites). Central to this discussion was his dating of the evidence. The earliest he could date Mandaeism was the second century A.D., much too late to be useful in source studies of the Gospel of John (contra Bultmann). Robert Grant of the University of Chicago wrote that Yamauchi's "restraint in an area where hypotheses have often overshadowed the evidence is highly welcome."[12]

By 1969, in addition to his monographs Yamauchi had produced a number of scholarly and popular articles. His work was respected by colleagues within and outside of evangelicalism. However, this did not earn him due advancement. Denied tenure by Rutgers University, where he had been an assistant professor of history since 1964, he was hired by Miami University (Ohio) in 1969 and promoted to full professor in 1973.

In Oxford, Ohio, Yamauchi greatly influenced local evangelicals. Together with Bill Wilson he helped establish the Oxford Bible Fellowship, an active church with a large campus ministry. He also served as advisor for InterVarsity Christian Fellowship and as coordinator for a group of faculty, graduate students, and staff members. He frequently gave public lectures on topics like "Easter—Myth, Hallucination, or History?"[13] Such work earned him the admiration and sometimes the scorn of the university community. More important was his influence on Miami students who rose to positions of evangelical leadership, including Michael Maudlin, managing editor of

9. Edwin M. Yamauchi, *Mandaic Incantation Texts,* American Oriental Series 49 (New Haven: American Oriental Society, 1967); see also Morton Smith, review of *Mandaic Incantation Texts,* by Edwin M. Yamauchi, *American Journal of Archaeology* 73 (Jan. 1969): 95–97; Edwin M. Yamauchi, "Aramaic Magic Bowls," *Journal of the American Oriental Society* 85 (1965): 511–23; idem, "A Mandaic Magic Bowl from the Yale Babylonian Collection," *Berytus* 17 (1967): 49–63.

10. Edwin M. Yamauchi, *Gnostic Ethics and Mandaean Origins* (Cambridge, Mass.: Harvard University Press, 1970), esp. 53–93; see also Kurt Rudolph, review of *Gnostic Ethics and Mandaean Origins,* by Edwin M. Yamauchi, *Theologische Literaturzeitung* 97 (Oct. 1972): 733–38.

11. Richard Reitzenstein, *Die hellenistischen Mysterienreligionen* (Leipzig: Teubner, 1910); Rudolf Bultmann, *Das Evangelium des Johannes* (Göttingen: Vandenhoeck and Ruprecht, 1964); Kurt Rudolph, *Die Mandäer,* 2 vols. (Göttingen: Vandenhoeck and Ruprecht, 1960–61).

12. Robert Grant, review of *Gnostic Ethics and Mandaean Origins,* by Edwin M. Yamauchi, *Journal of Biblical Literature* 91 (1972): 281; see also George MacRae, review of *Gnostic Ethics and Mandaean Origins,* by Edwin M. Yamauchi, *Theological Studies* 32 (1971): 730: "It is important to have a position like this so clearly argued at a time when the hypothesis of a pre-Christian Western origin of Mandaeism risks becoming a dogma of the history of religions."

13. Edwin M. Yamauchi, "Easter—Myth, Hallucination, or History?" *Christianity Today* 18.12 (March 15, 1974): 4–7; 18.13 (March 29, 1974): 12–14, 16.

Christianity Today, and Dorothy Chappell, dean of the faculty at Gordon College.[14]

In 1972 Yamauchi published *The Stones and the Scriptures: An Introduction to Biblical Archaeology,* outlining his convictions that archeology produces confirmation as well as difficulties for the biblical texts.[15] He warns against fundamentalist abuses of archeology but at the same time emphasizes its strengths, which were sufficient to bring about William F. Albright's shift from a critical position to acceptance of biblical authenticity and William Ramsay's dramatic affirmation of Luke's accuracy on the basis of archeological data from Asia Minor.[16] In this work Yamauchi affirms that, though the evidence is often limited, an accurate analysis including the three spheres of archeological material, inscriptions, and tradition will produce a better understanding of the religious and cultural environments of the Hebrews and early Christians.[17]

The central theme of *The Stones and the Scriptures* is a critique of higher-critical (literary or source) theory in contrast to lower (textual) criticism. Here Yamauchi affirms the values of limited critical techniques in ascertaining the text and background of the Bible, but refuses to accept approaches that include literary analysis unsupported by the evidence. He sternly warns against theories that argue from silence. He criticizes the Tübingen school and the theories of religious evolution affirmed by the history-of-religions school.[18] For Yamauchi, the presupposition that the biblical text is always inaccurate causes essential errors. He suggests that no classicist, no Orientalist, no Egyptologist would approach a text the way in which biblical scholars handle their data.[19]

The Major Work on Gnosticism

In 1973 appeared Yamauchi's most important work, *Pre-Christian Gnosticism: A Survey of the Proposed Evidences.*[20] The central question addressed in this monograph is whether Gnostic systems existed prior to and gave

14. Edwin M. Yamauchi, "God's Work at Miami U," *Christianity Today* 37.7 (June 21, 1993): 13.

15. Edwin M. Yamauchi, *The Stones and the Scriptures: An Introduction to Biblical Archaeology* (Philadelphia: Lippincott, 1972); see also idem, "The Archaeological Confirmation of Suspect Elements in the Classical and the Biblical Traditions," in *The Law and the Prophets,* ed. John H. Skilton (Nutley, N.J.: Presbyterian and Reformed, 1974), 54–70.

16. Yamauchi, *Stones,* 24–25, 95–96.

17. Ibid., 20–22, 25–26, 158–65.

18. Yamauchi was influenced by Carsten Colpe, *Die religionsgeschichtliche Schule: Darstellung und Kritik ihres Bildes vom gnostischen Erlösermythus* (Göttingen: Vandenhoeck and Ruprecht, 1961); see also Edwin M. Yamauchi, "History-of-Religions School," in *New Dictionary of Theology,* ed. Sinclair B. Ferguson et al. (Downers Grove, Ill.: InterVarsity, 1988), 308–9.

19. Yamauchi, *Stones,* 27–31, 92–97; idem, *Composition,* 32–37; see also Martha M. Wilson, review of *The Stones and the Scriptures,* by Edwin M. Yamauchi, *Library Journal* 97 (Sept. 1972): 2742.

20. Edwin M. Yamauchi, *Pre-Christian Gnosticism: A Survey of the Proposed Evidences* (Grand Rapids: Eerdmans, 1973; 2d ed., Grand Rapids: Baker, 1983); see also Edwin M. Yamauchi, "Some Alleged Evidences for Pre-Christian Gnosticism," in *New Dimensions in New Testament Study,* ed. Richard N. Longenecker and Merrill C. Tenney (Grand Rapids: Zondervan, 1974), 46–70.

Christianity its "redeemer myth" (among other elements), as claimed by Reitzenstein and Bultmann, or whether proto-Gnostic components were drawn
together by Christians and Jews into full-fledged Gnostic systems after the
first century.[21] A related question is whether non-Christian Gnostic evidence
necessarily points to a pre-Christian Gnostic presence. In opposition to scholarly orthodoxy, Yamauchi rejects the notion of a pre-Christian Gnosticism.[22]

The inability of scholars to define the word *Gnostic* is among Yamauchi's
many points of contention.[23] More important is the dating of Gnosticism. All
definitive data concerning Christian and non-Christian Gnostic systems
come from the second to eighth centuries A.D. For scholars to establish a pre-
Christian Gnosticism, they have to extrapolate backwards from post–first
century A.D. evidence. Among the data Yamauchi addresses are patristic
sources, hermetic literature, Manichaeism, Syriac evidence, Coptic (Nag
Hammadi) evidence, the Mandaic data, and Judaic sources.[24] In each case
Yamauchi reviews various theories and the failure to discover definite evidence of any pre-Christian Gnostic systems.[25]

First-century sources support Yamauchi's position. The New Testament
(particularly the Johannine literature) and apocryphal texts certainly include Gnostic tendencies, but by no means point to a Gnostic system.[26] The
Dead Sea Scrolls also come up for discussion, for they seem to teach a Gnos-
tic-like cosmological dualism (light vs. dark). Further, the baptismal elements found at Qumran have been seen as Gnostic influences on John the
Baptist and early Christianity. Yamauchi points out, however, that Gnostic
thought was manifestly anti-Jewish, including a non-Judaic dualism. In addition, Gnostic systems give evidence of only a limited knowledge of the Hebrew Scriptures (mainly Genesis). Consequently, whatever Gnostic elements
the Dead Sea Scrolls and, indeed, any of the first-century evidence contain,
are only a small part of the great variety of proto-Gnostic components found
throughout the Mediterranean milieu from which Gnostic systems arose.
So, then, the scrolls, while illuminating ancient Christianity, in no way reflect a pre-Christian Gnostic system at Qumran.[27] Yamauchi concludes by
questioning the misuse of data and the generally poor methodology of his
fellow scholars.[28]

---

21. Yamauchi, *Pre-Christian Gnosticism,* 163–70.
22. Ibid., 13–28.
23. Ibid., 18. Of particular import was the Messina conference, "The Origins of Gnosticism," in
1966; see George MacRae, "Gnosis in Messina," *Catholic Biblical Quarterly* 28 (1966): 332. Even
major proponents were frustrated; see James M. Robinson and Helmut Koester, *Trajectories through
Early Christianity* (Philadelphia: Fortress, 1971), 115–16.
24. See also Edwin M. Yamauchi, "Jewish Gnosticism? The Prologue of John, Mandaean Parallels, and the Trimorphic Protennoia," in *Studies in Gnosticism and Hellenistic Religions,* ed. R. van
den Broek and M. J. Vermaseren (Leiden: Brill, 1981), 467–97.
25. Yamauchi, *Pre-Christian Gnosticism,* 56–142.
26. Ibid., 29–55.
27. Ibid., 152–56.
28. Ibid., 151–62, 184–86.

Reviews of *Pre-Christian Gnosticism* were positive, affirming the critique of both general theory and methodology. Elaine Pagels stated that Yamauchi "has cleared the way for revaluation of the basic issue, the relation of Gnosticism and NT Christianity. Whoever takes up this issue should find in his book an incisive account of the history of scholarship and a challenge to rethink critically one's own approach to the sources."[29] Of course, no paradigm shift occurred. So in 1983 Yamauchi published a second edition with a new chapter entitled "Pre-Christian Gnosticism Reconsidered a Decade Later."[30] Here he discusses the continued scholarly frustration regarding a definition for the word *Gnostic*, the failure to discover any pre-Christian Gnostic documents, and the fact that the Nag Hammadi texts present only a vague notion of Gnosticism.[31] Acknowledging that there is only limited support for his position, he exhorts his readers to consider the evidence and the work of other scholars who doubt pre-Christian Gnosticism.[32]

Among the supporters of Yamauchi's position was Alan Segal, whose *Two Powers in Heaven* examined reports by rabbis who were "among the closest, most expert, and most concerned contemporary observers of Christianity and Gnosticism."[33] He concluded that they attributed dualistic sentiments ("two powers") to both Gnostics and early Christians. But "the evidence is that [rabbinic] opposition to Christian exegesis preceded opposition to extreme gnostic exegesis." Indeed, the controversy led to a Gnostic self-definition: "The radicalization of gnosticism [the concept of the two powers as antagonistic] was a product of the battle between the rabbis, the Christians and various other 'two powers' sectarians who inhabited the outskirts of Judaism."[34] Thus Gnosticism arose later than Christianity.

29. Elaine Pagels, review of *Pre-Christian Gnosticism*, by Edwin M. Yamauchi, *Theological Studies* 35 (1974): 776; other reviews include those of Hall Partrick, *Church History* 43 (1974): 97; John D. Turner, *Journal of Biblical Literature* 93 (1974): 482–84; R. McL. Wilson, *Expository Times* 84 (1972–73): 379; Gilles Quispel, *Louvain Studies* 5.2 (1974): 211–12; George MacRae, *Catholic Biblical Quarterly* 36 (1974): 296–97.

30. Yamauchi, *Pre-Christian Gnosticism*, 2d ed., 187–249; see also Birger A. Pearson, review of *Pre-Christian Gnosticism*, by Edwin M. Yamauchi, *Religious Studies Review* 11.1 (Jan. 1985): 75.

31. See also Edwin M. Yamauchi, "Pre-Christian Gnosticism in the Nag Hammadi Texts?" *Church History* 48 (1979): 129–41; idem, "The Word from Nag Hammadi," *Christianity Today* 22.7 (Jan. 13, 1978): 19–22; idem, review of *The Nag Hammadi Library in English*, by James M. Robinson, *Christianity Today* 23.1 (Oct. 6, 1978): 36–40, 42–43; idem, review of *The Gnostic Gospels*, by Elaine Pagels, *Eternity* 31 (Sept. 1980): 66–67, 69; idem, review of *Zur Sprache und Literatur der Mandäer*, by Rudolf Macuch, Kurt Rudolph, and Eric Segelberg, *Journal of the American Oriental Society* 100 (1980): 79–82; idem, review of *The Gnostic Dialogue*, by Pheme Perkins, *Christian Scholar's Review* 11 (1982): 171; idem, "Pre-Christian Gnosticism, the New Testament and Nag Hammadi in Recent Debate," *Themelios* 10.1 (1984): 22–27; idem, "Gnosticism: Has Nag-Hammadi Changed Our View?" *Evangel* 8.2 (Summer 1990): 4–7.

32. Yamauchi, *Pre-Christian Gnosticism*, 2d ed., 248–49.

33. Alan F. Segal, *Two Powers in Heaven: Early Rabbinic Reports about Christianity and Gnosticism* (Leiden: Brill, 1977), 29.

34. Ibid., 262, 265; see also Edwin M. Yamauchi, "The Descent of Ishtar, the Fall of Sophia, and the Jewish Roots of Gnosticism," *Tyndale Bulletin* 29 (1978): 140–71; idem, "Christians and the Jewish Revolts against Rome," *Fides et Historia* 23 (1991): 11–30.

Among European scholars Yamauchi found support in Simone Pétrement, a friend and biographer of the Catholic mystic Simone Weil.[35] Yamauchi frequently cited Pétrement, who had long contested the critical approach to Gnostic studies. In turn her 1984 work *Le Dieu séparé: Les Origines du gnosticisme* (Eng. trans., 1990) cited Yamauchi as support for her contention that Gnosticism must have emerged from Christianity.[36]

Yamauchi's work was also acknowledged by an invitation to participate in the Second International Congress of Mithraic Studies, convened by the empress of Iran during September of 1975. His paper *"The Apocalypse of Adam, Pre-Christian Gnosticism, and Mithraism"* continued the critique of his contemporaries.[37] By this time his work in Mandaic studies, general Gnostic theory, and archeology had made Yamauchi an important voice within biblical and early Christian scholarship.

The 1980s: A Sense of Balance

During the 1980s Yamauchi began his work as a consultant for Scholars Press, the publisher for the Society of Biblical Literature and the American Academy of Religion. He also served on the editorial boards of several journals: *Bulletin for Biblical Research, Fides et Historia, Journal of the Evangelical Theological Society,* and *Journal of the American Scientific Affiliation.* Thus his influence was being felt within and outside of evangelical circles.

Most of Yamauchi's efforts during this period focused on biblical archeology.[38] He produced *The Archaeology of New Testament Cities in Western Asia Minor*[39] and *Harper's World of the New Testament.*[40] In lectures at Western Conservative Baptist Seminary in 1980 he critiqued the work of various archeologists and reviewed the general field of Old Testament archeology: "In the eight years since I published *The Stones and the Scriptures* the trends have not all been positive in confirming the Scriptures as I had antic-

35. Simone Pétrement, "La Notion de gnosticisme," *Revue de métaphysique et de morale* 65 (1960): 385–421; idem, "Le Colloque de Messine et le problème du gnosticisme," *Revue de métaphysique et de morale* 72 (1967): 344–73; idem, "Sur le problème du gnosticisme," *Revue de métaphysique et de morale* 85 (1980): 145–77; idem, *Simone Weil: A Life* (New York: Pantheon, 1976).

36. Simone Pétrement, *A Separate God: The Christian Origins of Gnosticism* (San Francisco: Harper and Row, 1990).

37. Edwin M. Yamauchi, "*The Apocalypse of Adam,* Pre-Christian Gnosticism, and Mithraism," in *Etudes mithriaques: Textes et mémoires,* ed. Jacques Duchesne-Guillemin (Liège: Bibliothèque Pahlavi, 1978), 4:537–63.

38. E.g., Edwin M. Yamauchi, "Ramsay's Views on Archaeology in Asia Minor Reviewed," in *The New Testament Student and His Field,* ed. John H. Skilton (Phillipsburg, N.J.: Presbyterian and Reformed, 1982), 27–40; idem, "Archaeology and the Gospels: Discoveries and Publications of the Past Decade (1977–1987)," in *The Gospels Today,* ed. John H. Skilton (Philadelphia: John H. Skilton, 1990), 1–12.

39. Edwin M. Yamauchi, *The Archaeology of New Testament Cities in Western Asia Minor* (Grand Rapids: Baker, 1980); this was republished in 1987 under the title *New Testament Cities in Western Asia Minor.* See also idem, "Recent Archaeological Work in the New Testament Cities of Western Anatolia," *Near East Archaeological Society Bulletin* 13 (1979): 37–116.

40. Edwin M. Yamauchi, *Harper's World of the New Testament* (San Francisco: Harper and Row, 1981).

ipated."[41] In this admission there was a note of frustration. However, there were also some positive trends which, along with the burgeoning digs at Ebla and other new finds, gave Yamauchi continued confidence that archeology would affirm the biblical accounts.[42] Despite the difficulties that the data sometimes presented to evangelical scholarship, insistence that theory be corroborated with evidence remained a central theme.[43]

An important balance to his negative evaluation of critical theory was Yamauchi's disavowal of idiosyncratic fundamentalist exegesis. He disapproved of the search for Noah's ark.[44] In response to apocalyptic exegesis as found in Hal Lindsey's *Late Great Planet Earth*,[45] he produced *Foes from the Northern Frontier*, a monograph clarifying various historical and geographical specifics of the Bible.[46] He discussed, for example, the location of Urartu (Ararat) and the anachronistic confusion of modern Russia with the ancient Scythians or Chaldeans.[47] When Saddam Hussein came to blows with the United Nations in 1990–91, Yamauchi again countered apocalyptic fervor with a solid review of John Walvoord's *Armageddon, Oil and the Middle East Crisis*.[48] Just as Yamauchi was willing to confront the poor methodology of some fellow scholars, he critiqued his fellow evangelicals as well.

A similar sense of balance was consistently reflected in Yamauchi's participation within evangelical scholarly spheres. He contributed to *The NIV Study Bible* and authored "Ezra-Nehemiah" in *The Expositor's Bible Commentary*.[49] Yamauchi also participated in the Institute for Biblical Research, an organization established by E. Earle Ellis in 1970 to encourage evangelical research in the Hebrew and Greek Scriptures. In its evolution the institute became a moderating body between the liberal Society for Biblical Literature and the conservative Evangelical Theological Society.[50] Yamauchi served on

41. Edwin M. Yamauchi, "Scriptures and Archaeology," Bueermann-Champion Lectures, Western Conservative Baptist Seminary, Portland, Oct. 1980, 1; see also idem, "Archaeology and the Scriptures," *Seminary Journal* 25 (1974): 163–241; Donald J. Wiseman and Edwin M. Yamauchi, *Archaeology and the Bible* (Grand Rapids: Zondervan, 1979).

42. Edwin M. Yamauchi, "Unearthing Ebla's Ancient Secrets," *Christianity Today* 25.9 (May 8, 1981): 18–21.

43. Edwin M. Yamauchi, "The Proofs, Problems and Promises of Biblical Archaeology," *Journal of the American Scientific Affiliation* 36.3 (1984): 129–38.

44. Edwin M. Yamauchi, "Critical Comments on the Search for Noah's Ark," *Near East Archaeological Society Bulletin* 10 (1977): 5–27; idem, "Is That an Ark on Ararat?" *Eternity* 28 (Feb. 1978): 27–32.

45. Hal Lindsey, *The Late Great Planet Earth* (Grand Rapids: Zondervan, 1970).

46. Edwin M. Yamauchi, *Foes from the Northern Frontier* (Grand Rapids: Baker, 1982).

47. See also Edwin M. Yamauchi, "The Scythians: Invading Hordes from the Russian Steppes," *Biblical Archaeologist* 46.2 (1983): 90–99.

48. Edwin M. Yamauchi, review of *Armageddon, Oil and the Middle East Crisis,* by John F. Walvoord, *Christianity Today* 35.5 (April 19, 1991): 50–51.

49. Edwin M. Yamauchi, "Ezra-Nehemiah," in *Expositor's Bible Commentary,* ed. Frank E. Gaebelein (Grand Rapids: Zondervan, 1988), 4:565–771; see also idem, "The Reverse Order of Ezra/Nehemiah Reconsidered," *Themelios* 5.3 (1980): 7–13.

50. It is important to note that Yamauchi has held office in the Evangelical Theological Society (chairman of the Eastern Section, 1965–66) and the related Near East Archaeological Society (board of directors, 1973–; vice-president, 1978–79).

the executive committee from 1974 to 1976; and as chairman from 1984 to 1989, he saw the organization double its membership from 150 to 300 fellows and associates. In the burgeoning inerrancy debate of the 1980s Yamauchi found that his position was more conservative than institutions like Fuller Seminary, but he was also comfortable with an eclectic and broadly defined doctrine of inerrancy. Though his work has always affirmed a strong confidence in Scripture, he has never published a position on this topic.

The 1990s: Continuity and New Interests

Yamauchi's work in the late 1980s and early 1990s reflected a continuity as well as movement in new directions. In 1990 he published *Persia and the Bible*,[51] the first volume of its kind since Robert North's *Guide to Biblical Iran*.[52] In this text Yamauchi brings together his work on Greek and Near Eastern contacts, a detailed analysis of Achaemenian history, a review of studies of Zoroastrianism and of the Magi,[53] as well as discussions of the confirmations, parallels, and difficulties that such studies have brought to the biblical text. Central to this monograph are continued confidence in classical texts, such as Herodotus, and defense of an early dating of Daniel.[54] While praising his scholarship, reviewers have often found fault with Yamauchi's conservative positions.[55]

In *Persia and the Bible* Yamauchi also delves deeply into the area of Mithraic studies. As in his work on Gnosticism, he confronts critical methodology, this time as represented by Franz Cumont's thesis that Mithraism had influenced early Christianity.[56] Though mainstream Mithraic studies have abandoned Cumont's analysis, Yamauchi provides a critique of the field, arguing that it is invalid to use data from the second and third centuries A.D. to postulate first-century influences on Christianity.[57] Possibly more than any of his previous studies *Persia and the Bible* illustrates Yamauchi's earlier emphasis (in *The Stones and the Scriptures*) that accurate analysis requires three spheres of evidence—tradition, inscriptions, and archeology.

During this period Yamauchi also developed an interest in ancient Africa. In 1991 he participated in multicultural dialogues at Miami University relating to Asian- and African-American relations. Yamauchi criticized both the

51. Edwin M. Yamauchi, *Persia and the Bible* (Grand Rapids: Baker, 1990).
52. Robert North, *Guide to Biblical Iran* (Rome: Pontifical Institute of Biblical Archaeology, 1956).
53. See also Edwin M. Yamauchi, "The Episode of the Magi," in *Chronos, Kairos, Christos: Nativity and Chronological Studies Presented to Jack Finegan*, ed. Jerry Vardaman and Edwin M. Yamauchi (Winona Lake, Ind.: Eisenbrauns, 1989), 15–39.
54. Yamauchi, *Persia*, 379–94.
55. Among the reviews of *Persia and the Bible* are Lester L. Grabbe, *Journal for the Study of Judaism* 22 (1992): 295–98; S. P. Brock, *Interpretation* 46 (Jan. 1992): 100–101; Joseph A. Fitzmyer, *Theological Studies* 52 (March 1991): 176; Paul-Alain Beaulieu, *Bibliotheca Orientalis* 50.3–4 (1993): 484–86; J. R. Russell, *Jewish Quarterly Review* 83 (1992): 256–61.
56. Franz Cumont, *The Mysteries of Mithra* (Chicago: Open Court, 1910).
57. Yamauchi, *Persia*, 502–4, 516–18.

racism of past European scholarship, which ignored Afro-Asian elements in classical culture, and Afrocentric trends that exaggerated these influences. Of particular importance was his reaction to Martin Bernal's *Black Athena*, which in overstating the Near Eastern and African elements within Greco-Roman culture made use of the work of Cyrus Gordon.[58] Yamauchi's efforts in this field included organizing a conference at Miami University on "Africa and Africans in Antiquity" and preparing the presentations for publication.[59] Exploring the often ignored or misinterpreted African elements in the biblical accounts, he also produced the monograph *Africa and the Bible*.[60]

In the mid–1990s, as an extension of his previous work in Mandaic and general Persian studies, Yamauchi began to research further the early developments of Christianity in the East.[61] His 1994 paper on "Adaptation and Assimilation in Asia," for example, discussed Hellenistic influences on Buddhist art in Gandhara as well as the movement of Manichaean Gnostic and Nestorian Christian missionaries along the Silk Road.[62] In this paper he also distinguished between assimilation and syncretism in reference to cultural and religious interaction, an important point in his overall view of the development and spread of early Christianity.

We have noted Yamauchi's interest in and ability to work with an extremely broad body of ancient evidence. To Miami University he has attracted graduate students interested in such wide-ranging fields as Mycenaean studies, ancient warfare, Judaica,[63] New Testament studies, and patristics.[64] His broad interests also served him well as a senior editor of *Christianity Today* from 1992 to 1994. His contributions in this capacity include an overview of the "power struggles, guerrilla publishing, and bizarre interpretations of the Dead Sea Scrolls."[65]

58. Martin Bernal, *Black Athena: The Afroasiatic Roots of Classical Civilization*, 2 vols. (New Brunswick, N.J.: Rutgers University Press, 1987, 1992).

59. *Africa and Africans in Antiquity*, ed. Edwin M. Yamauchi (East Lansing: Michigan State University Press, forthcoming); the conference was held on 1–2 March 1991.

60. Edwin M. Yamauchi, *Africa and the Bible* (Grand Rapids: Baker, forthcoming); idem, "The Archaeology of Biblical Africa: Cyrene in Libya," *Archaeology of the Biblical World* 2 (1992): 6–18; idem, "Afrocentric Biblical Interpretations," *Journal of the Evangelical Theological Society*, forthcoming.

61. See Edwin M. Yamauchi, review of *A History of Christianity in Asia*, vol. 1, by Samuel H. Moffett, *American Historical Review* 99 (April 1994): 617.

62. Edwin M. Yamauchi, "Adaptation and Assimilation in Asia" (paper presented to the Association of Ancient Historians, Dayton, 6–8 May 1994); see also Edwin M. Yamauchi, "Hellenistic Bactria and Buddhism," *Humanitas* 18.3 (Winter 1995): 5–10.

63. See, e.g., Edwin M. Yamauchi, "Josephus and the Scriptures," *Fides et Historia* 13.1 (1980): 42–63.

64. See, e.g., Edwin M. Yamauchi, "The Crucifixion and Docetic Christology," *Concordia Theological Monthly* 46.1 (1982): 1–20.

65. Thomas Jones, "Scroll Hype," interview with Edwin M. Yamauchi, *Christianity Today* 37.11 (Oct. 4, 1993): 28–31. Interest in the scrolls is also evident in Yamauchi, "Qumran and Colosse," *Bibliotheca Sacra* 121 (1964): 141–52; idem, "The Teacher of Righteousness from Qumran and Jesus of Nazareth," *Christianity Today* 10.16 (May 13, 1966): 12–14; idem, review of *The Dead Sea Scrolls and the New Testament*, by William S. LaSor, *Christianity Today* 17.25 (Sept. 28, 1973): 34–35; idem, review of *Qoumrân: L'Établissement Essénien des bords de la Mer Morte*, by E.-M. Laperrousaz, *American Historical Review* 83 (1978): 136–37.

Continued willingness to address issues of biblical scholarship[66] has brought Yamauchi into conflict with the Jesus Seminar of the Westar Institute, which published a monograph entitled *The Five Gospels: The Search for the Authentic Words of Jesus.* This work, which represents an extreme of higher-critical methodology, makes an overall judgment as to which of the *logia* (sayings) in the four canonical Gospels and the Gnostic Gospel of Thomas are authentic words of the historical Jesus.[67] Yamauchi's response was published in *Jesus under Fire,* a work representing a general evangelical rejoinder.[68] Here he deals with the Jewish, Roman, and early Christian evidence of Jesus. Crucial to his arguments is the fact that the "Fellows of the Seminar were equally skeptical about the logia of *Thomas.* They considered only three of its sayings that have no canonical parallels worthy of serious consideration."[69] Despite such evidence as Yamauchi outlines, the Jesus Seminar insists that the "sayings of Jesus in the Gospels were freely invented by the church."[70] In his conclusion Yamauchi applies a sharp critique to the seminar's methodology and presuppositions, likening them to the eccentric and idiosyncratic speculations of John Allegro, who claimed that early Christianity was rooted in a mushroom cult.[71]

In 1994 Yamauchi returned again to the field of Gnostic studies with an article for the anthology *Hellenization Revisited.*[72] As in his earlier treatments he maintained that "the more analytic approach sees only a rudimentary, inchoate Gnosticism at the end of the first century, and concludes that the developed system cannot be understood apart from its parasitic relationship to Christianity."[73] This article was immediately followed by a most interesting critique by Michel Desjardins: Yamauchi's scholarship, while highly admirable, creates a false dilemma by oversimplifying the question. His distinction between full-blown Gnosticism and proto-Gnostic elements is too sharp; it does not allow a middle ground of a developing Gnosticism alongside early Christianity.[74] Desjardins then goes a step further by critiqu-

66. Edwin M. Yamauchi, "The Current State of Old Testament Historiography," in *Faith, Tradition, and History: Old Testament Historiography in Its Near Eastern Context,* ed. A. R. Millard, J. K. Hoffmeier, and D. W. Baker (Winona Lake, Ind.: Eisenbrauns, 1994), 1–35; idem, "Political Background of the Old Testament," in *Foundations for Biblical Interpretation,* ed. David S. Dockery, Kenneth A. Mathews, and Robert B. Sloan (Nashville: Broadman and Holman, 1994), 306–27.

67. *The Five Gospels: The Search for the Authentic Words of Jesus,* ed. Robert W. Funk and Roy W. Hoover (New York: Macmillan, 1993), 1–34.

68. Edwin M. Yamauchi, "Jesus outside the New Testament: What Is the Evidence?" in *Jesus under Fire: Modern Scholarship Reinvents the Historical Jesus,* ed. Michael J. Wilkins and J. P. Moreland (Grand Rapids: Zondervan, 1995), 207–29.

69. Ibid., 218.

70. Ibid., 219.

71. Ibid., 222; see also Edwin M. Yamauchi, review of *The Sacred Mushroom and the Cross,* by John Allegro, *Eternity* 22 (Nov. 1971): 54–55.

72. Edwin M. Yamauchi, "Gnosticism and Early Christianity," in *Hellenization Revisited: Shaping a Christian Response within the Greco-Roman World,* ed. Wendy Helleman (Lanham, Md.: University Press of America, 1994), 29–61.

73. Ibid., 30.

74. Michel Desjardins, "Yamauchi and Pre-Christian Gnosticism," in *Hellenization Revisited,* ed. Helleman, 64–66.

ing Yamauchi's conservative Protestant presuppositions: Yamauchi "does not view the material with a disinterested eye. Gnosticism for him was a dangerous perversion of the Christian understanding of God, the Bible, and Christ; humanity is better served by its absence."[75]

The close reader of Yamauchi's work will acknowledge that Desjardins is essentially correct on both points. First, Yamauchi, like Pétrement, has always maintained that Gnostic systems emerged specifically from first-century Christian and Jewish groups. For Yamauchi this "cut-and-dried" position is sustainable because it best matches the evidence. On the second point it should be noted that as early as 1966 Yamauchi had touched on the matter of faith.[76] And in *The Stones and the Scriptures* he was quite bold regarding his position: "The [Christian] will be encouraged to know that the biblical traditions are not a patchwork of legends but are reliable records of men and women who have responded to the revelation of God in history. . . . Archaeology may show to us the nature of Christ's tomb. But it can never be a substitute for that personal faith which carries the believer beyond the empty tomb to a living relationship with [Christ]."[77] That Yamauchi has consistently communicated his position stands in sharp contrast to the many scholars who have claimed objectivity while working from a subjective agenda. Even Leopold von Ranke, the German historian whose American followers claimed an ideal *Objectivität,* understood history as pointing toward a metaphysical teleology informing the nature of reality.[78] From 1966 Edwin Yamauchi has worn the hats of a historian, biblical scholar, classicist, Orientalist, archeologist, innovator, spoiler, and apologist. And he has never been shy about the faith that has informed the entirety of this work.

Primary Sources

Yamauchi, Edwin M. *Composition and Corroboration in Classical and Biblical Studies.* Philadelphia: Presbyterian and Reformed, 1966.

———. "Ezra-Nehemiah." In *Expositor's Bible Commentary,* edited by Frank E. Gaebelein, 4:565–771. Grand Rapids: Zondervan, 1988.

———. *Foes from the Northern Frontier.* Grand Rapids: Baker, 1982.

———. *Gnostic Ethics and Mandaean Origins.* Cambridge, Mass.: Harvard University Press, 1970.

———. *Greece and Babylon: Early Contacts between the Aegean and the Near East.* Grand Rapids: Baker, 1967.

———. *Harper's World of the New Testament.* San Francisco: Harper and Row, 1981.

75. Ibid., 66.
76. Yamauchi, *Composition,* 37–38.
77. Yamauchi, *Stones,* 165–66.
78. Leopold von Ranke, "Idee der Universalhistorie," *Historische Zeitschrift* 178 (1954): 290–301; idem, "Einleitung zu einer Vorlesung über Universalhistorie," *Historische Zeitschrift* 178 (1954): 304–7; see also Georg G. Iggers, *The German Conception of History* (Middletown, Conn.: Wesleyan University Press, 1968), 63–89.

————. *Mandaic Incantation Texts.* American Oriental Series 49. New Haven: American Oriental Society, 1967.

————. *New Testament Cities in Western Asia Minor.* Grand Rapids: Baker, 1987.

————. *Persia and the Bible.* Grand Rapids: Baker, 1990.

————. *Pre-Christian Gnosticism: A Survey of the Proposed Evidences.* 2d ed. Grand Rapids: Baker, 1983.

————. *The Stones and the Scriptures: An Introduction to Biblical Archaeology.* Philadelphia: Lippincott, 1972.

Yamauchi, Edwin M., and Donald J. Wiseman. *Archaeology and the Bible.* Grand Rapids: Zondervan, 1979.

Peter C. Craigie

Lyle Eslinger

Peter Craigie was born in Lancaster, England, on August 18, 1938. The second of three sons, Craigie grew up in Edinburgh, where he attended a private school, the Edinburgh Academy. Reared in an evangelical Anglican tradition, he grew dissatisfied with it in his university days and began to explore the traditions of other evangelical churches in Scotland. Through contacts made with Baptist and Evangelical Free churches, he became involved in the Inter-Varsity Fellowship and summer Bible camps. In the end his explorations brought him back to the Anglicanism of his childhood, and he remained in that tradition for the rest of his life.

From an early age, Craigie planned to become a pilot in the Royal Air Force. He enlisted when he was only seventeen. The Royal Air Force promised flying, travel, and exotic locations—all dear to a young man with a wanderlust that would never leave him. The thought of a quiet life behind a desk in a seminary or university was nowhere in sight at this time. But the Bible, the book that would occupy Craigie at a desk for most of his adult years, was already becoming a more important part of his life. In the preface to his commentary on the Book of Deuteronomy, Craigie indicates that he first became interested in serious biblical study during his stint in the Royal Air Force.[1] Sadly, Craigie's dream of traveling the world as a pilot was, to the good fortune of his many readers, doomed to fail. Testing proved that he was color-blind; he would never fly as a pilot. His main purpose defeated, Craigie left the military as soon as he had fulfilled the minimum two years of national service. But he still had no interest in university education, let alone the idea of pursuing something so bookish, to a young adventurer, as academic biblical studies.

Academic Training and Career

Immediately after leaving the Royal Air Force, Craigie set off for Canada to study at the Prairie Bible Institute in Three Hills, Alberta. He had chanced on a copy of the school's paper, *The Prairie Overcomer,* and decided that this

---

1. Peter C. Craigie, *The Book of Deuteronomy* (Grand Rapids: Eerdmans, 1976), 9.

was the school for him. Prairie Bible Institute had a strong missions emphasis, and Craigie hoped to combine religious and travel aspirations by becoming a missionary. As a bonus, the trip to Canada got him out of Scotland to
a remote location. Far-off destination aside, a small Bible college isolated on
the Prairies seems an odd place to begin what would become an academic career in the study of the Hebrew Bible. But the career as a biblical scholar was
still beyond the horizon. Prairie Bible's theological stance was and remains
normative evangelicalism, affirming the authority of the Bible in matters of
faith, biblical inerrancy, and traditional ascriptions such as the Mosaic authorship of most of the Pentateuch. This conservative stance on the Bible
fixed an indelible imprint on Craigie, who had been accustomed to it in his
church environment from childhood on. Though his later writings show increasing tolerance of historical criticism, he always approached the "established results" with a skepticism that took inspiration from Prairie Bible's
stance. The choice of Prairie Bible as the institution from which to begin,
then, seems to have been well suited to Craigie's personal theological incli-
nations.

After studying in Alberta for two years, Craigie went home on vacation
and did not return to complete the third year of his program. Instead, his father persuaded him that he ought to be in a university.[2] So Peter stayed on to
enrol in a bachelor's program at the University of Edinburgh.

Back in Scotland, at the New College, University of Edinburgh, Craigie's
specific interest in Semitics was sparked by an optional Hebrew course being
offered by Norman Porteous. Craigie's own remark on his reason for beginning the study of Hebrew was that the course just happened to suit his time-
table.[3] This chance beginning kindled his interest, and Craigie enrolled in an
M.A. honors program in Semitics, completing it five years later in 1965.
A Semitics degree at that time often included the study of Arabic. So Craigie
did three years of Arabic, which he completed by spending the summer of 1963
in Lebanon at the Middle East Centre for Arabic Studies. His linguistic skills,
among others, earned him the respect of fellow students and teachers alike.
Craigie's work at Edinburgh was rewarded by a Vans Dunlop Scholarship in
Hebrew and Oriental Languages (1965–66). And later, John C. L. Gibson of
the University of Edinburgh would assign his former student two commentaries in the Daily Study Bible series—*Ezekiel* and *Twelve Prophets*. Commenting
on the eleven authors that he had selected for the series, Gibson said, "I can
assure those who use these commentaries that they are in the hands of competent teachers who know what is of real consequence in their subject."[4]

---

2. Idestrom, "Peter C. Craigie and the Old Testament" (M.R. thesis, Wycliffe College, 1990), 91.
This thesis, and especially its collection of comments from interviews shortly after Craigie's death, is
a useful resource for those interested in Craigie's conservative approach to biblical studies.

3. Peter C. Craigie, *The Old Testament: Its Background, Growth, and Content* (Nashville: Abingdon, 1986), 10.

4. John C. L. Gibson, general preface to Peter C. Craigie, *Twelve Prophets*, 2 vols. (Philadelphia:
Westminster, 1984–85), 2:5.

Following his Semitics degree, Craigie began a two-year diploma in theology at St. John's College in the University of Durham. The program was a broad-based one designed to prepare for ordination as an Anglican priest. But early in his studies at Durham he began to think increasingly about pursuing an academic rather than a pastoral career. To make the decision, he had to go through a great deal of soul searching; in the end he resolved in favor of academia. This period of self-examination served him often in his later career, when he had to make decisions about whether to take up positions in theological or secular institutions. He remained committed to a nonconfessional working environment, though he was just as thoroughly committed to the improvement and defense of conservative Christianity. So now he had consciously realigned the career goal of his religious studies twice: from evangelical missionary (Prairie Bible) and now from Anglican priest to academic biblical scholar. He graduated from Durham in 1967 with distinction.

Making the rounds of universities, Craigie moved on to the University of Aberdeen. There he did another master's degree, this time in theology. His study at Aberdeen, where John Gray was his supervisor, was supported by a Bruce and Fraser Scholarship in Divinity (1967–68). Gray would later recall "precious memories of many stimulating hours in our post-graduate work together in the University of Aberdeen, where Peter left a very distinctive impression both on staff and students."[5] Gray's own interests at the time were the earliest stages of Hebrew poetry and comparative philology as a tool to illuminate the Hebrew Bible. Gray's influence is clear in the title of Craigie's thesis, "Ancient Semitic War Poetry (with Particular Attention to Judges 5)."[6] Craigie graduated from Aberdeen in 1968 with an M.Th.

Craigie's formal training concluded where he began, back in Canada. In the light of his background and training thus far, McMaster University might seem as odd a place to end as Prairie Bible Institute had been to begin. He started in the cloistered setting of a conservative Bible school and finished in the virtual confessional pluralism of the religious studies department of a secular university. But the university years in the United Kingdom had expanded his theological horizons, and the training at McMaster would allow Craigie to continue evolving his own unique vision, which saw conservative Christianity (and its unique flavor of biblical scholarship) as a full and equal partner in the pluralist department. The change to a religious studies environment marks the third and final contextual shift in Craigie's academic development. Though he would have tempting offers to return to a confessional environment, the liberalizing pattern established through his school years solidified his preference for a secular work environment.

5. John Gray, "Israel in the Song of Deborah," in *Ascribe to the Lord: Biblical and Other Studies in Memory of Peter C. Craigie,* ed. Lyle Eslinger and J. Glen Taylor (Sheffield: Sheffield Academic, 1988), 421.
6. It is noteworthy that Gray chose to contribute to the 1988 memorial volume for Craigie an essay on Judges 5 ("Israel in the Song of Deborah") as a memento of their work together on that text.

Craigie had developed considerable expertise in comparative philology, especially as to how the Ras Shamra Ugaritic texts bear on our understanding of the Bible. But until Craigie arrived at McMaster in 1968 nobody there had such interests or expertise.[7] Either Aberdeen with John Gray or Edinburgh with John Gibson would have seemed a more obvious choice. Craigie's choice of McMaster was pragmatic: he had nearly exhausted all available sources of funding for graduate study in Britain, and McMaster was offering attractive funding. Harvard University was also a possibility, but did not make an offer competitive with McMaster's. At the time, McMaster was strongly flavored by the presence and influence of the Canadian political thinker George Grant. Under Grant's influence and that of Eugene Combs, Craigie began to consider the Bible in the light of political philosophy, especially that of Baruch Spinoza.[8] Though Combs had been trained in standard historical-critical biblical methods, his interests had broadened well beyond biblical studies by the time Craigie came to McMaster. Combs's influence on Craigie was in the area of broader philosophical issues and in his demand of a careful and close reading of the biblical text. For the standard issues of critical biblical scholarship, Craigie was left to rely on his previous training. Fortunately, he had been well prepared for independent study; it seems that he had already done much of the research for what was to be his Ph.D. thesis. He completed his Ph.D., which included comprehensive examinations in his minor area, Buddhism/Hinduism, in only two years and graduated in 1970. His McMaster thesis continued the trend toward comparative study of the oldest poetic pieces in the Bible: "Earliest Israelite Religion: A Study of the Song of the Sea (Exodus 15:1–18)."

Following his schooling, Craigie took an appointment as an assistant professor at Carleton University. He spent only one year there (1970–71) before he was offered a similar position at McMaster University. He kept the post at McMaster until 1974, when he returned, this time with a family, to the province where he had begun, Alberta. The shift from McMaster to the University of Calgary was a gamble, since he had tenure at McMaster while Calgary offered only an untenured, limited-term position that was partly funded by the Christian and Jewish communities (Calgary Interfaith). He spent much of his time, in the early years at Calgary, giving lectures outside the academic context. The many talks on seemingly dull and arcane topics like the laws of Deuteronomy and Ugaritic philology were always enthusiastically received. The religious community honored his work with a D.D. (St. Stephen's College, University of Alberta) and a canonship in the Anglican diocese of Calgary. Calgary Interfaith's support for the young religious studies depart-

---

7. Eugene Combs, who would be Craigie's supervisor at McMaster, had done his doctoral work on Exodus 15, the text that Craigie would work on for his Ph.D. thesis. But Combs did not have the training in comparative philology nor the broad interest in the most ancient Hebrew poetry that Craigie's M.Th. supervisor, John Gray, had.

8. Peter C. Craigie, "The Influence of Spinoza in the Higher Criticism of the Old Testament," *Evangelical Quarterly* 50 (1978): 23–32.

ment at the university was a success as Craigie mediated the results of scholarship to the lay community.

Success in the lay community was matched by progress in the university. Craigie's personal warmth and sincerity, along with his leadership skills, moved him up the ladder quickly. He began at Calgary, not even tenured, in 1974; in 1977 he became head of the religious studies department; in 1979, dean of the faculty of humanities; in 1984, associate vice-president (academic); and, in 1985, vice-president (academic). He seemed the obvious candidate for the next president of the university.

The one obstacle that stood in the path of the presidency was something that no one could foresee: in September of 1985, just a few months after taking on his new job as vice-president, Peter Craigie was involved in a serious automobile accident. He survived the crash, but his life would last only a little longer. Within the university community Craigie was widely admired and respected. In the days between the crash and his death the university community rallied round this favorite son. Prayer meetings were held on the campus and at the university hospital. But his injuries were too severe and he died on September 26, 1985. At the university memorial service which followed, President Norman Wagner tried to express the university community's loss and sorrow.[9] No speech, especially in that kind of official forum, could capture the personal grief that struck so broad a path through Peter's university colleagues and friends. Months and even years passed before the impact of this loss was erased from the daily life of the campus.

The Attempt to Balance Conservative Assumptions and Critical Methods

In the space of his brief career Craigie's overarching emphasis was the need for a balance between the dictates of reason, in the form of historical-critical scholarship, and the traditional conception of revelation, in particular, the views of the Old Testament espoused by conservative Protestant Christianity. Craigie's work on a balanced conservative hermeneutic took place on the eve of the critique of historical-critical methods that mushroomed into the methodological and hermeneutical ferment of the late 1980s and the 1990s. For him, the historical method remained the scholarly approach to the Old Testament, and that was what a conservative scholar had to wrestle with.[10] What he tried to create in his own approach was a melding of conservative theological interests and assumptions with the scientific methods of modern biblical criticism. Adapting a hyphenated term from Spinoza *(Tractatus Theologico-Politicus)*, he said that his approach could be characterized as "theological-

9. Norman Wagner, "Reflections: A Memorial Service for Peter Craigie," in *Ascribe to the Lord*, ed. Eslinger and Taylor, 599–601.

10. For Craigie, "scientific" and "historical" were synonymous positive adjectives describing the enterprise of biblical scholarship ("The Role and Relevance of Biblical Research," *Journal for the Study of the Old Testament* 18 [1980]: 21).

historical" or "theological-scientific."[11] All of Craigie's formal training was in the older, traditional methods of historical criticism. In the contexts of the departments at Edinburgh and Aberdeen, source and form criticism would have been taken for granted and, with them, the disarray of biblical literature as it has come down to us and the need to unravel that disarray. Craigie's published work right to the end shows an uneasy acceptance of these methods and literary-historical assumptions. Nevertheless, his work also shows a growing attraction to new literary approaches that were just coming into prominence in the late 1970s and early 1980s. Had his life not been cut short, it seems likely that he would have pursued his attraction to the new emphases on the Bible as literature and on analyzing it in its final form.[12]

In practical terms, Craigie's emphasis on balance translated into an effort to distill and interpret the incredible detail of biblical scholarship for the community of faith. The conservative Christian community is a ready-made audience with a keen interest in the Bible. Why not try to convey to it all the hard, often overly technical labor of the biblical scholars over the past two centuries? Such was Craigie's self-appointed mandate. To serve it in accord with the spirit of conservative assumptions about the Bible, he consciously opened himself and his work to criticism from mainstream biblical scholarship. So, for example, his decision to argue a modified traditional view that Moses wrote the Pentateuch, specifically the Book of Deuteronomy, was panned by Ernest Nicholson, a respected Deuteronomy scholar.[13] Craigie took such barbs as part of the course of mediating between critical biblical scholarship and the believing community. His resolve to tackle the job of mediating biblical scholarship to a conservative popular audience was a steadfast decision that shaped all of his scholarly output. A second support for his conservatism was skepticism about historical criticism and its hermeneutical principles.[14] Craigie's desire to address a popular audience, rather than restricting his work to the cloistered world of biblical scholars (and even more so that of Ugaritologists), also led him to try to bring his biblical scholarship

---

11. Craigie, *Deuteronomy*, 77.

12. See Peter C. Craigie, *Psalms 1–50* (Waco: Word, 1983), 48, for brief comments on the positive influence of Nicolaas H. Ridderbos, who offered an early, somewhat crude form of structural and rhetorical analyses of the Psalms (*Die Psalmen: Stilistische Verfahren und Aufbau mit besonderer Berücksichtigung von Ps 1–41*, Beiheft zur Zeitschrift für die alttestamentliche Wissenschaft 117 [Berlin: de Gruyter, 1972]).

13. Ernest W. Nicholson, "Once More Moses and Deuteronomy: Review of *Deuteronomy* [by Peter C. Craigie]," *Expository Times* 89 (1978): 153: "His commentary offers frequent insights which will be found helpful. But his approach and presuppositions are unmistakably 'fundamentalist.'" Inasmuch as Craigie's position was that conservative biblical scholarship is relevant primarily to the community of faith that shares its assumptions ("Role and Relevance," 30), Nicholson's characterization, while pejorative, is banal.

14. E.g., against those who would exorcise the historical Jeremiah from the book named after him, Craigie, *Old Testament*, 162, said that the redactors called in to replace the prophet are more elusive as historical figures than is the traditional author they are adduced to replace. Here skepticism combines with conservatism, as Craigie counted himself among those who reckoned the bulk of the book as authentic.

to bear on the larger theological issues. Too much scholarly energy, he thought, is consumed by historical and philological technicalities. Little if any energy is left over to work out the biblical implications for faith, preaching, or even life itself.[15]

As a self-consciously conservative biblical scholar operating in the pluralism of a religious studies department, Craigie made certain assumptions that he thought characteristic of conservative Christianity. These assumptions, he believed, give the conservative scholar a distinct role and relevance. Pared to a minimum, these assumptions "pertain to the inspiration and truth of Scripture, and to its absolute authority within life, thought, and behavior."[16] This statement, which was published in a nonconservative, nonevangelical journal, reflects a conviction that a strong conservative position is a full equal in the world of scholarly pluralism. Craigie's attempts to balance his conservative assumptions with the critical methods of that world are evident in his treatment of four topics that regularly recur in his writing: the traditional ascriptions of biblical authorship; the problem of the moral offensiveness of parts of the Old Testament; the contradiction between the miraculous in the Bible and the conclusions arrived at by historical analogy and empiricism; and the negligible role of archeological discovery as vindication of the Bible's truth.

The Traditional Ascriptions of Biblical Authorship

On questions of authorship, Craigie's stance was a combination of conservatism about traditional ascriptions and skepticism for the conclusions of modern scholarship. His premise, reiterated in numerous public lectures and books, was that if there is no compelling contrary evidence, traditional ascriptions are all that we have. Craigie's earliest monograph sets out this position most controversially, arguing a Mosaic provenance for the Book of Deuteronomy.[17] He maintains the same line of reasoning regarding Davidic authorship of at least some psalms.[18] The historicity of the prophet Ezekiel

---

15. Craigie, "Role and Relevance," 26.
16. Ibid., 29.
17. Craigie, *Deuteronomy*, 28, 78.
18. Craigie's position on the psalm titles, evidence that might warrant acceptance of Davidic authorship, is indicative of his principled conservatism. Where the psalm titles do suggest authorship, they do so with an ambiguous preposition *(le-)* that might mean written "by" or "for" the person named. The consensus (see James Limburg, "Psalms, Book of," in *Anchor Bible Dictionary*, ed. David Noel Freedman, 6 vols. [New York: Doubleday, 1992], 5:528) is that these ascriptions merely reflect the fact that as the psalm tradition developed, the tendency was to ascribe more and more of the psalms to David. The result was that David was eventually held to be the author in the same way that Moses was eventually considered to be the author of the Pentateuch. Craigie's reading of the ambiguous psalm titles is that, though the preposition need not entail authorship, the books of Samuel do suggest that David was something of a balladeer, and so there is a possibility that at least some of the psalms ascribed to David do in fact go back to him. Though Craigie's final statement on the issue is that acknowledgment of ignorance about authorship is the most honest position (and one that does not materially affect the moral applicability of the psalms), he refuses to abandon the principle that if traditional authorship is possible, then, in the absence of contrary evidence, we are best served by tradition. And, without any published evidence to the contrary, it seems safe to assume, on the same principle, that Craigie himself accepted this position and was not simply soothing the troubled minds of a conservative biblical readership.

is undergirded by modern Jewish traditions about his tomb,[19] and the complete authenticity of the book that goes by his name is an unwritten assumption throughout Craigie's Daily Study Bible commentary. In regard to the Minor Prophets, the conservative principle led Craigie to accept the traditional ascriptions for the books of Micah, Nahum, and Habakkuk.[20] In the case of the Book of Zephaniah, the most that Craigie is willing to concede is that a subsequent redactor arranged the prophecies in an unchronological sequence—the oracles themselves are authentic.[21] Craigie's judgment on the Book of Haggai is that it is a collection of the prophet's oracles combined with editorial comments on the prophet.[22] But Craigie defers to the now conventional distinction between Zechariah 1–8 and 9–14. His conservatism here is expressed as a rather weak nod toward the recent appreciation of the book's thematic unity and the fact that our earliest textual witness shows no awareness of a division into two parts.[23]

Even though in his later words on authorship Craigie seemed to move closer to the mainstream of self-conscious agnosticism on the subject, he continued to maintain his basic conservative principle.[24] In his introduction to the Old Testament, for instance, Craigie notes that the Bible makes no claims regarding the authorship and date of the Pentateuch.[25] But he also argues that the tradition of Mosaic authorship combined with references within the Bible to Moses' sometime role as scribe or author suggests "that there may be a 'Mosaic base' to the literature of the Pentateuch."[26] Furthermore, Craigie's views on the authorship and integrity of Micah, Nahum, and Habakkuk remained essentially unaltered.[27]

Craigie's hermeneutic on the troubling issue of authorship and traditional ascriptions contained an ironic twist. First he admitted, alongside modern critical scholarship, that the traditional claims for authorship are frequently unsupported or not even staked within the biblical text itself. Second, he would take critical skepticism to its logical conclusion regarding traditional claims: in nearly all of the disputed cases, the Bible itself says little or nothing about authorship. Third, since modern critical principles do not lead to indisputable certainty about authorship, one might reconsider the traditional ascriptions. These might be the traces of ancient recollections of who the authors were; the traditional ascriptions are also supported, sometimes, by tangential details in the Bible itself. For example, while the pentateuchal books have neither titles nor superscriptions attributing them to Moses, we do read

19. Peter C. Craigie, *Ezekiel* (Philadelphia: Westminster, 1983), 4.
20. Craigie, *Twelve Prophets*, 2:2–3, 60, 78.
21. Ibid., 107.
22. Ibid., 136.
23. Ibid., 156.
24. See Peter C. Craigie, *Jeremiah 1–25* (Dallas: Word, 1991), xxxi–xli, for a thorough exploration of both sides of the question of the authorship of the Book of Jeremiah.
25. Craigie, *Old Testament*, 105–6.
26. Ibid., 123.
27. Ibid., 190, 194, 196.

that God commanded Moses to write (Exod. 24:4; 34:27) and that Moses recorded events in Israel's travels (Num. 33:2).

From the biblical evidence itself, then, there is little support for a defense of the traditional ascriptions. The concern to defend them issues instead from postbiblical theological assumptions about the nature of Scripture, scriptural authority, and the credibility of the traditional authors. Craigie often alluded to the fact that the Bible is little concerned with these issues, which have their roots in the notions of Scripture and canonicity developed in early Judaism. Many conservative scholars now choose to adopt the Bible's own reticence on the matter of authorship. As Craigie himself said on the Psalms: "The absence of precise information concerning authorship is not a serious setback with respect to understanding the Psalms, for their theme is the relationship between a person and God, and their variations on that central theme have a universality and timelessness which transcend the particularities of authorship."[28]

Why, then, does a focus on authorship run through most of Craigie's biblical commentary? First, it was part of his missionary zeal to bring the positive results of critical scholarship to conservative Christianity. The strategy was to show that something as weak as the traditional claims about authorship was yet defensible against the alternatives offered by critical scholarship. Now if conservatives have nothing to fear even on this sandy soil, they might then go bravely on to learn from and debate with the critics whose weaknesses Craigie so frequently indicated. Second, the focus on authorship was an extrapolation, though not a necessary one, from his assumption about biblical authority. If, given the biblical evidence, the question of authorship is truly moot, why not decide for an authoritative figure such as Moses, to whom the Pentateuch is traditionally attributed, rather than a faceless conglomerate of nameless redactors working down through the centuries?[29]

The Moral Offensiveness of Parts of the Old Testament

Biblical scholarship is a large and technically demanding field, requiring the mastery of many languages and exegetical techniques. For many people, the inevitable specialization often means leaving behind the theological issues that first interested them. Craigie fought that tendency as being detrimental to the discipline's and its practitioners' best interests.[30] He chose to

---

28. Craigie, *Psalms 1–50*, 35. In this and other remarks on the traditional ascriptions, Craigie echoes the spirit of Origen's comment on the belief that Paul wrote the Book of Hebrews: "If then some church considers that this epistle was written by Paul, let it be honored also for that. For it is not by chance that the ancients have transmitted it under the name of Paul. But who wrote the epistle? God knows the truth" (fragment quoted by Eusebius *Ecclesiastical History* 6.25).

29. That a hermeneutical leap of faith is being made here will be obvious to anyone who compares Craigie's open admission of the failings of the tradition of Mosaic authorship (*Old Testament*, 116) with his rationally thin, assumptively thick defense of that tradition a few pages later (122–23).

30. Craigie, "Role and Relevance," 26.

wrestle with those aspects of the Bible that modern-day Christians find problematic or even offensive. His book on the so-called sacred warfare in the Old Testament is an unshirking exploration of the shameless advocacy of violence and aggression in the wars of conquest.[31] Calls to violence and revenge, such as the exhortation to infanticide in Psalm 137:8–9, are disturbing to a Christian morality that finds them in the same inspired Scripture as Jesus' call to turn the other cheek.

Craigie's solution to this problem is the hazardous road of positing a canon within the canon. Some parts of the Bible are more inspiring (inspired?) than others. He adds a novel twist to this tightrope hermeneutic by speaking of the different voices that are found in the Bible. The psalmist's exhortations to villainy, for example, are not oracles of God, neither are they sanctified by inclusion in Scripture. They are the pained reactions of the psalmist to Israel's historical experience and must be judged evil, though they are part of the life of the soul bared before God.[32] Unfortunately, Craigie does not pursue his insight about our ability to discriminate the different voices on the basis of explicit indications. Instead, Craigie says that we might view such an outburst as a kind of confession of sin, even though it is not phrased as such. With that suggestion, which interprets the biblical expression in a way that is at variance with the context, the awkwardness of Craigie's stance is obvious. Instead of following his original aim of presenting a reasoned apology for a particular "deficiency" of the Bible, he ends up converting that deficiency into a sentiment in accord with modern Christian morality.

The Contradiction between Biblical Miracles and the Empiricism of Historical Criticism

Another recurring theme is Craigie's critique of the unexamined naturalistic empiricism often found in critical biblical studies. In general, Craigie was willing to allow that accepting the possibility of supernatural interventions in human history is a radically different hermeneutic based in a faith shared with the ancient writers.[33] Modern secular historians will go their own way, interpreting events without accepting theological assumptions about the possibility of divine intervention in history. But to understand the biblical philosophy of history, Craigie contended, one has to allow for intervention in mundane events by a transcendent God. Central to that philosophy of history is the exodus event, though Craigie acknowledged that the biblical record thereof cannot be called historical in the "modern scientific sense. This does not mean that 'it didn't happen'; but it means that the essence of the Exodus was an act of God, which by its very nature is trans-historical in relation to a modern concept of history."[34]

---

31. Peter C. Craigie, *The Problem of War in the Old Testament* (Grand Rapids: Eerdmans, 1978).
32. Craigie, *Psalms 1–50*, 41.
33. Craigie, *Old Testament*, 257.
34. Craigie, *Deuteronomy*, 40.

The Role of Archeology in Vindicating the Bible

Craigie's primary training was in the area of comparative philology and the Hebrew Bible. The broad goal of this area of biblical scholarship is to elucidate the text and culture of the Bible by drawing on parallels between Israel's literature, the Old Testament, and the literature of its ancient Near Eastern neighbors. Underlying this comparative approach is the belief that there is a cultural gap between the modern world and the biblical world. Comparative study tries to provide the modern reader with some access to the ancient cultural context within which the Bible's historical record came into being. That effort has often been extended to include the belief that archeological discoveries, especially of written artifacts, will somehow prove the Bible's authenticity and even the accuracy of its historical narratives.

Craigie's characteristic caution set him as much against that brand of fideistic bibliolatry as it did against the speculations of historical criticism. Every new discovery has brought new claims that the Bible has finally been vindicated by the archeological facts. In writing about the discoveries at Ebla, Craigie pointed out the weaknesses of such claims, based as they often are in a desire for vindication of the Bible. Bowing to the modern myth of scientific objectivism, such evidence mongering is contrary to faith. The quest for proof is sadly ironic because it can never be consummated: "To prove that the historical narrative of the Old Testament is accurate, if such were possible, does not prove the essential truth of the Bible—namely, what it says about God. That must always remain both the subject and the object of faith."[35] Craigie's clear conviction was that the material remains of places like Ebla can be useful only as a cultural context for the study of the Bible.

Craigie's primary field of research was the literature and civilization not of Ebla but of Ugarit. The ancient kingdom of Ugarit was discovered in 1928 by Mahmoud Mella az-Zir, a plowman. The field in which he unearthed the first Ugaritic discovery has proven rich enough for scholars to spend their entire careers working with its material artifacts. Though important in its own right for our understanding of ancient Mediterranean civilization and culture, the Ugaritic legacy has been most enlightening for students of the Bible. As Craigie suggests, the Ugaritic artifacts and texts help us to understand the cultural and historical milieu that, somewhat later, also produced ancient Israel and its religious literature, the Old Testament.[36]

In his introduction to the Ugaritic materials Craigie provides several illustrations of the light that the Ugaritic texts seem to shed on difficult biblical passages. The strange prohibition against boiling a kid in its mother's milk (Deut. 14:21) has long troubled readers of the Bible. The discovery of the same phrase on a Ugaritic clay tablet seemed to provide an answer. If, as some scholars have suggested, that particular tablet was used in or describes

35. Peter C. Craigie, *Ugarit and the Old Testament* (Grand Rapids: Eerdmans, 1983), 98.
36. Ibid., 67.

ritual sexuality in the Canaanite cult, then the prohibition in Deuteronomy might be an abbreviated polemic. Readers ignorant of the Canaanite cultural context now provided by Ugarit would inevitably misunderstand what would have been obvious to the Israelite audience, who knew of the Canaanite practice. In spite of his belief in the importance of Ugaritic studies for the Bible, however, Craigie was not a "pan-Ugariticist" who found Ugaritic allusions in every corner of the Bible. In his discussion of the prohibition in Deuteronomy 14:21, for example, he goes on to rehearse arguments against the suggested interpretation of the Ugaritic text and thus against its supposed elucidation of the Deuteronomic law. His typically cautious conclusion is that mistaken parallels will occasionally be drawn, but the rewards of comparative research outweigh such risks.[37]

By 1985 Craigie's academic career was in full swing. He had several important publication contracts and was hard at work on a volume *(Jeremiah 1–25)* for the Word Biblical Commentary series. The busy writing schedule was paralleled by his new tasks as academic vice-president at the University of Calgary. But bright prospects sometimes go unfulfilled, and so it was for Peter Craigie. The automobile accident took the achievement of his goals from Peter, the husband and father from his family, and a beloved biblical commentator from evangelical Christianity.

Primary Sources

Craigie, Peter C. *The Book of Deuteronomy.* New International Commentary on the Old Testament. Grand Rapids: Eerdmans, 1976.

———. *Ezekiel.* Daily Study Bible. Philadelphia: Westminster, 1983.

———. *Jeremiah 1–25.* Word Biblical Commentary. Dallas: Word, 1991.

———. *The Old Testament: Its Background, Growth, and Content.* Nashville: Abingdon, 1986.

———. *The Problem of War in the Old Testament.* Grand Rapids: Eerdmans, 1978.

———. *Psalms 1–50.* Word Biblical Commentary. Waco: Word, 1983.

———. *Twelve Prophets.* Daily Study Bible. 2 vols. Philadelphia: Westminster, 1984–85.

———. *Ugarit and the Old Testament.* Grand Rapids: Eerdmans, 1983.

37. Ibid., 76; see also Craigie, *Psalms 1–50,* 55–56.

D. A. Carson

Andreas J. Köstenberger

While many know D. A. Carson for his mind and his impressive scholarly writings, few people know the heart that produces those works. It is especially obvious in *How Long, O Lord? Reflections on Suffering and Evil* and *A Call to Spiritual Reformation: Priorities from Paul and His Prayers*, which give evidence of a deeply personal faith.

Though Carson is a very private person, his friends attest to his devotion to family and his true pastor's heart. The noted scholar Colin Hemer, a personal friend, died in Carson's arms. Carson's eulogy for Hemer was a moving testimony to his own deep care for the spiritual welfare of those close to him.[1] Similarly, after hearing of the death of his mentor, Barnabas Lindars, Carson was genuinely moved, reminiscing at the beginning of a class for quite a while about his studies and personal conversations with Lindars while at Cambridge. The intensity of his beliefs is evident in an autobiographical section of *How Long, O Lord?* where Carson writes, "I would rather die than end up unfaithful to my wife; I would rather die than deny by a profligate life what I have taught in my books; I would rather die than deny or disown the gospel."[2] To understand the true depth of D. A. Carson's faith, it is important to recount in some detail his godly heritage.

A Godly Heritage

The second of three children, Donald Arthur Carson was born on December 21, 1946, to Thomas Donald McMillan Carson and his wife Elizabeth Margaret (née Maybury). In *How Long, O Lord?* Carson describes the "just under the poverty line" type of family in which he grew up:

> The father and mother love each other. They serve the Lord in a low-paying job where they feel they can exercise real ministry. Their modest (and rented) home is characterized by gratitude; their children are disciplined for ingratitude

---

1. D. A. Carson, "Colin John Hemer: *In Memoriam,*" *Forum for the Association of Christians in Higher Education,* Fall 1987, pp. 56–60.
2. D. A. Carson, *How Long, O Lord? Reflections on Suffering and Evil* (Grand Rapids: Baker, 1990), 120.

and shown by example how the Lord provides for his own. There is time to read and think and discuss. There is moral and emotional support (and sometimes material support as well) from the local church, and even an adventurous challenge to see how much can be invested in the "bank of heaven" (Matt. 6:19–21). I grew up in such a home. I did not find out how "poor" we were until I left home to go to university (funded by scholarships and part-time work; my parents certainly could not afford to send me).[3]

Carson's father had been born in Carrickfergus, near Belfast, Northern Ireland, and had immigrated with his family to Ottawa, Canada, in 1913. There Tom Carson, D. A.'s father, grew up under the influence of Calvary Baptist Church. In 1933, at the height of the Great Depression, he entered Toronto Baptist Seminary. During his seminary years, Tom Carson developed an interest in evangelism and church planting in the province of Quebec. He graduated in 1937 and married in 1938. After a few years of service in an English-speaking congregation, Tom Carson moved to Drummondville in 1948, where he established a bilingual church, Faith Baptist Church. The fifteen years spent in ministry in Drummondville were years of persecution, hardships, and a scarcely visible harvest. From 1963 until his death in 1992, Tom Carson continued serving in various forms of local church ministry, primarily at the Montclair Church in Hull, where the Carsons had moved.

In his moving tribute on the occasion of his father's funeral, D. A. Carson expressed his gratitude for his father's perseverance, his life of prayer, his uncomplaining spirit, and his generosity. "When Dad died," Carson wrote, "there were no crowds outside the hospital, no notice in the papers, no announcements on the television, no mention in Parliament, no notice in the nation. In his hospital room there was only the quiet hiss of oxygen, vainly venting because Dad had stopped breathing and would never need it again. But on the other side, all the trumpets sounded. Dad won admittance to the only throne-room that matters, not because he was a good man or a great man, but because he was a forgiven man."[4]

Career to Date

D. A. Carson attended McGill University in Montreal from 1963 to 1967, graduating with a bachelor's degree in chemistry and mathematics. He then earned a master's in divinity from Central Baptist Seminary in Toronto. From 1970 to 1972 he pastored Richmond Baptist Church in Richmond, British Columbia, where he was ordained in 1972. The years 1972–75 were spent in doctoral studies at Cambridge University under Barnabas Lindars. Carson's doctoral dissertation bore the title "Predestination and Responsi-

3. Ibid., 56; see also D. A. Carson, "Growing Up a 'PK,'" *Evangel* 2.4 (1984): 16–18.
4. D. A. Carson, "Thomas Donald McMillan Carson: A Tribute," *Banner of Truth* 356 (May 1993): 24.

bility: Elements of Tension-Theology in the Fourth Gospel against Jewish Background."[5]

During his time in Cambridge, Carson, like another well-known author before him, was "surprised by Joy." To the amazement of Carson's friends, who thought him too devoted to serious scholarship to be sidetracked by romance, Carson's attraction to Joy Wheildon, a British schoolteacher, quickly grew, and on August 16, 1975, the two were married in Cambridge. For the next three years Carson served at Northwest Baptist Theological College in Vancouver, the first year as associate professor of New Testament, the following two years as the founding dean of the seminary.

A significant turn of events occurred when Kenneth Kantzer, the dean of Trinity Evangelical Divinity School in Deerfield, Illinois, heard Carson present a paper at a theological conference and asked him to join the Trinity faculty. From 1978 until 1982 as an associate professor, from 1982 until 1991 as professor, and from 1991 as research professor of New Testament, Carson bloomed into one of the most respected evangelical scholars at the dawn of the twenty-first century. The breadth of his writing is apparent in the bibliography at the end of this article. In addition, Carson has held editorial posts with the *Trinity Journal* (editor, 1980–86) and the *Journal of the Evangelical Theological Society* (book review editor, 1979–86), and recently began work as the editor of New Studies in Biblical Theology, a multivolume update of the Studies in Biblical Theology series. Besides being the editor of the Pillar Commentary series and the founding chairperson of the GRAMCORD Institute (a research and educational institution designed to develop computer-related tools for research into the Bible), he has served as cochair of the Biblical Greek and Linguistics section of the Society of Biblical Literature (1991–96).[6]

The Reception of Carson's Biblical Scholarship

C. S. Lewis once remarked, "A man is ill-advised to write a book on any living author. There is bound to be at least one person and there are probably several who inevitably know more about the subject than ordinary research will discover. Far better to write about the unanswering dead."[7] Reasons why the present essay is preliminary and limited could be multiplied. Accordingly, the reader should not view with any degree of finality our attempt to assess D. A. Carson's contribution to evangelical biblical scholarship.

Mark Noll, in his survey of evangelical scholarship, singles out Richard Longenecker and D. A. Carson as doing "the most seminal New Testament

---

5. A revised and simplified form was published as D. A. Carson, *Divine Sovereignty and Human Responsibility: Biblical Perspectives in Tension* (Atlanta: John Knox, 1981).

6. The best papers of these consultations are published in three volumes, each coedited with Stanley E. Porter: *Biblical Greek Language and Linguistics* (1993); *Discourse Analysis and Other Topics in Biblical Greek* (1995); and *Linguistics and the New Testament* (forthcoming).

7. Quoted in Brian Sibley, *C. S. Lewis through the Shadowlands* (Old Tappan, N.J.: Revell, 1985), 11.

work by contemporary evangelicals."[8] This assessment becomes increasingly justified by the year. Carson's productivity is made possible in part by Trinity's generous sabbatical policies, which have allowed him to spend every third year at Tyndale House, a research center for biblical studies in Cambridge which Carson regards as his ultimate academic home. Apart from affording Carson time and opportunity to write, these sabbaticals also enable him to maintain a truly international scope for his teaching and scholarship. He blends well into the academic setting in Britain and is accepted and sought after in university circles there. This involvement, together with his worldwide travels, enables him to surmount the isolation from the rest of the world that plagues much of North American biblical scholarship.

Some have voiced concerns that Carson's prodigious output ("he makes us all look like sluggards," one of his colleagues at Trinity, himself a respected author, has remarked) may at times limit his scholarship. True, Carson has not yet produced the kind of technical monograph that proves singularly influential in a given field, though his *Syntactical Concordance to the Greek New Testament* is eagerly awaited by many. And one looks forward as well to a major work on the relationship between the Testaments and perhaps even a treatment of Johannine theology.[9]

Others object to Carson's confrontational, direct manner, both in writing and in person. It should be realized, however, that what may appear as glibness in Carson's dealing with opposing views could actually be a reflection of his quickness in sizing up an opponent and his sharp penetration to the heart of an issue. But whether these criticisms are warranted or not, they reveal a certain ambiguity with which Carson has been received by his colleagues. Many scholars who do not share Carson's conservative evangelical views on Scripture apparently believe they can safely ignore his writings. Others, perhaps voicing the concerns just mentioned, do not give Carson's views the attention they deserve. Overall, it seems that Carson is only beginning to get the kind of exposure and attention due a man of his scholarly stature.

The reception of Carson's commentary on John's Gospel illustrates the varied responses to his work. Hailed in evangelical circles as an epitome of lucidity and thorough scholarship,[10] the work has been less well received by scholars in the larger Christian community.[11] However, it should be expected that any effort to defend the fourth Gospel's historicity will be criticized in our day.[12] Moreover, it does not endear Carson to many of his col-

---

8. Mark A. Noll, *Between Faith and Criticism*, 2d ed. (Grand Rapids: Baker, 1991), 136.

9. Important forthcoming works include the two-volume *Paul and Variegated Nomism* and a dictionary on the use of the Old Testament in the New, for both of which Carson is serving as coeditor.

10. See, e.g., Moisés Silva, review of *The Gospel according to John*, by D. A. Carson, *Westminster Theological Journal* 54 (1992): 376–78.

11. See, e.g., David Ball, "Some Recent Literature on John: A Review Article," *Themelios* 19.1 (Oct. 1993): 13–18.

12. See Ben Witherington, review of *Jesus as God*, by Murray Harris, *Themelios* 19.1 (Oct. 1993): 28–29.

leagues that he gives short shrift to source and redaction theories,[13] and that he maintains a healthy skepticism regarding the many contemporary literary techniques invading biblical scholarship.[14] Thus Carson has criticized such Johannine scholars as R. Alan Culpepper[15] and J. Louis Martyn, disputing the validity of their "mirror" and "two-level" readings of the fourth Gospel.[16] As a result, some in the academic world see Carson as hyperconservative and as part of the extreme right in evangelical scholarship. As one Oxford professor commented, "He is too clever to be a fundamentalist" but still "far too conservative" to be taken seriously by scholars in certain circles. Also very revealing is a correspondence with a senior British scholar on the nature of Scripture.[17]

Although Carson is viewed by most of his scholarly colleagues as very conservative, this label does not describe him accurately in every respect. He is often unconventional and very open to the breaking of new ground. For example, he essentially embraced the "verbal aspect theory" that one of his students, Stanley Porter (Carson was his external examiner at Sheffield), forcefully advocated at a time when few colleagues had even heard of this theory on the function of the Greek verb. Carson's forthcoming commentary on the Johannine Epistles promises to be the first consistent effort to integrate verbal aspect theory into a full-fledged commentary. As the general editor of a series entitled Studies in Biblical Greek, Carson has also had the opportunity to be involved in the publication of seminal studies by Porter and K. L. McKay.[18]

D. A. Carson may one day be remembered as one of the last great Renaissance men in evangelical biblical scholarship. In an age of increasing specialization and fragmentation, Carson, to the admiring disbelief of many of his colleagues, persistently refuses to limit his interests. His publications cover a vast range of subjects: New Testament Greek, Bible translation, hermeneutics, contextualization, the use of the Old Testament in the New, preaching,

13. See D. A. Carson, "Current Source Criticism of the Fourth Gospel: Some Methodological Questions," *Journal of Biblical Literature* 97 (1978): 411–29; idem, "Historical Tradition and the Fourth Gospel: After Dodd, What?" in *Gospel Perspectives*, ed. R. T. France and David Wenham, vol. 2 (Sheffield: JSOT, 1981), 83–145; and for more general treatments see idem, "Redaction Criticism: On the Legitimacy and Illegitimacy of a Literary Tool," in *Scripture and Truth*, ed. D. A. Carson and John D. Woodbridge (Grand Rapids: Zondervan, 1983), 119–46; and D. A. Carson et al., "Redaction Criticism: Is It Worth the Risk?" *Christianity Today* 29.15 (Oct. 18, 1985): 1–10.
14. See Carson's survey articles on Johannine studies in *Themelios* 9.1 (Sept. 1983): 8–18; and 14.2 (Jan.-Feb. 1989): 57–64; or "Gundry on Matthew: A Critical Review," *Trinity Journal*, n.s., 3 (1982): 71–91.
15. D. A. Carson, review of *Anatomy of the Fourth Gospel*, by R. Alan Culpepper, *Trinity Journal*, n.s., 4 (1983): 119–21; idem, *The Gospel according to John* (Grand Rapids: Eerdmans, 1991), 63–68.
16. D. A. Carson, review of *Overcoming the World*, by David Rensberger, *Themelios* 17.1 (Oct.-Nov. 1991): 27–28; and idem, review of *Peter and the Beloved Disciple*, by Kevin Quast, *Themelios* 17.2 (Jan.-Feb. 1992): 21–22.
17. See D. A. Carson, *The Gagging of God: Christianity Confronts Pluralism* (Grand Rapids: Zondervan, 1996), 158–63.
18. Stanley E. Porter, *Verbal Aspect in the Greek of the New Testament* (New York: Peter Lang, 1989); K. L. McKay, *A New Syntax of the Verb in New Testament Greek* (New York: Peter Lang, 1994).

various aspects of New Testament and biblical theology, major commentaries on Matthew and John, and even poetry. Carson's fielding of questions subsequent to a presentation at the 1993 annual meeting of the Institute for Biblical Research showed glimpses of his competence in an array of fields. As a reviewer of one of his books put it, "Professor Carson possesses qualities which are not often found in combination. He is a New Testament scholar who sees the Bible as a whole; a biblical scholar with a concern for both the theological and the practical implications of the Bible's teaching; a blunt writer with a pastoral heart; and (perhaps rarest of all) an academic with a clear, vigorous, occasionally even slangy style."[19]

In the light of these qualities, it is understandable that some compare Carson favorably with other evangelical scholars such as F. F. Bruce and I. Howard Marshall. While Bruce, unlike Carson, had a background in classical Greek, Carson may exceed Bruce in his exegetical and theological grasp. Significantly, Carson is not just a New Testament exegete but a biblical theologian who synthesizes materials that other scholars leave unrelated. Moreover, he is abreast of the latest developments in computer technology and linguistics. At the same time, some see Carson as taking over the mantle from John Stott as an evangelical leader and spokesman respected worldwide. That Carson can be compared with evangelical figures as diverse and influential as Bruce, Marshall, and Stott is in itself a tribute to his versatility and increasing stature.

Characteristics of Carson's Biblical Scholarship

An International Ministry

Carson grew up in the Baptist tradition. To this day, while in England he associates with and worships in a Baptist church. However, during his doctoral studies and his regular sabbaticals at Tyndale House he has functioned in an interdenominational context. He moves freely in Anglican circles in Britain and in Australia, and his counsel is sought on a wide range of biblical and pastoral issues by church leaders from various confessional backgrounds. Ultimately, Carson's ministry is not channeled through denominations but through individuals and institutions that invite him to minister in their respective contexts.

In this connection we note that Carson served for a number of years with the Faith and Church Study Unit of the Theological Commission of the World Evangelical Fellowship, an involvement that is indicative of his concern for the universal church and of his commitment to cooperation among evangelicals worldwide. His contacts in Britain and the fact that his command of French enables him to function as a liaison to French-speaking Africa place Carson in a strategic position to facilitate such collaboration. He

19. Paul Ellingworth, review of *How Long, O Lord?* by D. A. Carson, *Evangelical Quarterly* 64 (1992): 361.

himself has lectured all over the world. Operating in a global context, with a commitment to first-rate evangelical scholarship, Carson has been engaged for a considerable amount of time in nurturing those who in turn train other Christian leaders. Indeed, Carson places a high priority on mentoring gifted students. Craig Blomberg, Stanley Porter, and many others can attest to his formative influence on their scholarly careers.

While Carson chaired the Faith and Church Study Unit, the group strove to make the ideal of a worldwide scope for the World Evangelical Fellowship a reality. Nigerians, Japanese, Indians, Indonesians, continental Europeans, and delegates from other parts of the world struggled to produce global solutions for important issues facing the church worldwide. In the past, those with adequate resources would have done all the writing. Under Carson's leadership, however, scholars from the Two-Thirds World, despite the lack of materials in their native contexts, were encouraged to participate fully in the discussions and writing. Carson ensured that every contributor was given bibliographical assistance and suggestions for improvement. Thus helpful insights on important subjects found their way to Japan, Hong Kong, Indonesia, and many other places. Eventually Carson would edit the submitted contributions for publication. In this way he promoted significantly both the coming of age of scholarship in the Two-Thirds World and global evangelical partnership.[20]

A High View of Scripture

As already indicated, it is difficult to assign D. A. Carson a distinct place in the field of evangelical theology. He himself has great admiration and respect for the fathers of the evangelical movement in the United States, Kenneth Kantzer and Carl Henry. Indeed, he had the privilege of interviewing these two men for the video series *Know Your Roots* in 1991. His own scholarly career has been characterized by a significant degree of independence from other scholars' views, a bedrock commitment to the authority of Scripture,[21] and use of all the resources available to the modern scholar to interpret it.

Carson considers a high view of the Scripture's integrity a nonnegotiable for his own work.[22] Thus in a speech given at a luncheon at Tyndale House he once remarked that anyone who arrives at a conclusion at odds with the traditional evangelical positions about the authority of the Bible should have

20. Peter O'Brien, interview by author, Sept. 1994. The volumes produced during Carson's term with the Faith and Church Study Unit include *Biblical Interpretation and the Church, The Church in the Bible and the World, Teach Us to Pray, Right with God,* and *Worship.*

21. See D. A. Carson, "Three Books on the Bible: A Critical Review," *Journal of the Evangelical Theological Society* 26 (1983): 337–67; idem, "Recent Developments in the Doctrine of Scripture," in *Hermeneutics, Authority, and Canon,* ed. D. A. Carson and John D. Woodbridge (Grand Rapids: Zondervan, 1986), 1–48.

22. D. A. Carson, "The Role of Exegesis in Systematic Theology," in *Doing Theology in Today's World,* ed. John D. Woodbridge and Thomas E. McComiskey (Grand Rapids: Zondervan, 1992), 54–56.

the integrity to stop claiming to be an evangelical.[23] At the same time, Carson is not a fundamentalist in the sense of interpreting Scripture fideistically and literalistically. He uses intelligent, detailed biblical study as the basis for theological construction and application. This general procedure was already visible in his dissertation on God's sovereignty and human responsibility. It has been refined over the years and was further elaborated upon in his lecture on biblical theology at the 1993 meeting of the Institute for Biblical Research.[24]

While Carson is committed to biblical theology, he does not therefore eschew systematic theology.[25] Moreover, he is highly concerned about the contextualization of the Christian faith in the pluralistic Western world of today as well as in cross-cultural contexts.[26]

Commitment and Ministry to the Church

For all his erudition, D. A. Carson insists that scholarship and personal faith must not be kept separate. Rather, a deep evangelical faith should undergird a person's effort to search the Scriptures as diligently and penetratingly as possible. Especially commendable is Carson's strong commitment to serve the needs of the evangelical church today. Indeed, Carson is a symbol for many that competent biblical scholarship and evangelical orthodoxy can go together. Pastors and other committed Christians can turn to his commentaries and biblical studies for help when interpreting difficult passages or confronting controversial issues. It is significant that several of his books are based on sermons or letters to a church or parachurch context (e.g., *The Sermon on the Mount* and *Showing the Spirit*). Carson's deep concern for the spiritual state of the church today can be seen in his *Call to Spiritual Reformation*, which begins with an impassioned plea for and practical tips on prayer.[27] He has also spoken out on the need for biblical expository preaching and regular time with God.[28]

Unafraid to speak out on controversial issues, Carson considers it his re-

23. Interview with Peter Comont, a former pastor at Eden Baptist Church in Cambridge.
24. D. A. Carson, "Current Issues in Biblical Theology: A New Testament Perspective," *Bulletin for Biblical Research* 5 (1995): 17–41.
25. See D. A. Carson, "Unity and Diversity in the New Testament: The Possibility of Systematic Theology," in *Scripture and Truth*, ed. Carson and Woodbridge, 65–95; idem, "Role of Exegesis," 39–76.
26. See especially D. A. Carson, "Christian Witness in an Age of Pluralism," in *God and Culture*, ed. D. A. Carson and John D. Woodbridge (Grand Rapids: Eerdmans, 1993), 31–66; idem, "Church and Mission: Reflections on Contextualization and the Third Horizon," in *The Church in the Bible and the World*, ed. D. A. Carson (Grand Rapids: Baker, 1987), 213–57; idem, "A Sketch of the Factors Determining Current Hermeneutical Debate in Cross-cultural Contexts," in *Biblical Interpretation and the Church*, ed. D. A. Carson (Grand Rapids: Baker, 1993), 11–29; idem, *Gagging of God;* and idem, ed., *Telling the Truth: Evangelizing Postmoderns* (forthcoming).
27. See also D. A. Carson, ed., *Teach Us to Pray* (Grand Rapids: Baker, 1990); and D. A. Carson, "A Church That Does All the Right Things, But . . .," *Christianity Today* 23.18 (June 29, 1979): 28–31.
28. D. A. Carson, "Accept No Substitutes: Six Reasons Not to Abandon Expository Preaching," *Leadership* 17 (1996): 87–88; idem, "Preaching That Understands the World," in *When God's Voice Is Heard*, ed. Christopher Green and David Jackman (Leicester: Inter-Varsity, 1995), 145–59; idem, *For the Love of God*, 2 vols. (Wheaton, Ill.: Crossway, 1998 and forthcoming); and idem, "The Difficult Doctrine of the Love of God," a four-part series starting in *Bibliotheca Sacra* 156 (1999): 3–12.

sponsibility to contribute discerningly and constructively to current debates within the church. In *Showing the Spirit* and in an essay on "The Purpose of Signs and Wonders in the New Testament,"[29] Carson addresses the contemporary charismatic movement; in "Reflections on Christian Assurance"[30] he deals with the "Lordship salvation" debate; in *How Long, O Lord?* he provides a courageous discussion of AIDS;[31] and in *The King James Version Debate* and *The Inclusive Language Debate* he seeks to adjudicate between two sides of important issues.[32] However, by maintaining a biblical focus Carson rises above mere polemics.

Perhaps one of Carson's greatest strengths is his ability to appreciate the merits of opposing views and to incorporate the best of both into a balanced mediating position. For example, on the issue of charismata, Carson is not a cessationist, arguing that 1 Corinthians 13 appears to preclude such a position. On the issue of divine sovereignty and human responsibility, Carson holds to "compatibilism"; on the issue of Christian assurance, Carson seeks to balance carefully the believer's security with the biblical injunctions for perseverance in the Christian faith.

Focus on the Gospel

What is not always understood but is nonetheless crucial for a true appraisal is that Carson, for all his scholarly writings, is first of all a minister of the gospel, not an academician. He is a gospel-centered man, not a theoretician. It appears that academia has not mastered him—he has mastered academia. Why then is Carson so deeply involved in scholarship? Doubtless he recognizes his God-given gifts and desires to be faithful to his calling. Also, Carson believes that people are built up by faithful exposition of the Scriptures and defense of the gospel. Well aware that too often liberals have held sway in the defining moments of discussion, he recognizes that the task of the evangelical is not exhausted by the assertion of truth but that it is also imperative to refute error.

But how would D. A. Carson himself like to be remembered? When his mother died and he struggled as to whether he should fulfil a commitment to speak at a large missionary conference, he was led to reflect on his priorities: "Sometimes when I look at my own children, I wonder if, should the Lord give us another thirty years, they will remember their father as a man of prayer, or think of him as someone distant who was away from home rather a lot and who wrote a number of obscure books."[33] It is appropriate to con-

---

29. D. A. Carson, "The Purpose of Signs and Wonders in the New Testament," in *Power Religion,* ed. Michael S. Horton (Chicago: Moody, 1992), 89–118.

30. D. A. Carson, "Reflections on Christian Assurance," *Westminster Theological Journal* 54 (1992): 1–29.

31. But see the critique by Ellingworth, review of *How Long, O Lord?* 362–63.

32. D. A. Carson, *The King James Debate* (Grand Rapids: Baker, 1979); idem, *The Inclusive Language Debate* (Grand Rapids: Baker, 1999).

33. D. A. Carson, *A Call to Spiritual Reformation* (Grand Rapids: Baker, 1992), 26.

clude with Carson's poem "The Finitude of Man," which puts the entire human quest to understand God in its proper perspective:

> I understand that matter can be changed
> To energy; that maths can integrate
> The complex quantum jumps that must relate
> The fusion of the stars to history's page.
> I understand that God in every age
> Is Lord of all; that matter can't dictate;
> That stars and quarks and all things intricate
> Perform his word—including fool and sage.
> But knowing God is not to know like God;
> And science is a quest in infancy.
> Still more: transcendence took on flesh and blood:
> I do not understand how this can be.
> The more my mind assesses what it can,
> The more it learns the finitude of man.[34]

Primary Sources

Carson, D. A. "Accept No Substitutes: Six Reasons Not to Abandon Expository Preaching." *Leadership* 17 (1996): 87–88.

———. *A Call to Spiritual Reformation: Priorities from Paul and His Prayers.* Grand Rapids: Baker, 1992.

———. *The Cross and Christian Ministry: An Exposition of Passages from 1 Corinthians.* Grand Rapids: Baker, 1993.

———. *Divine Sovereignty and Human Responsibility: Biblical Perspectives in Tension.* Atlanta: John Knox, 1981.

———. *Exegetical Fallacies.* 2d ed. Grand Rapids: Baker, 1996.

———. *The Farewell Discourse and Final Prayer of Jesus: An Exposition of John 14–17.* Grand Rapids: Baker, 1980.

———. *For the Love of God.* 2 vols. Wheaton, Ill.: Crossway, 1998 and forthcoming.

———. *From Triumphalism to Maturity: An Exposition of 2 Corinthians 10–13.* Grand Rapids: Baker, 1984.

———. *The Gagging of God: Christianity Confronts Pluralism.* Grand Rapids: Zondervan, 1996.

———. *The Gospel according to John.* Grand Rapids: Eerdmans, 1991.

———. *Greek Accents: A Student's Manual.* Grand Rapids: Baker, 1985.

———. *Holy Sonnets of the Twentieth Century.* Grand Rapids: Baker, 1994.

———. *How Long, O Lord? Reflections on Suffering and Evil.* Grand Rapids: Baker, 1990.

———. *The Inclusive Language Debate.* Grand Rapids: Baker, 1999.

———. *The King James Version Debate: A Plea for Realism.* Grand Rapids: Baker, 1979.

———. "Matthew." In *Expositor's Bible Commentary*, edited by Frank E. Gaebelein, 8:1–599. Grand Rapids: Zondervan, 1984.

---

34. D. A. Carson, *Holy Sonnets of the Twentieth Century* (Grand Rapids: Baker, 1994), 97.

————. *New Testament Commentary Survey.* 4th ed. Grand Rapids: Baker, 1993.

————. "Preaching That Understands the World." In *When God's Voice Is Heard,* edited by Christopher Green and David Jackman, 145–59. Leicester: Inter-Varsity, 1995.

————. *The Sermon on the Mount: An Evangelical Exposition of Matthew 5–7.* Grand Rapids: Baker, 1978.

————. *Showing the Spirit: A Theological Exposition of 1 Corinthians 12–14.* Grand Rapids: Baker, 1987.

————. *When Jesus Confronts the World: An Exposition of Matthew 8–10.* Grand Rapids: Baker, 1987.

Carson, D. A., ed. *Biblical Interpretation and the Church: Text and Context.* Grand Rapids: Baker, 1993.

————. *The Church in the Bible and the World: An International Study.* Grand Rapids: Baker, 1988.

————. *From Sabbath to Lord's Day.* Grand Rapids: Zondervan, 1982.

————. *Right with God: Justification in the Bible and the World.* Grand Rapids: Baker, 1992.

————. *Teach Us to Pray: Prayer in the Bible and the World.* Grand Rapids: Baker, 1990.

————. *Worship: Adoration and Action.* Grand Rapids: Baker, 1993.

Carson, D. A., Leon Morris, and Douglas J. Moo. *An Introduction to the New Testament.* Grand Rapids: Zondervan, 1991.

Carson, D. A., and Stanley E. Porter, eds. *Biblical Greek Language and Linguistics: Open Questions in Current Research.* Sheffield: JSOT, 1993.

————. *Discourse Analysis and Other Topics in Biblical Greek.* Sheffield: JSOT, 1995.

————. *Linguistics and the New Testament: Critical Junctions.* Sheffield: JSOT, forthcoming.

Carson, D. A., and H. G. M. Williamson, eds. *It Is Written: Scripture Citing Scripture.* New York: Cambridge University Press, 1988.

Carson, D. A., and John D. Woodbridge, eds. *God and Culture.* Grand Rapids: Eerdmans, 1993.

————. *Hermeneutics, Authority, and Canon.* Grand Rapids: Zondervan, 1986.

————. *Scripture and Truth.* Grand Rapids: Zondervan, 1983.

Nicholas Thomas Wright

John J. Hartmann

N. T. (Tom) Wright was born in Morpeth, Northumberland, England, on December 1, 1948. Wright came to a personal realization of God's love in Christ by the age of seven and of a calling to Christian service by age ten. This sense of a personal relationship with God would grow in his teen years through prayer, Scripture reading, and involvement in Christian youth fellowships. While focusing on classics in his formal education, Wright also privately studied New Testament Greek and ancient history. These areas of study would lay the foundation for his later work as a Christian theologian and apologist.

Wright was subsequently educated at Oxford, where he studied for the B.A. in classics (1971), trained for ordination as a priest (B.A., Wycliffe Hall, 1971–73), and read for the D.Phil. in the New Testament (1974–80). During his undergraduate years he was challenged to think through complex philosophical issues and their implications for Christian faith. Theological training exposed him to views which unnecessarily posed a dichotomy between the historical Jesus and the Jesus of faith; his response was to press for a more rigorous synthesis of history and theology. His doctoral thesis on Romans would articulate the seminal insight that Paul thought of the Messiah as representing and summing up the whole people of God in himself (representative and incorporative messiahship).[1] Wright has since held posts as an assistant professor of New Testament at McGill University, Montreal (1981–86), and as a lecturer in New Testament at Oxford University (1986–92), where he also served as a fellow, tutor, and chaplain of Worcester College. He is presently the dean of Lichfield Cathedral, a post he has held since 1993.

Wright has written on a wide span of topics, at both a popular and a scholarly level. His more popular writings include books and articles on Jesus, Paul, the mission of the church, the Spirit, the authority of Scripture, and the question of God in general. Though in no sense lacking in depth, these writings are highly accessible to all readers and reflect Wright's faith and commitment to God, the church, and Christian mission. Of highest pri-

---

1. N. T. Wright, "The Messiah and the People of God" (D.Phil. diss., Oxford University, 1980).

ority are his commitment to evangelical faith and his concern that orthodoxy not follow the mistake of first-century Judaism in losing its sense of calling and mission to the world.[2]

In the 1990s Wright emerged as a notable contributor to the scholarly study of Jesus and Paul and their relationship to first-century Judaism. His magnum opus is a projected six-volume study that addresses the subject of Christian origins and the contemporary question of God. Volume 1, *The New Testament and the People of God*, deals with hermeneutical theory (how we study the New Testament as literature, history, and theology), New Testament backgrounds (the history and "story" of ancient Judaism), and the emergence of early Christianity. Volume 2, *Jesus and the Victory of God*, places the mission and message of Jesus in the first-century context of the Jewish expectation of the kingdom of Israel's God. While the third volume has yet to be released, Wright has already set forth his innovative interpretation of its topic (Pauline theology) in several essays, his doctoral thesis, the scholarly monograph *The Climax of the Covenant*, and *What St. Paul Really Said*. In this article we will summarize Wright's views on hermeneutical theory, Judaism, Jesus, and Paul.

Hermeneutical Theory

In *The New Testament and the People of God*, Wright proposes to integrate literary criticism, historical reconstruction, and theology as a means of clarifying the message of the New Testament.[3] Over against modern and postmodern views of what is really knowable, Wright adopts an epistemology of critical realism. This approach acknowledges (1) the independent reality of objects external to the knower (hence "realism"), (2) the possibility of knowing that reality through dialogue between the knower and the thing known (hence "critical"), and (3) the provisional nature of all that the knower comes to know (hence a hermeneutic of humility and love).[4] More importantly, Wright observes that "story" is the vehicle through which meaning is brought to the facts and events uncovered in the study of New Testament literature, history, and theology.[5] Stories articulate the worldviews through which societies and individuals perceive all reality. By encapsulating worldviews which claim to make sense of the whole of reality, stories function to modify and subvert other stories and the worldviews which they articulate. They also provide a narrative framework for analyzing the literary, historical, and theological dimensions of the New Testament, which represents the writings of a group of first-century Jews who retold and subverted the basic

2. Conversation with the author, 13 February 1997.
3. N. T. Wright, *The New Testament and the People of God,* vol. 1 of *Christian Origins and the Question of God* (Minneapolis: Fortress, 1992), 27.
4. Ibid., 31–46.
5. Ibid., 47–144.

Jewish story by claiming that its climax had arrived in the life, death, and resurrection of Jesus.

In his integration of literature, history, and theology Wright points out
that *literature* involves "the telling of stories which bring worldviews into ar-
ticulation."[6] That both Jewish and Christian writings employ story forms indicates that the debate between Judaism and Christianity was not a controversy about abstract doctrines, but "about different tellings of the story of
Israel's God, his people, and the world."[7] *Written history,* Wright continues,
involves "meaningful narrative of events and intentions."[8] The historian
must consider the wider worldview that lies beneath the narration of historical events and produce historical reconstructions which (1) incorporate all
the evidence, (2) simplify the overall picture, and (3) clarify related issues.[9]
Within the larger narrative framework of the biblical story, the *theology* of
the New Testament involves explicit debate about basic and consequent beliefs that derive from the unexpressed Jewish worldview.[10] The Gospels are
literary works of the early church which offer a *theological* interpretation of
real events in *history,* telling how Israel's God had at last acted in the Messiah
Jesus.[11]

The Jewish Story: Exile and Restoration

For Wright, the New Testament represents a continuation and, with its climax in Jesus, a subversive retelling of the Jewish story.[12] Fundamental to the
Jewish story is the belief that the Creator God had called Israel to be the people through whom he would deal with the problem of evil produced by
Adam's sin. Though the promises to Abraham came to an initial climax in
the exodus, Israel's sin-laden history would ultimately lead to a divided kingdom, rejection of the prophets, and enactment of the covenant curse in the
exile. Israel's failure did not mean that the covenant purpose was abandoned,
but led instead to another fundamental belief: God would restore his exiled
people to their rightful place as his true humanity in order that they might
fulfil their original calling in relation to the rest of the world.[13] Since, however, the return from Babylon (538 B.C.) resulted in only a partial restoration
(Israel remained subject to foreigners, and her God did not return to the temple), the Old Testament period ended with "a story in search of a conclusion."[14] Most Jews of the intertestamental period viewed the exile as an ongoing reality to be ended only when Israel's God acted again for his people's

6. Ibid., 65.
7. Ibid., 76.
8. Ibid., 82.
9. Ibid., 103, 464.
10. Ibid., 121–43.
11. Ibid., 78–79, 91.
12. For Wright's full description of the Jewish story see *New Testament,* 147–338.
13. Ibid., 259–72.
14. Ibid., 217.

restoration.[15] In the extended exile the covenant God was justly punishing Israel for her disobedience and in forbearance allowing time for more to repent. But the hope was never abandoned that he would yet manifest his righteousness (covenant faithfulness) and vindicate those who had remained faithful to the covenant by keeping the Torah.

This Jewish worldview came to expression in fundamental beliefs and symbols. The three basic beliefs were monotheism, election, and eschatological hope.[16] Monotheism and election represented the first level of God's covenant purpose: the Creator God would deal with the world's evil through his covenant people Israel. The second level of covenant purpose was articulated in the teaching that the covenant God would restore his exiled people to their rightful place as his true humanity. During the period of waiting, Israel had to hold fast to the Torah, since her God was coming to vindicate those who remained faithful to the covenant.[17] The four basic symbols were the temple (representing the presence of God), the land (the place where God would bless his people), the Torah (the covenant charter regulating Israel's way of life), and the racial identity that marked Israel off from the other peoples.[18] Israel's eschatological hope focused on the restoration of these symbols in a renewed world: the temple would be rebuilt and the Torah observed by a regathered Israel in a cleansed land.[19]

In the intertestamental period, the Maccabean revolt (167–164 B.C.) decisively reinforced the belief that God would again act to deliver his people, while dissatisfaction with the ensuing Hasmonean dynasty (164–63 B.C.) gave rise to various sectarian groups (e.g., Essenes, Pharisees) that viewed Jerusalem as the center of a corrupt and illegitimate regime.[20] After Rome occupied Jerusalem (63 B.C.), Jewish revolutionary movements developed in response to the Roman backing of Herod the Great (37–4 B.C.) and continued to increase in the period after Herod's death until the Jewish war of A.D. 66–70 broke out. The revolutionary groups of this period were connected by a tradition of active zeal, which traced its genesis through the Maccabees to Elijah and Phinehas the priest. The political agenda which looked for restoration of Israel's sovereignty arose from beliefs about Israel's destiny (Dan. 7), but also represented a response to Roman taxation and disregard for the sanctity of the temple. The Sadducees, an aristocratic group closely associated with the priests and chief priests, maintained the status quo and acted as a liaison between Rome and the Jewish populace.

---

15. Ibid., 268–72.

16. For full discussion see N. T. Wright, *The Climax of the Covenant: Christ and the Law in Pauline Theology* (Minneapolis: Fortress, 1991), 1; idem, *New Testament,* 259–72.

17. Wright, *New Testament,* 222. Wright notes that the Jews of this period kept the Torah not to gain salvation after death, but to preserve their distinct identity as God's people and to guarantee personal vindication when God acted on a national level to restore Israel's sovereignty (pp. 168–70, 238–39).

18. Wright, *New Testament,* 224–32.

19. Ibid., 280.

20. For this paragraph see Wright, *New Testament,* 167–214.

The Historical Jesus

The Jewish story of exile and restoration provides Wright with the framework for understanding the life of Jesus. Twentieth-century research into the life of Jesus has followed either William Wrede's thoroughgoing skepticism (the Gospels are an ahistorical theological creation of the early church) or Albert Schweitzer's thoroughgoing eschatological approach (the Gospels tell of the historical Jesus who looked for the long-awaited kingdom of Israel's God).[21] In *Jesus and the Victory of God* Wright takes the latter path and argues that Jewish eschatology provides the fundamental framework for understanding Jesus' proclamation and activity.[22] Jesus' warnings about imminent judgment constituted a prophetic call to national repentance in the face of sociopolitical events that represented the climactic moment in Israel's history.[23] In terms of the contemporary discussion, Wright criticizes the Jesus Seminar for removing Jesus from the context of Jewish eschatological expectation in favor of the unverifiable hypothesis that Jesus was a Cynic who invited the underprivileged to follow him in rejecting the social structures of his day.[24]

Wright thus maintains that Jesus functioned within his first-century Jewish context as a "leadership prophet" who announced the arrival of the kingdom of God, warned of imminent judgment, and summoned the people of Israel to an immediate change of heart. In word and deed he claimed that the traditional expectation for Israel's restoration was being fulfilled.[25] His parables redefined the traditional understanding of the kingdom of God and brought it to birth by both inviting the repentant into the new world that was dawning and warning the unrepentant of the coming judgment.[26] His mighty works functioned within the context of his prophetic proclamation as signs that the kingdom of God was coming to birth; on the other hand, they were viewed as subversive by those who resisted his program. Many of his healings signified a renewal of the covenant for those whose diseases banned them from fellowship in the covenant community (lepers, the blind, lame, deaf and dumb).[27] Other mighty works (calming storms, feeding multitudes) pointed

21. N. T. Wright, "Quest for the Historical Jesus," in *Anchor Bible Dictionary*, ed. David Noel Freedman, 6 vols. (New York: Doubleday, 1992), 3:796–802; idem, *Jesus and the Victory of God*, vol. 2 of *Christian Origins and the Question of God* (Minneapolis: Fortress, 1996), 3–82.

22. Wright, *Jesus and the Victory*, 81–124; see also idem, *New Testament*, 1–2, 5–6, 100; and idem, "Jesus, Israel and the Cross," in *SBL 1985 Seminar Papers*, ed. K. H. Richards (Chico, Calif.: Scholars, 1985), 75–95.

23. Wright strongly disagrees with Schweitzer's claim that "apocalyptic" signifies an imminent end of the world and with his views about the end result of Jesus' mission. See Wright, "Jesus, Israel," 78–83; idem, *New Testament*, 268–338; and idem, *Jesus and the Victory*, 96–97, 162–72.

24. Wright, *Jesus and the Victory*, 29–82; see also idem, "Taking the Text with Her Pleasure: A Post-Post-Modernist Response to J. Dominic Crossan *The Historical Jesus: The Life of a Mediterranean Jewish Peasant* (with Apologies to A. A. Milne, St Paul and James Joyce)," *Theology* 96 (1993): 303–10.

25. Wright, *Jesus and the Victory*, 162–72.

26. Ibid., 173–82.

27. Ibid., 186–96.

to the renewal of all creation that was to occur at Israel's restoration, while the casting out of demons signified a head-on war with Satan that was already in the process of being won.

Jesus redefined Israel's plight by claiming that the real enemy was not Rome, but Satan.[28] In the Jewish worldview, evil powers had usurped the authority of Yahweh, who would reestablish his rightful rule by means of a great final battle that would crush the evil Gentile powers presently in control. Jesus employed this cosmic language to describe his conflict with the powers of darkness: Satan's house was being plundered, and those not joining Jesus in this battle were fighting on the other side (Matt. 12:29–30; Mark 3:27; Luke 11:22–23; see also 10:18). This victory was initially won in the wilderness temptations and continued throughout Jesus' ministry. The decisive climax, however, came in Jesus' death, which was "the actual victory of the kingdom, by which the enemy of the people would finally be defeated."[29] All who would repent Jesus welcomed to participate in the restoration he was bringing, while those who presumed upon Jewish ancestry were warned of the coming judgment. His table fellowship with sinners was a controversial symbolic enactment of the messianic banquet to which all (including Gentiles) were invited, and from which those who refused his call were excluded. And thus, correcting Israel's nationalistic understanding of the people of God, Jesus redefined them as those who respond to his announcement of the kingdom. Similarly, the expectation for a restored Israel in the land he redefined in terms of his mighty works in restored human beings (Isa. 35).[30]

Jesus also attacked the standard symbols of the Jewish worldview.[31] This evoked hostility from the Pharisees, whose zeal for the Torah and purity was closely tied to their political agenda for national liberation. Because this policy was leading to ruin, Jesus relativized the boundary markers which symbolized Israel's national aspirations (laws concerning the Sabbath, food, and purity). Rather, the hour had arrived for a restored Israel to fulfil her true vocation in relation to the rest of the world. But the symbol which finally brought Jesus into conflict with the Jewish and Roman authorities was the temple.[32] The temple functioned as the site of God's presence and of purification from sin through the sacrificial system, and also carried political significance for those invested with authority over the nation. Jesus' proclamation of the forgiveness of sins indicated the arrival of the eschatological restoration and thus was clearly subversive to those in charge of the temple. Jesus further subverted the temple ideology by claiming that the anticipated rebuilding of the temple and return of Yahweh to Zion were actually occur-

---

28. Ibid., 446–63.
29. Ibid., 466; see also 463–67.
30. Ibid., 428–30.
31. Ibid., 369–442.
32. Ibid., 413–28, 510–19.

ring in and through his work. In addition, he carried out symbolic prophetic actions that served as signs of the destruction of Jerusalem and the temple.

Finally, Jesus went to Jerusalem to die as the messianic representative of God's people.[33] His cleansing of the temple was a symbolic enactment of Yahweh's judgment on the temple; and the Last Supper, a symbolic enactment of the Passover and exodus, indicated that Jesus' death for the redemption of God's people was the climactic moment of the whole Jewish story and that those sharing in this meal were the people of the renewed covenant.[34] His final journey to Jerusalem, which climaxed in these two events, was itself a symbolic enactment of Israel's greatest hope, the promise of Yahweh's victorious return to Zion to judge and save.[35]

The early Christian mission was motivated by the conviction that Israel's hope of redemption had been realized in Jesus' death and resurrection, and that the time had arrived for the Gentiles to be incorporated into the people of God.[36] The coming of the Spirit was interpreted as evidence that the age of restoration had arrived. Replacing the exodus and the celebration of Passover, baptism and the Eucharist became the defining symbols of the new community. Early Christians were united by the belief that Israel's restoration had been realized in her messianic representative, who had dealt with the sin of the world.

Within this new setting the Gospels tell of how the original Jewish story came to completion in Jesus and the restored covenant people.[37] Luke retells Israel's story as coming to its climax in the promised Davidic descendant who ended the exile and secured redemption. Matthew begins with an announcement that Israel's exile has been ended by a new Davidic descendant who has saved his people "from their sins" (1:21); the book ends with this good news going out into all the nations (28:19). Mark's "Christian apocalypse" portrays the story of Jesus' messiahship and crucifixion as a subversion of Jewish nationalistic hopes: it leads to the desolation of Jerusalem and the destruction of the temple.

Pauline Theology

Jesus' Representative and Incorporative Messiahship

The Jewish story also provides the narrative framework for understanding Paul's theology. Wright maintains that Paul thinks of the Messiah as the representative of the whole people of God.[38] The death of Jesus, who was acting

33. Ibid., 540–611.
34. Ibid., 612–53.
35. Ibid., 631.
36. Wright, *New Testament*, 359–70, 444–64.
37. Ibid., 371–443.
38. N. T. Wright, "Messiah and the People of God"; idem, *Climax of the Covenant*, 18–55; idem, "Romans and the Theology of Paul," in *Pauline Theology*, ed. E. Elizabeth Johnson and David M. Hay (Minneapolis: Fortress, 1995), 3:34.

as Israel's messianic representative, marked the end of Israel's exile; his resurrection marked the creation of a new Israel which was continuous with the
covenant promise that Abraham would have a worldwide family characterized by faith. Israel's destiny came to completion in the death and resurrection of Jesus the Messiah; all of her privileges were then passed on to him and
his people, the new Abrahamic family comprising all nations and defined by
faith in the God who raised Jesus.

For Paul, the Messiah takes Israel's place as the last Adam. In the Jewish
story Israel was destined to regain Adam's lost dominion and glory (Ps. 8:4–
6; Manual of Discipline 4:23). As the last Adam eschatological Israel would
take Adam's place as God's obedient humanity, ruling over the nations (Dan.
7).[39] But, according to Paul, Israel's failure necessitated the transferral of her
destiny as the last Adam to Jesus her messianic representative. The Messiah
represents his people; they are summed up in him. The idea that the Messiah
sums up his people and acts as their representative derives from the Old Testament understanding that "the king and the people are bound together in
such a way that what is true of one is true in principle of the other."[40] In passages such as Romans 6–8 and Galatians 3 Paul makes particularly clear that
Jesus the Messiah "sums up his people in himself, so that what is true of him
is true of them."[41] According to 1 Corinthians 15:20–28, 45, Christ, as the
last Adam, took on the eschatological task of Israel in his obedient death on
a cross, and in resurrection became the life-giving source for the future resurrection of those who belong to him.[42] And according to Romans 5:12–21
Jesus not only replaced Israel as God's true humanity, but has redeemed humanity "in Adam" from the reign of sin and death that followed from Adam's
transgression; Jesus has procured justification for those who were without defense before God.[43] Jesus' obedience was the act of Israel's representative, un-
doing the effects of Adam's sin and restoring God's original intention for humanity, realized both partially now and fully in the age to come.[44]

Jesus' representative messiahship constitutes the basic line of thought in
Romans.[45] Israel's fall into evil (Rom. 1:18–3:20) and failure to be a light to
the world (2:17–29) meant that God had to find an obedient humanity
through whom he could accomplish his purposes for the world's redemption.
Jesus the Messiah through his obedient death achieved God's covenant purpose for the world's redemption (3:21–31). This revelation of God's cove-

---

39. Wright, *Climax of the Covenant*, 21.
40. Ibid., 46; see also Wright, "Messiah and the People of God," ch. 1. In *The Climax of the Covenant*, 41–55, Wright insists that Paul retains Χριστός in its titular sense of "Messiah." Thus the term
carries incorporative significance for Paul: the Messiah is the representative of God's people, the one
in whom they are summed up. When understood against this background, Paul's "in Christ" terminology essentially amounts to "belonging to the people of the Messiah."
41. Wright, *Climax of the Covenant*, 48.
42. Ibid., 35.
43. Ibid., 37.
44. Ibid., 38–40.
45. Wright, "Messiah and the People of God"; idem, "Romans."

nant faithfulness in Jesus the Messiah has excluded Jewish boasting in ethnic privilege and brought the Abrahamic promises to fruition by creating a family embracing all nations that is defined not by ethnic boundaries but by faith (3:27–4:25). Israel's privileges have been transferred to the Messiah and his people (Rom. 5–8; 9:4–5), who, as God's true eschatological humanity, inherit all the glory of Adam (5:2; cf. Manual of Discipline 4:23). Israel's present rejection represents a paradoxical outworking of God's faithfulness to the Abrahamic promises; the result is salvation for the world in much the same way that Israel's rejection of her Messiah accomplished reconciliation for all humankind (Rom. 5:10; 11:15).[46] In God's merciful purpose, however, the inheritance of Israel's blessings by the Gentiles will provoke Israel to jealousy and lead to her participation in the renewed covenant through acceptance of the Messiah (11:11–32).

Christological Monotheism

In the matter of Christology, Wright focuses on three passages which confirm that Paul thought of Jesus "as ranking alongside of Israel's God."[47] (1) Philippians 2:5–11 speaks of Jesus' self-humiliation and obedience to the death of the cross, which fulfils Israel's calling to be the last Adam. In reversing the first Adam's failure he has inherited the rulership envisaged in Genesis 1:26; Psalms 8 and 110; and Daniel 7:14–18. Christ's divinity appears in the claims that he preexisted as equal with God (Phil. 2:6) and that he has now received the title and accolades which properly belonged to Israel's God (vv. 10–11; cf. Isa. 45:23). (2) The poem of Colossians 1:15–20 echoes Jewish wisdom traditions which insist that God is both Creator and Redeemer.[48] Paul here identifies Christ as the God active in creation and redemption; at the same time, however, Paul distinguishes him from God the Father. (3) In 1 Corinthians 8:6 Paul lays the foundation for christological monotheism by equating Jesus with "Lord" in the Hebrew *Shema* (Deut. 6:4–5).[49] While Paul did not formulate the doctrine of the Trinity, he did bequeath to his later interpreters "a manner of speaking and writing about God which made it, or something very like it, almost inevitable."[50]

The Law and Justification by Faith

E. P. Sanders's revisionary arguments about the covenantal structure of first-century Judaism have shaped the recent discussion of Paul's theology.[51] Sanders argues that the Judaism known to Paul was not a legalistic religion of works-righteousness, but one in which salvation rested on remaining in

46. Wright, *Climax of the Covenant*, 231–57; idem, "Romans," 56–62.
47. Wright, *Climax of the Covenant*, 55–136.
48. Ibid., 108.
49. Ibid., 121, 129, 136.
50. Ibid., 117.
51. E. P. Sanders, *Paul and Palestinian Judaism: A Comparison of Patterns of Religion* (Philadelphia: Fortress, 1977).

the covenant already established by God's grace. Remaining in the covenant depended, in turn, on obedience to the law and repenting of transgressions. Sanders's thesis has challenged the Reformation view that Paul's doctrine of justification by faith was set in opposition to Jewish attempts to earn salvation by doing the law. Wright has been at the forefront of expanding Sanders's thesis into a new view of Paul's thought. For Wright, the "works of the law" to which Paul opposes the doctrine of justification by faith do not refer to Jewish attempts to earn salvation through works, but to those ethnocentric badges (circumcision, Sabbath keeping, and dietary laws) by which Jews defined their membership in the covenant. Paul does not attack Jewish legalism, but the pursuit of national righteousness, that is, "the belief that fleshly Jewish descent guarantees membership of God's true covenant people."[52]

Paul's view of the Mosaic law was determined by his understanding of Israel's covenant role in relation to the world's redemption. As God's agent for the world's salvation, Israel had to become the place where sin was gathered together so that it might then be passed on to the Messiah alone. The law was given to facilitate this saving design: through the Torah the sin of all humanity was gathered together in one place (Israel) and from there transferred to the Messiah, who dealt with it on the cross (Rom. 5:20; 7:7–8:11). In God's wider purposes of redemption, Israel, through the Torah, had become a vessel of wrath. Having fulfilled this role, Israel was to let go of the Torah as that which defined her as God's covenant people. Paul's critique of the law and of his Jewish contemporaries focuses on the fact that Israel, in clinging to the Torah as the key symbol of ethnic privilege, was mistakenly attempting to establish her own national righteousness at the very hour in which she should have embraced the righteousness of God now revealed in the Messiah (Rom. 9:30–10:4).

Wright regards Paul's doctrine of justification by faith as an eschatological and covenantal idea: God declares "that those who believe the gospel are his covenant people."[53] In the Jewish hope those who had been faithful to the covenant were to be resurrected and vindicated in a great law-court scene in which God would act as the righteous and impartial Judge who punishes sin and vindicates the helpless.[54] Paul appropriated this framework and declared "that the verdict had already been announced in the death and resurrection of Jesus."[55] Jesus in his resurrection received from God the vindication that properly belongs to the faithful of Israel at the end of the age. In Paul's teaching on justification, this *past* verdict pronounced over Jesus in his resurrection is brought forward and pronounced in the *present* over those joined to

52. N. T. Wright, "The Paul of History and the Apostle of Faith," *Tyndale Bulletin* 29 (1978): 64–65; see also idem, *New Testament*, 238–41.
53. Wright, *Climax of the Covenant*, 214.
54. N. T. Wright, "Justification: The Biblical Basis and Its Relevance for Contemporary Evangelicalism," in *The Great Acquittal: Justification by Faith and Current Christian Thought*, ed. G. Reid (London: Collins, 1980), 13–37; idem, *New Testament*, 334–38; idem, *What St. Paul Really Said: Was Paul of Tarsus the Real Founder of Christianity?* (Oxford: Lion, 1997), 95–133.
55. Wright, *New Testament*, 458.

Jesus, all of this in anticipation of the *future* verdict to be pronounced at the final judgment.[56] Since justification is essentially God's pronouncement that one is now a member of the covenant, the doctrine of justification by faith signifies that the badge of covenant membership is no longer the Torah, circumcision, or race, but faith in the God who raised Jesus from the dead. In terms of our law-court metaphor, the righteousness of faith conferred upon humans when God declares them to be covenant members is simply the favorable verdict of the court. It is not to be equated with the righteousness of God, a quality that cannot be transferred from the judge to the defendant.[57]

Wright's historical and theological project represents a fresh and innovative attempt to bring coherence to the message of the New Testament. His six-volume project engages questions related to epistemology, interpretive method, the proper use of biblical criticism, biblical theology, and the problem of conveying the Christian message in a postmodern culture. The theological and historical views advanced in his various writings will no doubt be found controversial on both ends of the critical spectrum. Certainly questions about the historical Jesus will continue for those doubting the historical credibility of the Gospels. Wright's interpretation of Jesus as an eschatological figure who announced the imminent dawn of the kingdom of God has the advantage of taking into account the basic Jewish framework of Jesus' life and mission. Of perhaps greater significance for Christian theology and proclamation, however, is Wright's claim that Paul's theology is fundamentally grounded not, as the Reformers had supposed, in an antithesis between Christian grace and Jewish legalism, but in the idea that Jesus' death and resurrection mark the fulfilment of Jewish hopes for God's covenant faithfulness and the beginning of a new humanity in him as the Second Adam. Wright attempts to do justice to the corporate and eschatological dimensions of the apostle's thought, though some may feel he has thereby given too little attention to those individualistic aspects of Paul's soteriology that were so critical for the Reformation's understanding of the gospel.[58] Wright's thesis demands consideration from those who base theology and proclamation in historical exegesis. We await anxiously his further work on the nature of Christian origins and of the gospel's birth in the context of a Jewish and Greco-Roman world.

Primary Sources

Wright, N. T. "A Biblical Portrait of God." In N. T. Wright with Keith Ward and Brian Hebblethwaite, *The Changing Face of God: Lincoln Lectures in Theology 1996*, 9–29. *Lincoln Studies in Theology 2.*

———. *The Climax of the Covenant: Christ and the Law in Pauline Theology.* Minneapolis: Fortress, 1991.

---

56. Wright, "Romans," 38–39; idem, *What St. Paul Really Said*, 143–44.
57. Wright, "Romans," 38–39; idem, *What St. Paul Really Said*, 96–103.
58. See in particular Wright, *What St. Paul Really Said*, 113–18.

————. *The Crown and the Fire.* Grand Rapids: Eerdmans, 1995.

————. *The Epistles of Paul to the Colossians and to Philemon.* Tyndale New Testament Commentaries. Rev. ed. Grand Rapids: Eerdmans, 1987.

————. *Following Jesus: Biblical Reflections on Discipleship.* Grand Rapids: Eerdmans, 1995.

————. "Gospel and Theology in Galatians." In *Gospel in Paul: Studies in Corinthians, Galatians and Romans for Richard N. Longenecker,* edited by L. Ann Jervis and Peter Richardson, 222–39. *Journal for the Study of the New Testament,* supplement 108. Sheffield: Sheffield Academic Press, 1994.

————. "Jesus." In *Early Christian Thought in Its Jewish Context,* edited by John Barclay, 43–58. New York: Cambridge University Press, 1996.

————. *Jesus and the Victory of God.* Vol. 2 of *Christian Origins and the Question of God.* Minneapolis: Fortress, 1996.

————. "Jesus, Israel and the Cross." In *SBL 1985 Seminar Papers,* edited by K. H. Richards, 75–95. Chico, Calif.: Scholars, 1985.

————. "Justification: The Biblical Basis and Its Relevance for Contemporary Evangelicalism." In *The Great Acquittal: Justification by Faith and Current Christian Thought,* ed. G. Reid, 13–37. London: Collins, 1980.

————. "The Law in Romans 2." In *Paul and the Mosaic Law,* edited by James D. G. Dunn, 131–50. Tübingen: J. C. B. Mohr (Paul Siebeck), 1994.

————. *The Lord and His Prayer.* Grand Rapids: Eerdmans, 1996.

————. "The Messiah and the People of God." D.Phil. diss., Oxford University, 1980.

————. *The New Testament and the People of God.* Vol. 1 of *Christian Origins and the Question of God.* Minneapolis: Fortress, 1992.

————. "The Paul of History and the Apostle of Faith." *Tyndale Bulletin* 29 (1978): 61–88.

————. "Quest for the Historical Jesus." In *Anchor Bible Dictionary,* ed. David Noel Freedman, 3:796–802. New York: Doubleday, 1992.

————. "Romans and the Theology of Paul." In *Pauline Theology,* edited by E. Elizabeth Johnson and David M. Hay, 3:30–67. Minneapolis: Fortress, 1995.

————. "Taking the Text with Her Pleasure: A Post-Post-Modernist Response to J. Dominic Crossan *The Historical Jesus: The Life of a Mediterranean Jewish Peasant* (with Apologies to A. A. Milne, St Paul and James Joyce)." *Theology* 96 (1993): 303–10.

————. "'That We Might Become the Righteousness of God': Reflections on 2 Corinthians 5:21." In *Pauline Theology,* ed. David M. Hay, 2:200–208. Minneapolis: Fortress, 1993.

————. *What St. Paul Really Said: Was Paul of Tarsus the Real Founder of Christianity?* Oxford: Lion, 1997.

————. *Who Was Jesus?* Grand Rapids: Eerdmans, 1992.

————, and Stephen Neill. *The Interpretation of the New Testament, 1861–1986.* New York: Oxford University Press, 1988.

————, and L. D. Hurst, eds. *The Glory of Christ in the New Testament: Studies in Christology in Memory of George Bradford Caird.* New York: Oxford University Press, 1987.

Walter A. Elwell is professor of biblical studies and theology at Wheaton College Graduate School. He has edited numerous works, including the *Evangelical Dictionary of Theology, Topical Analysis of the Bible,* and *Handbook of Evangelical Theologians.* J. D. Weaver is editorial director of academic and reference books at Baker Book House.